A Dictionary of Linguistics and Phonetics

Fourth Edition

THE LANGUAGE LIBRARY

EDITED BY DAVID CRYSTAL

The Articulate Computer	*Michael McTear*
The Artificial Language Movement	*Andrew Large*
Children's First School Books	*Carolyn D. Baker & Peter Freebody*
Children's Writing and Reading	*Katharine Perera*
A Child's Learning of English	*Paul Fletcher*
Clichés and Coinages	*Walter Redfern*
A Companion to Old and Middle English Studies	*A. C. Partridge*
A Dictionary of Literary Terms (third edition)	*J. A. Cuddon*
Early Modern English	*Charles Barber*
A Dictionary of Linguistics and Phonetics (fourth edition)	*David Crystal*
The Foreign-Language Barrier	*J. A. Large*
A History of the English Language	*G. L. Brook*
A History of Foreign-Language Dictionaries	*R. L. Collison*
How Conversation Works	*Ronald Wardhaugh*
An Informal History of the German Language	*W. B. Lockwood*
Language and Class in Victorian England	*K. C. Phillipps*
The Language of *1984*	*W. F. Bolton*
Language, Society and Identity	*John Edwards*
Languages in Competition	*Ronald Wardhaugh*
Modern Englishes: Pidgins and Creoles	*Loreto Todd*
Non-Standard Language in English Literature	*N. F. Blake*
Oral Cultures Past and Present	*Viv Edwards and Thomas J. Sienkewicz*
Puns	*Walter Redfern*
Rhetoric: The Wit of Persuasion	*Walter Nash*
Seeing Through Language	*Ronald Carter and Walter Nash*
Sense and Sense Development (revised)	*R. A. Waldron*
The Study of Dialect	*K. M. Petyt*
Swearing	*Geoffrey Hughes*
Thomas Hardy's English	*Ralph W. V. Elliott*
The Treatment of Sounds in Language and Literature	*Raymond Chapman*
Words in Time	*Geoffrey Hughes*
The Writing Systems of the World	*Florian Coulmas*

A Dictionary of Linguistics and Phonetics

Fourth Edition

David Crystal

First published by André Deutsch 1980
Reprinted 1983
Second edition published by Basil Blackwell 1985
Reprinted 1988, 1989, 1990
Third edition 1991
Reprinted 1992, 1993, 1994, 1995, 1996
Fourth edition published by Blackwell Publishers Ltd 1997
Reprinted 1997 (twice)

Blackwell Publishers Ltd
108 Cowley Road
Oxford OX4 1JF, UK

Blackwell Publishers Inc
350 Main Street
Malden, Massachusetts 02148, USA

British Library Cataloguing in Publication Data
A CIP catalogue record for this book is available from the British Library

Library of Congress Cataloging in Publication Data
Crystal, David 1941–
A dictionary of linguistics and phonetics/David Crystal—4th ed.
p. cm.—(The language library)
ISBN 0–631–20096–7 — ISBN 0–631–20097–5 (pbk)
1. Linguistics—Dictionaries. I. Title. II. Series.
P29.C65 1997 90–7651
410'.3—dc20 CIP

Phototypeset in Times 9 on 11pt
by Intype London Ltd
Printed and bound in Great Britain by
MPG Books Ltd, Bodmin, Cornwall

This book is printed on acid-free paper

Preface to the First Edition

When I took the first survey of my undertaking, I found our speech copious without order, and energetick without rules: wherever I turned my view, there was perplexity to be disentangled, and confusion to be regulated; choice was to be made out of boundless variety, without any established principle of selection; adulterations were to be detected, without a settled test of purity; and modes of expression to be rejected or received, without the suffrages of any writers of classical reputation or acknowledged authority.

Samuel Johnson, Preface to *A Dictionary of the English Language*

One sign of immaturity [in a science] is the endless flow of terminology. The critical reader begins to wonder if some strange naming taboo attaches to the terms that a linguist uses, whereby when he dies they must be buried with him.

Dwight Bolinger, *Aspects of Language*, p. 554

What is needed, of course, is a comprehensive lexicographical survey, on historical principles, of twentieth-century terminology in linguistics and phonetics. One could use the techniques, well established, which have provided dictionaries of excellence, such as the OED and Merriam Webster's. The painstaking scrutiny of texts from a range of contexts, the recording of new words and senses on slips, and the systematic correlation of these as a preliminary to representing patterns of usage: such steps are routine for major surveys of general vocabulary and could as readily be applied for a specialized vocabulary, such as the present undertaking. Needless to say, it would be a massive task – and one which, for linguistics and phonetics, has frequently been initiated, but never completed. I am aware of several attempts to work along these lines, in Canada, Great Britain, Japan and the United States, sometimes by individuals, sometimes by committees. All seem to have foundered, presumably for a mixture of organizational and financial reasons. I tried to initiate such a project myself, twice, but failed both times, for the same reasons. The need for a proper linguistics dictionary is thus as urgent now as it ever was; but to be fulfilled it requires a combination of academic expertise, time, physical resources and finance which so far have proved impossible to attain.

But how to cope, in the meantime, with the apparently 'endless flow of terminology' which Bolinger, among many others, laments? And how to deal with the enquiries from the *two* kinds of consumer of linguistic and phonetic terms? For this surely is the peculiar difficulty which linguists nowadays have to face – that their subject, despite its immaturity, carries immense popular as well as academic appeal. Not only, therefore, is terminology a problem for the academic linguist and phonetician; these days, such people are far outnumbered by those who, for private or professional reasons, have developed more than an incidental interest in the subject. It is of little use intimating that the interest of the outside world is premature, as has sometimes been suggested. The interest exists, in a genuine, responsible and critical form, and requires a comparably responsible academic reaction. The present dictionary is, in the first instance, an attempt to meet the popular demand for information about linguistic terms, pending the fuller, academic evaluation of the subject's terminology which one day may come.

The demand has come mainly from those for whom a conscious awareness of language is an integral part of the exercise of a profession, and upon whom the influence of linguistics has been making itself increasingly felt in recent years. This characterization includes two main groups: the range of teaching and remedial language professions, such as foreign-language teaching and speech therapy; and the range of academic fields which study language as part of their concerns, such as psychology, sociology, literary criticism and philosophy. It also includes an increasing number of students of linguistics – especially those who are taking introductory courses in the subject at postgraduate or in-service levels. In addition, there are the many categories of first-year undergraduate students of linguistics and phonetics. My aim, accordingly, was to provide a tool which would assist these groups in their initial coming to grips with linguistic terminology, and it is this which motivated the [original] title of this book: a *first* dictionary. . . .

Coverage

Once a decision about readership had been made, the problem of selecting items and senses for inclusion simplified considerably. It is not the case that the whole of linguistic terminology, and all schools of thought, have proved equally attractive or useful to the above groups. Some terms have been used (and abused) far more than others. For example, COMPETENCE, LEXIS, GENERATE, STRUCTURALISM, MORPHOLOGY and PROSODY are a handful which turn up so often in these students' early experience of the subject that their exclusion would have been unthinkable. On the other hand, *anthropophonics, allolog, bahuvrihi, hyperplexon* and *paraphonology* are unlikely to cause any problems for my intended readership, as they will not encounter them in their initial contact with linguistic ideas. Likewise, some linguistic theories and descriptions have achieved far more popularity than others – generative grammar, most obviously, and (in Great Britain) Hallidayan linguistics and the Quirk reference grammar, for example. The terminology of phonetics, also, is so pervasive that it is a priority for special attention. On the other hand, despite their considerable relevance to the formation of ideas in linguistic theory, the detailed terminology of, say, glossematics, or stratificational grammar, has not made so direct an impact on the general consciousness of the above groups. While I have included several of the more important theoretical terms from these less widely used approaches, therefore, I have not presented their terminology in any detail. Similarly, theoretical terminology which has developed since the mid-1970s will not be found [but see prefaces to the second and third editions, below]. The biases of this dictionary, I hope, will be seen to be those already present in the applied and introductory literature – with a certain amount of systematization and filling-out in places, to avoid gaps in the presentation of a topic (for example, whereas many introductory texts selectively illustrate DISTINCTIVE FEATURES, this topic has been systematically covered in the present book).

Bearing in mind the background of the above groups helped to simplify the selection of material for inclusion in a second main way: only terms or senses which have arisen because of the influence of twentieth-century linguistics and phonetics have been included. This dictionary is therefore in contrast with several which have appeared in recent years, where the aim seems to have been to cover the whole field of language, languages and communication, as well as linguistics and phonetics. My attitude here is readily summarized: one does not need to include such terms as *alphabet, abbreviation* and *acronym*, because these are terms whose general sense any good dictionary would handle routinely; *as terms*, they owe nothing to the development of ideas in linguistics. Similarly, while such terms as *reinforcement, rhyme-scheme* and *runic* are more obviously technical, their special ranges of application derive from conceptual frameworks other than linguistics. None of these terms therefore has any place in the present dictionary. Likewise, proper names of languages and language families (such as *Chinese, Indo-European*) and any associated fields of study (e.g. *Chinese linguistics*) have been excluded. On the other hand, I devote a great deal of space to the many 'harmless-looking' terms which are used by linguists, where an apparently everyday word has developed a special sense, often after many years of linguistic debate, e.g. FORM, FUNCTION, FEATURE, ACCENT, WORD, SENTENCE. These are terms which, perhaps on account of their less technical appearance, cause especial difficulty at an introductory level. Particular attention is paid to them in this dictionary, therefore, alongside the more obvious technical terms, such as PHONEME, BILABIAL, ADJUNCTION, MORPHOPHONEMIC and HYPONYMY.

Several other constraints on coverage have been introduced, to preserve the dictionary's coherence. In particular, four categories of terminology have been excluded:

(a) The technical terms of traditional language studies (i.e. pre-twentieth century), unless they have been the focus of attention in linguistics and phonetics. For example, classical rhetorical terms are not included, such as *anaptyxis, prosiopesis* and *alliteration*. Similarly, most of the *detailed* terms of traditional grammatical description have been excluded as separate entries (though many of them are referred to as part of some larger entry), e.g. *masculine, feminine, neuter* (but cf. GENDER).

(b) The technical terms that properly belong to other disciplines, unless linguistics or phonetics have introduced a special sense, or a fresh dimension to their use. Acoustic phonetics, for example, uses many terms from physics (*spectrum, amplitude,* etc.), but, as no special sense is involved, these terms have been excluded. A similar principle applied in relation to the terms of information theory (e.g. *noise*), audiology (e.g. *audiogram*), and the detailed terminology belonging to logical and philosophical analysis of language. On the other hand, the formalization of linguistic ideas initiated by Chomsky has introduced several terms from philosophy, logic and mathematics which have become fundamental to thinking in grammar and semantics (AXIOM, ALGORITHM, PROPOSITION, CALCULUS, etc.), and thus the more important of these have been included.

(c) Terms which relate primarily to the various fields of applied language studies, such as foreign-language teaching (e.g. *transfer*) and language pathology (e.g. *aphasia*).

(d) The classical terminology of comparative philology (e.g. *umlaut, ablaut*).

There are no proper names in the dictionary, save in a few cases where major schools of thought have developed, e.g. CHOMSKYAN, BLOOMFIELDIAN, PRAGUE SCHOOL.

On this basis, the first edition of this dictionary contained just over 1,000 entries (boldface headwords). Within an entry, technical phrases involving the headword appeared, and these accounted for a further 1,000 boldface items. [Second and third edition statistics are given below.]

Treatment

I remain doubtful even now whether the most appropriate title for this book is 'dictionary'. The definitional parts of the entries, by themselves, were less illuminating than one might have expected; consequently it proved necessary to introduce in addition a more discursive approach, with several illustrations, to capture the significance of a term. Most entries accordingly contain encyclopedic information, about such matters as the historical context in which a term was used, or the relationship between a term and others from associated fields. At times, owing to the absence of authoritative studies of terminological development in linguistics, I have had to introduce a personal interpretation in discussing a term; but I hope this has been balanced by the further context provided through bibliographical references at the end of every entry – a chapter from one of a small number of basic textbooks [no longer present in the fourth edition; see preface below]. I have used several well-established introductory texts, as well as a few more advanced ones. These references do not usually constitute the original sources of terms but act as a convenient locus where one may obtain further information about the framework of ideas from which the terms derive their significance. That is why the references are to chapters and not to pages.

Each entry is self-contained: that is, there are no obligatory cross-references to other entries to complete the exposition of a sense. Nor have I made use of the convention 'See Y' following an entry. Given the interdependence of so much terminology (COMPETENCE–PERFORMANCE, DEEP STRUCTURE–SURFACE STRUCTURE, etc.), to put all the information under one of these terms, with a mere 'See . . .' under the other, involves an arbitrariness of organization that can cause a reader much frustration. I have preferred to work on the principle that, as most dictionary-users open a dictionary with a *single* problematic term in mind, they should be given a satisfactory account of that term as immediately as possible. I therefore explain *competence* under COMPETENCE, *performance* under PERFORMANCE, and so on. As a consequence of the interdependence of these terms, however, this procedure means that there must be some repetition: at least the salient characteristics of the term *performance* must be incorporated into the entry for COMPETENCE, and vice versa. This repetition would be a weakness if the book were read from cover to cover; but a dictionary should not be used as a textbook, and, while the result has been a somewhat longer volume than would have been the case if the 'See . . .' convention had been used, I remain convinced of the greater benefits of look-up convenience and entry coherence.

Within an entry, the main terms being defined are printed in boldface (along with their main inflectional variants). Any other terms and phrases, less central to the exposition of the headword, are printed in quotation marks. Terms defined elsewhere in this dictionary are printed in small capitals – but only on their *first* appearance within an entry, and only where their technical status is important for an appreciation of the sense of the entry.

Acknowledgements

I have been fortunate in having several colleagues in my department who have given generously of their time to read the text of this dictionary, in whole or in part, advised me on how to proceed in relation to several of the above problems, and pointed out places where my own biases were intruding too markedly. I have benefited enormously from their comments, and I wish only that there had been more time to go into the large number of points of interpretation which emerged in the process. Such discussions have confirmed me in my view that there is an urgent need for the job to be done properly. In the meantime, I thank them all for their perseverance, and apologize if I have not done their comments justice in my revisions. I would dearly like to have had all my errors eliminated in this way: the responsibility for those that may be left is mine, and I would welcome comments from readers about weaknesses which might be taken account of in any future edition. I am most grateful, accordingly, to Ron Brasington, Paul Fletcher, Michael Garman, Arthur Hughes, Frank Palmer and Irene Warburton, for all their help. And to my wife, lastly, who typed the entire manuscript (much of it, more than once), and who still claims she enjoyed it: her support and encouragement have been crucial.

David Crystal
Reading, December 1978

Preface to the Second Edition

More than any other form of publication, dictionaries date. In the present case, the datedness of the first edition is apparent, even after only five years, not so much in the terms it included but in those excluded. Topics which a few years ago would have seemed out of place in a *first* dictionary of linguistics and phonetics are now obligatory candidates for entry, as they are increasingly being encountered in courses and textbooks. I have continued to use my three-year-rule – only to include something if it is still being talked about three years later! – but even the rigorous application of this rule permits the inclusion of 125 new boldface head words or abbreviations and a further 100 or so boldface terms within entries; a further 100 or so entries have also been expanded to take account of new senses. Perhaps surprisingly, I was unable to find cases where I could delete a term on the grounds that it was no longer used. In short, the second edition is about a sixth larger than the first, in terms of entry coverage. It won't go on like this, will it?

More specifically, most of the new entries will be seen to cover such areas of (relatively) recent development as transformational grammar of the late 1970s (e.g. filters, binding, X-bar syntax), alternatives to TG (e.g. co-representational grammar, generalized phrase-structure grammar), phonological theory, pragmatics, discourse analysis and text linguistics. I was surprised to find hardly anything to add in the field of phonetics. Thanks to the critical eyes of reviewers and colleagues, I have been able to make good some stupid omissions and inconsistencies from the first edition, and made innumerable modifications to points of phrasing within individual entries, which I hope have sharpened the dictionary's cutting edge. I have expanded the number of bibliographical references a little, but I have not changed my policy of citing only secondary sources – a policy which some reviewers have criticized. The purpose of the references, however, is pedagogical, not lexicographical – to point the student in the direction of relevant further reading, and not to provide information about the original historical source of a term, for which a much larger dictionary would be required. [These references have been dropped from the fourth edition: see preface below.]

It is therefore a pleasure to acknowledge the assistance of those reviewers, colleagues and students of mine who have provided me with suggestions for the improvement of this dictionary – in particular, K. V. T. Bhat, Colin Biggs, Georges Bourcier, René Dirven, Dušan Gabrovšek, Gerald Gazdar, Francisco Gomez de Matos, Lars Hermerén, Rodney Huddleston, Neil Smith, Irene Warburton, John Wood and Walburga von Raffler Engel. In the light of their comments, and having recently trawled again the depths of the linguistics journals to see what terms I could catch, I remain more than ever convinced of the need for a major terminology project on historical principles, which I referred to in my first preface. The need for standardization is as urgent now as it ever was – perhaps even more so these days, given the multiple directions in which fields such as semantics and pragmatics are moving. It is the development of novel, idiosyncratic terminology which worries me most – especially when authors seem unaware of previous terms and senses which deal with the same phenomena. This dictionary is only an introductory one, but I hope it nonetheless will continue to draw people's attention to the existence of the problem, and thus contribute a little to its solution.

It will perhaps be noted that the word 'first' has been dropped from the title of the book, at the suggestion of the publisher. No alteration of level or scope is reflected in the change, but simply the view that, in the absence of a 'second-level' dictionary with which it might be compared, the adjective was unnecessary. I have concurred, as my use of the word was intended only to make a point (p. vi), and now that the dictionary has come to be used quite widely, it is probably no longer necessary to lay stress upon it.

David Crystal
Holyhead, October 1984

Preface to the Third Edition

Yes, it will (to answer my own question at the end of the first paragraph of the second edition Preface). In the five years since the second edition, I have continued to keep an eye open for new terms and senses, helped this time by the indexes to the quarterly *Linguistics Abstracts*, and the coverage of the various encyclopedias of linguistics which have also been appearing at regular intervals. For the new edition, I have introduced a further 300 new terms, abbreviations, or senses, over two-thirds of them requiring separate entries. Particular attention has been paid to the terminology of government-binding theory and to the proliferation of terms which identifies current work in phonology, especially in metrical phonology and autosegmental phonology. All old entries have been read again, and revised in the light of current developments. Several new items have been added to the bibliography, as supportive reading. For the convenience of the reader a table showing the International Phonetic Alphabet has been included, opposite the first page of the dictionary proper.

The dictionary is getting large – much larger than I originally expected. To save space, therefore, I have relaxed my principle of entry autonomy, emphasized in the first edition, and brought in a few 'cf.' and 'X see Y' references. I have also increased the number of 'clerical' cross-references, so that it is possible to locate all boldface terms which occur in parenthesis following a headword – previous editions did not, for example, cross-refer all terms beginning with *non-* (e.g. *non-factive, non-restrictive*), and this has evidently misled some readers into thinking that these terms have not been covered.

The increasing size of the exercise has had a further consequence; it has proved necessary to call in the cavalry, in the form of Ewa Jaworska, who along with Bob Borsley read through the entries in syntactic theory, and provided many up-dating suggestions, as well as drafts of supplementary material on the terminology of government-binding theory. Their help has proved invaluable, and I am most grateful to them for their input to the current edition.

As ever, all suggestions for additions and modifications will be most welcome.

David Crystal
Holyhead, April 1990

Preface to the Fourth Edition

This new edition has in some ways been easier to prepare than previous editions, and in some ways it has been more difficult. Any lexicographer is greatly assisted when surveys of a subject appear, and in linguistics the 1990s has certainly proved to be the decade of the survey, with the appearance of several major encyclopedic projects – notably the *International Encyclopedia of Linguistics* (OUP, 1992) and *The Encyclopedia of Language and Linguistics* (Pergamon, 1993). These books have been invaluable indications of new terms and senses. An additional helpful source has been the series of Blackwell Handbooks in Linguistics, chiefly the compilations on phonology and semantics. I have again scanned the indexes of recent years of *Linguistics Abstracts* for new terminology. The role of these works, and their many contributors, is hereby acknowledged.

That is the good news. The bad news, for a small-scale enterprise like the present dictionary, is that the availability of such wide-ranging sources has brought to light huge numbers of new terms and senses – well over 600, for the new edition. The field of non-linear phonology alone has been responsible for dozens of new items, and there has been a similar expansion in semantics. Not all of these terms are ready for inclusion in this dictionary, of course. In many cases, a term is a nonce-usage coined for the idiosyncratic purpose of a particular model (e.g. the many ad hoc designations for constraints and conditions), and its life may not extend beyond the article (often just a working paper) in which it first appeared. Only those items which have lived on beyond their originator, and which have become genuine institutionalized terms, are allowed in. However, it is sometimes difficult to know how generally used a term is. Fashion is everywhere, and just because a term is on everyone's lips in 1996 does not mean that it will be around in 1997. I have been fairly cautious in my approach, and as a rule of thumb have included only those items which I have seen used in at least two sources, one of which is not the originator's. The major handbooks help, of course, in sharpening my sense of general usage, as do letters from this dictionary's users, who have occasionally been kind enough to write to point out omissions.

It is a tricky balancing act, and I am conscious of having made some arbitrary decisions. Even so, the size of the present edition has increased dramatically – by some 15 per cent. There are now over 1,400 terms dealt with as main entries in the book, and a further 1,400 handled as boldface items within entries. Special senses, distinctive collocations (generally shown by phrases being placed in inverted commas), and usage guidance is given on a further 1,200 items. In round terms, the dictionary now contains information on the specialized usage of some 4,000 items in linguistics and phonetics. The flavour of the new terminology can be suggested by the following selection from the new boldface items handled in this new edition: *bootstrapping*, *bracketing paradox*, *charm*, *cognitive metaphor*, *connectionism*, *de dicto/de re*, *defaults*, *discourse attachment*, *dynamic semantics*, *feature geometry*, *greed*, *grinding*, *hidden Markov model*, *interactional sociolinguistics*, *lambda*, *ludling*, *minimalist programme*, *non-linear phonology*, *optimality theory*, *percolation*, *procrastinate*, *qualia*, *underspecification*, *unification*.

Looking back over the first edition preface, I see I am now including items which I originally said I would not. Well, times have changed. For instance, progress in speech synthesis and recognition now brings basic acoustics terminology more frequently before the linguist, and I have often been asked to increase the coverage of terms in that area. Similarly, increased interest in the history of linguistic ideas has prompted me to include some of the core terms of traditional grammar. However, the new edition is not solely a matter of new entries. There have been many changes within entries to take account of fresh theoretical developments. I have also greatly increased the number of cross-references in the new edition, so that it is easier to find items buried within longer entries. And it has proved too cumbersome to continue with the practice of referring an entry to a general location in a textbook or other source for follow-up reading. Some readers have asked me for more precise information about the originator of a term, but (apart from in a few cases) this proves remarkably difficult to summarize briefly. Only a fully fledged historical account, using citations, can perform that service – and that exercise is no nearer now than it was twenty years ago, when the first edition of this dictionary was being prepared.

David Crystal
Holyhead, February 1996

THE INTERNATIONAL PHONETIC ALPHABET (revised to 1989)

CONSONANTS

	Bilabial	Labiodental	Dental	Alveolar	Postalveolar	Retroflex	Palatal	Velar	Uvular	Pharyngeal	Glottal
Plosive	p b			t d		ʈ ɖ	c ɟ	k ɡ	q ɢ		ʔ
Nasal	m	ɱ		n		ɳ	ɲ	ŋ	ɴ		
Trill	ʙ			r					ʀ		
Tap or Flap				ɾ		ɽ					
Fricative	ɸ β	f v	θ ð	s z	ʃ ʒ	ʂ ʐ	ç ʝ	x ɣ	χ ʁ	ħ ʕ	h ɦ
Lateral fricative				ɬ ɮ							
Approximant		ʋ		ɹ		ɻ	j	ɰ			
Lateral approximant				l		ɭ	ʎ	ʟ			
Ejective stop	pʼ			tʼ		ʈʼ	cʼ	kʼ	qʼ		
Implosive	ɓ̥ ɓ			ɗ̥ ɗ			ʄ̊ ʄ	ɠ̊ ɠ	ʛ̥ ʛ		

Where symbols appear in pairs, the one to the right represents a voiced consonant. Shaded areas denote articulations judged impossible.

VOWELS

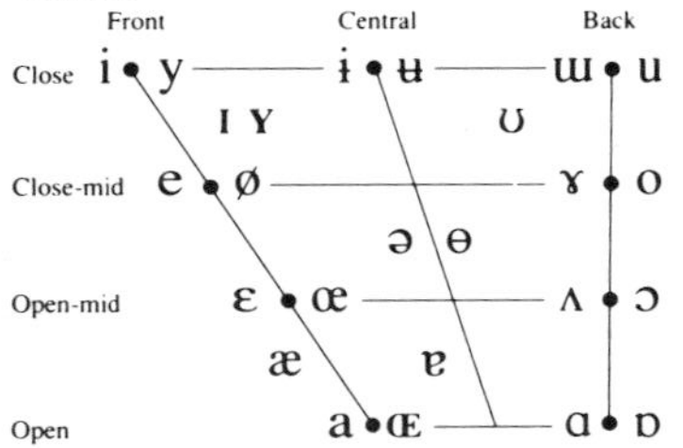

	Front		Central		Back
Close	i • y		ɨ • ʉ		ɯ • u
		ɪ ʏ		ʊ	
Close-mid	e • ø		ɘ ɵ		ɤ • o
			ə		
Open-mid	ɛ • œ		ɜ ɞ		ʌ • ɔ
		æ	ɐ		
Open		a • ɶ			ɑ • ɒ

Where symbols appear in pairs, the one to the right represents a rounded vowel.

OTHER SYMBOLS

ʍ Voiceless labial-velar fricative

w Voiced labial-velar approximant

ɥ Voiced labial-palatal approximant

ʜ Voiceless epiglottal fricative

ʢ Voiced epiglottal fricative

ʡ Epiglottal plosive

ɕ ʑ Alveolo-palatal fricatives

ɜ Additional mid central vowel

ʘ Bilabial click

ǀ Dental click

ǃ (Post)alveolar click

ǂ Palatoalveolar click

ǁ Alveolar lateral click

ɺ Alveolar lateral flap

ɧ Simultaneous ʃ and x

Affricates and double articulations can be represented by two symbols joined by a tie bar if necessary. k͡p t͡s

DIACRITICS

̥ Voiceless	n̥ d̥	̹ More rounded	ɔ̹	ʷ Labialized	tʷ dʷ	̃ Nasalized	ẽ
̬ Voiced	s̬ t̬	̜ Less rounded	ɔ̜	ʲ Palatalized	tʲ dʲ	ⁿ Nasal release	dⁿ
ʰ Aspirated	tʰ dʰ	̟ Advanced	u̟	ˠ Velarized	tˠ dˠ	ˡ Lateral release	dˡ
̤ Breathy voiced	b̤ a̤	̠ Retracted	i̠	ˤ Pharyngealized	tˤ dˤ	̚ No audible release	d̚
̰ Creaky voiced	b̰ a̰	̈ Centralized	ë	̴ Velarized or pharyngealized	ɫ		
̼ Linguolabial	t̼ d̼	̽ Mid-centralized	e̽	̝ Raised	e̝ (ɹ̝ = voiced alveolar fricative)		
̪ Dental	t̪ d̪	̩ Syllabic	ɹ̩	̞ Lowered	e̞ (β̞ = voiced bilabial approximant)		
̺ Apical	t̺ d̺	̯ Non-syllabic	e̯	̘ Advanced Tongue Root	e̘		
̻ Laminal	t̻ d̻	˞ Rhoticity	ə˞	̙ Retracted Tongue Root	e̙		

SUPRASEGMENTALS

ˈ Primary stress

ˌ Secondary stress ˌfoʊnəˈtɪʃən

ː Long eː

ˑ Half-long eˑ

̆ Extra-short ĕ

. Syllable break ɹi.ækt

| Minor (foot) group

‖ Major (intonation) group

‿ Linking (absence of a break)

↗ Global rise

↘ Global fall

TONES & WORD ACCENTS

LEVEL		CONTOUR	
e̋ or ˥	Extra high	ě or ˩˥	Rising
é ˦	High	ê ˥˩	Falling
ē ˧	Mid	e᷄ ˦˥	High rising
è ˨	Low	e᷅ ˩˨	Low rising
ȅ ˩	Extra low	e᷈ ˧˦˧	Rising-falling etc.
↓ Downstep			
↑ Upstep			

Reproduced by courtesy of the International Phonetic Association.

A An abbreviation sometimes used for ADJECTIVE (especially in GENERATIVE GRAMMAR), and sometimes for ADVERB(IAL) (especially in grammars written within the STRUCTURALIST tradition). In GOVERNMENT-BINDING THEORY it stands for ARGUMENT.

abbreviation (1) The everyday sense of this term has been refined in LINGUISTICS as part of the study of WORD FORMATION, distinguishing several ways in which words can be shortened. **Initialisms** or **alphabetisms** reflect the separate pronunciation of the initial letters of the constituent words (*TV*, *COD*); **acronyms** are pronounced as single words (*NATO*, *laser*); **clipped forms** or **clippings** are reductions of longer forms, usually removing the end of the word (*ad* from *advertisement*), but sometimes the beginning (*plane*), or both beginning and ending together (*flu*); and **blends** combine parts of two words (*sitcom*, *motel*).

(2) (**abbreviatory**) The term also appears within LINGUISTICS and PHONETICS as part of the phrase **abbreviatory convention** – any device used in a formal analysis which allows rules that share common elements to be combined (cf. BRACKETING (2)), thus permitting greater economy of statement.

abducted see VOCAL CORDS

A-binding and **A-bar-binding** see BINDING THEORY

ablative In languages which express GRAMMATICAL relationships by means of INFLECTIONS, a term referring to the FORM taken by a NOUN PHRASE (often a single NOUN or PRONOUN), typically used in the expression of a range of LOCATIVE or INSTRUMENTAL meanings. English does not have an 'ablative CASE', as did Latin, but uses other means (the PREPOSITIONS *with*, *from* and *by* in particular) to express these notions, e.g. *He did it* ***with*** *his hands*.

ablaut see GRADATION (2)

abrupt A term sometimes used in the DISTINCTIVE FEATURE theory of PHONOLOGY, as part of the phrase **abrupt release**: it refers to a sound RELEASED suddenly, without the acoustic turbulence of a FRICATIVE, as in PLOSIVE CONSONANTS. Its opposite is DELAYED release, used to characterize AFFRICATES.

absolute (1) A term used in TRADITIONAL GRAMMATICAL DESCRIPTION, and occasionally in LINGUISTICS, to refer to a SENTENCE CONSTITUENT which is isolated from or abnormally connected to the rest of the sentence. English displays an absolute use of ADVERBS and ADJECTIVES in sentence-INITIAL position, e.g. ***However**, he arrived later*, ***Happy**, she went to sleep*. In Latin, there are such EXOCENTRIC constructions as the 'ABLATIVE absolute', as in *hoc facto* (= 'this having been done').

(2) In linguistic theory, the term refers to a type of UNIVERSAL. An **absolute universal** is one which characterizes all languages, without exception; it contrasts with RELATIVE universal.

(3) See RELATIVE (3).

absolutive A term used in the GRAMMATICAL DESCRIPTION of some languages, such as Eskimo and Georgian, where there is an ERGATIVE system. In this system, there is a FORMAL parallel between the OBJECT of a TRANSITIVE VERB and the SUBJECT of an intransitive one (i.e. they display the same CASE), and these are referred to as 'absolutive': the subject of the transitive verb is then referred to as 'ergative'.

accent (1) The cumulative auditory effect of those features of pronunciation which identify where a person is from, regionally or socially. The LINGUISTICS literature emphasizes that the term refers to pronunciation only, and is thus distinct from DIALECT, which refers to GRAMMAR and VOCABULARY as well. **Regional accents** can relate to any locale, including both rural and urban communities within a country (e.g. 'West Country', 'Liverpool') as well as national groups speaking the same language (e.g. 'American', 'Australian'), and our impression of other languages ('foreign accent', 'Slavic accent'). **Social accents** relate to the cultural and educational background of the speaker. Countries with a well-defined traditional social-class system, such as India and Japan, reflect these divisions in language, and accent is often a marker of class. In Britain, the best example is the regionally neutral accent associated with a public-school education, and of the related professional domains, such as the Civil Service, the law courts, the Court and the BBC – hence the labels 'Queen's English', 'BBC English', and the like. RECEIVED PRONUNCIATION (RP) is the name given to this accent, and because of its regional neutrality RP speakers are sometimes thought of as having 'no accent'. This is a misleading way of putting it, however: linguistics stresses that everyone must have an accent, though it may not indicate regional origin. The popular label 'broad' accent refers to those accents that are markedly different from RP.

(2) (**-ed, -ual, -uation**) The emphasis which makes a particular WORD or SYLLABLE stand out in a stream of speech – one talks especially of an **accented** sound/word/syllable, or the **accent(ual) pattern** of a PHRASE/SENTENCE. The term is usually found in a discussion of metre (METRICS), where it refers to the 'beats' in a line of poetry – the accented syllables, as opposed to the **unaccented** ones. But any style of spoken language could be described with reference to the relative weight (**accentuation**) of its syllables: one might talk of the 'strongly accented' speech of a politician, for instance.

Technically, accent is not solely a matter of LOUDNESS but also of PITCH and DURATION, especially pitch: comparing the VERB *record* (as in *I'm going to record the tune*) and the NOUN (*I've got a record*), the contrast in **word accent** between *re***cord** and **re***cord* is made by the syllables differing in loudness, length and pitch movement. The notion of **pitch accent** has also been used in the PHONOLOGICAL analysis of these languages, referring to cases where there is a restricted distribution of tone within words (as in Japanese). A similar use of these variables is found in the notion of **sentence accent** (also called 'contrastive accent'). This is an important aspect of linguistic analysis, especially of INTONATION, because it can affect the ACCEPTABILITY, the MEANING, or the PRESUPPOSITIONS of a sentence, e.g. *He was wearing a red **hat*** could be heard as a response to *Was he wearing a red coat*?, whereas *He was wearing a **red** hat* would respond to *Was he wearing a green hat*? The term STRESS, however, is often used for contrasts of this kind (as in the phrases 'word stress' and 'contrastive stress'). An analysis in terms of pitch accent is also possible (cf. PITCH).

The total SYSTEM of accents in a language is sometimes called the **accentual system**, and would be part of the study of PHONOLOGY. The coinage 'accentology' for the study of accents is sometimes found in European linguistics.

acceptability (un-acceptable) The extent to which linguistic DATA would be judged by NATIVE-SPEAKERS to be possible in their language. An 'acceptable UTTERANCE' is one whose use would be considered permissible or normal. In practice, deciding on the acceptability of an utterance may be full of difficulties. Native-speakers often disagree as to whether an utterance is normal, or even possible. One reason for this is that INTUITIONS differ because of variations in regional and social backgrounds, age, personal preferences, and so on. An utterance may be normal in one DIALECT, but **unacceptable** in another, e.g. *I ain't, I be, I am*. Much also depends on the extent to which people have been brought up to believe that certain forms of LANGUAGE are 'correct' and others are 'wrong': many do not accept as desirable those sentences which the PRESCRIPTIVE approach to GRAMMAR would criticize, such as *I will go tomorrow* (for *I shall go . . .*), or *This is the man I spoke to* (for *. . . to whom I spoke*). To a LINGUIST, all such utterances are acceptable, in so far as a section of the community uses them consistently in speech or writing. The analytic problem is to determine which sections of the community use which utterances on which occasions. Within a DIALECT, an utterance may be acceptable in one CONTEXT but unacceptable in another.

Linguistics has devised several techniques for investigating the acceptability of linguistic data. These usually take the form of experiments in which native-speakers are asked to evaluate sets of utterances containing those language features over whose acceptability there is some doubt (**acceptability tests**). It is necessary to have some such agreed techniques for judging acceptability as, especially in speech, very many utterances are produced whose status as sentences is open to question. In one sample of data, someone said, *I think it's the money they're charging is one thing*. The job of the linguist is to determine whether this was a mistake on the speaker's part, or whether this is a regular feature of a speech SYSTEM; if the latter, then whether this feature is idiosyncratic, or characteristic of some social group; and so on. Such investigations by their nature are inevitably large-scale, involving many INFORMANTS and sentence patterns; they are therefore very time-consuming, and are not often carried out.

An utterance which is considered unacceptable is marked by an asterisk; if **marginally acceptable**, usually by a question mark, as follows:

*the wall was arrived before
?the wall was arrived before by the army sent by the king

These conventions are also used to indicate ungrammatical or marginally grammatical sentences. In linguistic theory, though, the difference between the acceptability and the GRAMMATICALITY of a sentence is important. A sentence may be grammatically correct, according to the RULES of the grammar of a language, but none the less unacceptable, for a variety of other reasons. For example, owing to the repeated application of a rule, the internal structure of a sentence may become too complex, exceeding the processing abilities of the speaker: these PERFORMANCE limitations are illustrated in such cases of multiple EMBEDDING as *This is the malt that the rat that the cat killed ate*, which is much less acceptable than *This is the malt that the rat ate*, despite the fact that the same grammatical operations have been used. In GENERATIVE linguistic theory, variations in acceptability are analysed in terms of performance; grammaticality, by contrast, is a matter of COMPETENCE.

accessibility (1) A term derived from psychology, and used in PSYCHOLINGUISTICS to refer to the extent to which a speaker can retrieve a linguistic unit from memory. Problems of accessibility are evident in 'tip-of-the-tongue' and TONGUE-SLIP phenomena, as well as in the varying times it takes someone to react to STRUCTURES involving different degrees of COMPLEXITY.

(2) In RELATIONAL GRAMMAR, the term is used as part of the phrase **accessibility hierarchy**, to refer to a postulated LINEAR series of DEPENDENCIES between NOMINAL entities, which controls the applicability of SYNTACTIC RULES. In the hierarchy, each entity in the series more freely undergoes syntactic rules than the items to the right. For example, the nominal operating as a SUBJECT is said to be 'more accessible' than that operating as DIRECT OBJECT; the direct object is more accessible than the INDIRECT object; and so on. The notion has been applied to several grammatical areas (e.g. RELATIVE CLAUSE formation, the use of REFLEXIVES, and QUANTIFIERS), but the full application of this principle remains to be explored.

accidence Most TRADITIONAL GRAMMARS recognize accidence as one of their main subdivisions, along with SYNTAX. It refers to the variations in WORD STRUCTURE which express grammatical MEANINGS, such as CASE, TENSE, NUMBER and GENDER. In English, for example, the reason for the difference betweeen *walk, walks, walking* and *walked* or between *boy, boys, boy's* and *boys'* would be described as part of the accidence section of a grammar. In LINGUISTICS, this term is rarely used, as these phenomena are handled under the heading of MORPHOLOGY, where they are seen as one process of WORD FORMATION alongside several others.

accommodation (accommodate) (1) A theory in SOCIOLINGUISTICS which aims to explain why people modify their style of speaking to become more like or less like that of their addressee(s). For example, among the reasons why people CONVERGE towards the speech pattern of their listener are the desires to identify more closely with the listener, to win social approval, or simply to increase the communicative efficiency of the interaction.

(2) In SEMANTICS, a term which refers to the extent to which a hearer shares the same premises as the speaker in order to interpret a sentence

('PRESUPPOSITIONAL accommodation'). The speaker presupposes a certain set of premises, and assumes that the hearer has been given adequate clues to retrieve the correct interpretation. For example, the sentence 'Can I introduce you to my daughter?' presupposes 'I have a daughter'. Because the presupposition is retrievable from the sentence, it is 'accommodated' without any difficulty.

accusative (accusativity, un-accusative) In languages which express GRAMMATICAL relationships by means of INFLECTIONS, this term refers to the FORM taken by a NOUN PHRASE (often a single noun or PRONOUN) when it is the OBJECT of a VERB. In Latin, for example, *I see the man* would be *Video hominem* and not **Video homo*, and *hominem* would be referred to as being 'in the accusative CASE'. LINGUISTS emphasize that it is not clear to use terms such as 'accusative' in languages which do not inflect words in this way. In English, for instance, whether a word is the object of the verb or not usually depends on WORD ORDER, as in *Dog bites postman*, where the recipient of the action is plainly the postman. Some traditional grammars would say here that *postman* is therefore 'accusative', but as there is no formal change between this word's use as object and its use as SUBJECT (*Postman bites dog*) linguists argue that this is a misleading use of the term, and avoid using it in such contexts. The only instance of a genuine accusative form of a word in English is in some PRONOUNS, e.g. *He hit **him***, *She saw **her***, *The man **whom** I saw*, and even here many linguists would prefer to use a neutral term, such as 'OBJECTIVE case', to avoid the connotations of TRADITIONAL GRAMMARS. A contrast is often drawn between 'accusative' and ERGATIVE languages; ergative verbs are sometimes called **unaccusative** verbs.

acoustic domain analog see SPEECH SYNTHESIS

acoustic feature/cue A characteristic of a speech sound when analysed in physical terms, e.g. FUNDAMENTAL frequency, amplitude, harmonic structure. Such analyses are provided by ACOUSTIC PHONETICS, and it is possible to make acoustic classifications of speech sounds based upon such features, as when one classifies VOWELS in terms of their FORMANT structure. The acoustic properties of a sound which aid its identification in speech are known as **acoustic cues**. In the DISTINCTIVE FEATURE theory of PHONOLOGY of JAKOBSON and Halle, acoustic features are the primary means of defining the BINARY oppositions that constitute the phonological SYSTEM of a language.

acoustic phonetics (acoustic(s)) The branch of PHONETICS, also known as **acoustics**, which studies the physical properties of speech sound, as transmitted between mouth and ear. It is wholly dependent on the use of instrumental techniques of investigation, particularly electronics, and some grounding in physics and mathematics is a prerequisite for advanced study of this subject. Its importance to the phonetician is that acoustic analysis can provide a clear, objective datum for investigation of speech – the physical 'facts' of utterance. In this way, acoustic evidence is often referred to when one wants to support an analysis being made in ARTICULATORY or AUDITORY PHONETIC terms. On the other hand, it is important not to become too reliant on acoustic analyses, which are subject to mechanical limitations (e.g. the need to calibrate measuring devices accurately), and which are often themselves open to multiple interpretations. Sometimes, indeed, acoustic and auditory analyses of a sound conflict – for example, in INTONATION studies, one may hear a speech melody as RISING, whereas the acoustic facts show the FUNDAMENTAL frequency of the sound to be steady. In such cases, it is for phoneticians to decide which evidence they will pay more attention to; there has been a longstanding debate concerning the respective merits of physical (i.e. acoustic) as opposed to psychological (i.e. auditory) solutions to such problems, and how apparent conflicts of this kind can be resolved.

acquisition (acquire) (1) In the study of the growth of LANGUAGE in children, a term referring to the process or result of learning a particular aspect of a language, and ultimately the language as a whole. **Child language acquisition** is the label usually given to the field of studies involved. The subject has involved the postulation of 'stages' of acquisition, defined chronologically, or in relation to other aspects of behaviour, which it is suggested apply generally to children; and there has been considerable discussion of the nature of the learning strategies which are used in the process of acquiring language, and of the criteria which can decide when a STRUCTURE has been acquired. Some theorists make a distinction between 'acquisition' and 'development', the former referring to the learning of a linguistic RULE (of GRAMMAR, PHONOLOGY, SEMANTICS), the latter to the further use of this rule in an increasingly wide range of linguistic and social situations. Others see no clear distinction between these two facets of language learning, and use the terms interchangeably. In GENERATIVE linguistics, the term **language acquisition device** (LAD) is used to refer to a model of language learning in which the infant is credited with an INNATE predisposition to acquire linguistic structure. This view is usually opposed to those where language acquisition is seen as a process of imitation-learning or as a reflex of cognitive development.

(2) 'Acquisition' is also used in the context of learning a foreign language: 'foreign' or 'second-language' acquisition is thus distinguished from 'first-language' or 'mother-tongue' acquisition. In this context, acquisition is sometimes opposed to 'learning': the former is viewed as a subconscious, natural process, which is the primary force behind foreign-language fluency; the latter is seen as a conscious process which monitors the progress of acquisition and guides the performance of the speaker.

acrolect(-al) A term used by some SOCIOLINGUISTS, in the study of the development of CREOLE languages, to refer to a prestige or STANDARD VARIETY (or LECT) to which it is possible to compare other lects. It is contrasted with MESOLECT and BASILECT.

acronym see ABBREVIATION

across-the-board phenomena A term used in various branches of LINGUISTICS for effects which apply to the whole of a designated linguistic system or subsystem. In particular, in language ACQUISITION it represents a view of PHONOLOGICAL development which asserts that, when children introduce a new pronunciation, the new form spreads to all the words in which it would be found in adult speech – for example, if /l/ and /j/ are at first both pronounced [j], and [l] is later acquired, it will be used only in adult words which contain /l/, and not /j/. There is no implication that the change takes place instantaneously. In

GENERATIVE grammar, the term has also been used to refer to phenomena which affect all the constituents in a CO-ORDINATE structure.

actant In VALENCY GRAMMAR, a FUNCTIONAL UNIT determined by the valency of the VERB; opposed to **circonstant**. Examples would include SUBJECT and DIRECT OBJECT.

active A term used in the GRAMMATICAL analysis of VOICE, referring to a SENTENCE, CLAUSE, or VERB FORM where, from a SEMANTIC point of view, the grammatical SUBJECT is typically the actor, in relation to the verb, e.g. *The boy wrote a letter.* It is contrasted with PASSIVE, and sometimes with other forms of the verb, e.g. the 'middle voice' in Greek.

actor–action–goal A phrase used in the GRAMMATICAL and SEMANTIC analysis of SENTENCE patterns, to characterize the typical sequence of FUNCTIONS within STATEMENTS in many languages. In the sentence *John saw a duck*, for example, *John* is the actor, *saw* the action, and *a duck* the GOAL. On the other hand, languages display several other 'favourite' sequences, such as Welsh, where the UNMARKED sequence is action–actor–goal. The phrase is widely used, but not without criticism, as the semantic implications of terms such as 'actor' do not always coincide with the grammatical facts, e.g. in *The stone moved*, the SUBJECT of the sentence is hardly an 'actor' in the same sense as *John* is above.

actualization (actualize) A term used by some linguists to refer to the physical EXPRESSION of an abstract LINGUISTIC unit; e.g. PHONEMES are 'actualized' in PHONIC SUBSTANCE as PHONES, MORPHEMES as MORPHS. Any UNDERLYING form may be seen as having a corresponding actualization in substance. REALIZATION is a more widely used term.

acute One of the features of sound set up by JAKOBSON and Halle in their DISTINCTIVE FEATURE theory of PHONOLOGY, to handle variations in PLACE OF ARTICULATION; its opposite is GRAVE. Acute sounds are defined articulatorily and ACOUSTICALLY as those involving a medial articulation in the VOCAL TRACT, and a concentration of acoustic energy in the higher frequencies; examples of [+acute] sounds are FRONT VOWELS, and DENTAL, ALVEOLAR and PALATAL CONSONANTS.

additive bilingualism see BILINGUALISM

address The general use of this term, in the sense of 'the manner of referring to someone in direct linguistic interaction', has provided SOCIOLINGUISTICS with a major field of study. **Forms of address** (or **terms of address**) have been analysed between different types of participant in different social situations, and RULES proposed to explain the speaker's choice of terms, e.g. governing the use of first names, titles, intimate PRONOUNS, etc. Social psychological concepts, such as power and solidarity, have been suggested as particularly significant factors in understanding **address systems**, i.e. the SYSTEM of RULES used by a speaker or group, governing their use of such forms as *tu* and *vous* (T FORMS and V FORMS).

adducted see VOCAL CORDS

adequacy (adequate) A term used in LINGUISTIC theory as part of the evaluation of levels of success in the writing of GRAMMARS. Several sets of distinctions based on this notion have been made. **External adequacy** judges a grammar in terms of how well it corresponds to the DATA (which are 'external' to the grammar); **internal adequacy** is a judgement based on the 'internal' characteristics of the grammar, such as its SIMPLICITY, elegance, etc. From a different point of view, grammars are said to be **weakly adequate** if they GENERATE some desired set of SENTENCES; they are **strongly adequate** if they not only do this but also assign to each sentence the correct STRUCTURAL DESCRIPTION. An alternative formulation recognizes three levels of achievement in grammars: **observational adequacy** is achieved when a grammar generates all of a particular sample (CORPUS) of data, correctly predicting which sentences are WELL FORMED; **descriptive adequacy**, when a grammar goes beyond this, and describes the INTUITIONS (COMPETENCE) of the language's speakers; **explanatory adequacy** is achieved when a principled basis is established for deciding between alternative grammars, all of which are descriptively adequate.

adessive A term used in GRAMMATICAL DESCRIPTION to refer to a type of INFLECTION which expresses the meaning of presence 'at' or 'near' a place. The adessive case is found in Finnish, for example, along with ALLATIVE, ELATIVE and several other cases expressing 'local' temporal and spatial meanings.

adjacency see ADJACENT

adjacency pair A term used in SOCIOLINGUISTIC analyses of conversational interaction to refer to a single stimulus-plus-response sequence by the participants. Adjacency pairs have been analysed in terms of their role in initiating, maintaining and closing conversations (e.g. the various conventions of greeting, leave-taking, topic-changing), and constitute, it has been suggested, an important methodological concept in investigating the ETHNOGRAPHY OF COMMUNICATION.

adjacency principle A principle in GOVERNMENT-BINDING THEORY which provides for the order of COMPLEMENTS. It requires that complements capable of being CASE-marked precede those complements which are not, and thus to be adjacent to the HEAD of the PHRASE in question. In English, for instance, the principle ensures that no CONSTITUENT intervenes between a VERB and its OBJECT NOUN phrase, e.g. *John read a book yesterday* v. **John read yesterday a book*.

adjacent (adjacency) An application of the general sense of this term in several areas of LINGUISTICS, especially in GENERATIVE models of language, where it refers specifically to neighbouring elements in a REPRESENTATION. For example, some phonological models require a 'LOCALITY condition': phonological rules apply only between elements which are next to each other on a given TIER. In FEATURE GEOMETRY, for instance, the neighbouring representation of features or NODES on a TIER are said to be **adjacent**, and those separated by other elements to be **non-adjacent**. In this context, the term is sometimes extended to include features on different tiers, which count as adjacent if they are linked to adjacent ROOT nodes. In METRICAL PHONOLOGY, the 'metrical locality principle' requires that rules refer only to elements at the same or adjacent layers of metrical structure. See also ADJACENCY PAIR, ADJACENCY PRINCIPLE.

adjective (adjectival) A term used in the GRAMMATICAL classification of WORDS to refer to the main set of items which specify the attributes of NOUNS. From a

FORMAL point of view, four criteria are generally invoked to define the class in English; they can occur within the noun PHRASE, i.e. they function in the 'attributive' position, e.g. *the **big** man*; they can occur in a post-verbal or 'predicative' position, e.g. *the man is **big**, he called it **stupid***; they can be PREMODIFIED by an INTENSIFIER, such as *very*, e.g. *the **very big** man*; and they can be used in a COMPARATIVE and SUPERLATIVE form, either by INFLECTION (e.g. *big, bigger, biggest*) or PERIPHRASTICALLY (e.g. *interesting, more interesting, most interesting*). However, not all adjectives satisfy all these criteria (e.g. *major*, as in *a major question*, does not occur predicatively – cf. **The question is major*), and the sub-classification of adjectives has proved quite complex. Both narrow and broad applications of the term 'adjective' will be found in grammars. In its broadest sense it could include everything between the DETERMINER and the noun, in such a phrase as *the vicar's fine old English garden chair*; but many linguists prefer to restrict it to the items which satisfy most or all of the above criteria (to include only *fine* and *old*, in this example), the other items being called 'adjective-like' or **adjectivals**. Adjectives may also be the HEADS of phrases (**adjective phrases**, such as *that's **very important***) and an adjectival function is sometimes recognized for certain types of CLAUSE (e.g. *he's the man **I saw***).

adjoin see ADJUNCTION

adjunct(-ival) A term used in GRAMMATICAL theory to refer to an optional or secondary element in a CONSTRUCTION: an adjunct may be removed without the STRUCTURAL identity of the rest of the construction being affected. The clearest examples at SENTENCE level are ADVERBIALS, e.g. *John kicked the ball **yesterday*** instead of *John kicked the ball*, but not **John kicked yesterday*, etc.; but other elements have been classed as **adjunctival**, in various descriptions, such as VOCATIVES and ADJECTIVES. Many adjuncts can also be analysed as MODIFIERS, attached to the HEAD of a phrase (as with adjectives, and some adverbs). The term may be given a highly restricted sense, as when it is used in QUIRK GRAMMAR to refer to a subclass of adverbials. In X-BAR syntax, an adjunct is one of the major components of a phrasal category (the others being HEAD, COMPLEMENT and SPECIFIER).

adjunction (adjoin) A basic SYNTACTIC operation in TRANSFORMATIONAL GRAMMAR (TG) referring to a RULE which places certain ELEMENTS of STRUCTURE in adjacent positions, with the aim of specifying how these structures fit together in larger UNITS. In classical TG, several types of adjunction were recognized. In **sister-adjunction** two elements were formally adjoined *under* a particular NODE and thus became sister CONSTITUENTS of that node. For example, in one formulation of the VERB PHRASE, the NEGATIVE PARTICLE was 'sister-adjoined' to the elements MODAL and TENSE, as in (1) below. (A different, but related, formal operation was known as **daughter-adjunction**.) **Chomsky-adjunction** provided an alternative way of handling this situation, and is now the only type of adjunction recognized in GOVERNMENT-BINDING THEORY. This suggestion involves adjoining an element to a node: a COPY of this node is then made immediately above it, and it is this which DOMINATES the adjoined elements. Under this analysis, the negative particle could be handled as in (2) below. This ensures that

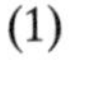

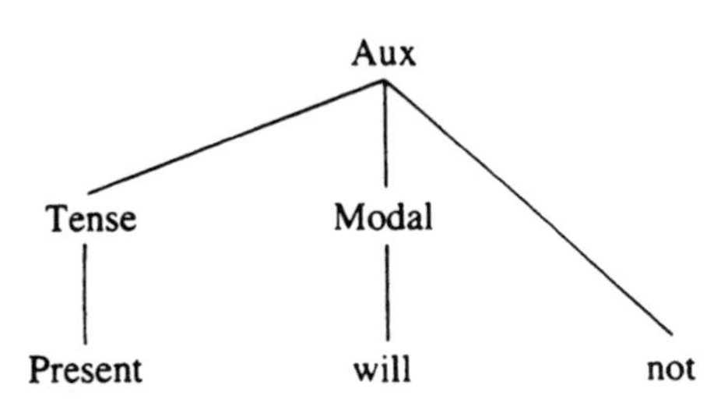

(2)

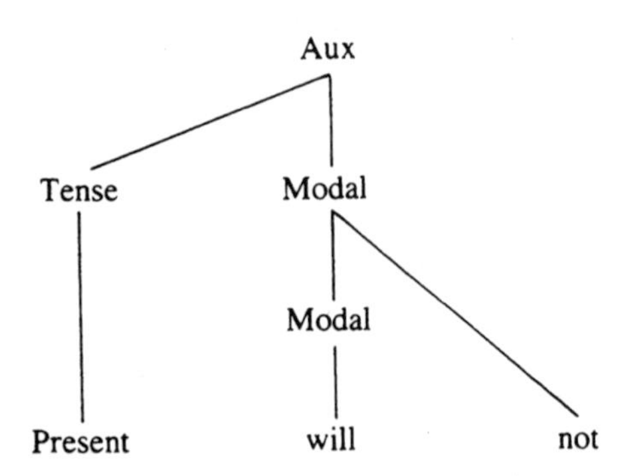

whatever happens to modal *will* also happens to *not* – for instance, CONTRACTED *not (n't)* needs to stay with the modal if the latter is moved, as in *won't he, can't he*, etc. It is thus claimed that this operation allows LINGUISTICALLY SIGNIFICANT GENERALIZATIONS to be made which might otherwise be missed, or which would be handled less ECONOMICALLY. In recent government-binding theory, MOVEMENT rules involve either (Chomsky-)adjunction or SUBSTITUTION. See also STRAY.

adnominal A term used by some GRAMMARIANS to refer to the elements in a NOUN PHRASE which MODIFY a noun (an analogy with ADVERBIAL), such as ADJECTIVES, PREPOSITIONAL phrases and 'possessive' nouns, e.g. *the **big** hat, the hat **in the box**, the **vicar's** hat*. The term is also used in the classification of RELATIVE CLAUSES (e.g. *the car which he bought* . . .).

adstratum A term sometimes used in SOCIOLINGUISTICS, referring to features in a language which have resulted from CONTACT with a neighbouring language. The process of CONVERGENCE may lead to the development of a linguistic AREA. A contrast is intended with SUBSTRATUM and SUPERSTRATUM, where a single language has been influenced by some other, thus further differentiating it from neighbouring languages.

adultomorphic (adultocentric) Labels sometimes used in language ACQUISITION studies to characterize an analysis of children's speech in terms which were originally devised for the study of the adult language, e.g. referring to *allgone* as an ELLIPTICAL SENTENCE, or describing babbling using the INTERNATIONAL PHONETIC ALPHABET. It is, of course, difficult to devise a terminology or NOTATION for child speech which is largely or totally free of adult values, but, it is argued, caution is nonetheless needed to avoid introducing too many adult assumptions, and as a consequence attributing to children a knowledge of language which they do not possess.

Adv or **ADV** An abbreviation of ADVERB(IAL), especially used in GENERATIVE linguistic studies.

advanced tongue root see ROOT (2)

advancement A term used in RELATIONAL GRAMMAR for a class of relation-changing PROCESSES. A NOUN PHRASE which bears a particular grammatical relation to some VERB comes to bear another grammatical relation to that verb, higher up the relational HIERARCHY, e.g. a process converting an OBJECT to a SUBJECT.

adverb(ial) A term used in the GRAMMATICAL classification of WORDS to refer to a heterogeneous group of items whose most frequent function is to specify the mode of action of the VERB. In English, many (by no means all) adverbs are signalled by the use of the *-ly* ending, e.g. *quickly*, but cf. *soon*. SYNTACTICALLY, one can relate adverbs to such QUESTIONS as *how, where, when* and *why*, and classify them accordingly, as adverbs of 'manner', 'place', 'time', etc.; but as soon as this is done the functional equivalence of adverbs, **adverb phrases**, PREPOSITIONAL PHRASES, NOUN phrases, and **adverb clauses** becomes apparent, e.g. A: *When is she going?* B: *Now/Very soon/In five minutes/Next week/When the bell rings.* An 'adverb phrase' (often abbreviated as AdvP) is a phrase with an adverb as its HEAD, e.g. *very slowly, quite soon*. The term **adverbial** is widely used as a general term which subsumes all five categories. 'Adverb' is thus a word-CLASS (along with NOUN, ADJECTIVE, etc.), whereas 'adverbial' is an ELEMENT of CLAUSE structure (along with SUBJECT, OBJECT, etc.). Within adverbials, many syntactic roles have been identified, of which verb MODIFICATION has traditionally been seen as central. A function of adverbials as SENTENCE modifiers or sentence CONNECTORS has been emphasized in linguistic studies, e.g. *However/Moreover/Actually/Frankly . . . I think she was right.* Several other classes of items, very different in DISTRIBUTION and FUNCTION, have also been brought under the heading of adverb(ial), such as INTENSIFIERS (e.g. *very, awfully*) and NEGATIVE PARTICLES (e.g. *not*); but often linguistic studies set these up as distinct word-classes. See also MANNNER (3), QUANTIFIER, RELATIVE (1).

adversative In GRAMMAR and SEMANTICS, a form or construction which expresses an antithetical circumstance. Adversative meaning can be expressed in several grammatical ways, such as through a CONJUNCTION (*but*), ADVERBIAL (*however, nevertheless, yet, in spite of that, on the other hand*), or PREPOSITION (*despite, except, apart from, notwithstanding*).

aerometry In PHONETICS, the measurement of air flow during speech; also called **electroaerometry**. Several instruments, such as the **electroaerometer**, have been designed to provide such data, using a special face mask which allows separate measures of air flow to be made from mouth and nose.

affect(ive) A term sometimes used in SEMANTICS as part of a classification of types of MEANING: it refers to the attitudinal element in meaning, as in the differing emotional associations (or CONNOTATIONS) of LEXICAL items (e.g. *a youth/youngster stood on the corner*) or the expression of attitude (or 'affect') in INTONATION. **Affective meaning** is usually opposed to COGNITIVE meaning. Alternative terms include EMOTIVE and ATTITUDINAL.

affected A term used by some LINGUISTS as part of the GRAMMATICAL or SEMANTIC analysis of a SENTENCE in terms of CASES or PARTICIPANT ROLES: it usually refers to an entity (ANIMATE or inanimate) which does not cause the happening denoted by the verb, but is directly involved in some other way. It is typically the role of the DIRECT OBJECT, e.g. *I kicked the ball.* PATIENT, OBJECTIVE and GOAL have sometimes been used in this sense, but alternative interpretations for these terms are common.

affirmative A term used in GRAMMATICAL description to refer to a type of SENTENCE or VERB which has no marker of NEGATION, i.e. it is expressing an assertion. The affirmative, or positive, 'pole' of this contrast is opposed to negative, and the grammatical SYSTEM involved is often referred to under the heading of POLARITY.

affix(-ation, -ing) The collective term for the types of FORMATIVE that can be used only when added to another MORPHEME (the ROOT or STEM), i.e. affixes are a type of 'bound' morpheme. Affixes are limited in number in a language, and are generally classified into three types, depending on their position with reference to the root or stem of the WORD: those which are added to the beginning of a root/stem (PREFIXES), e.g. ***un**happy*; those which follow (SUFFIXES), e.g. *happi**ness***; and those which occur within a root/stem (INFIXES). Less common terms include 'circumfix' or 'ambifix', for a combination of prefix and suffix (as in *en-light-en*). The morphological process whereby GRAMMATICAL or LEXICAL information is added to a stem is known as **affixation** ('prefixation', 'suffixation', 'infixation'). From an alternative point of view, affixes may be divided into INFLECTIONAL and DERIVATIONAL types. The number of affixes in a word has been suggested as one of the criteria for classifying languages into types (the **affix(ing) index**). Languages which express grammatical relationships primarily through the use of affixes are known as **affixing languages**, e.g. a 'prefixing' language (as in Bantu), or a 'suffixing' language (as in Latin or Greek).

In GENERATIVE grammar, the term 'affix' applies to such notions as 'present' and 'past', as well as *-ing, be, have*, etc., in the formulation of RULES. **Affix-hopping**, in this approach, is an OBLIGATORY TRANSFORMATIONAL rule which attaches an affix to the appropriate formative in a STRING: the affix 'hops' over the VERB, which is adjacent to it, e.g. *-ing+go* becoming *go+-ing*. **Affixal morphology** is an approach which claims that the only permissible morphological operation is the combining of affixes and stems (other alternations, such as GRADATION or DELETION, are part of the PHONOLOGY); this restriction is absent in **non-affixal morphology**.

affricate(-d, affrication) A term used in the classification of CONSONANT sounds on the basis of their MANNER OF ARTICULATION: it refers to a sound made when the air-pressure behind a complete CLOSURE in the VOCAL TRACT is gradually released; the initial RELEASE produces a PLOSIVE, but the separation which follows is sufficiently slow to produce audible friction, and there is thus a FRICATIVE element in the sound also. However, the DURATION of the friction is usually not as long as would be the case of an independent fricative sound. If it is very brief indeed, the term **affrication** is used; in some English DIALECTS, such as Cockney, **affricated** plosives may be heard, such as [tˢ] and [dᶻ], the auditory brevity of the friction element being indicated in the TRANSCRIPTION by the small symbols. It is, then, the combination of plosion and friction which identifies an affricate. In English, only [t] and [d] are released in this way, as in *ch-* [ʧ] of *chip* and *j-* [ʤ] of *just*. German examples are [pf-] *pfennig*, 'penny' and [ts] *zu*, 'to'. While affricates are PHONETICALLY easy to define, it is often a problem for PHONOLOGICAL analysis to decide whether a sequence of plosive and fricative elements constitutes a single functional unit, or is best analysed as two separate units. English [ʧ], for example, occurs initially, medially and finally in a word, readily contrasting with other PHONEMES, e.g. *chip/sip, richer/ripper, patch/pat*. On the other hand [tr], while occurring initially and medially (*trip/sip, petrol/petal*), does not occur finally. Further, [tθ] only occurs finally (*eighth/eight*). Phonetically, all could be considered affricates; but, phonologically, there would be difference of opinion as to whether those with a restricted DISTRIBUTION could usefully be identified in this way.

agentive (agent-less) A term used in GRAMMATICAL description to refer to a FORM or CONSTRUCTION whose typical FUNCTION in a SENTENCE is to specify the 'agent' or means whereby a particular action came about. In some languages, the term is used as one of the CASES for NOUNS, along with ACCUSATIVE, etc. In English, the term has especial relevance with reference to the PASSIVE construction, where the agent may be expressed or unexpressed (**agentless**) (e.g. *the man was bitten* [***by a snake***]). In active constructions in English, the agent is usually the grammatical SUBJECT, but in some sentences (and often in some other languages) a more complex statement of agentive function is required (as in such sentences as *The window broke* (cf. ERGATIVE) and *We ran the car out of petrol*). 'Agentive' (later, 'agent') has a special status in several linguistic theories, such as CASE grammar and GOVERNMENT-BINDING THEORY, where it is defined similarly to the above, but is seen as one of a fixed set of SEMANTIC cases or roles (THETA ROLES), along with OBJECTIVE, DATIVE, etc. The term COUNTER-AGENT is also used in the context of case grammar.

agglutinative (agglutinat-ing, -ion) A type of language established by COMPARATIVE LINGUISTICS using STRUCTURAL (as opposed to DIACHRONIC) criteria, and focusing on the characteristics of the WORD: in **agglutinative** or **agglutinating languages**, words typically contain a linear sequence of MORPHS – as seen in English *dis/establish/ment* – and thus contrast with ISOLATING and INFLECTIONAL languages. As always in such classifications, the categories are not clear-cut: different languages will display the characteristic of 'agglutination' to a greater or lesser degree. Languages which display agglutination to a major extent include Turkish and Japanese.

AGR An abbreviation in GOVERNMENT-BINDING THEORY for AGREEMENT, especially for the agreement features in the I(NFL) category in a FINITE CLAUSE.

agrammatism A term traditionally used in LANGUAGE pathology, as part of the study of aphasia, referring to a type of SPEECH production characterized by TELEGRAPHIC SYNTACTIC structures, the loss of FUNCTION WORDS and INFLECTIONS, and a generally reduced grammatical range. There may also be problems of comprehension. The notion has come to attract research interest in NEUROLINGUISTICS and PSYCHOLINGUISTICS as part of the study of the way the brain processes language. A distinction was traditionally drawn between agrammatism (the omission of items) and **paragrammatism** (the deviant replacement of items), but as both types of symptoms are often found in the same patient, in varying degrees, the dichotomy is now felt to obscure rather than clarify the nature of the phenomenon.

agreement A traditional term used in GRAMMATICAL theory and description to refer to a formal relationship between ELEMENTS, whereby a FORM of one WORD requires a corresponding form of another. In Latin, for example, agreement between elements is of central importance, being one of the main means of expressing grammatical relationships, in the absence of fixed patterns of WORD ORDER. The term CONCORD has been more widely used in linguistic studies, but in recent GENERATIVE LINGUISTICS 'agreement' has resurfaced with a new range of application. In GOVERNMENT-BINDING THEORY, **agreement marking** (AGR) of person, gender or number in FINITE VERBS plays an important role in BINDING THEORY and CASE theory. In GENERALIZED PHRASE-STRUCTURE GRAMMAR, the **control agreement principle** (CAP) is a semantically based principle governing the distribution of agreement marking.

airstream mechanism A term used in PHONETICS for a physiological process which provides a source of energy capable of being used in SPEECH sound PRODUCTION. Air is moved inwards or outwards by the movement of this mechanism, producing respectively an INGRESSIVE and an EGRESSIVE airflow. The main initiator of air movement is the lungs (the PULMONIC airstream), which underlies the majority of human speech sounds. The 'glottalic' airstream mechanism, as its name suggests, uses the movement of the glottis (the aperture between the VOCAL CORDS) as the source of energy (cf. GLOTTAL). The 'velaric' airstream mechanism, also as its name suggests, involves an airflow produced by a movement of the BACK of the TONGUE against the velum (cf. VELAR). It is also possible to start air vibrating using other movable parts of the vocal tract, such as the cheeks or the oesophagus, but these are not methods used in normal speech production. The use of the cheeks produces a 'buccal' voice (the basis for the Donald Duck effect); the 'oesophageal' voice is characteristic of the speech taught to people who have had their larynx surgically removed.

Aktionsart see ASPECT

alethic A term derived from modal logic and used by some LINGUISTS as part of a theoretical framework for the analysis of MODAL VERBS and related STRUCTURES in LANGUAGE. **Alethic modality** is concerned with the necessary or contingent truth of propositions, e.g. the use of the modals in sentences such as *The car must be ready*, i.e. 'It follows from what is known (e.g. that the car is outside) that it is ready.' It contrasts with EPISTEMIC and DEONTIC modality, which would interpret this sentence respectively as 'It is surely the case that the car is ready' and 'I oblige you to ensure that the car is ready'.

algorithm An application in LINGUISTICS and PHONETICS of the general use of this term in cybernetics, computing, etc., referring to a procedure devised to carry out a complicated operation by breaking it down into a precisely specified sequence of simpler operations, as in the flow chart of a computer program. The main use of this reasoning in linguistics is found in the analytic statements of a GENERATIVE GRAMMAR.

alienable A term used in GRAMMATICAL analysis to refer to a type of possessive relationship formally MARKED in some languages (e.g. Chinese). If a possessed item is seen as having only a temporary or non-essential dependence on a possessor, it is said to be 'alienable', whereas if its relationship to the possessor is a permanent or necessary one, it is **inalienable**. Distinctions of **alienable possession** are not MORPHOLOGICALLY marked in English, but SEMANTICALLY the contrast can be seen in *the boy's book* (alienable) and *the boy's leg* (inalienable).

allative A term used in GRAMMATICAL DESCRIPTION to refer to a type of INFLECTION which expresses the meaning of motion 'to' or 'towards' a place. The allative CASE is found in Finnish, for example, along with ILLATIVE, ADESSIVE and several other cases expressing 'local' temporal and spatial meanings.

allo- A prefix used generally in LINGUISTICS to refer to any noticeable variation in the FORM of a linguistic UNIT which does not affect that unit's FUNCTIONAL identity in the language. The formal variation noted is not linguistically distinctive, i.e. no change of MEANING is involved. The written language, for example, consists of a series of letters, or GRAPHEMES, but each of these graphemes can be written in several different ways, depending on such matters as linguistic CONTEXT, choice of type, handwriting variation, and so on, e.g. 'a letter A' may appear as *A, a,* a, *a*, etc. Each of these possibilities is a graphic VARIANT of the abstract grapheme ⟨A⟩: they are all **allographs** of the grapheme ⟨A⟩. The identity of the word *cat* stays the same, regardless of whether it is written *cat, cAt, cat*, etc. (though not all of these would be equally acceptable).

The first relationship of this kind to be established was in PHONOLOGY, viz. the relationship of **allophones** to PHONEMES. The phonemes of a language are abstractions, and the particular phonetic shape they take depends on many factors, especially their position in relation to other sounds in a sentence (cf. COMPLEMENTARY DISTRIBUTION). The English phoneme /t/ for example, is usually articulated in ALVEOLAR position (as in *eight*), but it may occur in DENTAL position, as in *eighth*, where it has been influenced by the place of articulation of the *th* sound following. We would thus talk of the alveolar and dental allophones of /t/ in this example. Many allophones are always in principle possible for any phoneme, given the wide range of idiosyncratic pronunciations which exist in a speech community (cf. FREE variation). Textbooks provide information about the major variants, viz. those clearly conditioned by linguistic or social (e.g. ACCENT) contexts. From a terminological point of view, one may also refer to the above phenomenon as an **allophonic variant** of a phoneme (sometimes simply a 'phonetic variant' or a 'sub-phonemic variant'). The relationship between allophones and phonemes is one of REALIZATION: a phoneme is 'realized' by its allophones. The differences between allophones can be stated using phonological RULES.

Later, the notion of variant units in GRAMMAR was established, on analogy with the allophone/phoneme distinction. Many of the MORPHEMES of the language appear in different forms, depending on the context in which they appear. The morpheme which expresses plurality in English, for instance, appears in several variants: *cap–caps, log–logs, force–forces, mouse–mice, sheep–sheep*, etc. Each of these variant forms – the voiceless [s] of *caps*, the voiced [z] of *logs*, the irregular shape of *mice*, and so on – would be said to be an **allomorph** of the plural morpheme. They have also been referred to as **morpheme** (or **morphemic) alternants.**

These are the main allo- terms which have been introduced, all opposed to an -emic term, and the suggestion has been made that this relationship, of allo- to -eme, is an important explanatory principle in linguistic analysis. Certainly many other such allo- relationships have been postulated since the terminology was first introduced in the 1930s. Some are **allochrone** (non-distinctive variant of a minimal unit of length, or CHRONEME), **allokine** (non-distinctive variant of a KINEME, i.e. a minimal unit of body movement, such as a gesture or facial expression) and **alloseme** (non-distinctive variant of a minimal unit of meaning, or SEMEME). None has proved to be as useful as allophone or allomorph, however, and the extent to which this terminology is helpful when applied to such other areas of linguistic analysis – and to behavioural analysis generally, as in the classification of units of dance, song, taste, movement – is disputed.

alphabetism see ABBREVIATION

alpha movement (α movement) An alternative term for MOVE ALPHA.

alpha notation A TRANSCRIPTIONAL convention in GENERATIVE LINGUISTICS which makes it possible to simplify the statement of a RULE by introducing a variable. In generative PHONOLOGY, for example, it is used in cases where there is a mutual predictability between sets of FEATURES, and avoids the necessity of having to make separate statements for the conditions of occurrence of each feature. For example, in order to state that a VOICED PLOSIVE in a language is always ROUNDED whereas a voiceless plosive is always unrounded, one can conflate the two rules by using the variable α to stand for the two possible correlations [+voice] ~ [+round] and [−voice] ~ [−round], viz. [α voice] ⇛ [α round]. Several developments of this convention will be encountered in this approach to phonology, including the use of other variables.

alternating (in metrical phonology) see METRICAL GRID

alternation (alternant) A term used in LINGUISTICS to refer to the relationship which exists between the alternative FORMS, or VARIANTS, of a linguistic UNIT. The usual symbol for alternation is ~. In PHONOLOGY, for example, the related VOWEL QUALITIES of such words as *telegraph ~ telegraphic, receive ~ reception* are sometimes described as alternants, as are the various ALLOphones of a PHONEME. The term has had particular currency in MORPHOLOGY, however, where 'morphemic/morpheme alternant' is another term for allomorph, and where various subtypes have been distinguished. For example, 'phonologically conditioned alternants' are illustrated in the various forms of the plural MORPHEME (/-s/, /-z/, /-ɪz/), which are predictable from the preceding phonological context ('MORPHOPHONEMIC alternants'). 'Grammatically conditioned alternants' are cases where there is no such rationale, the occurrence of an alternant depending entirely on the particular morphemes which occur in its environment, as in the various forms of the past participle in English (*frozen, jumped*, etc.). SUPPLETION is another category of alternation, referring to a morpheme lacking *any* regular phonological correspondence with other forms in a PARADIGM, as in *go* ~ *went*. In SYNTAX, examples of sets of alternants can be seen in the various grammatical CATEGORIES, such as TENSE (e.g. present ~ past ~ future).

alveolar A term in the classification of CONSONANT sounds on the basis of their PLACE OF ARTICULATION: it refers to a sound made by the BLADE of the TONGUE (or the TIP and blade together) in contact against the **alveolar ridge** (or 'alveolum'), which is the bony prominence immediately behind the upper teeth. A number of sounds are given an alveolar articulation in English – [t], [d], [l], [n], [s] and [z]. If the sound is articulated towards the back of the alveolar ridge, near where the palate begins, the term **post-alveolar** can be used. In English the *r* in *red, trip, drill* is articulated in POST-alveolar position.

alveo(lo)-palatal A term used in the PHONETIC classification of speech sounds on the basis of their PLACE OF ARTICULATION: it refers to a sound made by the FRONT of the TONGUE a little in advance of the PALATAL articulatory area, i.e. in the direction of ALVEOLAR articulations. Only two such sounds are distinguished in the INTERNATIONAL PHONETIC ALPHABET, the FRICATIVES [ɕ] and [ʑ], which occur for example in Polish.

ambifix see AFFIX

ambiguity (ambiguous) The general sense of this term, referring to a WORD or SENTENCE which expresses more than one MEANING, is found in LINGUISTICS, but several types of ambiguity are recognized. The most widely discussed type in recent years is **grammatical** (or **structural**) **ambiguity**. In PHRASE-STRUCTURE ambiguity, alternative CONSTITUENT STRUCTURES can be assigned to a CONSTRUCTION, as in *new houses and shops*, which could be analysed either as *new* [*houses and shops*] (i.e. both are new) or [*new houses*] *and shops* (i.e. only the houses are new). In TRANSFORMATIONAL ambiguity, the alternative SEMANTIC representations can be shown only by relating the ambiguous sentence to different structures. For example, *Visiting speakers can be awful* is relatable to either *It is awful to visit speakers* or *Speakers who visit are awful*. A sentence with more than two structural interpretations is said to be **multiply ambiguous**. An analysis which demonstrates the ambiguity in a sentence is said to DISAMBIGUATE the sentence. Ambiguity which does not arise from the grammatical analysis of a sentence, but is due solely to the alternative meanings of an individual LEXICAL ITEM, is referred to as **lexical ambiguity**, e.g. *I found the table fascinating* (='object of furniture' or 'table of figures' – cf. POLYSEMY). In semantic discussion, a distinction is sometimes drawn between 'ambiguity' and 'vagueness': an ambiguous sentence is formulated as having more than one distinct structure; a vague sentence, on the other hand, permits an unspecifiable range of possible interpretations (i.e. is unstateable in syntactic or PHONOLOGICAL terms). For example, deciding on the implications of a NEGATIVE sentence such as *He didn't hit the dog* is a matter of vagueness, in this view, in that it is not possible to state specifically a fixed number of different underlying structures involved in its interpretation. (*What* **did** *he hit? Did he do something else to the dog?*) See also SCOPE.

ambisyllabicity (ambisyllab-ic, -ify, -ification) A principle in models of NON-LINEAR PHONOLOGY (notably, METRICAL PHONOLOGY) which allows INTERVOCALIC CONSONANTS to be members of both adjacent SYLLABLES, in the UNDERLYING syllabification of a LANGUAGE, while conforming to the language's syllable structure TEMPLATE.

amelioration In HISTORICAL LINGUISTICS, a term used in the classification of types of SEMANTIC change, referring to the loss of an earlier SENSE of disapproval in a LEXICAL item; opposed to DETERIORATION. For example, *mischievous* has lost its strong sense of 'disastrous' and now means the milder 'playfully annoying'.

amplitude A term derived from the study of the physics of sound, and used in ACOUSTIC PHONETICS, referring to the extent to which an air particle moves to and fro around its rest point in a sound wave. The greater the amplitude, the greater the INTENSITY of a sound, and (along with other factors, such as FUNDAMENTAL FREQUENCY and DURATION) the greater the sensation of LOUDNESS.

anacoluthon A traditional rhetorical term, sometimes encountered in LINGUISTIC studies of conversational speech. It refers to a SYNTACTIC break in the expected GRAMMATICAL sequence within a SENTENCE, as when a sentence begins with one CONSTRUCTION and remains unfinished, e.g. *The man came and – are you listening?* 'Anacolutha' have come to be especially noticed in recent linguistic studies as an area of PERFORMANCE features which a grammar of a language would aim to exclude.

analogy A term used in HISTORICAL and COMPARATIVE LINGUISTICS, and in LANGUAGE ACQUISITION, referring to a process of regularization which affects the exceptional forms in the GRAMMAR of a language. The influence of the REGULAR pattern of plural formation in English, for example, can be heard in the treatment of irregular forms in the early UTTERANCES of children, e.g. *mens, mans, mouses*: the children are producing these forms 'on analogy with' the regular pattern. DIALECTS also often illustrate analogical processes at work, which the STANDARD language has so far resisted, e.g. *goed/seed/knowed* for *went/saw/knew*, etc., and this process is, of course, common in the ERRORS of foreign learners of the language. Processes of 'analogical creation' are one of the main tendencies in the history of languages, as when VERBS which had an irregular past TENSE form in Old English came to be produced with the regular *-ed* ending, e.g. *healp* becoming *helped*.

analysable (un-) A term used in GENERATIVE GRAMMAR to refer to the characteristic of a STRING in relation to a TRANSFORMATION. If the string meets the STRUCTURAL DESCRIPTION (SD) of the transformational RULE, it is said to be 'analysable', and the rule is thereby applicable. For example, for the PASSIVE rule to operate (in one formulation), the following SD is required: NP–Aux–V–NP. A string such as *the boy is kicking the ball* would thus be 'analysable', with respect to this rule; *the boy has gone*, on the other hand, would not meet the SD of the rule, and would thereby be **unanalysable**.

analysis-by-synthesis A theory of SPEECH PERCEPTION which credits listeners with an internal, language-specific mechanism that responds to incoming speech by selecting certain ACOUSTIC cues, and then attempting to synthesize a replica of the input. When this is achieved, the synthesis has, in effect, carried out an analysis of the input. Such a procedure, it is argued, has the merit of being able to explain how listeners resolve the acoustic variability in signals, stemming from the differences between speakers, contexts, etc.

analytic(ity) (1) A type of language established by COMPARATIVE LINGUISTICS using STRUCTURAL (as opposed to DIACHRONIC) criteria, and focusing on the characteristics of the WORD: in 'analytic' languages, all the words are invariable (and SYNTACTIC relationships are shown primarily by WORD ORDER). The term is seen in opposition to SYNTHETIC (and sometimes also POLYSYNTHETIC) languages (which include AGGLUTINATIVE and INFLECTING types), where words typically contain more than one MORPHEME. Several languages of South-East Asia illustrate analyticity in their word structure. As always in such classifications, the categories are not clear-cut: different languages will display the characteristic of analyticity to a greater or lesser degree.

(2) Considerable use is made in SEMANTICS of the sense of 'analytic' found in logic and philosophy, where an **analytic proposition/sentence** is one whose GRAMMATICAL FORM and LEXICAL MEANING make it necessarily true, e.g. *Spinsters are unmarried women*. The term contrasts with SYNTHETIC, where the truth of the proposition is established using empirical criteria.

anaphor A term used in recent GOVERNMENT-BINDING THEORY to refer to a type of NOUN PHRASE which has no independent REFERENCE, but refers to some other sentence CONSTITUENT (its ANTECEDENT). Anaphors include REFLEXIVE PRONOUNS (e.g. *myself*), RECIPROCAL pronouns (e.g. *each other*), and NP-TRACES. Along with PRONOMINALS and LEXICAL noun phrases (R-EXPRESSIONS), anaphors are of particular importance as part of a theory of BINDING: in this context, an anaphor must be bound in its GOVERNING category. The term has a more restricted application than the traditional term ANAPHORIC.

anaphora (anaphoric) A term used in GRAMMATICAL description for the process or result of a linguistic UNIT deriving its interpretation from some previously expressed unit or meaning (the ANTECEDENT). **Anaphoric reference** is one way of marking the identity between what is being expressed and what has already been expressed. In such a sentence as *He did that there*, each word has an anaphoric reference (i.e. they are **anaphoric substitutes**, or simply **anaphoric words**): the previous sentence might have been *John painted this picture in Bermuda*, for instance, and each word in the response would be anaphorically related to a corresponding unit in the preceding CONTEXT. Anaphora is often contrasted with CATAPHORA (where the words refer forward), and sometimes with DEIXIS or EXOPHORA (where the words refer directly to the extralinguistic SITUATION). It may, however, also be found subsuming both forwards- and backwards-referring functions. See also ZERO.

anaptyxis (anaptyctic) A term used in COMPARATIVE PHILOLOGY, and sometimes in PHONOLOGY, to refer to a type of INTRUSION, where an extra VOWEL has been inserted between two CONSONANTS; a type of EPENTHESIS. **Anaptyctic vowels** are also known as **parasite vowels** or **svarabhakti vowels** (the latter term reflecting the occurrence of this phenomenon in Sanskrit). An example is the pronunciation of *film* as [ˈfɪləm] in some dialects of English.

anchor(-ing, -ed) In NON-LINEAR PHONOLOGY, an application of the general use of this term to refer to a UNIT on which some other unit depends. For example, ROOT NODES are said to serve as 'anchors' for the FEATURES which define a SEGMENT, and a segment to which another segment ASSOCIATES is said to be its 'anchor'. A unit which is not 'anchored' may be said to be FLOATING. The term has a special application in PROSODIC MORPHOLOGY, in the context of the phonological analysis of REDUPLICATION, where 'anchoring' is a CONSTRAINT which places a structural restriction on the relation between the base (B) and the reduplicant (R): in R+B sequences, the initial element in R is identical to the initial element in B; and in B+R sequences, the final element in R is identical to the final element in B.

animate (in-, -ness) A term used in the GRAMMATICAL classification of words (especially NOUNS) to refer to a subclass whose REFERENCE is to persons and animals, as opposed to inanimate entities and concepts. In some languages, distinctions of **animateness** are made MORPHOLOGICALLY, as a contrast in GENDER. In English, the distinction can be made only on SEMANTIC grounds, apart from a certain correspondence with personal and relative PRONOUNS (*he/she/who v. it/which*). In adjectives expressing the concept 'old', for example, *elderly* is animate, *antique* inanimate; *old* is neutral, being applicable to either category.

antecedent A term taken over from TRADITIONAL GRAMMAR by some grammarians, and used for a linguistic UNIT from which another unit in the SENTENCE derives its interpretation (ANAPHORIC REFERENCE), typically a later unit. In particular, personal and relative PRONOUNS are said to refer back to their antecedents, as in *The car* ***which*** *was parked . . .* ***It*** *was . . .*

anterior One of the features of sound set up by CHOMSKY and Halle in their DISTINCTIVE FEATURE theory of PHONOLOGY, to handle variations in PLACE OF ARTICULATION (CAVITY features). Anterior sounds are defined articulatorily as those produced with a STRICTURE in front of the PALATO-ALVEOLAR area in the mouth. LABIAL and DENTAL consonants are [+anterior] (abbreviated as [+ant]). Its opposite is **non-anterior**, referring to sounds produced without such a stricture, as in VELAR, GLOTTAL and VOWEL sounds, which are [−anterior] ([−ant]).

anthropological linguistics A branch of LINGUISTICS which studies language variation and use in relation to human cultural patterns and beliefs, as investigated using the theories and methods of anthropology. For example, it studies the way in which linguistic features may identify a member of a (usually primitive) community with a social, religious, occupational or kinship group. The term overlaps to some degree with ETHNOLINGUISTICS and SOCIOLINGUISTICS, reflecting the overlapping interests of the correlative disciplines involved – anthropology, ethnology and sociology. It is also known as **linguistic anthropology**.

anthropophonics A term suggested by Polish linguist Jan Baudoin de Courtenay (1845–1929) for the study of the physical potential for sound production in the human vocal apparatus. The field includes the physical comparison of VOCAL TRACTS and individual ARTICULATING organs in ethnic or racial populations, to determine whether anatomical differences (e.g. TONGUE size) have any PHONETIC or PHONOLOGICAL consequences. Differences between the sexes and changes with age are also included. One of the general aims of the field is to determine the principles on which the selection of the sounds in individual languages might be based in the course of human evolution. The term is not used by all phoneticians, many of whom see its subject-matter as simply a part of phonetics.

anticipation A term used by some PSYCHOLINGUISTS to refer to a type of TONGUE-SLIP where a later LINGUISTIC UNIT is anticipated, as when *catch the ball* might become *batch the call.*

anticipatory (1) A term used in PHONETICS and PHONOLOGY as part of the classification of types of ASSIMILATION. In **anticipatory** (or 'regressive') **assimilation**, a sound changes because of the influence of the following sound, as when [t] becomes [k] in *hot cakes.* It is opposed to PROGRESSIVE and COALESCENT assimilations.

(2) The term is also used with reference to the commonest type of COARTICULATION (**anticipatory coarticulation**), wherein an ARTICULATOR not involved in a particular sound begins to move in the direction of a TARGET articulation needed for a later sound in the UTTERANCE. An example is the NASALIZATION which can be heard on VOWELS followed by a nasal CONSONANT, when the soft PALATE begins to lower in anticipation of the consonant during the articulation of the vowel.

(3) In GRAMMAR, the term is sometimes used for the kind of *it* found in EXTRAPOSITION, where it corresponds to a later item in the SENTENCE, e.g. ***It** was nice to see her.* This **anticipatory *it*** (or 'anticipatory SUBJECT') is also referred to as 'extrapositive' or 'preparatory' *it*, and is distinguished from the PROP or DUMMY *it* found in *It was raining*, etc. The term is also occasionally used for the use of *there* in EXISTENTIAL sentences (**anticipatory *there***), e.g. ***There** were several people in the room.*

antipassive In GRAMMAR, a term used to characterize a type of VOICE in ERGATIVE languages (e.g. Dyirbal) which is the functional equivalent of the PASSIVE in non-ergative languages. In these languages, the TOPIC of a clause is usually the PATIENT, not (as in English) the ACTOR, and the antipassive construction handles cases where the actor is chosen as topic. Antipassive forms are formally more complex than the corresponding ergative forms, with the VERB marked by a derivational SUFFIX.

antonym(y) A term used in SEMANTICS as part of the study of oppositeness of MEANING. 'Antonymy' is one of a set of SENSE relations recognized in some analyses of meaning, along with SYNONYMY, HYPONYMY, INCOMPATIBILITY and others. In its most general sense, it refers collectively to all types of semantic oppositeness, with various subdivisions then being made (e.g. between **graded antonyms**, such as *big* ~ *small*, where there are degrees of difference, and **ungraded antonyms**, such as *single* ~ *married*, where there is an either/or contrast). Some linguists (e.g. the British linguist John Lyons (b. 1932)) have reserved the term for a particular type of oppositeness: graded antonyms are referred to as 'antonyms', the other type just illustrated being referred to as COMPLEMENTARIES. It is a matter of controversy how many types of opposites one should usefully recognize in semantic analysis, and the use of the term 'antonym' must always be viewed with caution.

aorist(ic) A term used in the GRAMMATICAL description of some languages, referring to a form of the verb with distinctive past TENSE or ASPECTUAL functions, especially expressing the lack of any particular completion, duration, or repetition. For example, in Ancient Greek, the aorist is chiefly a past tense in the INDICATIVE MOOD, but expresses aspectual meanings in other moods. In the TRADITIONAL grammar of some modern languages (e.g. Bulgarian) it is restricted to perfectivity in the past tense. The term **aoristic** is sometimes used in place of 'perfective' as part of the cross-linguistic discussion of aspect.

A-over-A A term introduced by Noam CHOMSKY (see *Language and Mind*, 1968) to characterize a CONDITION imposed on the operation of certain GRAMMATICAL TRANSFORMATIONS. The **A-over-A principle** (or **condition**) states that if a transformation applies to a STRUCTURE of the form $[_S \ldots [_A \ldots]_A \ldots]_S$ then for any category A it must be interpreted as applying to the maximal PHRASE of the type A. For example, the SENTENCE *John kept the car in the garage* is AMBIGUOUS: it can mean either 'It was in the garage that John kept the car' or 'The car in the garage was kept by John' (cf. 'the car in the street by Mary', etc.). The sentence can be DISAMBIGUATED by such INTERROGATIVES as *How much did the car in the garage cost?*, which relates only to the second of these, i.e. to the sentence where the phrase *in the garage* is part of the larger NOUN phrase. The A-over-A principle claims that any transformational operation applying to *car* will also apply to *garage*. The reference given above illustrates other types of construction which evidence the need for a condition of this sort. However, the application of the principle has encountered several types of exception, and its generality has turned out to be more restricted than had been expected.

aperiodic see PERIOD

aperture A term used in various models of NON-LINEAR PHONOLOGY to handle CONTRASTS involving OPENNESS of ARTICULATION. In PARTICLE PHONOLOGY, for example, aperture is a PRIVATIVE feature (particle) representing openness, and symbolized by [a]. Differences in vowel height are characterized by combinations of aperture particles: for example, combining [a] with palatal [i] results in a relatively open PALATAL vowel, such as [e]. In a CONSTRICTION model of phonology, aperture refers to the degree of constriction imposed on a VOCOID (a VOWEL or a GLIDE), which dominates vowel height features. It is one of the two main parameters of classification for vocoids (the other being PLACE). The superordinate node is called the **aperture node**. In some approaches, CONTOUR segments have been analysed as sequences of aperture nodes. A threefold classification is recognized: the total absence of oral airflow (as in oral STOPS), a degree of aperture sufficient to produce air turbulence (as in FRICATIVES), and a degree of aperture insufficient to produce turbulence (as in oral SONORANTS).

apex (apic-al, -o) A term used in PHONETICS for the end point of the TONGUE (also known as the TIP), used in the ARTICULATION of a few speech sounds, such as the TRILLED [r], or some varieties of DENTAL (sc. 'apico-dental') sounds. Such sounds could then be classified as **apical**.

aphaeresis (aphesis, aphetic) A term used in COMPARATIVE PHILOLOGY, and sometimes in modern PHONOLOGY, to refer to the DELETION of an INITIAL sound in a WORD; often contrasted with SYNCOPE and APOCOPE. Examples include the historical loss of /k/ in *knife* and such contractions as *I've*. **Aphesis** is a type of aphaeresis – the loss of an unstressed vowel at the beginning of a word (*'gain*).

apico- see APEX

apocope A term used in COMPARATIVE PHILOLOGY, and sometimes in modern PHONOLOGY, to refer to the DELETION of the final element in a WORD; often contrasted with APHAERESIS and SYNCOPE. Examples include the pronunciation of *an* as /ən/ or of *of* as /ə/ in such phrases as *snakes and ladders* or *cup of tea*.

apodosis In TRADITIONAL GRAMMAR, and sometimes now in SEMANTICS, a term which refers to the consequence or result expressed in the MAIN CLAUSE of a CONDITIONAL sentence; opposed to **protasis**. In the sentence *We shall get in if we queue, we shall get in* is the apodosis, *if we queue* is the protasis.

appellative see EPONYM

appendix see EXTRASYLLABIC (1)

application (applicab-le, -ility) (1) A term used by some LINGUISTS to refer to the overall relationship which exists between LANGUAGE and non-linguistic entities, situations, etc. The 'application' of a linguistic UNIT is its use in a specific CONTEXT; a unit is said to be 'applicable' to that context. For example, a LEXICAL ITEM may be applied to a range of situations (none of which would constitute part of its normal DENOTATION OF REFERENCE), e.g. *heap* being applied to a car, a house, a sculpture. The term is particularly useful in the context of translation, where pairs of apparently equivalent terms turn out to have different ranges of application; e.g. the use of *merci* in French differs from the use of *thank you* in English. If items from different languages totally correspond in the range of situations where they may be used, they are said to have the same application.

(2) **Applicational grammar** is the name given to a type of CATEGORIAL GRAMMAR proposed by the Russian linguist S. K. Šaumjan (b. 1916). Its basic units are term (α) and sentence (β).

applicative In GRAMMAR, a type of double-OBJECT construction in some languages (roughly corresponding to the DIRECT/indirect object construction in English). An applicative AFFIX on the verb encodes as objects a range of ROLES, such as BENEFACTIVE and LOCATIVE. The construction can be analysed as a type of VOICE, in which the focus is on the types of object rather than on the relationship between SUBJECT and object. Applicatives are widely found in Bantu languages.

applied linguistics A branch of LINGUISTICS where the primary concern is the application of linguistic theories, methods and findings to the elucidation of LANGUAGE problems which have arisen in other areas of experience. The most well-developed branch of applied linguistics is the teaching and learning of foreign languages, and sometimes the term is used as if this were the only field involved. But several other fields of application have emerged in recent years, including the linguistic analysis of language disorders (CLINICAL LINGUISTICS), the use of language in mother-tongue education (EDUCATIONAL LINGUISTICS), and developments in LEXICOGRAPHY, translation and STYLISTICS. There is an uncertain boundary between applied linguistics and the various interdisciplinary branches of linguistics, such as SOCIOLINGUISTICS and PSYCHOLINGUISTICS, especially as several of the latter's concerns involve practical outcomes of a plainly 'applied' kind (e.g. planning a national language policy). On the other hand, as these branches develop their own theoretical foundations, the distinction between 'pure' and 'applied' is becoming more apparent, and the characterization of research as being in 'applied psycholinguistics', etc., is now more regularly encountered. See also PRAGMATICS.

apposition(al) A traditional term retained in some models of GRAMMATICAL description for a sequence of units which are CONSTITUENTS at the same grammatical LEVEL, and which have an identity or similarity of REFERENCE. In *John Smith, the butcher, came in*, for example, there are two NOUN PHRASES; they have identity of reference; and they have the same SYNTACTIC function (as indicated by the omissibility of either, without this affecting the sentence's ACCEPTABILITY, e.g. *John Smith came in/The butcher came in*). There are, however, many theoretical and methodological problems in defining the notion of apposition, because of the existence of several constructions which satisfy only some of these criteria, and where other SEMANTIC or syntactic issues are involved, as in titles and other designations (*the number six , my friend John*, etc.). Sometimes the term **appositive relative** is used as an alternative to non-RESTRICTIVE RELATIVE.

appropriate(ness) An application of the general sense of this term in LINGUISTICS, and especially in SOCIOLINGUISTICS, PRAGMATICS and STYLISTICS, to refer to a linguistic VARIETY or FORM which is considered suitable or possible in a given social situation. For example, ELLIPTICAL and CONTRACTED forms (e.g. *I'll, isn't, going to lunch?*, etc.) are appropriate for relatively informal conversational situations; forms such as *thou, vouchsafe*, etc., are appropriate for some kinds of religious situations. The point of the term is to provide an alternative to the absolute implications of CORRECTNESS encountered in PRESCRIPTIVE approaches to language, where linguistic forms are held to be either right or wrong, no reference being made to the different expectations of different situations. In pragmatics, appropriateness conditions for sentences are generally referred to as FELICITY CONDITIONS.

approximant A general term used by some PHONETICIANS in the classification of speech sounds on the basis of their MANNER OF ARTICULATION, and corresponding to what in other approaches would be called FRICTIONLESS CONTINUANTS, i.e. [w], [j], [r], [l], and all VOWELS. The term is based on the ARTICULATIONS involved, in that one articulator approaches another, but the degree of narrowing involved does not produce audible friction. In some analyses, [h] would also be considered an approximant (i.e. the voiceless equivalent of the VOWEL following).

arbitrariness (arbitrary) A suggested defining property of human LANGUAGE (contrasting with the properties of other SEMIOTIC systems) whereby LINGUISTIC

FORMS are said to lack any physical correspondence with the entities in the world to which they refer. For example, there is nothing in the word *table* which reflects the shape, etc., of the thing. The relationship between sound and meaning is said to be 'arbitrary' – or 'conventional', as classical tradition puts it. By contrast, some words in a language may be partly or wholly ICONIC, i.e. they do reflect properties of the non-linguistic world, e.g. onomatopoeic expressions, such as *splash, murmur, mumble.*

arbitrary reference A term used in GENERATIVE GRAMMAR, especially in GOVERNMENT-BINDING THEORY, in connection with the understood SUBJECT of certain INFINITIVES, represented by big PRO. For example, in *It's easy PRO to annoy John*, the infinitive has an empty PRO subject which is not CONTROLLED (i.e. it is not CO-REFERENTIAL with some other NOUN PHRASE in the SENTENCE), but is interpreted as 'for anyone'. The reference in such a case is arbitrary.

arboreal A term sometimes used in GENERATIVE LINGUISTICS to describe a TREE structure. In METRICAL PHONOLOGY, an **arboreal grid** is a modification of the metrical TREE in which HEADS are vertically aligned with their mother constituent NODES, resulting in a grid-like HIERARCHICAL configuration of heads.

arc A convention used in RELATIONAL GRAMMAR to represent a directional DEPENDENCY relation between a SYNTACTIC UNIT (or GOVERNOR) and the entities which constitute the relational STRUCTURE of that unit. The 'arcs' in a 'relational network' are represented by curved arrows; alternatively, the dependency relations can be shown as a dependency TREE. Arcs are also an important device in NETWORK grammars. Relationships can be postulated between pairs of arcs, and these pairs of arcs can then in turn be interrelated in 'pair networks' (as is found in **arc-pair grammar**, a formalized development of relational grammar proposed in the mid-1970s).

archiphoneme A term used in PHONOLOGY referring to a way of handling the problem of NEUTRALIZATION (i.e. when the CONTRAST between PHONEMES is lost in certain positions in a WORD). In such cases as PLOSIVES following initial /s-/, where there is no OPPOSITION (e.g. there is no **sgin* to contrast with *skin*), the problem for the phonologist is how to analyse the second element of these words. To choose either the voiceless TRANSCRIPTION /skɪn/ or the voiced one /sgɪn/ would be to attribute the element with a contrastive status it does not possess. The solution suggested by the PRAGUE SCHOOL phonologist Nikolai Trubetskoy (1890–1939) was to set up a new category for such cases, which he called an archiphoneme, and to transcribe it with a different symbol. A capital letter is sometimes used, e.g. /sKɪn/. Alternative ways of analysing the problem have been suggested, as in MORPHOPHONEMIC approaches.

archistratum A term sometimes used in SOCIOLINGUISTICS, referring to a privileged VARIETY of language from which a community draws its cultured or intellectual vocabulary. For example, Classical Arabic is used as an archistratum throughout the Islamic world.

area(l) A term used in DIALECTOLOGY for any geographical region isolated on the basis of its LINGUISTIC characteristics. The study of the linguistic properties of 'areas' – the analysis of the divergent FORMS they contain, and their historical antecedents – is known as **areal linguistics**. An **areal classification** would establish **areal types** (or **groups**), such as the Scandinavian languages, or the London-influenced dialects – cases where it is possible to show certain linguistic features in common as a result of the proximity of the SPEECH communities. Such a classification often cuts across that made on purely historical grounds. It is often possible to identify a **focal area** – the region from which these linguistic characteristics have spread to the area as a whole (as in the case of London) – and several other significant parts of an area have been terminologically distinguished, e.g. the **transitional areas** which occur between adjacent areas, the **relic areas** which preserve linguistic features of an earlier stage of development. Areal linguistics is contrasted with **non-areal** differences in language use, e.g. contrasts between male and female speech, and between some social VARIETIES. The German term *Sprachbund* ('language league') is also widely used in the sense of a 'linguistic area'.

argument A term used in PREDICATE calculus, and often found in the discussion of SEMANTIC theory, to refer to the relationship of a name to the simple PROPOSITION of which it is a part. For example, in the proposition, *the boy is naughty, the boy* is an 'argument' of the proposition. In CASE GRAMMAR, each underlying proposition is analysed in terms of a predicate word and an unordered set of argument slots, each of which is labelled according to its semantic ('case') relationship with the predicate word. In recent GENERATIVE GRAMMAR, the term is used to refer to any NOUN PHRASE POSITION within a sentence (i.e. functioning as SUBJECT, OBJECT, etc.). In GOVERNMENT-BINDING THEORY, an argument is an expression with a THETA ROLE, and the position to which a theta role can be assigned is called an **A(rgument)-position**. The preservation of argument structure under morphological operations is termed **inheritance** (e.g. verb-derived nouns in *-ing* allow inheritance of all the input verb's arguments, as in *the putting of the ladder against the wall*). A **preferred argument structure** is a demonstrable DISCOURSE preference in a language for the use of a particular syntactic structure – for example, a tendency for lexical NPs to appear as the subject of an intransitive verb rather than of a transitive verb.

arrangement A term used in LINGUISTICS to refer to any SEQUENCE of linguistic ELEMENTS in terms of their relative position, or DISTRIBUTION, e.g. the possible combinations of PHONEMES within SYLLABLES and WORDS, or of MORPHEMES within words and SENTENCES. This notion is fundamental to the ITEM-AND-ARRANGEMENT model of linguistic description.

article A term used in the GRAMMATICAL classification of WORDS, referring to a subclass of DETERMINERS which displays a primary role in differentiating the uses of NOUNS, e.g. *the/a* in English. Many languages have no article system (e.g. Russian). Of those which do, a distinction is usually made into **definite** and **indefinite** (or 'non-definite') types, partly on SEMANTIC and partly on grammatical grounds. Articles may appear before the noun (as in English), or after (as in Swedish). See also ZERO.

articulation (articulat-e, -or(y)) (1) The general term in PHONETICS for the physiological movements involved in modifying an airflow to produce the various types of speech sounds, using the VOCAL TRACT above the LARYNX. Sounds are classified in terms of their PLACE and MANNER OF ARTICULATION in the vocal apparatus. Reference is usually made to the nature of the AIRSTREAM MECHANISM, the action of the VOCAL CORDS, the position of the soft PALATE, and the other organs in the mouth – TONGUE and lips in particular. Any specific part of the vocal apparatus involved in the production of a sound is called an **articulator**. Two kinds of articulators are distinguished: 'active' articulators are the movable parts of the vocal apparatus, such as the lips, tongue and lower jaw; 'passive' articulators are those parts of the vocal tract which cannot move, but which provide the active articulators with points of reference, e.g. the roof of the mouth, the upper teeth.

In recent years, the study of articulation using instrumental techniques has emphasized the importance of seeing articulation not as a sequence of independently articulated sounds but as a continuum of sound production. This principle is obscured through the use of phonetic TRANSCRIPTION. The transcription [kæt] suggests the existence of three DISCRETE segments: what it obscures is the existence of the TRANSITIONS between segments, as the several articulators, working simultaneously, gradually move from one articulatory position to the next. Forms of transcription which draw attention to these continuously varying (DYNAMIC) parameters are devisable, but they are complex, and lack the immediate readability of the SEGMENTAL transcription.

Several types of articulation can be distinguished. Most sounds are produced with a single point of articulation. Sounds may, however, be produced involving two points of articulation (COARTICULATION), in which case two articulatory possibilities emerge: the two points of articulation both contribute equally to the identity of the sound ('double articulation' or 'co-ordinate coarticulation'); or one point of articulation may be the dominant one (the 'primary (co-) articulation'), the other having a lesser degree of stricture (the 'secondary (co-) articulation'). Examples of secondary articulation are PALATALIZATION, VELARIZATION, PHARYNGEALIZATION and LABIALIZATION.

(2) There is a second use of the phrase **double articulation**, within the linguistic theory associated with the French linguist André Martinet (b. 1908). He used the term to refer to the two LEVELS of STRUCTURE in which LANGUAGE is organized: speech can be analysed into the meaningful FORMS of language (i.e. MORPHEMES, WORDS, etc.), and this constitutes a 'first' articulation; these units are then capable of further analysis into the meaningless sound units of language (i.e. PHONEMES), and this constitutes a 'second' articulation. A corresponding term in more widespread use is DUALITY OF STRUCTURE.

articulator-based feature theory In PHONOLOGY, a development of FEATURE theory in which speech is modelled in terms of a series of independently functioning ARTICULATORS (lips, tongue front, tongue body, tongue root, soft palate, larynx), represented by NODES on separate TIERS. Articulator features are also called 'place' features, because they are grouped under the place CONSTITUENT in the feature HIERARCHY. LABIAL, CORONAL and DORSAL nodes represent single-valued features. **Articulator-bound features** depend on a specific feature for their execution, further specifying the nature of a CONSTRICTION formed by an articulator (e.g. APICAL and LAMINAL articulations are distinguished under the coronal node through the use of the features [ANTERIOR] and [DISTRIBUTED]). **Articulator-**

free features (or 'stricture features') are not restricted to a specific articulator; they identify the degree of stricture of a sound independent of the articulators involved (e.g. [+continuant] sounds represent a continuous airflow through the centre of the oral tract, regardless of the location of the major stricture). Among the claims made for this model are its ability to offer an integrated account of vowel and consonant articulation in terms of place of articulation and stricture: for example, in one model, features such as back, high, and low, as tongue-body features, are linked under the dorsal node, and rounding under the labial node.

articulator model A theory which aims to integrate PHONETICS and PHONOLOGY into a single model, providing a FEATURE analysis related to the muscular activity underlying the movements of individual ARTICULATING organs. The approach developed in the 1980s, and has influenced several later conceptions of phonology, notably feature geometry.

articulatory analog see SPEECH SYNTHESIS

articulatory phonetics The branch of PHONETICS which studies the way in which speech sounds are made ('articulated') by the VOCAL ORGANS. It derives much of its descriptive terminology from the fields of anatomy and physiology, and is sometimes referred to as 'physiological phonetics'. This area has traditionally held central place in the training of phoneticians, the movements involved being reasonably accessible to observation and, in principle, under the control of the investigator. The classification of sounds used in the INTERNATIONAL PHONETIC ALPHABET, for example, is based on articulatory variables. In recent years, there has been much progress in the development of instrumental techniques for observing and measuring such factors as TONGUE, lip, PALATE and VOCAL CORD movement, such as the palatograph, which displays tongue contact with the palate, the electro-aerometer, which measures the relative flow of air from mouth and nose, and ELECTROMYOGRAPHY, for the measurement of muscular movement while speaking. Using such techniques, a far more detailed understanding of articulation is possible than using traditional visual and kinaesthetic methods.

articulatory phonology A theory which aims to integrate PHONETICS and PHONOLOGY, using basic units of CONTRAST defined as 'gestures' – abstract characterizations of ARTICULATORY events, with an intrinsic time dimension. Utterances are modelled as organized patterns ('constellations') of gestures, in which the gestural units may overlap in time. The resulting phonological structures provide a HIERARCHY of articulatorily based natural classes, which are used to describe the phonological structure of specific languages and to account for phonological variation.

articulatory setting In PHONETICS, a global configuration of all the ARTICULATORS in relation to each other, which one adopts and maintains during speech; also called a **phonetic setting**. This accounts for some of the broad qualitative differences between LANGUAGES and DIALECTS, e.g. a characteristic NASAL twang, or marked degree of lip-ROUNDING. **Phonatory setting** is sometimes distinguished: a habitual setting of the LARYNX which results in such VOICE QUALITIES as whispery or CREAKY PHONATION. In the most general application, 'phonetic setting' refers to any tendency towards co-ordination underlying the production of a chain of speech SEGMENTS, so that a particular configuration of the vocal apparatus is maintained. It thus subsumes COARTICULATION, ASSIMILATION, VOWEL HARMONY and other such segmental features, as well as the NON-SEGMENTAL effects noted in relation to PARALANGUAGE and voice quality.

artificial language A LANGUAGE which has been invented to serve some particular purpose. Artificial languages include those which have been devised to facilitate international communication (where they are a type of AUXILIARY language, such as Esperanto), programming languages (e.g. BASIC), languages which communicate with computers or robots in artificial intelligence (e.g. SHRDLU), and simplified languages which are used by people with learning difficulties (e.g. Bliss symbols).

ascension A term used in RELATIONAL GRAMMAR for a class of relation-changing PROCESSES in which a NOUN PHRASE which is part of a larger noun phrase comes to bear the grammatical relation previously borne by the larger noun phrase.

ascriptive A term used in GRAMMATICAL analysis to refer to a SENTENCE of the type *The cat is angry*, where there is an attributive identity between the pre- and post-verbal ELEMENTS, but no permutability (unlike the otherwise similar EQUATIVE sentence – cf. **Angry is the cat*, but *Freda is the leader/The leader is Freda*). Sentences of the type *Freda is a doctor* are also sometimes called ascriptive, but are more problematic to analyse.

aspect(ual, -izer) A category used in the GRAMMATICAL description of VERBS (along with TENSE and MOOD), referring primarily to the way the grammar marks the duration or type of temporal activity denoted by the verb. A well-studied 'aspectual' CONTRAST, between PERFECTIVE and IMPERFECTIVE, is found in many Slavic languages: in Russian, for example, there is a perfective/imperfective contrast – the former often referring to the completion of an action, the latter expressing duration without specifying completion (cf. the perfective form *on pročital*, 'he read (something)', and the imperfective form *on čital*, 'he used to read/was reading (something)'. The English verb PHRASE makes a formal distinction which is usually analysed as aspectual: the contrast between PROGRESSIVE (or 'continuous') and 'non-progressive' (or SIMPLE) duration of action. The contrast between *I was living* and *I have been living*, and other uses of the *have* auxiliary, are also often analysed in aspectual terms, but this analysis is more controversial. Other English constructions have sometimes been analysed in terms of aspect, e.g. involving HABITUAL contrasts (as in *used to*); and in other languages further aspectual distinctions may be found, e.g. 'iterative' or 'frequentative' (referring to a regularly occurring action), 'inchoative' or 'inceptive' (referring to the beginning of an action). Aspectual oppositions are sometimes viewed generally as SEMANTIC distinctions, but sometimes the notion is restricted to those oppositions which have achieved a grammaticalized status in a language. In this respect, a contrast is often drawn between aspect and **Aktionsart** (German, plural **Aktionsarten**, 'kinds of action'), aspect referring to instances where the opposition has been grammaticalized, Aktionsart to instances where it has been lexicalized (especially, in Slavonic linguistics, to instances where the contrast is expressed using the language's DERIVATIONAL MORPHOLOGY). The term **aspectualizer** is sometimes used (in GENERATIVE grammar) for a formative which marks an aspectual relation. See also REALIS.

Aspects model/theory A commonly used abbreviation for the approach to GENERATIVE GRAMMAR expounded in Noam CHOMSKY's 1965 book, *Aspects of the Theory of Syntax*; also known as the STANDARD THEORY. MODELS similar in principle to this one are 'Aspects-type' models.

aspiration (aspirated) A term in PHONETICS for the audible breath which may accompany a sound's ARTICULATION, as when certain types of PLOSIVE CONSONANT are released. It is usually symbolized by a small raised [^{h}] following the main symbol. In examples such as English *pin* [p^hɪn], the aspiration may be felt by holding the back of the hand close to the mouth while saying the word; the contrast with *bin*, where there is no aspiration, is noticeable. Some languages, such as Hindi, have contrasts of aspiration applying to both voiceless and VOICED STOPS, viz. a four-way contrast of [p-], [p^h-], [b-], and [b^h-]. In some phonetic environments the aspiration effect varies, as when in English the PLOSIVES are followed by /l, r, w, j/: here the aspiration devoices these consonants, as in *please, twice, queue*. Following initial /s/, the aspiration contrast is lost altogether, as in [spɪn]. Sounds other than plosives may be aspirated, but they are less commonly encountered. In a more detailed analysis, **pre-aspiration** (aspiration before the consonant) can be distinguished from **post-aspiration** (aspiration after the consonant); both features occur, for example, in Scottish Gaelic.

ASR The abbreviation for 'automatic SPEECH recognition'.

assign(ment) A term used in GENERATIVE linguistics to refer to the action of rules; rules attribute, or 'assign', structure to SENTENCES. By the use of REWRITE RULES, a STRING OF ELEMENTS is introduced as a series of stages, each stage being associated with a pair of LABELLED BRACKETS, e.g.

$$\begin{array}{ll} S \rightarrow NP + VP & [NP + VP]_{S} \\ VP \rightarrow V + NP & [NP + [V + NP]_{VP}]_{S} \\ NP \rightarrow D + N & [[D + N]_{NP} + [V + [D + N]_{NP}]_{VP}]_{S} \end{array}$$

In such a way, the structure of NOUN PHRASE, VERB phrase, etc., can be assigned to any sentence to which these rules apply; e.g. [[*the man*] [*saw*[*the dog*]]].

assimilation A general term in PHONETICS which refers to the influence exercised by one sound segment upon the ARTICULATION of another, so that the sounds become more alike, or identical. The study of assimilation (and its opposite, DISSIMILATION) has been an important part of HISTORICAL LINGUISTIC study, but it has been a much neglected aspect of SYNCHRONIC speech analysis, owing to the traditional manner of viewing speech as a sequence of DISCRETE WORDS. If one imagines speech to be spoken 'word at a time', with PAUSES corresponding to the spaces of the written language, there is little chance that the assimilations and other features of CONNECTED SPEECH will be noticed. When passages of natural conversation came to be analysed, however, assimilation emerged as being one of the main means whereby fluency and RHYTHM are maintained.

Several types of assimilation can be recognized. It may be 'partial' or 'total'.

In the phrase *ten bikes*, for example, the normal form in colloquial speech would be /tem baɪks/, not /ten baɪks/, which would sound somewhat 'careful'. In this case, the assimilation has been partial: the /n/ has fallen under the influence of the following /b/, and has adopted its BILABIALITY, becoming /m/. It has not, however, adopted its PLOSIVENESS. The phrase /teb baɪks/ would be likely only if one had a severe cold! The assimilation is total in *ten mice* /tem maɪs/, where the /n/ is now identical with the /m/ which influenced it.

Another classification is in terms of whether the change of sound involved is the result of the influence of an adjacent sound or of one further away. The common type is the former, as illustrated above: this is known as 'contiguous' or 'contact' assimilation. An example of the opposite, 'non-contiguous' (or 'distance') assimilation, occurs in *turn up trumps*, where the /-n/ of *turn* may be articulated as /-m/ under the influence of later sounds. It also occurs in languages displaying VOWEL harmony, where a vowel in one part of a WORD may influence other vowels to be articulated similarly, even though there may be other sounds between them.

A further classification is in terms of the direction in which the assimilation works. There are three possibilities: (a) **regressive** (or **anticipatory**) assimilation: the sound changes because of the influence of the following sound, e.g. *ten bikes* above: this is particularly common in English in ALVEOLAR consonants in word-FINAL position; (b) **progressive** assimilation: the sound changes because of the influence of the preceding sound, e.g. *lunch score* articulated with the *s-* becoming /ʃ/, under the influence of the preceding *-ch*; but these assimilations are less common; (c) **coalescent** (or **reciprocal**) assimilation: there is mutual influence, or FUSION, of the sounds upon each other, as when *don't you* is pronounced as /ˈdəʊntʃʊ/ – the *t* and the *y* have fused to produce an AFFRICATE.

In standard GENERATIVE PHONOLOGY, assimilation is characterized through the notion of FEATURE COPYING: SEGMENTS copy feature specifications from neighbouring segments. In NON-LINEAR models, a FEATURE or NODE belonging to one segment (the trigger) is viewed as SPREADING to a neighbouring segment (the target). The assimilation is UNMARKED when a rule spreads only features not already specified in the target (a 'feature-filling' mode); if the rule applies to segments already specified for the spreading features (thereby replacing their original values), it is said to apply in a 'feature-changing' mode. Further types of assimilation can be recognized within this approach, based on the identity of the spreading node: if a ROOT node spreads, the target segment acquires all the features of the trigger (**total** or **complete assimilation**); if a lower-level class node spreads, the target acquires only some of the features of the trigger (**partial** or **incomplete assimilation**); and if only a TERMINAL feature spreads, just one feature is involved (**single-feature assimilation**).

association (associative) The general senses of this term are often found in linguistic discussion – the non-linguistic feelings (cf. CONNOTATIONS) which a LEXICAL ITEM gives rise to, or the range of psychologically connected items which come to mind (i.e. the 'sense associations'). Some LINGUISTS have used the term with a more restricted definition, however. For example, the SAUSSUREAN conception of PARADIGMATIC relationships was referred to as **associative relations**. Some linguists use the term **associative field** (or **association group**) to refer to a set of lexical items which display a specific similarity of FORM or SENSE.

association line A term used in NON-LINEAR PHONOLOGY for a line drawn between UNITS on different LEVELS. The notion has been especially developed as a means of linking TIERS in AUTOSEGMENTAL PHONOLOGY. From a PHONETIC viewpoint, these lines represent temporal simultaneity, indicating the relationship in time between the FEATURES represented at each tier, such as TONES and VOWELS. Segments which associate between tiers are considered **freely associating** segments; segments which do not freely associate would be ignored, in the application of an autosegmental RULE. Once an association line has been established, the **association convention** is used to relate the remaining features: when **unassociated** features (e.g. vowels and tones) appear on the same side of an association line, they are automatically associated in a one-to-one way, radiating outward from the association line. Unbroken association lines indicate associations that already exist; broken association lines (– – – –) indicate a STRUCTURAL CHANGE following a rule. Association lines in a given representation may not cross (the 'no-crossing constraint'). An 'X' (or similar convention, such as =) through an association line indicates that the line is to be DELETED by a rule. A circle round a segment means that it is not associated to any segment on the facing tier. For example, the following diagram represents a shift in a high tone from the first vowel (in the input to the rule) to the second.

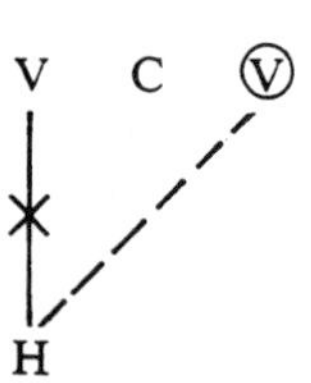

Such shifts in association are known as **reassociations**. **Multiple associations** relate a unit to more than one V or C slot. Because autosegmental phonology allows a different number of elements in each tier and does not require that the boundaries between them coincide, the notion of association lines emerges as central.

asterisk(ed) (1) In LINGUISTICS, a linguistic construction that is UNACCEPTABLE or UNGRAMMATICAL is marked thus by the use of an initial asterisk, e.g. **the man do been go*. An **asterisked form** (or 'starred form') is a form which cannot occur in a language, e.g. **walkedn't*.

(2) In X-BAR SYNTAX, the asterisk is an operator used to indicate any number of instances of a category (including zero). For example, YP* means 'any number of phrases of any type'.

(3) In linguistic theory, non-CONFIGURATIONAL LANGUAGES are also known as W* ('W-star') languages.

(4) In HISTORICAL linguistics, asterisks are used to indicate a form which has been RECONSTRUCTED, there being no written evidence for its existence, as in the sounds and words postulated for Indo-European, e.g. **s*, **penk^{w}e* ('five').

(5) In early AUTOSEGMENTAL PHONOLOGY, an asterisk (also called a 'star')

marked a segment with a priority ASSOCIATION, resistant to modification by later RULES. The convention is also seen in some approaches to INTONATION, where it identifies a BOUNDARY TONE associated with a stressed syllable: H*, L*.

asymmetric rhythmic theory An approach to METRICAL PHONOLOGY based on an inventory of FOOT TEMPLATES in which IAMBIC and TROCHAIC styles of ALTERNATION do not display symmetrical properties. ITERATIVE iambic systems use feet whose members are of uneven DURATION; iterative trochaic systems use feet whose members tend towards even duration.

asyndeton see SYNDETON

atelic A term used in the GRAMMATICAL analysis of ASPECT, to refer to an event where the activity has no clear terminal point. Atelic verbs include *look, play* and *sing* (in such contexts as *he's singing*, etc.). They contrast with TELIC verbs, such as *kick*, where there is a clear end point.

ATN The abbreviation for 'augmented TRANSITION NETWORK' GRAMMAR.

ATR The abbreviation for 'advanced tongue root' (cf. ROOT (2)).

attenuative A term sometimes used in GRAMMAR and SEMANTICS, referring to a reduced quality or quantity of the state or activity expressed by the VERB ('a little', 'less'). In some languages (e.g. Hungarian) the contrast is a formal part of the ASPECT system.

attested A term used in LINGUISTICS to refer to a lingustic FORM for which there is evidence of present or past use. In HISTORICAL linguistics, for example, **attested forms** are those which appear in written texts, as opposed to the 'RECONSTRUCTED forms' arrived at by a process of deduction. In studies of contemporary speech, the term is used to refer to actual recorded usage, compared with the hypothetical predictions of GRAMMAR or the INTUITIVE (but otherwise unsupported) observations of the linguist.

atomic phonology see PHONOLOGY

attitudinal A term sometimes used in SEMANTICS as part of a classification of types of MEANING: it refers to the emotional element in meaning, as in the different attitudes expressed by varying the INTONATION or loudness of a sentence, e.g. anger, sarcasm. In the context of PROSODY, 'attitudinal meaning' is usually distinguished from GRAMMATICAL. Alternative terms include AFFECTIVE and EMOTIVE; opposed terms include COGNITIVE and REFERENTIAL.

attribute (attributive) (1) A term derived from auditory perception and used in AUDITORY PHONETICS to refer to an isolatable characteristic of sound sensation, e.g. the attributes of PITCH, LOUDNESS and TIMBRE.

(2) **(attribution)** In GRAMMATICAL description, the term is normally used to refer to the role of ADJECTIVES and NOUNS when they occur as MODIFIERS of the HEAD of a noun PHRASE. For example, *red* has **attributive** function in *the red chair*, as has *Jane's* in *Jane's hat*. The term contrasts with the PREDICATIVE function of these words, as in *the chair is red, the hat is Jane's*. Some MODELS of grammatical description have extended the use of this term to include such COMPLEMENT structures as *he is* ***my uncle,*** *I called him* ***a fool***, and this usage

can include the adjectival use above (i.e. in *she is happy* the adjective's SEMANTIC role in relation to *she* is one of **attribution**). Ambiguity in this context is thus a real possibility.

audible friction see FRICTION

auditory phonetics The branch of PHONETICS which studies the perceptual response to speech sounds, as mediated by ear, auditory nerve and brain. It is a less well-studied area of phonetics, mainly because of the difficulties encountered as soon as one attempts to identify and measure psychological and neurological responses to speech sounds. Anatomical and physiological studies of the ear are well advanced, as are techniques for the measurement of hearing, and the clinical use of such study is now established under the headings of audiology and audiometry. But relatively little pure research has been done into the attributes of speech-sound sensation, seen as a phonetic SYSTEM, and the relationship between such phonetic analyses and PHONOLOGICAL studies remains obscure.

augmentative A term used in MORPHOLOGY to refer to an AFFIX with the general meaning of 'large', used literally or metaphorically (often implying awkwardness or ugliness). Examples include *-one* in Italian and *-ón* in Spanish (e.g. *sillón* 'armchair', cf. *silla* 'chair'). The term is usually contrasted with DIMINUTIVE.

augmented transition network grammar see TRANSITION NETWORK GRAMMAR

autohyponym see HYPONYM

autolexical syntax An approach to GRAMMAR, developed in the early 1990s, which proposes autonomous systems of RULES co-ordinated via the LEXICON. SYNTACTIC, SEMANTIC and MORPHOLOGICAL modules (formalized as context-free PHRASE-STRUCTURE GRAMMARS) are interrelated by a series of interface principles which limit the degree of structural discrepancy between the REPRESENTATIONS. An expression must satisfy the independent requirements of each module to be WELL-FORMED.

automatic A term used in LINGUISTICS to refer to a MORPHOLOGICAL variation which is motivated by the PHONOLOGICAL rules of a language. For example, the ALTERNATION of /-s/, /-z/ and /-ɪz/ in English PLURALS, POSSESSIVES and VERBS is automatically determined by the phonology: forms ending in a SIBILANT are followed by /-ɪz/; non-sibilant VOICELESS CONSONANTS are followed by /-s/; and non-sibilant voiced consonants are followed by /-z/. More complex automatic alternations are illustrated by SANDHI phenomena.

automatic speech recognition see SPEECH RECOGNITION

automaton (automata) A term taken from mathematics, where it refers to the FORMALIZATION of a set of rules for a computation, and used in theoretical and computational LINGUISTICS as part of the frame of reference for classifying languages which can be formally GENERATED (cf. CHOMSKY HIERARCHY). Automata (such as computers) can be modelled in abstract terms as a series of inputs, outputs, states, and rules of operation. They typically perform operations on an input tape by moving through a series of 'states' (or 'configurations'), each state being linked to the next by a 'transition function'. The most general automata are known as 'Turing machines' (named after British mathematician Alan Mathison Turing (1912–54), who in 1936 devised a logical machine which defined computable numbers by working in this way). The most restricted kinds of automata are **finite automata** (also called 'Markov sources' or 'simple TRANSITION NETWORKS'), which consist of a finite number of states and state-transitions, and an input tape which can be read only in one direction, one symbol at a time. FINITE-STATE LANGUAGES belong to the class of finite automata.

autonomous (1) An adjective often used in discussing the status of LINGUISTICS as a science: the implication is that the subject of language is now studied in its own terms, no longer being dependent on the incidental interest of scholars from other disciplines, such as logic, literary criticism, or history.

(2) In PHONOLOGY, the term is used to characterize the notion of a PHONEME when no reference is made to its relationships with GRAMMATICAL (especially WORD) STRUCTURE. The **autonomous phoneme**, in this sense, is contrasted with the MORPHOPHONEME, or the SYSTEMATIC PHONEME of GENERATIVE linguistics, where other factors than the strictly phonemic are allowed into the analysis.

(3) **Autonomous syntax** is the view propounded by the STANDARD THEORY of generative grammar that the SYNTACTIC COMPONENT of the grammar is independent ('autonomous') of SEMANTICS, i.e. the factors which determine the GRAMMATICALITY of a SENTENCE operate without reference to those which determine the sentence's MEANING. This view was attacked in GENERATIVE SEMANTICS, but prevails in modern linguistic theory.

(4) See **idioglossia**.

autosegment A term used in AUTOSEGMENTAL PHONOLOGY for a SEGMENT considered to be autonomous and represented on its own TIER. The notion is applied particularly to TONES, which are viewed as segments in their own right, independent of the CONSONANT and VOWEL segments represented on the SKELETAL TIER.

autosegmental phonology A term used in recent PHONOLOGICAL theory to refer to an approach which contrasts with strictly SEGMENTAL theories of phonology. The segmental approach is seen as a set of REPRESENTATIONS which consist of a LINEAR arrangement of segments (or unordered sets of FEATURES) and BOUNDARIES that are dependent on MORPHOLOGICAL and SYNTACTIC criteria. By contrast, the autosegmental approach sees phonology as comprising several TIERS, each tier consisting of a linear arrangement of segments; these are linked to each other by association lines which indicate how they are to be COARTICULATED. Originally devised to handle TONAL phenomena, the approach has now been extended to deal with other features whose scope is more than one segment, especially VOWEL and CONSONANT HARMONY.

aux The usual abbreviation for AUXILIARY.

auxiliary (aux) (1) A term used in the GRAMMATICAL classification of VERBS to refer to the set of verbs, subordinate to the main LEXICAL verb, which help to make distinctions in MOOD, ASPECT, VOICE, etc. In English the main auxiliaries are *do*, *be* and *have*, e.g. *she **is** coming*, ***does** she know*, *she **has** taken*. The MODAL auxiliaries include *can/could*, *may/might*, *shall/should*, *will/would*, *must*, *ought* *to* and *used to*. The class of auxiliaries is distinguished grammatically from lexical verbs in several ways; for instance, they have a special NEGATIVE form (e.g. *isn't, hasn't, can't*, as opposed to **walkn't*), and they can be used with SUBJECT INVERSION (e.g. *is he, does he, will they*, as opposd to **walks he*). 'Marginal' or 'semi-auxiliaries', i.e. verbs which display some but not all of the properties of the auxiliary class, include *dare* and *need*.

(2) In SOCIOLINGUISTICS, an **auxiliary language** is one which has been adopted by different SPEECH communities for purposes of communication, trade, education, etc., it being the native language of none of them. English and French are auxiliary languages for many communities in Africa, for example; Swahili is used thus in parts of East Africa. This sense is unrelated to the use of the term 'auxiliary language' to mean an artificially constructed language, such as Esperanto.

avalent see VALENCY

avoidance languages In LINGUISTICS, a term used to characterize LANGUAGES which permit communication between a person and others with whom there is a social taboo; sometimes loosely called **mother-in-law languages**. The concept relates chiefly to Australian Aboriginal languages, where there may be strict taboos between certain relatives, such as a man and his wife's mother and maternal uncles. In Dyirbal, for example, the everyday language is known as Guwal, and the avoidance language as Dyalnguy, which would be used whenever a taboo relative was within earshot.

axiom(atic) An application in LINGUISTICS of the general use of this term in the branch of logic known as **axiomatics**. It refers to a set of initial propositions (or **axioms**) which a theory assumes to be true. Further propositions (or 'theorems') are then deduced from these by means of specific rules of inference (to which the term 'transformational rule' is sometimes applied). The full statement of an axiomatic system will contain a 'syntax', which determines the WELL-FORMEDNESS of its propositions, and a 'vocabulary', which lists the terms of the system. The application of these ideas in LINGUISTICS has come mainly from the influence of CHOMSKYAN ideas, concerning the FORMALIZATION of LANGUAGE, and is central to MATHEMATICAL linguistics. In pre-GENERATIVE attempts at systematizing ideas about language, the weaker term POSTULATES was usually used. A specifically non-generative approach is **axiomatic functionalism**, a paradigm of enquiry developed in the 1960s by J(ohannes) W(ilhelmus) F(ranciscus) Mulder (1919–), in which linguistics is presented as a formal axiomatic-deductive system within a broad SEMIOTIC frame of reference. The approach applies a network of postulates, supporting definitions, and associated theorems to the structural analysis of core areas of language as well as to areas which are conventionally handled under other headings (such as PRAGMATICS).

axis (1) A term sometimes used in LINGUISTICS to refer to intersecting dimensions of linguistic analysis, especially those introduced by the Swiss linguist Ferdinand de SAUSSURE. The distinction between SYNCHRONIC and DIACHRONIC is characterized as the 'axis of simultaneities' *v.* the 'axis of successions'. Likewise the SYNTAGMATIC/PARADIGMATIC distinction may be referred to in terms of axes ('syntagmatic axis', 'axis of chain relationships', etc.).

(2) In some MODELS OF GRAMMATICAL classification, the term refers to the second ELEMENT in an EXOCENTRIC CONSTRUCTION, the other being the DIRECTOR, e.g. *in* ***the garden***, *see* ***the car***.

B

baby-talk (BT) An extension in LANGUAGE ACQUISITION studies of the traditional sense of this term, to refer to the whole range of DISTINCTIVE LINGUISTIC characteristics found in adult speech addressed to young children. Baby-talk thus includes far more than the often stereotyped use of endearing pronunciations and words (such as *doggie*, /den/ for *then*, etc.) and is primarily characterized with reference to the use of simplified SENTENCE STRUCTURES, and certain types of linguistic interaction (such as the expansion of a child's sentence into a full adult form, e.g. *Dadda gone* → *Yes, daddy's gone*). The study of baby-talk, or 'language input', became a major focus of language acquisition studies in the early 1970s, a particular stimulus coming from SOCIOLINGUISTICS. The term is now uncommon in PSYCHOLINGUISTICS because of its apparent restriction to babies (as opposed to young children generally) and its ambiguity (talk *by* babies as well as *to* babies). In recent years it has tended to be replaced by MOTHERESE, or by more general notions such as **caregiver speech**.

back (sounds) Classification of back speech sounds are of two types: (a) those articulated in the back part of the mouth; and (b) those articulated with the back part of the TONGUE. In many cases, these two criteria coincide: back VOWELS are 'back' in both senses, as in English *hard, talk, show, got*, as are the back CONSONANTS heard at the beginning of *go, car* and *way*. Consonants made in the LARYNX or PHARYNX, however, such as [h], are 'back' in sense (a) only. Back vowels are contrasted, in traditional PHONETIC classifications, with FRONT and CENTRAL VOWELS.

In the traditional classifications, sounds made at the back of the mouth are distinguished from those made at the front; and those made by the back of the tongue are opposed to those made further forward, by the TIP and BLADE (or front) of the tongue. In the DISTINCTIVE FEATURE analysis of sounds proposed by CHOMSKY and Halle, the equivalent of 'front' is ANTERIOR, and of 'tip/blade' is CORONAL. Back sounds as a whole, in their terminology, are a type of CAVITY feature (specifically, a TONGUE-BODY feature); they are contrasted with **non-back** sounds, i.e. sounds produced without any retraction of the tongue from the neutral position. Back vowels and consonants are more difficult to control consciously, because of the relative lack of feeling in that area of the mouth.

backchannelling A term used in PRAGMATICS and SOCIOLINGUISTICS, as part of the study of listener behaviour in an INTERACTION, referring to the reactions given to a speaker by way of FEEDBACK. They include monosyllabic responses (*mhm*), short phrases (*I guess so*), utterance repetitions and sentence completions, as well as non-verbal cues (e.g. nodding, gaze variation).

back-formation A term used in historical studies of MORPHOLOGY to refer to an abnormal type of WORD FORMATION where a shorter word is derived by deleting an imagined AFFIX from a longer form already present in the language. *Edit*, for example, comes from *editor*, and not the other way round. This DERIVATION presumably took place because NATIVE-SPEAKERS saw an ANALOGY between *editor* and other words where a normal derivational process had taken place, e.g. *credit/creditor, inspect/inspector, act/actor*, the NOUNS being in each case formed from the VERBS. The derivation of *edit* thus reverses the expected derivational pattern, hence the term 'back-formation'.

backgrounding see FOREGROUNDING

backlooping A term in TAGMEMIC GRAMMAR for the inclusion of higher-LEVEL CONSTRUCTIONS within the SLOTS of a lower-level construction, as in the use of RELATIVE CLAUSES within the NOUN PHRASE (e.g. *the lady who was talking*...); sometimes referred to as **loopback**. It is distinguished from LEVEL-SKIPPING and LAYERING.

bar A mode of CLASSIFICATION of syntactic categories in X-BAR SYNTAX. Most commonly, **zero-bar** categories are word-level categories; **single-bar** and **double-bar** categories are PHRASAL. SINGLE BARS and DOUBLE BARS are often represented by a bar over a category symbol (e.g. $\bar{N}$, $\bar{\bar{N}}$). The alternative ways of representing bar(s) include primes (e.g. N′, N″), and numerical symbols (e.g. N1, N2 or N^1, N^2). Zero-bar categories are sometimes represented as N0 or N^0. In GENERALIZED PHRASE-STRUCTURE GRAMMAR, bar is a multi-valued category feature which can take 0, 1 or 2 as its value. See also PROJECTION, VARIABLE (3).

barrier A term used in GOVERNMENT-BINDING THEORY to refer to categories whose boundaries restrict certain phenomena. A barrier is a NODE which blocks the syntactic processes of MOVEMENT and GOVERNMENT: one barrier blocks government; two barriers block movement. The principle that movement cannot cross more than one barrier is known as SUBJACENCY. A is considered to be a barrier for B if A is a 'blocking category' for B: to be a blocking category, A must not be THETA-marked by a LEXICAL (L) category, and A must dominate B. Anything can be a barrier, apart from IP (INFLECTION-phrase). Other nodes can also become barriers for B if they dominate non-L-marked nodes dominating B or if they dominate the nearest governor of B (the 'MINIMALITY condition'). The notion became increasingly important in SYNTACTIC theory following the publication of Noam Chomsky's *Barriers* (1986). Barriers are also encountered in PHONOLOGY, where they refer to any unit (e.g. a BOUNDARY SYMBOL, a SEGMENT) within a STRING which blocks the application of a phonological RULE to that string.

base (basic) (1) A term used in MORPHOLOGY as an alternative to ROOT or STEM: it refers to any part of a WORD seen as a UNIT to which an operation can be applied, as when one adds an AFFIX to a root or stem. For example, in *unhappy* the **base form** is *happy*; if *-ness* is then added to *unhappy*, the whole of this item would be considered the base to which the new affix is attached. Some analysts, however, restrict the term 'base' to be equivalent to 'root', i.e. the part of a word remaining when all AFFIXES have been removed. In such an approach, *happy* would be the base form (the highest common factor) of all its DERIVATIONS – *happiness, unhappy, unhappiness*, etc.

(2) In a more abstract approach to GRAMMAR (SYNTAX as well as morphology), the term **basic form** is used to refer to any abstract unit which has been set up in order to allow a range of FORMS to be interrelated, i.e. seen as VARIANTS. In morphology, for example, the basic or CANONICAL form of a MORPHEME might be identified as one of its ALTERNANTS (e.g. the **basic form** (or 'basic alternant') of the morpheme *man* is the morph *man*, with *men* being DERIVED from this in some way), or it might be a unit underlying both (e.g. a unit [mVn], where both *man* and *men* are derived by some process of VOWEL (V) replacement). Similarly in syntax a SENTENCE can be seen as having a basic form from which other sentences are derived (e.g. ACTIVE underlying PASSIVE sentences, POSITIVES underlying NEGATIVES), or related structures can be seen as being derived from a common UNDERLYING form. GENERATIVE grammar is the approach which has exploited the potential of such analyses most fully. This sense of 'basic', it should be clear, is different from that used in language teaching or learning situations, where (possibly in addition to the above) the implication is that basic patterns of vocabulary are easier to learn, or are more useful for communication.

(3) As part of the STANDARD model of generative grammar, the term is used in the phrase **base component** (or 'sub-component'), which is one of the two main divisions of the grammar's syntactic COMPONENT, the other being the TRANSFORMATIONAL (sub-)component. In Noam CHOMSKY's *Syntactic Structures* (1957), the alternative term was 'phrase-structure component', which specified the PHRASE-STRUCTURE RULES of the grammar. In *Aspects of the Theory of Syntax* (1965), the same distinction (between base and transformational sub-components) is made, but the roles of the two differ from the earlier version, in relation to the theory as a whole. In *Aspects*, the base contains a 'categorial' component (specifying the CATEGORIES, S, NP, VP, etc.) and a 'lexical' component (consisting of LEXICAL entries made up of such FEATURES as 'animate', 'human', etc.). Taken together, the information in these components specifies the DEEP STRUCTURE of sentences. In later versions of generative grammar, the role of the base component receives further modifications, as the relationship between syntax and SEMANTICS is investigated. See also UNIVERSAL.

basilect(al) A term used by some SOCIOLINGUISTS, in the study of the development of CREOLE LANGUAGES, to refer to a linguistic VARIETY (or LECT) most remote from the prestige language (the 'matrilect' or ACROLECT). It is also contrasted with the intermediate varieties, known as MESOLECTS.

beat A term used by some METRICAL PHONOLOGISTS for the grid marks at the second or higher LEVEL in a METRICAL GRID; the marks at the bottom level are referred to as **demibeats**. The distinction corresponds in part to the STRONG/WEAK FORM or STRESSED/unstressed distinction: beats or demibeats that coincide with a beat at a higher level are strong; those which do not are weak.

behaviourism In LINGUISTICS, the influence of this school of psychology (the study of observable and measurable behaviour) has been most marked in the work of the American linguist Leonard BLOOMFIELD. It can be seen in the Bloomfieldian insistence on rigorous DISCOVERY PROCEDURES, and most notably in his behaviourist account of MEANING in terms of observable stimuli and responses made by participants in specific situations. The limitations of behaviourist (or 'mechanistic') accounts of LANGUAGE (especially that associated with the work of the American psychologist B(urrhus) F(rederic) Skinner (1904–90) were criticized by Noam CHOMSKY in the late 1950s, in writings which anticipate the development of MENTALISTIC ideas in linguistics.

benefactive A term used in some GRAMMATICAL descriptions to refer to a CASE FORM or CONSTRUCTION whose FUNCTION in a SENTENCE is to express the notion 'on behalf of' or 'for the benefit of'. This sense of 'intended RECIPIENT' is often introduced by a *for* phrase in English, e.g. *I've got a book for you.*

bidialect(al)ism In its most general sense, the term refers to proficiency in the use by a person or a community of two DIALECTS of a language, whether regional or social. Several kinds of 'bidialectal' situation have been studied, one of the best known being the switching from a casual to a FORMAL VARIETY of speech (DIGLOSSIA). More specifically, it is a principle propounded in SOCIOLINGUISTICS and EDUCATIONAL LINGUISTICS wherein different dialects are attributed equal linguistic validity and recommended for use in their appropriate social settings. The principle is of particular importance in relation to educational policy in schools, where the differences between the non-standard and the STANDARD forms of a language can lead to considerable conflict. Bidialectalism recommends that both non-standard and standard dialects should be encouraged in the educational process, along with the fostering of children's abilities to use CODE-switching, thus developing a greater degree of understanding and control over the varieties of their language than would otherwise be the case.

bidirectionality see ITERATIVITY

bilabial A term in the classification of CONSONANT sounds on the basis of their PLACE OF ARTICULATION: it refers to a sound made by the coming together of both lips. Examples are the initial sounds in *pin, bin, mat*; a non-English bilabial would be the initial sound in Welsh *mhen* 'my head'. The term is restricted to consonantal ARTICULATION; the active use of the lips in the articulation of VOWELS is discussed in terms of ROUNDING and SPREADING. The only common speech sounds in which a single lip is the primary articulator are known as LABIO-DENTALS. 'Monolabial' is not found as a technical term; 'quadrilabial' exists only in humour, as part of the PHONETICIAN's technical description of a kiss!

bilateral (1) A type of OPPOSITION recognized in PRAGUE SCHOOL PHONOLOGY, distinguished from MULTILATERAL. The opposition betwen English /t/ and /d/, for example, is bilateral, because these are the only UNITS in the SYSTEM which are ALVEOLAR/PLOSIVE, and they are differentiated by the single feature of VOICING; the opposition between, say, /t/ and /v/, however is multilateral, because there are other possibilities involving the same set of FEATURES, e.g. /d/ *v.* /f/.

(2) A LATERAL sound in which air escapes around both sides of the tongue, as in the usual ARTICULATION of [l]; opposed to 'unilateral'.

bilingual(ism) The general sense of this term – a person who can speak two LANGUAGES – provides a pre-theoretical frame of reference for linguistic study, especially by SOCIOLINGUISTS, and by APPLIED LINGUISTS involved in foreign- or second-language teaching. The focus of attention has been on the many kinds and degrees of 'bilingualism' and 'bilingual situations' which exist. Definitions of bilingualism reflect assumptions about the degree of proficiency people must achieve before they qualify as bilingual (whether comparable to a monolingual NATIVE-SPEAKER, or something less than this, even to the extent of minimal knowledge of a second language). Several technical distinctions have been introduced, e.g. between COMPOUND and CO-ORDINATE bilingualism (based on the extent to which the bilingual sees the two languages as SEMANTICALLY equivalent or non-equivalent), between the various methods of learning the two languages (e.g. simultaneously or in sequence in childhood, or through formal instruction), and between the various levels of abstraction at which the linguistic systems operate – bilingualism being distinguished from BIDIALECTISM and DIGLOSSIA. Of particular importance is the way in which studies of bilingualism involve the analysis of social, psychological and national (e.g. in the case of Welsh and Flemish) concerns – such as the social status of the different languages, and their role in identifying speakers with particular ethnic groups. In 'additive' or 'elite' bilingualism, a majority group learns a second language without this being a threat to its first language (e.g. English-speaking Canadians learning French); in 'subtractive' or 'folk' bilingualism, the second language comes to replace the first (a common situation with minority languages).

bimoraic see MORA

binary feature A property which can be used to classify linguistic UNITS in terms of two mutually exclusive possibilities, such as in PHONOLOGY the presence versus the absence of VOCAL-CORD vibration, or lip-ROUNDING. Binary features are a major organizational principle of DISTINCTIVE FEATURE theories of phonology, where it is conventional to mark the OPPOSITION using +/− in square brackets; e.g. a sound is characterized as [+ voice] or [− voice]. Binary features are also established in GRAMMATICAL and SEMANTIC analyses of LEXICAL ITEMS, within GENERATIVE grammar, where the same TRANSCRIPTIONAL convention is used, e.g. NOUNS have such properties as [+ common], [− common]. Binary features stand in contrast to 'unary' and 'multi-valued' ('n-valued' or 'n-ary') features. For example, in 'unary component theory' in recent phonology, binary notions (e.g. [+/− round]) are replaced by single elements (e.g. [round]).

Binarity, or **binarism**, in this sense is relatable to the principles of binary coding used in INFORMATION theory, but the status of such contrasts in language is often controversial, as it is not always clear whether the linguistic possibilities available in phonology, grammar and semantics are best seen as a series of **binary choices**. In IMMEDIATE CONSTITUENT analysis, for example, which uses a binary technique for splitting SENTENCES into smaller parts, it is sometimes impossible to decide where a binary division should be made, as in the case of ADJECTIVE sequence (e.g. *nice old red chair* is not really divisible into *nice* + *old* *red*, or *nice old* + *red*). It has sometimes been suggested that binary BRANCHING is the norm in a PHRASE-MARKER. In cases where binary features are used, it is sometimes possible to see one of the features as neutral, or unmarked, and the other as positive, or MARKED.

bind(ing) A term used in GOVERNMENT-BINDING THEORY to refer to a series of CONDITIONS which formally relate, or 'bind', certain elements of a sentence. Two kinds of binding are distinguished: **A-binding** and **A-bar-binding** (**Ā-binding**). The former obtains if a category (an ANAPHOR) is CO-INDEXED with a C-COMMANDING NOUN PHRASE in an A-position (= ARGUMENT-position). The latter obtains if a category (e.g. a variable such as a *WH*-MOVEMENT TRACE) is co-indexed with a c-commanding category which is in an A-bar position (a position other than subject, object, and object of a preposition), e.g. the clause-initial position occupied by a *wh*-phrase. The extension (or generalization) of the approach from the former to the latter is known as **generalized binding**. Elements which are not bound are FREE. **Binding theory** is one of the (sub-) theories of government-binding theory. It is primarily concerned with the distribution of NPs in a sentence, determining the situations in which they can or must be co-indexed with other NPs. The NPs are classified into ANAPHORS, PRONOMINALS and R-EXPRESSIONS ('referring expressions'). The three principles of binding theory – binding conditions A, B and C – are: (a) an anaphor is A-bound in its governing category; (b) a pronominal is A-free in its governing category; (c) an R-expression is A-free (everywhere). The **binding inheritance principle** is a reinterpretation of the FOOT-feature principle of GENERALIZED PHRASE-STRUCTURE GRAMMAR within HEAD-DRIVEN PHRASE-STRUCTURE GRAMMAR.

binomial A term from mathematics (where it refers to an expression consisting of two elements connected by a plus or minus sign) which is sometimes used in LEXICOLOGY to characterize two-element idiomatic COLLOCATIONS such as *spick and span* or *rack and ruin*.

biolinguistics A developing branch of LINGUISTICS which studies the biological preconditions for language development and use in human beings, from the viewpoints of both the history of language in the race, and the development of language in the individual. It is also known as **biological linguistics**. Topics of common interest to the two subject-areas involved include the genetic transmission of language, neurophysiological models of language production, the anatomical parallels between human and other species, and the development of pathological forms of language behaviour (cf. CLINICAL LINGUISTICS).

bioprogram(me) hypothesis A hypothesis in the study of CREOLE LANGUAGES that creoles are the inventions of the children growing up in the forts or on the plantations of the newly formed colonies. These children, who would hear only the highly simplified structures of PIDGINS around them, used their INNATE linguistic capacities to transform the pidgins into a natural language. This account, introduced by Derek Bickerton, claims to be able to explain the similarity and simplicity of creole languages: they are similar because the innate capacity applied was UNIVERSAL, and they are simpler because only the most basic language structures were represented. The study of creole languages, in this view, provides special insight into the character of universal grammar.

biopositionality In some models of NON-LINEAR PHONOLOGY, the REPRESENTATION of CONSONANT or VOWEL LENGTH in two positions on the TIER at which phonological QUANTITY is represented (e.g. the CV-tier, X-tier). A long consonant or vowel is represented as a ROOT NODE linked to two units of quantity.

biuniqueness A principle in some approaches to PHONOLOGY which states that any sequence of PHONEMES will be represented by a unique sequence of PHONES, and vice versa – in other words, there is a one-to-one (or 'reversible') correspondence between phones and phonemes. For example, in the word *bin*, the relationship between the two LEVELS of analysis can be shown as

/b/ + /ɪ/ + /n/
↕ ↕ ↕
[b] [ɪ] [n]

There are, however, several cases where this straightforward correlation does not apply, and where the notion of a phoneme as a unique class of sounds consequently is invalid. In such cases (cf. OVERLAPPING), one phone is assigned to more than one phoneme, depending on the CONTEXT. The **biuniqueness condition**, along with the conditions of LINEARITY and INVARIANCE, on which it depends, was particularly criticized by GENERATIVE phonologists, as part of their general attack on TAXONOMIC phonemics.

bivalent see VALENCY

black English vernacular see VERNACULAR

blade The part of the TONGUE between TIP and CENTRE, and which lies opposite the teeth and ALVEOLAR ridge when the tongue is in neutral position. Also known as the LAMINA, it is used in the articulation of several speech sounds, such as [t] and [s].

bleaching A term sometimes used in SEMANTICS to refer to a perceived loss or dilution of MEANING in a word as a result of semantic change. Examples are the use of *you know* and *I mean* as PRAGMATIC particles.

bleeding (bleed, counter-) A term used in GENERATIVE linguistic analysis of RULE-ordering, and originally introduced in the context of DIACHRONIC PHONOLOGY, to refer to a type of FUNCTIONAL relationship between rules; opposed to FEEDING. A bleeding relationship is one where a rule (A) removes a STRUCTURAL REPRESENTATION to which another rule (B) would otherwise have applied, and thus reduces the number of forms which can be generated. If rule B is of the form X → Y, then rule A must be of the form W → not X. In these circumstances, rule A is called a **bleeding rule** in relation to B, and the LINEAR ORDER of these rules is called a **bleeding order**. If the rules are applied in the reverse order, A is said to **counter-bleed** B. Counter-bleeding results in a non-affecting interaction in which a rule fails to realize its potential to reduce the number of forms to which another rule applies.

blend(ing) A process found in the analysis of GRAMMATICAL and LEXICAL CONSTRUCTIONS, in which two ELEMENTS which do not normally co-occur, according to the RULES of the language, come together within a single LINGUISTIC UNIT (a **blend**). In GRAMMAR, the process is illustrated by such **syntactic blends** as *It's his job is the problem*, a combination of the SENTENCES *It's his job* and *His job is the problem*. In LEXIS, 'blending' is a common source of new WORDS through ABBREVIATION (though not all become standard), e.g. *brunch, Interpol* and *Eurovision*. The term is also used by some PSYCHOLINGUISTS for a type of TONGUE-SLIP involving the FUSION of two target words, e.g. *swurse* for *swear* + *curse*. See also LOAN.

block(-ed, -ing) A term used in classical TRANSFORMATIONAL GRAMMAR to refer to the non-application of a transformational RULE. A rule is said to be 'blocked' if it cannot be applied to a DERIVATION because of the occurrence of a specific property in the PHRASE-MARKER. The term is also used in GOVERNMENT-BINDING THEORY to formalize the notion of what can act as a BARRIER. To be a **blocking category**, A must not be THETA- marked by a LEXICAL (L) category, and A must dominate B.

block language A term used in some GRAMMATICAL DESCRIPTIONS to refer to the use of abbreviated structures in restricted COMMUNICATIVE CONTEXTS, especial use being made of the WORD or PHRASE, rather than the CLAUSE or SENTENCE. Common examples include: *No smoking, Exit, One way*, and 'headlinese', e.g. *Prime Minister shock*.

Bloomfieldian(ism) Characteristic of, or a follower of, the linguistic approach of the American linguist Leonard **Bloomfield** (1887–1949), as exemplified in his book *Language*, published in 1933. **Bloomfieldianism** refers particularly to the school of thought which developed between the mid-1930s and 1950s, especially in America, and which was a formative influence on STRUCTURAL LINGUISTICS. It was especially characterized by its behaviouristic principles for the study of MEANING, its insistence on rigorous DISCOVERY PROCEDURES for establishing linguistic units, and a general concern to make linguistics AUTONOMOUS and scientific (in a BEHAVIOURIST sense). A reaction against Bloomfieldian tenets was a powerful force in producing GENERATIVE grammar. Though Bloomfieldianism is no longer fashionable, some of its methods are still widely used in field studies.

Boolean A term from mathematical logic (where it characterizes a type of algebra in which logical symbols are used to represent relations between sets; named after George Boole (1815–64), and widely used in COMPUTATIONAL LINGUISTICS and certain kinds of SEMANTICS, where it elucidates PROPOSITIONS linked by the three fundamental logical operations *and, or*, and *not*. It is especially relevant in cases which deal with mutually exclusive alternatives, such as BINARY features.

bootstrap(ping) In the study of child language ACQUISITION, a suggested DISCOVERY PROCEDURE whereby children make deductions about the SEMANTICS or SYNTAX of a language from their observations of language use. In 'semantic bootstrapping', children are thought to use semantic information to make deductions about syntax – for example, knowing something about the meaning of a VERB (e.g. that *give* involves a giver, a gift and a receiver) may help them to work out semantic ROLES and thus syntactic REALIZATIONS. In 'syntactic bootstrapping', the child uses syntactic or morphological information to make deductions about semantics – for example, using INFLECTIONAL clues to distinguish types of WORD, thus providing a means of assigning preliminary meanings to unfamiliar words. The term derives from mythology (where Baron Münchhausen saves himself by lifting himself up by his own bootstraps) and computing (where it refers to a short program used to load a longer program from disk into the computer, thus enabling the longer program to operate the computer).

borrow(ing) A term used in COMPARATIVE and HISTORICAL linguistics to refer to linguistic FORMS being taken over by one language or DIALECT from another; such **borrowings** are usually known as 'loan words' (e.g. *restaurant, bonhomie, chagrin*, which have come into English from French), and several types have been recognized (cf. LOAN). Less commonly, sounds and GRAMMATICAL STRUCTURES may be borrowed, e.g. the pronunciation of the above loan words with a French or quasi-French accent, or the influence of English grammar often found in European languages, e.g. using an English plural *-s* for a noun, as in *drinks, ski-lifts, goals, girls*.

bottom-up In several branches of LINGUISTICS, a term which informally characterizes any procedure or MODEL which begins with the smallest functional UNITS in a HIERARCHY and proceeds to combine these into larger units; opposed to **top-down**, which begins with the analysis of a high-level unit into progressively smaller units. For example, in GRAMMAR, models which begin with MORPHEMES or WORDS are 'bottom-up grammars', those which begin with SENTENCE, CLAUSE, or some DISCOURSE unit are 'top-down grammars'. The distinction is also used in the analysis of text structure in textlinguistics and STYLISTICS, in some approaches to NON-LINEAR PHONOLOGY, in the teaching of reading (phonics *v.* whole word), and also in relation to models of mental PROCESSING in PSYCHOLINGUISTICS.

bound (1) A term used as part of the classification of MORPHEMES; opposed to FREE. A **bound morpheme** (or **bound form**) is one which cannot occur on its own as a separate WORD, e.g. the various AFFIXES *de-, -tion, -ize*, etc.

(2) A term in the BINDING sub-theory of GOVERNMENT-BINDING THEORY referring to CONSTITUENTS which have been FORMally related through CO-INDEXING: X is bound if it is an ARGUMENT CO-INDEXED with a C-COMMANDING argument. Its opposite is FREE. Some constituents (specifically, ANAPHORS) must be bound (A-bound) in their GOVERNing category, and some (variables and R-EXPRESSIONS) must be free, otherwise the structures are ILL FORMED. Variables must be A-bar bound – co-indexed with a c-commanding element in an A-bar position.

(3) See FORMULAIC LANGUAGE.

boundary-symbol/-marker Symbols used in TRANSFORMATIONAL GRAMMAR to indicate the boundaries between STRUCTURAL UNITS, e.g. the ELEMENTS of a STRING (+), or the boundaries of strings (#), e.g. *#the+man+pres+have+en-+kick+the+ball#*. The notion has a central role in some models of PHONOLOGY, where the DOMAINS of phonological RULES can be expressed in terms of phonological boundary symbols. Boundary strength is quantitative, expressed by the number of symbols present. A given phonological rule specifies only the minimal boundary strength across which it cannot apply.

boundary tone In some analyses of INTONATION, a TONE typically positioned at the

EDGE of a PHRASAL CONSTITUENT. High (H) and Low (L) tones are recognized as having important boundary roles, expressing such functions as assertion, question, and continuation. An asterisk is used to identify a tone that is realized on the STRESSED SYLLABLE (H*, L*), and a % symbol is used to show that a tone ASSOCIATES with the EDGE syllable of a phrase (H%, L%). The notion, applied to a wide range of languages, subsumes effects which are usually handled separately (e.g. NUCLEAR tone, syllabic accent, PITCH ACCENT). Utterance spans which are dominated by boundary tones are intonational phrases. 'Medial' boundary tones are also recognized, positioned at certain points within a CONSTITUENT, marking an intermediate-level phrase.

bounded foot see FOOT (1), BOUNDEDNESS

boundedness In METRICAL PHONOLOGY, a FOOT-shape PARAMETER which governs the DISTRIBUTION of STRESSES. **Bounded feet** contain no more than two SYLLABLES, and stresses fall within limited distances from each other and from word EDGES. Unbounded feet have no restriction in size or on stress distribution.

bounding theory One of the (sub-) theories of GOVERNMENT-BINDING THEORY, which sets limits on the domain of MOVEMENT rules. Its chief principle is SUBJACENCY, which states that no movement operation can cross more than one BARRIER. In EXTENDED STANDARD THEORY and early GB theory, barriers to movement were known as **bounding nodes**, commonly assumed to be NP and S.

bracketing (brackets) (1) A technique used in LINGUISTICS to display the internal (HIERARCHICAL) structure of a STRING OF ELEMENTS, in a similar manner to that used in mathematics and symbolic logic. In the SENTENCE *The cat saw the king*, for example, the various intuitively motivated divisions it is possible to make are each associated with the imposition of a pair of brackets on to the sentence, e.g. distinguishing *the cat* from *the king* would lead to the representation *[the cat] [saw] [the king]*. Each pair of brackets may be associated with a label which indicates the GRAMMATICAL reason for their presence (a 'labelled' bracketing), for example:

$$[\text{the cat}]_{\substack{\text{Subject}\\ \text{NP}}}\ [\text{saw}]_{\text{Verb}}\ [\text{the king}]_{\substack{\text{Object}\\ \text{NP}}}$$

In a more sophisticated analysis, the order in which the pairs of brackets are applied is also made explicit, as in PHRASE-STRUCTURE GRAMMAR (here illustrated without labelling), for example:

Sentence unit [the cat saw the king]
SUBJECT/PREDICATE (or NP + VP) [[the cat] [saw the king]]
VERB/OBJECT (or V + NP) [[the cat][[saw][the king]]]

It is plain that, as sentences become more complex, the sets of brackets within brackets will become increasingly difficult to read. The TREE diagram display is the most widely used convention to overcome this difficulty.

(2) Many of the abbreviating conventions used in writing a grammar involve brackets. In GENERATIVE grammar, the following kinds of brackets are widely used to conflate RULES:

(a) **parenthesis notation (round brackets)** ( ) encloses OPTIONAL elements, e.g.

a rule involving D(Adj)N refers to the potential occurrence of two STRUCTURES, DN and D Adj N;

(b) **brace notation (curly brackets)** { } encloses alternative elements, e.g. a rule involving $D\begin{Bmatrix}\text{Adj}\\ \text{N}\end{Bmatrix}N$ refers to the selection of only one of the two structures, *either* D Adj N *or* DNN. In other approaches these brackets are used to indicate MORPHEMES, or MORPHOPHONEMIC forms;

(c) **bracket notation** [ ] requires that elements be matched along the same horizontal row, e.g. $\begin{bmatrix}\text{A}\\ \text{B}\end{bmatrix} \rightarrow \begin{bmatrix}\text{C}\\ \text{D}\end{bmatrix}$ reads that 'A becomes C' and 'B becomes D';

(d) **angled brackets notation** ⟨ ⟩ signals an interdependency between optional features in generative PHONOLOGY, e.g. $\begin{bmatrix}+\text{A}\\ \langle+\text{B}\rangle\end{bmatrix} \rightarrow \begin{bmatrix}+\text{C}\\ \langle+\text{D}\rangle\end{bmatrix}$ reads that 'feature A becomes feature C, and if feature B is present it becomes feature D'. In other approaches these brackets may be used to indicate GRAPHEMES.

(3) In PHONETICS, there are two main uses of brackets: square brackets enclose a SEGMENTAL phonetic TRANSCRIPTION or a DISTINCTIVE FEATURE notation (e.g. [+grave]); slashes / / enclose PHONEMIC transcription.

(4) Square brackets are also used to enclose FEATURES at a GRAMMATICAL or SEMANTIC LEVEL, e.g. [+common], [−countable], [+male], [−female].

bracketed grid see METRICAL GRID

bracketing paradox In GENERATIVE PHONOLOGY, a term used for cases in which two incompatible ways of ORDERING RULES are both well motivated. A rule can be applied to a SUBSTRING containing the MORPHEMES [A B], as part of a STRING [A B C], even though the corresponding morphological CONSTITUENT structure [A [B C]] does not identify [A B] as a WELL-FORMED constituent. A much-discussed example is the constituency of the word *ungrammaticality*, represented morphologically as [[*un*[*grammatical*]$_{\text{ADJ}}$]$_{\text{ADJ}}$] *ity*]$_{\text{N}}$. Because *un-* is a PREFIX which attaches to ADJECTIVES, and not NOUNS, it needs to be shown to attach to the STEM before the *-ity* SUFFIX applies. However, phonologically, the opposite situation obtains. Here, the representation has to be [*un*[[*grammatical*]*ity*]$_1$]$_2$, because the *-ity* suffix triggers a STRESS shift (and other changes) in the stem, and thus has to apply first; *un-*, which causes no such effects, should apply second.

branch(ing) A term used in LINGUISTICS to refer to the descending linear connections which constitute the identity of a TREE diagram (see example on p. 49). PHRASE STRUCTURE RULES which generate such trees are sometimes called **branching rules**. The S, the first NP, and the VP in the diagram are **branching nodes**; the other NODES are **non-branching**. It has sometimes been suggested that binary branching is the norm in a PHRASE-MARKER. See also BINARY FEATURE.

breath group A stretch of UTTERANCE produced within a single expiration of breath. Where and how often one breathes while speaking can be of significance for the LINGUIST, in that the breathing pattern will impose a series of PAUSES on the utterance, and these will need to be related to PHONOLOGICAL, GRAMMATICAL and

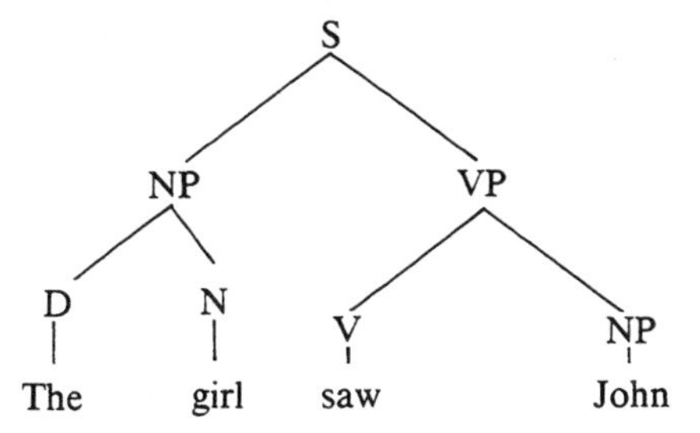

[**branch(ing)**, p. 48]

SEMANTIC structure. Within each breath group, also, it is possible that certain regularities exist, such as a predictable pattern of PROMINENCE or RHYTHM, and some investigators have used this notion as part of their study of a language's PROSODY (though terms such as TONE UNIT are here more widely used). More recently, the term has been used as a means of identifying the earliest VOCALIZATION units in infants.

breathy A term used in the PHONETIC classification of VOICE QUALITY, on the basis of ARTICULATORY and AUDITORY criteria. It refers to a vocal effect produced by allowing a great deal of air to pass through a slightly open GLOTTIS: this effect is also sometimes called **murmur**. Some speakers do have an abnormally breathy voice quality, as a permanent feature of their speech. What is of particular significance for linguistic analysis is that breathy effects may be used with CONTRASTIVE force, communicating a PARALINGUISTIC meaning: the whole of an UTTERANCE may be thus affected, as in an extremely shocked pronunciation of *Oh really!* 'Breathy voice', or 'breathy phonation', is also sometimes encountered as a PHONOLOGICAL characteristic, as in Gujarati, where there is an opposition between breathy and non-breathy VOWELS.

broad A term used in the classification of types of PHONETIC TRANSCRIPTION. A 'broad' transcription is less detailed than a 'narrow' transcription.

BT an abbreviation sometimes used in LANGUAGE ACQUISITION studies to refer to BABY-TALK.

buccal A term occasionally used in ARTICULATORY PHONETICS as an alternative to ORAL (as in 'buccal cavity'), but more often with reference to sounds made specifically within the cavity of the cheek. A well-known 'buccal voice' is that produced by Donald Duck.

bunching A term used in ARTICULATORY PHONETICS to refer to a TONGUE position in which the body of the tongue is held high and tense during the production of a sound, as in CLOSE VOWELS (e.g. [i], [u]), and FRICATIVES articulated in the PALATAL-ALVEOLAR area (e.g. [ʃ]).

bundle A term used in PHONOLOGY to characterize one conception of the PHONEME: in the approach of the PRAGUE SCHOOL the phoneme is seen as a 'bundle' of PHONETIC DISTINCTIVE FEATURES. The English phonome /s/, for example, can be seen as a result of the combination of the features of ALVEOLARITY, FRICTION, VOICELESSNESS, etc.

burst A term used in ACOUSTIC PHONETICS, referring to a sudden, short peak of acoustic energy which occurs in the production of certain sounds, such as at the release stage of PLOSIVES, and in some FLAPS and TRILLS.

C An abbreviation in recent GOVERNMENT-BINDING THEORY for the category COMPLEMENTIZER, generally abbreviated in earlier work as COMP. This abbreviation is associated with the idea that complementizer is a HEAD of PHRASE category broadly similar to NOUN, VERB, ADJECTIVE and PREPOSITION, with associated SINGLE-BAR and DOUBLE-BAR categories, C′ and C″. C″, usually referred to as CP, is the largest unit of GRAMMATICAL analysis (the initial symbol), equivalent to S′ in earlier government-binding theory, LEXICAL FUNCTIONAL GRAMMAR and GENERALIZED PHRASE-STRUCTURE GRAMMAR.

CA The usual abbreviation for 'CONVERSATION ANALYSIS' or 'CONTRASTIVE analysis'.

calculus see PREDICATE (2), PROPOSITION

calque (from French *calquer*, to trace) A term used in COMPARATIVE and HISTORICAL linguistics to refer to a type of BORROWING, where the morphemic constituents of the borrowed WORD or PHRASE are translated ITEM by item into equivalent MORPHEMES in the new language. Such 'loan translations' are illustrated in English *power politics* from German *Machtpolitik, Superman* from *Übermensch.*

canonical An application in LINGUISTICS and PHONETICS of the general sense of this term, to refer to a linguistic FORM cited as a NORM or standard for purposes of comparison. In PHONOLOGY, for example, the normal syllabic combinations of sounds in a LANGUAGE (or in language as a whole) are often referred to as 'canonical', e.g. a CONSONANT-VOWEL (CV) or CVC structure constitutes a 'canonical SYLLABLE' pattern; an averaged waveform in automatic SPEECH RECOGNITION may be described as a 'canonical waveform'. In MORPHOLOGY the term is used sometimes to refer to the typical phonological shape of MORPHEMES in a language (e.g. CVCV in Polynesian), and sometimes for the basic form in which a MORPHEME is cited (e.g. *-s* for the plural morpheme in English). In SYNTAX, canonical STRUCTURES (such as WORD ORDER) have been postulated, e.g. SUBJECT–VERB–OBJECT, but this is an extended sense of the term. In some SOCIOLINGUISTIC and PSYCHOLINGUISTIC studies, the normal positions of human beings in relation to each other while conversing (i.e. face-to-face, etc.) is called a 'canonical encounter' or 'orientation'. See also TEMPLATE.

CAP The abbreviation for CONTROL AGREEMENT PRINCIPLE.

capacity A term used in GENERATIVE linguistics to refer to the generative POWER of

GRAMMARS. If a series of grammars generates an identical set of STRINGS (SENTENCES), they are said to have the same 'weak generative capacity'. If in addition they assign the same STRUCTURAL DESCRIPTIONS to these strings, then they have the same 'strong generative capacity'.

cardinal A TRADITIONAL term retained in some models of GRAMMATICAL description, referring to the class of numerals *one, two*, etc., by contrast with the ORDINAL numbers *first, second*, etc.

cardinal vowels A set of standard reference points, devised by the British PHONETICIAN Daniel Jones (1881–1967), to provide a precise means of identifying the VOWEL sounds of a language. The cardinal vowel system is based on a combination of ARTICULATORY and AUDITORY judgements. Four theoretical levels of TONGUE height are recognized: (a) the highest position to which the tongue can be raised without producing audible FRICTION; (b) the lowest position the tongue is capable of achieving; (c) and (d), two intermediate levels, which divide up the intervening space into areas that are articulatorily and auditorily equidistant. Using the FRONT of the tongue, and without rounding the lips, four **primary** vowel types are produced, and these are given the symbols (from HIGH to LOW [i], [e] [ɛ] and [a]. Using the BACK of the tongue, four more primary vowel types are recognized, symbolized as (from low to high) [ɑ], [ɔ], [o] and [u] – the last three involving lip-ROUNDING. In addition, each of these primary values is coded numerically, from 1 to 8 respectively.

By reversing the lip position, a **secondary** series of vowel types is produced: rounding the lips for the front vowels produces (from high to low) [y], [ø], [œ] and [Œ]; [ɒ] is the rounded equivalent of cardinal 5, and [ʌ], [ɤ] and [ɯ] are the unrounded equivalents of cardinals 6, 7 and 8 respectively. The numerical code for the secondary series runs from 9 to 16. Two further cardinal vowels represent the highest point the centre of the tongue can reach: these are symbolized by [ɨ] for the unrounded vowel and by [ʉ] for the rounded vowel, coded 17 and 18 respectively. The entire system is usually shown in the form of the 'cardinal vowel diagram', or 'cardinal vowel quadrilateral', in which the aim is to give an approximate picture of the degree and direction of tongue movement involved. Additional lines help to delimit the area in which central vowel sounds are made. It should be emphasized that the cardinal vowels are not real vowels: they are invariable reference points (available as a recording), which have to be learned by rote. Once learned, phoneticians can use them in order to locate the position of the vowels of a LANGUAGE or to compare the vowels of different languages or DIALECTS. They can be sure that the vowels will all fall somewhere within the boundaries of the cardinal area. DIACRITIC marks can then be used to plot vowel positions more accurately, e.g. a hook beneath the vowel means that the articulation is more open than the cardinal value (as in [o̜]), a dot beneath the vowel means that the articulation is closer (as in [ẹ]).

Several other suggestions have been made concerning the best way of dividing up the vowel articulation area, but Daniel Jones's system is still the most widely used.

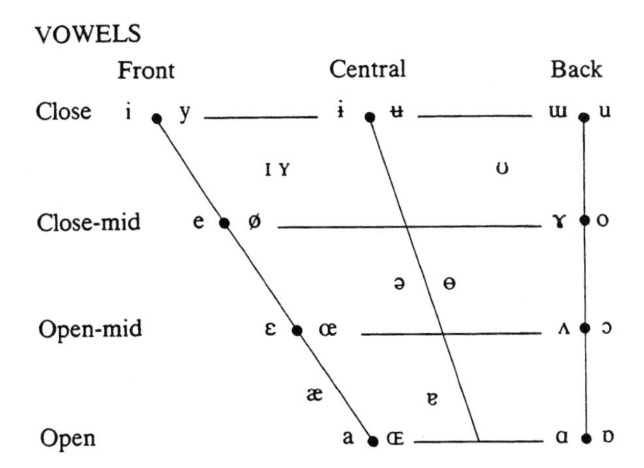

Where symbols appear in pairs, the one to the right represents a rounded vowel.

caregiver/caretaker speech see MOTHERESE

Cartesian linguistics A term used by some linguists to refer to any LINGUISTIC theories or methods which, it is claimed, illustrate the influence of the French philosopher René Descartes (1596–1650) and the GRAMMARIANS of PORT ROYAL. The discussion of UNIVERSALS in GENERATIVE linguistics, in particular, draws certain parallels with Cartesian views concerning the relationship between language and thought. This interpretation of the history of linguistic thought has remained controversial, since its initial statement by Noam CHOMSKY (cf. *Language and Mind* (1968)).

case (1) A GRAMMATICAL CATEGORY used in the analysis of WORD classes (or their associated PHRASES) to identify the SYNTACTIC relationship between words in a SENTENCE, through such contrasts as NOMINATIVE, ACCUSATIVE, etc. The traditional CLASSIFICATION, such as is found in Latin GRAMMAR, is based on variations in the MORPHOLOGICAL forms of the word (a set of such forms constituting a PARADIGM, as in Latin *puella, puellam, puellae, puella*, the singular case forms of 'girl' – respectively nominative/VOCATIVE, accusative, genitive/DATIVE and ABLATIVE). Each form is analysed in terms of a specific range of meaning; e.g. nominative is primarily the case of the grammatical SUBJECT of the sentence, genitive refers to such notions as possession, origin, and so on. In languages which lack morphological variations of this kind, the term 'case', as traditionally used, does not apply. In English, for example, the only case form which is so marked is the genitive (as in *boy's* or *boys'*); all other forms have no ending, the remaining case 'meanings' being expressed using PREPOSITIONS (as in *with a boy, to the boy*) or word order (as in the *cat chases mouse/mouse chases cat* contrast). A great deal of space in introductions to LINGUISTICS has been devoted to this point, in particular to criticism of TRADITIONAL grammars of English which insisted nonetheless on analysing the English noun in terms of cases. In some languages, highly complex morphological SYSTEMS are encountered –

according to some, Finnish can be analysed as having sixteen cases, for example – along with a correspondingly complex descriptive terminology (using such terms as INESSIVE ('in' a place), ELATIVE ('from inside' a place) and ILLATIVE ('into' a place)).

(2) **Case grammar** refers to an approach to grammatical analysis devised by the American linguist Charles Fillmore (b. 1929) in the late 1960s, within the general orientation of GENERATIVE grammar. It is primarily a reaction against the STANDARD-THEORY analysis of sentences, where notions such as SUBJECT, OBJECT, etc., are neglected in favour of analyses in terms of NP, VP, etc. By focusing on syntactic FUNCTIONS, however, it was felt that several important kinds of SEMANTIC relationship could be represented, which it would otherwise be difficult or impossible to capture. A set of sentences such as *The key opened the door, The door was opened by/with the key, The door opened, The man opened the door with a key*, etc., illustrate several 'stable' semantic roles, despite the varying SURFACE grammatical STRUCTURES. In each case the key is 'instrumental', the door is the entity affected by the action, and so on. Case grammar FORMALIZES this insight using a MODEL which shows the influence of the PREDICATE calculus of formal logic: the DEEP STRUCTURE of a sentence has two CONSTITUENTS, MODALITY (features of TENSE, MOOD, ASPECT and NEGATION, relating to the sentence as a whole) and PROPOSITION (within which the VERB is considered central, and the various semantic roles that ELEMENTS of structure can have are listed with reference to it, and categorized as cases). The term 'case' is used because of the similarity with several of the traditional meanings covered by this term (cf. (1) above), but the deep-structure cases recognized by the theory do not systematically correspond with anything in the surface morphology or syntax. The original proposal set up six cases (AGENTIVE, INSTRUMENTAL, DATIVE, FACTITIVE, LOCATIVE and OBJECTIVE) and gave rules for their combination in defining the use of verbs, e.g. a verb like *open* can be used with an objective and instrumental case (e.g. *The key opened the door*), or with an additional agent (e.g. *The man opened the door with a key*). Later, other cases were suggested (SOURCE, GOAL, COUNTER-AGENT), some cases were reinterpreted and relabelled (cf. EXPERIENCER, RESULT), and certain cases came to be given special study, it being claimed that they were more fundamental (location and direction, in particular). In a locative or LOCALIST case theory, for example, structures such as *there is a table, the table has legs, the table's legs*, and many more, could each be analysed as having an underlying locational feature. The problems in formalizing this conception of linguistic structure have remained very great, and case grammar came to attract somewhat less interest in the mid-1970s; but it has proved to be influential on the terminology and classification of several later theories. See also FRAME.

(3) (**Case**) When written with a capital C, the term refers to an abstract notion which is distinct from the MORPHOLOGICALLY marked case described under (1) above. Abstract **Case** (or **deep Case**) is present even in languages (such as Chinese) which lack morphological case on NOUN PHRASES; it is usually assumed to be CONGRUENT with morphological case when such features are present. **Case theory** is one of the (sub-)theories of GOVERNMENT-BINDING THEORY: it deals with the assignment of abstract Case and its morphological realizations, restricting the distribution of LEXICAL NPs at S-STRUCTURE. **Struc-**

tural Case is assigned to NPs at S-structure; **inherent Case** is assigned to NPs in D-STRUCTURE. **Case-marking rules** assign structural Case to certain NP positions (e.g. OBJECTIVE, where the NP is GOVERNED by a TRANSITIVE VERB or PREPOSITION), and the **Case filter** restricts the range of SENTENCES which can be generated in this way, making MOVEMENT obligatory in PASSIVES, and preventing the appearance of an ADVERBIAL between a verb and its object. Case theory in this sense must be clearly distinguished from that outlined under (2) above.

cataphora (cataphoric) A term used by some GRAMMARIANS for the process or result of a LINGUISTIC UNIT referring forward to another unit. **Cataphoric reference** is one way of marking the identity between what is being expressed and what is about to be expressed: for example, *I said this/the following* . . . , where the meaning of *this* and *the following* must be specified in the subsequent CONTEXT. *Here is the 9 o'clock news* shows the cataphoric function of *here.* **Cataphoric words** (or 'substitutes') are usually contrasted with ANAPHORIC words (which refer backwards), and sometimes with EXOPHORIC words (which refer directly to the EXTRALINGUISTIC SITUATION).

categorical perception A term used in PHONETICS and PSYCHOLINGUISTICS to refer to a class of discontinuities in the labelling and discrimination of items along ACOUSTIC PHONETIC continua. Subjects perceive differences in stimuli only between those items that are labelled as belonging to different categories.

category (categor-ize, -ization, -ial, recategorize) A general term used in LINGUISTICS at varying levels of abstraction. At its most general level, **categorization** refers to the whole process of organizing human experience into general concepts with their associated linguistic labels; the linguistic study of this process (in SEMANTICS) overlaps with that of philosophers and psychologists. In the field of GRAMMAR, categorization refers to the establishment of a set of classificatory UNITS or properties used in the description of language, which have the same basic DISTRIBUTION, and which occur as a structural unit throughout the language. In the course of language change, there may be alterations in the category status of a unit (**recategorization**). The term **category** in some approaches refers to the CLASSES themselves, e.g. NOUN, VERB, SUBJECT, PREDICATE, noun PHRASE, verb phrase (any associated abbreviations being referred to as **category symbols**). More specifically, it refers to the defining properties of these general units: the categories of the noun, for example, include NUMBER, GENDER, CASE and COUNTABILITY; of the verb, TENSE, ASPECT, VOICE, etc. A distinction is often made between **grammatical categories**, in this second sense, and grammatical FUNCTIONS (or **functional categories**), such as SUBJECT, OBJECT, COMPLEMENT.

While both of these senses of 'category' are widespread, several specific applications of the term have developed within individual theories. Most distinctive of all, perhaps, is the special status given to the term in theories of **categorial grammar**, a type of FORMAL GRAMMAR developed by several linguists and logicians in the 1950s (in particular, the linguist Yehoshua Bar Hillel (b. 1915)), the most developed of which operates in terms of two fundamental 'categories', SENTENCE and NOUN. All other categories are derived from these, the operations being based on an analysis of their SYNTACTIC DISTRIBUTION.

In SCALE-AND-CATEGORY GRAMMAR, the term is used primarily to refer to the notions of CLASS, SYSTEM, UNIT and STRUCTURE, which the theory recognized as basic. In GENERATIVE grammar, the set of PHRASE-STRUCTURE RULES in a grammar may be referred to as the **categorial component**, i.e. that part of the BASE component of the grammar which specifies such syntactic categories as S, NP, VP. A **categorial rule** is a RULE which EXPANDS a category into other categories. Also, in some MODELS of generative grammar, the term **category feature** is used to refer to a type of CONTEXTUAL feature, i.e. a syntactic feature which specifies the conditions relating to where in a DEEP STRUCTURE a LEXICAL ITEM can occur. Category features specify which NODE will be the one to DOMINATE directly the lexical item, once it is introduced into the PHRASE-MARKER (replacing the corresponding EMPTY (DELTA) symbol, e.g. [+N], [+Det], [+V]. A **category variable** is a symbol which stands for any lexical category. A related term in this model is **strict sub-categorization**, referring to features which specify further restrictions on the choice of lexical items in deep structure. See also EMPTY (1), GOVERN (2), HIGHER CATEGORY.

catenative A term used in some GRAMMATICAL descriptions of the VERB phrase to refer to a LEXICAL verb which governs the non-FINITE form of another lexical verb, as in one possible analysis of *she **likes** to go, she **wants** to see, she **hates** waiting*, etc. In GENERATIVE GRAMMAR, such constructions are known as CONTROL and RAISING CONSTRUCTIONS.

causative A term used in GRAMMATICAL description to refer to the causal relationship between alternative versions of a SENTENCE. For example, the pair of sentences *The cat killed the mouse* and *The mouse died* are related, in that the transitive *kill* can be seen as a 'causative' version of the intransitive *die*, viz. 'cause to die' (*The cat caused the mouse to die*); similarly, some AFFIXES have a causative role, e.g. *-ize*, as in *domesticize* (= 'cause to become domestic'). This is a relationship which is clearly established in the MORPHOLOGICAL STRUCTURE of some LANGUAGES (e.g. Japanese, Turkish), where an AFFIX can systematically distinguish between **non-causative** and causative uses of a VERB (e.g. 'she eats', 'she causes (someone) to eat', which is similar to English *she makes him eat*). Some linguists have also tried to apply the notion of causative systematically to English, seeing it as an abstract UNDERLYING category from which sets of 'surface' verbs (such as *kill* and *die*) can be derived.

cavity (1) In PHONETICS, this term refers to any of the anatomically defined chambers in the VOCAL TRACT which are the principal formative influences on the character of a sound. The main cavities are: (a) the OESOPHAGEAL cavity, from oesophagus to stomach, which is used only in abnormal speech production, such as following a laryngectomy operation; (b) the PULMONIC cavity, made up of the lungs and trachea, which is the normal source of speech sounds; (c) the PHARYNGEAL cavity, from the LARYNX to the point where the soft PALATE makes contact with the back of the throat; (d) the ORAL cavity, made up of the whole of the mouth area, and the main means of modifying the RESONANCE of the sound produced at the larynx; sometimes referred to as BUCCAL; (e) the NASAL cavity, made up of the nose and the part of the pharynx above the point of soft palate closure.

(2) In CHOMSKY and Halle's DISTINCTIVE FEATURE theory of PHONOLOGY, **cavity**

features constitute one of the five main dimensions in terms of which speech sounds are analysed (the others being MAJOR CLASS FEATURES, MANNER OF ARTICULATION features, SOURCE FEATURES, and PROSODIC features). The features subsumed under this heading, all analysed as OPPOSITIONS, are CORONAL, ANTERIOR, TONGUE-BODY FEATURES (HIGH/LOW/BACK), ROUNDED, DISTRIBUTED, COVERED, GLOTTAL constrictions, and SECONDARY APERTURES (NASAL and LATERAL). In some models of FEATURE GEOMETRY, an **oral cavity node** is introduced, corresponding to the articulatory notion of an oral cavity CONSTRICTION. It is represented between the ROOT NODE and the PLACE node, thus DOMINATING place and [+/− continuant] nodes.

c-command The usual abbreviation for 'constituent command'. See COMMAND (2).

CD An abbreviation for 'COMMUNICATIVE dynamism', as used by the PRAGUE SCHOOL.

ceneme (1) **(cene-matics, -tics)** A term used in GLOSSEMATICS to refer to the minimal UNIT in a language's PHONOLOGICAL system. **Cenematics** and **cenetics** are the terms used to refer to the analysis of cenemes at LEVELS corresponding to those of phonology and PHONETICS respectively.

(2) **(cenemic)** In the study of writing systems, a SIGN which denotes only linguistic FORM; opposed to **plereme**, where MEANING is also involved. There are two main types: syllabaries (e.g. Japanese kana) and alphabets. Systems of cenemic signs are more economical in their use of elementary units, and are often thought to represent a more advanced state of writing.

centre (central-ize, -ization) (1) The top part of the TONGUE, between FRONT and BACK, and used especially in the production of 'central VOWELS' (also called 'neutral' vowels), such as the [ə] sound which opens the word *asleep* and closes the word *sofa*. In a sense, when compared with the theoretical extremes of vowel ARTICULATION which define the CARDINAL VOWELS in PHONETICS, *all* real LANGUAGE vowels are **centralized**; but the term is usually used to refer to cases where a vowel normally articulated in the periphery of the vowel area comes to be produced nearer the centre of the mouth, as when *bacon and* [= and] *eggs* becomes, in normal colloquial speech, *bacon* [ənd] *eggs*. Several degrees of this process of **centralization** can be heard. Markedly 'centralized vowels' are common in several urban British DIALECTS, for example. A DIPHTHONG which involves a GLIDE towards the centre of the mouth may be referred to as a 'centring' diphthong.

(2) The most SONOROUS part of a SYLLABLE may be referred to as the 'centre' (or NUCLEUS), e.g. the [uː] in the word *boot* [buːt].

(3) In those types of grammatical PHRASE where several words depend on one HEAD word (ENDOCENTRIC constructions), the head is often referred to as the 'centre' of the phrase.

centre-embedding see SELF-EMBEDDING

centum language An Indo-European LANGUAGE in which the VELAR STOP /k/ of Proto-Indo-European was retained in such words as Latin *centum* 'hundred'; opposed to a **satem** language, where this sound changed to an alveolar fricative /s/ in such words as Avestan *satem* 'hundred'. Celtic, Romance, and Germanic languages are among the centum group; Balto-Slavonic and Indo-Iranian languages are among the satem group.

chain (1) In COMMUNICATION studies, a term used to describe a MODEL which presents the communicative act as an interrelated sequence of stages between a speaker and a receiver. With reference to speech (the **speech chain**), the model usually distinguishes psychological, neurological, physiological and anatomical stages of sound production, an acoustic stage of transmission, and anatomical, physiological, neurological and psychological stages of sound reception.

(2) In GOVERNMENT-BINDING THEORY, a MOVED CONSTITUENT and its CO-INDEXED TRACES form a **movement chain**.

(3) In historical PHONOLOGY, a situation where a series of sound changes take place, each one influencing the next. Two directions of movement are possible. When the process begins at the top or front end of an ARTICULATORY dimension, empty slots are left in the chain which other sounds move up to fill: a **drag chain**. When the process begins at the bottom or back end of the chain, each sound 'pushes' the next one out of place: a **push chain**. The Great Vowel Shift in English is often cited as a classical example of a chain movement (or **chain shift**) in operation.

(4) In SYNTAX, a term used to describe CLAUSE combinations in languages where the distinction between CO-ORDINATION and SUBORDINATION does not easily apply. In a **clause-chaining language** (such as the Papuan language, Hua), identity or lack of identity between the SUBJECTS of successive clauses is marked by verb INFLECTION (cf. SWITCH REFERENCE).

(5) (**chaining**) In SOCIOLINGUISTICS, a continuing sequence of QUESTION/answer exchanges in a conversation.

chain/choice A pair of terms used by some LINGUISTS to refer to the two main AXES of linguistic organization, corresponding to the distinction between SYNTAGMATIC ('chain') and PARADIGMATIC ('choice'). This sense of 'choice' is more restricted than that found in some discussions of SEMANTICS, where a widely held conception of MEANINGfulness is based on the ability of the speaker/hearer to 'choose' from a selection of linguistic alternatives, which provide the information-carrying contrasts prerequisite for communication.

charm (-ed, -less) In GOVERNMENT PHONOLOGY, a term adapted from particle physics, and used to refer to a property of the combinatorial possibilities of the primitive elements which form phonological SEGMENTS. Segments may be positively **charmed** (e.g. VOWELS) or negatively charmed (e.g. PLOSIVES), or they may be neutral (**charmless**, e.g. LIQUIDS). Charmed segments may govern; charmless segments may be governed. Positively charmed segments may not occur in non-NUCLEAR positions; negatively charmed segments may not occur in nuclear positions.

chart (1) A term used in PHONETICS to refer to the INTERNATIONAL PHONETIC ASSOCIATION's classification of the sounds of LANGUAGE presented in matrix form: the 'IPA chart'. See p. xvii of this dictionary.

(2) A term used in AUTOSEGMENTAL PHONOLOGY for a pair of TIERS along with the set of ASSOCIATION LINES which relates them.

checked (1) One of the features of sound set up by JAKOBSON and Halle in their DISTINCTIVE FEATURE theory of PHONOLOGY, to handle SECONDARY ARTICULATIONS – in this case, glottalization. Checked CONSONANTS are defined, both articulatorily and acoustically, as those sounds produced with accompanying GLOTTAL activity, involving a rapid energy discharge in a short time interval. EJECTIVES and IMPLOSIVES, in this view, are [+ checked]. The opposite term is **unchecked**, which applies to all non-glottalized sounds, signalled acoustically by a lower energy discharge over a larger time interval.

(2) The term is also found as an alternative to CLOSED, in the description of SYLLABLES: a **checked syllable** is one ending in a consonant, and a **checked vowel** is a vowel occurring in such a syllable.

checking (1) A term sometimes used in GRAMMATICAL description to refer to a subtype of TAG QUESTIONS: a **checking tag** is one which reverses the positive or negative value of the main-CLAUSE VERB, and whose function is seen as one of confirmation, or 'checking', e.g. *he's coming, is he*. Other types of tag would be referred to as 'copy' tags.

(2) In the MINIMALIST PROGRAMME, a procedure which determines whether a LEXICAL element has the appropriate FEATURES before it is used in a position in SENTENCE STRUCTURE. It is a basic relation which allows one element to LICENSE another by checking off the features with which the latter is associated. The set of positions to be checked is called the **checking domain**.

cherology (chereme) In LINGUISTICS, a term sometimes used for the study of SIGN language. It was coined on analogy with PHONOLOGY to refer to the study of the smallest CONTRASTIVE units (**cheremes**) which occur in a sign language. Signs are analysed into such features as the location of the signing space in which a sign is made, the hand configuration used, and the action of the active hand.

chest pulse A term used in PHONETICS to refer to a contraction of those muscles of the chest which are involved in the exhalation of air from the lungs. For the production of emphatic speech, these pulses are said to be 'reinforced' or 'stressed'. The chest pulse has been suggested as a central explanatory concept in one account of SYLLABLE production ('chest pulse theory'), but this view presents several problems.

child language acquisition see ACQUISITION (1)

choice see BINARY FEATURE

chômeur A term used in RELATIONAL GRAMMAR, derived from the French word meaning 'unemployed', to refer to a NOMINAL item which has its role in a CLAUSE taken over (or 'usurped') by another nominal; abbreviated as **cho**. For example, in a PASSIVE SENTENCE, the UNDERLYING SUBJECT is seen as having its subject FUNCTION usurped by the DIRECT OBJECT from the ACTIVE sentence; as a result, the subject of the active sentence becomes demoted into a chômeur. By seeing such STRUCTURES in terms of RULES which alter relations (rather than in terms of a TRANSFORMATION of one PHRASE-MARKER into another), it is hoped that a more UNIVERSAL formulation of such rules will be obtained.

Chomskyan (Chomskian) Characteristic of, or a follower of, the linguistic principles of (Avram) Noam **Chomsky** (b. 1928), Professor of Modern Languages and Linguistics at the Massachusetts Institute of Technology. His theory of LANGUAGE STRUCTURE known as TRANSFORMATIONAL-generative grammar revolutionized work in LINGUISTICS in 1957, with the publication of his monograph *Syntactic Structures*. Later, major publications on technical linguistic topics included *Current Issues in Linguistic Theory* (1964) and *Aspects of the Theory of Syntax* (1965). The latter publication introduced a new direction into GENERATIVE theory and became the orthodoxy for several years. His main publication on phonology was *The Sound Pattern of English* (1968), with Morris Halle, referred to in this dictionary as 'Chomsky and Halle'. Later developments in his linguistic thinking in book form may be found in *Reflections on Language* (1976), *Rules and Representations* (1980), *Knowledge of Language* (1986), *Barriers* (1986) and *The Minimalist Program* (1995).

By the mid-1960s Chomsky had come to stress the role of language as a key means to the investigation of the human mind. The view that linguistics can be profitably seen as a branch of cognitive psychology is argued especially in *Language and Mind* (1968), and it is this aspect of his thinking which has attracted a wide readership outside linguistics, especially among philosophers and psychologists.

Chomsky has also been actively involved in politics and has written widely on US involvement in Indo-China, the Middle East and Central America, e.g. *American Power and the New Mandarins* (1969), *The Fateful Triangle* (1983), and *Turning the Tide* (1985).

Chomsky-adjunction (-adjoin) A type of SYNTACTIC operation in TRANSFORMATIONAL GRAMMAR, referring to a RULE which places certain elements of STRUCTURE in adjacent POSITIONS, with the aim of specifying how these structures fit together in larger units. To 'Chomsky-adjoin' elements, a CONSTITUENT A is adjoined to B by creating a new B NODE which immediately DOMINATES both A and B. (See ADJUNCTION for TREE diagrams.)

Chomsky hierarchy A label applied to the series of increasingly powerful classes of FORMAL languages which can be generated by formal GRAMMARS (as first demonstrated by Noam CHOMSKY, using notions partly derived from AUTOMATA theory). **Type 3** grammars are FINITE-STATE GRAMMARS (also called 'right-linear grammars'); **Type 2** grammars are CONTEXT-free grammars; **Type 1** grammars are context-sensitive grammars; and **Type 0** grammars are RECURSIVE or recursively enumerable grammars.

chroneme (chrone) An abstract unit, used by some PHONOLOGISTS as a means of describing phonologically CONTRASTIVE differences in the LENGTH of speech sounds. Both VOWELS and CONSONANTS may display PHONEMIC contrasts in length: long and short vowels are found in German, long and short consonants in Lithuanian. The vowel-length differences in English, such as in *bit* and *beat*, also involve differences in QUALITY, and the term chroneme is thus not applicable. Those who use this terminology would refer to the ETIC unit of duration as a **chrone**.

chunk(ing) In PSYCHOLINGUISTICS, the breaking up of an utterance into units (**chunks**) so that it can be more efficiently PROCESSED. For example, the use of

PROSODY to chunk a sequence of digits enables the digits to be remembered more easily (cf. /3, 7, 4, 1, 9, 8, 5, 7, 6, 2/ *v.* /3, 7, 4, 1, 9 / 8, 5, 7, 6, 2/). Chunking is also used as a teaching technique in speech pathology and foreign language teaching.

circonstant In VALENCY GRAMMAR, a non-essential DEPENDENT UNIT, not determined by the valency of the VERB; opposed to **actant**. Examples would include MODIFIERS and most uses of ADVERBIALS.

circumfix see AFFIX

circumscription (circumscribe) In PROSODIC MORPHOLOGY, a term used to characterize a core principle of the approach: 'prosodic circumscription' asserts that the DOMAIN to which morphological operations apply is defined by prosodic criteria (as well as by the traditionally recognized morphological criteria). In AFFIXATION, for example, the operation of assigning a PREFIX to a BASE is traditionally carried out on purely grammatical grounds, whereas in prosodic circumscription the base form is delimited prosodically. The notion makes it possible to give an account of such phenomena as the locus of INFIXATION in prosodic terms. See also TEMPLATE (2).

citation form The FORM of a LINGUISTIC UNIT when it is cited in isolation, for purposes of discussion. More specifically, the term refers to the pronunciation given to a word when it is produced in isolation, and not in CONNECTED SPEECH.

The term **citation** is also used in a general sense in LINGUISTICS, referring to the use of an UTTERANCE or piece of TEXT for quotation or reference purposes. In LEXICOGRAPHY, **citation slips** are used to provide the evidence on which the dictionary's entries are selected and organized.

clashing (in metrical phonology) see METRICAL GRID

class(-ification, -ifier) (1) An application in LINGUISTICS and PHONETICS of the general use of this term, to refer to a set of entities sharing certain FORMAL or SEMANTIC properties. Its most widespread use is in relation to the classification of MORPHEMES into **form-classes** and WORDS into **word-classes** (other syntactic UNITS being less likely to be referred to in terms of classes). A major distinction is sometimes drawn between OPEN and CLOSED classes of words. The term **class cleavage** is sometimes used where a word is analysable into different classes, e.g. *round* in *It's your round, round the corner*, etc. Some GRAMMARIANS refer to COUNTABLE NOUNS as 'class nouns'. 'Class' has a special status in HALLIDAYAN LINGUISTICS, where it is one of the four main CATEGORIES recognized by that theory (the others being STRUCTURE, UNIT and SYSTEM). Here, classes are any set of ITEMS having the same possibilities of operation in structure, e.g. the class of 'nominal groups' can operate as SUBJECT, OBJECT, etc., in CLAUSE structure.

Morphemes whose function is to indicate the formal or SEMANTIC class to which items belong are sometimes called **classifiers**, e.g. *-ly* is an ADVERB classifier, *-ess* is a 'femininity' classifier. The marking of LEXICAL items as belonging to the same semantic class is an important feature of many languages (e.g. Chinese, Vietnamese, Hopi), and sometimes quite unexpected bases of classifications are found, in terms of shape, size, colour, movability, animacy, status, and so on.

Classification is a feature of STRUCTURALIST linguistics, where PHONES were classified into PHONEMES, MORPHS into MORPHEMES, etc. The perceived limitations of this TAXONOMIC approach to language provided a main argument for the development of GENERATIVE linguistics. However, the notion of a NATURAL CLASS is central to some recent models of PHONOLOGY; for example, in FEATURE geometry, features of the same kind are grouped together under **class nodes**.

(2) In SOCIOLINGUISTICS, the term **class dialects** is sometimes used to refer to VARIETIES of language which correlate with divisions of social class – alternatively known as 'social DIALECTS'.

classeme A term used by some European LINGUISTS (e.g. Eugene Coseriu (b. 1921)), to refer to the relatively abstract SEMANTIC FEATURES shared by LEXICAL items belonging to different semantic FIELDS, e.g. ANIMATE/inanimate, adult/child. In this approach, the term contrasts with the irreducible semantic features (SEMES) which work, at a very particular level, within a particular semantic field, e.g. *table* being identified in terms of 'number of legs', 'shape', etc.

classifier (1) See CLASS (1).

(2) In SIGN-language studies, a term used for a handshape which functions PRONOMINALLY for a class of objects, e.g. 'vehicle'.

clause (clausal) A term used in some models of GRAMMAR to refer to a UNIT of grammatical organization smaller than the SENTENCE, but larger than PHRASES, WORDS or MORPHEMES. The traditional classification is into **main** (or **superordinate**) and **subordinate** (or **dependent**) clauses, e.g. *The girl arrived | after the rain started*. Some grammars distinguish FINITE and non-finite types of clause, depending on the FORM of the VERB used, and further subdivisions are sometimes made (e.g. a reduced 'verbless' clause, as in ***when ripe***, *these apples will be lovely*). A more detailed subclassification would take into account the FUNCTION of clauses within the sentence, e.g. as ADVERBIAL, NOUN or ADJECTIVE. It would also analyse clauses into formal ELEMENTS of structure, such as SUBJECT, VERB, OBJECT, COMPLEMENT and adverbial. Derived terms include ***wh*-clauses**, such as *I wonder* ***when they will leave; that*-clauses**, such as *They decided* ***that the journey was too far***; and **small clauses**, a term used in GOVERNMENT-BINDING THEORY for clauses which contain neither a finite verb nor an INFINITIVAL *to*, such as *I saw* [***him do it***]. Mainstream GENERATIVE GRAMMAR makes no formal distinction between clauses and sentences: both are symbolized by S/S′ (or equivalents such as IP/CP). Some grammarians make use of the notion of **kernel clause**: such a clause forms a sentence on its own; is structurally complete, not ELLIPTICAL; is DECLARATIVE, not IMPERATIVE, INTERROGATIVE or EXCLAMATIVE; is POSITIVE, not NEGATIVE; and is UNMARKED with respect to all the THEMATIC systems of the clause. It should be noted that this is not an alternative term for the early generative grammar notion of 'KERNEL sentence'. See also CHAIN (4), SERIAL VERB.

clause-mate A term used in early GENERATIVE GRAMMAR to refer to a type of relationship between the ELEMENTS of a SENTENCE STRUCTURE within a PHRASE-MARKER. Elements are clause-mates if they are DOMINATED by exactly the same S NODES. For example, in a TREE partially illustrated by

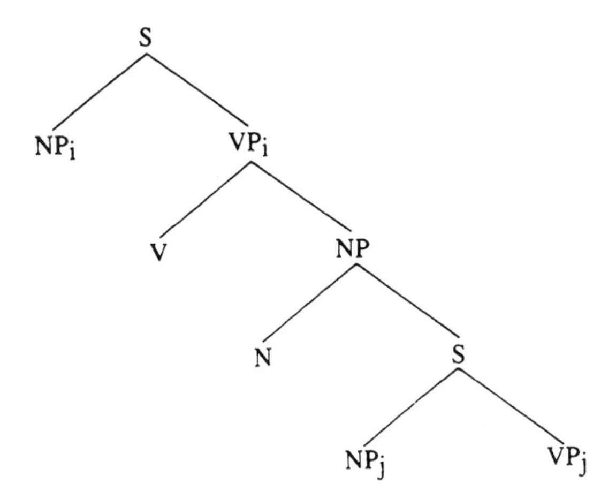

the elements NP_i and VP_i are clause-mates, as are the elements NP_j and VP_j; but NP_i is not a clause-mate of VP_j. The notion permits a certain economy of statement in discussing the properties of TRANSFORMATIONAL rules; SELECTIONAL RESTRICTIONS, for example, apply only to clause-mates.

clause-wall A term used in NON-DISCRETE GRAMMAR, to refer to the different degrees of DEPENDENCY existing between CLAUSES. Clauses which have a relatively high clause-wall between them are more independent than those which are separated by a relatively low clause-wall.

clear *l* An impressionistic but commonly used term for a variety of LATERAL sounds where the RESONANCE is that of a front VOWEL of an [i] quality, as in the standard pronunciation of /l/ before vowels and /j/ in English, e.g. *leap, lamp*. It is opposed to DARK *L*.

cleft sentence A term used in GRAMMATICAL description to refer to a CONSTRUCTION where a single CLAUSE has been divided into two separate sections, each with its own VERB. For example, the sentence *Mary is driving a new car* can be 'cleft' in various ways, e.g. *It's Mary who is driving a new car, It's a new car that Mary is driving*. The VARIANTS affect the distribution of emphasis within the SENTENCE, and correlate closely with patterns of INTONATIONAL PROMINENCE. Cleft sentences, and the associated PSEUDO-CLEFT SENTENCES, have attracted particular attention in TRANSFORMATIONAL grammar, because of the DERIVATIONAL problems they pose.

click (1) A term used in the classification of CONSONANT sounds on the basis of their MANNER OF ARTICULATION: it is a shorthand way of referring to the series of sounds produced by using the velaric AIRSTREAM MECHANISM (cf. VELAR). In English, click sounds may be heard in the 'tut tut' sound of disapproval, in some types of kiss, and in the noise used to signal appreciation or to 'gee up' horses. In some languages (e.g. Zulu, Xhosa), clicks have PHONEMIC status. The range of clicks includes BILABIAL [ʘ], dental [ǀ] formerly [ʇ], alveolar [!] formerly [ʗ], and lateral [ǁ] formerly [ʖ]. COARTICULATIONS with clicks are called 'click accompaniments'.

(2) In PSYCHOLINGUISTIC experiments on SPEECH PERCEPTION and COMPREHENSION, a 'click' refers to a BURST of ACOUSTIC noise introduced extraneously into one ear while the listener attends to speech in the other. For example, by varying the position of the click in relation to the GRAMMATICAL STRUCTURE of the speech, information can be gained concerning the way in which grammatical units are perceived and organized by the brain. In one series of experiments, when the click occurred at a grammatical boundary, it was recalled as occurring there; but when it occurred within a CONSTITUENT, it was recalled as occurring towards the constituent boundary ('click displacement'). Such findings can then be interpreted in terms of the perceptual or cognitive reality of constituent boundaries.

cline A term used in HALLIDAYAN LINGUISTICS to refer to a continuum of potentially infinite gradation, e.g. the range of possible contrasts between FALLING and RISING PITCH levels, or the degrees of contrast capable of being drawn along a time scale. Since its original use in SCALE-AND-CATEGORY GRAMMAR, the term has come to be used in other fields than linguistics, often unnecessarily, as a synonym for 'continuum'.

clinical linguistics A term sometimes used for the application of LINGUISTIC theories, methods and descriptive findings to the analysis of medical conditions or settings involving a disorder of language. This application involves the linguist working in collaboration with SPEECH pathologists/therapists, audiologists and others in helping to assess, diagnose and remediate disorders of the PRODUCTION and COMPREHENSION of spoken or written language – disorders which may of course occur in educational as well as clinical settings. The relevance of PSYCHOLINGUISTICS, NEUROLINGUISTICS and language ACQUISITION studies to this end is noteworthy.

clipped form see ABBREVIATION

clitic(-ize, -ization) A term used in GRAMMAR to refer to a FORM which resembles a WORD, but which cannot stand on its own as a normal UTTERANCE, being structurally dependent upon a neighbouring word in a CONSTRUCTION. (The term 'clitic' comes from the Greek word for 'leaning'.) Examples are the CONTRACTED forms of *be*, such as *I'm* and *he's*. The ARTICLES of English, French, etc., are sometimes referred to as clitics: a form like *the* cannot stand on its own in normal utterance, but it would be called a word nonetheless by NATIVE-SPEAKERS. Such clitic words ('clitics') can be classified into **proclitics** (i.e. they depend upon a following word, as in the case of the articles) and **enclitics** (i.e. they depend upon a preceding word, as in the attachment (**cliticization**) of some PRONOUNS to the end of a VERB form in Italian or Spanish). The processes are also referred to as **proclisis** and **enclisis** respectively.

close (1) A term used in the four-level classification of vertical TONGUE movement in VOWEL sounds based on the CARDINAL VOWEL system, the others being 'half-close', 'half-open' and 'open'. It refers to a vowel made with the tongue in the highest position possible without causing audible FRICTION, as in the

ARTICULATION of [i] and [u]: the closest vowels in English are in words like *seat* and *shoot*. The area of articulation immediately below 'close' is known as **half-close** or **mid-close**, as in [e] and [o] (the nearest sounds in English are in words like *say* and *so* respectively). In a three-level classification of vowel sounds, the highest group are known as 'high' vowels (as opposed to 'low' and 'mid').

(2) A term used in the classification of types of JUNCTURE or TRANSITION, referring to the normal transitions operating between the sounds in a word. 'Close juncture' is opposed to 'open' or 'plus' juncture; 'close transition' to 'open transition'.

(3) A term used in the classification of types of JAW SETTING, referring to a jaw position in which the teeth are brought closer together than normal; opposed to 'open' jaw settings.

closed (1) A term sometimes used in the GRAMMATICAL classification of WORDS to refer to one of two postulated major word-CLASSES in language, the other being OPEN. A **closed class** is one whose membership is fixed or limited. New ITEMS are not regularly added, as is the case with 'open-class' items. PRONOUNS, PREPOSITIONS, CONJUNCTIONS, ARTICLES, etc., are all closed class or **closed system** items, the term 'system' here reflecting the fact that the membership of such classes is finite, the members displaying an interdependence of MEANING and use.

(2) A term used in the two-way classification of SYLLABLE structure, referring to a syllable ending in a CONSONANT; its opposite is OPEN, where the syllable ends in a vowel. This feature is sometimes referred to as a CHECKED or blocked syllable.

closure A general term used in PHONETICS to refer to an ARTICULATION where the contact between active and passive articulators obstructs the airstream through the mouth and/or nose. A 'complete closure' exists in the case of PLOSIVES, AFFRICATES and NASALS, and in the glottalic and velaric AIRSTREAM MECHANISMS. An 'intermittent closure' exists in the case of ROLLS, FLAPS and TAPS. A 'partial closure' exists in the case of LATERALS. Some phoneticians would include FRICATIVES under the heading of 'partial' or 'incomplete' closure. A narrowing of the VOCAL TRACT where there is *no* articulatory contact is usually called a STRICTURE.

cluster A term used in the analysis of CONNECTED SPEECH to refer to any sequence of adjacent CONSONANTS occurring INITIALLY or FINALLY in a SYLLABLE, such as the initial [br-] of *bread*, or the final [-st] of *best*. Not all possible combinations of consonants occur in a LANGUAGE. Initially in syllables in English, for example, clusters are not possible with [ð], [ʧ], [ʤ] or [z]. Up to three consonants can occur initially, as in [spr-], [spl-], [skw-]; up to four can occur finally, as in *glimpsed* [-mpst] and *twelfths* [-lfθs]. See also REDUCE.

coalesce(nce) (1) A term used in LINGUISTICS, especially in HISTORICAL studies, to refer to the coming together of linguistic UNITS which were originally distinguishable. ALLOphones of a PHONEME may coalesce, as may different phonemes and different MORPHEMES. Many CASES of Modern English /ʒ/, for example, are the result of coalescence of /z/ and /j/, e.g. *occasion, measure*; in WORDS like *forma-*

tion, one could analyse the AFFIX as a coalescence of the morphemes *-ate* + *-tion*. Analogous terms include SYNCRETISM, MERGER, FUSION and NEUTRALIZATION.
(2) (**-nt**) A term used in PHONETICS and PHONOLOGY as part of the classification of types of ASSIMILATION. In **coalescent** (or 'reciprocal') **assimilation**, each of two adjacent ARTICULATIONS influences the other. An example is the FUSION of [d] and [j] to produce [ʤ] in such phrases as *could you*.

coarticulation An ARTICULATION which takes place involving in a simultaneous or overlapping way more than one point in the VOCAL TRACT, as in the co-ordinate STOPS [k͡p], [g͡b], [p͡t] and [b͡d] often heard in West African languages. In **anticipatory coarticulation**, an articulator not involved in a particular sound begins to move in the direction of an articulation needed for a later sound in the UTTERANCE (its TARGET). An example is the *sh-* of *shoe*, which is normally pronounced with lip-ROUNDING, anticipating the influence of the following [uː]. Coarticulation may also be seen when a sound retains a characteristic deriving from an earlier articulation. See also ANTICIPATORY (2).

cocktail party phenomenon An everyday effect studied scientifically in PSYCHOLINGUISTICS as part of a theory of SPEECH PERCEPTION. It refers to the process of SELECTIVE LISTENING, whereby people listening to several conversations at once are able to attend consciously to one of them, and to ignore the others.

coda A term used in PHONETICS and PHONOLOGY to refer to the ELEMENT of a SYLLABLE which may follow the syllabic NUCLEUS, e.g. the /p/ of /kʌp/. A distinction is sometimes drawn between 'simple' syllabic codas (containing only one segment) and 'complex' codas (containing more than one segment). Restrictions on the segments or features which may occur in coda position are known as **coda constraints**.

code The general sense of this term – a set of conventions for converting one signalling system into another – enters into the subject-matter of SEMIOTICS and COMMUNICATION theory rather than LINGUISTICS. Such notions as 'encoding' and 'decoding' are sometimes encountered in PHONETICS and linguistics, but the view of language as a 'code' is not one which figures greatly in these subjects. The term has come to the fore in SOCIOLINGUISTICS, where it is mainly used as a neutral label for any system of communication involving language – and which avoids sociolinguists having to commit themselves to such terms as DIALECT, LANGUAGE or VARIETY, which have a special status in their theories. The linguistic behaviour referred to as **code-switching**, for example, can be illustrated by the switch BILINGUAL speakers may make (depending on who they are talking to, or where they are) between STANDARD and regional forms of English, between Welsh and English in parts of Wales, or between occupational and domestic varieties. **Code-mixing** involves the transfer of linguistic elements from one language into another. On the other hand, several sociologists and sociolinguists have given 'code' a more restricted definition. For example, codes are sometimes defined in terms of mutual intelligibility (e.g. the language of a private or professional group). But the most widespread special use of the term was in the theory of communication codes propounded by the British sociologist Basil Bernstein (b. 1924). His distinction between ELABORATED and RESTRICTED codes was part of a theory of the nature of social systems, concerned in particular with the kinds of meanings people communicate, and how explicitly they do this, using the range of resources provided by the language.

codification (codify) A term used in LANGUAGE planning (CORPUS planning), referring to the compilation of a systematic statement of the RULES and conventions governing the use of a language VARIETY, typically the STANDARD language of a community. When a language has been codified, its products include spelling and pronunciation guides, grammars, dictionaries, style manuals, and guides to correct usage.

cognate (1) A language or a LINGUISTIC FORM which is historically derived from the same source as another language/form, e.g. Spanish/Italian/French/Portuguese are 'cognate languages' (or simply 'cognates'); *père/padre*, etc. ('father') are 'cognate words' or cognates.

(2) The term is also applied to the description of some kinds of SYNTACTIC RELATIONS: a 'cognate OBJECT' is one which has the same historical derivation as the VERB which governs it (or, more loosely, is SEMANTICALLY dependent upon the action of the verb), e.g. *to run a race, live a good life, ask a question*; a cognate SUBJECT–VERB–OBJECT sequence is illustrated by such sentences as *Employers employ employees.*

cognise see COGNIZE

cognitive (meaning) A term sometimes used in SEMANTICS as part of a classification of types of MEANING. It refers to those aspects of meaning which relate directly to DENOTATIONS of LEXICAL items and the PROPOSITIONAL content of SENTENCES, and thus corresponds to an intellectually objective level of interpretation, as opposed to one where emotional or subjective interpretation is involved. Alternative terms include DENOTATIVE and REFERENTIAL; opposite terms include EMOTIVE and CONNOTATIVE.

cognitive grammar A LINGUISTIC theory which sees language as an integral part of cognition, a means whereby cognitive content is given structure; originally called **space grammar**. In this approach, the basic function of language is to symbolize conceptualization by means of PHONOLOGY. GRAMMAR is seen as an inherently meaningful (or 'symbolic') component of the theory, linking SEMANTICS (viewed in conceptualist terms) and phonology. This pairing of FORMS and MEANINGS sets up connections between established ('entrenched') patterns of neurological activity ('units'), which serve as TEMPLATES for categorizing expressions. Each unit (semantic, phonological, symbolic) corresponds to an aspect of STRUCTURE, and WELL-FORMED expressions are 'conventionally' constructed using a series of units. Grammatical CLASSES and CONSTRUCTIONS are analysed as configurations of symbolic structures: a basic distinction is drawn between 'nominals' (things, e.g. NOUN PHRASES) and 'relational expressions' (relationships, e.g. VERBS, PREPOSITIONS, ADJECTIVES, CLAUSES); grammatical RULES are characterized as abstract 'constructional schemas'. See also COGNITIVE SEMANTICS.

cognitive metaphor A theory in which metaphor is viewed as performing an essential role in human LANGUAGE and cognition, encoding world-views in all forms of linguistic activity, including everyday conversation ('conceptual metaphors'). Higher-level concepts such as causality, time, and the emotions are seen to be SEMANTICALLY grounded in lower-level domains of physical experience, as in such expressions as *life is a journey* or the interpretation of causation in family terms (*X is the father of modern physics*). 'Poetic metaphors' are seen as extensions or novel combinations of everyday metaphors. This approach thus contrasts with the traditional account of metaphor (with its distinction between literal and figurative MEANING, and its focus on rhetorical and literary contexts), which is felt to be of limited relevance to a fully linguistic account of grammatical and semantic structure.

cognitive semantics A SEMANTIC theory, part of COGNITIVE GRAMMAR, which identifies MEANING with conceptualization – the structures and processes which are part of mental experience. It operates with an encyclopedic view of meaning, not recognizing a clear boundary between linguistic and extralinguistic worlds; everything that is known about an entity is allowed to contribute to its meaning. LEXICAL ITEMS are therefore typically POLYSEMOUS, and analysed as a network of related SENSES. A central notion is how a conceptual content is 'construed': the construal of a lexical item depends on several factors, including the 'cognitive domains' in which it appears (e.g. space, time, colour) and variations in perspective and salience.

cognize A term suggested by Noam CHOMSKY as an alternative to 'know'. Speakers are said to cognize not only the linguistic facts which they consciously know (e.g. that a particular SENTENCE has a particular interpretation), but also the mentally represented RULES from which these facts derive and the INNATE principles underlying these rules.

coherence An application of the general use of this term in DISCOURSE analysis, referring to the main principle of organization postulated to account for the underlying FUNCTIONAL connectedness or identity of a piece of spoken or written LANGUAGE (TEXT, discourse). It involves the study of such factors as the language users' knowledge of the world, the inferences they make, and the assumptions they hold, and in particular of the way in which communication is mediated through the use of SPEECH ACTS. In this context, coherence is usually contrasted with COHESION, which refers to the SYNTACTIC or SEMANTIC CONNECTIVITY of linguistic FORMS at a SURFACE-STRUCTURE LEVEL of analysis.

cohesion (cohesive(ness)) (1) A term often used in GRAMMAR to refer to a defining property of the WORD, seen as a grammatical UNIT. The criterion states that new ELEMENTS cannot usually be inserted into words in normal speech, but only at word boundaries. An alternative name for this criterion is 'uninterruptability'. The criterion works well for English (apart from such examples as *abso-blooming-lutely*), but has to be modified if applied to languages where INFIXES are used.

(2) The term is used by some linguists to refer to the property of larger units than the MORPHEME to bind together in CONSTRUCTIONS, e.g. ARTICLE + NOUN. In this use, any group of words which acts as a CONSTITUENT of a larger unit can be said to be internally cohesive. In the HALLIDAYAN approach to grammatical analysis, cohesion is a major concept, referring to those SURFACE-STRUCTURE features of an UTTERANCE or TEXT which link different parts of SENTENCES or

larger units of DISCOURSE, e.g. the cross-referencing function of PRONOUNS, ARTICLES and some types of ADVERB (as in ***The** man went to town. **However,** he did not stay long ...*). A distinction is usually drawn with the notion of a text's UNDERLYING COHERENCE.

co-hyponyms see HYPONYM

co-indexing (co-index) A term used in recent GENERATIVE LINGUISTIC theory to refer to the process of assigning the same subscript letter or numeral to a series of CONSTITUENTS; superscripts are sometimes used. In particular, these numerals mark the identity of constituents in the DEEP STRUCTURE of a SENTENCE. For example, in the deep structure of *I persuaded Mary*$_1$ PRO$_1$ *to leave*, where the PRO convention is used, the numerals show that *Mary* is co-indexed with (co-REFERENTIAL with) PRO, and is thus the SUBJECT of *leave*. Co-indexing is also used in the TRACE theory of MOVEMENT RULES.

collapse A term used in GENERATIVE GRAMMAR to refer to the notational conflation of two RULES into one, in the interests of a simpler and more general statement, e.g. NP → D N and NP → D Adj N, being replaced by NP → D(Adj)N, where the BRACKETS refer to the optional use of the adjective.

collective A term used in GRAMMATICAL DESCRIPTION to refer to a NOUN which denotes a group of entities, and which is FORMALLY differentiated from other nouns by a distinct pattern of NUMBER contrast (and, in some languages, MORPHOLOGICALLY). **Collective nouns** (e.g. *government, army, club, jury, public*) fall into several grammatical subclasses, but their distinctive characteristic is their ability to co-occur in the singular with either a singular or a plural VERB, this correlating with a difference of interpretation – the noun being seen as a single collective entity, or as a collection of individual entities (cf. *the committee is wrong v. the committee are wrong*). In some languages, 'collective' (*v.* **non-collective**) refers to a type of plural formation in which a number of individuals is seen as forming a coherent set; for example, a plural SUFFIX A attached to *house* might express the notion of a 'village' (collective), whereas suffix B might refer to any random group of houses (non-collective).

colligation (colligate) A term in FIRTHIAN LINGUISTICS for the process or result of grouping a set of WORDS on the basis of their similarity in entering into SYNTAGMATIC GRAMMATICAL RELATIONS. For example, a set of VERBS which take a certain kind of COMPLEMENT CONSTRUCTION would be said to be 'in colligation with' that construction, e.g. *agree, choose, decline, manage*, etc. **colligate** with *to*+infinitive constructions, as opposed to *-ing* forms, as *I agree to go v. *I agree going*. Colligation is usually contrasted with COLLOCATION.

collocation (colloc-ate, -ability) A term used in LEXICOLOGY by some (especially FIRTHIAN) LINGUISTS to refer to the habitual co-occurrence of individual LEXICAL ITEMS. For example, *auspicious* 'collocates' with *occasion, event, sign*, etc.; and *letter* collocates with *alphabet, graphic*, etc., on the one hand, and *postman, pillar-box*, etc., on the other. Collocations are, then, a type of SYNTAGMATIC lexical relation. They are linguistically predictable to a greater or lesser extent (e.g. the bond between *spick* and *span* is stronger than that between *letter* and *pillar-box*), and this differentiates them from SENSE ASSOCIATIONS which tend to include idiosyncratic connections (e.g. *mother-in-law* associating with *hippopotamus*). Some words have no specific **collocational restrictions** – grammatical words such as *the, of, after, in*. By contrast, there are many totally predictable restrictions, as in *eke* + *out, spick* + *span*, and these are usually analysed as IDIOMS, clichés, etc. Another important feature of collocations is that they are FORMAL (not SEMANTIC) statements of co-occurrence; e.g. *green* collocates with *jealousy* (as opposed to, say, *blue* or *red*), even though there is no REFERENTIAL basis for the link. Lexical items which are 'collocated' are said to be **collocates** of each other; the potential of items to collocate is known as their **collocability** or **collocational range**. A related notion is 'semantic prosody' (cf. SEMANTICS). Collocational restrictions are analogous to the notion of SELECTIONAL RESTRICTIONS in GENERATIVE GRAMMAR.

colouring (colour) In PHONETICS, a perceived slight change in the quality of a VOWEL sound due to the influence of some nearby sound. For example, '*r*-colouring' occurs when a vowel is affected by the RESONANCE of a following *r*-type sound, most noticeably a RETROFLEX; a following /h/ can cause '*h*-colouring'.

combinatorial A fundamental function of LINGUISTIC UNITS to 'combine' with one another to produce more complex patterns. The 'combinatorial properties' or 'relations' of CONSONANTS and VOWELS, for example, can be used as a definition of SYLLABLE (vowel as NUCLEUS, consonants as MARGINS). Combination, in this sense, is a SYNTAGMATIC relation, and opposed to the PARADIGMATIC notion of CONTRAST.

command (1) A term used in the classification of SENTENCE FUNCTIONS, and defined sometimes on GRAMMATICAL and sometimes on SEMANTIC or SOCIOLINGUISTIC grounds. SYNTACTICALLY a command is a sentence which typically has no SUBJECT, and where the VERB is in the IMPERATIVE MOOD, e.g. *Come here!* Semantically it is primarily used to tell someone to do (or not do) something. From a SPEECH ACT point of view, the function of command may be expressed using other forms, e.g. *that boy will stand up*, or by a dominant INTONATION. The term is usually contrasted with three other major sentence functions: STATEMENT, QUESTION, EXCLAMATION. In grammatical discussion, commands are usually referred to as 'imperative' in form.

(2) In recent GENERATIVE grammar, the term is used in the phrase **constituent-command**, invariably abbreviated to **c-command**, and **maximal-command**, invariably abbreviated to **m-command**. C-command is the relationship between an element and the other elements it is superior to in the PHRASE-MARKER, but which it does not dominate. A CONSTITUENT X is said to m-command Y if the first maximal PROJECTION which DOMINATES X also dominates Y, and X does not dominate Y, and Y does not dominate X. Thus, in the TREE

N''
Det N'
N P''

N m-commands Det although it does not c-command it. In the tree

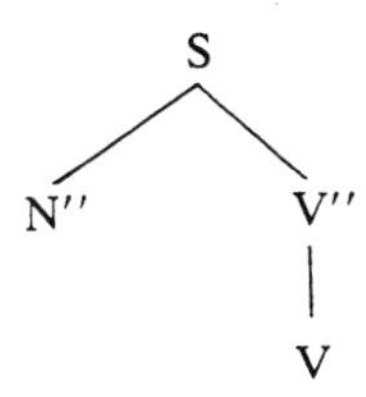

V does not m-command N″ although it c-commands it. C-commanding is an important notion in the explication of GOVERNMENT.

comment (1) A term used in SEMANTICS and GRAMMAR as part of an alternative binary characterization of SENTENCE structure to that traditionally found in the SUBJECT/PREDICATE distinction; the opposite term is TOPIC. The topic of a sentence is the person or thing about which something is said, whereas the comment is that part of the sentence which says something further about the topic. In the sentence *The book was on the table, the book* is the topic, and the remainder of the sentence is the comment. English does not mark this distinction as clearly as in some languages, where grammatical PARTICLES, WORD-order contrasts or INFLECTIONS may help to show the contrast. An analogous distinction is made using the terms THEME and RHEME, by some linguists.

(2) A type of CLAUSE recognized in QUIRK GRAMMAR, referring to an optional structure whose function is to add a parenthetic comment to another clause. There is a wide range of **comment clauses** in English, e.g. *you know, to be honest, they say, generally speaking*. Several of these act as STEREOTYPED conversation fillers, with several complex functions, e.g. *you see, mind you, I see.*

commissive A term used in the theory of SPEECH ACTS to refer to a type of UTTERANCE where the speaker makes a commitment to a future course of action, as in *I promise/I guarantee. . . .*

common (1) A term used in GRAMMATICAL description to refer to the UNMARKED MORPHOLOGICAL form of a grammatical CATEGORY. In English, for example, the form of the NOUN other than the GENITIVE could be called the 'common CASE' form. Similarly, one might use 'common GENDER' in a language where only one contrast is made (e.g. feminine *v.* masculine/neuter, etc.), or where sex is indeterminate out of context (as in French *enfant*, 'child'). In TRADITIONAL grammar, 'common nouns' were a SEMANTICALLY defined subclass of nouns (referring to 'general concepts') contrasted with PROPER nouns (names of individuals, etc.); LINGUISTIC approaches tend to emphasize the FORMAL distinctions that can be made between such subclasses (e.g. different patterns of ARTICLE usage).

(2) The phrase **common core** is used in some SOCIOLINGUISTIC and STYLISTIC studies, referring to the range of linguistic features common to all VARIETIES, DIALECTS, etc., of a language. A usage such as *thou* in English, for example, would not be part of this common core, as it is restricted to certain dialects and religious CONTEXTS.

communication (communicat-e, -ive) A fundamental notion in the study of behaviour, which acts as a frame of reference for LINGUISTIC and PHONETIC studies. Communication refers to the transmission and reception of INFORMATION (a 'message') between a source and receiver using a signalling system: in linguistic contexts, source and receiver are interpreted in human terms, the system involved is a LANGUAGE, and the notion of response to (or acknowledgement of) the message becomes of crucial importance. In theory, communication is said to have taken place if the information received is the same as that sent: in practice, one has to allow for all kinds of interfering factors, or 'noise', which reduce the efficiency of the transmission (e.g. unintelligibility of ARTICULATION, idiosyncratic ASSOCIATIONS of WORDS). One has also to allow for different levels of control in the transmission of the message: speakers' purposive selection of signals will be accompanied by signals which communicate 'despite themselves', as when VOICE QUALITY signals the fact that a person has a cold, is tired/old/male, etc. The scientific study of all aspects of communication is sometimes called **communication science**: the domain includes linguistics and phonetics, their various branches, and relevant applications of associated subjects (e.g. acoustics, anatomy).

Human communication may take place using any of the available sensory modes (hearing, sight, etc.), and the differential study of these modes, as used in communicative activity, is carried on by SEMIOTICS. A contrast which is often made, especially by psychologists, is between **verbal** and **non-verbal communication** to refer to the linguistic *v.* the non-linguistic features of communication (the latter including facial expressions, gestures, etc., both in humans and animals). However, the ambiguity of the term 'verbal' here, implying that language is basically a matter of 'words', makes this term of limited value to linguists, and it is not usually used by them in this way.

The term 'communicative' is often used in a restricted sense. In the phrase **communicative competence**, for instance, it is in contrast with 'linguistic', a distinction being made between the NATIVE-SPEAKERS' awareness of the FORMAL patterning of their language, on the one hand (their 'linguistic competence'), and of the situational APPROPRIATENESS of their language, on the other. This emphasis on functional appropriateness also characterizes several uses of the term in the field of foreign-language teaching (**communicative grammar, communicative syllabus**, etc.). **Communicative dynamism** (or CD) is a fundamental concept of the modern PRAGUE SCHOOL theory of LINGUISTICS (cf. FUNCTIONAL SENTENCE PERSPECTIVE), whereby an UTTERANCE is seen as a process of gradually unfolding MEANING, each part of the utterance contributing variously ('dynamically') to the total communicative effect. Some parts of an utterance will contribute little to the meaning, because they reflect only what has already been communicated: these 'thematic' aspects would be considered to have the lowest degree of CD. By contrast, 'rhematic' aspects have the highest degree of CD, containing new information which advances the communicative process. Other aspects are also recognized.

commutation A term used by some PHONOLOGISTS to refer to a process of sound SUBSTITUTION to show CONTRASTIVITY. It is especially encountered in the phrase **commutation test**, which is a systematic use of the substitutability technique of MINIMAL PAIRS for establishing PHONEMES. Some LINGUISTIC theories have used the term in a more restricted sense: in GLOSSEMATICS, for example, it is contrasted with 'substitution', and refers only to one type of relationship between the members of a PARADIGM.

comp An abbreviation for COMPACT, COMPLEMENT and COMPARATIVE; also, in recent GENERATIVE LINGUISTICS, as **Comp** or **COMP**, an abbreviation for COMPLEMENTIZER.

compact One of the features of sound set up by JAKOBSON and Halle in their DISTINCTIVE FEATURE theory of PHONOLOGY, to handle variations in PLACE OF ARTICULATION, its opposite being DIFFUSE. Compact sounds are defined articulatorily and acoustically, as those which involve a STRICTURE relatively far forward in the mouth, and a relatively high concentration of ACOUSTIC energy in a narrow, central part of the sound spectrum. For example, OPEN VOWELS are [+compact] (abbreviated as [+comp]; HIGH or MID vowels are [−compact] ([−comp]). The feature is replaced by LOW in CHOMSKY and Halle's system.

comparative (1) A term used to characterize a major branch of LINGUISTICS, in which the primary concern is to make statements comparing the characteristics of different LANGUAGES (DIALECTS, VARIETIES, etc.), or different historical states of a language. During the nineteenth century, the concern for comparative analysis was exclusively historical, as scholars investigated the relationships between such FAMILIES of languages as Sanskrit, Greek, Latin, their hypothetical antecedents (i.e. the PROTO-language from which such families developed), and the subsequent processes which led to the formation of the language groups of the present day. This study became known as **comparative philology** (or simply PHILOLOGY) – sometimes as **comparative grammar**. The phrase **comparative method** refers to the standard comparative philological technique of comparing a set of forms taken from COGNATE languages in order to determine whether a historical relationship connects them. If there were such a relationship, this analysis would then be used to deduce the characteristics of the ancestor language from which they were assumed to have derived (a process of 'comparative' or 'internal' RECONSTRUCTION).

Early twentieth-century linguistics switched from a DIACHRONIC to a SYNCHRONIC emphasis in language analysis, and, while not excluding historical studies, comparative linguistics these days is generally taken up with the theoretical and practical analysis of the STRUCTURAL correspondences between living languages, regardless of their history, with the aim of establishing general types of language ('TYPOLOGICAL comparison', or 'typological linguistics') and ultimately the UNIVERSAL characteristics of human language.

(2) A term used in the three-way GRAMMATICAL description of ADJECTIVES and

ADVERBS into DEGREES, specifying the extent of their application. The **comparative form** is used for a comparison between two entities, and contrasts with SUPERLATIVE, for more than two, and POSITIVE, where no comparison is implied. In English, there is both an INFLECTION (*-er*) and a PERIPHRASTIC construction (*more*) to express this notion (e.g. *nicer, more beautiful*). The construction which may follow the use of a comparative is called a 'comparative clause' or 'comparative sentence', e.g. *He is bigger* ***than I am***.

compensatory lengthening In PHONOLOGY, an effect in which the DELETION of one SEGMENT is accompanied by an increase in the LENGTH of another, usually adjacent to it, thus preserving SYLLABLE weight. Typically, a VOWEL is lengthened when a syllable-final segment is lost, as in Old English *gōs* 'goose', which comes from Germanic *gans* through the loss of the NASAL and the lengthening of the preceding vowel. The phenomenon is of importance in phonological theories which recognize the role of syllabic weight (such as AUTOSEGMENTAL PHONOLOGY).

competence A term used in LINGUISTIC theory, and especially in GENERATIVE GRAMMAR, to refer to speakers' knowledge of their language, the SYSTEM of RULES which they have mastered so that they are able to produce and understand an indefinite number of SENTENCES, and to recognize grammatical mistakes and AMBIGUITIES. It is an idealized conception of language, which is seen as in opposition to the notion of PERFORMANCE, the specific UTTERANCES of speech; the SAUSSUREAN distinction between LANGUE and PAROLE is similar, but there are important differences between the definitions of competence and *langue*. According to CHOMSKY, linguistics before generative grammar had been preoccupied with performance in a CORPUS, instead of with the UNDERLYING competence involved. As a general conception, this distinction has been widely accepted, but there has been criticism from linguists who feel that the boundary between the two notions is not as clear-cut as their definitions would lead one to believe. There are problems, often, in deciding whether a particular speech feature is a matter of competence or performance (e.g. a feature of INTONATION, or DISCOURSE).

A particularly strong line of criticism emerged in the notion of **communicative competence**, which focuses on the NATIVE-SPEAKERS' ability to produce and understand sentences which are appropriate to the CONTEXT in which they occur – what speakers need to know in order to communicate effectively in socially distinct settings. Communicative competence, then, subsumes the social determinants of linguistic behaviour, including such environmental matters as the relationship between speaker and hearer, and the pressures which stem from the time and place of speaking. If speakers have a tacit awareness of such communicative CONSTRAINTS, it is argued, then a linguistic theory ought to aim to provide an explicit account of these factors, in so far as these are systematic within a community, and not restrict itself to the analysis of STRUCTURE in purely FORMAL terms (as in the notion of 'linguistic' competence). This view has received a wide measure of acceptance, but to date relatively little progress has been made over the question of how to model this broader conception of competence in precise terms. More recently, an analogous notion of **pragmatic competence** has been proposed. See also GRAMMAR (5), PRAGMATICS.

complement(-ation) A term used in the analysis of GRAMMATICAL FUNCTION, to refer to a major CONSTITUENT of SENTENCE or CLAUSE STRUCTURE, traditionally associated with 'completing' the action specified by the VERB. In its broadest sense, complement therefore is a very general notion, subsuming all obligatory features of the PREDICATE other than the verb, e.g. OBJECTS (e.g. *She kicked* ***the ball***) and ADVERBIALS (e.g. *She was* ***in the garden***). In some approaches, the complement is given a more restricted definition, e.g. to refer only to the 'completing' function of structures following the verb *to be* (or similar verbs) – in such an analysis, *She kicked the doctor* would be SUBJECT–Verb–Object, whereas *She is a doctor* would be Subject–Verb–Complement. A further distinction is sometimes made between complements of the subject and those of the object, as in *She is* ***a doctor*** (**subject complement**) and *She called me* ***a fool*** (**object complement**). **Complement clauses** of various kinds are recognized, this notion sometimes being interpreted as any kind of SUBORDINATE clause, sometimes as only one type of subordinate clause (e.g. a clause following *be*, such as *That is* ***what I said***). However, the domain of **complementation** remains an unclear area in linguistic analysis, and there are several unresolved issues, e.g. whether the PARTICLES in phrasal verbs (e.g. *come* ***in***) should be subsumed under this heading. In GENERATIVE grammar, a complement is a SISTER constituent of a ZERO-level category. Categories other than the verb are also sometimes said to take complements, e.g. in *a student of physics, of physics* is said to be the complement of *student*. In X-BAR SYNTAX, the term is used in opposition to ADJUNCT (cf. *a student with long hair*). See also WH-.

complementary (1) A term used primarily in PHONOLOGY in the phrase **complementary distribution**, referring to the mutual exclusiveness of a pair of sounds in a certain PHONETIC ENVIRONMENT. In English, for example, the voiceless ALLophone of the /l/ phoneme occurs after initial /s-/, as in *sleep*, and the VOICED allophone is excluded; conversely, [l] is used initially when no /s-/ proceeds. [l̥] and [l] are thus said to be 'in complementary DISTRIBUTION' in this environment. The term is also used analogously in MORPHOLOGY, with reference to the distribution of pairs of FORMS in GRAMMATICAL environments (e.g. the selection of alternative forms of plural MORPHEME in English).

(2) (**complementarity**) In SEMANTICS, the term is often used to refer to a category of SENSE relation between LEXICAL ITEMS. **Complementary terms** (or **complementaries**) display a type of oppositeness of MEANING, illustrated by such pairs as *single/married* and *boy/girl. Single* is said to be 'the complementary of' *married*, and vice versa. In such a relationship, the assertion of one of the items implies the denial of the other: an entity cannot be both at once. The relationship of complementarity is characterized by the lack of any gradability between the items (there is no continuum of gradation between *boy* and *girl*, such that one can be **less boy*, **very boy*, and so on). In this respect, the term contrasts with the technical sense of ANTONYMY, where gradations between the opposites are possible (cf. *big, bigger, very big*, etc. *v. small, smaller*, etc.), and also with CONVERSENESS, where the opposites presuppose each other (e.g. *husband/wife*). The term CONTRADICTORY is an alternative preferred by some analysts.

complementizer (abbreviated **Comp, COMP, C**) In GENERATIVE SYNTAX, a term used to refer to SUBORDINATING CONJUNCTIONS which mark an EMBEDDED sentence of a COMPLEMENT type, e.g. *that* in *I said that he was leaving*. It is also used, in X-BAR syntax, to refer to a position in CLAUSE (S′) structure, symbolized by COMP or C, which may be filled (for example) by a complementizer or by a clause-initial *WH*-phrase. In GOVERNMENT-BINDING THEORY, COMP (or C) is a ZERO-level category whose maximal PROJECTION C″ (or CP) is, like the initial symbol, the highest-level GRAMMATICAL construction. Within this approach, *WH*-MOVEMENT, for example, is a movement to the specifier-of-C position.

complete feedback see FEEDBACK

complex(ity) The general sense of this term is found in LINGUISTICS, with reference to both the FORMAL internal structuring of linguistic UNITS and the psychological difficulty in using or learning them. The factors which contribute to the notion of complexity are a major topic in PSYCHOLINGUISTICS, both in studies of adult COMPREHENSION and PRODUCTION, and in child language ACQUISITION. A central theme is the nature of the interaction between levels of difficulty in cognitive and linguistic STRUCTURES, and especially the way this affects the order of emergence of language patterns in children. However, it has not yet proved feasible to establish independent measures of complexity defined in purely linguistic terms (such as the number of TRANSFORMATIONS in a SENTENCE DERIVATION, or the number of FEATURES in the specification of a linguistic unit. cf. SIMPLICITY METRIC), largely because of controversy over the nature of the linguistic measures used, and the interference stemming from other psychological factors, such as the language user's attention and motivation.

Several restricted senses are also used (mostly contrasting with the term 'simple'), e.g. 'complex SENTENCE' (in two senses: either a sentence consisting of more than one CLAUSE, or one consisting of a main clause and at least one SUBORDINATE clause), 'complex PREPOSITION' (a preposition consisting of more than one word), 'complex word' (i.e. one containing a free MORPHEME and at least one bound morpheme), 'complex tone' (an INTONATIONAL NUCLEUS with two distinct PITCH movements), 'complex stop' (a PLOSIVE with two points of ARTICULATION), 'complex nucleus' (a SYLLABIC peak with two distinct VOWEL qualities), 'complex SEGMENT' (a segment with two or more simultaneous oral tract CONSTRICTIONS, in some models of FEATURE theory), and so on. In GENERATIVE GRAMMAR, a 'complex NP' is a NOUN PHRASE with a clause as a COMPLEMENT (e.g. *the assumption that the engine is working*) or ADJUNCT (e.g. *the assumption that he made*). The 'complex NP constraint' in classical transformational grammar states that no element can be extracted out of a complex NP – in other words, such constructions are syntactic ISLANDS.

complex symbol A term used in some MODELS of GENERATIVE GRAMMAR (cf. ASPECTS) to refer to a symbol in a PHRASE-MARKER which has an internal structure of its own. It consists of an unordered set of SYNTACTIC FEATURES, e.g. [N], [+Abstract], [+Animate], and (in some accounts) the MORPHEME which the set of features specify, e.g.

$$\begin{bmatrix} \text{+N} \\ \text{+Human} \\ \text{–Proper} \\ \textit{man} \end{bmatrix}$$

component(ial) (1) A term used in GENERATIVE LINGUISTICS to refer to the main sections into which a generative GRAMMAR is organized. In Noam CHOMSKY'S *Syntactic Structures* (1957), three components are recognized: the PHRASE-STRUCTURE component (which generates a set of UNDERLYING STRINGS), the TRANSFORMATIONAL component (which acts on these strings in various OPTIONAL and OBLIGATORY ways, introducing SEMANTIC changes), and the MORPHOPHONEMIC component (which converts each syntactic string into a string of PHONOLOGICAL UNITS). In *Aspects of the Theory of Syntax* (1965), the model is radically altered. The phrase-structure component is replaced by a **base component**, which generates the underlying PHRASE-MARKERS representing the DEEP STRUCTURE of SENTENCES, i.e. all semantically relevant grammatical notions. The base component contains the CATEGORIAL and LEXICAL components (or **sub-components**) of the grammar. Two things then happen to these markers: (a) they are semantically interpreted, using the rules of the **semantic component** (which has no equivalent in the *Syntactic Structures* model), and (b) they are converted into SURFACE structures through the **transformational component** (which contains largely obligatory RULES, the optional ones now being handled by choices made in the base rules). Lastly, a **phonological component** operates on the surface structures, providing them with a PHONETIC interpretation.

(2) In SEMANTICS, the term refers to an irreducible FEATURE in terms of which the SENSE of LEXICAL ITEMS can be analysed, e.g. *girl* can be analysed into the components 'human', 'female', 'child', etc. **Componential analysis** is a semantic theory which has developed from a technique for the analysis of kinship vocabulary devised by American anthropologists in the 1950s. It claims that all lexical items can be analysed using a finite set of components (or 'semantic features'), which may, it is felt, be UNIVERSAL. Certainly, several sets of lexical items exist to show the strengths of the approach (e.g. the correspondences between *boy/girl, man/woman, ram/ewe*, etc., can be stated in terms of [+male] *v.* [−male] or [−female] *v.* [+female]. There are several limitations to the componential models of analysis so far suggested, such as the extent to which BINARY analyses are possible for many lexical items, the claimed universality of components, and the justification for selecting one value rather than the other for a possible component (e.g. whether the above example should be analysed in terms of [+male] or [−female]).

'Componential analysis' is also found in a general sense in linguistics, especially in Europe, referring to any approach which analyses linguistic units into components, whether in PHONOLOGY, grammar or semantics. In this view, PRAGUE SCHOOL phonological analysis is componential, as are the analyses of WORD-AND-PARADIGM MORPHOLOGY.

(3) In some recent approaches to PHONOLOGY (e.g. DEPENDENCY PHONOLOGY), a term for a FEATURE represented as a single ('unary') element, rather than as a BINARY opposition. The term is given special status in 'unary component theory'.

composition(-al(ity), de-compos-e, compos-ite) A term used in LINGUISTICS to refer to a HIERARCHICAL MODEL of linguistic STRUCTURE in which larger UNITS are seen as being 'composed' of smaller units. For example, in GRAMMATICAL analysis, the relationship between SENTENCE, CLAUSE, PHRASE, WORD, and MORPHEME is sometimes described as one of **composition** (CONSTITUENCY, or RANK), the units of higher rank being analysable (**decomposable**) into units of lower rank. One might subsequently analyse such structures in terms of their **compositional meaning**. Compositional models are to be found especially in SCALE-AND-CATEGORY, TAGMEMIC, STRATIFICATIONAL and PHRASE-STRUCTURE GRAMMARS. In relation to WORD FORMATION, the term is used both in the general sense of 'processes of compounding', and sometimes in a restricted sense, referring to a particular type of compound. In TRANSFORMATIONAL grammar, PHRASAL VERBS (e.g. *switch on, take off*) may be referred to as **composite verbs**. In SEMANTICS, compositionality is the view that the MEANINGS of individual words can be used to build up the meanings of larger units: the meaning of the whole is the sum of the meaning of its parts. The notion is important in, for example, MONTAGUE GRAMMAR.

compound(ing) (1) A term used widely in DESCRIPTIVE LINGUISTIC studies to refer to a linguistic UNIT which is composed of ELEMENTS that function independently in other circumstances. Of particular currency are the notions of compounding found in 'compound WORDS' (consisting of two or more free MORPHEMES, as in such 'compound NOUNS' as *bedroom, rainfall* and *washing machine*) and 'compound SENTENCES' (consisting of two or more main CLAUSES); but other applications of the term exist, as in 'compound VERBS' (e.g. *come in*), 'compound TENSES' (those consisting of an AUXILIARY + LEXICAL verb), 'compound SUBJECTS/OBJECTS', etc. (where the clause element consists of more than one noun PHRASE or PRONOUN, as in *the boys and the girls shouted*) and 'compound PREPOSITIONS' (e.g. *in accordance with*).

(2) The term is also used by some linguists in the classification of BILINGUALISM. **Compound bilinguals** are those who attribute identical MEANINGS to corresponding LEXICAL UNITS in the two languages – a distinction here being made with CO-ORDINATE bilingualism, where there is no such identity.

comprehension The general sense of this term is found in LINGUISTICS, referring to the ability to understand and interpret spoken and written language; it is opposed to PRODUCTION. In PSYCHOLINGUISTICS, the analysis of the process of speech comprehension is a major theme, encompassing such topics as the strategies used by children in language ACQUISITION, the strategies adults use in interpreting different types of SENTENCE (e.g. AMBIGUITY, NEGATION, QUESTIONS), the role of the EXTRALINGUISTIC SITUATION, and the role of cognitive factors (such as memory, attention and perception) in arriving at the interpretation of sentences and DISCOURSES.

computational linguistics A branch of LINGUISTICS in which computational techniques and concepts are applied to the elucidation of linguistic and PHONETIC problems. Several research areas have developed, including NATURAL LANGUAGE PROCESSING, SPEECH synthesis, speech recognition, automatic translation, the making of concordances, the testing of GRAMMARS, and the many areas where statistical counts and analyses are required (e.g. in literary textual studies).

computational system In the MINIMALIST PROGRAMME, a term used for the set of operations required by the process of SENTENCE composition (DERIVATION). Computation involves the SYNTACTIC combination of LEXICAL items and the construction of REPRESENTATIONS in LOGICAL FORM and PHONETIC FORM. The system builds structures by selecting elements from the NUMERATION and combining them in various ways to form individual subtrees; these are ultimately combined ('merged') into a single TREE. The computational process is constrained by various ECONOMY principles, such as shortest MOVE, PROCRASTINATE and GREED.

conative A term used by some linguists to refer to a general type of LINGUISTIC FUNCTION – the use of language in order to achieve a result in an addressee, in accord with the speaker's wishes. Its use is illustrated by a range of DIRECTIVE functions (e.g. COMMANDS, VOCATIVES), but its precise sense needs to take into account the range of other functions recognized by the theory in which it is used – in particular, the contrast which is often made between conative and EXPRESSIVE (personal) and REFERENTIAL (situational) functions.

concessive In GRAMMAR, referring to a word or construction which expresses the meaning of 'concession'. The point expressed in the MAIN CLAUSE continues to be valid despite the point being made in the SUBORDINATE clause (the **concessive clause**). In English, the most widely used markers of concession are *although* and *though*.

concatenation A term used in the FORMAL representation of LINGUISTIC STRUCTURES, and especially in GENERATIVE GRAMMAR, to refer to a process for forming STRINGS of ELEMENTS, the elements being seen in a relation of linear succession, e.g. X + Y + Z or X⁀Y⁀Z (i.e. X is 'concatenated with' or 'chained together with' Y, etc.).

concord A term used in GRAMMATICAL theory and description to refer to a formal relationship between ELEMENTS, whereby a FORM of one WORD requires a corresponding form of another. In English, for example, a singular SUBJECT co-occurs with the third-person singular form of the VERB in the present TENSE, e.g. *he walks* (*v. they walk*); in Latin, there is concord between the NUMBER, GENDER and CASE of ADJECTIVES and NOUNS. This formal correspondence was traditionally referred to as AGREEMENT (the adjective 'agrees' with the noun, etc.), and is usually contrasted in grammatical discussion with the notion of GOVERNMENT.

condition A term used in LINGUISTICS to refer to any factors which, it might be argued, need to be taken into account in evaluating a theory, a GRAMMAR, or an individual analysis, e.g. such conditions as external ADEQUACY, GENERALITY, SIMPLICITY. More specifically, it refers to any criterion which must be met before a particular analysis may be carried out. In SYSTEMIC grammar, for example, the ENTRY conditions specify the structural criteria which must be satisfied in order for a particular grammatical system to become operative. In TRANSFORMATIONAL grammar, the STRUCTURAL DESCRIPTION which provides the input to a transformational RULE specifies the conditions which must be met before the rule can operate. More recently, in this theory, the term has been used to refer to the factors which constrain the application of transformations, in such contexts as MOVEMENT rules. For example, one condition states that a moved CONSTITUENT can only be substituted for an EMPTY category; another, that a moved constituent leaves behind a CO-INDEXED TRACE of itself. The 'ISLAND condition' asserts that

SUBJECTS and ADJUNCTS, but not COMPLEMENTS, are islands, i.e. constituents can be extracted out of complement phrases, but not out of subject/adjunct phrases. Since the late 1970s, conditions on transformations have largely been replaced by conditions on various levels of REPRESENTATION, e.g. BINDING THEORY (a set of conditions on surface structures and/or logical form) replaced several conditions on rules of grammar proposed during the 1970s. See also ENTRY (2), FELICITY CONDITIONS, NOMINATIVE.

conditional A term used in GRAMMATICAL DESCRIPTION to refer to CLAUSES whose SEMANTIC role is the expression of hypotheses or conditions. In English, these are introduced by *if, unless*, and a few other CONJUNCTIONS (e.g. *if John asks, tell him* . . .). The TRADITIONAL grammatical notion of 'conditional TENSE' (using *would, should*) is usually interpreted in terms of ASPECTUAL or MODAL VERB forms in analyses of English, though this is MORPHOLOGICALLY expressed in many languages (e.g. French).

conditioned/conditioning A term used in LINGUISTICS to refer to the FORM a linguistic UNIT takes when this is partly or wholly determined by the linguistic CONTEXT in which it occurs. For example, in English PHONOLOGY, the ALVEOLAR /t/ PHONEME predictably becomes DENTAL when followed by /θ/, as in *eighth*, i.e. [t̪] is a **conditioned variant** of /t/; in MORPHOPHONOLOGY, the indefinite ARTICLE *a* becomes *an* when followed by a VOWEL. The concept of ALLO- is the most succinct way of referring to phonological and GRAMMATICAL 'conditioning', and other terms are sometimes used for the same phenomenon, e.g. 'contextual/positional/combinatory/automatic' variants. The term 'conditioning' is also sometimes used with reference to the influence of the social/cultural situation on the choice of linguistic forms ('environmental conditioning').

configuration (1) (**-al**) A term used to refer to the STANDARD MODEL of GENERATIVE GRAMMAR, seen in contrast with RELATIONAL theories of grammar. In the former, PHRASE-MARKERS are seen as clusters ('configurations') of SYNTACTIC CATEGORIES, arranged in LINEAR ORDER.

(2) The term is also used generally in LINGUISTICS and PHONETICS for any formally identifiable ARRANGEMENT of ELEMENTS. It has been used, for example, with reference to the sequence of TONES which constitute an INTONATION CONTOUR (a 'tonal configuration') and to the set of SYNTACTIC FUNCTIONS which depend upon a particular VERB, as in CASE grammar (a 'configuration of cases'). See also AUTOMATON.

configurational languages Languages with fairly fixed WORD ORDER and HIERARCHICAL CONSTITUENT structure, e.g. English and Hebrew. Such languages are contrasted with NON-CONFIGURATIONAL LANGUAGES. Both types have received a great deal of attention in GOVERNMENT-BINDING THEORY as subject to PARAMETRIC variation. However, the typology is not unequivocally accepted.

congruence (congruent) A term used in LINGUISTICS to refer to a correspondence between the decisions made at one LEVEL of analysis (PHONOLOGY, GRAMMAR or SEMANTICS) and those made at another. The SENTENCE is the UNIT where there is maximum **congruence of levels**, in that criteria of identification at each level tend to coincide: certain classes of exception aside, a sentence is a grammatically, semantically and phonologically autonomous unit. The notion of WORD, by contrast, displays less congruence: phonological (and orthographic), MORPHOLOGICAL, SYNTACTIC and semantic criteria often conflict in word identification and CLASSIFICATION.

conj A common abbreviation for CONJUNCTION or 'CO-ORDINATING conjunction'.

conjoin(ing, -ed) A term used in GENERATIVE GRAMMAR to refer to a CONSTRUCTION where two or more SENTENCES, PHRASES or WORDS are CO-ORDINATED ('conjoined'). Conjoining processes are distinct from EMBEDDING ones. The linking of CLAUSES using *and, but*, etc., would be carried out using conjoining (e.g. *The man fed the cat and the lady fed the dog*).

conjugation (conjugate) In GRAMMAR, a traditional term for a CLASS of VERBS in an INFLECTING language which occur with the same range of FORMS. Latin verbs, for example, belonged to four conjugations. Forms of the 'first conjugation', for example, were traditionally illustrated using the verb *amare* ('to love'), which in the ACTIVE INDICATIVE PRESENT TENSE had the endings *amo, amas, amat, amamus, amatis, amant* (for 'I/you/he-she/we/you/they' persons respectively). 'Fourth conjugation' verbs, illustrated by *audire* ('to hear'), conjugated differently; *audio, audis, audit, audimus, auditis, audiunt* (for the same persons). The term is not usually found in modern LINGUISTIC analysis (which talks in terms of word classes), but will be encountered in studies of LINGUISTIC HISTORIOGRAPHY.

conjunction (conjunct) A term used in the GRAMMATICAL classification of WORDS to refer to an ITEM or a process whose primary function is to connect words or other CONSTRUCTIONS. The conventional subclassification of these 'connective' items distinguishes CO-ORDINATING conjunctions (e.g. *and, or, but*) and SUBORDINATING conjunctions (e.g. *because, when, unless*) – also referred to as 'co-ordinators' and 'subordinators' respectively. Certain types of ADVERBIAL (those whose function is primarily connective) are also sometimes referred to as 'conjunctive', or simply as 'conjuncts', e.g. *however, moreover, indeed*. A process of conjunction is also recognized in TRANSFORMATIONAL accounts (as in formal logic), this normally being referred to as a CONJOINING transformation; the conjoined elements may also be referred to as **conjuncts**.

conjunctive A term used in GENERATIVE PHONOLOGY to refer to a principle affecting the ORDERING of RULES. **Conjunctive ordering** is found in the use of the brace NOTATION, which indicates an OBLIGATORY selection of one member of a set of alternatives. If a SEQUENCE of rules is abbreviated using this notation – e.g.

$$X \left\{ \begin{matrix} Y \\ Z \\ W \end{matrix} \right\} P$$

, which stands for (a) XYP, (b) XZP or (c) XWP

– then this sequence forms a conjunctively ordered block, i.e. one or other of (a), (b) or (c) must apply. It is distinguished from DISJUNCTIVE ordering.

connected speech A term used in LINGUISTICS to refer to spoken language when analysed as a continuous sequence, as in normal UTTERANCES and conversations. Its significance lies in the contrast implied with studies of linguistic UNITS seen in isolation, such as an individual sound, WORD or PHRASE, which were the subject-matter of much traditional linguistic enquiry. It is now realized that important changes happen to these units when they are used in connected speech, as demonstrated by such processes as ASSIMILATION and ELISION, e.g. *and* becoming /n/ in such phrases as *boys and girls.*

connection A term used by some FIRTHIAN linguists, as part of the phrase **renewal of connection**, referring to a way of validating an analysis predictively: an analysis made on the basis of a set of data (S_1) is applied again to a further sample (S_2) and is found to be adequate, in that in S_2 one meets again the EXPONENTS of the abstract UNITS originally postulated in S_1 (i.e. there has been a 'renewal of connection').

connectionism (connectionist) An application in LINGUISTICS of a computational framework for modelling cognitive functions, based on numerical computation rather than symbol manipulation. A **connectionist network** (or **neural network**) is devised which models the kinds of structures and processes thought to operate in the brain: the processing units in the network are called 'neurons' (in an abstract sense) or 'nodes', each being excited or inhibited (according to certain numerical formulae) by information obtained from the other units to which it is connected. The pattern of neuronal activity represents the data being processed by the network. A particular interpretation (e.g. of speech input data) is likely to depend on the activity pattern of a large number of related units ('distributed representation'), the properties of which can be demonstrated only through statistical analysis. Because all the processing units compute at the same time, the approach is also known as **parallel distributed processing**. This approach contrasts with the view that people process sentences by TRANSFORMING REPRESENTATIONS according to a set of RULES, and rejects the notion that speakers INTERNALIZE grammars, in the GENERATIVE sense. Areas of application include the modelling of the non-DISCRETE and statistical properties of language use, and the study of language processing within PSYCHOLINGUISTICS, NEUROLINGUISTICS, and COMPUTATIONAL LINGUISTICS (e.g. automatic SPEECH RECOGNITION).

connective (connect-ivity, -or) A term used in the GRAMMATICAL classification of WORDS to characterize words or MORPHEMES whose function is primarily to link LINGUISTIC UNITS at any LEVEL. CONJUNCTIONS are the most obvious types (e.g. *and, or, while, because*), but several types of ADVERB can be seen as connective ('conjuncts' such as *therefore, however, nevertheless*), as can some VERBS (the COPULAS *be, seem*, etc.). One type of EXOCENTRIC construction is also referred to as 'connective', e.g. *was happy, stayed quiet*, where the first element is the connector, and the second a predicative ATTRIBUTE. See also ZERO.

connotation (connotative) A term used in SEMANTICS as part of a classification of types of MEANING; opposed to DENOTATION. Its main application is with reference to the emotional associations (personal or communal) which are suggested by, or are part of the meaning of, a LINGUISTIC UNIT, especially a LEXICAL ITEM. Denotation, by contrast, covers the relationship between a linguistic unit and the non-linguistic entities to which it refers. (The traditional philosophical use of 'connotation' and 'denotation' is quite different: here, the meanings involved largely correspond to the distinction between SENSE and REFERENCE, the former being concerned with the relationships of equivalence between terms and

PROPOSITIONS, the latter with their external-world status and truth-value.) For example, the connotations of the lexical item *December* might include 'bad weather', 'dark evenings', etc. (for north Europeans, at least), or 'parties', 'Christmas', etc. Alternative terms for 'connotative meaning' include AFFECTIVE and EMOTIVE.

consonant(al) One of the two general CATEGORIES used for the classification of speech sounds, the other being VOWEL. Consonants can be defined in terms of both PHONETICS and PHONOLOGY. Phonetically, they are sounds made by a CLOSURE or narrowing in the VOCAL TRACT so that the airflow is either completely blocked, or so restricted that audible FRICTION is produced. Consonant ARTICULATIONS are relatively easy to feel, and as a result are most conveniently described in terms of PLACE and MANNER of articulation. In addition, a routine phonetic description of consonants would involve information about the mode of vibration of the VOCAL CORDS (see VOICING), and it is often necessary to specify the DURATION of the sound, the AIRSTREAM MECHANISM involved and the direction of airflow (EGRESSIVE or INGRESSIVE). From a phonological point of view, consonants are those UNITS which function at the MARGINS of SYLLABLES, either singly or in CLUSTERS.

Usually, phonetic and phonological criteria coincide: [f], for example, is a consonant in that there is audible friction and the sound occurs marginally, as in *fat, leaf*. In sounds such as [l], [r], [w] and [j], however, there is a conflict between the two criteria. Phonologically, these sounds are consonants, because their role in syllables is the same as that taken by [f], [p], etc., e.g. *lip, rip, wet, yet*. But, phonetically, they lack the friction required by the above definitions: they are vowel-like in character. Such sounds as a result are often called 'semi-vowels' or **semi-consonants** (cf. APPROXIMANT).

The trouble arises from having only one term to do two jobs (phonetic and phonological descriptions). Several terminological solutions have been suggested, the most well-known one being the suggestion of the American linguist K. L. Pike (b. 1912) to reserve the term 'consonant' for the phonological level of analysis, and to introduce CONTOID for the phonetic level (as opposed to VOCOID). In this way, [p] would be consonant and contoid, and [l], etc., consonant and vocoid.

Consonantal is used in a general adjectival sense, and also has separate technical status in the DISTINCTIVE FEATURE theory of phonology, where 'consonantal' and **non-consonantal** constitute one of the major CLASS FEATURES in terms of which speech sounds are analysed. Consonantal sounds may be defined either articulatorily or acoustically in this approach: they are produced with a major obstruction in the middle of the vocal tract, and have low ACOUSTIC energy. Non-consonantal sounds lack this obstruction, and have high acoustic energy. Consonants in the above phonological sense would be analysed as having the feature [+consonantal]: vowels would be [−consonantal].

consonant harmony see HARMONY

conspiracy (conspire) A term used in GENERATIVE PHONOLOGY to refer to any set of RULES which can be seen as acting together, or 'conspiring', to produce a specific result, which it would not be possible or economical to state as a single rule.

constant A type of OPPOSITION recognized in PRAGUE SCHOOL PHONOLOGY, distinguished from NEUTRALIZABLE. A constant opposition exists when all its members can occur in all possible positions, e.g. wherever /p/ might be found in a LANGUAGE, a contrast with /b/ will also be found. A DISTINCTION such as English /t/ *v.* /d/, however, is neutralizable because, in some positions, the CONTRAST disappears (as in /t/ following INITIAL /s/).

constative A basic term used in the theory of SPEECH ACTS: it refers to UTTERANCES which are DESCRIPTIVE STATEMENTS, capable of being analysed in terms of truth-values. 'Constative utterances' are contrasted with PERFORMATIVE utterances, where the function is one of 'doing' rather than 'saying'.

constituent (constituency) (1) A basic term in GRAMMATICAL analysis for a LINGUISTIC UNIT which is a functional component of a larger CONSTRUCTION. Based on a combination of intuitive and FORMAL (e.g. DISTRIBUTIONAL) criteria, a SENTENCE can be analysed into a series of constituents, such as SUBJECT + PREDICATE, or NP+VP, etc. These units thus produced can, in turn, be analysed into further constituents (e.g. a NOUN PHRASE might consist of a DETERMINER and a noun), and this **constituent analysis** process can be continued until no further subdivisions are possible. The major divisions that can be made within a construction, at any level, are known as the **immediate constituents** (ICs) of that construction. The irreducible ELEMENTS resulting from such an analysis are known as the **ultimate constituents** (UCs) of the construction. So, in analysing the sentence *The clock has stopped*, the ICs would be *the clock* and *has stopped* (how these constituents are to be LABELLED is a separate decision-making process). *The clock* has *the* and *clock* as its ICs. The ICs of *has stopped* are *has* and *stopped*. And *stopped* can be broken down further into *stop* and *-ed*. The process is often drawn in the form of a TREE diagram, as follows:

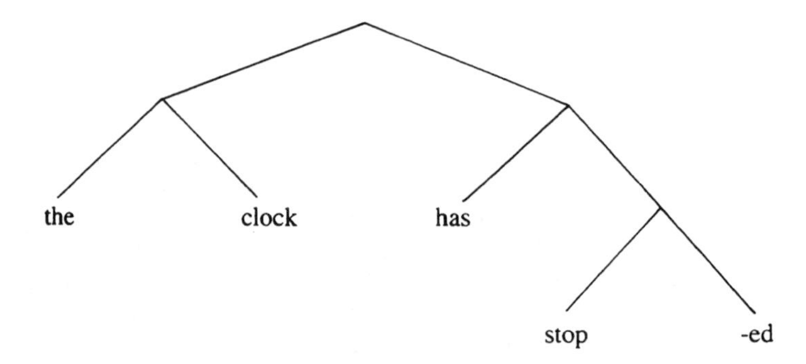

This **constituent structure** may also be represented using BRACKETS, each analytic decision being represented by the imposition of a pair of square brackets at the appropriate points in the construction, e.g. [[*the clock*] [*has stop*[*-ed*]]]. A grammar which analyses sentences wholly in this way, i.e. in terms of a HIERARCHY of structural layers, is sometimes called a **constituent-structure gram-**

mar; in classical GENERATIVE linguistics, such an analysis is carried on by the PHRASE-STRUCTURE COMPONENT of the grammar. The term **constituency grammar** will also be encountered, as will the term **constituent sentence**, referring to an EMBEDDED sentence. **Constituent-base** grammars need to be distinguished from those which do not recognize constituents, such as DEPENDENCY grammar and WORD GRAMMAR.

The limitations of IC analysis have been much discussed in the linguistics literature, especially in relation to the greater POWER of TRANSFORMATIONAL grammars. IC analysis, for example, is unable to make explicit the relationships between formally connected sets of sentences (such as ACTIVE and PASSIVE), nor can it demonstrate the AMBIGUITY involved in several kinds of construction (a much-discussed example here being *it is too hot to eat*). But some kind of constituent analysis is an important feature of most grammatical systems. See also C-STRUCTURE.

(2) In NON-LINEAR PHONOLOGY, a term which describes a group of FEATURES which regularly FUNCTION together as a UNIT in phonological RULES. In this approach, SEGMENTS are REPRESENTED as a HIERARCHY of NODE configurations, in which intermediate nodes are constituents and terminal nodes are feature values. Elements are grouped into constituents using ASSOCIATION LINES. Only feature sets which form constituents may function together in phonological rules. The approach uses the usual TREE terminology of GENERATIVE grammar: dependents are viewed as 'daughters' of a higher constituent node, and 'sisters' of other nodes at the same level within the hierarchy.

constraint (constrain) A term used in LINGUISTICS, and especially in GENERATIVE GRAMMAR, to refer to a CONDITION which restricts the application of a RULE, to ensure that the sentences generated are WELL FORMED. For example, in generative PHONOLOGY, a distinction can be made between 'simultaneous' and 'sequential' constraints: the former states the restrictions on the simultaneous occurrence of FEATURES, e.g. a SEGMENT cannot be at once [+high] and [+low]; the latter states the restrictions on sequences of features, e.g. whether a language permits CONSONANT CLUSTERS. In generative SYNTAX there are also several constraints which have to be imposed in order to prevent the DERIVATION of ILL-FORMED PHRASE-MARKERS, e.g. constraints on the ORDERING of rules. For example, 'surface structure' constraints (FILTERS, or 'OUTPUT conditions') refer to conditions where a characteristic of SURFACE STRUCTURE decides which phrase-markers are well formed; e.g. no phrase-marker containing an internal boundary symbol can qualify as a well-formed surface structure. Other examples include ISLAND constraints and the CO-ORDINATE structure constraint. Recent generative studies have aimed to find constraints which apply to large classes of derivations (i.e. the constraints have a greater EXPLANATORY power) – a trend which contrasts with the local application of the constraints proposed in the 1960s. 'Constraints', in this work, are distinguished from 'filters': the former are conditions affecting two successive phrase-markers in a derivation: the latter are conditions on a single level of structure, which serves as the output of a given set of rules.

The term is also used more generally in generative linguistics with reference to theory construction. A linguistic theory needs to be constrained, in order to restrict the class of potential grammars. In this sense, the main aim of linguistics is said to be the provision of an explanatorily ADEQUATE theory which is maximally constrained.

constriction (constricted) A general term used in ARTICULATORY PHONETICS to refer to a narrowing within the VOCAL TRACT. The different kinds and degrees of constriction are the basis of the articulatory classification of sound QUALITIES. The term 'constricted' is sometimes used in a restricted sense, referring to GLOTTALIZED sounds. 'Constriction' has developed a central role in recent PHONOLOGICAL theory, especially in some models of FEATURE GEOMETRY. A **constriction model** aims to unify the description of VOCOIDS (VOWELS and GLIDES) and CONSONANTS in terms of their characteristic constriction, defined by the parameters of **constriction degree** (a CONTINUANT node for consonants and an APERTURE node for vocoids) and **constriction location** (a PLACE node, represented by 'C-place' for consonants and 'V-place' for vocoids, and defined in terms of the active articulator involved). Constrictions are represented by a separate node in the feature HIERARCHY, and degree and location are separate nodes linked under the constriction node. The definition of DORSAL, for example (involving a constriction formed by the back of the TONGUE) is equally applicable to consonants and vocoids, thus avoiding the 'two-mouth' descriptions of traditional approaches. The three main types of correspondence proposed are: between LABIAL consonants and ROUNDED or labialized vocoids; between CORONAL consonants and FRONT vocoids; and between dorsal consonants and BACK vocoids.

construction (construct) (1) In its most general sense in LINGUISTICS, 'construction' refers to the overall process of internal organization of a GRAMMATICAL UNIT – a SENTENCE, for example, being 'constructed' out of a set of MORPHEMES by the application of a set of RULES. More specifically, it refers to the SYNTAGMATIC result of such a process, a particular type of construction (a 'constructional type' or 'pattern') being defined as a sequence of units which has a FUNCTIONAL identity in the grammar of a LANGUAGE, such as SUBJECT+VERB+OBJECT (with reference to CLAUSES), or DETERMINER+NOUN (with reference to PHRASES). Most specifically, it refers to a token of a constructional type, in the sense of STRING, e.g. *the+man+is+walking*. It is constructions of this last kind which are analysed into CONSTITUENTS, as in IMMEDIATE-CONSTITUENT analysis. Constituents forming a syntactic relationship are said to be 'in construction with' each other. **Constructional homonymity** refers to a grammatical string with more than one interpretation in terms of the patterns of construction it contains (as defined, say, by a PHRASE-STRUCTURE grammar). In more traditional grammatical terms, the string would be said to be 'structurally ambiguous'. For example, *men and women in coats* could be analysed as *men and* [*women in coats*] (i.e. only the women have coats) or as *men and women* [*in coats*] (they all have coats).

(2) In PSYCHOLINGUISTICS, the term is often used as part of a theory of COMPREHENSION, to refer to the psychological process of 'constructing' an interpretation of sentences, based on the ability to identify and interrelate the various ELEMENTS and LEVELS of MEANING involved.

construe (construal) A TRADITIONAL term in GRAMMATICAL analysis, which refers to the process of FORMALLY arranging words into CONSTRUCTIONAL relationships, and to the study and interpretation of these relationships. It has received a new lease of life in recent GENERATIVE SYNTAX, where it is used to define the relationships which are formed between certain types of CONSTITUENTS (ANTECEDENTS and ANAPHORS) as a consequence of applying a TRANSFORMATIONAL RULE (**rules of construal**). See also COGNITIVE SEMANTICS.

consultant see INFORMANT

contact (1) A term used in SOCIOLINGUISTICS to refer to a situation of geographical continuity or close social proximity (and thus of mutual influence) between LANGUAGES or DIALECTS. The result of 'contact situations' can be seen linguistically, in the growth of LOAN words, patterns of PHONOLOGICAL and GRAMMATICAL change, mixed forms of language (such as CREOLES and PIDGINS), and a general increase in BILINGUALISM, of various kinds. In a restricted sense, languages are said to be 'in contact' if they are used alternately by the same persons, i.e. bilinguals. The term **contact language** or **contact vernacular** is also sometimes used to refer to a pidgin.

(2) A term used by some GRAMMARIANS to describe a type of RELATIVE CLAUSE with no relative PRONOUN, and where the clause is thus directly 'in contact' with the HEAD NOUN (e.g. *the book I bought*): a **contact clause** or **contact relative**. In the context of GENERATIVE grammar, these clauses have no OVERT COMPLEMENTIZER nor an overt *WH*-PHRASE.

content(ive) The general sense of this term – referring to the MEANING of an expression – is found pre-theoretically in LINGUISTICS, but some linguists have given it a technical status, by analysing language into two major dimensions, distinguishing a 'content plane' from an 'expression plane' (analogous to the SAUSSUREAN distinction between the MEANING and FORM of linguistic SIGNS). More specifically, some approaches to WORD CLASSIFICATION recognize a class of **content words** or **contentives**, defined as words which have stateable LEXICAL meaning – the majority of words in the LANGUAGE, in fact, apart from the few FUNCTION words, whose role is primarily to express GRAMMATICAL relationships. Alternative terms include LEXICAL and FULL words.

context(-ual-ization) (1) A general term used in LINGUISTICS and PHONETICS to refer to specific parts of an UTTERANCE (or TEXT) near or adjacent to a UNIT which is the focus of attention. The occurrence of a unit (e.g. a sound, WORD) is partly or wholly determined by its context, which is specified in terms of the unit's relations, i.e. the other features with which it combines as a sequence. The everyday sense of the term is related to this, as when one 'puts a word in context', in order to clarify the MEANING intended, as in dictionary entries. Providing a context in this way is referred to as **contextualization**. Words, it is suggested, have meaning only when seen in context.

The specification of FORMAL contexts is a particular characteristic of the formulation of rules in GENERATIVE linguistics, where forms can be classified in terms of whether they occur only within a specific context ('context-sensitive/restricted/dependent' rules) or are independent of context ('context-free' rules). A **context-free grammar** is one in which all the rules apply regardless of context, i.e. they would be all of the type 'Rewrite X as Y', no further conditions being specified. A **context-sensitive** grammar contains some rules of the type A → B/ C—D, where the oblique line means 'in the context of', and the horizontal line indicates the place in the structure where A is rewritten as B – in this case, between C and D. In some GENERATIVE MODELS (cf. ASPECTS), **contextual features** refer to one of the types of (BINARY) FEATURES which are contained in a LEXICAL entry (the others being INHERENT and RULE features); such features provide information as to where in a DEEP-STRUCTURE REPRESENTATION a lexical item can occur. Three types of contextual features are recognized: CATEGORY features, STRICT SUB-CATEGORIZATION features and SELECTIONAL features.

Variants of sound, GRAMMAR, etc., which are dependent on context for their occurrence are sometimes called **contextual variants** (or 'conditioned variants'); an example is the allophone (cf. ALLO-). An analysis in these terms is sometimes called a **contextual analysis**. Some scholars use the term CO-TEXT for context in sense (1), reserving the latter term for sense (2) below.

(2) A term referring to the features of the non-linguistic world in relation to which linguistic units are systematically used. The term 'situation' is also used in this sense, as in the compound term **situational context**. In its broadest sense, situational context includes the *total* non-linguistic background to a text or utterance, including the immediate situation in which it is used, and the awareness by speaker and hearer of what has been said earlier and of any relevant external beliefs or PRESUPPOSITIONS. Others restrict the term to what is immediately observable in the co-occurring situation. Further distinctions are usually made in SEMANTICS and STYLISTICS, distinguishing, for example, REFERENTIAL and EMOTIVE meaning from **contextual meaning**, i.e. information signalled about the kind of use a linguistic unit has in its social context, e.g. whether it has a 'restricted' use (as in social pleasantries, or religious settings), or how it relates to such factors as age, sex or class of the speakers.

(3) **Context of situation** is a specific term in FIRTHIAN linguistic theory, deriving from the work of the anthropologist Bronislaw Malinowski (1884–1942). In this theory, meaning is seen as a multiple phenomenon, its various facets being relatable on the one hand to features of the external world, and on the other hand to the different LEVELS of linguistic analysis, such as PHONETICS, grammar and semantics. Context of situation refers to the whole set of external-world features considered to be relevant in the analysis of an utterance at these levels.

(4) Other related senses may be found. For example, the general term **context of utterance** is sometimes used to refer to all the factors which systematically determine the FORM, MEANING or appropriateness of UTTERANCES (i.e. including both sense (1) and sense (2) of this entry). 'Context' is also used in HALLIDAYAN linguistics, but in a restricted sense, as the name of an INTER-LEVEL of language organization which relates linguistic form to extralinguistic SITUATION – it is thus equivalent to SEMANTICS.

continuant One of the features of sound set up by CHOMSKY and Halle in their DISTINCTIVE FEATURE theory of PHONOLOGY, to handle variations in MANNER OF ARTICULATION. Continuant sounds have been defined articulatorily and acoustically, as those produced with an incomplete CLOSURE of the VOCAL TRACT. All VOWELS and FRICATIVES are [+continuant] (abbreviated as [+cont]). The opposite term in JAKOBSON and Halle's approach is DISCONTINUOUS; in Chomsky and Halle's later system, it is **non-continuant** or STOP: these are sounds produced with a complete closure of the vocal tract, and thus characterized acoustically by a silence, as in PLOSIVES [−continuant] [−cont]. The term INTERRUPTED is also sometimes used.

continuity hypothesis see DISCONTINUOUS (3)

continuous A term used in GRAMMATICAL description of VERB FORMS, referring to a CONTRAST of a temporal or a durative kind, and thus handled sometimes under the heading of TENSE and sometimes under ASPECT. The usual contrast recognized is between 'continuous' or PROGRESSIVE (e.g. *I am going*) and **non-continuous**, SIMPLE, or 'non-progressive' (e.g. *I go*). Linguists prefer an aspectual analysis here, because of the complex interaction of durational, completive and temporal features of meaning involved; TRADITIONAL grammars, however, merely refer to 'continuous tense', etc., and thus imply a meaning which is to some degree an oversimplification.

contoid A term invented by the American phonetician Kenneth Pike (b. 1912) to help distinguish between the PHONETIC and the PHONOLOGICAL notions of CONSONANT. Phonetically, a consonant is defined with reference to a complete CLOSURE in the VOCAL TRACT, or a narrowing sufficiently great to cause audible FRICTION. Phonologically, it is a unit which FUNCTIONS at the MARGINS of SYLLABLES. But there are cases where these criteria do not coincide, such as [l], [r], [w] and [j], which function as consonants in syllables, but which are phonetically VOWEL-like. To handle such cases, Pike proposed that separate terms be used for the phonetic and the phonological definitions of all sounds: 'contoid' refers to the phonetic characterization of a consonant, as defined above; 'consonant' is reserved for the phonological sense. Its opposite is VOCOID.

contour (1) A term used in SUPRASEGMENTAL PHONOLOGY, particularly by those phonologists working within an American tradition, to refer to a distinctive CONFIGURATION of PITCHES, TONES or STRESSES in an UTTERANCE. Several types of contour are recognized, e.g. 'primary', 'secondary' and 'terminal' contours, which relate to major patterns in the analysis of INTONATION, or the notion of **stress contour** in GENERATIVE phonology, which refers to a sequence of stresses assigned through the application of the transformational CYCLE. Rising and falling tones are sometimes referred to as **contour tones**. A contour tone system is used in some tone languages (e.g. Thai) where the critical feature is the direction of tonal movement rather than the relative level of the tone (a CONTOUR TONE LANGUAGE as opposed to a REGISTER TONE LANGUAGE).

(2) In some models of NON-LINEAR PHONOLOGY, a sequence of different FEATURES which belong to a SEGMENT in a HIERARCHICAL feature representation. Such segments (e.g. AFFRICATES, prenasalized STOPS) are known as **contour segments**. Such segments display phonological EDGE effects, in that the segment behaves as though it has the feature [+F] with regard to segments on one side and [−F] with regard to those on the other.

contraction (contracted) A term used in LINGUISTICS to refer to the process or result of PHONOLOGICALLY reducing a linguistic FORM so that it comes to be attached to an adjacent linguistic form, or FUSING a sequence of forms so that they appear as a single form. The first kind of **contracted form** (or **contraction**) can be illustrated by *I've* from *I have, haven't* from *have not*, and WANNA-CONTRACTION. The second kind is seen in French *du, des* from **de le* and **de les* respectively.

contradictory A term sometimes used in SEMANTICS to refer to a SENSE relation between LEXICAL ITEMS. 'Contradictory terms' (or 'contradictories') display a type of oppositeness of MEANING, illustrated by such pairs as *male/female* and *single/married*. Because of the technical use of this term in logic (where it refers to a relationship between two propositions such that they cannot both be true or both false), some semanticists prefer to use COMPLEMENTARITY to refer to the LINGUISTIC relationship involved in such opposites.

contrafactive A term used in the classification of VERB–COMPLEMENT constructions, in which the PROPOSITION expressed in the complement CLAUSE is PRESUPPOSED to be false. e.g. *I wish John would go*, where it is presupposed that John has not gone. Contrafactive verbs are usually distinguished from FACTIVE and 'non-factive' verbs.

contrary A term sometimes used in SEMANTICS to refer to a SENSE relation between LEXICAL ITEMS. 'Contrary terms' (or 'contraries') display a type of oppositeness of MEANING, illustrated by such pairs as *big/little, happy/sad*. Because of the technical use of this term in logic (where it refers to the relationship between two propositions such that they both cannot be true, though both can be false), some semanticists prefer to use ANTONYMY to refer to the LINGUISTIC relationship involved in such opposites.

contrast(iv-e, -ity) (1) A term used in LINGUISTICS for a difference between units, especially one which serves to distinguish MEANINGS in a language. Such differences are also referred to as DISTINCTIVE, FUNCTIONAL or SIGNIFICANT. The principle of contrast is considered fundamental to linguistic analysis. It can be illustrated with reference to the notions of PHONEME (in particular), DISTINCTIVE FEATURE, MORPHEME, etc., which may all be defined as 'minimally contrastive units' at some LEVEL of analysis. Examples in PHONOLOGY are the contrast between English /p/ and /b/, or VOICED *v.* voiceless; in GRAMMAR, between INFLECTIONAL endings, or the various possibilities of WORD ORDER. Many linguists use the term OPPOSITION in the same way, but in some approaches this term is given separate definition, referring only to the PARADIGMATIC differences between units ('contrast' being reserved for SYNTAGMATIC differences).

(2) The phrase **contrastive analysis (CA)** also identifies a general approach to the investigation of language, particularly as carried on in certain areas of APPLIED LINGUISTICS, such as foreign-language teaching and translation. In a contrastive analysis of two languages, the points of STRUCTURAL difference are identified, and these are then studied as areas of potential difficulty (INTERFERENCE or 'negative transfer') in foreign-language learning. The claim that these differences are the source of difficulty in foreign-language learning, and thus govern the progress of the learner, is known as the **contrastive analysis hypothesis**. Although strongly influential (motivating audio-lingual methods of language teaching), by the 1980s the validity of the hypothesis had been seriously questioned, especially following research into the nature of

INTERLANGUAGE and into the cognitive contribution which individuals themselves bring to the learning task. Contrastive analyses are SYNCHRONIC; analogous 'contrastive' studies of two states in the history of a language would be grouped under a different heading, such as COMPARATIVE or HISTORICAL LINGUISTICS.

contrastive accent see ACCENT (2)

contrastive stress see STRESS

control(ler) A term used in one of the (sub-) theories of GOVERNMENT-BINDING THEORY (**control theory**), which determines the potential for REFERENCE of the abstract pronominal element PRO. For example, a PRO which is the SUBJECT of an EMBEDDED INFINITIVE CLAUSE is said to be under the 'control' of the MAIN-clause subject (its **controller**), after a VERB like *promise*; but after a verb like *persuade* it is controlled by the OBJECT of that verb (it is 'non-subject-controlled'): compare *I_1 promised John PRO_1 to go* and *I persuaded $John_2$ PRO_2 to go*. Still other uses of PRO are 'uncontrolled' (that is, they have ARBITRARY reference, and do not take their reference from an ANTECEDENT NP). **Control sentences** subsume the EQUI NP DELETION sentences of classical TRANSFORMATIONAL GRAMMAR; they are often contrasted with RAISING sentences. Sometimes, control constructions are referred to as CATENATIVE constructions.

control agreement principle (CAP) A term used in GENERALIZED PHRASE-STRUCTURE GRAMMAR to refer to a principle which is introduced to account for AGREEMENT phenomena.

convention(al) LINGUISTICS uses this term in its general sense – referring to any accepted practice in the use of LANGUAGE (e.g. the 'convention' of using certain formulae upon leave-taking), or in developing a MODEL of language (e.g. it is 'conventional' to transcribe PHONEMES using / / brackets). But there is also a restricted sense, where it refers to the ARBITRARY nature of the relationship between linguistic EXPRESSIONS and their MEANINGS: one says that the relationship between the LEXICAL ITEM *table* and the thing 'table' is 'conventional', the term here being used in a traditional philosophical sense which dates from Plato.

conventional implicature see IMPLICATURE

converge(nce) (1) A term used in SOCIOLINGUISTICS to refer to a process of DIALECT change in which the dialects become more like each other (or 'converge'). This usually happens when a non-standard dialect falls under the influence of the STANDARD, but it may happen the other way round – as in the current development of modified forms of RECEIVED PRONUNCIATION in English. Geographically adjacent SPEECH communities are sometimes referred to as 'convergence areas'. The opposite effect is known as DIVERGENCE. 'Convergence' also has a currency in HISTORICAL linguistic studies, referring to the MERGING of FORMS which at an earlier stage of a LANGUAGE were CONTRASTIVE.

(2) In the MINIMALIST PROGRAMME, a DERIVATION is said to 'converge' if a STRUCTURAL DESCRIPTION is interpretable at the level of PHONETIC FORM or at the level of LOGICAL FORM. For this to happen, there should be no semantic infor-

mation in the phonetic REPRESENTATION and no phonetic information in the semantic representation. If these conditions are not met, the derivation is said to **crash**.

conversation analysis (CA) A term used in LINGUISTICS and associated disciplines to refer to a method of studying the sequential STRUCTURE and COHERENCE of conversations (in their everyday sense), usually employing the techniques of ETHNOMETHODOLOGY. The approach studies recordings of real conversations, to establish what properties are used in a systematic way when people linguistically interact. Conversation analysis is basically an empirical, inductive study, and a contrast is often drawn with the deductive approach characteristic of DISCOURSE analysis.

conversational implicature see IMPLICATURE

conversational turn see TURN

converse(ness) A term often used in SEMANTICS to refer to a SENSE relation between LEXICAL ITEMS. **Converse terms** display a type of oppositeness of MEANING, illustrated by such pairs as *buy/sell, parent/child, employer/employee* and *above/below*. *Buy* is said to be 'the converse of' *sell*, and vice versa. In such a relationship, found especially in the definition of reciprocal social roles, spatial relationships, and so on, there is an interdependence of meaning, such that one member of the pair presupposes the other member. In this respect, 'converseness' contrasts with COMPLEMENTARITY, where there is no such symmetry of dependence, and with the technical sense of ANTONYMY, where there is a gradation between the opposites.

conversion A term used in the study of WORD FORMATION to refer to the DERIVATIONAL process whereby an ITEM comes to belong to a new WORD-CLASS without the addition of an AFFIX, e.g. VERBS/NOUNS: *smell/taste/hit/walk/bottle/brake*; ADJECTIVES/verbs: *dirty/empty/lower*. Some GRAMMARS distinguish between 'full conversion' and 'partial conversion' – the latter being cases where only some of the characteristics of the new word-class are adopted (e.g. *the rich*). Other terms used for this phenomenon, which is very common in English, include 'ZERO derivation' and 'FUNCTIONAL shift'.

co-occur(rence) A term used in LINGUISTICS and PHONETICS to refer to the permitted SYNTAGMATIC combination of UNITS, according to the GRAMMATICAL and LEXICAL RULES of a LANGUAGE. For example, *a* 'co-occurs' with *boy*, but not with *information; eke* co-occurs with *out*, but not with *in*. The CONSTRAINTS involved are known as 'co-occurrence relations' or 'restrictions', and are often specified in the form of CONTEXT-sensitive or TACTIC rules. The dependencies involved may be unidirectional (e.g. ADVERBS co-occurring with VERBS, but not necessarily the other way round), bidirectional (e.g. TRANSITIVE verbs and OBJECTS), and mutually exclusive (e.g. *a* cannot co-occur with *an* in the same NOUN PHRASE).

co-operative principle A term derived from the work of the philosopher H. P. Grice (1913–88) and now frequently used in LINGUISTICS as part of the study of conversational structure. At its simplest, the principle states that speakers try to co-operate with each other when communicating: they will, in particular, attempt to be informative, truthful, relevant and clear (MAXIMS of 'quantity', 'quality', 'relation' and 'manner' respectively). Listeners will normally assume that a speaker is following these criteria. Speakers may break these maxims (in lying, sarcasm, etc.) but conversation proceeds on the assumption that they do not. It is then possible to deduce implications from what *has* been said concerning what has *not* been said (conversational IMPLICATURES), though the extent to which this can be done consistently and generally is somewhat controversial.

co-ordination (co-ordinat-(iv)e, -ing, -or) (1) A term in GRAMMATICAL analysis to refer to the process or result of linking LINGUISTIC UNITS which are usually of equivalent SYNTACTIC status, e.g. a series of CLAUSES, or PHRASES, or WORDS. (In this respect, it is usually distinguished from SUBORDINATE linkage, where the units are not equivalent.) **Co-ordinate clauses** are illustrated in the sentence *John walked and Mary ran*: the marker of linkage is *and*, a **co-ordinating conjunction** (or **co-ordinator**). Constructions may also be analysed as co-ordinate without any explicit marker (a phenomenon sometimes referred to as 'asyndetic co-ordination'), as in *There was an awkward, depressing silence*, where the 'co-ordinative' role of the two adjectives can be tested by the insertion of *and* between them. The **co-ordinate structure constraint** in GENERATIVE GRAMMAR asserts that no RULE may affect a CONJUNCT in a co-ordinate structure, nor may any element in a conjunct be affected by a rule.

(2) **Co-ordinate** is also used by some linguists in the classification of BILINGUALISM. 'Co-ordinate bilinguals' are those who attribute partly or wholly different MEANINGS to corresponding LEXICAL units in the two LANGUAGES – a distinction here being made with COMPOUND bilingualism, where the meanings are seen as identical.

Copenhagen School A group of LINGUISTS who constituted the Copenhagen Linguistic Circle in the mid-1930s, and who developed an approach to linguistics known as GLOSSEMATICS. Largely through the work of their main theoretician, Louis Hjelmslev (1899–1965), the school developed a philosophical and logical basis for linguistic theory which was not to be surpassed until the FORMALIZATION introduced by GENERATIVE GRAMMAR.

copula(tive) A term used in GRAMMATICAL description to refer to a linking VERB, i.e. a verb which has little independent MEANING, and whose main function is to relate other elements of CLAUSE structure, especially SUBJECT and COMPLEMENT. In English, the main copulative verb is *be*, e.g. *She **is** a doctor*, and the term is often restricted to this verb; but there are many others which have a similar function, e.g. *she **feels** angry, that **looks** nice, he **fell** ill.*

copying (copy) A basic SYNTACTIC operation within the framework of TRANSFORMATIONAL GRAMMAR which adds a duplicate of a CONSTITUENT in a PHRASE-MARKER to some other part of the phrase-marker. For example, to make a RULE deriving TAG QUESTIONS from such SENTENCES as *He is a doctor*, the VERB is taken and 'copied' to the right of the sentence (changing its status from POSITIVE to NEGATIVE); the tag-SUBJECT is a PRONOMINAL copy of the main subject, placed to the right of this verb. This would be one way of generating the sentence *He is a doctor, isn't he?* The verb is copied only if it is AUXILIARY or COPULA, and replaced by a form of *do* otherwise (e.g. *John knows the answers, doesn't he*).

Outside GENERATIVE LINGUISTICS, some linguists use **copy tags** to refer to a subtype of tag questions, viz. only those which retain the same POSITIVE or NEGATIVE value as the main-CLAUSE verb (the others being referred to as CHECKING tags), e.g. *He's coming, is he?*

core (1) (**non-**) In the phrase **core grammar**, the term is used in recent GENERATIVE LINGUISTICS to refer to the UNIVERSAL set of linguistic principles which characterize all the UNMARKED grammatical principles found in LANGUAGE. A RULE which conforms to these principles is a **core rule**; one which does not is a **non-core rule**. A core grammar can be developed for an individual language or for language in general (a 'theory of core grammar').

(2) In the phrase **common core**, the term refers to the set of linguistic features which are shared by all VARIETIES of a language.

(3) In PHONOLOGY, the term is sometimes used for a CONSTITUENT of SYLLABLE structure comprising the NUCLEUS and CODA, more usually referred to as the RHYME (as in METRICAL PHONOLOGY).

(4) In ROLE AND REFERENCE GRAMMAR, a term used to identify one of the two basic concepts used in analysing CLAUSE structure; opposed to **periphery**. The core layer contains the VERB NUCLEUS and associated ARGUMENTS.

co-referential(ity) A term used in LINGUISTICS, and especially in GENERATIVE GRAMMAR, to refer to CONSTITUENTS in a SENTENCE that have the same REFERENCE. For example, in the sentence *I said I would leave*, the two SUBJECTS are co-referential; in *He said he would go* it is unclear whether co-referentiality applies, as the second *he* might refer to someone else. The distinction can be formulated using referentiality indices (CO-INDEXING), e.g. *She*$_i$ *said she*$_i$ *would go* (co-referential) *v. She*$_i$ *said she*$_j$ *would go* ('non co-referential').

co-representational grammar A LINGUISTIC theory developed in the 1970s as an alternative to TRANSFORMATIONAL GRAMMAR, which aims to relate SURFACE STRUCTURE directly to SEMANTIC structure. The approach proposes a single structure which 'co-represents' both the SYNTACTIC and the semantic aspects of a SENTENCE's internal relations. The single LEVEL of surface syntactic structure contains only information about CLASS membership, LINEAR SEQUENCE and NOUN-PHRASE HIERARCHY; the semantic structure contains only information about the relations between PREDICATES and their ARGUMENTS.

coronal One of the features of sound set up by CHOMSKY and Halle in their DISTINCTIVE FEATURE theory of PHONOLOGY, to handle variations in PLACE OF ARTICULATION (CAVITY features). Coronal sounds are defined ARTICULATORILY, as those produced with the BLADE of the TONGUE raised from its neutral position. ALVEOLAR, DENTAL and PALATO-ALVEOLAR CONSONANTS are [+coronal] (abbreviated as [+cor]. Its opposite is NON-CORONAL, referring to sounds produced with the tongue blade in neutral position, as in LABIAL and VELAR consonants [−coronal] ([−cor]). The term has continued to be used in later phonological theory, especially in various NON-LINEAR models. For example, in ARTICULATOR-BASED FEATURE models, it refers to a single-valued NODE involving the tongue front as an active articulator. In CONSTRICTION-based models, it is defined as a constriction formed by the front of the tongue. **Coronalization** is a term used to express several kinds of relationship between coronal consonants and front VOWELS (cf. PALATALIZATION); for example, the process of VELAR consonants becoming coronal, or ANTERIOR consonants becoming coronal, before front vowels.

corpus (corpora) (1) A collection of LINGUISTIC DATA, either written texts or a TRANSCRIPTION of recorded speech, which can be used as a starting-point of linguistic description or as a means of verifying hypotheses about a LANGUAGE (**corpus linguistics**). Linguistic DESCRIPTIONS which are 'corpus-restricted' have been the subject of criticism, especially by GENERATIVE GRAMMARIANS, who point to the limitations of corpora (e.g. that they are samples of PERFORMANCE only, and that one still needs a means of PROJECTING beyond the corpus to the language as a whole). In fieldwork on a new language, or in HISTORICAL study, it may be very difficult to get beyond one's corpus (i.e. it is a 'closed' as opposed to an 'extendable' corpus), but in languages where linguists have regular access to NATIVE-SPEAKERS (and may be native-speakers themselves) their approach will invariably be 'corpus-based', rather than corpus-restricted. Corpora provide the basis for one kind of COMPUTATIONAL LINGUISTICS. A **computer corpus** is a large body of machine-readable texts. Increasingly large corpora (especially of English) have been compiled since the 1980s, and are used both in the development of natural language processing software and in such applications as lexicography, speech recognition, and machine translation.

(2) In SOCIOLINGUISTICS, the term refers to one of the two major types of LANGUAGE planning. **Corpus planning** deals with the way language NORMS are chosen and codified, as when a VARIETY is selected to be a national language, a spelling system is reformed, campaigns for plain or non-sexist language are launched, and literacy programmes are introduced. It contrasts with **status planning**, which deals with the standing of one language in relation to others. Status planning is thus more concerned with the social and political implications of choosing a language, and with such matters as language attitudes, national identity, international use, and minority rights. For example, the relative standing of French and English in Canada, and such matters as the law governing their use in official documents, is a matter of status planning; the choice of which variety of French is to be taught as a standard in Canadian schools, and the provision of relevant teaching materials, is a matter of corpus planning.

correct(ness) A term usually encountered in LINGUISTICS in the context of criticism of PRESCRIPTIVE attitudes to LANGUAGE. The judgements of TRADITIONAL grammarians that usages were either 'right' or 'wrong' has been replaced by a concern to describe the observable facts of linguistic usage, without reference to value judgements, and to replace absolute notions of correctness by an emphasis on the relative APPROPRIATENESS of language to social settings. Similarly, the question of evaluating GRAMMAR in terms of correctness (as in a decision PROCEDURE) has given way to a concern over the relative merits of competing grammars, bearing in mind their purpose (as in an evaluation procedure). See also ACCEPTABILITY.

correlation A term used in PRAGUE SCHOOL PHONOLOGY to refer to a systematic relationship between two SERIES of sounds. For example, the series of voiceless and voiced FRICATIVES in English are related by a 'correlation' of VOICE; voice is thereby the 'mark of correlation'.

correlative In GRAMMAR, referring to a construction which uses a pair of CONNECTING words. Constructions of this kind in English include *either . . . or . . . , not only . . . but also . . .* and *if . . . then . . . .*

correspond(ence) (1) A term used in LINGUISTICS to refer to any similarity of FORM between WORDS or STRUCTURES in related LANGUAGES. For example, there is a stateable relationship between the sound structure of such words as *fish* and *piscis* (Latin); /f/ and /p/, for example, can be shown to be in systematic correspondence, because of the nature of the sound changes which took place in the history of English.

(2) The notion is often encountered in SEMANTIC discussion, deriving from the common philosophical view of truth, that a PROPOSITION is true only if it denotes an actual state of affairs which verifies it. The classical **correspondence theory** of MEANING argued that there is a direct relationship between a linguistic form and the entity it denotes, as shown, for example, by the existence of onomatopoeic words (such as *splash* and *murmur*). Because the vast majority of the words in a language demonstrate only the arbitrariness of the relationship between 'words' and 'things', however, this view is therefore often called the **correspondence fallacy**.

(3) The **correspondence hypothesis** attracted considerable PSYCHOLINGUISTIC interest in the 1960s, especially with reference to language ACQUISITION studies. It states that the sequence of RULES used in the GRAMMATICAL DERIVATION of a SENTENCE corresponds to the sequence of psychological processes that takes place in SPEECH PRODUCTION and SPEECH PERCEPTION. Evidence in its favour came from several experiments which showed that the time it took for speakers to process sentences with more COMPLEX derivations was longer than their less complex counterparts (e.g. PASSIVES as opposed to ACTIVES, NEGATIVES as opposed to AFFIRMATIVES). Further experimental evidence, in the late 1960s, was less convincing, however, and methodological problems were raised (e.g. how one separates out effects due to length and meaning, as well as TRANSFORMATIONAL history); there have also been radical theoretical changes in the notions of transformation involved. As a result, the correspondence hypothesis is no longer influential as a research PARADIGM.

cost A term used metaphorically in GENERATIVE PHONOLOGY in discussing the relative SIMPLICITY or NATURALNESS of phonological analyses. Increasing the complexity of an analysis (e.g. by adding FEATURES or RULES) is said to add to its cost, and vice versa. The principle involved here is a general one, sometimes discussed with reference to the notion of 'diminishing returns': as more CLASSES of LINGUISTIC UNIT are set up, each class comes to subsume fewer DATA, and, while this permits an increase in the ability of the GRAMMAR to handle exceptions, there is a consequential drop in generality. There is thus plenty of room for controversy over where the least costly cut-off point in an analysis would be, in trying to reconcile generality with depth of descriptive detail.

co-text A term used by some British LINGUISTS in an attempt to resolve the AMBIGUITY of the term CONTEXT, which can refer to both LINGUISTIC and

SITUATIONAL ENVIRONMENTS. The practice is to reserve 'co-text' for the former, and 'context' for the latter.

count(un-count-able, -ability) A term used in the GRAMMATICAL classification of NOUNS; opposed to 'uncountable' or MASS. This 'countability' distinction was often unrecognized in TRADITIONAL grammars, but it has been a focus of attention in LINGUISTIC analyses of the NOUN PHRASE, because of the way it can explain the DISTRIBUTION of nouns in relation to the use of such ITEMS as ARTICLES and QUANTIFIERS. **Countable** nouns are those denoting what the LANGUAGE treats as separable entities, by using them with such forms as *a, many, two, three*, etc.; **uncountable** or **non-count** nouns are treated as continuous entities, having no natural bounds, by being used with such forms as *much, some*. The contrast can be seen in *a boy v. *much boy*, and **an information v. much information*. Many nouns can be used in both contexts, e.g. *a cake/many cakes/much cake*.

counter-agent A term used in later CASE GRAMMAR to refer to the force or resistance against which an action is carried out.

counter-bleeding see BLEEDING

counter-example LINGUISTICS and PHONETICS use this term in its general sense, referring to the process of constructing or encountering a piece of DATA which falsifies a hypothesis, and thus leads to revision in an analysis. As in other sciences, there is frequent discussion of whether a suggested counter-example is real or apparent, i.e. able to be analysed in such a way that one's hypothesis can be salvaged.

counter-factual A term used in GRAMMAR and SEMANTICS to refer to a type of CONDITIONAL SENTENCE which refers to a totally hypothetical situation, such as *If she had taken the train, she would have arrived on time*. Counter-factual or 'unreal' statements are usually contrasted with such 'real' conditional statements as *If she took the train, she will have arrived on time*. Both types of sentence can be discussed with reference to the notion of FACTIVITY.

counter-feeding see FEEDING

counter-intuitive(ness) A term used to characterize an implausible analysis, according to the INTUITION of the NATIVE-SPEAKER or the LINGUIST. For example, an analysis which derives STATEMENTS from QUESTIONS is felt to be less natural than one which derives questions from statements, and these feelings can be to some degree supported experimentally (e.g. by showing differences in reaction times). Obtaining intuitive reactions from native-speakers in a systematic, verifiable way is not easy, however, and is not often done; and the dangers of circularity are evident, especially when native-speaker and linguist are the same person (as is usually the case in much of the work done in theoretical linguistics): it is very easy to allow one's intuitions as a native-speaker to be swayed by the purpose of one's analysis as a linguist. The problems inherent in the counter-intuitiveness criterion have been satirically summarized in one definition (by the British linguist Angus MacIntosh (b. 1914)): 'going against everything that suits my theory or purpose, and don't ask me to explain why!'

covered One of the features of sound set up by CHOMSKY and Halle in their

DISTINCTIVE FEATURE theory of PHONOLOGY, to handle variations in PLACE OF ARTICULATION (CAVITY features). It is a tentative categorization, referring to sounds produced with a narrowed, tensed PHARYNX and raised LARYNX, as may occur in some West African languages on tensed VOWELS. Its opposite is **non-covered**, where there is no such narrowing and tensing of the pharynx.

covert (1) A term used in LINGUISTIC analysis to refer to the relationships between linguistic FORMS which are not observable in the SURFACE STRUCTURE of a SENTENCE, but emerge only when sets of sentences are brought into relationship with each other; opposed to OVERT. Examples of covert relations include SUBSTITUTABILITY (as in the notion of WORD-CLASS) and TRANSFORMATIONAL equivalence. 'Covert *WH*-MOVEMENT' involves the movement of a phonologically NULL element, as occurs with *that*-RELATIVES or COMPARATIVES in GOVERNMENT-BINDING THEORY.

(2) In the MINIMALIST PROGRAMME, a term describing the subsystem (the **covert component**) which, following the operation of SPELL-OUT, continues the computation of a sentence to LOGICAL FORM; it contrasts in this model with the 'phonological component', which leads to a representation in phonetic form.

(3) A term used in SOCIOLINGUISTICS as part of the analysis of the way linguistic FORMS carry social prestige: in **covert prestige**, forms belonging to VERNACULAR DIALECTS are positively valued, emphasizing group solidarity and local identity. This kind of prestige is covert, because it is usually manifested subconsciously between members of a group, unlike the case of OVERT prestige, where the forms to be valued are publicly recommended by powerful social institutions.

CP An abbreviation in recent GOVERNMENT-BINDING THEORY for COMPLEMENTIZER PHRASE, the maximal PROJECTION of C (C″). CP is the largest unit of GRAMMATICAL analysis (the initial symbol), equivalent to S′ in earlier GB, and in LEXICAL FUNCTIONAL GRAMMAR and GENERALIZED PHRASE-STRUCTURE GRAMMAR.

C-place see PLACE

cps see CYCLE (3)

crash see CONVERGE

creak(y) A term used in the PHONETIC classification of VOICE QUALITY, on the basis of ARTICULATORY and AUDITORY PHONETIC criteria. It refers to a vocal effect produced by a very slow vibration of only one end of the VOCAL CORDS. Some speakers do have an abnormally creaky voice quality, as a permanent feature of their speech. What is of particular significance for linguistic analysis is that creaky effects may be used with contrastive force, communicating a PARALINGUISTIC MEANING: in RECEIVED PRONUNCIATION, for example, it is often heard to help to express disparagement, when a phrase such as *Oh I don't know* is pronounced at a very low PITCH level. 'Creaky voice', or simply 'creak', is also sometimes encountered as a phonological characteristic, as in Hausa, where there is an opposition between creaky and non-creaky PLOSIVES. Creaky sounds are also called 'laryngealized'.

creativity (creative) An application in LINGUISTICS of the usual sense of this term to refer to the capacity of LANGUAGE users to produce and understand an indefinitely large number of SENTENCES, most of which they will not have heard or used before. Seen as a property of language, it refers to the 'open-endedness' or PRODUCTIVITY of patterns, whereby a finite set of sounds, STRUCTURES, etc., can be used to produce a potentially infinite number of sentences. In contrast with studies of animal communication, linguistic creativity is considered to be a species-specific property: the creation of new sentences is not a feature of animal communication systems. The notion of creativity has a long history in the discussion of language, but it has become a central feature of contemporary studies since the emphasis placed upon it by CHOMSKY. One of the main aims of linguistic enquiry, it is felt, is to explain this creative ability, for which such constructs as GENERATIVE RULES have been suggested. Care must, however, be taken to avoid confusing this sense of 'creative' with that found in artistic or literary contexts, where notions such as imagination and originality are central.

creole (creolize, de-creoliz-ation) A term used in SOCIOLINGUISTICS to refer to a PIDGIN LANGUAGE which has become the mother-tongue of a SPEECH community, as is the case in Jamaica, Haiti, Dominica, and in several other ex-colonial parts of the world. The process of **creolization** expands the STRUCTURAL and STYLISTIC range of the pidginized language, such that the **creolized language** becomes comparable in FORMAL and FUNCTIONAL COMPLEXITY to other languages. A process of **decreolization** takes place when the STANDARD language begins to exert influence on the creole, and a POST-CREOLE CONTINUUM emerges.

criteria In LINGUISTICS and PHONETICS this term is used with reference to the FORMAL justification of an analysis or description – why one carries out a linguistic analysis in a particular way. The criteria may result from general considerations of the purpose of one's analysis (e.g. whether pure or applied, theoretical or descriptive, SYNCHRONIC or DIACHRONIC), or may relate to the range of specific factors felt to be relevant to a restricted problem. For example, in the setting up of WORD-CLASSES, decisions must be made as to whether purely **linguistic criteria** will be used (e.g. PHONOLOGICAL, GRAMMATICAL, SEMANTIC), or whether reference will be made to **non-linguistic criteria** (e.g. logical, NOTIONAL, aesthetic). Linguistics has generally emphasized two principles: that criteria should always be made EXPLICIT, and should as far as possible be based on formal considerations, e.g. of grammar or phonology. The term is also used with reference to the levels of ADEQUACY ('criteria of adequacy') of a grammatical theory.

critical linguistics A developing branch of LINGUISTICS which aims to reveal hidden power relations and ideological processes at work in spoken or written texts. Critical linguists criticize mainstream linguistics for its FORMALIST preoccupations, lacking adequate social explanations, and obscuring ideological and political issues. The study includes such topics as the social context of texts, grammar production, and language policy. In recent years the notion has been extended to such areas as PRAGMATICS and SOCIOLINGUISTICS, and specifically to the study of DISCOURSE. **Critical discourse analysis** is a perspective which studies the relationship between discourse events and sociopolitical and cultural factors, especially the way discourse is ideologically influenced by and can itself influence power relations in society.

cross-over A term used in GENERATIVE GRAMMAR, referring to a principle restricting the operation of certain TRANSFORMATIONS which move a NOUN PHRASE (as in PASSIVES, REFLEXIVES, TOUGH MOVEMENT). In an early formulation, the principle states that a transformation cannot apply to a PHRASE-MARKER if it would result in one noun phrase crossing another with which it is CO-REFERENTIAL. The 'cross-over constraint' or 'principle' would be used, for example, to explain why passivization cannot apply to structures of the type *John washed himself*: given an UNDERLYING STRUCTURE *John*$_i$ *washed John*$_i$, to derive a passive *John*$_i$ *was washed by John*$_i$ would involve a violation of this principle. In later formulations, more specific CONSTRAINTS on the application of this principle are introduced.

cross-sectional An application of the general use of this term in the field of child language ACQUISITION, referring to one of the two main procedures used in order to study the process of LANGUAGE development. In a cross-sectional study, the language of a group of children of the same or different ages is compared at a given point in time. This method contrasts with a LONGITUDINAL study, which follows the course of language acquisition in a single child or group over a period of time.

cryptophasia see IDIOGLOSSIA

c-structure An abbreviation in LEXICAL-FUNCTIONAL GRAMMAR for CONSTITUENT-structure. This is essentially the SURFACE STRUCTURE of a SENTENCE, and contrasts with F-STRUCTURE (or functional structure), which provides an analysis of the sentence in terms of grammatical FUNCTIONS such as SUBJECT and OBJECT.

cue see ACOUSTIC FEATURE

culminativity (culminative) In METRICAL GRID theory, a FOOT-shape PARAMETER which constrains every CONTENT word to contain one STRESSED SYLLABLE. This is a consequence of the nature of the PROSODIC HIERARCHY, and of the EXHAUSTIVITY condition, which requires every syllable to be included in metrical structure. More generally, any prosodic process which makes certain syllables more prominent is described as **culminative**.

cultural transmission A suggested defining property of human LANGUAGE (contrasting with the properties of many other SEMIOTIC systems), whereby the ability to speak a language is transmitted from generation to generation by a process of learning, and not genetically. This is not to deny that children may be born with certain INNATE predispositions towards language, but it is to emphasize the difference between human language, where environmental learning has such a large role to play, and animal systems of communication, where instinct is more important.

cupping A term sometimes used in PHONETICS for one of the transverse ARTICULATIONS which may be made by the TONGUE: specifically, it refers to the way the tongue body is able to adopt a concave, hollowed shape during an articulation, by allowing the mid-line of the tongue to drop lower than the sides. The effect is common in the formation of RETROFLEX consonants. A contrast can be drawn with GROOVING.

CV, CVC, etc. (1) Abbreviations for CONSONANT and VOWEL sequences, used especially in describing the types of SYLLABLE which exist in a LANGUAGE; e.g. in English the statement of the PHONOTACTIC possibilities will include the information that it is possible to have CCCV- INITIALLY, as in *splice*, and -VCCCC FINALLY, as in *sixths*.
(2) CV is also a commonly used abbreviation for CARDINAL VOWEL.

CV phonology A term used in PHONOLOGY for a MODEL which adds a CONSONANT (C) and VOWEL (V) TIER to the SYLLABIC and SEGMENTAL tiers previously recognized in AUTOSEGMENTAL PHONOLOGY. The addition of this tier removes the need for the feature [syllabic] at the SKELETAL TIER.

CV rule see ONSET (1)

cycle (cyclic-al, -ity) (1) A principle in TRANSFORMATIONAL GENERATIVE GRAMMAR that allows RULES to apply in a repeated ordered way to sections of a PHRASE-MARKER where a particular STRUCTURAL DESCRIPTION is met, instead of in a single scan to the phrase structure as a whole. This application of the rules is referred to as **cyclic**, and the whole process is known as the **transformational cycle** or **cyclic principle**. Its FORMALIZATION requires that the rules apply first to the UNDERLYING SENTENCE most deeply EMBEDDED in a phrase-marker (the first cycle), and then to the next highest sentence (the second cycle), until the MATRIX sentence is arrived at. On each application, at a given level, in this view, the rules may not take into account information higher up the phrase-marker. This principle allows for a less complicated analysis to be assigned to sentences with 'repeated' elements, such as *The man seems to want to try a second time.* Various types of **cyclic rules** have been suggested, e.g. 'last-cyclic' rules, which apply only to the highest level in a DERIVATION. Cyclic TRANSFORMATIONS reduce in number in later versions of TRANSFORMATIONAL GRAMMAR – ultimately reducing to a single rule of (ALPHA) MOVEMENT – and are constrained by several CONDITIONS on their applicability (such as the SUBJACENCY condition, the SPECIFIED-SUBJECT CONDITION and the TENSED-subject condition). **Post-cyclic rules** are also recognized in the EXTENDED STANDARD THEORY, to refer to a type of transformation which applies after cyclic transformations have been completed, as might be suggested for handling INVERSION, the initial placement of QUESTION words in English (e.g. ***where*** *did John say that he was going?*), or in TAG formation. A **successive cyclic** analysis is one where superficially unbounded movement processes are analysed as involving a succession of bounded processes, e.g. in *What did you say that you would do?*, where *WH*-movement would be applied in successive steps, crossing a single INFLECTION PHRASE boundary in each of its applications.

In generative PHONOLOGY, the cyclic principle was established by CHOMSKY and Halle to account for the variations in STRESS contrast in relation to VOWEL QUALITY within WORDS and SENTENCES. It is argued that the place of a word's main stress, and the remaining stresses in a POLYSYLLABIC word, are explainable by referring to the SYNTACTIC and the SEGMENTAL phonological structure of an UTTERANCE. The SURFACE STRUCTURE of a sentence, in this view, is seen as a string of FORMATIVES which are bracketed together in various ways, the BRACKETS reflecting the grammatical structure ASSIGNED to the sentence, such as sentence, NOUN PHRASE, VERB PHRASE, e.g. [[the [elephant]] [[kick[ed]] [the [ball]]]]. The cyclic principle makes the phonological rules apply first to the maximal STRINGS that contain no brackets; once applied, the brackets surrounding these strings are then erased. The phonological rules then apply again to the maximal strings without brackets produced by this first procedure, and again the innermost brackets are erased. The procedure continues until all brackets have been removed. Various types of rule have been devised to make this cyclical procedure work, such as the Compound Rule and the Nuclear Stress Rule, both of which are ways of assigning main degrees of stress to the various CONSTITUENTS of a sentence (the first in relation to compound items, the second to sequences of items in phrases). In later phonological theory, the **strict cycle condition** (**SCC**) is a constraint governing the proper application of cyclic rules: it states in essence that cyclic rules apply only to DERIVED representations.

(2) In SEMANTICS, the term is sometimes used to refer to a type of SENSE relationship between LEXICAL ITEMS (a subtype of INCOMPATIBILITY). **Lexical cycles** (or 'cyclical sets') are sets of items organized in terms of successivity, but lacking any fixed end-points, e.g. days of the week, months of the year. 'Serial' ordering, by contrast, displays fixed end-points, as in military ranks.

(3) A term derived from the study of the physics of sound, and used in ACOUSTIC PHONETICS, referring to a single to-and-fro movement (oscillation) of an air particle in a waveform around its point of rest. FREQUENCY used to be measured in **cycles per second** (**cps**), but this unit has now been replaced by the **Hertz** (**Hz**).

D

D An abbreviation for DEEP, in such contexts as D-STRUCTURE, and for DETERMINER in the context of DP (DETERMINER PHRASE).

DA The usual abbreviation for 'DISCOURSE analysis'.

DAF The usual abbreviation for delayed auditory FEEDBACK.

dark *l* An impressionistic but commonly used term for a variety of LATERAL sound, where the RESONANCE is that of a back vowel of an [u] quality, as in the standard-English pronunciation of /l/ after VOWELS, before CONSONANTS, and as a SYLLABIC sound, e.g. *pull, altar, bottle*; it is opposed to CLEAR *L* Alternatively, one might refer to this quality as a 'velarized' /l/ (cf. VELAR), transcribing it [ɫ].

data The term is used in its general sense in LINGUISTICS, referring to the phenomena which constitute the subject-matter of enquiry (viz. linguistic behaviour). There have, however, been two distinct views concerning the nature of this behaviour, which are usually seen in opposition to each other. The traditional conception of linguistic data is limited to the observable patterns of speech and writing, especially when recorded and gathered together in a CORPUS; GENERATIVE linguistic theory, on the other hand, goes beyond this, including as part of the raw data for analysis the language user's judgements (INTUITIONS) about the language. Much controversy has been generated by these opposed views (which are related to the more basic divergences between BEHAVIOURIST and MENTALIST philosophies), and the issue is still prominent, criticisms being made of the limited reliability and generality of observable data, and of the uncertain verifiability and objectivity of mentalistic data, as evidence of linguistic SYSTEM. In language ACQUISITION, the term 'primary linguistic data' refers to the language input to the child, deriving from parents, siblings, etc.

dative One of the FORMS taken by a NOUN PHRASE (often a single NOUN or PRONOUN) in LANGUAGES which express GRAMMATICAL relationships by means of INFLECTIONS. The dative CASE typically expresses an INDIRECT OBJECT relationship, or a range of meaning similar to that covered by *to* or *for* in English: but there is a great deal of variation between languages in the way this case is used. English itself does not have a dative case form, but expresses the notion of indirect object using PREPOSITIONS and WORD ORDER, e.g. *he gave a book to the boy* or *he gave the boy a book*. In classical TRANSFORMATIONAL GRAMMAR, the **dative movement transformation** related DITRANSITIVE constructions of this kind. The term is given special status in CASE grammar, where it refers to the case of the ANIMATE being affected by the VERB's state or action (later, EXPERIENCER). A frequently used alternative is RECIPIENT.

daughter A relation between two NODES in a PHRASE-MARKER. If one node X immediately DOMINATES another node Y, then X is the 'mother' of Y, and Y is the 'daughter' of X.

daughter adjunction see ADJUNCTION

daughter-dependency grammar An approach to GRAMMATICAL analysis based on a system of SYNTACTIC FEATURES and DEPENDENCY relations, in which there is a single LEVEL of syntactic REPRESENTATION, TRANSFORMATIONS not being required. The 'vertical' CONSTITUENCY relations between NODES are referred to in terms of 'daughter-dependency'; the 'horizontal' dependencies (of SUBJECT-VERB, etc.) are referred to in terms of 'sister-dependency'. All nodes in this approach are complexes of BINARY features (as opposed to the unitary CATEGORIES of earlier models of transformational grammar). Classification RULES define the permissible combinations of features to construct categories; **dependency rules** specify the structures in which these categories appear. All constituents are defined in terms of a notion of relative peripherality: given any two constituents, one will be more peripheral than the other. A notion of syntactic FUNCTION (e.g. subject, TOPIC) is assigned to nodes, whose main function is to determine SURFACE-STRUCTURE WORD ORDER.

Davidsonian semantics see SEMANTICS

death (of language) see LANGUAGE

debuccalized (debuccalization) A term used in some models of NON-LINEAR PHONOLOGY to refer to CONSONANTS which lack an ORAL PLACE feature, such as GLOTTAL STOP or [h]. The process through which such consonants are formed is called **debuccalization** (also **deoralization**): examples include [t] > [ʔ] and [s] > [h].

declaration A term used in the theory of SPEECH ACTS to refer to a type of UTTERANCE where the speaker's words bring about a new situation in the external world, as in *I name this ship/child . . . , I resign.*

declarative A term used in the GRAMMATICAL classification of SENTENCE types, and usually seen in contrast to IMPERATIVE, INTERROGATIVE, etc., MOODS. It refers to VERB FORMS or sentence/CLAUSE types typically used in the expression of STATEMENTS, e.g. *the man is walking*. The term 'indicative' is also sometimes used in this sense.

declension In GRAMMAR, a traditional term for a CLASS of NOUNS, ADJECTIVES, or PRONOUNS in an INFLECTING language, which occur with the same range of FORMS. In Latin, for example, the 'first declension' refers to nouns whose endings are *-a, -am*, or *-ae*, in the various cases in the SINGULAR (e.g. *insula* 'island', *poeta* 'poet'). There are a further four declensions with different types of ending, as well as several nouns which decline in an IRREGULAR way. The term is not usually found in modern LINGUISTIC analysis (which talks in terms of 'word classes'), but will be encountered in studies of LINGUISTIC HISTORIOGRAPHY).

declination see DOWNSTEP

decode see CODE

deconstruction see LOGOCENTRISM

decreolization see CREOLE

de dicto/de re Terms used in philosophy and logic which have been invoked in the SEMANTIC analysis of sentences expressing such MODAL meanings as 'It is possible that...' or 'X believes that...' *De dicto* (Latin 'about the saying') denotes knowledge acquired through language rather than through an experience of the situation to which the language refers. If I have never been to Mauritius, I can still say 'I know that Mauritius is a nice place', from what I have heard people say about it. *De re* ('about the thing') denotes knowledge acquired by experience of the situation itself (e.g. from having been to Mauritius), rather than through any linguistic account I may have received of it. The relevance of this distinction is that it helps elucidate the alternative logical interpretations of such sentences as 'P believes that Y is a doctor': (a) there is an object Y such that it is believed by P to be a doctor; (b) there is not necessarily any object Y such that it is believed by P to be a doctor. In the former case, there is a Y in reality (the *de re* interpretation); in the latter case, it is a matter of what P believes (the *de dicto* interpretation).

deep structure A central theoretical term in TRANSFORMATIONAL GRAMMAR; opposed to SURFACE STRUCTURE. 'Deep structure' (or 'deep grammar') is the abstract SYNTACTIC REPRESENTATION of a SENTENCE – an UNDERLYING LEVEL of structural organization which specifies all the factors governing the way the sentence should be interpreted. (The basic notion has also been referred to, in various theoretical contexts, as D-STRUCTURE, UNDERLYING structure, BASE structure, REMOTE STRUCTURE and INITIAL structure.) This level provides information which enables us to distinguish between the alternative interpretations of sentences which have the same surface form (i.e. they are AMBIGUOUS), e.g. *Flying planes can be dangerous*, where *flying planes* can be related to two underlying sentences, *Planes which fly*... and *To fly planes*... It is also a way of relating sentences which have different surface forms but the same underlying MEANING, as in the relationship between ACTIVE and PASSIVE structures, e.g. *The panda chased the man* as opposed to *The man was chased by the panda*. Transformational grammars would derive one of these alternatives from the other, or perhaps both from an even more abstract ('deeper') underlying structure. The various grammatical relations in such sentences can then be referred to as the 'deep SUBJECT', 'deep OBJECT', etc. (contrasted with 'surface subject', etc.). It is also possible to compute the 'depth' at which a transformation operates, by referring to the number of stages in a DERIVATION before it applies, and some attempt has been made to correlate this notion with the COMPLEXITY of a sentence.

In some generative studies, the role of deep structure has been called into question, it being suggested that a separate level of underlying syntactic organization between surface structure and meaning is unnecessary and misleading (cf. GENERATIVE SEMANTICS). It is also possible to find the term used in the general sense of 'underlying structural interpretation', without commitment to a specific interpretation in terms of transformational grammar. Indeed, the original use of this term, by the American linguist Charles Hockett (b. 1916), antedates its CHOMSKYAN application.

default The application of the general use of this term in several domains of linguistics and phonetics, to refer to cases where a previously specified value is automatically introduced into an analysis when certain conditions apply. In some recent models of PHONOLOGY, for example, it refers to an UNMARKED mode of operation of a RULE. A case in point is in radical UNDERSPECIFICATION theory, where for each FEATURE one value (the phonologically active value) is specified in the lexical REPRESENTATION, and the other is filled in at some later stage by a **default rule** (or **default specification**) which assigns an unmarked value to the feature. The default rule may become activated by a phonological rule, or it may stay passive throughout the derivation. The notion is also important in some SEMANTIC lexical analyses, such as certain models of TYPED FEATURE structures.

defective (1) In GRAMMAR, a traditional description of WORDS which do not follow all the rules of the CLASS to which they belong. The English MODAL VERBS, for example, are defective in that they do not permit the usual range of verb INFLECTIONS: **musted, *cans, *shalling*, etc. Because of its pejorative connotations, the term is not usually found in modern LINGUISTIC analysis (which talks more in terms of IRREGULAR forms and exceptions to RULES), but will be encountered in studies of LINGUISTIC HISTORIOGRAPHY.

(2) In PHONOLOGY, descriptive of any pattern which fails to show all the properties of the class to which it belongs. For example, a SEGMENT with a 'defective DISTRIBUTION' does not appear in all the ENVIRONMENTS possible for other members of its class (e.g. the distribution of English /h/ is defective, compared with other FRICATIVES, because it cannot appear syllable-finally).

deficit hypothesis In SOCIOLINGUISTICS and EDUCATIONAL LINGUISTICS, the name given to the view that some children, especially those belonging to an ethnic minority or with a working-class background, lack a sufficiently wide range of GRAMMATICAL constructions and vocabulary to be able to express complex ideas, such as will be needed for success in school. An unfashionable hypothesis in the intellectual climate of the present-day, it is contrasted with the **difference hypothesis** – the view that the language used by such children is simply different from that found in middle-class children, though its social standing is lower. The difference hypothesis views all DIALECTS as intrinsically equal and able to express ideas of any complexity, though children who speak non-STANDARD dialects may not have had the same kind of opportunity or motivation to use their language in demanding educational contexts.

defining (*v.* non-defining) see RELATIVE

defining vocabulary In several areas of APPLIED LINGUISTICS, a fixed set of words used as part of the definition of other words. The notion is found in such contexts as foreign language teaching, the teaching of reading, and LEXICOGRAPHY. These days, several dictionaries intended for the non-native user have a limited vocabulary – for example, 2,000 words – in order to define the meanings of all their lexical entries.

definite(ness) A term used in GRAMMAR and SEMANTICS to refer to a specific, identifiable entity (or class of entities); it is usually contrasted with INDEFINITE (less often 'non-definite'). Definiteness in English is generally conveyed through the use of definite DETERMINERS (such as *this, my*), and especially through the definite ARTICLE, *the*. Definite NOUN PHRASES are often referred to, especially in the PHILOSOPHICAL LINGUISTIC literature, as **definite descriptions** – referents which are identifiable not only by their name but by a description which is sufficiently detailed to enable that referent to be distinguished from all others, e.g. *the present Queen of England*.

defooting see FOOT (1)

deforestation A principle proposed in GENERATIVE PHONOLOGY whereby, before applying any RULES on a phonological CYCLE, all PROSODIC structure in the DOMAIN of that cycle is erased. The principle was introduced to handle WORDS which are subject to processes of DERIVATIONAL MORPHOLOGY due to AFFIXATION (e.g. *sensation, sensationality*).

degenerate foot see FOOT (1)

degree A GRAMMATICAL CATEGORY used to specify the extent of a comparison between ADJECTIVES or ADVERBS. A three-way contrast of GRADATION is usually recognized (POSITIVE *v.* COMPARATIVE *v.* SUPERLATIVE), but other possibilities are sometimes distinguished, e.g. an 'equative' degree (as in *as big as*). In English, both MORPHOLOGICAL and SYNTACTIC means are used in the expression of degree, e.g. *bigger/biggest* but *more fascinating/most fascinating*.

deixis (deictic) A term used in LINGUISTIC theory to subsume those features of LANGUAGE which refer directly to the personal, temporal or locational characteristics of the SITUATION within which an UTTERANCE takes place, whose MEANING is thus relative to that situation; e.g. *now/then, here/there, I/you, this/that* are **deictics** ('deictic' or EXOPHORIC words). Deixis is analogous to the philosophical notion of INDEXICAL EXPRESSION. The term is also used for words which refer backwards or forwards in DISCOURSE (ANAPHORA and CATAPHORA respectively), e.g. *that, the following, the former*. This is sometimes known as **discourse** (or **text**) **deixis**, which should be distinguished from **social deixis**, the encoding of social distinctions that relate to PARTICIPANT ROLES (speaker-addressee, etc.), as encountered in such matters as PRONOUNS, HONORIFICS, VOCATIVES and forms of ADDRESS. The notion of deixis has proved to be fruitful in several areas of LINGUISTICS, especially in PRAGMATICS, and in language ACQUISITION studies, where some investigators view the learning of these ITEMS by children as constituting a significant feature of early development.

delayed One of the features of sound set up by CHOMSKY and Halle in their DISTINCTIVE FEATURE theory of PHONOLOGY, as part of the phrase **delayed release**, to handle variations in MANNER OF ARTICULATION, specifying the nature of a sound's RELEASE. Delayed release sounds are defined both ARTICULATORILY and

ACOUSTICALLY, as those sounds where a sound is produced with a gradual release sufficient to make a sound similar to a FRICATIVE, as in AFFRICATES. Affricates are all [+delayed release] ([+del rel]). Its opposite is INSTANTANEOUS or ABRUPT release, referring to a sound released suddenly and without the ACOUSTIC turbulence of a fricative, as in PLOSIVES.

deletion (delete) A basic operation within the framework of TRANSFORMATIONAL GRAMMAR, which eliminates a CONSTITUENT of an input PHRASE-MARKER. In classical TG, it accounted for IMPERATIVE SENTENCES, for example (where the SUBJECT and AUXILIARY VERB of an UNDERLYING sentence is deleted, as in *kick the ball* from ***You will*** *kick the ball*). Other applications of the notion can be found in the transformational treatment of DUMMY symbols, and in several specific transformational operations (e.g. EQUI NP DELETION). Several formal CONSTRAINTS on the use of deletion transformations have been suggested, especially that the deleted elements must be RECOVERABLE, i.e. the deletion transformation must specify the elements to be deleted, and in the output phrase-marker the effects of the deletion must be clearly indicated. If this were not the case, there would be several unfortunate consequences; e.g. a single surface structure could be related to an indefinite number of deep structures, as in *He's been hit*, derivable from *Someone/John/A bullet . . . hit him*.

delicacy (delicate) In HALLIDAYAN LINGUISTICS, this term is used to refer to one of the scales of analysis which interrelates the CATEGORIES of the theory, viz. the dimension which recognizes increasing depth of detail. An increasingly 'delicate' analysis of the notion of CLAUSE, for example, might recognize AFFIRMATIVE *v.* INTERROGATIVE types; interrogative clauses could then be analysed into several QUESTION types; and so on. Other scales in this approach are labelled RANK and EXPONENCE.

delimitative A term sometimes used in GRAMMAR and SEMANTICS, referring to a limitation on the duration of the state or activity expressed by the VERB ('for a little while'). In some languages (e.g. Russian) the contrast is a formal part of the ASPECT system.

delinking see SPREADING

delta A symbol Δ used in some MODELS of TRANSFORMATIONAL GRAMMAR (cf. ASPECTS), which acts as a DUMMY element in the generation of DEEP STRUCTURES. The purpose of the **delta symbols** is to mark the places in an initial PHRASE-MARKER (a PRE-LEXICAL structure) where LEXICAL items are later to be inserted: lexical insertion RULES then replace each 'empty' delta by a COMPLEX SYMBOL containing the SYNTACTIC FEATURES which will be used to define the deep structures of the grammar.

demibeat see BEAT

demonstrative see PRONOUN

demotion A term used in RELATIONAL GRAMMAR for a class of relation-changing PROCESSES in which a NOUN PHRASE bearing a particular grammatical relation to some VERB comes to bear another grammatical relation to that verb, which is lower down the relational HIERARCHY. An example would be a process which converted a SUBJECT to an OBJECT.

denasalized see NASAL

denominal A term used in GRAMMAR for an element which originates as a NOUN but is used in some other way in sentence structure. For example, in *the garden fence, garden* could be described as a 'denominal adjective'.

denotation (denotative) A term used in SEMANTICS as part of a classification of types of MEANING; opposed to CONNOTATION. 'Denotative meaning' involves the relationship between a LINGUISTIC UNIT (especially a LEXICAL ITEM) and the non-linguistic entities to which it refers – it is thus equivalent to REFERENTIAL meaning. For example, the denotation of *dog* is its dictionary definition of 'canine quadruped', etc.; its connotations might include 'friend', 'helper', 'competition', etc.

dental A term in the PHONETIC classification of CONSONANT sounds on the basis of their PLACE OF ARTICULATION: it refers to a sound made by the tongue TIP and RIMS against the teeth. 'Apico-dental' is a more explicit but less used description of such sounds, 'apico-' being derived from APEX, an alternative term for tongue tip. Usually the upper teeth are the ones involved, as in the [d̪], [t̪] and [n̪] of some English DIALECTS, such as Irish English (this contrasts with the ALVEOLAR articulation of [d] and [t] in RECEIVED PRONUNCIATION); but both upper and lower teeth may be in contact with the tongue during the articulation, as in the *th-* sounds of *thin* [θ] and *this* [ð]. In [θ] and [ð], moreover, the tip of the tongue is usually slightly between the teeth, in which cases the more precise term INTERDENTAL can be used. If the sound is articulated towards the back of the upper teeth, close to the alveolar ridge, the term 'POST-dental' can be used. 'Denti-alveolar' identifies the place of articulation at the junction of the upper teeth and alveolar ridge. The phonetic symbol for 'dental articulation' is [̪], placed underneath the symbol for the consonant in question, as above.

deontic A term derived from modal logic and used by some LINGUISTS as part of a theoretical framework for the analysis of MODAL VERBS and related STRUCTURES in LANGUAGE. **Deontic modality** is concerned with the logic of obligation and permission, e.g. the use of the modals in SENTENCES such as *The car must be ready*, i.e. 'I oblige you to ensure that the car is ready'. It thus contrasts with ALETHIC and EPISTEMIC modality, which would interpret this sentence respectively as 'It follows that the car is ready' and 'It is surely the case that the car is ready'.

deoralization see DEBUCCALIZATION

dependency grammar A type of FORMAL GRAMMAR, developed by several LINGUISTS in the 1950s (in particular, the French linguist Lucien Tesnière (1893–1954)), which establishes types of dependencies between the ELEMENTS of a CONSTRUCTION as a means of explaining grammatical relationships. SYNTACTIC STRUCTURE is represented using **dependency trees** – sets of NODES whose inter-connections specify structural RELATIONS. Every tree contains a GOVERNOR and a set of **dependents**, each of which bears a specific relation to the governor. For example, in a CLAUSE, the VERB is seen as governor, and the dependents are NOUN PHRASES, which are assigned numerical values depending on the VALENCY attributed to the verb. In a PREPOSITIONAL phrase, such as *on the box*, the preposition governs the noun, and the noun governs the ARTICLE. Dependencies are usually displayed as ARCS, which relate words (rather than CONSTITUENTS). The statements which specify the governing and dependent relations which each class of unit may enter into are known as **dependency rules**. Dependencies are of particular importance in several recent grammatical theories (such as DAUGHTER-DEPENDENCY GRAMMAR). The term 'dependency' is also used in several frameworks to express types of relationship between phrases, e.g. UNBOUNDED DEPENDENCY.

dependency phonology An approach to PHONOLOGY which makes use of the principles of DEPENDENCY GRAMMAR to set up a model of the internal relational STRUCTURE of SEGMENTS. The SYLLABLE is seen as a dependency structure, with a GOVERNOR (or HEAD) and dependents (or MODIFIERS). A syllabic ELEMENT (a VOWEL or a syllabic CONSONANT) is the minimal obligatory component of the syllable, other elements being marginal, governed by their syllabic. Degree of dependency is represented vertically in a **dependency graph**, the governor being 'degree zero', with other levels 'degree one', etc., as in the graph for *cat*:

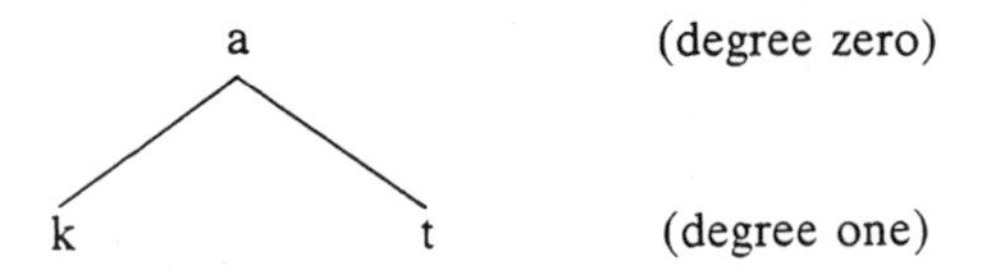

Within the segment, all features are viewed as unary, and are generally referred to as 'components'. The notion of dependency has also come to be used by some other NON-LINEAR PHONOLOGICAL models to denote any kind of relation which may be represented asymmetrically, especially with reference to segment-internal structure. For example, headedness may be seen in the relative PROMINENCE of sequences of strong and weak segments in METRICAL PHONOLOGY, or between SONOROUS and non-sonorous consonants, or between the elements of a consonant CLUSTER. In FEATURE GEOMETRY, the dependency relation holds between features on different TIERS ('feature dependency' or 'dependent tier ordering').

dependent A general term used in GRAMMATICAL analysis as part of the classification of CLAUSE types: opposed to MAIN, and synonymous with SUBORDINATE. The term has a specific application in DEPENDENCY GRAMMAR.

depth hypothesis A hypothesis proposed by the American LINGUIST Victor Yngve (b. 1920) in the early 1960s as an explanation of the psychological differences between the two categories of linguistic CONSTRUCTION: LEFT-BRANCHING (e.g. *the man's hat*) and RIGHT-BRANCHING (e.g. *the hat of the man*). He argued that left-branching structures add more to the psychological COMPLEXITY (or transformational 'depth') of a SENTENCE, because the processing of such structures takes up more space in short-term memory than does the processing of right-branching structures. The hypothesis has been criticized on various grounds, particular reference being made to other important types of construction which complicate the issue, such as SELF-EMBEDDING.

de re see *DE DICTO/DE RE*

derivation(-al, derive(d)) (1) A term used in MORPHOLOGY to refer to one of the two main categories or processes of WORD FORMATION (**derivational morphology**), the other being INFLECTION(AL), also sometimes called **derivatology**. These terms also apply to the two types of AFFIX involved in word formation. Basically, the result of a derivational process is a new word (e.g. *nation* → *national*), whereas the result of an inflectional process is a different form of the same word (e.g. *nations, nationals*). The distinction is not totally clear-cut, however (e.g. how best to analyse *-ly* in English). **Derivational affixes** change the grammatical CLASS of MORPHEMES to which they are attached (as in SUFFIXATION, e.g. *-tion* is a noun-forming derivational suffix); they also usually occur closer to the ROOT morpheme than do inflections, e.g. *nation-al-ize+-ing/-s/-d*. Often they have independently stateable LEXICAL MEANINGS (e.g. *mini-, sub-*), though these are not always easy to identify (e.g. *-er*). The combination of root and derivational affixes is usually referred to as the STEM of the word, i.e. the ELEMENT to which inflections are attached; several modes of classification are available in the literature on this subject.

(2) In GENERATIVE GRAMMAR, the term refers to the set of formally identifiable stages used in generating a SENTENCE from an INITIAL SYMBOL to a TERMINAL STRING, i.e. the whole set of PHRASE-STRUCTURE, TRANSFORMATIONAL, etc., RULES which have applied. In a more restricted context, a **derived structure** refers to the form of an output PHRASE-MARKER, after a transformational rule has applied.

(3) In HISTORICAL LINGUISTICS, the term is used to refer to the origins or historical development of a LANGUAGE or linguistic form. Sounds, words (cf. ETYMOLOGY) and structures are said to be 'derived' from corresponding FORMS in an earlier state of a language.

derived environment In some models of PHONOLOGY, a term used to characterize a CONSTRAINT on the application of certain phonological RULES: the **derived environment constraint** or **condition** asserts that certain kinds of rules (e.g. obligatory NEUTRALIZATION rules) apply only in DERIVED environments – that is, derived either through MORPHOLOGICAL composition or the application of a phonological rule. The DOMAINS which exhibit this constraint are CYCLIC.

description (descriptiv-e, -ism, -ist) The general sense of this term is found in LINGUISTICS, identifying one of the main aims of the subject – to give a comprehensive, systematic, objective and precise account of the patterns and use of a specific LANGUAGE or DIALECT, at a particular point in time. This definition suggests several respects in which 'descriptive' is in contrast with other conceptions of linguistic enquiry. The emphasis on objectivity, systematicness, etc., places it in contrast with the PRESCRIPTIVE aims of much TRADITIONAL GRAMMAR: the aim of **descriptive linguistics** is to describe the facts of linguistic usage as they are, and not how they ought to be, with reference to some imagined ideal state. The emphasis on a given time places it in contrast with HISTORICAL LINGUISTICS, where the aim is to demonstrate linguistic change: descriptive linguistics aims to describe a language SYNCHRONICALLY, at a particular time (not necessarily the present – one can describe the linguistic patterns of any period). The emphasis on 'a' language distinguishes the subject from COMPARATIVE linguistics, as its name suggests, and also from GENERAL linguistics, where the aim is to make theoretical statements about language as a whole. It ought not to be forgotten, of course, that there is an interdependence between these various branches of the subject: a description is the result of an analysis, which must in turn be based on a set of theoretical assumptions. But in descriptive linguistics the theory is only a means to an end, viz. the production of a **descriptive grammar** (or one of its subdivisions, e.g. PHONOLOGY, LEXICON, SYNTAX, MORPHOLOGY). An approach which is characterized by an almost exclusive concern with description, in the above sense, is known as **descriptivism**, and its proponents as **descriptivists**. In linguistics, the term is usually applied to American anthropological and STRUCTURALIST studies before the 'generativist' approach of the late 1950s. Within GENERATIVE grammar, also, the phrase **descriptive adequacy** adds a special dimension to the use of the term: it refers to an account of the NATIVE-SPEAKER's linguistic COMPETENCE (and not merely to an account of a CORPUS of DATA, as would be intended by the earlier use of 'description').

desiderative A term used in the GRAMMATICAL CLASSIFICATION of SENTENCE types, and usually seen in contrast to INDICATIVE, IMPERATIVE, etc., MOODS. It refers to VERB FORMS or sentence/CLAUSE types used for the expression of wants and desires – approximately translatable by '*I want*+sentence', but often LEXICALIZED, e.g. *to want to eat* → *to hunger*.

designated terminal element (DTE) A term used in METRICAL PHONOLOGY for the most PROMINENT element in a STRING, DOMINATED only by relatively strong (*s*-)NODES. For example, *egg* is the DTE in the phrase *the hard-boiled egg*.

destressing see STRESS

det or **DET** The usual abbreviations for DETERMINER.

deterioration In HISTORICAL LINGUISTICS, a term used in the classification of types of SEMANTIC change, referring to the development of a SENSE of disapproval in a LEXICAL item; also called **pejoration**, and opposed to AMELIORATION. For example, *notorious* once meant 'widely known', and now means 'widely and unfavourably known'.

determiner (det, DET, D) A term used in some models of GRAMMATICAL description, referring to a class of ITEMS whose main role is to CO-OCCUR with NOUNS to express a wide range of SEMANTIC contrasts, such as QUANTITY or NUMBER. The ARTICLES, when they occur in a LANGUAGE, are the main subset of determiners (e.g. *the/a* in English); other WORDS which can have a determiner function in English include *each/every, this/that, some/any*, all of which have a DISTRIBUTION which includes the article position, e.g. *the/this/some . . . cake*. Some LINGUISTS extend the application of this term to include other types of word within the noun PHRASE (e.g. ADJECTIVES, PREdeterminers), and sometimes even to include MODIFIERS in other parts of the sentence. In some GENERATIVE GRAMMAR theories, determiner is regarded as the head in combination with a noun, to produce a **determiner phrase** (DP).

developmental linguistics A branch of LINGUISTICS concerned with the study of the ACQUISITION of LANGUAGE in children. The subject involves the application of linguistic theories and techniques of analysis to child language DATA, in order to provide a precise description of patterns of development and an explanation of the norms and variations encountered, both within individual languages and UNIVERSALLY. In relation to the task of explanation, particular attention is paid to the role of non-linguistic factors, such as cognition, social background, the nature of the experimental task, and so on, and as a consequence there has been an increasingly multidisciplinary approach to the problem. Because of the particular relevance of psychological factors, the subject is sometimes referred to as **developmental psycholinguistics**.

deverbal A term used in GRAMMAR for an element which originates as a verb but is used in some other way in sentence structure. For example, in *the singing policeman, singing* could be described as a 'deverbal adjective'.

deviance (deviant) A term used in LINGUISTIC analysis to refer to a SENTENCE (or other UNIT) which does not conform to the RULES of a GRAMMAR (i.e. it is ILL FORMED). Deviant sentences are conventionally marked with an initial ASTERISK, i.e. **Is they be going*.

device A term derived from mathematics and used especially in GENERATIVE LINGUISTICS to refer to an abstract design specifically constructed to enable an analysis to be made. A GRAMMAR, in this sense, can be seen as a device for generating SENTENCES. The notion is sometimes encountered in child language studies, where, in the CHOMSKYAN view, children are credited with a 'language ACQUISITION device' (LAD) which enables them to work out the correct grammatical analysis of sentences on the basis of the speech DATA presented to them.

devoiced see **voice**

dia- A commonly used PREFIX, derived from the term DIALECT, and used in LINGUISTIC studies whenever a dialectal frame of reference is required. **Dialinguistics** is sometimes used to refer to the study of the range of dialects and LANGUAGES used in a speech community. A **diatype** is a term used by some SOCIOLINGUISTS to refer to a VARIETY of language defined according to its use or purpose. It thus contrasts with **dialect**, which is a variety defined in terms of regional or social groups of users. Alternative terms include VARIETY and REGISTER. A **diasystem** is a network of FORMAL relationships which shows the common linguistic SYSTEM assumed to underlie two or more dialects, as a framework for displaying their STRUCTURAL differences. The notation used for this purpose includes formulae which display structural correspondence, e.g.

$$\begin{matrix} X \\ Y \end{matrix} \; \frac{i \sim \text{ɨ}}{i} \approx e \approx \frac{a}{a \sim e}$$

etc., where X and Y are the names of two areas, ~ indicates a contrast which is relevant for one dialect only, ≈ for two (or more) dialects. Within such a framework, diasystemic UNITS can be identified: a **diaphone** is an abstract PHONOLOGICAL unit set up to identify an equivalence between the sound system of different dialects, e.g. the diaphone /ei/, as in English *mate*, is realized as [ei], [ai] etc.; a **diamorph** displays equivalences between MORPHOLOGICAL units; and so on.

diachronic One of the two main temporal dimensions of LINGUISTIC investigation introduced by the Swiss linguist, Ferdinand de SAUSSURE, the other being SYNCHRONIC. In 'diachronic linguistics', LANGUAGES are studied from the point of view of their historical development – for example, the changes which have taken place between Old and Modern English could be described in phonological, grammatical and semantic terms ('diachronic PHONOLOGY/SYNTAX/SEMANTICS'). An alternative term is HISTORICAL LINGUISTICS. The earlier study of language in historical terms, known as COMPARATIVE PHILOLOGY, does not differ from diachronic linguistics in subject-matter, but in aims and method. More attention is paid in the latter to the use of synchronic description as a preliminary to historical study, and to the implications of historical work for linguistic theory in general.

diacritic In PHONETICS, a mark added to a symbol to alter its value, e.g. the various ACCENTS (´ ` ^ etc.), the signs of DEVOICING [̥] and NASALIZATION [˜]. In GENERATIVE PHONOLOGY, **diacritic features** are introduced into the DERIVATION of FORMATIVES to account for the apparently exceptional behaviour of SEGMENTS. A readjustment RULE introduces the feature [D], e.g. to handle the exceptional STRESS pattern of words like *mómentary* (cf. the more regular *eleméntary*). [+D] would be inserted *ad hoc* at an early stage in their derivation. See also FEATURE.

diagramming see PARSING (1)

dialect(-al, -ology) A regionally or socially distinctive VARIETY of language, identified by a particular set of WORDS and GRAMMATICAL STRUCTURES. Spoken dialects are usually also associated with a distinctive pronunciation, or ACCENT. Any LANGUAGE with a reasonably large number of speakers will develop dialects, especially if there are geographical barriers separating groups of people from each other, or if there are divisions of social class. One dialect may predominate as the official or STANDARD form of the language, and this is the variety which may come to be written down.

The distinction between 'dialect' and 'language' seems obvious: dialects are subdivisions of languages. What linguistics (and especially SOCIOLINGUISTICS) has done is to point to the complexity of the relationship between these notions. It is usually said that people speak different languages when they do not understand each other. But the so-called 'dialects' of Chinese (Mandarin, Cantonese, etc.) are mutually unintelligible in their spoken form. (They do, however, share the same written language, which is the main reason why one talks of them as 'dialects of Chinese'.) And the opposite situation occurs: Swedes, Norwegians and Danes are generally able to understand each other, but their separate histories, cultures, literatures and political structures warrant their being referred to as different languages.

The systematic study of all forms of dialect, but especially regional dialect, is called **dialectology**, also 'linguistic geography' or **dialect geography**. Traditionally dialectology studies commenced in the late nineteenth century, and have taken the form of detailed surveys using questionnaires and (more recently) tape-recorded interviews. Regionally distinctive words (distinct in FORM, SENSE or pronunciation) were the centre of attention, and collections of such words were plotted on maps and compiled in a **dialect atlas** (or 'linguistic atlas'). If a number of DISTINCTIVE ITEMS all emerged as belonging to a particular area, then this would be the evidence for saying that a dialect existed. It was often possible to show where one dialect ended and the next began by plotting the use of such items, drawing lines around their limits of use (ISOGLOSSES), and, where a 'bundle' of such isoglosses fell together, postulating the existence of a **dialect boundary**. On one side of the bundle of isoglosses, a large number of word forms, senses and pronunciations would be used which were systematically different from the equivalent items used on the other side. Dialect boundaries are not usually so clear-cut, but the principle works well enough. Traditional dialectological methods of this kind have more recently been supplemented by the methods of **structural dialectology**, which tries to show the patterns of relationship which link sets of forms from different dialects. The SYSTEMS of STRUCTURAL correspondence published by this approach are known as 'DIASYS-tems'. **Dialectometry** is a statistical method of dialect analysis, developed in the 1970s, which measures the linguistic 'distance' between localities in a dialect region by counting the number of contrasts in a large sample of linguistic features.

Dialects which identify where a person is from are called **regional dialects**, though other terms are used, e.g. 'local', 'territorial', 'geographical'. It is sometimes thought that dialects of this type are dying out, but this is happening only in some rural areas. Urban dialects are becoming more in evidence, especially with the growth of major conurbations. Within cities such as New York and London, it is possible to isolate local dialect areas, such as Brooklyn or the East End.

Dialects which identify where a person is in terms of social scale are called **social dialects** or **class dialects**. More recently, the term SOCIOLECT has been used. Some languages are highly stratified in terms of social divisions, such as class, professional status, age and sex, and here major differences in social dialect are apparent. In English, the differences are not so basic, but it is possible to point to usages in vocabulary, grammar and pronunciation which are socially based, e.g. *ain't*, which has in its time identified both working-class and upper-class (e.g. Lord Peter Wimsey) types. Such variants were generally ignored in regional dialectology, and would these days tend to be studied under the heading of SOCIOLINGUISTICS. **Social dialectology** is the application of dialectological methods to the study of social structure, focusing on group membership as a determinant of dialectal competence.

'Dialect' is also sometimes applied to the linguistically distinct historical stages through which a language has passed, and here the term **historical** or **temporal dialect** might be used, e.g. Elizabethan English, seventeenth-century British English. 'Dialect' has further been used to refer to the distinctive language of a particular professional group (**occupational dialect**), but more recent terms have come to be used to refer to social variations of this kind (e.g. REGISTER, DIAtype, VARIETY). The popular application of the term to the unwritten languages of developing countries (cf. 'there are many dialects in Africa', and the like) is not a usage recommended in linguistics.

dialinguistics, diamorph, diaphone, diasystem, diatype see DIA-

DICE The abbreviation for DISCOURSE IN COMMON SENSE ENTAILMENT.

difference hypothesis see DEFICIT HYPOTHESIS

differential see SEMANTICS

diffuse One of the features of sound set up by JAKOBSON and Halle in their DISTINCTIVE FEATURE theory of PHONOLOGY, to handle variations in PLACE OF ARTICULATION; its opposite is COMPACT. Diffuse sounds are defined ARTICULATORILY and ACOUSTICALLY, as those which involve a STRICTURE relatively far back in the mouth, and a relatively low concentration of acoustic energy in non-central parts of the sound spectrum. CLOSE VOWELS and FRONT CONSONANTS are [+diffuse] (abbreviated as [+diff]): MID or LOW vowels and PALATAL or VELAR consonants are [−diffuse] ([−diff]). This feature is replaced by HIGH in CHOMSKY and Halle's system.

diffusion see LANGUAGE

diglossia (diglossic) A term used in SOCIOLINGUISTICS to refer to a situation where two very different VARIETIES of a LANGUAGE CO-OCCUR throughout a SPEECH community, each with a distinct range of social function. Both varieties are STANDARDIZED to some degree, are felt to be alternatives by NATIVE-SPEAKERS and usually have special names. Sociolinguists usually talk in terms of a high (H) variety and a low (L) variety, corresponding broadly to a difference in FORMALITY: the high variety is learnt in school, tends to be used in church, on radio programmes, in serious literature, etc., and as a consequence has greater social prestige; the low variety in family conversations, and other relatively informal settings. Diglossic situations may be found, for example, in Greek (High: Katharevousa; Low: Dhimotiki), Arabic (High: classical; Low: colloquial), and some varieties of German (H: Hochdeutsch; L: Schweizer-deutsch, in Switzerland).

digraph A term used in PHONETICS/PHONOLOGY and GRAPHETICS/GRAPHOLOGY to refer to a GRAPHIC UNIT in which two symbols have combined to function as a single ELEMENT in a SYSTEM, e.g. [æ] for the vowel in RECEIVED PRONUNCIATION *cat*, or the linked *æ* or *œ* in the classical spelling of some English words (e.g. *encyclopædia, onomatopœia*).

diminutive A term used in MORPHOLOGY to refer to an AFFIX with the general meaning of 'little', used literally or metaphorically (as a term of endearment). Examples include *-ino* in Italian, *-zinho* in Portuguese, and *-let* in English. The term is usually contrasted with AUGMENTATIVE.

diphthong(-al, ization, -ize) A term used in the PHONETIC classification of VOWEL sounds on the basis of their MANNER OF ARTICULATION: it refers to a vowel where there is a single (perceptual) noticeable change in quality during a SYLLABLE, as in English *beer, time, loud*. Related terms are MONOPHTHONG, where no qualitative change is heard, and TRIPHTHONG, where two such changes can be heard. Diphthongs, or 'gliding vowels', are usually classified into phonetic types, depending on which of the two elements is the more SONOROUS: 'falling' (or 'descending') diphthongs have the first element STRESSED, as in the English examples: 'rising' (or 'ascending') diphthongs have the second element stressed, as in a possible analysis of English *cue* [kiu].

Other classifications of 'diphthongal' types exist, in terms of the extent of their movement (e.g. whether it is 'wide' or 'narrow') and their direction (whether the diphthong is 'centring' or not, i.e. ending with a CENTRAL vowel). **Diphthongization** is the term used to describe a process where a monophthong has become a diphthong (has been 'diphthongized'), as in cases of historical or DIALECT change. Diphthongs are transcribed using symbols which represent the extremes of vowel movement between the two positions, as in [ai] for the vowel in *fine*.

direct (1) A term used in GRAMMATICAL description to refer to one of the two types of OBJECT ELEMENT which can function in CLAUSE STRUCTURE, the other being labelled INDIRECT. The relationship between the two is illustrated by such SENTENCES as *The man gave the boy a book*, where *a book* is the **direct object** (*What did the man give?*) and *the boy* is the **indirect object**. The direct object is the more central in clause structure, indirect objects requiring a direct object to relate to (cf. **The man gave the boy*). This distinction is not always recognized in linguistic theories: for example, in GENERATIVE grammar (especially in RELATIONAL GRAMMAR and LEXICAL FUNCTIONAL GRAMMAR), the indirect object without *to* is regarded as a direct object.

(2) The opposition between direct and indirect is also used to identify the two main ways of reflecting a person's speech: **direct speech** refers to the use of actual UTTERANCE, with no grammatical MODIFICATION, e.g. '*Is he coming?' John asked* is a **direct question**, whereas *John asked if he was coming* is an **indirect question**.

directionality (1) In METRICAL PHONOLOGY, a PARAMETER which determines the direction in which foot construction scans the STRESS DOMAIN. This may happen right-to-left, starting at the right EDGE, or vice versa. The notion applies to both TREES and METRICAL GRIDS.

(2) In SEMANTICS, a term used to describe the relationship between two SENSES of a LEXICAL item, when one can be shown to be DERIVED from the other, as in the case of *violin* (the instrument) and *violin* (the player – as in *She is first violin*). Cases of sense extension generally proceed from the more to the less conventionalized, but often perceived directionality is unclear.

directive (1) In some classifications of SPEECH ACTS, a 'directive' is an UTTERANCE whose purpose is to get other people to do something for the speaker. The LINGUISTIC means may be GRAMMATICAL (e.g. COMMANDS), SEMANTIC (appropriate vocabulary, e.g. *please*) or PHONOLOGICAL (e.g. persuasive INTONATION patterns).

(2) (**director, directed**) A term used in some MODELS of GRAMMATICAL CLASSIFICATION to refer to a type of EXOCENTRIC CONSTRUCTION in which the initial ELEMENT is referred to as a 'director', and the 'directed element' as the AXIS. For example, in *kicked the ball, kicked* is the director, *the ball* the axis; in *in the box, in* is the director (or 'directive PARTICLE'), *the box* is the axis.

disambiguate A term used in LINGUISTICS, and especially in TRANSFORMATIONAL

GRAMMAR, to refer to an analysis which demonstrates the alternative STRUCTURAL interpretations of an AMBIGUOUS SENTENCE, e.g. by ASSIGNING BRACKETS or specifying a transformational relationship. For example, the SENTENCE *It is too hot to eat* can be 'disambiguated' by showing how it can be related to such sentences as *The food is too hot to eat, The weather is too hot to allow eating* and *The girl is too hot to eat anything.*

discontinuous (1) A term used by JAKOBSON and Halle in their DISTINCTIVE FEATURE theory of PHONOLOGY to refer to sounds produced with a complete CLOSURE of the VOCAL TRACT, as in PLOSIVES. Its opposite is CONTINUANT, used to characterize FRICATIVES, VOWELS, etc.

(2) (**discontinuity**) In GRAMMATICAL analysis, discontinuity refers to the splitting of a CONSTRUCTION by the insertion of another grammatical UNIT. **Discontinuous constructions** or **constituents** are illustrated by the way the PARTICLE in some PHRASAL VERBS may be separated from the LEXICAL ELEMENT, e.g. *switch on* → ***switch** the light **on***, by the double NEGATIVE system in some languages (French *ne . . . pas*, Welsh *nid . . . ddim*, etc.), or by the separation of AUXILIARY verb and main verb in QUESTION forms in English (e.g. *is he coming*?). Some analysts make use of the notion of a 'discontinuous morph(eme)', as when Arabic ROOT forms are identified by the CONSONANTS they contain, each of which is separated by a VOWEL (e.g. *k-t-b* 'write'). A **discontinuity grammar** is a logic grammar FORMALISM which allows relationships between widely separated constituents to be stated within a single grammatical RULE; there are several types (e.g. extraposition grammars, gapping grammars, static discontinuity grammars).

(3) In language ACQUISITION, the term refers to the view, primarily proposed by the American linguist Roman JAKOBSON, that the sounds of babbling bear no direct relationship to later PHONOLOGICAL development. It is opposed to a 'continuity' hypothesis, which argues that languages gradually select from the range of sounds used in babbling. The term is also used in child language acquisition (especially in relation to PHONOLOGY) to describe a situation where new learning (e.g. acquiring a new phonological RULE) interferes with established ability, causing a temporary disturbance in the development of speech production.

discourse A term used in LINGUISTICS to refer to a continuous stretch of (especially spoken) LANGUAGE larger than a SENTENCE – but, within this broad notion, several different applications may be found. At its most general, a discourse is a behavioural UNIT which has a pre-theoretical status in linguistics: it is a set of UTTERANCES which constitute any recognizable SPEECH event (no reference being made to its linguistic STRUCTURING, if any), e.g. a conversation, a joke, a sermon, an interview. A classification of discourse functions, with particular reference to type of subject-matter, the situation, and the behaviour of the speaker, is often carried out in SOCIOLINGUISTIC studies (of primitive societies, in particular), e.g. distinguishing dialogues *v.* monologues, or (more specifically) oratory, ritual, insults, narrative, and so on. In recent years, several linguists have attempted to discover linguistic regularities in discourses (**discourse analysis** or **DA**), using GRAMMATICAL, PHONOLOGICAL and SEMANTIC criteria (e.g. COHESION, ANAPHORA, inter-sentence CONNECTIVITY). Special attention has been focused on **discourse**

markers – sequentially dependent elements which demarcate units of speech, such as *oh, well,* and *I mean*. It is now plain that there exist important linguistic dependencies between sentences, but it is less clear how far these dependencies are sufficiently systematic to enable linguistic units higher than the sentence to be established. The methodology and theoretical orientation of discourse analysis (with its emphasis on WELL-FORMEDNESS and RULES governing the sequence of permissible units, in both spoken and written TEXTS) are often contrasted with those of CONVERSATION ANALYSIS. The term **discourse grammar** has also come to be used by those seeking to develop an alternative to the GENERATIVIST conception of an autonomous FORMAL grammar, which would incorporate principles of a FUNCTIONAL, COMMUNICATIVE kind. Some linguists adopt a broader, PSYCHOLINGUISTIC perspective in studying discourse, which they view as a dynamic process of expression and comprehension governing the performance of people during linguistic interaction. Some adopt a sociolinguistic perspective, in which the purpose or function of the discourse is emphasized. These emphases distance the subject from 'TEXT linguistics', when this is seen as the formal account of the linguistic principles governing the structure of texts. But there is considerable overlap between the domains of discourse analysis and text linguistics (for example, the notion of cohesion is prominent in both), and any attempt at a principled distinction would be premature.

In semantics, some use is made of the logical term **universe of discourse**, viz. the range of entities, topics, situations, etc., within which a particular speech event makes reference. In this sense, the universe of discourse of sermons, for example, will be predictably different (usually) from the universe of discourse of commercial advertising. See also FORMULAIC LANGUAGE, MANNER (2), MODE (1).

discourse attachment A term used in SEMANTICS and DISCOURSE ANALYSIS to refer to a process of modelling PRAGMATIC knowledge resources to infer which RHETORICAL relations hold between two given discourse CONSTITUENTS. It represents the rhetorical relations which underlie a TEXT, given the reader's background knowledge, in relation to a theory of discourse structure.

discourse in common sense entailment (DICE) A theory of DISCOURSE ATTACHMENT which uses a logic called 'common sense entailment' to handle the ability to reason with conflicting knowledge resources. It supplies a logical consequence relation for resolving conflict among the knowledge resources available during the interpretation of a discourse, in order to explain how linguistic STRINGS can be interpreted differently in different discourse contexts.

discourse representation theory A SEMANTIC theory which seeks to extend MODEL-THEORETIC SEMANTICS to accommodate sequences of SENTENCES, and in particular to accommodate ANAPHORIC dependencies across sentence boundaries. Central to the theory is an intermediate level of semantic REPRESENTATION called a **discourse-representation structure (DRS)**. An initial DRS is derived by an ALGORITHM from the SYNTACTIC STRUCTURE of sentences. Further RULES then determine how an initial DRS can be enriched to identify various anaphoric dependencies. **Segmented discourse representation theory** is an extension of

DRT: it is a semantically based theory of discourse structure which represents the rhetorical relations that hold between the propositions introduced in a text.

discovery A term used in LINGUISTICS to refer to a type of PROCEDURE used in carrying out an analysis. A **discovery procedure** is a set of techniques which can be automatically or 'mechanically' applied to a sample of LANGUAGE and which will produce a correct GRAMMATICAL analysis. Attempts to develop such procedures characterized the work of many BLOOMFIELDIAN linguists, and were strongly criticized in early formulations of GENERATIVE grammar. It is argued that it is never possible to identify with certainty all the factors which lead a linguist in the direction of a particular analysis. Nor is it desirable to seek such a procedure, as the analysis itself can be evaluated regardless of the means by which it was obtained.

discrete(ness) A suggested defining property of human LANGUAGE (contrasting with the properties of other SEMIOTIC SYSTEMS), whereby the ELEMENTS of a signal can be analysed as having definable boundaries, with no gradation or continuity between them. A system lacking 'discreteness' is said to be 'continuous' or **non-discrete** (cf. NON-DISCRETE GRAMMAR). The term is especially used in PHONETICS and PHONOLOGY to refer to sounds which have relatively clear-cut boundaries, as defined in ACOUSTIC, ARTICULATORY or AUDITORY terms. It is evident that speech is a continuous stream of sound, but speakers of a language are able to SEGMENT this continuum into a finite number of discrete UNITS, these usually corresponding to the PHONEMES of the language. The boundaries of these units may correspond to identifiable acoustic or articulatory features, but often they do not. The minimal discrete units in phonetics are known as PHONES.

disharmony, disharmonicity see HARMONY

disjunction (disjunct(ive)) A term in formal logic now encountered as part of the theoretical framework of several areas in LINGUISTICS, especially SEMANTICS. It refers to the process or result of relating two PROPOSITIONS such that they are in an 'either-or' relationship, e.g. (*Either*) *Mary is late or John is early.* With disjunction, it is usual to distinguish **inclusive** and **exclusive** interpretations: with the former, the disjunction is true if either, or both, of the propositions is true; with the latter, the disjunction is true only if one or other of the propositions is true (but not both). Under the exclusive interpretation, therefore, the above disjunction would be false, if both Mary was late and John was early; whereas, under the inclusive interpretation, the disjunction would be true.

In some GRAMMATICAL descriptions, the term is adapted to refer to a process whose primary function is to mark a relationship of contrast or comparison between STRUCTURES, using such 'disjunctive' ITEMS as *or* and *but.* (Some approaches, such as QUIRK GRAMMAR, use the term **disjunct**, in a highly restricted sense, to refer to a subclass of ADVERBIALS (such as *seriously, frankly, really*), which contrasts with CONJUNCTS, SUBJUNCTS and ADJUNCTS on SYNTACTIC and SEMANTIC grounds.) The two disjunctions above are often referred to as the 'exclusive *or*' and the 'inclusive *or*'. In GENERATIVE grammar, the notion is applied as a principle affecting the order of RULES. **Disjunctive ordering** is found in the use of the parenthesis NOTATION, which indicates OPTIONAL ELEMENTS. If a SEQUENCE of rules is abbreviated by using this notion (e.g. X → Y/Z(P)Q, which stands for the sequence (a) X → Y/ZPQ and (b) X → Y/ZQ), then this sequence forms a disjunctively ordered block, i.e. if (a) applies, (b) is not permitted to apply. It is distinguished from CONJUNCTIVE ordering.

displacement (displaced) A suggested defining property of human LANGUAGE (contrasting with the properties of many other SEMIOTIC systems), whereby language can be used to refer to CONTEXTS removed from the immediate situation of the speaker (i.e. it can be 'displaced'). For example, if someone says *I was afraid*, it is not necessary that the speaker still is afraid; whereas animal calls seem generally tied to specific situations, such as danger or hunger, and have nothing comparable to **displaced speech** (unless this is artificially taught to them, as some experiments with chimpanzees have tried to do).

dissimilation A general term in PHONETICS and PHONOLOGY to refer to the influence exercised by one sound SEGMENT upon the ARTICULATION of another, so that the sounds become less alike, or different. Such changes have mainly been noticed in HISTORICAL LINGUISTIC studies, where the effects have manifested themselves over a long period of time (e.g. *pilgrim* from Latin *peregrinus*, with the first *r* 'dissimilating' to *l*), but SYNCHRONIC dissimilations are also possible, as when we avoid a sequence of identical sounds (cf. the difficulty of tongue-twisters such as *Will will willingly* . . .). As with the opposite effect, ASSIMILATION, it is possible to classify dissimilations into types, based on the place, degree and direction of the changes involved.

distinctive(ness) A term used in LINGUISTICS for any feature of speech (or writing) which enables a CONTRAST to be made between PHONOLOGICAL, GRAMMATICAL or SEMANTIC UNITS. Such contrasts might also be labelled 'relevant', FUNCTIONAL or SIGNIFICANT. The main use of the term has been in phonology, as part of the phrase **distinctive feature**, where it refers to a minimal contrastive UNIT recognized by some linguists as a means of explaining how the sound SYSTEM of languages is organized. Distinctive features may be seen either as part of the definition of PHONEMES, or as an alternative to the notion of the phoneme. The first of these views is found in the approach of the PRAGUE SCHOOL, where the phoneme is seen as a BUNDLE of PHONETIC distinctive features: the English phoneme /p/, for example, can be seen as the result of the combination of the features of BILABIAL, VOICE, PLOSIVE, etc. Other phonemes will differ from /p/ in respect of at least one of these features. In distinctive feature theories of phonology, however, the phoneme is not considered to be a relevant unit of explanation: symbols such as *p, b*, etc., are seen simply as convenient abbreviations for particular sets of FEATURES. It is the features which are the minimal units of phonological analysis, not the phonemes. It is argued that, by substituting features for phonemes in this way, generalizations can be made about the relationships between sounds in a language, which would otherwise be missed. Moreover, because features are phonetic units, it should be possible to make inter-language (e.g. DIACHRONIC and DIALECTAL) and cross-language comparisons, and ultimately statements about phonological UNIVERSALS, more readily than by using a phonemic model of phonology.

Distinctive feature analysts claim that there are several advantages over the traditional phonetic alphabet approach to phonological description, which describes UTTERANCES as a sequence of SEGMENTS. For example, it was originally suggested that a relatively small set of abstract feature OPPOSITIONS (a dozen or so) would account for all the phonological contrasts made in languages: it would not then be necessary to recognize so much phonetic classificatory detail, as exists on, say, the IPA chart, where the phonological status of the segments recognized is not indicated. In fact, it has turned out that far more features are required, as new languages come to be analysed. Another advantage, it is suggested, is that CONSONANTS and VOWELS can be characterized using the same set of phonetic features (unlike traditional 'two-mouth' descriptions, where the classificatory terminology for vowels – HIGH, LOW, etc. – is quite different from that used for consonants – LABIAL, PALATAL, etc.).

By using a system of this kind, some quite specific predictions can be made about the sound systems of languages. For example, using the JAKOBSON and Halle system below enables one to distinguish phonologically two degrees of FRONT/BACK contrast in the consonant system and three degrees of vowel height. But what follows from this is a universal claim – that no languages permit more than these numbers of contrasts in their phonological systems. These are empirical claims, of course, and in recent years much effort has been spent on investigating these claims and modifying the nature of the feature inventory required.

Two major statements concerning the distinctive feature approach were influential: one by Roman Jakobson and Morris Halle, in *Fundamentals of Language* (1956), the other by Noam CHOMSKY and Morris Halle, in *The Sound Pattern of English* (1968). The Jakobson and Halle approach set up features in pairs, defined primarily in ACOUSTIC terms (as could be detected on a SPECTROGRAM), but with some reference to ARTICULATORY criteria. Examples of their features include VOCALIC *v.* non-vocalic, CONSONANTAL *v.* non-consonantal, COMPACT *v.* DIFFUSE, GRAVE *v.* ACUTE, NASAL *v.* ORAL, discontinuous *v.* CONTINUANT, STRIDENT *v.* MELLOW, FLAT *v.* SHARP/PLAIN and VOICED *v.* voiceless. The emphasis in this approach is firmly on the nature of the oppositions between the UNDERLYING features involved, rather than on the description of the range of phonetic REALIZATIONS each feature represents. In the Chomsky and Halle approach, more attention is paid to the phonetic realizations of the underlying features recognized, and a different system of feature classification is set up. Some of the earlier features are retained (e.g. voice, consonantal, tense, continuant, nasal, strident), but many are modified, and new features added, some of which overlap with the earlier approach (e.g. SONORANT *v.* OBSTRUENT, DELAYED *v.* INSTANTANEOUS RELEASE, ANTERIOR *v.* non-anterior, CORONAL *v.* non-coronal, DISTRIBUTED *v.* non-distributed, SYLLABIC *v.* non-syllabic). The application of these features to languages is not without controversy, and in recent years further suggestions have been forthcoming as to the need for additional features, such as LABIAL.

In recent phonological theory, features have become a focus of attention in their own right, and are widely viewed as the basic unit of phonological REPRESENTATION. The merits of UNARY (single-valued) as opposed to binary analyses have been presented by some models (e.g. DEPENDENCY PHONOLOGY). In addition to questions of feature identification and definition, however, recent research has focused on the nature of feature organization within phonological representations, as part of NON-LINEAR PHONOLOGY. In particular, **feature geometry** looks especially at the non-linear relationship between features, and at the way they can be grouped into a HIERARCHICAL array of functional CLASSES. Several formalisms have been devised to handle the relationships between features in particular phonological contexts, and terminology has begun to develop accordingly. For example, in the study of ASSIMILATION, a rule which spreads only features not already specified in the target is said to be operating in a **feature-filling** mode; if the rule applies to segments already specified for the spreading features (thereby replacing their original values), it is said to apply in a **feature-changing** mode.

distinguisher A term used by some GENERATIVE LINGUISTS as part of a (controversial) two-way classification of the SEMANTIC COMPONENTS of LEXICAL ITEMS. 'Distinguishers' were said to be those components which are needed to keep apart the different meanings of HOMONYMS, but which are unsystematic in a LANGUAGE; that is, they have no general role to play in the statement of SELECTIONAL and other restrictions. For example, in one of the items originally analysed in this way, *bachelor*, one distinguisher is the component [having the academic degree conferred . . .]. Components which do operate systematically (e.g. [old], [male], [animate]) were known as MARKERS.

distributed One of the features of sound set up by CHOMSKY and Halle in their DISTINCTIVE FEATURE theory of PHONOLOGY to handle variations in PLACE OF ARTICULATION (CAVITY features) in FRICATIVE sounds. Distributed sounds are defined ARTICULATORILY, as those produced with a STRICTURE which extends for a considerable distance along the direction of the airflow, as in BILABIAL and PALATO-ALVEOLAR fricatives. Its opposite is **non-distributed**, referring to sounds produced with a relatively short stricture, as in DENTAL and RETROFLEX fricatives.

distributed representation see CONNECTIONISM

distribution(al) A general term used in LINGUISTICS to refer to the total set of linguistic CONTEXTS, or ENVIRONMENTS, in which a UNIT (such as a PHONEME, a MORPHEME or a WORD) can occur. Every linguistic unit, it is said, has a characteristic distribution. A **distributional analysis** would plot the places in larger linguistic units where smaller units occur, such as the distribution of phonemes within a SYLLABLE or word, or of words within a SENTENCE. Distributional ideas were originally developed in PHONOLOGY, but were later extended to other linguistic units. In some approaches, the notion of distribution became a major explanatory principle, being seen as a possible way of grouping sounds into phonemes without reference to the meaning or grammatical properties of the words in which they appear – or even, to the PHONETIC similarities existing between them. On this basis, for instance, [h] and [ŋ] in English might be considered members of the same phoneme, because they never share the same set of environments. In phonemic phonology, the most important continuing use of the term is in the phrase **complementary distribution**, which refers to the status of related sounds (or ALLOPHONES) when they are found in mutually exclusive environments, as in the use of a DENTAL *v.* an ALVEOLAR allophone of /t/ in English, e.g. *eight v. eighth*. (In GENERATIVE phonology, on the other hand, distributional statements of this kind are handled by a formulation in terms of phonological RULES.)

disyllable (disyllabic) A term used in PHONETICS and PHONOLOGY to refer to a UNIT consisting of two SYLLABLES. A 'disyllabic' form is distinguished from MONOSYLLABIC, trisyllabic, etc., forms.

ditransitive A term used by some LINGUISTS to refer to a VERB which can take two OBJECTS, e.g. *give* (*I gave him a book*). It is usually distinguished from 'monotransitive' verbs, such as *kick*.

divergence A term used in SOCIOLINGUISTICS to refer to a process of DIALECT change in which the dialects become less like each other (or 'diverge'). This process (sometimes called 'dialectalization') is only likely to happen in the absence of geographical and social links between populations within a SPEECH community, lines of communication thereby being few or difficult, and a STANDARD dialect probably being non-existent. The opposite effect is known as CONVERGENCE. 'Divergence' also has a currency in HISTORICAL linguistic studies, referring to the splitting of a FORM into two CONTRASTIVE UNITS.

DO An abbreviation sometimes used for DIRECT OBJECT.

docking see FLOATING

***do*-deletion/insertion/support** A set of RULES in GENERATIVE SYNTAX which determine the use of the EMPTY AUXILIARY VERB *do*. '*Do*-insertion' or '*do*-support' inserts the verb *do* into a place in a STRUCTURE, as part of the DERIVATION of a sentence. An example is in some types of TAG QUESTIONS, where to form a tag from the sentence *It wants cleaning* a *do* needs to be introduced, viz . . . *doesn't it*. It is primarily used where a TENSE-marker has no verb FORMATIVE to attach to, as with tense variation in question forms (e.g. ***did** X happen*). '*Do*-deletion' would apply if a *do* form previously generated by the rules for a given sentence were to be deleted.

domain (1) An extension of the general meaning of this WORD by some LINGUISTS to refer to the realm of application of any linguistic construct, e.g. the 'domain' of a RULE in a GRAMMAR would refer to the range of STRUCTURES to which that rule was applicable. In GENERATIVE linguistics, the term refers specifically to the parts of a TREE diagram deriving from any one NODE, i.e. the structure which the node DOMINATES. There are several applications, e.g. the 'CYCLIC domain' in PHONOLOGY (i.e. the constituents internal to the word to which phonological rules apply); the 'harmonic domain' in vowel or consonant HARMONY.

(2) A term used by some SEMANTICS to refer to the area of experience covered by the set of terms in a particular SEMANTIC FIELD, e.g. colour terms, kinship terms.

(3) In SOCIOLINGUISTICS the term refers to a group of institutionalized social situations typically constrained by a common set of behavioural rules, e.g. the domain of the family is the house, of religion is the church, etc. The notion is seen as of particular importance in the analysis of MULTILINGUAL settings involving several participants, where it is used to relate variations in the individuals' choice and topic of language to broader sociocultural norms and expectations of interaction.

domination (domin-ate, -ance) A term in GENERATIVE LINGUISTICS for one type of vertical relationship between NODES in a TREE diagram ('X dominates Y'). If no nodes intervene between X and Y, one says that X 'directly' or 'immediately' dominates Y. For example, in the diagram of the sentence *The king saw the cat* the T and N are directly dominated by NP, the first NP is directly dominated by 'Sentence', and the second by the VP. It is by the use of this notion that

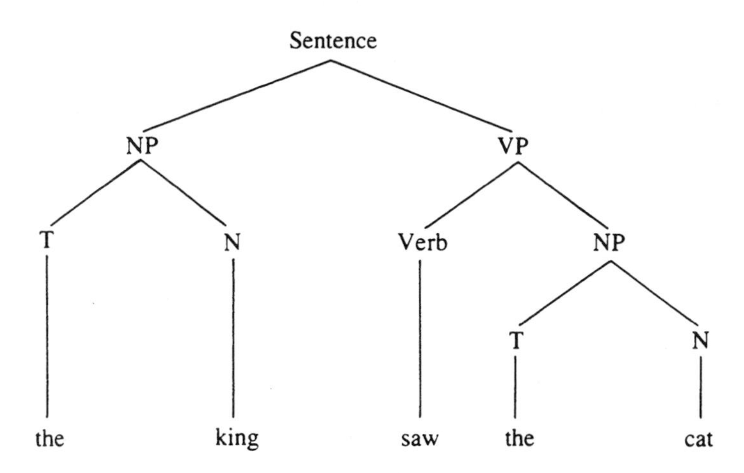

distinctions such as SUBJECT and OBJECT can be made using this model, viz. the Subject is that NP directly dominated by Sentence, the Object is that NP directly dominated by VP. A further notion is that of 'exhaustive' dominance: a node A exhaustively dominates a string of words if and only if it dominates those words and no other words. A node A is also said to exhaustively dominate a node B if it immediately dominates B and no other node. The 'vertical' dimension of **dominance** should be distinguished from the 'horizontal' notion of PRECEDENCE. **Immediate-dominance rules** are one of the components of a GENERALIZED PHRASE-STRUCTURE GRAMMAR. The notion is also important in several models of PHONOLOGY. For example, in later METRICAL PHONOLOGY **foot dominance** is a PARAMETER which determines the side of the FOOT where the HEAD is located: in 'left-dominant' feet, all left nodes are dominant and right nodes RECESSIVE; in 'right-dominant' feet all right nodes are dominant and left nodes recessive. In the phonological analysis of SIGN language, the term is used to characterize handedness: a signer is linguistically either left-hand or right-hand dominant, depending on which hand typically executes one-handed signs.

donkey sentence A type of problematic SENTENCE, typically illustrated by *Every man who owns a donkey beats it*, in which the PRONOUN must be construed as dependent upon the NOUN PHRASE *a donkey*, without allowing that phrase to have wider scope than the universal QUANTIFICATION expressed by *every*. Such sentences have been given detailed study in DISCOURSE REPRESENTATION THEORY.

dorsal (dorsum) A term sometimes used in the PHONETIC classification of speech sounds, referring to a sound made with the BACK, or dorsum, of the TONGUE in contact with the roof of the mouth, as in VELAR (sc. 'dorso-velar') or PALATAL (sc. 'dorso-palatal') sounds. Some authors include other parts of the tongue under this heading. The term has developed a special status in recent PHONOLOGICAL theory, especially in various NON-LINEAR models. For example, in ARTICULATOR-BASED FEATURE THEORY, it refers to a single-valued NODE involving the tongue body as an active articulator. In CONSTRICTION-based models, it is defined as a constriction formed by the back of the tongue.

double articulation see ARTICULATION (2)

double-bar In the most widely assumed version of X-BAR SYNTAX, a full PHRASAL category (the maximal PROJECTION of a ZERO-level category). It is distinguished from a SINGLE-BAR category, which is a 'small' phrasal category.

double-base A type of TRANSFORMATIONAL RULE recognized in early MODELS of GENERATIVE GRAMMAR, where the rule operates with an input of two or more TERMINAL STRINGS. Double-base transformations are also known as GENERALIZED transformations, and are opposed to 'single-base' types, where only one string is involved.

doubly filled COMP filter A FILTER proposed within EXTENDED STANDARD THEORY to rule out such SENTENCES as **I wonder who that John saw*, in which two items (*who* and *that*) occupy the COMP position.

downdrift see DOWNSTEP

downgrading (downgraded) A term used by some LINGUISTS to refer to a GRAMMATICAL process in which a UNIT in the grammatical HIERARCHY is EMBEDDED within a unit from a lower LEVEL. For example, the clause *I don't care* is used as the equivalent of a WORD in the SENTENCE *That's a very I-don't-care attitude*; it has thus been 'downgraded' (cf. the notion of RANK shift).

downstep(-ped) A term used in the PHONOLOGY of TONE languages, referring to a lowering process which applies to the second of two high-tone SYLLABLES. A downstepped high tone would be slightly lower than the preceding high tone, but not so low as to be equivalent to a low tone. The process has been widely observed in African languages. Less commonly, the opposite effect, **upstep**, has been noted, where successive high tones become progressively higher. Downstep is phonologically CONTRASTIVE, and is usually distinguished from **downdrift**, a sequential process whereby high tones after low tones become progressively less high throughout an intonational unit. These effects have been described more generally as 'register lowering' or 'key lowering'. **Declination** is often used as an equivalent for downdrift, but this term also has a more general phonetic use ('F_0 declination'), referring to a gradual descent of pitch level and narrowing of pitch range throughout an utterance, partly as a result of reduction in air pressure at the glottis, as speakers use up the breath in their lungs. Such effects, of course, are not restricted to tone languages.

DP The abbreviation for DETERMINER PHRASE.

drag chain see CHAIN (3)

DRS The abbreviation for 'discourse representation structure' in DISCOURSE REPRESENTATION THEORY.

drum language In LINGUISTICS, a term used to characterize a type of LANGUAGE in which a drum is used to simulate selected features of speech (primarily, TONES and RHYTHMS). The signals consist mainly of short, FORMULAIC utterances, but are used to build up quite elaborate systems of communication, especially in Africa, both within villages and between communities.

D-structure A term used in recent TRANSFORMATIONAL GRAMMAR to refer to an alternative conception of DEEP STRUCTURE, which is related to S-STRUCTURE (SURFACE STRUCTURE) through the use of EMPTY elements such as TRACES and PRO.

DTE An abbreviation in METRICAL PHONOLOGY for DESIGNATED TERMINAL ELEMENT.

dual see NUMBER

dualism (dualist) A term used to characterize a theory of MEANING which postulates that there is a direct, two-way relationship between LINGUISTIC FORMS and the entities, states of affairs, etc., to which they refer (i.e. REFERENTS). Such theories are usually contrasted with TRIADIC theories of meaning, which postulate a threefold relationship, namely between forms, referents and SENSE.

duality (of patterning/structure) A suggested defining property of human LANGUAGE (contrasting with the properties of other SEMIOTIC SYSTEMS), which sees languages as being STRUCTURALLY organized in terms of two abstract LEVELS. At the first, higher level, language is analysed in terms of combinations of (meaningful) UNITS (such as MORPHEMES, WORDS); at another, lower level, it is seen as a sequence of SEGMENTS which lack any MEANING in themselves, but which combine to form units of meaning. These two levels are sometimes referred to as ARTICULATIONS – a 'primary' and 'secondary' articulation respectively.

dummy A term used in LINGUISTICS to refer to a FORMAL GRAMMATICAL ELEMENT introduced into a STRUCTURE or an analysis to ensure that a grammatical SENTENCE is produced. Apart from their formal role, 'dummy elements' have no meaning – they are SEMANTICALLY empty, e.g. *there* in *there were many people at the club, it* in *it's raining*. When this element acts as a locus for grammatical CONTRASTS, it is referred to as a 'dummy carrier', e.g. *do* in QUESTION forms is a 'dummy auxiliary', which carries the TENSE/NUMBER contrast for the VERB PHRASE (*do/did you know, do/does he know*). Notions involving ZERO (e.g. 'zero morpheme') could also be considered types of dummy. In TRANSFORMATIONAL GRAMMAR, 'dummy symbols' are sometimes introduced into the DEEP STRUCTURE of a sentence, to facilitate the DERIVATION of CLASSES of sentence, but they never appear in the sentence's surface structure, e.g. the various kinds of BOUNDARY symbol, or the DELTA ($\triangle$) symbol which acts as a 'place-holder' for LEXICAL ITEMS (specified as COMPLEX SYMBOLS). In GOVERNMENT-BINDING THEORY, the term refers to elements in A-position (usually in subject position) with no THETA ROLE; they are also known as 'expletives'.

duration A term used in PHONETICS, to refer to the LENGTH of time involved in the

ARTICULATION of a sound or SYLLABLE. Distinctions between relatively 'long' and relatively 'short' durations are measured in units of time, such as the millisecond (msec). In speech, the absolute duration of sounds is dependent to a considerable extent on the overall TEMPO of speaking. Issues which need reference to duration include the study of rhythm (cf. ISOCHRONY), CONSONANT articulation (cf. VOICE onset time), and JUNCTURE.

durative (durativity) A term used in the GRAMMATICAL analysis of ASPECT, to refer to an event involving a period of time (cf. CONTINUOUS, PROGRESSIVE); it contrasts with 'non-durative' or PUNCTUAL.

dynamic (1) A term used in GRAMMATICAL classification, referring to one of the two main ASPECTUAL categories of VERB use; the other is STATIVE or STATIC. The distinguishing criteria are mainly SYNTACTIC; for example, dynamic verbs occur in the PROGRESSIVE form (e.g. *I'm running, He's playing*) and in the IMPERATIVE (e.g. *Run!*). The SEMANTICS of this class covers a wide range, including activity, process (e.g. *change, grow*), bodily sensation (e.g. *feel, hurt*), etc.

(2) A term used by some SOCIOLINGUISTS to characterize a view of LANGUAGE (**dynamic linguistics**) in which a temporal dimension is introduced into the study of language variation: SYNCHRONIC states are seen in terms of the processes ('waves') of change which produce and affect them, as defined in terms of such notions as relative rate and direction of change. A similar introduction of the temporal dimension into an otherwise 'static' view of a subject is found in parametric PHONETICS (**dynamic phonetics**), and in several contemporary instrumental techniques for the study of ARTICULATION, as in myodynamic (muscular movement) and aerodynamic (airflow) investigations. Phonological approaches which incorporate parametric phonetic principles are characterized as **dynamic phonology**.

(3) A term sometimes used in PHONOLOGY for a TONE which varies in PITCH range, e.g. rising or falling. Dynamic tones are usually contrasted with STATIC tones.

(4) **(dynamism)** A term used in FUNCTIONAL SENTENCE PERSPECTIVE, as part of the phrase 'communicative dynamism', whereby an utterance is seen as a process of gradually unfolding meaning, in which each part contributes variously ('dynamically') to the total communicative effect.

(5) A term used to describe a formal approach to SEMANTICS which characterizes the MEANING of a sentence as its potential to change INFORMATION states in a language user (**dynamic semantics**). It is opposed to a 'static' model, in which meaning is viewed as equivalent to the TRUTH CONDITIONAL content of sentences. An information state is seen as a set of possibilities – an encoding of information about the possible DENOTATIONS of the expressions of the language and about the possible values of variables used in these expressions (ANAPHORA). These states are used to define the information change potential of expressions – the change which is brought about by the utterance of a sentence. The analysis involves a continuous process of updating interpretations, as information states come to be extended through the addition of new discourse information and the elimination of certain possibilities, and as a result the approach is also referred to as **update semantics**. The approach has been particularly used in explicating PRONOUN COREFERENCE.

dynamic time warping see SPEECH RECOGNITION

E

e In GENERATIVE GRAMMAR, an abbreviation for a category with no PHONOLOGICAL content (i.e. a GAP).

ear-training A technique used in PHONETICS whereby aspiring practitioners of the subject are trained to discriminate and identify the whole range of human speech sounds. The correlative technique of producing the sounds is known as PERFORMANCE.

echo (non-) A term used in some GRAMMATICAL descriptions, notably QUIRK GRAMMAR, to refer to a type of SENTENCE which repeats, in whole or in part, what has just been said by another speaker. Such 'echo utterances' include 'echo QUESTIONS' (e.g. A: *I saw a ghost.* B: *You saw what?*) and EXCLAMATIONS (e.g. A: *Have you been to the office?* B: *Have I been to the office!*). Questions which do not echo in this way are sometimes referred to as **non-echo** questions.

eclectic(ism) The application of this general term in LINGUISTICS is found mainly in relation to MODELS of DESCRIPTION which have been built from a combination of features originating in more than one linguistic theory. For example, QUIRK GRAMMAR is eclectic in that it makes use of concepts and procedures deriving from STRUCTURALIST, TRANSFORMATIONAL and other approaches. Eclectic accounts are justified by the multiple insights they can provide into an area of LANGUAGE. Their main weakness is the difficulty of developing a coherent theoretical framework within which the various descriptive components can be interrelated.

ECM The abbreviation in GOVERNMENT-BINDING THEORY for EXCEPTIONAL CASE MARKING.

economy A criterion in LINGUISTICS which requires that, other things being equal, an analysis should aim to be as short and use as few terms as possible. It is a measure which permits one to quantify the number of FORMAL constructs (symbols, RULES, etc.) used in arriving at a solution to a problem, and has been used, explicitly or implicitly, in most areas of linguistic investigation. This application of Occam's razor is a major feature of the proposals for evaluating analyses made by GENERATIVE GRAMMAR (cf. EXPLANATORY ADEQUACY), and it has become a central tenet of the MINIMALIST PROGRAMME. In generative PHONOLOGY, in particular, it has been claimed that the preferred analysis is one which is overall the simpler, i.e. it uses fewer FEATURES and RULES. On the other hand, it has been argued that it will not always be the case that the simpler solution, in this quantitative sense, will be the intuitively more ACCEPTABLE one, or the one which allows the most informative LINGUISTICALLY SIGNIFICANT GENERALIZATIONS to be made.

Linguistic economy is a difficult criterion to work with: simplification made in one part of an analysis may cause difficulties elsewhere. And, until a total description is made, any suggestions concerning economy are necessarily tentative. But generative theory argues that this notion is of major theoretical importance, and several attempts have been made to provide a formal account of what is involved in it, as in the notion of a SIMPLICITY METRIC.

A simple example of relative economy of statement can be found in the opening rules of a generative grammar, if one were to make these apply in a linear order:

(1) S → NP + VP (2) V → V + NP (3) NP → Det + N

A reason for this particular ordering becomes clear when one considers what would have happened had rule (3) been used before rule (2): the NP in rule (3) would then REWRITE that introduced in rule (1), and the NP in rule (2) would still need to be expanded, thus requiring an additional rule (4), as follows (with subscripts added, for clarity):

(1) S → NP_1 + VP (2) NP_1 → Det + N
(3) VP → V + NP_2 (4) NP_2 → Det + N

The first ordering would thus seem to be superior, in terms of economy.

ECP The abbreviation in GOVERNMENT-BINDING THEORY for EMPTY CATEGORY PRINCIPLE.

***-ed* form** A term used in English GRAMMATICAL description to refer to the simple past-TENSE FORM of the VERB, e.g. *I walked, she jumped.* It does not necessarily end in this form (e.g. *I ran, she saw*), which should be seen solely as a mnemonic device, useful mainly in writing RULES succinctly. The *-ed* ending is, however, also a common form of the past PARTICIPLE (e.g. *she has walked*), and the potential AMBIGUITY has to be borne in mind.

edge In some models of NON-LINEAR PHONOLOGY, the application of the everyday sense of this term to identify phonological effects which apply at the margins of a linguistic unit, such as at the beginning or end of a WORD or SYLLABLE. For example, some models talk about **edge effects**, where a given SEGMENT behaves as though it bears the FEATURE [+F] with regard to segments on one side and [−F] with regard to those on the other side, as in the case of PRENASALIZED STOPS. Segments which do not display these effects are then said to show 'anti-edge effects', as in the analysis of AFFRICATES, which behave as stops with respect to following segments and/or as FRICATIVES with respect to preceding segments. The **edge-marking parameter** is cited in some approaches to METRICAL structure: this places a parenthesis at one edge of a sequence of marks (a left parenthesis to the left of the leftmost element in a STRING, or a right parenthesis to the right of the rightmost element). The **phrase edge prominence** constraint states that an edge CONSTITUENT will be more prominent than that of a constituent not located at an edge. In the analysis of REDUPLICATION in PROSODIC MORPHOLOGY, phonological constraints suggest that the two components (the base form and the reduplicant) must share an edge element – initial in PREFIXING reduplication, and final in SUFFIXING reduplication.

educational linguistics A term sometimes used for the application of LINGUISTIC theories, methods and descriptive findings to the study of the teaching/learning of a native language, in both spoken and written forms, in schools or other educational settings; more broadly, to *all* teaching contexts; also called **pedagogical linguistics**. Specific topics of interest include the study of reading and writing, ACCENT and DIALECT, oracy (cf. ORAL), language VARIETY across the curriculum, and the teaching of linguistics, GRAMMAR, etc. in schools.

egressive A term used in the PHONETIC classification of speech sounds, referring to all sounds produced using an outwards-moving AIRSTREAM MECHANISM. The opposite category is INGRESSIVE, which is an uncommon mode for speech production. The vast majority of speech sounds are made with egressive air from the lungs (PULMONIC air). A few CONSONANTS are produced using an egressive airflow originating at the LARYNX: these are known as EJECTIVE or 'glottalic' sounds (see GLOTTAL), such as [t', s', ʧ'].

ejective A term used in the PHONETIC classification of CONSONANT sounds on the basis of their MANNER OF ARTICULATION; it refers to the SERIES of sounds produced by using the glottalic AIRSTREAM MECHANISM. Air is compressed in the mouth or PHARYNX while the GLOTTIS remains closed, and then released. Ejective PLOSIVES are quite common in LANGUAGES (as in many languages of Africa and the Americas, e.g. Quechua, Amharic), and ejective FRICATIVES may also be found. These sounds are transcribed with a small raised GLOTTAL stop, or an apostrophe, following the segment involved, e.g. [p'], [s']. They are also referred to as 'glottalic' sounds, and occasionally as 'glottalized' sounds.

elaborated A term used by the sociologist Basil Bernstein (b. 1924) to refer to one of two VARIETIES (or CODES), of LANGUAGE use, introduced as part of a general theory of the nature of social systems and social rules, the other being RESTRICTED. **Elaborated code** was said to be used in relatively FORMAL, educated situations; not to be reliant for its meaningfulness on extralinguistic CONTEXT (such as gestures or shared beliefs); and to permit speakers to be individually creative in their expression, and to use a range of linguistic alternatives. It was said to be characterized linguistically by a relatively high proportion of such features as SUBORDINATE CLAUSES, ADJECTIVES, the PRONOUN *I*, and PASSIVES. Restricted code, by contrast, was said to lack these features. The correlation of elaborated code with certain types of social-class background, and its role in educational settings (e.g. whether children used to a restricted code will succeed in schools where elaborated code is the norm – and what should be done in such cases), brought this theory considerable publicity and controversy, and the distinction has since been reinterpreted in various ways.

E-language An abbreviation for **externalized language**, a term suggested by Noam CHOMSKY to refer to a collection of SENTENCES understood independently of the properties of the mind, and in this sense contrasted with I-LANGUAGE. It subsumes the notion of LANGUAGE as a system of utterances or forms paired with meanings, which it is the purpose of a GRAMMAR to describe.

elative A term used in GRAMMATICAL DESCRIPTION to refer to a type of INFLECTION which expresses the meaning of motion 'away from (inside)' a place. The elative CASE is found in Finnish, for example, along with ALLATIVE, ADESSIVE, and several other cases expressing 'local' temporal and spatial meanings. 'Elative' is often contrasted with ABLATIVE – from inside *v.* from outside.

electroaerometry see AEROMETRY

electrokymograph(-y, -ic) An instrument used in ARTICULATORY PHONETICS to enable a record to be made of the changes in ORAL and NASAL airflow during speech. **Electrokymography** involves the use of a face-mask which can differentiate the two kinds of flow, and associated equipment which can measure air volume and velocity, and record it visually (as an **electrokymogram**).

electromyograph(-y, -ic) (EMG) An instrument used in PHONETICS to observe and record muscular contractions during speech. **Electromyography** involves the application of electrodes (surface pads or needles) to the muscles involved in the VOCAL TRACT, and the analysis of the electromyographic traces produced visually (**electromyogram**).

electropalatograph(-y, -ic) (EPG) An instrument used in ARTICULATORY PHONETICS to enable a continuous record to be made of the contacts betwen TONGUE and PALATE during speech. **Electropalatography** involves the use of an artifical palate containing several electrodes, which register the tongue contacts as they are made: the results are presented visually as **electropalatograms**.

element A term used in LINGUISTICS, sometimes in the general sense of 'part', but often restricted, especially in GRAMMATICAL analysis, to refer to the IMMEDIATE CONSTITUENTS of a UNIT in a HIERARCHY. For example, SUBJECT/VERB, etc., are FUNCTIONAL elements of CLAUSE STRUCTURE: AFFIXES are FORMAL 'elements' of WORD structure.

elicitation (elicit) A term used in LINGUISTICS and PHONETICS to refer to the method of obtaining reliable linguistic DATA from speakers (INFORMANTS) – either actual UTTERANCES, or judgements about utterances (e.g. their ACCEPTABILITY). Several ingenious 'elicitation techniques' have been suggested to obtain ('elicit') this information in an indirect and unselfconscious way, e.g. asking informants to perform linguistic tasks which, though apparently irrelevant to the purpose at hand, will bring to light features of direct interest to the analyst.

elision A term used in PHONETICS and PHONOLOGY to refer to the omission of sounds in CONNECTED SPEECH. Both CONSONANTS and VOWELS may be affected, and sometimes whole SYLLABLES may be elided. UNSTRESSED GRAMMATICAL WORDS, such as *and* and *of*, are particularly prone to be elided, as when the *f* is dropped in *cup of tea* (cf. *cuppa tea*), or the *a* and *d* are dropped in *boys 'n' girls*. Within POLYSYLLABIC words, the vowels and consonants in unstressed syllables regularly elide in conversational speech of normal speed, e.g. *camera* (/ˈkamrə/), *probably* (/ˈprɒblɪ/), *February* (/ˈfebrɪ/). Complex consonant CLUSTERS are also often reduced, e.g. *twelfths* becoming /twelθs/ or /twelfs/. Several intricate patterns of influence can be demonstrated.

Traditional rhetoric was much concerned with the phenomenon of elision, because of the implications for constructing well-formed metrical lines, which would scan well. In rhetorical terminology, an elision in word-INITIAL position was known as *aphaeresis* or *prosiopesis*, in word-MEDIAL position as *syncope*, and in word-FINAL position as *apocope*. A similar classification was made for the opposite of elision, INTRUSION.

ellipsis (elide, ellipt-ed, -ical) A term used in GRAMMATICAL analysis to refer to a SENTENCE where, for reasons of economy, emphasis or style, a part of the STRUCTURE has been omitted, which is recoverable from a scrutiny of the CONTEXT. TRADITIONAL grammars talk here of an ELEMENT being 'understood', but LINGUISTIC analyses tend to constrain the notion more, emphasizing the need for the 'elided' (or 'ellipted') parts of the sentence to be unambiguously specifiable. For example, in the sequence A: *Where are you going?* B: *To town*, the 'full' FORM of B's sentence is predictable from A's sentence ('I am going to town'). But in such sentences as *Thanks, Yes*, etc., it is generally unclear what the full form of such sentences might be (e.g. 'Thanks is due to you'? 'I give you thanks'?), and in such circumstances the term 'ellipsis' would probably not be used. 'Elliptical' constructions are an essential feature of everyday conversation, but the rules governing their occurrence have received relatively little study. They are also sometimes referred to as REDUCED, CONTRACTED or 'abbreviated' constructions.

elsewhere condition A principle used in LEXICAL PHONOLOGY which states that, when two principles of operation are in conflict at a certain point in a DERIVATION, the one whose domain of operation is more restricted has priority of action. For example, if all OBSTRUENTS are VOICELESS in a language, and all AFFRICATES are VOICED, the latter statement will have priority over the former, in the case of a particular ALVEO-PALATAL affricate. The second statement, being more specific, has priority over the more general statement, which thus applies only in contexts where the specific statements do not obtain – in other words, 'elsewhere'.

embed(-ding, -ded) A term used in GENERATIVE GRAMMAR to refer to the process or CONSTRUCTION where one SENTENCE is included ('embedded') in another, i.e. in SYNTACTIC SUBORDINATION. 'Embedding' is distinct from CONJOINING (CO-ORDINATING). A RELATIVE CLAUSE within a NOUN PHRASE is an example of embedding, e.g. *The man who has a suitcase is in the bar*. In a process view, this sentence could be derived from *The man has a suitcase*, which is embedded within the MATRIX sentence *The man is in the bar*. Embedded clauses can also be COMPLEMENTS, as in *the discussion of his new book*. A derivative notion is SELF-EMBEDDING (or 'centre-embedding').

EMG see ELECTROMYOGRAPH(Y)

emic/etic A pair of terms which characterize opposed approaches to the study of LINGUISTIC DATA. An 'etic' approach is one where the physical patterns of LANGUAGE are described with a minimum of reference to their function within the language SYSTEM. An 'emic' approach, by contrast, takes full account of

FUNCTIONAL relationships, setting up a CLOSED system of abstract CONTRASTIVE UNITS as the basis of a DESCRIPTION. Emic is in fact derived from such terms as PHONEME and MORPHEME, where *-eme* refers to the minimal DISTINCTIVE units involved. An emic approach to INTONATION, for example, would describe only those features of the PITCH pattern which are used by a language to signal MEANINGS; an etic approach, on the other hand, would describe the UTTERANCE's pitch movements much more minutely, regardless of whether the features described were being used by the language to signal MEANINGS or not. The distinction is a central feature of the American linguist Kenneth Pike's (b. 1912) theory of language, known as TAGMEMICS.

emotive A term sometimes used in SEMANTICS as part of a CLASSIFICATION of types of MEANING. The 'emotive meaning' of an expression refers to its emotional effect on the listener, as in the 'emotive content' of propaganda speeches, advertising language, etc. Alternative terms include AFFECTIVE and CONNOTATIVE; opposed terms include COGNITIVE and REFERENTIAL.

emphatic consonant In PHONOLOGY, a type of CONSONANT, associated particularly with the Semitic languages (and much studied in Arabic), which is articulated in the PHARYNGEAL or UVULAR regions of the vocal tract, or which has a COARTICULATION in those regions (such as pharyngealization and VELARIZATION). Emphasis often spreads to a string of adjacent SEGMENTS, and the phenomenon is thus widely analysed as a PROSODIC or 'long' component of word structure.

empty (1) A term used in some GRAMMATICAL descriptions to refer to a meaningless ELEMENT introduced into a structure to ensure its GRAMMATICALITY. There is an empty use of *it*, for example, in such sentences as *it's raining*, and EXISTENTIAL *there* is sometimes regarded in this way (e.g. *there are mice in the larder*). Such elements have also been called PROP words, or DUMMY elements. In GENERATIVE grammar, empty elements (**empty nodes**) are displayed in phrase markers as DELTAS filled by dummies or **empty categories**. Empty categories include PRO, PRO, and TRACE (in GOVERNMENT-BINDING THEORY) and the SLASH categories of GENERALIZED PHRASE-STRUCTURE GRAMMAR.

(2) The term is also sometimes used in the grammatical CLASSIFICATION of WORDS to refer to one of two postulated major word classes in LANGUAGE, the other being FULL. **Empty words** are said to be words which have no LEXICAL MEANING, and whose function is solely to express grammatical relationships, e.g. *to, the, in, of.* The distinction has been criticized, on the grounds that there are degrees of meaning in most grammatical words, few (if any) being really devoid of CONTENT. The term is still used, however – though not as widely as some other terms (such as GRAMMATICAL word, FUNCTION WORD).

(3) A term used in MORPHOLOGY, in the phrase **empty morph**, to refer to a FORMAL FEATURE in a word which cannot be allocated to any MORPHEME. A well-discussed example in English is the word *children*, where a possible analysis is into ROOT *child* and plural SUFFIX *-en* (cf. *oxen*); the residual /r/ left by this analysis is then seen as an empty morph without which the word would not be exhaustively analysed at the morphemic LEVEL.

empty category principle (ECP) A principle of the GOVERNMENT (sub-)theory of GOVERNMENT-BINDING THEORY. It requires a TRACE to be properly governed, i.e.

to be governed either by a LEXICAL CATEGORY or by a category with the same INDEX (its ANTECEDENT).

enclitic see CLITIC

encode see CODE

endearment, terms of In SOCIOLINGUISTICS, forms of address used between people who mutually perceive their relationship to be one of intimacy. Examples in English include *love, dear, honey, mate.* Such forms can also be used asymmetrically, when only one participant uses them (as in service encounters, when a customer uses one but a clerk does not, or vice versa).

endocentric A term used in GRAMMATICAL analysis as part of a two-way classification of SYNTACTIC constructions using DISTRIBUTIONAL criteria: it refers to a group of syntactically related WORDS where one of the words is FUNCTIONALLY equivalent to the group as a whole (i.e. there is a definable 'centre' or HEAD inside the group, which has the same distribution as the whole); it is opposed to EXOCENTRIC. Endocentric constructions include NOUN PHRASES and VERB phrases (as traditionally defined), where the CONSTITUENT items are SUBORDINATE to the head, e.g. *the big* ***house, the cake*** *with icing, will be* ***going***, and also some types of CO-ORDINATION, e.g. *boys and girls.*

endoglossic In SOCIOLINGUISTICS, a term referring to a LANGUAGE which is the native language of most (or all) of the population in a geographical area; contrasts with **exoglossic**. English, for example, is endoglossic for most of Australia and England, but exoglossic for Quebec and Singapore.

endophoric (endophora) A term used by some LINGUISTS to refer to the relationships of COHESION which help to define the STRUCTURE of a TEXT; it is contrasted with EXOPHORIC relationships, which do not play a part in cohesion, and where the interpretation requires reference to the EXTRALINGUISTIC SITUATION. Endophoric relations are divided into ANAPHORIC and CATAPHORIC types.

-en **form** A term used in English GRAMMATICAL description to refer to the past PARTICIPLE FORM of the VERB, e.g. *I have* ***taken***. It does not necessarily have this ending, which should be seen solely as a mnemonic device, useful mainly in writing RULES succinctly. The *-ed* ending is also common in this function (e.g. *I have walked*), and may be seen as an alternative symbol.

engineering (linguistic) see LANGUAGE

entailment A term derived from formal logic and now often used as part of the study of SEMANTICS. It refers to a relation between a pair of SENTENCES such that the truth of the second sentence necessarily follows from the truth of the first, e.g. *I can see a dog – I can see an animal.* One cannot both assert the first and deny the second. In recent semantic discussion, entailment has come to be contrasted with PRESUPPOSITION, on the grounds that different consequences follow from either of the sentences being false. For example, if *I can see a dog* is false, then the notion of entailment requires that *I can see an animal* may be true or false; but the notion of presupposition requires that, if the first sentence is false, the second must be true, as in *He has stopped buying videos* presupposes *He has bought videos.*

entry (1) A term used in GRAMMATICAL description to refer to the accumulated STRUCTURAL information concerning a LEXICAL item as formally located in a LEXICON or dictionary. A dictionary is seen as a set of **lexical entries**.

(2) In SYSTEMIC GRAMMAR, the phrase **entry condition** refers to the criterion which must be met in order for a particular grammatical system to become operative. For example, in order to operate the system which contains the choices DECLARATIVE ~ INTERROGATIVE ~ IMPERATIVE, the entry condition requires that the input be a main CLAUSE. The whole of LANGUAGE is viewed as a network of systems of this kind.

environment (1) A general term used in LINGUISTICS and PHONETICS to refer to specific parts of an UTTERANCE (or TEXT) near or adjacent to a UNIT which is the focus of attention. Features of the linguistic environment may influence the selection of a particular unit, at a given place in an utterance, and thus restrict its occurrence, or DISTRIBUTION. For example, in PHONOLOGY, whether a CONSONANT PHONEME is lip-ROUNDED or not may depend on the presence of a rounded VOWEL in its phonetic environment. Sounds are referred to as being 'conditioned' by their environment. In GRAMMAR, the term is used similarly; e.g. the occurrence of one MORPHEME may depend on the prior use of another in its environment, as with *cran-*, which occurs only in the grammatical environment of *-berry*. In recent years, the term CONTEXT has come to be widely used in this sense. The symbol / (in such contexts as A → B/C 'rewrite A as B in the context of C') is called an **environment bar**. See also DERIVED ENVIRONMENT.

(2) Particularly in the phrase **linguistic environment**, the term refers to the SOCIOLINGUISTIC situation in relation to which a particular observation is being made. In language ACQUISITION, for example, a particular STRUCTURE might be said to appear at age two, 'regardless of the linguistic environment of the child', i.e. disregarding the kind of language the child is used to hearing in its social situation. The term CONTEXT is sometimes used in this sense also.

epenthesis (epenthetic) A term used in PHONETICS and PHONOLOGY to refer to a type of INTRUSION, where an extra sound has been inserted in a WORD; often subclassified into PROTHESIS and ANAPTYXIS. The phenomenon is common both in HISTORICAL change and in CONNECTED SPEECH (e.g. *incredible* as /ɪŋkᵊredɪbl/).

EPG see ELECTROPALATOGRAPH(Y)

epicene A term from TRADITIONAL GRAMMAR, and now with some use in SOCIOLINGUISTICS, referring to a NOUN which can relate to either sex without changing its FORM. The term is from Greek *epikoinos* 'common to many', and was used in Latin and Greek grammar for nouns which stayed in the same GENDER regardless of the sex of the being referred to (e.g. Latin *vulpes* 'fox/vixen'). English examples include *teacher* and *doctor*. The notion is perceived to be relevant to contemporary discussion of language and gender.

epistemic A term derived from modal logic and used by some LINGUISTS as part of a theoretical framework for the analysis of MODAL VERBS and related STRUCTURES in LANGUAGE. 'Epistemic logic' is concerned with the logical structure of statements which assert or imply that PROPOSITIONS are known or believed, e.g. the use of modals in SENTENCES such as *The car must be ready*, i.e. 'It is surely the case that the car is ready'. It contrasts with ALETHIC and DEONTIC modality, which would interpret this sentence respectively as 'It follows that the car is ready' and 'I oblige you to ensure that the car is ready'.

eponym(ous) The name of a person after whom something (such as an invention or a place) is named; also called an **appellative**. Examples include *cardigan, biro* and *sandwich*. Place names in some countries are also often eponymous (*Washington, Sydney, Gorky*).

equative (equational) (1) A term used in GRAMMATICAL analysis to refer to a type of SENTENCE where a verb places two NOUN PHRASES into a relationship of identity, e.g. *Jo is the leader*. The VERB which links these ELEMENTS may be called an **equational verb** (or a verb with 'equative' function) – usually in English a form of the COPULA verb *be*. Some LANGUAGES (e.g. Russian) have equative sentences where the copula is not present – cf. the stereotyped language of film primitives (*him Tarzan*, etc.).

(2) Some grammatical descriptions recognize an 'equative' DEGREE, in analysing comparison between ADJECTIVES or ADVERBS, e.g. *as big as*.

equi NP deletion An OBLIGATORY RULE in classical TRANSFORMATIONAL GRAMMAR, usually abbreviated to **Equi**, which deletes a NOUN PHRASE from a COMPLEMENT CLAUSE in a SENTENCE when it is identical in meaning (CO-REFERENTIAL) with another noun phrase in the main clause of the same sentence. An example is *John wants to see the film*, where the underlying subject of *see* is *John*. In later approaches, this transformation was eliminated, and these constructions, along with RAISING constructions, were referred to as CONTROL sentences. In GOVERNMENT-BINDING THEORY, the missing subject is analysed as PRO.

equipollent (1) A type of OPPOSITION recognized in PRAGUE SCHOOL PHONOLOGY, distinguished from PRIVATIVE and GRADUAL. An equipollent opposition is one where the members are seen as logically equivalent to each other, contrasted neither gradually nor by a BINARY FEATURE: e.g. the DISTINCTION between /p/ and /k/ cannot be analysed, according to Nikolai Trubetskoy, as a difference along a single PHONETIC continuum, nor can /p/ be seen as 'non-VELAR', or /k/ as 'non-BILABIAL'.

(2) In some recent phonological models, a term used to characterize a FEATURE where both values are needed (cf. BINARY); opposed to PRIVATIVE.

equivalence (non-equivalent) A relationship of equality of POWER between GRAMMARS. Grammars which GENERATE the same set of SENTENCES are said to be 'equivalent' or 'weakly equivalent'. Grammars which generate the same set of PHRASE-MARKERS are 'strongly equivalent', i.e. they generate not only the same sentences but assign the same STRUCTURAL DESCRIPTIONS to each. Grammars which display differences in the LABELLING or BRACKETING of structures, or which generate differents sets of sentences, are said to be **non-equivalent**. The term is also used in other SYNTACTIC and SEMANTIC contexts, e.g. 'DISTRIBUTIONAL equivalence' (between units with the same distribution), 'semantic equivalence' (i.e. SYNONYMY).

erasure see STRAY

ergative (ergativity) A term used in the GRAMMATICAL description of some languages, such as Eskimo and Basque, where a term is needed to handle CONSTRUCTIONS where there is a formal parallel between the OBJECT of a TRANSITIVE VERB and the SUBJECT of an intransitive one (i.e. they display the same CASE). The subject of the transitive verb is referred to as 'ergative' whereas the subject of the intransitive verb, along with the object of the transitive verb, are referred to as ABSOLUTIVE. In some languages this kind of case marking is displayed only under certain circumstances, with ACCUSATIVE patterns being used elsewhere (**split ergativity**). For example, in Yucatec Mayan, in the PERFECT, the absolutive marks both the subject of an intransitive verb and the object of a transitive verb, while the ergative marks the subject of transitives. In the imperfect, the absolute marks only transitive objects, while the ergative marks the subjects of both transitives and intransitives. The concept of 'ergativity' has also been applied to English and other languages by some LINGUISTS, though the formal markers of the relationships involved are less clear. In this approach, SENTENCES such as *The window broke* and *The tree broke the window* would be analysed 'ergatively': the subject of the intransitive use of *broke* is the same as the object of its transitive use, and the AGENT of the action is thus said to appear as the 'ergative subject'. Ergative verbs are also known as UNACCUSATIVE verbs, especially in RELATIONAL GRAMMAR.

error (1) A term used in PSYCHOLINGUISTICS referring to mistakes in spontaneous speaking or writing attributable to a malfunctioning of the neuromuscular commands from the brain. It is thus distinct from the traditional notion of error, which was based on the LANGUAGE user's ability to conform to a set of real or imagined standards of expression. Several types of psycholinguistic error have been recognized. 'Speaker's errors', involving difficulties with the timing or sequence of commands, will lead to the addition, deletion or substitution of sounds and MORPHEMES – and is most noticeable in the phenomenon labelled 'slips of the tongue' (relabelled by some psycholinguists 'slips of the brain'), and in the false starts, PAUSES, and other non-fluencies of everyday speech. 'Hearer's errors' are particularly noticeable in language ACQUISITION, as when a child mis-analyses an adult SENTENCE (e.g. A: *He's got his hat on.* C: *Where's his hat on?*), and in the history of language, where new forms have come from a re-analysis (or 'metanalysis') of older ones (e.g. *a napron* → *an apron*). The distinction between 'errors' of PRODUCTION and PERCEPTION is sometimes hard to draw, however – especially as often the only evidence for the latter is the former – and, generally, the term 'error' should be used with caution, especially in language acquisition studies, where it can be easily confused with the pedagogical notion of 'error' (in the context of essay-marking, etc.).

(2) In language teaching and learning, **error analysis** is a technique for identifying, classifying and systematically interpreting the unacceptable forms produced by someone learning a foreign language, using any of the principles and procedures provided by LINGUISTICS. Errors are assumed to reflect, in a systematic way, the level of COMPETENCE achieved by a learner; they are contrasted with 'mistakes', which are PERFORMANCE limitations that a learner would be able to correct.

esophageal An alternative spelling for OESOPHAGEAL.

essential conditions see FELICITY CONDITIONS

essive A term used in GRAMMATICAL DESCRIPTION to refer to a type of INFLECTION which expresses a state of being. The essive CASE is found in Finnish, for example, along with ADESSIVE, INESSIVE, and several other cases expressing 'local' temporal and spatial meanings.

EST The usual abbreviation for EXTENDED STANDARD THEORY.

état de langue A term introduced into LINGUISTICS by the Swiss linguist Ferdinand de SAUSSURE, referring to a 'state of language' seen as if at a particular point in time, regardless of its antecedents or subsequent history. An *état de langue* is therefore the primary subject-matter of SYNCHRONIC linguistic study.

ethnolinguistics (ethnography of communication/speaking) A branch of LINGUISTICS which studies LANGUAGE in relation to the investigation of ethnic types and behaviour. The term overlaps to some degree with ANTHROPOLOGICAL LINGUISTICS and SOCIOLINGUISTICS, reflecting the overlapping interests of the correlative disciplines involved – ethnology, anthropology and sociology. The phrase **ethnography of communication** or **ethnography of speaking** has been applied by sociolinguists to the study of language in relation to the entire range of extralinguistic variables which identify the social basis of communication, the emphasis being on the description of linguistic interaction. The student of such matters is known as an 'ethnolinguist'. **Ethnosemantics** (or **ethnographic semantics**) takes further the anthropological perspective in relation to cognitive science, studying the way meaning is structured in different cultural settings (e.g. in relation to the expression of kinship, colour, or the DISCOURSE structure of SPEECH EVENTS) and the principles governing culturally conditioned SEMANTIC variation.

ethnomethodology (ethnomethodologist) A term referring to a movement that developed in American sociology of the early 1970s, which led to the development of CONVERSATION ANALYSIS in LINGUISTICS. The approach proposed to replace the predominantly deductive and quantitative techniques of previous sociological research, with its emphasis on general questions of social structure, by the study of the techniques (= 'methods') which are used by people themselves (curiously referred to as 'ethnic') when they are actually engaged in social (and thus linguistic) interaction. The emphasis is on how individuals experience, make sense of and report their interactions; and ethnomethodological data therefore consist of tape-recordings of natural conversation, and their associated TRANSCRIPTIONS.

ethnopoetics The study of oral art forms (including poetry) practised by indigenous peoples. It focuses especially on the expressive vocal effects and COHESIVE structural features of artistic oral DISCOURSE, and on methods of TRANSCRIPTION and written presentation. Particular attention is paid to the identification of 'lines', metrical patterns, and other recurring linguistic or STYLISTIC features, in relation to a typology of oral literature. See also POETICS.

etic see EMIC

etymology (etymo-n, -logical) The term traditionally used for the study of the origins and history of the FORM and MEANING of WORDS. In so far as etymology derives its methods from LINGUISTICS (especially SEMANTICS), it may be seen as a branch of HISTORICAL LINGUISTICS. The linguistic form from which a later form derives is known as its **etymon**. A **folk etymology** occurs when a word is assumed to come from a particular etymon, because of some association of form or meaning, whereas in fact the word had a different DERIVATION, e.g. *spit and image* becomes *spitting image*. The **etymological fallacy** is the view that an earlier (or the oldest) meaning of a word is the correct one (e.g. that *history* 'really' means 'investigation', because this was the meaning the etymon had in classical Greek). This view is commonly held, but it contrasts with the attitude of the linguist, who emphasizes the need to describe the meanings of modern words as they are now, and not as they once may have been in some earlier state of the language (the 'oldest' state, of course, being unknown).

eurhythmy (eurhythmic) A principle proposed in METRICAL PHONOLOGY for the interpretation of METRICAL GRIDS, indicating which grids are possible and preferable. In particular, it ensures that STRINGS result in a preferred grid configuration (PERIODICITY), such as the tendency in English towards a particular spacing of STRESSED SYLLABLES (cf. the more general notion of ISOCHRONY). The values of a RHYTHMIC structure can be computed from the grid by a set of RULES of eurhythmy; for example, these rules might require the equal spacing of grid marks at all levels, promoting a regular alternation. The status of the principle as an evaluative process is controversial.

evaluative A term used in SEMANTICS for a type of MODALITY where PROPOSITIONS express the speaker's attitude (e.g. surprise, regret) towards what is being said. For example, Menomini has a pair of SUFFIXES which express the evaluative notions 'despite our expectations, X will happen' and 'despite our expectations, X will not happen'.

eventive A term used by some LINGUISTS as part of the GRAMMATICAL or SEMANTIC analysis of a SENTENCE in terms of CASES or participant roles. It usually refers to an element which expresses an action, accompanying a verb which is relatively 'empty' of meaning, e.g. ***The invasion** happened in 1944* (eventive subject), *They are having **a row*** (eventive object).

evidential(ity) A term used in SEMANTICS for a type of EPISTEMIC MODALITY where PROPOSITIONS are asserted that are open to challenge by the hearer, and thus require justification. Evidential constructions express a speaker's strength of commitment to a proposition in terms of the available evidence (rather than in terms of possibility or necessity). They add such nuances of meaning to a given sentence as 'I saw it happen', 'I heard that it happened', 'I have seen evidence that it happened (though I wasn't there)', or 'I have obtained information that it happened from someone else'. Tuyuca (Brazil) has a complex system of five evidentials; English, by contrast, has none, relying instead on judgements (propositions which are asserted with doubt, and for which challenge and evidence is irrelevant).

exceptional case marking (ECM) A term used in GOVERNMENT-BINDING THEORY in connection with certain VERBS and the constructions in which those verbs appear.

In general, it applies to the class of subject-to-object RAISING verbs of classical TRANSFORMATIONAL GRAMMAR, such as *believe* and *consider*, which take some kind of CLAUSAL COMPLEMENT (e.g. *Mary believes Bill to be a fool, Mary considers Bill a fool*). The exceptional nature of these verbs is in their ability to assign (objective) CASE to NOUN PHRASE subjects of complement INFINITIVAL clauses or SMALL CLAUSES.

exclamation (exclamatory) A term used in the classification of SENTENCE FUNCTIONS, and defined sometimes on GRAMMATICAL and sometimes on SEMANTIC or SOCIOLINGUISTIC grounds. Traditionally, an exclamation referred to any emotional UTTERANCE, usually lacking the grammatical structure of a full sentence, and marked by strong INTONATION, e.g. *Gosh! Good grief!* In QUIRK GRAMMAR, **exclamatory sentences** have a more restricted definition, referring to constructions which begin with *what* or *how* without a following INVERSION of SUBJECT and VERB, e.g. *What a fool he was!, How nice!* These sentences are sometimes called **exclamatives**. Semantically, the function is primarily the expression of the speaker's feelings – a function which may also be expressed using other grammatical means, e.g. *What on earth is she doing?* (when it is obvious what is being done). The term is usually contrasted with three other major sentence functions: STATEMENT, QUESTION and COMMAND.

exclusive (1) With reference to PRONOUNS, a term used (in contrast with INCLUSIVE) to refer to a first-PERSON role where the addressee (or someone else) is not included along with the speaker, e.g. *we* = 'me but not you'.

(2) In SEMANTICS, a term derived from formal logic (in contrast with INCLUSIVE) to refer to a type of DISJUNCTION: in an exclusive interpretation, the disjunction is true only if one or other of the PROPOSITIONS is true. In *Either X is happening or Y is happening*, it is not the case that both X and Y could be happening at the same time.

exhaustiveness A principle of LINGUISTIC analysis whereby the aim is to specify totally the linguistic CONTRASTS in a set of DATA, and ultimately in the LANGUAGE as a whole. It is often cited as one of three scientific principles to be adhered to in linguistics, the others being logical self-consistency and ECONOMY.

exhaustivity In METRICAL PHONOLOGY, a FOOT-shape PARAMETER which requires that every SYLLABLE in a word must be included in metrical structure.

existential A term used in the GRAMMATICAL description of CLAUSE or SENTENCE types, referring to a type of STRUCTURE commencing with the unstressed word *there* followed by a form of the verb *be*, the notion of existence thereby being expressed, e.g. *there's plenty to do, there are three cats on the wall.* The relationship between such sentences and others (cf. *three cats are on the wall, the wall has three cats on it*, etc.) has attracted particular interest in LINGUISTICS, especially in GENERATIVE grammar. Several types of existential sentences have been recognized (including some where other forms than *there* and *be* are involved, e.g. *she has a meal ready* and *there exist several such figures*), and the relationship between these and other SEMANTIC categories (such as location and possession) is considered to be an important aspect of the investigation of UNIVERSAL grammatical FUNCTIONS. See also QUANTIFIER.

exocentric A term used in GRAMMATICAL analysis as part of a two-way classification of SYNTACTIC CONSTRUCTIONS using DISTRIBUTIONAL criteria: it refers to a group of syntactically related WORDS where none of the words is FUNCTIONALLY equivalent to the group as a whole (i.e. there is no definable 'centre' or HEAD inside the group); it is opposed to ENDOCENTRIC. The English basic SENTENCE structure of SUBJECT + PREDICATE is exocentric, by this definition (a 'PREDICATIVE exocentric construction'), as neither part can substitute for the sentence structure as a whole, e.g. *the man fell* cannot be replaced by either *the man* or by *fell* alone. Other types include 'DIRECTIVE constructions', such as PREPOSITION + NOUN PHRASE sequences (e.g. *on the table*), where the ADVERBIAL function of the whole is not equivalent to any of its parts; VERB + OBJECT sequences (e.g. *kick the ball*); and 'CONNECTIVE constructions', where a connector ELEMENT is followed by an ATTRIBUTIVE element (e.g. *seemed angry*).

exoglossic see ENDOGLOSSIC

exophora (exophoric) A term used by some LINGUISTS to refer to the process or result of a linguistic UNIT referring directly (i.e. DEICTICALLY) to the EXTRALINGUISTIC SITUATION accompanying an UTTERANCE, e.g. *there, that, her.* 'Exophoric reference' is usually contrasted with ENDOPHORIC reference, subclassified into ANAPHORIC and CATAPHORIC reference.

expansion (expand) A GRAMMATICAL process in which new ELEMENTS are added to a CONSTRUCTION without its basic STRUCTURE being affected, e.g. the addition of ADJECTIVES before a NOUN, or AUXILIARIES before a VERB. In GENERATIVE grammar, REWRITE RULES are sometimes called 'expansion rules', by virtue of the fact that a single symbol is 'expanded' into a STRING of symbols which represent its CONSTITUENT structure (e.g. VP → V+NP). The term is also found in broader senses, referring to any process whereby an initial LINGUISTIC STATE is enlarged, e.g. in historical SEMANTICS a WORD's earlier meaning may come to be 'expanded' to cover a wider range of REFERENTS (e.g. Modern English *gay*); in SOCIOLINGUISTICS, a LANGUAGE or VARIETY may come to be used in new situations, thus 'expanding' its influence (e.g. through LOAN words).

experiencer A term used in later versions of CASE GRAMMAR (cf. earlier use of DATIVE) to refer to the case of an entity or person affected by the action or state expressed by the VERB, as in ***The dentist*** *heard a bang, The book interested* ***her***.

experimental phonetics see PHONETICS

explanatory A term used in GENERATIVE LINGUISTICS to refer to a level of achievement in the writing of GRAMMARS. **Explanatory adequacy** is achieved when a principled basis is established for deciding the relative merits of alternative grammars, all of which are DESCRIPTIVELY ADEQUATE (i.e. they account for the NATIVE-SPEAKER'S COMPETENCE). Several criteria have been suggested for FORMALIZING this notion, of which relative SIMPLICITY is the most investigated.

expletive An alternative label for DUMMY elements in GOVERNMENT-BINDING THEORY.

explicit(ness) A characteristic of formulations in LINGUISTICS – and especially a primary goal of GENERATIVE analysis – whereby all the properties of a RULE and the conditions under which it operates are specified fully and precisely. In this sense, explicit descriptions contrast with several found in TRADITIONAL grammar, which were often ambiguous, or needed prior knowledge on the part of the NATIVE-SPEAKER to be interpreted (as in the definition of NOUNS as names of persons, places and things, where it is up to the LANGUAGE user to decide whether a particular ITEM qualifies).

exponent (exponence) A concept in a HIERARCHICAL LINGUISTIC analysis, referring to the relationship of correspondence between linguistic UNITS at a higher LEVEL of analysis and units at a lower level. For example, WORDS can be said to have PHONOLOGICAL units (such as PHONEMES) as their 'exponents', and the exponents of the latter are PHONETIC features. The term REPRESENTATION is equivalent. In this sense, abstract units are expounded by other abstract units or by physical units.

An alternative emphasis restricts the application of the term to the physical expression of any abstract unit (i.e. at any LEVEL), e.g. a MORPH being the exponent of a MORPHEME, a PHONE of a PHONEME, a particular FORMATIVE (such as *-s*) of a SYNTACTIC CATEGORY (such as 'plural'), the item *going* of the LEXEME *go*. There are plainly many possible types of exponence relationships (e.g. to handle the 'fusion' or 'overlapping' of exponents). This sense of the term receives a specific technical status in HALLIDAYAN linguistic theory (cf. SYSTEMIC grammar), referring to one of the SCALES of analysis which interrelates the CATEGORIES of the theory, viz. the relationship postulated between these categories and the raw DATA. For example, the LEXICAL item *table* is an instance of (an 'exponent' of) the CLASS of NOUNS. Other scales in this approach are labelled RANK and DELICACY.

expression (1) This term is used in a general sense in LINGUISTICS, referring to a STRING OF ELEMENTS treated as a UNIT for the purposes of analysis and discussion: expressions have both a GRAMMATICAL and a LEXICAL character, and are definable in terms of both, e.g. the expression *so be it* can be analysed as a sequence both of FORM-CLASSES and of lexical ITEMS. Expressions can then be investigated in terms of their SEMANTIC properties, as is carried on in philosophical and logical discussion (through such notions as 'referring' and 'predicative expression'), and as is increasingly the case in linguistics. See also INDEXICAL (2).

(2) The term is also found in the SAUSSUREAN distinction between expression (or FORM) and CONTENT (or MEANING): 'expression' here refers to all aspects of linguistic FORM, i.e. sounds and their grammatical SEQUENCES. A more restricted sense equates 'expression' solely with the LEVEL of linguistic organization of SUBSTANCE, i.e. PHONOLOGY and GRAPHOLOGY. The abstract formal UNITS which are realized either in PHONIC or in GRAPHIC SUBSTANCE are sometimes referred to as **expression elements**, e.g. the expression element /s/ is realized PHONETICALLY as [s] and GRAPHETICALLY as *s*, *ss*, etc. In FUNCTIONAL GRAMMAR, **expression rules** play an important role in the final stage of sentence generation.

expressive A term sometimes used in SEMANTICS as part of a classification of types of MEANING. The **expressive meaning** of an EXPRESSION refers both to its emotional CONTENT and to any identity it might have in terms of the personality or individual creativity of the user (as in much poetic LANGUAGE). It is usually contrasted with DESCRIPTIVE and 'social' meaning. Other terms which overlap with 'expressive' include AFFECTIVE, CONNOTATIVE and EMOTIVE. The term is also used in the theory of SPEECH ACTS to refer to a type of UTTERANCE where the speaker expresses his or her feelings, e.g. *I apologize/sympathize/regret.*

extended standard theory (EST) The name given to a MODEL of GENERATIVE GRAMMAR which developed in the early 1970s out of that expounded in Noam CHOMSKY's *Aspects of the Theory of Syntax* (1965) (the STANDARD THEORY). The 'extension' is primarily due to the range of the SEMANTIC RULES, some of which Chomsky suggested should now be allowed to operate with SURFACE STRUCTURE as input. Features of surface structure relevant to the semantics include various functions of STRESS and INTONATION, aspects of QUANTIFICATION, and the FOCUS in a sentence which provides information concerning the sentence's PRESUPPOSITIONS. In other words, it was no longer the case that only the DEEP STRUCTURE was the determinant of the semantic REPRESENTATION of a sentence. In a later development of this view, it is argued that perhaps the notion of deep structure can be dispensed with altogether, in relation to the semantics, this being determined by a developed notion of surface structure. (See further the REVISED EXTENDED STANDARD THEORY.)

extension(1)(**-al**) A term in philosophy and logic, and now often used as part of a theoretical framework for LINGUISTIC SEMANTICS, to refer to the class of entities to which a WORD is correctly applied. For example, the extension (or 'extensional meaning') of the term *flower* would be a list of all the entities referred to by the term, e.g. *daffodil, rose, fuchsia . . .* 'Extension' is opposed to INTENSION, which includes only the defining properties of terms.

(2) In HISTORICAL LINGUISTICS, a term used in the classification of types of SEMANTIC change, referring to a widening of meaning in a LEXICAL item; opposed to NARROWING. For example, in Latin 'virtue' was a male quality (cf. *vir* 'man'), but today it applies to both sexes.

extensive A term used in some GRAMMATICAL analyses to refer to structures where there is no close SEMANTIC relationship between elements of structure, such as SUBJECT and OBJECT (e.g. *he stroked the dog*) or DIRECT and INDIRECT object (e.g. *he gave me a letter*). **Extensive verbs** are either TRANSITIVE or intransitive, and are contrasted with INTENSIVE verbs, such as *be.*

external adequacy see ADEQUACY

externalized language see E-LANGUAGE

extralinguistic In its most general sense, this term refers to anything in the world (other than LANGUAGE) in relation to which language is used – the 'extralinguistic situation'. The term 'extralinguistic features' is used both generally, to refer to any properties of such situations, and also specifically, to refer to properties of communication which are not clearly analysable in LINGUISTIC terms, e.g. gestures, tones of voice. Some linguists refer to the former class of features as METALINGUISTIC; others refer to the latter class as PARALINGUISTIC.

extrametricality A principle in METRICAL PHONOLOGY which allows certain ELEMENTS in a given STRING not to count when assigning metrical structure, i.e. the RULES of STRESS ASSIGNMENT ignore such elements; also called **extraprosodicity**. Proposals for English include **consonant extrametricality** (applying to the final CONSONANT in a word), **noun extrametricality** (applying to the final SEGMENT in certain types of NOUN, such as *museum* and *elephant*), and **adjective extrametricality** (applying to certain ADJECTIVE SUFFIXES). Extrametricality, which is restricted to PERIPHERAL elements, enables the analysis to avoid rare or unknown FOOT types at word EDGES, to handle the stresslessness of peripheral syllables, and to mark exceptions to the stress RULES.

extraposition (extrapose) A term used in GRAMMATICAL analysis to refer to the process or result of moving (or 'extraposing') an ELEMENT from its normal position to a position at or near the end of the SENTENCE, e.g. *That the boy came in late upset the teacher*, compared with *It upset the teacher that the boy came in late*. The *it* which is introduced in such sentences is known as **extrapositive *it***.

extraprosodicity see EXTRAMETRICALITY

extrasyllabic(ity) A term used in AUTOSEGMENTAL PHONOLOGY with two different but related applications.

(a) It may refer to SEGMENTAL material appearing in word-FINAL position which cannot be SYLLABIFIED according to the principles that appear to hold word-internally; this material has also been called a **termination** or an **appendix**. Extra statements are required which may add or remove restrictions on what can appear word-finally. Because this situation reflects the stable status of word-final segments, it is sometimes called **licensed extrasyllabicity**, as opposed to the contingent notion described below.

(b) The term is also used to handle a situation where CONSONANTS fail to become syllabified during the syllabification procedure, and remain unattached to any syllable until a later point in a DERIVATION. This unstable situation is often called **contingent extrasyllabicity**, to distinguish it from the more general notion referred to under (a).

extrinsic A term used in GENERATIVE GRAMMAR referring to a type of constraint imposed on the ORDERING of RULES (as opposed to a condition where such rules are allowed to apply in a random order). An **extrinsic ordering** is one where the SEQUENCE of rules is motivated solely by a consideration of the facts of a LANGUAGE and not by considerations of a logical kind: it is a specific ordering which is required to ensure that only GRAMMATICAL sentences are generated. Extrinsic rules are held by many to be of particular importance in organizing the TRANSFORMATIONAL rules in grammar, but the nature of these CONSTRAINTS is controversial, such as how much extrinsic ordering there ought to be, and how many times the rules in an ordered sequence should apply. It is opposed to INTRINSIC.

F

face In PRAGMATICS and interactional SOCIOLINGUISTICS, a term used in the analysis of politeness phenomena. **Positive face** is the desire to show involvement with others; **negative face** is the desire not to offend others. These factors can be used to analyse the kind of rapport which exists in an INTERACTION: for example, a speaker may choose to phrase something differently in order not to offend. Face helps to account for different types of interactive STYLE – for example, associated with the expression of distance, deference, or friendliness – whose proposed UNIVERSALITY is a topic of current research.

factitive A term used in GRAMMATICAL description to refer to a CONSTRUCTION or FORM (usually a VERB) denoting an action in which a cause produces a result: e.g. *make, kill, choose, elect* could be called 'factitive verbs'. In early CASE grammar, the term has special status, where it refers to the SEMANTIC case of the entity resulting from the verb's action, or understood as part of the verb's meaning, and is contrasted with AGENTIVE, DATIVE, etc. (cf. later use of RESULT, in this theory).

factive (factivity) A term used in the CLASSIFICATION of VERBS, referring to a verb which takes a COMPLEMENT CLAUSE, and where the speaker PRESUPPOSES the truth of the PROPOSITION expressed in that clause. For example, *know, agree, realize,* etc. are 'factive verbs': in *she knows that the cat is in the garden*, the speaker presupposes that the cat is in the garden. 'Factive predicators' may involve other classes than verbs: ADJECTIVES and NOUN CONSTRUCTIONS, for example, may display 'factivity', as in *it's surprising that he left, it's a shame that he left.* By contrast, **non-factive** constructions do not commit the speaker to the truth of the proposition expressed in the complement clause, e.g. *believe, think* as in *she thinks that the cat is in the garden.* **Contrafactive** constructions presuppose the falsity of the proposition expressed in the complement clause, e.g. *wish, pretend,* as in *I pretended the cat was in the garden.*

falling/fall (1) A term used in classifying the linguistic uses of PITCH, referring to a movement from relatively high to relatively low. Falling tones of various kinds (e.g. 'high/low falling', 'falling-rising') may be encountered in the study of INTONATION systems and of TONE LANGUAGES.

(2) A term used in a two-way classification of DIPHTHONGS (opposed to

RISING), referring to cases where the first ELEMENT of the diphthong receives the maximum PROMINENCE.

family (sub-) A term used in HISTORICAL LINGUISTIC studies to characterize a GENETIC MODEL of the relationships between LANGUAGES. A 'family' of languages is the set of languages deriving from a common ancestor, or 'parent', e.g. the Indo-European family consists of the 'daughter' languages Sanskrit, Greek, Latin, etc., which all developed out of Proto-Indo-European. Groupings within a family may be referred to as 'sub-families' (e.g. the Romance sub-family within the Italic family). The **family tree** is a representation of these relationships devised by COMPARATIVE PHILOLOGISTS in the nineteenth century. As COMPARATIVE studies grew to include larger numbers of potentially related languages, the term 'family' came to be used with increasing generality, often applied to cases where a genetic relationship was impossible to demonstrate. Usage varies greatly, but there is now a trend to avoid this term for language groups with only a remote degree of relationship, or where a clear ancestor language is unknown. 'Phylum' (plural 'phyla') has come to be widely used in such cases – with 'macro-phylum' available for still less definite groupings. Many scholars therefore now talk of the 'Australian phylum' (of Aboriginal languages), though in popular usage 'family' will still be heard. Proposed clusters of languages within phyla are variously called 'groups', 'sub-groups', or 'branches', with no fixed usage. 'Stock' is also found as an alternative to 'family'.

fatherese see MOTHERESE

favourite (non-) A term used by some LINGUISTS in the CLASSIFICATION of SENTENCE types to refer to the most PRODUCTIVE sentence pattern in a LANGUAGE. In English, the SUBJECT + PREDICATE (NP+VP) pattern is the favourite (or MAJOR) type, other types being referred to as **non-favourite** (or MINOR).

feature A term used in LINGUISTICS and PHONETICS to refer to any typical or noticeable property of spoken or written LANGUAGE. Features are classified in terms of the various LEVELS of linguistic analysis, e.g. 'PHONETIC/PHONOLOGICAL/GRAMMATICAL/SYNTACTIC features' or in terms of dimensions of DESCRIPTION, e.g. 'ACOUSTIC/ARTICULATORY/AUDITORY features'. At the most general level, features may be classified as linguistic (or 'intralinguistic') as opposed to 'non-linguistic' (EXTRALINGUISTIC or METALINGUISTIC). At the most specific level, certain types of feature may be set up as the minimal UNITS of a theory, as in **distinctive feature** theories of phonology. In GENERATIVE grammatical analysis, the term has come to be associated with the way in which words are classified in the LEXICON in terms of their grammatical properties, such as [animate], [common], [masculine], [countable]. Such features are usually considered to be BINARY, as were phonological features, and analysed as [+animate], [−animate], etc. SEMANTIC features, likewise, can be handled in binary terms, as in the analysis of *spinster* as [+human], [+adult], [+never married] and [+female] (or perhaps, [−male]). Non-binary ('unary' and 'multi-valued') features are also recognized. Features are sometimes referred to as COMPONENTS, especially in semantic analysis. In recent grammatical theories, especially in PHRASE-STRUCTURE grammars, grammatical CATEGORIES are defined in terms of **feature specifications** – ordered pairs containing a feature and a feature value – which rules can access. As part of its method, this approach requires a statement of 'feature-co-occurrence restrictions' and 'feature-specification defaults'. Recent semantic theory has also developed the notion of feature in several directions, notably in the use of **feature structures** which represent TYPES of lexical information organized HIERARCHICALLY. Features (e.g. 'cause', 'change', 'force' as part of the representation of *push*) are here seen as MODAL operators that label arcs between the NODES in a lattice framework. See also CONTEXT, DIACRITIC, DISTINCTIVE FEATURE, SYNTAX.

feature geometry In NON-LINEAR PHONOLOGY, a model of the ways in which FEATURES are organized in phonological representations. Approaches to feature geometry look especially at the non-linear relationship between features, and at the way they can be grouped into a HIERARCHICAL array of functional CLASSES. Feature values are arrayed on separate TIERS (levels, planes, layers . . .), where they may enter into non-linear relations with each other. At the same time, features are organized into hierarchical arrays, in which each CONSTITUENT functions as a single unit in phonological rules. Several models of feature theory have been proposed, such as ARTICULATOR-BASED FEATURE THEORY, CONSTRICTION theory, and UNDERSPECIFICATION.

feedback An extension of the technical use of this term in COMMUNICATION theory, referring to the process whereby the sender of a message obtains a reaction from the receiver which enables a check to be made on the efficiency of the communication. More specifically, some LINGUISTS have suggested it as a defining property of human LANGUAGE (contrasting with the properties of other SEMIOTIC SYSTEMS), whereby speakers are able to monitor their own PERFORMANCE (both by self-observation, and by observing the response-signals of others). The term **complete feedback** is usually used for this property, when it is seen as a 'design feature' of language. In PHONETICS, speakers' awareness of their own production of sound is also referred to as feedback; this may be AUDITORY (via the ear), kinaesthetic (via the internal sensation of ARTICULATORY movement) or vibratory (via bone conduction). **Delayed auditory feedback (DAF)** takes place when a delay is artificially introduced into the transmission of speech between mouth and ear, so that the signal reaches the ear somewhat later than is normally the case. Certain periods of delay cause marked alteration in one's ability to speak with normal fluency; conversely, the speech of stammerers can sometimes be improved by using this technique.

feeding (feed, counter-) A term used in GENERATIVE LINGUISTIC analysis of RULE-ordering and originally introduced in the context of DIACHRONIC PHONOLOGY, to refer to a type of FUNCTIONAL relationship between rules; opposed to BLEEDING. A feeding relationship is one where the application of one rule (A) creates a STRUCTURAL REPRESENTATION to which another rule (B) is applicable, and thus increases ('feeds') the number of forms which can be generated. If rule B is X → Y, then rule A must be of the form W → X. In these circumstances, rule A is called a **feeding rule** in relation to B, and the LINEAR ORDER of these rules is called a **feeding order**. If the rules are applied in the reverse order, A is said to **counter-feed** B. Counter-feeding results in a non-affecting interaction in which a rule fails to realize its potential to increase the number of forms to which another rule applies.

feet see FOOT

felicity conditions A term used in the theory of SPEECH ACTS to refer to the criteria which must be satisfied if the speech act is to achieve its purpose. Several kinds of felicity conditions have been suggested. 'Preparatory conditions' relate to whether the person performing a speech act has the authority to do so (e.g. not everyone is qualified to fine, christen, arrest, etc.). 'Sincerity conditions' relate to whether the speech act is performed sincerely (e.g. the speaker is not lying). 'Essential conditions' relate to the way the speaker is committed to a certain kind of belief or behaviour, having performed a speech act (e.g. accepting an object that one has just requested). For example, felicity conditions which have been suggested for the analysis of indirect requests include the speaker's believing that the hearer has the ability to carry out the request, and the existence of good reasons for making the request in the first place. An UTTERANCE which does not satisfy these conditions cannot function as a valid instance of the type of speech act to which they apply, e.g. *will you drive?* is inappropriate as a request if the speaker knows that the hearer has not learned to drive, and the mutual awareness of this inappropriateness would lead to an interpretation of a different order (e.g. as a joke, as sarcasm, etc.). Such utterances are said to be **infelicitous**.

field (1) A term used in SEMANTICS to refer to the vocabulary of a LANGUAGE viewed as a SYSTEM of interrelated LEXICAL networks, and not as an inventory of independent ITEMS. The theory of **semantic fields** (**field theory**) was developed in Europe in the 1930s (especially by Jost Trier (b. 1894), and later Johann Weisgerber (b. 1899)). Conceptual fields (e.g. colour, kinship) are isolated, and the lexical items used to refer to the various features of these fields are analysed in terms of a network of SENSE relations. This network constitutes the lexical STRUCTURE of the semantic (or 'lexical') field. Several interpretations of this notion can be found in the semantics literature of the period.

(2) In HALLIDAYAN linguistics, **field of discourse** (or simply, 'field') refers to a classification of REGISTERS in terms of subject-matter, e.g. the 'fields' of chemistry, religion, advertising.

(3) The usual sense of the term **fieldwork** (or **field study**) is also used in LINGUISTICS referring to the principles and procedures of obtaining linguistic DATA from INFORMANTS, especially in their home environment.

(4) In TAGMEMICS, the term refers to the analysis of linguistic UNITS in terms of their DISTRIBUTION – as distinct from their status as PARTICLES (physically DISCRETE items) or WAVES (their VARIANT forms).

filled pause A term used by some LINGUISTS to refer to a non-silent PAUSE, i.e. a hesitation which has been 'filled' by *er*, *erm*, or some such VOCALIZATION.

filler A term used in some MODELS of LINGUISTIC analysis, especially TAGMEMICS, to refer to a FORM which can be used at a given place, or SLOT, in a STRUCTURE.

filter (1) A process first recognized in the STANDARD THEORY of GENERATIVE GRAMMAR (cf. ASPECTS), whereby in a DERIVATION only certain BASE PHRASE-MARKERS are transformed into SURFACE STRUCTURES, others being 'filtered out' by the application of various CONSTRAINTS (specified, for example, by the non-lexical TRANSFORMATIONS). It assumes a more central role in GOVERNMENT-BINDING THEORY, where it refers to a type of CONDITION which prevents the generation of UNGRAMMATICAL SENTENCES. Filters state simply that any structure of type X is ILL FORMED. They are also known as 'OUTPUT constraints' or 'surface-structure constraints'. For example, a 'FOR–FOR filter' has been proposed, which states that any surface structure containing the sequence *for–for* is ungrammatical; this thereby excludes the generation of sentences in which VERBS like *hope for* are used along with their *for*+INFINITIVE COMPLEMENTS (cf. *What she is hoping for is for John to win*), as in the ungrammatical **She is hoping for for John to win*.

It is important in recent discussion to distinguish 'filters' from 'constraints': the former apply solely to the structure which is the output of a given set of RULES; the latter apply to two successive stages within a derivation. Filters are claimed to be more general, more UNIVERSAL and more constraining on theory construction than the constraints which restrict the application of specific rules: a filter BLOCKS the generation of a sentence (S), regardless of the set of rules which have applied in generating that sentence, whereas a constraint blocks the application of a *specific* set of rules to produce S (thus allowing the possibility that S might nonetheless be generated by the application of other sets of rules).

(2) See SOURCE (2).

filtered speech In PHONETICS, speech which has been passed through filters (devices which only allow signals of certain FREQUENCIES to pass) to alter its acoustic characteristics. The distorted speech produced is often used in research into SPEECH perception – for example, determining the extent to which words can still be recognized after certain frequencies have been removed.

final The usual way of referring to the last ELEMENT in a LINGUISTIC UNIT, especially in PHONOLOGY. For example, the PHONEME /t/ occurs 'in final position' (or 'finally') in the WORD *cat*; the MORPHEME of plurality occurs in final position in English words. Other positions are referred to as INITIAL and MEDIAL.

finite A term used in the GRAMMATICAL classification of types of VERBS and CLAUSES. A finite verb (PHRASE) is a form that can occur on its own in an independent SENTENCE (or MAIN clause); it permits FORMAL CONTRASTS in TENSE and MOOD. **Non-finite** forms of the verb, on the other hand, occur on their own only in DEPENDENT clauses, and lack tense and mood contrasts. All forms except the INFINITIVES and PARTICIPLES (*-ing* and *-en* forms) are finite, e.g. *is walking, have walked, walks*. Clauses which contain a finite verb are **finite clauses** (these in English always contain a SUBJECT, except in the case of COMMANDS); otherwise, they are non-finite clauses (e.g. *walking down the street, to kick the ball*).

finite-state grammar (finite-state language) A type of GRAMMAR discussed by Noam CHOMSKY in his book *Syntactic Structures* (1957) as an illustration of a simple GENERATIVE DEVICE. Finite-state grammars generate by working through a SENTENCE 'from left to right'; an INITIAL ELEMENT is selected, and thereafter the possibilities of occurrence of all other elements are wholly determined by the nature of the elements preceding them. For example, in the sentence *The* *cat saw the dog*, the grammar would start by specifying the first WORD (i.e. selecting one of the set of possible first words for a sentence in English), would proceed from this 'initial state' to specify the next word (i.e. one of the set of words which can follow *the*), and continue this process until the 'final state' of the sentence has been arrived at. Chomsky shows how this extremely simple kind of grammar is incapable of accounting for many important processes of sentence formation, as in DISCONTINUOUS CONSTRUCTIONS, e.g. *The boys who saw John are going*, where the grammatical relationship of *boys* to *are* cannot be handled in a finite-state grammar. Alternative grammars are discussed by Chomsky which improve on this MODEL in several respects (cf. PHRASE-STRUCTURE and TRANSFORMATIONAL grammars). Finite-state grammars, also called 'one-sided linear grammars', 'regular grammars' and 'Type-3 grammars' (cf. CHOMSKY HIERARCHY), generate **finite-state languages**, which in terms of AUTOMATA theory comprise the smallest class of denumerably infinite languages.

first language see LANGUAGE

Firthian Characteristic of, or a follower of, the LINGUISTIC principles of J(ames) R(upert) **Firth** (1890–1960), Professor of General Linguistics in the University of London (1944–56), and the formative influence on the development of linguistics in Great Britain (the 'London School' of linguistics). A central notion is POLYSYSTEMICISM, an approach to linguistic analysis based on the view that LANGUAGE patterns cannot be accounted for in terms of a single system of analytic principles and categories (MONOSYSTEMIC linguistics), but that different SYSTEMS may need to be set up at different places within a given LEVEL of DESCRIPTION. Other central Firthian notions include his CONTEXTUAL theory of MEANING, with its strong emphasis on the social CONTEXT OF SITUATION; PROSODIC (as opposed to PHONEMIC) PHONOLOGY, and COLLOCATION. Relatively little of Firth's teaching was published, but many of his ideas have been developed by a **neo-Firthian** group of scholars, whose main theoretician is M. A. K. Halliday, Professor of General Linguistics in the University of London from 1965 to 1970 (cf. HALLIDAYAN).

'fis' phenomenon A commonly used name for a behaviour recognized in language ACQUISITION, in which children refuse to accept an adult's IMITATION of their own mispronunciation. The name derives from the first report of this behaviour in the early 1960s, since when several other such names have been used (e.g. the 'wabbit' phenomenon). An investigator referred to a child's toy fish as his /fɪs/, imitating the child's form; the child refused to accept the adult's pronunciation of /fɪs/, despite the fact that his own version was identical. Such phenomena are interpreted as evidence for a more well-developed PERCEPTUAL than PRODUCTIVE LINGUISTIC ability in the young child, some investigators concluding that it is in fact the adult PHONOLOGICAL form which is stored in the child's brain.

fission In some recent models of PHONOLOGY, one of two formal processes used to represent the relationship between MONOPHTHONGS and DIPHTHONGS. In particular, in PARTICLE PHONOLOGY, fission refers to the process which splits one ROOT NODE into two, thus providing a mechanism for handling diphthongization and other types of 'breaking' phenomena.

fixed (1) A term used in LINGUISTICS and PHONETICS to refer to an unchanging aspect of the STRUCTURE of a linguistic UNIT; opposed to FREE. It occurs in such phrases as 'fixed STRESS' (i.e. the stress always falling on a particular SYLLABLE in a WORD, e.g. the penultimate syllable in Welsh), and 'fixed word ORDER' (i.e. languages with word order patterns that cannot be altered without a change of MEANING, e.g. English). See also FORMULAIC LANGUAGE.

(2) See LATENT CONSONANT.

flap(ped) A term used in the PHONETIC classification of CONSONANT sounds on the basis of their MANNER OF ARTICULATION; it refers to any sound produced by a single rapid contact between two organs of articulation (excluding VOCAL CORD vibration). The usual occurrence of this is in the production of types of *r* sound, as when in English *very* the *r* is produced by the TIP of the TONGUE in a 'flapped' articulation against the ALVEOLAR ridge (transcribed [ɾ]). The main PHONETIC contrast is between this sound and the TRILL, where several vibrations are involved. Some phoneticians distinguish systematically between flaps and TAPS, on the grounds that in the case of flaps the articulator which makes the contact is returning to a position of rest, whereas in the case of taps this is not so, and the contact resembles a very rapid STOP articulation. Such a distinction has been cited for Hausa and Tamil, but it is not common.

flat (1) A term used in LINGUISTICS to refer to a structure which has no HIERARCHICAL constituency. For example, in GRAMMATICAL theory, SENTENCES have a flat structure if they lack the NP–VP configuration. NON-CONFIGURATIONAL LANGUAGES with free WORD ORDER are analysed as having a flat structure. In PHONOLOGY, a flat analysis of the word *cat* would be *c+a+t*, ignoring possible intermediate notions such as ONSET, RHYME, etc.

(2) One of the features of sound set up by JAKOBSON and Halle in their DISTINCTIVE FEATURE theory of PHONOLOGY, to handle lip-ROUNDING, the opposite being PLAIN. Flat sounds are defined ARTICULATORILY and ACOUSTICALLY, as those involving a relatively narrow mouth opening with accompanying velarization (cf. VELAR), and a weakening of the high-frequency components of the sound spectrum. Lip-ROUNDED sounds all have the feature [+flat], as would RETROFLEX, velarized and pharyngealized (cf. PHARYNX) sounds; unrounded sounds are [−flat], as are all sounds lacking these SECONDARY ARTICULATIONS.

(3) See SLIT.

floating (flotation) (1) In GENERATIVE LINGUISTICS, a term referring to an element which has no fixed association with a place in a DERIVATION. In particular, it is used in some models of NON-LINEAR PHONOLOGY for a unit which is not ASSOCIATED to some higher level of PROSODIC structure (i.e. it is not prosodically LICENSED). For example, LATENT CONSONANTS (e.g. French LIAISON) have no SKELETAL slot, and are therefore floating, whereas fixed consonants are ANCHORED. A 'floating TONE' is one which has been separated from a SYLLABLE following the application of a phonological RULE, and now has no association with any particular tone-bearing unit in the representation. The term 'docking' is sometimes used to refer to the process whereby a floating unit is re-attached to a REPRESENTATION: for example, a floating tone would 'dock' with a syllable if it were assigned to a VOWEL already carrying a tone or to a toneless vowel.

In AUTOSEGMENTAL PHONOLOGY, the term 'floating trace' is used with two applications: to a MORPHEME whose UNDERLYING representation is composed of SEGMENTS only on a tonal TIER; and to a segment which, at a given point in a DERIVATION, is not ASSOCIATED with any vowel (as a consequence of a vowel becoming DELETED).

(2) The term is also used in GENERATIVE SYNTAX for an element which is able to move from one position to another in a SENTENCE STRUCTURE. The best-known examples are 'floating QUANTIFIERS' like *all* and *both*, as in *Both the cars have been painted* / *The cars have both been painted.*

focal area see AREA

focus A term used by some LINGUISTS in a two-part analysis of SENTENCES which distinguishes between the INFORMATION assumed by speakers, and that which is at the centre (or 'focus') of their communicative interest; 'focus' in this sense is opposed to PRESUPPOSITION. (The CONTRAST between GIVEN and NEW information makes an analogous distinction.) For example, in the sentence *It was* ***Mary*** *who came to tea, Mary* is the focus (as the INTONATION contour helps to signal). Taking such factors into account is an important aspect of inter-sentence relationships: it would not be possible to have the above sentence as the answer to the question *What did Mary do?*, but only to *Who came to tea?*

folk etymology see ETYMOLOGY

foot (1) (**de-**) A term used by some PHONETICIANS and PHONOLOGISTS to describe the UNIT of RHYTHM in LANGUAGES displaying ISOCHRONY, i.e. where the STRESSED SYLLABLES fall at approximately regular intervals throughout an UTTERANCE. It is an extension of the term used in traditional studies of metrical verse structure, where the many regular patterns of stressed/unstressed syllable sequence were given a detailed classification (e.g. 'iambic' for an unstressed+stressed (˘/) pattern: 'trochaic' for a stressed+unstressed (/˘) pattern; 'spondaic' for a pattern of two stresses; 'dactylic' for /˘˘; 'anapaestic' for ˘˘/). In a more general phonological sense, the notion is applied to any utterance in a STRESS-TIMED language, not just verse. The rhythm of an utterance, in this approach, is analysed first in terms of INTONATION units, and these are analysed into feet, e.g. /the ˈman is ˈwalking in the gàrden/ is a single TONE UNIT consisting of three feet. The term has particular relevance in several models of NON-LINEAR PHONOLOGY, such as METRICAL PHONOLOGY, where it refers to an underlying unit of metrical structure (or **stress-foot**), consisting of syllable RHYMES, and organized into CONSTITUENTS that make up phonological WORDS. Feet are classified as 'left-headed' (the leftmost rhyme is stressed) or 'right-headed' (the rightmost rhyme is stressed). Feet no longer than two syllables in length are **bounded feet**; a foot containing only one syllable is called a **degenerate foot**; the DELETION of a foot from a REPRESENTATION is sometimes called **defooting**. In later metrical theory, **foot dominance** is a foot-shape PARAMETER which determines the side of the foot where the head is located: in left-DOMINANT feet, all left nodes are dominant and right nodes RECESSIVE; in right-dominant feet, the reverse situation obtains. In PROSODIC MORPHOLOGY, the foot is a member of the prosodic HIERARCHY of MORA, syllable, foot and (prosodic) word.

(2) In the phrase **foot-feature principle**, the term is used in GENERALIZED

PHRASE-STRUCTURE GRAMMAR: it refers to a principle governing the DISTRIBUTION of FEATURES which express information that CONSTITUENTS are missing or have to be bound to some constituent (cf. BINDING).

foregrounding (foreground) A term used in STYLISTICS (especially POETICS) and sometimes in PRAGMATICS and DISCOURSE analysis, to refer to relative prominence in discourse, often involving deviance from a linguistic NORM; the analogy is of a figure seen against a background (and the rest of the text is often referred to as **backgrounding**). The deviant or prominent feature is said to have been 'foregrounded'. For example, the use of rhyme, alliteration and metrical regularity are examples of foregrounding operating at the level of PHONOLOGY.

foreign language see LANGUAGE

forensic linguistics In LINGUISTICS, the use of linguistic techniques to investigate crimes in which language data forms part of the evidence, such as in the use of GRAMMATICAL or LEXICAL criteria to authenticate police statements. The field of **forensic phonetics** is often distinguished as a separate domain, dealing with such matters as speaker identification, voice line-ups, speaker profiling, tape enhancement, tape authentication, and the decoding of disputed utterances.

form(al) One of the most widely used terms in LINGUISTICS, with a correspondingly wide range of meanings. Its main areas of application are:

(1) **form** *v.* **meaning/function**. In its most general sense, it refers to the abstract PHONOLOGICAL and/or GRAMMATICAL characterization of LANGUAGE, as opposed to its MEANING, as in such phrases as 'linguistic form', 'grammatical form'. More specifically, it refers to the phonological/grammatical/LEXICAL characteristics of linguistic UNITS, such as SENTENCES, MORPHEMES, LEXEMES, NOUNS, etc., these being referred to as **linguistic forms**. The term here is often contrasted with FUNCTION: one can study a unit such as the noun PHRASE from both formal and functional points of view (e.g. its internal syntactic structure *v.* its role as SUBJECT, OBJECT, etc., in a clause). More specifically still, it refers to a particular instance of a grammatical CATEGORY, as in such phrases as 'the analysis of the forms *be, seem, have* . . .' A set of forms displaying similar or identical grammatical FEATURES is said to constitute a **form-class**, e.g. *walk, come, see* are part of the form-CLASS of VERBS because they have similar MORPHOLOGICAL characteristics and SYNTACTIC DISTRIBUTION. Phonological/grammatical criteria which identify units and classes are known as **formal criteria**. 'Formal' here is also contrasted with the 'notional' approach of TRADITIONAL grammar, where attempts were made to characterize linguistic units in terms of UNIVERSAL notions, as in the definition of a sentence as 'the expression of a complete thought'.

(2) **form** *v.* **substance**. Here, the term refers to the overall linguistic organization, or STRUCTURE, of speech or writing, as opposed to the physical REALIZATION of language in PHONIC or GRAPHIC SUBSTANCE. In this sense, SEMANTIC structure is included, along with grammar and phonology/GRAPHOLOGY, being part of the abstract language system.

(3) **form** *v.* **substance** and **meaning**. HALLIDAYAN linguistic theory models language in terms of three interdependent LEVELS: the level of 'form' (comprising the grammatical and lexical organization of language) is distinguished from the levels of SUBSTANCE and CONTEXT.

(4) **forms** (of a unit). The variant realizations of a linguistic unit are referred to as 'forms' of the unit, i.e. the members of a set of PARADIGMATIC alternatives. For example, the forms of the verb *walk* are *walk, walking, walks*, etc.

(5) The critical characteristics of a linguistic theory, especially as stated in the FORMALIZED terms of logic or mathematics, are referred to as the 'form' of that theory. In GENERATIVE grammar, the formal characteristics of linguistic theory have received special attention, especially in the notion of 'formal UNIVERSALS'. **Formal semantics** refers to analysis (in terms of truth conditions, etc.) of a logical system, such as PROPOSITIONAL calculus – an approach which has come to be applied to the study of natural languages (cf. MONTAGUE GRAMMAR).

(6) **formal(ity)** In STYLISTIC and SOCIOLINGUISTIC studies, **formal** is opposed to such terms as **informal**, 'intimate', 'familiar', etc., as part of a system of 'formality' of expression, referring to a level of language considered APPROPRIATE to socially formal situations.

formalist A term applied in STYLISTICS to any approach which regards a TEXT as a FORMAL object of study, with an internal STRUCTURE that can be objectively and formally identified. Such approaches have been primarily associated with East European STRUCTURAL linguists.

formalize (formalism, formalization) A characteristic of formulations in LINGUISTICS – and especially a primary goal of GENERATIVE analyses – whereby the RULES, PRINCIPLES, CONDITIONS, etc. governing an analysis are capable of being specified in a precise and rigorous way. Ultimately it ought to be possible, in any **formalization**, for a linguistic analysis to be FORMALLY interpreted in logical or mathematical terms, and a calculus developed. A 'formalized' account of an area of LANGUAGE, in this sense, is opposed to an 'informal' one. A specific feature, or set of features, used as part of the process of formalization, is known as a **formalism**.

formant A term in ACOUSTIC PHONETICS of particular value in the classification of VOWELS and vowel-like sounds, and of TRANSITIONAL features between vowels and adjacent sounds. A formant is a concentration of acoustic energy, reflecting the way air from the lungs vibrates in the VOCAL TRACT, as it changes its shape. For any vowel, the air vibrates at many different frequencies all at once, and the most dominant frequencies combine to produce the distinctive vowel QUALITIES. Each dominant band of frequencies constitutes a formant, which shows up clearly in a record produced by a sound SPECTROGRAPH as a thick black line. Three main formants provide the basis of vowel description: the 'first formant' is the lowest, and the 'second' and 'third formants' are respectively higher. Other formants are less significant for linguistic analysis. The formants can be related to the ARTICULATORY DESCRIPTIONS of vowels, as represented, say, by the CARDINAL VOWEL diagram. The first formant, for example, decreases in its frequency as one moves from low to high (e.g. *sat* → *set* → *seat*). In the case of CONSONANTS, similar correlations can be established: for example, in the transition from VELAR consonants, the second and third formants come very close together.

formation rule A term used in relation to the GENERATIVE SEMANTICS MODEL of

LINGUISTICS to refer to the initial set of RULES which generate the semantic REPRESENTATIONS of SENTENCES.

formative A formally identifiable, irreducible GRAMMATICAL ELEMENT which enters into the construction of larger LINGUISTIC UNITS, such as WORDS and SENTENCES. It has come to be used especially in GENERATIVE grammar, as an alternative to the term MORPHEME, for the TERMINAL elements in a SURFACE-STRUCTURE REPRESENTATION of a sentence. Several types of formative can be distinguished, depending on their role in sentence structure, e.g.'inflectional formatives' (viz. INFLECTIONAL endings, etc.), 'lexical formatives' (viz. forms which enable one LEXICAL item to be derived from another, e.g. *-tion*).

form of address see ADDRESS

formulaic language A term used in some theoretical and DESCRIPTIVE studies of GRAMMAR to refer to UTTERANCES which lack normal SYNTACTIC OR MORPHOLOGICAL characteristics. (It may also be used, literally, to mean 'language containing formulae', or special symbols, as in scientific writing.) Sentences such as *God save the Queen, The more the merrier, How do you do?* and *Many happy returns* do not contrast in the usual way with other sentences in the language, e.g. *Few happy returns, How will you do?* Such FOSSILIZED structures, often used in limited social situations, have also been called 'bound', 'fixed', 'frozen', 'set', 'prefabricated' or 'STEREOTYPED expressions'. The notion can be broadened from individual utterances to larger spoken or written events. **Formulaic discourse** refers to any fixed form of words which serves a particular social purpose, such as greeting exchanges, skipping rhymes, or the words of a marriage ceremony; it contrasts with **free discourse**.

form word A term sometimes used in WORD classification for a word whose role is largely or wholly grammatical, e.g. ARTICLES, PRONOUNS, CONJUNCTIONS. Several such terms exist for this notion (e.g. FUNCTION WORD, GRAMMATICAL word, FUNCTOR); all contrast with the LEXICAL words in a language, which carry the main SEMANTIC content.

fortis A term used in the PHONETIC classification of CONSONANT sounds on the basis of their MANNER OF ARTICULATION: it refers to a sound made with a relatively strong degree of muscular effort and breath force, compared with some other sound (known as LENIS). The distinction between TENSE and LAX is used similarly. The labels 'strong' and 'weak' are sometimes used for the contrast involved, but these are more prone to AMBIGUITY. In English, it is the VOICELESS consonants ([p], [t], [f], [s], etc.) which tend to be produced with fortis articulation (their voiced counterparts being relatively weak), and often, when the voicing distinction is reduced, it is only the degree of articulatory strength which maintains a contrast between sounds. The term 'fortis' is sometimes used loosely to refer to strong VOWEL articulation also, but this is not a standard practice.

fortition A term used in PHONOLOGY to refer to a strengthening in the overall force of a sound, whether DIACHRONICALLY or SYNCHRONICALLY; opposed to **lenition**. Typically, fortition involves the change from a FRICATIVE to a STOP, an APPROXIMANT to a fricative, or a VOICED to a voiceless sound (as in the devoicing of final OBSTRUENTS in German).

fossilized (fossilization) (1) A term used in GRAMMAR and LEXICOLOGY to refer to a type of CONSTRUCTION which is no longer PRODUCTIVE in a LANGUAGE. In English, for example, fossilized SENTENCES include *So be it, Long live the Queen* and *Least said, soonest mended*; fossilized LEXICAL items include such REDUPLICATIVE forms as *goody-goody, hocus-pocus*, and several types of IDIOM.

(2) In the acquisition of a foreign language, the stabilization of a level of achievement in the use of a linguistic form which falls short of the norms of the target language. No further learning takes place, and the form becomes a fossilized error in the usage of the learner, part of the learner's INTERLANGUAGE.

frame A term used in some MODELS of GRAMMATICAL DESCRIPTION to refer to the STRUCTURAL CONTEXT within which a CLASS OF ITEMS can be used. For example, the frame *She saw – box* provides an ENVIRONMENT for the use of DETERMINERS (*the, a, my*, etc.). The terms **syntactic frame** and **substitution frame** are also used. In GENERATIVE grammar, **sub-categorization frames** are used to specify the range of SISTER CONSTITUENTS which a LEXICAL item takes. In CASE grammar, the array of cases which specifies the structural context for VERBS is known as a **case frame**. In LEXICAL entries for verbs, in this theory, abbreviated statements called **frame features** indicate the set of case frames into which the various verbs may be inserted. In SEMANTIC theory, frames are structures that encode knowledge about STEREOTYPED kinds of objects or situations, with special provision for the roles played by their parts or participants.

free A term used in a range of LINGUISTIC contexts to refer to a PHONOLOGICAL or GRAMMATICAL feature lacking a specific type of FORMAL CONSTRAINT. For example, a 'free FORM' or 'free MORPHEME' is a minimal grammatical UNIT which can be used as a WORD without the need for further MORPHOLOGICAL modification (opposed to BOUND); 'free word order' occurs when the word ORDER in a LANGUAGE can be altered without a consequent change of MEANING (opposed to FIXED); 'free STRESS' occurs whenever there is a fixed place for the primary stress to fall in a POLYSYLLABIC word; 'free discourse' is spoken or written expression which makes no use of FORMULAIC LANGUAGE, unlike 'formulaic discourse.' In the GENERATIVE linguistic theory of BINDING, the term is applied to CONSTITUENTS which are not BOUND, i.e. they are not formally related through CO-INDEXING to a C-COMMANDING ARGUMENT.

The main use of the term is in the phrase **free variation** in phonology, referring to the SUBSTITUTABILITY of one sound for another in a given ENVIRONMENT, with no consequent change in the word's MEANING, as when a speaker articulates a word like *sit* with an unreleased or a released PLOSIVE, or different pronunciations are given to *either* (/iːðə/ *v.* /aɪðə/). These different phonetic realizations of a PHONEME are called 'free variants' (opposed to the 'contextual variants' found in cases of COMPLEMENTARY DISTRIBUTION). In traditional phonological study, free variation has been considered to be an area of little importance; but in recent SOCIOLINGUISTIC studies it is suggested that free variants need to be described, in terms of the frequency with which they occur, because the choice of one variant rather than another may be made on sociological grounds, as when one 'chooses' a careful rather than a 'casual' speech style.

The term 'free variation' is occasionally applied analogously in grammar and SEMANTICS, as when SYNONYMOUS expressions might be said to be in 'free variation'.

frequency A term derived from the study of the physics of sound, and used in ACOUSTIC PHONETICS, referring to the number of complete CYCLES of VOCAL CORD vibration in a unit of time (per second). It is measured in Hertz (Hz), a term which has replaced the older 'cycles per second'. An increase in the frequency of a sound correlates with an auditory sensation of higher PITCH. See also FUNDAMENTAL.

frequentative A term sometimes used in the GRAMMATICAL classification of VERBS to refer to the expression of repeated action. In some LANGUAGES (e.g. Russian) the CLASS may be marked MORPHOLOGICALLY, but in English the MEANING is normally expressed through ADVERBIALS of frequency, e.g. *again, regularly, often*.

fricative A term used in the PHONETIC classification of CONSONANT sounds on the basis of their MANNER OF ARTICULATION: also sometimes called **spirant**, it refers to sounds made when two organs come so close together that the air moving between them produces audible FRICTION. There is no complete CLOSURE between the organs (in which case a PLOSIVE articulation would be produced): there is simply a STRICTURE, or narrowing. There are several such sounds in English, both VOICED and voiceless, as in *fin* [f], *van* [v], *thin* [θ], *this* [ð], *sin* [s], *zoo* [z], *ship* [ʃ], *measure* [ʒ], *hoop* [h]. Other fricative sounds may be heard in English, in restricted CONTEXTS or speech STYLES, such as the PALATAL fricative [ç], and several other fricatives may be heard in other languages, e.g. a voiceless VELAR fricative [x] in Welsh or German, a voiceless PHARYNGEAL fricative [ħ] in Arabic, a voiced BILABIAL fricative [β] in Spanish. The fricative manner of articulation produces a wider range of speech sounds than any other. They are sounds with a potential for considerable DURATION (e.g. *s-s-s*), and, from this point of view, the opposite of fricative (i.e. a continuant sound lacking friction) is called a FRICTIONLESS CONTINUANT. The term 'spirantization' is sometimes used for the process of deriving a fricative from some other type of articulation.

friction A term used in PHONETICS to refer to the sound produced when air passes a CONSTRICTION made in the VOCAL TRACT. The occurrence of **audible friction** is part of the phonetic definition of CONSONANTS; the phonetic definition of VOWELS requires that they be FRICTIONLESS. Various types of friction can be identified, in terms of anatomical point of origin, e.g. BILABIAL friction, PHARYNGEAL friction; friction above the GLOTTIS may be referred to as SUPRAGLOTTAL friction.

frictionless (continuant) A general term used in the PHONETIC classification of speech sounds on the basis of their MANNER OF ARTICULATION: it refers to any sound functioning as a CONSONANT but which lacks the CLOSURE or FRICTION which identifies most consonantal articulations. In RECEIVED PRONUNCIATION, /r/ is often articulated in this way, with no audible friction. From a PHONETIC point of view, all VOWELS and vowel-like sounds are also technically 'frictionless' and 'continuant', but it is usual to restrict the term to those sounds which are consonantal in function. All NASALS and LATERALS are thus classifiable under this heading, as well as many varieties of /r/. In received pronunciation, the POST-AVEOLAR /r/ is often articulated in this way, without audible friction, and is often described specifically as a 'post-alveolar frictionless continuant'. Some phoneticians use the term APPROXIMANT to refer to these sounds.

front(-ing, -ed) In PHONETICS, classifications of front speech sounds are of two types: (a) those ARTICULATED in the front part of the mouth (as opposed to the BACK); (b) those articulated by the front part (or BLADE) of the TONGUE. Front sounds which satisfy both criteria would be front VOWELS, as in *see, bit, pet, cap*, and such front CONSONANTS as the initial sound of *two, do, see, zoo, this, thin*. Consonants such as those in *pay* and *bay* are, however, front in sense (a) only. Front vowels, it should be noted, are in traditional phonetic classification contrasted with CENTRAL and BACK vowels. In DISTINCTIVE FEATURE analyses of sound SYSTEMS, front in sense (a) is referred to as ANTERIOR, in sense (b) is referred to as CORONAL.

In some analyses of sound patterns, it is useful to talk about **fronting**, a process common in historical sound change, and when children are learning to speak, whereby a sound (or group of sounds) may come to be articulated further forward in the mouth than the accepted adult norms. It is also often useful to analyse one sound as being 'fronted' when compared with a back variant of the same PHONEME: for example the /k/ phoneme in English has both front and back VARIANTS (as in *key* and *car* respectively) owing to the influence of the following vowel. The analogous terms 'backing'/'backed', are not commonly used.

(2) **Fronting** is also a term used in TRANSFORMATIONAL GRAMMAR referring to any transformation which transposes a CONSTITUENT from the middle or end of a STRING to initial position. For example, the rule of '*Wh*-fronting' places a WH-PHRASE (e.g. *where, which books*) in initial position, transposing it from the underlying non-initial position (cf. *John walked there* → *John walked where* → *where did John walk*).

frozen expression see FORMULAIC LANGUAGE

FSP The usual abbreviation for FUNCTIONAL SENTENCE PERSPECTIVE.

f-structure An abbreviation in LEXICAL-FUNCTIONAL GRAMMAR for **functional structure**, a REPRESENTATION of a SENTENCE in terms of grammatical FUNCTIONS such as SUBJECT and OBJECT. It contrasts with C-STRUCTURE (or constituent structure), the SURFACE STRUCTURE of the sentence.

full A term sometimes used in the GRAMMATICAL CLASSIFICATION of WORDS to refer to one of two postulated major classes in LANGUAGE, the other being EMPTY. 'Full words' are said to be those which contain LEXICAL MEANING (e.g. *table, man, go, red*) as opposed to empty words, which have a purely grammatical role. The distinction has come under criticism, largely on the grounds that the boundary between 'full' and 'empty' words is not as clear-cut as is suggested. Words like *while, but, in*, etc., are considered to be grammatical words, but they plainly do have some independently stateable meaning.

'Full' may also be encountered as part of the specification of types of grammatical UNIT, e.g. 'full verb' (i.e. the lexical VERB in the verb PHRASE), 'full sentence' (i.e. a MAJOR SENTENCE type, consisting of SUBJECT and PREDICATE), 'full predication' (in FUNCTIONAL GRAMMAR).

function(al) One of the most widely used terms in LINGUISTICS, with a correspondingly wide range of meanings. There are three main areas of application.

(1) The relationship between a linguistic FORM and other parts of the linguistic pattern or SYSTEM in which it is used. In GRAMMAR, for example, the NOUN PHRASE can 'function' in CLAUSE structure as SUBJECT, OBJECT, COMPLEMENT etc., these roles being defined distributionally. **Syntactic functions** (or 'syntactic relations' or 'grammatical relations') of this kind are a major feature of several MODELS of linguistic analysis, including the approaches of the PRAGUE SCHOOL, GLOSSEMATICS, RELATIONAL GRAMMAR and LEXICAL FUNCTIONAL GRAMMAR, and the terms **functional analysis** and **functional linguistics** have been used to characterize theories which treat the notion of function as central (cf. also FUNCTIONAL SENTENCE PERSPECTIVE, FUNCTIONAL GRAMMAR). In GOVERNMENT-BINDING THEORY and PHRASE-STRUCTURE grammars, grammatical functions are notions defined in terms of the position in clause structure of a constituent; in relational and lexical functional grammars they are PRIMITIVES. Functional explanations of grammatical phenomena are also to be found in COMMUNICATIVE and DISCOURSE-based grammars. More specifically, the term functional is used of an ELEMENT which is DISTINCTIVE, or CONTRASTIVE, within a language system, as in one definition of PHONOLOGY as **functional phonetics**. See also AXIOM, CATEGORY.

(2) The use made of a linguistic contrast in a SYSTEM is sometimes referred to as its **functional load** or **yield**. The term is usually used with reference to phonology, where in English, for example, the contrast between /p/ and /b/ would be said to have a higher functional load than between /ʃ/ and /ʒ/: the former contrast distinguishes many MINIMAL PAIRS, whereas the latter contrast distinguishes only a few. Several criteria are used in making such quantitative judgements, such as the position within a WORD at which the contrast is found, and the frequency of occurrence of the words in the language.

(3) The role language plays in the context of society or the individual is also referred to by the term 'function' (**social function**). For example, language is used ('functions') to communicate ideas, to express attitudes, and so on. It may also be used to identify specific SOCIOLINGUISTIC situations, such as informality or intimacy, or VARIETIES of language such as science and law: in such cases, one might talk, for instance, of the 'function' of scientific language being to express a certain mode of experience in a certain way, and so on. Several detailed classifications of the social functions of language have been made, especially in HALLIDAYAN linguistics, and in relation to PRAGMATICS and the theory of SPEECH ACTS. The traditional classification of SENTENCE functions falls between grammatical and SPEECH-ACT theory: sentences are said to 'function' as STATEMENTS, QUESTIONS, COMMANDS, etc. In narratology, the term is used in the analysis of plots for a type of action performed by one or more types of character, such as 'Villain harms member of family'. See also NARRATIVE.

functional grammar A LINGUISTIC theory which was devised in the 1970s as an alternative to the abstract, FORMALIZED view of LANGUAGE presented by TRANSFORMATIONAL GRAMMAR, and relying instead on a PRAGMATIC view of language as social interaction. The approach focuses on the RULES which govern verbal interaction, seen as a form of co-operative activity, and on the rules (of SYNTAX, SEMANTICS and PHONOLOGY) which govern the linguistic expressions that are used as instruments of this activity. In this approach, a PREDICATE is taken to be the basic element of a 'predication'; it is listed in the LEXICON in the form of a 'predicate frame', specified for the number of ARGUMENTS it takes (AGENT, GOAL, etc.). From predicate frames, 'NUCLEAR predications' are formed by inserting appropriate terms into the argument positions. 'Full predications' are formed from nuclear predications through the use of SATELLITES (e.g. MANNER, LOCATIVE). Syntactic functions (interpreted semantically) and pragmatic functions are then ASSIGNED to elements of predication, and expressed in SENTENCES through the use of 'expression rules' (which deal with such matters as CASE, AGREEMENT, ORDER and INTONATION).

functional sentence perspective (FSP) A theory of LINGUISTIC analysis associated with the modern exponents of the PRAGUE SCHOOL of linguistics. It refers to an analysis of UTTERANCES (or texts) in terms of the INFORMATION they contain, the role of each utterance part being evaluated for its SEMANTIC contribution to the whole. The notion of 'COMMUNICATIVE dynamism' has been developed as an attempt to rate these different LEVELS of contribution within a structure, particularly with reference to the concepts of RHEME and THEME.

functional structure see F-STRUCTURE

function word A term sometimes used in WORD classification for a word whose role is largely or wholly grammatical, e.g. ARTICLES, PRONOUNS, CONJUNCTIONS. Several such terms exist for this notion (e.g. FORM WORD, GRAMMATICAL word, FUNCTOR, EMPTY word); all contrast with the LEXICAL words in a language, which carry the main SEMANTIC content.

functor A term sometimes used in WORD classification for words and BOUND MORPHEMES whose role in language is largely or wholly grammatical, such as PREPOSITIONS, ARTICLES, PRONOUNS, CONJUNCTIONS. Several such terms relate to this notion (e.g. FUNCTION WORD, GRAMMATICAL word, FORM word, EMPTY word); all contrast with the LEXICAL words in a language, which carry the main SEMANTIC content.

fundamental (frequency) A term derived from the study of the physics of sound, and used in ACOUSTIC PHONETICS, referring to the lowest FREQUENCY component in a complex sound wave (other components being known as the 'harmonics'). The 'fundamental', or F_0 ('f nought'), is of particular importance in studies of INTONATION, where it displays a reasonably close correspondence with the PITCH movements involved.

fusion In some recent models of PHONOLOGY, a type of RULE which accounts for various processes of FEATURE COALESCENCE; also called **merger**, and contrasted with **fission**. In particular, in PARTICLE PHONOLOGY, fusion is a process which merges two ROOT NODES into one, thus providing a mechanism for handling MONOPHTHONGIZATION.

fusional (fuse, fusion) A type of LANGUAGE sometimes distinguished in COMPARATIVE LINGUISTICS using STRUCTURAL (as opposed to historical) criteria, and focusing on the characteristics of the WORD: in **fusional languages**, words typically contain more than one MORPHEME, but there is no one-to-one correspondence between these morphemes and the linear SEQUENCE of MORPHS the words contain. Languages such as Latin and Sanskrit represent this type, also known as INFLECTING languages. For example, in Latin *amicus* ('friend'), this form 'fuses' the features masculine, NOMINATIVE and singular, in addition to the ROOT, in a manner which makes the word extremely difficult to segment morphologically (except by WORD-AND-PARADIGM techniques). As always in such classifications, the categories are not clear-cut: different languages will display the characteristic of 'fusion' to a greater or lesser degree.

The term is also used, independently of this classification, to refer to the merging of exponents within a linguistic unit, especially a word; e.g. *took* represents the 'fusion' of *take+past*; sounds may be 'fused' in some types of ASSIMILATION.

future tense In GRAMMAR, a TENSE form which refers to future time, as in French *J'irai* 'I'll go'. English has no INFLECTIONAL future tense, but has many ways of referring to future time, such as through the use of the MODAL verbs *will/shall*, future-time ADVERBIALS (*tomorrow, next week*), and such verbs as *be about to*. The *will/shall* forms are usually called 'future tenses' in TRADITIONAL grammar, but many linguists consider this to be misleading, as these forms express several other meanings than future time (such as timelessness in *Stones will sink in water*). Analogously, the use of *will/shall have* was called the **future perfect tense** (or the 'future in the past') in traditional grammar.

fuzzy A term derived from mathematics and used by some LINGUISTS to refer to the INDETERMINACY involved in the analysis of a linguistic UNIT or PATTERN. For example, several LEXICAL ITEMS, it is argued, are best regarded as representing a SEMANTIC CATEGORY which has an INVARIANT core with a variable (or 'fuzzy') boundary, this allowing for flexibility of APPLICATION to a wide range of entities, given the appropriate CONTEXT. The difficulty of defining the boundaries of *cup* and *glass* has been a well-studied example of this indeterminacy. Other items which lend 'fuzziness' to language include *sort of, rather, quite*, etc. (and see also SQUISH). **Fuzzy grammars**, advocated in the early 1970s, were grammars capable of generating sentences with specific degrees of assigned grammaticality. The notion is seen as particularly important in NON-DISCRETE GRAMMAR.

G

gap A term used in LINGUISTICS to refer to the absence of a linguistic UNIT at a place in a pattern of relationships where one might have been expected. The term occurs especially in SEMANTICS, where a 'LEXICAL gap' can be illustrated by the absence of a male *v.* female distinction within the term *cousin* (cf. *brother/ sister, uncle/aunt*, etc.). An example of a PHONOLOGICAL 'gap' or 'hole in the pattern' would be a LANGUAGE where the PHONEMIC CONTRASTS /p/, /b/ and /t/, /d/ were not matched by a corresponding velar pair, only /k/ being found. An example of a SYNTACTIC 'gap' would be the UNDERLYING DIRECT OBJECT position in *Who did you invite—?*. Gaps are often assumed to contain phonologically EMPTY categories (symbolized as *e*). A PARASITIC GAP is postulated when the presence of a syntactic gap depends on the prior existence of another gap in the structure of the sentence. See also PATTERN.

gapping A term proposed in GENERATIVE GRAMMAR to refer to the absence of a repeated VERB in CLAUSES which have been CONJOINED – a 'gap' appears in the reduced clause, e.g. *she went to London and he to New York.*

GB The abbreviation for GOVERNMENT-BINDING THEORY.

geminate (gemination) A term used in PHONETICS and PHONOLOGY for a SEQUENCE of identical adjacent SEGMENTS of a sound in a single MORPHEME, e.g. Italian *notte* /nɔtte/ ('night'). Because of the SYLLABLE division, a geminate sequence cannot be regarded as simply a 'long' CONSONANT, and TRANSCRIPTIONAL differences usually indicate this, e.g. [-ff-] is geminate, [-fː] is long. The special behaviour of geminates has been a particular focus in some approaches to NON-LINEAR PHONOLOGY, as a part of the discussion of the way in which QUANTITATIVE phenomena should be represented. Those long segments which cannot be separated by EPENTHETIC vowels ('true' geminates, represented with multiple ASSOCIATION) are said to display geminate 'inseparability' or 'integrity'. Those which fail to undergo rules because only one part of the structure satisfies the structural description are said to display geminate 'inalterability'. True geminates are contrasted with 'fake' or 'apparent' geminates, where identical segments have been made ADJACENT through morphological CONCATENATION.

gender A GRAMMATICAL CATEGORY used for the analysis of WORD-CLASSES displaying such CONTRASTS as masculine/feminine/neuter, ANIMATE/inanimate, etc. Discussion of this concept in LINGUISTICS has generally focused upon the need to distinguish **natural gender**, where items refer to the sex of real-world entities, and **grammatical gender**, which has nothing to do with sex, but which has an important role in signalling grammatical relationships between words in a SENTENCE (ADJECTIVES agreeing with NOUNS, etc.). The gender SYSTEMS of French, German, Latin, etc., are grammatical, as shown by the FORM of the ARTICLE (e.g. *le* v. *la*) or of the noun (e.g. nouns ending in *-a* are feminine). Grammatical gender is not a feature of English, though some parts of the language can be analysed in such terms (e.g. the correlation between PRONOUNS, *he/she* co-occurring with *who/whose*, etc., whereas *it* co-occurs with *which*). English gender contrasts are on the whole natural, viz. *he* refers to male people, animals, etc. The few cases of other kinds of usage (e.g. *a ship* being referred to as *she*) pose interesting problems which have attracted considerable discussion in linguistics.

genealogical classification see GENETIC CLASSIFICATION

general (1) A commonly used characterization of LINGUISTICS, when one wants to emphasize the UNIVERSAL applicability of linguistic theory and method in the study of LANGUAGES. **General linguistics** thus includes the theoretical, DESCRIPTIVE and COMPARATIVE biases of the subject. It is sometimes seen in contrast with those branches of linguistics where there is an interdisciplinary or applied orientation (as in SOCIOLINGUISTICS, APPLIED LINGUISTICS). A similar use of the term is in the phrase **general grammar** found in several early language studies (e.g. the PORT ROYAL GRAMMAR), and often used in GENERATIVE linguistic contexts in the sense of 'UNIVERSAL grammar'. **General phonetics** emphasizes the applicability of phonetic methods of analysis to all human speech sounds. **General semantics**, by contrast, has nothing to do with linguistics in its modern sense, referring to a philosophical movement developed in the 1930s by the American scholar Alfred Korzybski (1879–1950), which aimed to make people aware of the conventional relationship between words and things, as a means of improving systems of communication and clear thinking.

(2) (**-ize(d), -ity, -ization**) A property of those linguistic analyses and descriptive statements which are applicable to a relatively wide range of DATA in a language, and which are expressed in relatively abstract terms. A statement which can be made only with reference to individual UNITS (e.g. LEXICAL ITEMS, sounds, CONSTRUCTIONS), or to small CLASSES of units, is said to 'lack generality'. The aim of the linguist is to make **generalizations** about data which need as few qualifications as possible (e.g. about exceptions, or restricted CONTEXTS of use), and which are MEANINGFUL to NATIVE-SPEAKERS (i.e. they are LINGUISTICALLY SIGNIFICANT GENERALIZATIONS). Likewise, linguistic theories should be as 'general' as possible, i.e. aiming to establish the universal characteristics of human language. Within this broad approach, the term has been given several specific applications, e.g. in GENERALIZED PHRASE-STRUCTURE GRAMMAR, or in the 'true generalization condition' of natural generative PHONOLOGY – a constraint which insists that all rules should express generalizations about the relationship between all SURFACE-STRUCTURE FORMS in the most direct and TRANSPARENT manner possible. Phonological rules should relate surface forms to each other, rather than to a set of abstract, UNDERLYING forms, as is required in traditional GENERATIVE phonology.

(3) In language ACQUISITION, 'generalization' refers to the process whereby

children extend their initial use of a linguistic feature to a class of items, as when, having learned to use an *-ing* ending on a VERB, the feature is 'generally' applied to the class of verbs. **Overgeneralization** takes place when the feature is extended beyond its limits in the adult grammar – as when the regular plural ending is applied to irregular FORMS, e.g. **mouses, *sheeps.*

(4) (**-ized**) A type of TRANSFORMATIONAL RULE recognized in early MODELS OF GENERATIVE grammar, where the rule operates with an input of two or more TERMINAL strings. Two types of **generalized transformation** are recognized: CONJOINING transformations handle CO-ORDINATION; EMBEDDING transformations handle SUBORDINATION.

General American A term used for the majority ACCENT of American English which conveys little or no information about the speaker's regional background. The accent is used, for example, by most radio and television presenters, and is not without some internal variation, but it is thought of as chiefly excluding speakers with eastern (New England) or southern backgrounds.

generalized phrase-structure grammar (GPSG) A LINGUISTIC theory which was developed as an alternative to TRANSFORMATIONAL accounts of language. GPSGs are weakly equivalent to a class of CONTEXT-FREE PHRASE-STRUCTURE GRAMMARS (PSGs). In GPSG, there are no transformations, and the SYNTACTIC structure of a SENTENCE is a single PHRASE-MARKER. Also, in traditional PSG, CATEGORY LABELS (e.g. NP, S) have no internal structure, whereas in GPSG a category is a set of FEATURE specifications (ordered pairs containing a feature and a feature value) which RULES can access. Instead of phrase-structure rules, GPSGs employ separate immediate DOMINANCE and linear PRECEDENCE rules. These interact with various general principles, feature CO-OCCURRENCE restrictions, and feature specification defaults to determine what local TREES (i.e. trees consisting of a NODE and its DAUGHTER or daughters) are well formed. This approach allows several generalizations to be captured in a way that is not possible with phrase-structure rules. GPSGs also employ METARULES, which derive immediate dominance rules from immediate dominance rules. An important offshoot of GPSG is HEAD-DRIVEN PHRASE-STRUCTURE GRAMMAR. A further generalization of this approach has been called **generalized generalized phrase-structure grammar (G^2PSG)**, in which the HEAD-feature convention, the FOOT feature principle, the CONTROL AGREEMENT PRINCIPLE, and the system of feature specification DEFAULTS are subsumed into a single mechanism – an extension of the feature co-occurrence restriction mechanism of standard GPSG.

generative (generate, generation, generativist) (1) A term derived from mathematics, and introduced by Noam CHOMSKY, in his book *Syntactic Structures* (1957), to refer to the capacity of a GRAMMAR to define (i.e. specifiy the membership of) the set of grammatical SENTENCES in a LANGUAGE. Technically, a **generative grammar** is a set of FORMAL RULES which PROJECTS a finite set of sentences upon the potentially infinite set of sentences that constitute the language as a whole, and it does this in an EXPLICIT manner, ASSIGNING to each a set of STRUCTURAL DESCRIPTIONS. Several possible MODELS of generative grammar have been formally investigated, following Chomsky's initial discussion of three types – FINITE-STATE, PHRASE-STRUCTURE and TRANSFORMATIONAL grammars. In recent years, the term has come to be applied to theories of several different kinds, apart from those developed by Chomsky, such as ARC-PAIR GRAMMAR, LEXICAL FUNCTIONAL GRAMMAR and GENERALIZED PHRASE-STRUCTURE GRAMMAR. There are two main branches of generative linguistics: **generative phonology** and **generative syntax**. The term 'generative semantics' is also used, but in a different sense (see (2) below). See also PHONOTACTICS.

(2) The **generative semantics** school of thought within generative LINGUISTIC theory was propounded by several American linguists (primarily George Lakoff (b. 1941), James McCawley (b. 1938), Paul Postal (b. 1936) and John Ross (b. 1938)) in the early 1970s; it views the SEMANTIC COMPONENT of a grammar as being the generative base from which SYNTACTIC structure can be derived. One proceeds in an analysis by first providing a semantic REPRESENTATION of a SENTENCE, and this single LEVEL is all that is needed to specify the conditions which produce WELL-FORMED SURFACE STRUCTURES. The subsequent syntactic RULES are solely INTERPRETIVE, and there is no intermediate level. This puts the approach plainly in contrast with the claims of Noam Chomsky and others (in the STANDARD THEORY) who argued the need for a level of syntactic DEEP STRUCTURE as well as a semantic level of analysis. 'Generative' in this phrase has, accordingly, a narrower sense than in 'generative grammar' as a whole, as it is specifically opposed to those MODELS which operate with a different, interpretative view of semantics. The proponents of this approach are known as 'generative semanticists'.

generic A term used in GRAMMATICAL and SEMANTIC analysis for a LEXICAL stem or PROPOSITION which refers to a CLASS of entities, e.g. ***the bat*** *is an interesting creature,* ***bats*** *are horrid, the English/French . . . , the poor/rich/good . . .*

genetic classification In HISTORICAL LINGUISTICS, the classification of languages according to a hypothesis of common origin; also called **genealogical classification**. Languages which are genetically related have a common ancestor. The terminology of description derives from that of the FAMILY tree of human relationships. Non-genetic links between languages can also be established using COMPARATIVE linguistic techniques.

Geneva School (1) In LINGUISTICS, the name given to those who have developed the views of the Swiss linguist Ferdinand de SAUSSURE, who taught linguistics at the University of Geneva between 1906 and 1911. Scholars such as Charles Bally (1865–1947) have expounded Saussurean theories and applied them to several new areas, e.g. literary LANGUAGE.

(2) In language ACQUISITION, the name given to those who have developed the views of the Swiss psychologist Jean Piaget (1896–1980). Particular attention has been paid to experimental techniques designed to extend Piaget's observations on LANGUAGE development in children to a wider range of DATA and CONTEXTS in a wider range of languages.

genitive One of the FORMS taken by a NOUN PHRASE (often a single NOUN or PRONOUN) in LANGUAGES which express GRAMMATICAL relationships by means of INFLECTIONS. The genitive CASE typically expresses a possessive relationship (e.g. *the boy's book*), or some other similarly 'close' connection (e.g. *a summer's day*); but there is a great deal of variation between languages in the way this case is used. The term may also apply to CONSTRUCTIONS formally related to the case form, as in the 'post-modifying' genitive with *of* in English, e.g. *the car of the general* (→ *The general's car*). In English LINGUISTICS, particular attention has been paid to the problems caused by the DISTRIBUTION of the genitive ending, as in *a book of my brother's* and *the King of England's hat.*

genre In SOCIOLINGUISTICS, DISCOURSE ANALYSIS and STYLISTICS, the generalization of a term well established in artistic and literary criticism for an identifiable category of literary composition (e.g. poetry, detective story). The extended use refers to any formally distinguishable VARIETY that has achieved a level of general recognition, whether in speech or writing, such as commercial advertising, jokes, and sermons. A genre imposes several identifiable characteristics on a use of language, notably in relation to subject-matter, purpose (e.g. narrative, allegory, satire), textual structure, form of argumentation, and level of formality. **Subgenres** can also be identified, as with types of novel or types of news story.

geographical linguistics The study of LANGUAGES and DIALECTS in terms of their regional distribution is sometimes collectively referred to by this label, though the terms DIALECTOLOGY and AREAL LINGUISTICS are more commonly used. 'Geographical dialect' is an alternative term for 'regional dialect'.

geolinguistics A branch of LINGUISTICS which studies the geographical distribution of LANGUAGES throughout the world, with reference to their political, economic and cultural status. More narrowly, the term is used in linguistics for an approach which combines the insights of DIALECT geography, urban dialectology and human geography in a SOCIOLINGUISTICALLY informed dialectology. This approach examines in particular the spread of innovations in a geographical area, using the notion of the linguistic VARIABLE.

geometry see FEATURE, TONE (1), TREE

gerund see PARTICIPLE

gesture A term used in PHONOLOGY for a MATRIX of FEATURES specifying a particular characteristic of a SEGMENT. For example, an 'oral gesture' would specify all SUPRAGLOTTAL characteristics (such as PLACE and MANNER OF ARTICULATION), and a 'laryngeal gesture' would specify characteristics of PHONATION. The notion is particularly used in DEPENDENCY PHONOLOGY, where 'categorial', 'articulatory' and 'initiatory' gestures are distinguished. Gestures, in turn, are analysed into **subgestures**; for example, the initiatory gesture is analysed into the subgestures of GLOTTAL STRICTURE, airstream direction and airstream source. See also ARTICULATORY PHONOLOGY, TIER.

ghost segment In PHONOLOGY, a SEGMENT in a REPRESENTATION which has a phonological effect, but which either never appears in SURFACE STRUCTURE or surfaces only in restricted contexts; also called a **phantom segment**. Examples include Polish YERS and English EPENTHETIC vowels.

given A term used by some LINGUISTS in a two-part analysis of UTTERANCES in terms of INFORMATION structure; 'given' information is opposed to NEW. (The contrast between FOCUS and PRESUPPOSITION makes an analogous distinction.) 'Given' refers to information already supplied by the previous linguistic CONTEXT whereas 'new' information, as its name suggests, has not been previously supplied. Given information will usually be relatively unstressed within the TONE UNIT: e.g. in the sequence A: *What are you looking at?* B: *I'm looking at a book*, all but the final phrase is given; in A: *What are you doing?* B: *I'm looking at a book*, the context shows that only the first part of the sentence is given. Complications arise when the new information is PROSODICALLY 'spread' throughout a tone unit, however, as in *your cóusin's had a bàby*, and analyses in these terms are not without controversy.

glide A term used in PHONETICS to refer to a TRANSITIONAL sound as the VOCAL ORGANS move towards or away from an ARTICULATION (**on-glide** and **off-glide** respectively). An example is the [j] glide heard in some pronunciations of words like *tune*, viz. [tʲuːn]. DIPHTHONGS are sometimes referred to as 'gliding vowels'.

global A term used in GENERATIVE LINGUISTIC theory in the early 1970s to refer to a type of RULE (**a global rule**) which extends over entire DERIVATIONS, or parts of derivations, and cannot be satisfactorily stated in terms of TRANSFORMATIONAL operations that define the conditions of WELL-FORMEDNESS on individual PHRASE-MARKERS or pairs of adjacent phrase-markers in a derivation. Global rules (or 'global derivational CONSTRAINTS') thus contrast with PHRASE-STRUCTURE and TRANSFORMATIONAL rules, as traditionally understood: they define the conditions of well-formedness on configurations of corresponding NODES in non-adjacent phrase-markers. Several topics in PHONOLOGY, SYNTAX and SEMANTICS have been analysed in these terms (e.g. CASE AGREEMENT, CONTRACTED forms, placement of contrastive STRESS).

glossematics An approach to LANGUAGE developed primarily by Louis Hjelmslev (1899–1965) and associates at the Linguistic Circle of Copenhagen in the mid-1930s (the COPENHAGEN SCHOOL). The novel name was a reflection of the originality of the school's intention to develop a theory which would be applicable, not just for language, but for general study of the humanities ('semiology', the study of symbolic systems in general; cf. SEMIOTICS). Language, in this view, was seen as one kind of symbolic system, whose special features would be clarified only when it was compared with other, non-linguistic symbolic systems (e.g. logic, dancing). The philosophical and logical basis of glossematic theory, especially as FORMALIZED by Hjelmslev in his *Prolegomena to a Theory of Language*, published in 1943, presenting language as a purely deductive system, is its most distinctive feature. The irreducible and invariant UNITS established by this procedure were called GLOSSEMES.

glosseme A term used in GLOSSEMATICS to refer to the abstract minimal invariant FORMS set up by the theory as the bases of explanation in all areas of LINGUISTIC analysis.

glossogenetics A term sometimes used in LINGUISTICS to refer to the study of the origins and development of LANGUAGE, both in the child and in the human race. It involves a wide range of contributing sciences, including biology, anthropology, psychology, semiotics, neurology and primatology, as well as linguistics.

glossolalia (glossolal-ist, -ic) A term used by some LINGUISTS to refer to the phenomenon of 'speaking in tongues', as practised by members of various religious groups. From a SOCIOLINGUISTIC perspective, glossolalic speech has a unique function, acting as a sign of the speakers' belief or as evidence of conversion, but lacking conventional REFERENCE. Its formal linguistic STRUCTURE is quite unlike that of ordinary languages, being simpler and more repetitive (notwithstanding the claims made that the speaker is articulating a real but unknown language). The written equivalent is **glossographia**.

glottal(-ic, -ize, -ization, glottis) A term in the classification of CONSONANT sounds on the basis of PLACE OF ARTICULATION: it is a sound made in the LARYNX, due to the CLOSURE or narrowing of the **glottis**, the aperture between the VOCAL CORDS. The audible release of a complete closure at the glottis is known as a **glottal stop**, transcribed [ʔ]. This is often used in English; e.g. it may be heard before a forcefully articulated VOWEL, as in ***are** you*, or between adjacent vowels as in *co-operate*. In several ACCENTS of English (e.g. those influenced by Cockney) the sound has PHONEMIC status, being used in some positions where RECEIVED PRONUNCIATION has a VOICELESS PLOSIVE ([t] and [k] especially), e.g. *bottle* /bɒʔl/ for /bɒtl/. Varying degrees of audible FRICTION may also originate at the glottis, as in whispered speech, or the [h] sound in English. Other glottal effects, due to the mode of vibration of the vocal cords, are an important feature of speech sounds, such as VOICING and PITCH variation, and BREATHY and CREAKY phonation.

Glottalization is a general term for any articulation involving a simultaneous glottal CONSTRICTION, especially a glottal stop. In English, glottal stops are often used in this way to reinforce a voiceless plosive at the end of a word, as in *what?* [wɒtʔ]. However, if the opening of the glottis is delayed until after the release of the glottalized sound, a different sound effect is created. Such sounds, made while the glottis is closed, are produced without the direct involvement of air from the lungs. Air is compressed in the mouth or PHARYNX above the glottal closure, and released while the breath is still held: the resultant sounds produced in this **glottalic** AIRSTREAM MECHANISM are known as EJECTIVE sounds. They are also called 'glottalic' or **glottalized** sounds (though the latter term is often restricted to sounds where the glottal feature is a SECONDARY ARTICULATION). They are transcribed with a following raised glottal stop sign or apostrophe, as in [p'], [t'], [s']. In English, such sounds have only STYLISTIC force (as when *I think* might be said in a clipped precise manner, producing an ejective [k'] in *think*), but in languages like Quechua and Hausa ejective consonants are used as phonemes. A further category of sounds involving a glottalic airstream mechanism is known as IMPLOSIVE.

In CHOMSKY and Halle's DISTINCTIVE FEATURE theory of PHONOLOGY, **glottal constrictions** constitute one of the types of sound set up to handle variations in place of articulation (CAVITY features). Glottal constrictions are formed by narrowing the glottis beyond its neutral position, as in the above sounds.

glottochronology A term used in LINGUISTICS, referring to the quantification of the extent to which LANGUAGES have diverged from a common source. Using a technique known as LEXICOSTATISTICS, one studies the extent to which the hypothetically related languages share certain basic WORDS (COGNATES) and deduces from this the distance in time since the languages separated. The theory and methods involved are in limited use, and are highly controversial.

GLOW The acronym for the organization **Generative Linguists of the Old World**, established by European linguists in the late 1970s, which meets annually at different university centres. It originally united adherents to the EXTENDED STANDARD THEORY, and is now oriented towards GOVERNMENT-BINDING THEORY.

goal A term used by some LINGUISTS as part of the GRAMMATICAL analysis of a SENTENCE: it refers to the entity which is affected by the action of the VERB, e.g. *the cat caught* **a mouse**. Several other terms have been used for this idea, e.g. 'patient', 'recipient'. In LOCALISTIC theories of MEANING, an entity takes a 'path' from a 'source' to a 'goal'. In CASE grammar, it refers to the place to which something moves.

God's truth A phrase coined in the 1950s to characterize one of two extreme states of mind of a hypothetical LINGUIST who sets up a DESCRIPTION of linguistic DATA; opposed to HOCUS-POCUS. A 'God's truth' linguist approaches data with the expectation that the LANGUAGE has a 'real' STRUCTURE which is waiting to be uncovered. The assumption is that, if one's procedure of analysis is logical and consistent, the same description would always emerge from the same data, any uncertainty being the result of defective observation or logic on the part of the analyst. In a hocus-pocus approach, by contrast, no such assumption is made.

govern (1) (**-ment**) A term used in GRAMMATICAL analysis to refer to a kind of SYNTACTIC linkage whereby one WORD (or word CLASS) requires a specific MORPHOLOGICAL FORM of another word (or class). For example, PREPOSITIONS in Latin are said to 'govern' NOUNS, making a certain case form obligatory (e.g. *ad* plus ACCUSATIVE). The notion is, accordingly, not readily applicable to a LANGUAGE like English, where case endings are few – to say that, in *the man kicked the ball, kicked* 'governs' *the ball* is true only in a loose SEMANTIC sense (and, even then, it is debatable whether this is a valid notion of government, when the relationship between other ELEMENTS is considered: almost any pairs of elements, e.g. *the man* and *kicked*, might be said to be displaying government, in this sense). The term is usually contrasted with AGREEMENT, where the form taken by one word requires a corresponding form in another.

(2) (**-ed, un-, -or**) In GENERATIVE grammar (cf. ASPECTS MODEL), the terms **governed** and **ungoverned** are used to refer to whether or not a RULE has LEXICAL exceptions. For example, because not all ACTIVE TRANSITIVE SENTENCES take the PASSIVE (e.g. *They have a car, The hat suits you*), the passivization rule would be said to be 'governed'. An example of an ungoverned rule is REFLEXIVIZATION (e.g. *I shaved myself*, etc.). In more recent generative grammar, the conditions which determine whether one CONSTITUENT governs another have been made more EXPLICIT. When several possible NODES C-COMMAND a constituent, the **governor** is the lowest of these nodes in the TREE (i.e. the 'minimal' node), as long as there is no intervening NOUN PHRASE or S-bar (cf. the conventions of X-BAR syntax). For example, in the tree representing *looked at John* (see p. 172), both *looked* and *at* c-command *John*; but only *at* is said to 'govern' *John* (*looked John* not being possible), i.e. to be the **governing node**. Governing nodes are noun, VERB, ADJECTIVE, preposition, TENSE and POSSESSIVE.

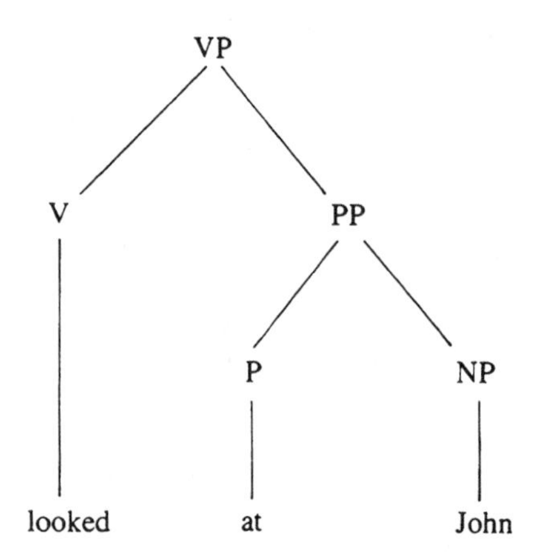

In relation to GOVERNMENT-BINDING THEORY, a **governing category** is the minimal structure (noun phrase or sentence) within which the relationships of binding obtain. X is the governing category for Y, where X is N, V, A, P, or AGR, if and only if X and Y are DOMINATED by exactly the same maximal PROJECTIONS (full phrasal categories). When an empty category is governed by a CO-INDEXED category, it is said to be 'antecedent governed' (important for the EMPTY CATEGORY PRINCIPLE). See also BARRIER, GOVERNMENT-BINDING THEORY, GOVERNMENT PHONOLOGY.

(3) (**-or**) In DEPENDENCY grammar, the **governor** refers to the superordinate NODE in a dependency tree, which 'governs' or 'controls' a set of 'dependent' nodes. Each combination of governor and dependent defines a specific structural relationship. For example, the verb is seen as the governor of the noun phrases occurring in CLAUSE STRUCTURE, and each verb/noun-phrase combination specifies a syntactic RELATION, e.g. SUBJECT, INDIRECT OBJECT. In the phrase *up the tree, up* governs *tree*, and *tree* governs *the.* Because of the possibility of ambiguity with sense (1) above, some linguists use the term 'controller' instead of 'governor'.

government-binding theory or **government and binding theory (GB)** A MODEL of GRAMMAR, a descendent of EXTENDED STANDARD THEORY and ultimately of classical TRANSFORMATIONAL grammar. It assumes that SENTENCES have three main levels of structure: D-STRUCTURE, S-STRUCTURE and LOGICAL FORM. S-structure is derived from D-structure, and logical form from S-structure, by a single transformation, MOVE ALPHA, which essentially means move anything anywhere. Various so-called sub-theories interact with this to allow just the right structures to be generated. The main sub-theories are X-BAR theory, THETA theory, CASE theory, BINDING theory, BOUNDING theory, CONTROL theory and GOVERNMENT theory. Because of the way these sub-theories interact, GB is commonly described as a 'modular' theory. Proponents of GB suggest that essentially the same principles of SYNTAX are operative in all languages, although they can take a slightly different form in different languages. For this reason, GB is often referred to as the 'PRINCIPLES and PARAMETERS' approach.

government phonology A model of NON-LINEAR PHONOLOGY in which the notion of GOVERNMENT is central; also called **government-based phonology** or **government and charm phonology**. 'Government' is here defined in terms of headedness – a BINARY asymmetric relation holding between two SKELETAL positions. Certain SEGMENTS within SYLLABLE structure are seen to have **governing** properties, and are ASSOCIATED to governing skeletal positions. Other segments are **governable**, and are associated to skeletal positions that are **governees**. Headedness is seen as local (i.e. between adjacent segments) and directional (head-initial). Syllabic CONSTITUENTS are thus defined as HEAD-initial governing domains. Government across constituent boundaries is called 'interconstituent government'. **Proper government** is a stronger form of government which asserts that the governor may not itself be governed, and that the domain of proper government may not include a governing domain. The approach is influenced by GOVERNMENT-BINDING THEORY, and advocates a constraining of phonology through the use of PRINCIPLES and PARAMETERS.

government theory One of the (sub-)theories of GOVERNMENT-BINDING THEORY. Its main principle is the EMPTY CATEGORY PRINCIPLE, which restricts the positions from which MOVEMENT can occur by requiring TRACES to be closely associated with either a LEXICAL category or a CO-INDEXED category.

GPSG The abbreviation for GENERALIZED PHRASE-STRUCTURE GRAMMAR.

gradability ((un)gradable) A term used in GRAMMAR and SEMANTICS to refer to an analysis of the SENSE relationship between LEXICAL items in terms of the possibility of comparison. In semantics, **gradable** terms are best illustrated by such opposites as *big/small, high/low* (cf. ANTONYMS). **Ungradable** terms can be illustrated by *single/married, north/south*, etc. In grammar, the term is used to refer to various types of grammatical MODIFICATION which can be used as criteria for comparative MEANINGS, e.g. *a piece/bit/chunk of . . . , a very/slightly/extremely . . .*

gradation (1) In GRAMMAR, the relationship between the forms of ADJECTIVES or ADVERBS when used in the expression of DEGREES of comparison. Languages typically express POSITIVE, EQUATIVE, COMPARATIVE and SUPERLATIVE forms, using MORPHOLOGICAL (e.g. English *-er*, *-est*) or SYNTACTIC (e.g. *more, most*) means.

(2) In HISTORICAL LINGUISTICS, the relationship between VERB forms based on variations in the root vowel, as in *sing, sang, sung*; more explicitly called **vowel gradation** or **ablaut**.

gradience A term used by some LINGUISTS to refer to areas of LANGUAGE where there are no clear boundaries between sets of analytic categories. PHONETIC continua provide clear examples (such as the set of possible CONTRASTS between FALLING and RISING INTONATION patterns), but the term is also found in SEMANTICS (as in the study of continua, such as colour terms, or GRADABLE ANTONYMS) and in GRAMMAR (where the boundaries between WORD-CLASSES are not clear-cut; e.g. noun-like words such as *rich, London, smoking, someone* make it difficult to circumscribe the class of NOUNS).

gradual A type of OPPOSITION recognized by PRAGUE SCHOOL PHONOLOGY, distinguished from PRIVATIVE and EQUIPOLLENT. A gradual opposition is one where degrees of difference in a LANGUAGE are recognized along a scale of some kind, as in a language with four FRONT VOWELS /i/, /e/, /ɛ/ and /a/ where (according to Nicolai Trubetskoy) it would not be desirable to analyse the four degrees of vowel height in terms of privative pairs, such as 'high' *v.* 'low'.

grammar (gramma-tical-ize, -rian) A central term in LINGUISTICS, but one which covers a wide range of phenomena. Several types of grammar can be distinguished.

(1) A **descriptive grammar** is, in the first instance, a systematic DESCRIPTION of a LANGUAGE as found in a sample of speech or writing (e.g. in a CORPUS of material, or as elicited from NATIVE-SPEAKERS). Depending on one's theoretical background, it may go beyond this and make statements about the language as a whole, and in so far as these statements are explicit and predictive of the speaker's COMPETENCE the grammar can be said to be 'descriptively adequate' and GENERATIVE. In the older tradition, 'descriptive' is in contrast to the PRESCRIPTIVE or NORMATIVE approach of grammarians who attempted to establish RULES for the socially or STYLISTICALLY CORRECT use of language. Comprehensive descriptions of the SYNTAX and MORPHOLOGY of a language are known as **reference grammars** or 'grammatical handbooks' (such as those produced this century by the North European grammarians, e.g. the Dane, Otto Jespersen (1860–1943), and more recently by Randolph Quirk et al. (see QUIRK GRAMMAR)).

(2) A **theoretical grammar** goes beyond the study of individual languages, using linguistic DATA as a means of developing theoretical insights into the nature of language as such, and into the categories and processes needed for successful linguistic analysis. Such insights include the distinction between 'DEEP grammar' and 'SURFACE grammar', the notion of 'grammatical CATEGORIES' and 'grammatical MEANING', and the study of 'grammatical RELATIONS' (the relationship between a verb and its dependents, such as 'subject of', 'direct object of'). In so far as grammar concentrates on the study of linguistic FORMS (their STRUCTURE, DISTRIBUTION, etc.), it may be referred to as **formal grammar** (as opposed to 'NOTIONAL grammar'); but formal grammar also refers to the use of the FORMALIZED techniques of logic and mathematics in the analysis of language.

(3) Other general notions include the distinction between DIACHRONIC and SYNCHRONIC grammars, based on whether or not grammars introduce a historical dimension into their analysis. **Comparative grammar**, which compares the forms of languages (or states of a language), relies on a combination of theoretical and descriptive methods. A 'pedagogical' or 'teaching grammar' is a grammar designed specifically for the purposes of teaching or learning a (foreign) language, or for developing one's awareness of the mother-tongue.

(4) The phrase **traditional grammar** is an attempt to summarize the range of attitudes and methods found in the pre-linguistic era of grammatical study. The term TRADITIONAL, accordingly, is found with reference to many periods, such as the Roman and Greek grammarians, Renaissance grammars, and (especially) the eighteenth- and nineteenth-century school grammars, in Europe and America. It is usually used with a critical ('non-scientific') implication, despite the fact that many antecedents of modern linguistics can be found in early grammars. Criticism is directed primarily at the PRESCRIPTIVE and PROSCRIPTIVE

recommendations of authors, as opposed to the descriptive emphasis of linguistic studies.

(5) In a restricted sense (the traditional sense in linguistics, and the usual popular interpretation of the term), grammar refers to a level of structural organization which can be studied independently of PHONOLOGY and SEMANTICS, and generally divided into the branches of SYNTAX and MORPHOLOGY. In this sense, grammar is the study of the way WORDS, and their component parts, combine to form SENTENCES. It is to be contrasted with a general conception of the subject, where grammar is seen as the entire system of structural relationships in a language, as in such titles as STRATIFICATIONAL grammar, SYSTEMIC grammar and (especially) GENERATIVE grammar. Here, 'grammar' subsumes phonology and semantics as well as syntax, traditionally regarded as separate linguistic LEVELS. 'A grammar', in this sense, is a device for generating a finite specification of the sentences of a language. In so far as a grammar defines the total set of RULES possessed by a speaker, it is a grammar of the speaker's competence (**competence grammar**). In so far as a grammar is capable of accounting for only the sentences a speaker has actually used (as found in a sample of output, or CORPUS), it is a **performance grammar**. The study of PERFORMANCE grammars, in a PSYCHOLINGUISTIC context, goes beyond this, however, attempting to define the various psychological, neurological and physiological stages which enter into the production and perception of speech. Investigations which go beyond the study of an individual language, attempting to establish the defining (UNIVERSAL) characteristics of human language in general, have as their goal a **universal grammar**.

Students of grammar are **grammarians**, and they carry out a **grammatical analysis** (the term here having no implications of WELL-FORMEDNESS, as it has in the notion of GRAMMATICALITY). When it is necessary to differentiate entities in one's analysis as belonging to a grammatical level of description as opposed to some other (e.g. semantic, phonological), the term 'grammatical' is often used attributively, as in 'grammatical CATEGORY' (e.g. GENDER, CASE, VOICE), 'grammatical gender' (as opposed to 'natural gender'), 'grammatical FORMATIVE/ITEM/UNIT' (e.g. an INFLECTIONAL ending), 'grammatical SUBJECT/OBJECT . . .' (as opposed to 'logical' or 'semantic' subjects/objects . . .), 'grammatical word' (as opposed to LEXICAL word). When a semantic contrast is expressed using grammatical forms, it is said to be **grammaticalized** (or **grammaticized**). See also AMBIGUITY, APPLICATION (2), ARC, CONSTITUENT, CORE, DISCOURSE, FUZZY, GENERAL (1).

grammaticality ((un)grammatical(ness)) In LINGUISTICS, the conformity of a SENTENCE (or part of a sentence) to the RULES defined by a specific GRAMMAR of a LANGUAGE. A preceding ASTERISK is commonly used to indicate that a sentence is **ungrammatical**, i.e. incapable of being accounted for by the rules of a grammar. In practice, deciding whether a sentence is grammatical or ungrammatical may cause difficulty, e.g. in cases such as *The bus he got off was a red one*, where NATIVE-SPEAKERS vary in their judgements. In GENERATIVE linguistics, the view is taken that a grammar is set up in the first instance to draw a dividing line between those sentences which are clearly grammatical and those which are clearly ungrammatical. Once this has been done, the cases of uncertainty can be investigated, and a decision made as to whether they can be incorporated into the grammar as they stand, and without further modification being introduced into the grammar. If they can, these sentences are thereby defined as grammatical, i.e. the grammar recognizes them as such. If not, they will be said to be ungrammatical, with reference to that grammar.

An alternative term for 'grammatical' in this context, is WELL FORMED (*v.* ILL FORMED): grammars adjudicate on the 'well-formedness' of sentences. Such decisions have nothing to do with the MEANING or ACCEPTABILITY of sentences. A sentence in this view may be well formed, but nonsensical (as in CHOMSKY's famous *Colourless green ideas sleep furiously*); it may also be well formed but unacceptable (for reasons of STYLISTIC inappropriateness, perhaps).

It should be emphasized that no social value judgement is implied by the use of 'grammatical', and this therefore contrasts with some popular uses of the term, as when sentences are said to be ungrammatical because they do not conform to the canons of the STANDARD language (as in the use of double NEGATIVES, such as *I haven't done nothing*). There is no PRESCRIPTIVE implication in the above use in linguistics.

graph A term used by some LINGUISTS to refer to the smallest DISCRETE SEGMENT in a stretch of writing or print – analogous to the notion of the PHONE in PHONETICS. The present line of type is composed of such graphs as *t, T, h, e,* and so on, as well as the punctuation marks. The linguistic analysis of these graphs into GRAPHEMES is the province of GRAPHOLOGY.

grapheme (graphemics) The minimal CONTRASTIVE UNIT in the writing SYSTEM of a LANGUAGE. The grapheme *a*, for example, is realized as several ALLOGRAPHS *A, a, a*, etc., which may be seen as units in COMPLEMENTARY DISTRIBUTION (e.g. upper case restricted to SENTENCE-initial position, proper names, etc.), or in FREE VARIATION (as in some styles of handwriting), just as in PHONEMIC analysis. 'Grapheme analysis' is the main business of **graphemics** (or GRAPHOLOGY).

graphetic(s) A term used by some LINGUISTS, on analogy with PHONETICS, for the analysis of the GRAPHIC SUBSTANCE of written or printed LANGUAGE. For example, it is theoretically possible to define a UNIVERSAL set of graphic features which enter into the formation of DISTINCTIVE letter shapes. There are also several properties of the written MEDIUM which exercise a considerable influence on communication, e.g. colour, size of writing or print, spacing. There is plainly an overlap here with the field of graphics and typography (and 'graphics' is in fact sometimes used as a label for this field). So far little analysis of TEXTS in these terms has taken place, and the relationship between GRAPHETICS and GRAPHOLOGY remains unclear.

graphic substance A term used by some LINGUISTS to refer to the written or printed form of LANGUAGE seen as a set of physically definable visual properties, i.e. marks on a surface. The analogous term for speech is PHONIC SUBSTANCE. The linguistic analysis of these graphic or GRAPHETIC features is sometimes referred to as GRAPHOLOGY, on analogy with PHONOLOGY.

graphology (graphological) A term used by some LINGUISTS to refer to the writing SYSTEM of a LANGUAGE – on analogy with PHONOLOGY. A 'graphological' analysis would be concerned to establish the minimal CONTRASTIVE UNITS of visual language – defined as GRAPHEMES, graphemic FEATURES, or without using EMIC terms – using similar techniques to those used in phonological analysis. Graphology in this sense has nothing to do with the analysis of handwriting to determine the psychological characteristics of the writer – an activity for which the same term is often popularly used.

grave One of the features of sound set up by JAKOBSON and Halle in their DISTINCTIVE FEATURE theory of PHONOLOGY, to handle variations in PLACE OF ARTICULATION; its opposite is ACUTE. Grave sounds are defined ARTICULATORILY and ACOUSTICALLY, as those involving a peripheral articulation in the VOCAL TRACT, and a concentration of acoustic energy in the lower frequencies. BACK VOWELS and LABIAL and VELAR CONSONANTS are [+grave]; FRONT VOWELS and DENTAL, ALVEOLAR and PALATAL consonants are [−grave].

greed In the MINIMALIST PROGRAMME, a general ECONOMY constraint which allows the MOVEMENT of an element only if it satisfies the requirements of the moved element. For example, an item can be moved to a particular position only if the MORPHOLOGICAL properties of the item would not otherwise be satisfied in the DERIVATION. An element may not move if its only motivation is to satisfy the requirements of some other element.

grid see METRICAL GRID

grinding (grinder, ground) In SEMANTICS, a term sometimes used in analysing the process of SENSE extension, notably that which creates UNCOUNTABLE NOUNS from COUNT nouns. The metaphor is that of a 'universal grinder' machine which would turn *a chicken*, for example, into the mass noun *chicken*. The analysis of 'ground nouns' aims to establish which types of noun allow conceptual grinding in a language (e.g. animal meat), and the extent to which languages employ different GRAMMATICAL means to encode grinding phenomena.

groove(-d, grooving) A term sometimes used in PHONETICS to refer to a type of FRICATIVE where the TONGUE is slightly hollowed (or 'grooved') along its central line, the passage of air producing a sound with a higher frequency than in other fricatives. In English, [s], [z], [ʃ] and [ʒ] are 'groove fricatives'. In SLIT (or 'flat') fricatives (e.g. [f], [θ]), there is no such groove. See also CUPPING.

group (1) A term used in HALLIDAYAN grammar to refer to a UNIT on the RANK scale intermediate between CLAUSE and WORD. For example, in the SENTENCE *The car was parked in the street, the car* is a 'NOMINAL group', *was parked* is a 'VERBAL group', and *in the street* is an 'ADVERBIAL group'. The term PHRASE is equivalent in most other approaches. See also PREPOSITION, STRESS, TONE GROUP.

(2) **A group genitive** is a general designation for the English CONSTRUCTION where the GENITIVE ending is added to the last ELEMENT in a NOUN PHRASE containing POST-modification or CO-ORDINATION, e.g. *the University of London's grant, Morecambe and Wise's humour.*

guttural In some models of FEATURE GEOMETRY, a NODE proposed to represent a NATURAL CLASS of sounds articulated between the LARYNX and the upper PHARYNX (GLOTTAL, pharyngeal, and UVULAR sounds). In some approaches, it is

H

H The abbreviation for the 'high' variety in DIGLOSSIA and for 'high' TONE in PHONOLOGY.

habitual A term used in the GRAMMATICAL analysis of ASPECT, referring to a situation in which an action is viewed as lasting for an extended period of time. English has a habitual aspect in the past TENSE, using *used to*, and habitual meaning is often expressed LEXICALLY, using ADVERBIALS (e.g. *often, frequently*). Many habitual uses express repeated action (*I visit my aunt regularly*), and in this function are often described as ITERATIVE, but the habitual is often non-iterative, as in *A castle used to stand at the top of that cliff.*

half-close see CLOSE (1)

half-open see OPEN (1)

Hallidayan Characteristic of, or a follower of, the linguistic principles of the British LINGUIST, M(ichael) A(lexander) K(irkwood) **Halliday** (b. 1925). Much of Halliday's early thinking can be traced back to the teaching of J. R. Firth, and his approach is accordingly often called 'neo-FIRTHIAN'. His original conception of LANGUAGE, SCALE-AND-CATEGORY GRAMMAR, was published in article form in 1961: this contained a MODEL of language organization in terms of LEVELS OF SUBSTANCE, FORM (GRAMMAR and LEXIS) and CONTEXT, and a theoretical model of grammar in terms of three SCALES (of RANK, EXPONENCE and DELICACY) and four CATEGORIES (of UNIT, CLASS, STRUCTURE and SYSTEM). The central role of the last two has led to an alternative label for this approach – 'system-structure theory'. In the 1970s, the notion of 'system' became the central construct in an alternative model known as 'systemic' grammar: here, grammar is seen as a network of interrelated systems of classes; ENTRY conditions define the choices which can be made from within each system, and these choices become increasingly specific ('delicate') as the analysis proceeds. The application of Hallidayan ideas has been widespread, e.g. in TEXT analysis (cf. COHESION), STYLISTICS (cf. REGISTER) and language ACQUISITION.

hand configuration A term used in some PHONOLOGICAL models of SIGN language, to refer to a separate TIER for handshape and orientation.

haplology A term used in PHONOLOGY, in both SYNCHRONIC and DIACHRONIC contexts, to refer to the omission of some of the sounds occurring in a sequence of similar ARTICULATIONS, as when *cyclists* is pronounced /ˈsaɪklɪsː/, *library* /ˈlaɪbrɪ/, etc. Some PSYCHOLINGUISTS also use the term to refer to a TONGUE-SLIP where an omission of this kind has taken place, e.g. *running jump* becoming *rump*.

hard consonant An impressionistic term sometimes used in the PHONETIC descriptions of particular LANGUAGES, referring to a CONSONANT which lacks PALATALIZATION. Russian is a language which has several such hard (as opposed to SOFT) consonants. In Russian, the ъ symbol ('hard sign') marks this lack of palatalization on the preceding consonant.

hard palate see PALATE

harmonic In ACOUSTIC PHONETICS, a regular (PERIODIC) waveform accompanying a FUNDAMENTAL FREQUENCY, which helps to identify a complex TONE; also called an **overtone**. Harmonics are whole-number multiples of the fundamental frequency; for example, if the fundamental is 200 Hz, the harmonics will be at 400 Hz, 600 Hz, and so on. The harmonics are numbered in sequence, and in phonetics the numbering starts with the first multiple of the fundamental (in this example, 400 Hz would be the 'first harmonic', 600 Hz the 'second harmonic', and so on). The combination of a fundamental frequency and the AMPLITUDE of its various harmonics combine to give a sound its characteristic tone and quality.

harmonic phonology In PHONOLOGY, an approach which recognizes three levels of REPRESENTATION working in parallel: MORPHOPHONEMIC ('M-level'), WORD/SYLLABLE tactics ('W-level'), and PHONETIC ('P-level'). Each level is characterized by a set of WELL-FORMEDNESS statements ('tactics') and a set of unordered 'intralevel' RULES which collectively define the paths an input representation has to follow in order to achieve maximum conformity to the tactics. This maximal well-formedness is called 'harmony'. The levels are related by 'interlevel' rules. The approach avoids the traditional conception of the organization of a GENERATIVE grammar in which each level of representation is seen to precede or follow another (as would be found in the ordered steps within a DERIVATION).

harmony (harmonic, dis-) A term used in PHONOLOGY to refer to the way the ARTICULATION of one phonological UNIT is influenced by (is 'in harmony' with) another unit in the same WORD or PHRASE. An analogous notion is that of ASSIMILATION. The two main processes are **consonant harmony** and **vowel harmony**. In the typical case of VOWEL harmony, for example, such as is found in Turkish or Hungarian, all the vowels in a word share certain FEATURES – for instance, they are all articulated with the FRONT of the TONGUE, or all are ROUNDED. The subsets of vowels which are affected differently by harmonic processes are **harmonic sets**. **Disharmony** (or **disharmonicity**) occurs when a vowel from set A is used (e.g. by SUFFIXATION) in words which otherwise have set B, thus forming a **harmonic island** (if TRANSPARENT) or a new **harmonic span** (if OPAQUE). The span within which harmony operates (usually the word) is the **harmonic domain**.

hash The symbol #, also sometimes called a 'double cross', used especially in GENERATIVE LINGUISTICS to represent a PHONOLOGICAL WORD boundary.

head (1)**(-ed)** A term used in the GRAMMATICAL description of some types of PHRASE (ENDOCENTRIC phrases) to refer to the central element which is DISTRIBUTIONALLY equivalent to the phrase as a whole. Such constructions are sometimes referred to as **headed** (as opposed to **non-headed**). The head also determines any relationships of CONCORD or GOVERNMENT in other parts of the phrase or SENTENCE. For example, the head of the NOUN phrase *a big man* is *man*, and it is the singular form of this ITEM which relates to the co-occurrence of singular verb forms, such as *is*, *walks*, etc.; the head of the VERB phrase *has put* is *put*, and it is this verb which accounts for the use of OBJECT and ADVERBIAL later in the sentence (e.g. *put it there*). In phrases such as *men and women*, either item could be the head. Since the early 1980s, the term has also been extended to the analysis of WORD FORMATION, such as in COMPOUNDS: the head of a word is the element which determines the grammatical properties of the whole word. In GENERALIZED PHRASE-STRUCTURE GRAMMAR, the term is used in a more abstract way, as a device which enables one to identify a cluster of related FEATURE specifications which need to be referred to for a particular purpose (such as N, V, AUX, PER (= person) and SLASH). The **head-feature convention**, in this context, refers to a principle which determines the feature specifications of the subconstituents of a phrase: it states that the head features on a mother category are the same as the head features on any daughter which is a head. The **head parameter** is a principle used in GENERATIVE SYNTAX, especially in relation to UNIVERSAL grammar, which concerns the position of heads within phrases. It asserts that a language has the heads on the same side in all phrases: **head-first languages** are represented by English, e.g. *kick the ball* (the verb in the verb phrase is to the left of the noun phrase) and *in the box* (the PREPOSITION in the prepositional phrase is to the left of the noun phrase); **head-last languages** are represented by Japanese or Korean, where the heads appear on the right (e.g. Korean *Seoul-eseo* 'in Seoul'). In METRICAL PHONOLOGY, **left-headed feet** are those where the leftmost RHYME of the FOOT is STRESSED; **right-headed feet** are those where the rightmost rhyme is stressed. In head-marked metrical NOTATION, these cases are distinguished by placing the NODE representing the foot CONSTITUENT geometrically above the head (i.e. on the rhyme that is stressed), as follows:

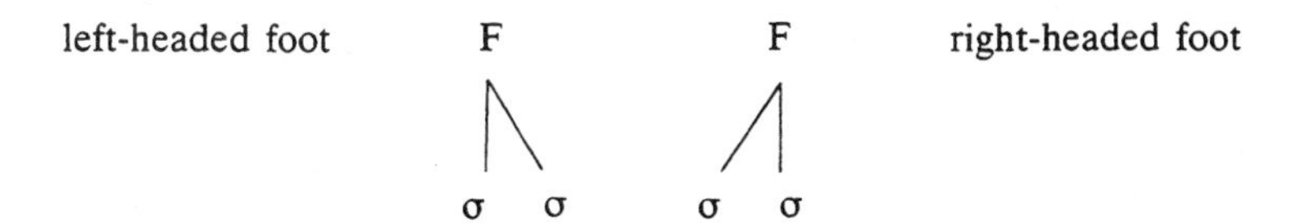

(2) A term used in some analyses of TONE GROUP structure, referring to the sequence of syllables between the first STRESSED syllable and the NUCLEAR tone; for example, in the tone group *there's a com'pletely 'new arràngement/* the head is *-pletely new a-*.

head-driven phrase-structure grammar (HPSG) A SYNTACTIC theory which builds on the insights of GENERALIZED PHRASE-STRUCTURE GRAMMAR, CATEGORIAL grammar and certain other approaches. A central feature is that categories incorporate information about the categories with which they combine. The consequence of this is that very few RULES are necessary, all important syntactic and SEMANTIC processes being driven by information contained in LEXICAL entries. For example, a single rule provides for all lexical category + COMPLEMENT structures. See also BINDING.

headword see LEMMA (1)

heavy (1) A term applying to a type of NOUN PHRASE recognized in GENERATIVE GRAMMAR, referring to a relatively long or complex ('heavy') CONSTITUENT in contrasting examples such as **John considers stupid my friends v. John considers stupid many of my best friends.* In classical TRANSFORMATIONAL grammar, the POSTPOSING of a heavy NP was called **heavy NP shift**.
(2) See WEIGHT.

hedge (noun/verb) An application in PRAGMATICS and DISCOURSE ANALYSIS of a general sense of the word ('to be non-committal or evasive') to a range of items which express a notion of imprecision or qualification. Examples include *sort of, more or less, I mean, approximately, roughly.* Hedges may also be used in combination: *something of the order of 10 per cent, more or less.*

heightened sub-glottal pressure One of the SOURCE FEATURES of sound set up by CHOMSKY and Halle in their DISTINCTIVE FEATURE theory of PHONOLOGY, to handle variations in sub-GLOTTAL pressure, as in the ASPIRATED STOPS of various LANGUAGES, such as Hindi.

Hertz see CYCLE (3)

hesitation The general sense of this term is used in LINGUISTICS, and especially in PSYCHOLINGUISTICS, where the phenomenon is subclassified into types, and the significance of 'hesitation phenomena' in terms of LANGUAGE-processing is discussed. Types of hesitation include silence, FILLED PAUSES (e.g. *er*, Japanese *ano*), elongated SYLLABLES (e.g. *we-e-ll*), repetitions (e.g. *the-the-thing . . .*), and so on. The DISTRIBUTION of these features is by no means random in speech, and it has been hypothesized that they occur at points where the speaker is planning new UTTERANCES. Based on the extent to which hesitations coincide with the boundaries between GRAMMATICAL, SEMANTIC, etc. CONSTITUENTS, the possibility has emerged that there may be more than one level of planning (e.g. syntactic, semantic, interactional) in SPEECH PRODUCTION.

heterography see HOMOGRAPHY (2)

heterorganic see HOMORGANIC

heteronym(y) A term sometimes used in SEMANTIC analysis to refer to words (LEXEMES) which display partial HOMONYMY, i.e. they differ in MEANING, but are identical in FORM in one MEDIUM only (viz. speech or writing). Examples would be the HOMOGRAPHS *row* (sc. a boat) and *row* (sc. noise), or the HOMOPHONES *threw* and *through*.

heuristic An application in LINGUISTICS and PHONETICS of the general use of this term in cybernetics, referring to a specific mode of investigation adopted as part of a process of discovery or problem-solving. In linguistics, the notion has been introduced mainly in the discussion of PROCEDURES of analysis, where BLOOMFIELDIAN DISCOVERY procedures are contrasted with the FORMAL analyses of GENERATIVE GRAMMAR. The term is also used in the looser sense of a 'working hypothesis', used to suggest or eliminate a possible explanation of events. A notion such as DISCOURSE, for example, cannot easily be given a formal or operational definition, but it can be seen as a 'heuristic device', and used as a pre-theoretical notion, thus enabling an investigation to proceed.

hidden Markov model In automatic SPEECH RECOGNITION, an approach which uses a SPECTRAL model of a word, viewed as a Markov model of the ACOUSTIC event (see MARKOV PROCESS). The pronunciation of a word, in all its variant forms, can be seen as a stochastic process: in a sequence of events (pronunciation here being modelled as a sequence of 'slices' through a speech SPECTROGRAM), the probabilities at each step depend on the outcome of previous steps. Each time the process is applied to the word, it generates a slightly different acoustic specification, within the limits of the model. Once a speech recognizer has been provided with Markov models for the words it contains, it can use these to evaluate the properties of a fresh speech event. When someone speaks a word into the recognition system, the acoustic event can be treated as if it were the output of a 'hidden' Markov model. The output of the model is known (i.e the event), but not the model itself (i.e. it is hidden), and the job of the recognizer is to reconstruct it.

hierarchy (hierarchical) A term derived from TAXONOMIC studies and applied in LINGUISTICS to refer to any CLASSIFICATION of linguistic UNITS which recognizes a series of successively subordinate LEVELS. **Hierarchical structure** can be illustrated from any branch of linguistics, e.g. the analysis of a SENTENCE into IMMEDIATE CONSTITUENTS, or the analysis of the LEXICON into semantic FIELDS of increasing specificity (as in *Roget's Thesaurus*). The relationship of inclusion which is involved can be seen in analyses of linguistic structure where DISCOURSES are said to 'consist of' sentences, which in turn consist of CLAUSES or PHRASES; these consist of WORDS, which in turn consist of MORPHEMES. The term has a special status in RELATIONAL GRAMMAR, as part of the phrase 'ACCESSIBILITY hierarchy', and has also been used with reference to CASE GRAMMAR ('case hierarchy'). In some models of NON-LINEAR PHONOLOGY, the 'PROSODIC hierarchy' shows the relationship between MORA, SYLLABLE, FOOT and WORD. See also CHOMSKY HIERARCHY, STRUCTURE, SONORITY.

high (1) One of the features of sound set up by CHOMSKY and Halle in their DISTINCTIVE FEATURE theory of PHONOLOGY, to handle variations in PLACE OF ARTICULATION (CAVITY features). High sounds are a type of TONGUE-BODY feature, and defined ARTICULATORILY as those produced by raising the TONGUE above the level it holds in neutral position; CLOSE VOWELS and PALATAL/VELAR CONSONANTS are [+high]. Its opposite is **non-high** [−high] or LOW, referring to sounds produced without any such raising, as in OPEN vowels and FRONT consonants.

(2) A term which describes the more formal variety in DIGLOSSIA; opposed to 'low'.

higher category A term used in GENERATIVE GRAMMAR to refer to a CATEGORY which is introduced into a SENTENCE DERIVATION earlier than a further instance of the same category. In a TREE-diagram representation of the derivation, the first instance of the category is seen to be higher up the tree than the other instance(s). For example, in the derivation of such sentences as *the idea that the man will resign surprises me*, the following (partial) tree might be used:

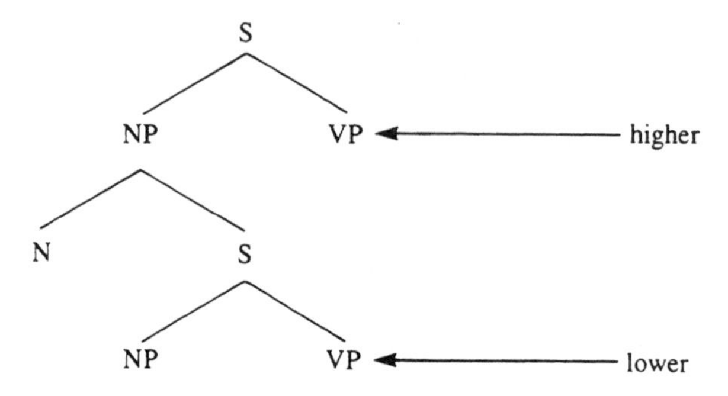

In this sentence, the 'higher VERB' is *surprise*, and the 'higher CLAUSE' or 'higher sentence' is *the idea surprises me.* Alternative terms are MATRIX and 'superordinate'. The usual term for the 'lower' verb/clause is EMBEDDED.

historical linguistics A branch of LINGUISTICS which studies the development of LANGUAGE and languages over time; also known as DIACHRONIC linguistics. The data of study are identical to that of COMPARATIVE PHILOLOGY, viz. the extant records of older states of languages; but the methods and aims are not the same. Historical linguistics uses the methods of the various schools of SYNCHRONIC linguistics (including SOCIOLINGUISTICS and PSYCHOLINGUISTICS, especially in considering the reasons for language change). One thus encounters such subfields as 'historical PHONOLOGY/MORPHOLOGY/SYNTAX', etc. It also aims to relate its findings to GENERAL linguistic theory.

hocus-pocus A phrase coined in the 1950s to characterize one of two extreme states of mind in a hypothetical LINGUIST who sets up a DESCRIPTION of linguistic DATA; opposed to GOD'S TRUTH. 'Hocus-pocus' linguists approach data in the expectation that they will have to impose an organization on it in order to show STRUCTURAL patterns. Different linguists, on this view, could approach the same data, and by virtue of their different backgrounds, INTUITIONS, PROCEDURES, etc., arrive at differing descriptions. In a 'God's truth' approach, by contrast, the aim is to demonstrate an underlying structure really present in the data over which there could be no dispute.

hodiernal In GRAMMAR, a category which marks how far a situation is from the moment of speaking (from Latin *hodie* 'today'); opposed to **prehodiernal**. For example, in many Bantu languages one verb form is used for 'today' events, and another for 'before today' events, regardless of their current relevance.

hold(ing) (1) A term used in describing the ARTICULATION of some types of sound, where the VOCAL ORGANS maintain their position for a definable period, as in the CLOSURE stage in the production of a PLOSIVE or a long CONSONANT (cf. LENGTH).

(2) In the PHONOLOGICAL analysis of SIGN language, a term referring to a static functional unit; also called **location**. Holds are distinguished from dynamic units, known as **movements**.

holophrase (holophras-tic, -is) A term used in language ACQUISITION to refer to a GRAMMATICALLY unstructured UTTERANCE, usually consisting of a single WORD, which is characteristic of the earliest stage of LANGUAGE learning in children. Typical **holophrastic** utterances include *dada, allgone, more, there*. Theoretical controversy centres on the extent to which these utterances may be analysed as SENTENCES ('one-word sentences'), or as a reduced version of a sentence, whose other ELEMENTS are 'understood' in the EXTRALINGUISTIC SITUATION (e.g. *daddy* means 'there is daddy', the *there is* being expressed by gesture, tone of voice, etc.). **Holophrasis** is also sometimes identified in adult utterances where there is no internal STRUCTURAL contrastivity, such as *thanks, please, sorry*.

homograph(-y, -ic) (1) A term used in SEMANTIC analysis to refer to WORDS (i.e. LEXEMES) which have the same spelling but differ in MEANING. Homographs are a type of HOMONYMY. **Homography** is illustrated from such pairs as *wind* (sc. blowing) and *wind* (sc. a clock). When there is AMBIGUITY on account of this identity, a **homographic clash** or 'conflict' is said to have occurred.

(2) The term **homography** is also used to refer to a type of orthography where there is a one-to-one correspondence between symbols and sounds, as in a PHONETIC TRANSCRIPTION, or the systematically devised alphabets of some languages. In this sense, it is opposed to **heterographic** systems, such as the spelling system of English, French, etc.

homonym(-y, -ic) A term used in SEMANTIC analysis to refer to LEXICAL ITEMS which have the same FORM but differ in MEANING. 'Homonymy' is illustrated from the various meanings of *bear* (= animal, carry) or *ear* (of body, of corn). In these examples, the identity covers both spoken and written forms, but it is possible to have partial homonymy (or HETERONYMY), where the identity is within a single MEDIUM, as in HOMOPHONY and HOMOGRAPHY. When there is AMBIGUITY between homonyms (whether non-deliberate or contrived, as in riddles and puns), a **homonymic clash** or 'conflict' is said to have occurred. In semantic analysis, the theoretical distinction between homonymy and POLYSEMY (one form with different meanings) provides a problem which has attracted a great deal of attention. See also CONSTRUCTION.

homophene A term sometimes used in the LINGUISTIC study of deaf communication, referring to WORDS which are visually identical when seen on the lips. Examples are *fan* and *van*.

homophone (homophon-y, -ic) A term used in SEMANTIC analysis to refer to WORDS (i.e. LEXEMES) which have the same pronunciation, but differ in MEANING. 'Homophones' are a type of HOMONYMY. **Homophony** is illustrated from such pairs as *threw/through* and *rode/rowed*. When there is AMBIGUITY on account of this identity, a **homophonic clash** or 'conflict' is said to have occurred.

homorganic A general term in the PHONETIC classification of speech sounds, referring to sounds which are produced at the same PLACE OF ARTICULATION, such as [p], [b] and [m]. Sounds involving independent articulations may be referred to as **heterorganic**. Sounds involving adjacent, and thus to some degree mutually dependent, articulations are also sometimes further distinguished as 'contiguous'.

honorific A term used in the GRAMMATICAL analysis of some LANGUAGES (e.g. Japanese) to refer to SYNTACTIC or MORPHOLOGICAL distinctions used to express LEVELS of politeness or respect, especially in relation to the compared social status of the participants. The PRONOUN system of several European languages expresses a contrast of this kind, e.g. French *tu* v. *vous*, Spanish *tú* v. *usted*.

hortative A term sometimes used in the GRAMMATICAL analysis of VERBS, to refer to a type of MODAL meaning in which an exhortation is made, as in the 'let us' construction in English (*let us pray*).

HPSG The abbreviation for HEAD-DRIVEN PHRASE-STRUCTURE GRAMMAR.

hypercorrection A term used in LINGUISTICS to refer to the movement of a linguistic FORM beyond the point set by the VARIETY of LANGUAGE that a speaker has as a target; also called **hyperurbanism** or **overcorrection**. The phenomenon usually takes place when speakers of a non-standard DIALECT attempt to use the STANDARD dialect and 'go too far', producing a version which does not appear in the standard, e.g. putting a long /ɑ/ in place of a short /æ/ in such words as *cap*, *mat*, etc. Analogous behaviour is encountered in second-language learning.

hypernasality see NASAL

hypernym see HYPONYM

hypersememic One of the strata recognized in STRATIFICATIONAL GRAMMAR, dealing with the conceptual or REFERENTIAL properties of LANGUAGE.

hyperurbanism see HYPERCORRECTION

hypocoristic A term used in LINGUISTICS for a pet name (e.g. Harry for Harold). Hypocoristics and similar phenomena have attracted special attention in some models of NON-LINEAR PHONOLOGY (notably, PROSODIC MORPHOLOGY), where they have been used as an illustration of TEMPLATE analysis and related procedures. One approach on these lines argues that a hypocoristic is the result of mapping a name onto a minimal word template.

hyponasality see NASAL

hyponym(y) A term used in SEMANTICS as part of the study of the SENSE relations which relate LEXICAL ITEMS. 'Hyponymy' is the relationship which obtains between specific and general lexical items, such that the former is 'included' in the latter (i.e. 'is a hyponym of' the latter). For example, a *cat* is a hyponym of *animal*, *flute* of *instrument*, *chair* of *furniture*, and so on. In each case, there is a superordinate term (sometimes called a **hypernym** or **hyperonym**), with reference to which the subordinate term can be defined, as is the usual practice in dictionary definitions ('a cat is a type of animal . . .'). The set of terms which are hyponyms of the same superordinate term are **co-hyponyms**, e.g. *flute*, *clarinet, trumpet.* A term which is a hyponym of itself, in that the same lexical item can operate at both superordinate and subordinate levels, is an **autohyponym**: for example, *cow* contrasts with *horse*, at one level, but at a lower level it contrasts with *bull* (in effect, 'a cow is a kind of cow'). Hyponymy is distinguished from such other sense relations as SYNONYMY, ANTONYMY and MERONYMY.

hypophonemic One of the strata recognized in STRATIFICATIONAL GRAMMAR, dealing with the PHONETIC properties of an UTTERANCE.

hypotactic (hypotaxis) A term used in TRADITIONAL GRAMMATICAL analysis, and often found in DESCRIPTIVE LINGUISTIC studies, to refer to DEPENDENT CONSTRUCTIONS, especially those where CONSTITUENTS have been linked through the use of SUBORDINATING CONJUNCTIONS. 'Hypotactic constructions' are opposed to PARATACTIC ones, where the linkage is conveyed solely by juxtaposition and punctuation/INTONATION. **Hypotaxis** is illustrated by *The keeper laughed when the dog barked* (cf. *the keeper laughed; the dog barked*).

Hz see CYCLE (3)

I

I The abbreviation in recent GOVERNMENT-BINDING THEORY for INFLECTION, previously abbreviated as INFL.

IA The usual abbreviation for an ITEM-AND-ARRANGEMENT MODEL of description in MORPHOLOGY.

iamb A traditional term in METRICS for a unit of poetic RHYTHM comprising a single pair of unstressed + STRESSED syllables (as in *leader*); also called an **iambic foot**. In METRICAL PHONOLOGY, the notion is used as an informal name for BOUNDED right-DOMINANT FEET, which display this rhythmical structure. See also TROCHEE.

iambic reversal see REVERSAL

IC The usual abbreviation for IMMEDIATE CONSTITUENT.

iconic(ity) A suggested defining property of some SEMIOTIC SYSTEMS, but not LANGUAGE, to refer to signals whose physical FORM closely corresponds to characteristics of the entities to which they refer. This is the normal state of affairs in animal communication, for example, where a call expressing fear is used only in a fear-producing context. In language, only a small number of ITEMS could be argued to possess such directly symbolic ('iconic') properties, e.g. onomatopoeic expressions such as *cuckoo, growl.*

ID The abbreviation in GENERALIZED PHRASE-STRUCTURE GRAMMAR for IMMEDIATE DOMINANCE.

idealization (ideal-ize) A term used in LINGUISTICS to refer to the degree to which linguists ignore certain aspects of the variability in their raw DATA, in order to arrive at an analysis that is as GENERALLY applicable as possible. Idealization is a major assumption of GENERATIVE linguistics, as it underlies the notion of COMPETENCE. A main aim of linguistics, in this view, is to account for the LANGUAGE of an 'ideal' speaker-hearer in an ideal (i.e. homogeneous) SPEECH community, who knows the language perfectly, and is unaffected by memory limitations, distractions, errors, etc., in actually using the language. While some degree of idealization is inevitable, if general statements are to be made, the decision as to what can be discounted in carrying out an analysis is often controversial.

ideational A term sometimes used in SEMANTICS as part of a classification of types of MEANING. It refers to that aspect of meaning which relates to the speaker's COGNITIVE awareness of the external world or (in a behavioural definition) to the objectively verifiable states of affairs in the external world, as reflected in LANGUAGE. This function of language, for the expression of CONTENT, is usually contrasted with INTERPERSONAL (or social), EXPRESSIVE and TEXTUAL meaning. Terms with similar meaning include 'conceptual' and COGNITIVE.

ideophone (ideophonic) A term sometimes used in LINGUISTICS and PHONETICS for any vivid representation of an idea in sound, such as occurs through onomatopoeia. In Bantu linguistics, it is the name of a particular WORD CLASS containing SOUND-SYMBOLIC words.

idioglossia A term sometimes used in LINGUISTICS for an invented form of speech whose meaning is known only to the inventor(s); also called **autonomous speech** or **cryptophasia**. An example is the idiosyncratic form of communication which sometimes emerges spontaneously between twins, and which is popularly labelled 'twin language' (though it is invariably only a deviant form of the local mother-tongue).

idiolect A term used in LINGUISTICS to refer to the linguistic SYSTEM of an individual speaker – one's personal DIALECT. A dialect can be seen as an abstraction deriving from the analysis of a large number of idiolects. Some linguists give the term a more restricted definition, referring to the speech habits of a person as displayed in a particular VARIETY at a given time.

idiom(atic) A term used in GRAMMAR and LEXICOLOGY to refer to a SEQUENCE of WORDS which is SEMANTICALLY and often SYNTACTICALLY restricted, so that they function as a single UNIT. From a semantic viewpoint, the MEANINGS of the individual words cannot be summed to produce the meaning of the 'idiomatic' expression as a whole. From a syntactic viewpoint, the words often do not permit the usual variability they display in other CONTEXTS, e.g. *it's raining cats and dogs* does not permit **it's raining a cat and a dog/dogs and cats*, etc. Because of their lack of internal CONTRASTIVITY, some linguists refer to idioms as 'ready-made UTTERANCES'. An alternative terminology refers to idioms as 'habitual COLLOCATIONS'. A point which has attracted considerable discussion is the extent to which degrees and kinds of idiomaticness can be established: some idioms do permit a degree of internal change, and are somewhat more literal in meaning than others (e.g. *it's worth her while/the job will be worth my while*, etc.). In GENERATIVE GRAMMAR, idiomatic constructions are used for testing hypotheses about structure. For example, the appearance of 'idiom chunks' in particular positions in a sentence is used to distinguish between CONTROL and RAISING sentences.

idiophone A term used by some LINGUISTS to refer to a speech sound identifiable with reference to a single IDIOLECT.

I-language An abbreviation for **internalized language**, a term suggested by Noam CHOMSKY to refer to LANGUAGE viewed as an element of the mind of a person who knows the language, acquired by the learner, and used by the speaker-hearer. It is seen in contrast with E-LANGUAGE.

illative A term used in GRAMMATICAL DESCRIPTION to refer to a type of INFLECTION which expresses the meaning of 'motion into' or 'direction towards' a place. The illative CASE is found in Finnish, for example, along with ALLATIVE, ELATIVE and several other cases expressing 'local' temporal and spatial meanings.

ill formed (ill-formedness) A term used in LINGUISTICS, especially in GENERATIVE GRAMMAR, to refer to the ungrammaticality ('ill-formedness' or DEVIANCE) of a SENTENCE. A sentence is ill formed if it cannot be generated by the RULES of a grammar; it is WELL FORMED if it can be. The term applies equally to SYNTAX, SEMANTICS and PHONOLOGY.

illocutionary A term used in the theory of SPEECH ACTS to refer to an act which is performed by the speaker by virtue of the UTTERANCE having been made. Examples of **illocutionary acts** (or **illocutionary force**) include promising, commanding, requesting, baptizing, arresting, etc. The term is contrasted with LOCUTIONARY (the act of 'saying') and PERLOCUTIONARY (where the act is defined by reference to the effect it has on the hearer).

imitation An application of the general sense of this term to LANGUAGE ACQUISITION, where it refers to children's behaviour in copying the language they hear around them. The importance of the notion is twofold. First, it has been shown that imitation cannot by itself account for the facts of language development (despite a popular view to the contrary – that children learn language by imitating their parents): FORMS such as **mouses* and **wented*, and SENTENCES such as **Me not like that*, show that some internal process of construction is taking place. Second, the skills children show when they are actually imitating are often different, in important aspects, from those they display in spontaneous SPEECH PRODUCTION, or in COMPREHENSION. The relationship between imitation, production and comprehension has been a major focus of experimental and descriptive interest in acquisition studies.

immediate constituent (IC) A term used in GRAMMATICAL analysis to refer to the major divisions that can be made within a SYNTACTIC CONSTRUCTION, at any LEVEL. For example, in analysing the SENTENCE *The boy is walking*, the immediate constituents would be *the boy* and *is walking*. These in turn can be analysed into immediate constituents (*the* + *boy*, *is* + *walking*), and the process continues until irreducible constituents are reached. The whole procedure is known as **immediate-constituent analysis** (or 'CONSTITUENT analysis'), and was a major feature of BLOOMFIELDIAN STRUCTURALIST linguistics.

immediate dominance (1) A term used in GENERATIVE LINGUISTICS for a type of relationship between NODES in a PHRASE-MARKER: a node A immediately DOMINATES a node B if and only if there is no node C such that it also dominates B and is dominated by A.

(2) An **immediate dominance (ID) rule** is a type of rule in GENERALIZED PHRASE-STRUCTURE GRAMMAR of the form X → Y, Z. It specifies that X can dominate Y and Z but does not specify the relative order of Y and Z. Together with LINEAR PRECEDENCE RULES and various general PRINCIPLES, ID rules generate phrase-markers of the classical type.

imperative A term used in the GRAMMATICAL classification of SENTENCE types, and usually seen in contrast to INDICATIVE, INTERROGATIVE, etc., MOODS. It refers to

VERB FORMS or sentence/CLAUSE types typically used in the expression of COMMANDS, e.g. *Go away!*

imperfect tense In GRAMMAR, a TENSE form used in some languages to express such meanings as duration or continuity in past time. Latin had an imperfect tense: *amabam* 'I was loving/used to love'.

imperfective A term used in the GRAMMATICAL analysis of ASPECT, referring to those FORMS of the VERB which mark the way in which the internal time structure of a situation is viewed. Imperfective forms contrast with PERFECTIVE forms, where the situation is seen as a whole, regardless of the time contrasts it may contain. The contrast is well recognized in the grammar of Slavic languages.

impersonal see PERSON

implicational scaling A model of language VARIATION which aims to account for the differential spread of changes in a population. Individual variation is represented as an alternation between old and new RULES, and differences between individuals are viewed as differences in rule inventories. An implicational table is used to display the spread of rules throughout a population. The approach contrasts with the VARIABLE rule model, in which variability is a property of the rules themselves.

implicational universal see UNIVERSAL

implicature A term derived from the work of the philosopher H. P. Grice (1913–88) and now frequently used in LINGUISTICS as part of the study of conversational structure. **Conversational implicatures** refer to the implications which can be deduced from the FORM of an UTTERANCE, on the basis of certain CO-OPERATIVE PRINCIPLES which govern the efficiency and normal ACCEPTABILITY of conversations, as when the sentence *There's some chalk on the floor* is taken to mean 'you ought to pick it up'. Several types of implicature have been discussed, in the context of the relationship between language and logical expression, and of the conditions which affect the APPROPRIATENESS of utterances. In particular, implicatures have been classified into **generalized** and **particularized** types – the former not being restricted to a particular context; the latter requiring a specific context. Also, a contrast has been drawn between conversational (or **non-conventional**) implicatures, which are inferences calculated on the basis of the MAXIMS OF CONVERSATION, and **conventional** implicatures, which are not derived from these principles but simply attached by convention to particular expressions. Examples of the latter which have been suggested include utterance-INITIAL *oh*, the use of *therefore, even* and *yet*, and sequences of the type *He is an Englishman; therefore he is brave.* However, relatively little detailed linguistic investigation has yet taken place into these matters, and several of the proposals are controversial.

implosive A term used in the PHONETIC classification of CONSONANT sounds on the basis of their MANNER OF ARTICULATION: it refers to the series of PLOSIVE sounds it is possible to make using an AIRSTREAM MECHANISM involving an inwards movement of air in the mouth (an INGRESSIVE airstream). A complete CLOSURE is made in the mouth, as with any plosive sound, but the air behind the closure is not compressed, ready for outwards release; instead, a downwards movement of the LARYNX takes place, and the air inside the mouth is accordingly rarefied. Upon release of the closure, air is then sucked into the mouth at the same time as the GLOTTIS is released, allowing lung air to produce some VOCAL CORD vibration. It is this combination of movements that results in the characteristically 'hollow' auditory effect of the implosive consonants. Such consonants are usually VOICED and occur PHONEMICALLY in such languages as Sindi and Ibo. They are transcribed with a right-facing hook attached to the consonant symbol, as in [ɠ], [ɗ], [ɓ]. Alternative terms are 'ingressive stop' and 'suction stop' consonants. There is no opposite technical term 'explosive'.

inalienable A term used in GRAMMATICAL analysis to refer to a type of possessive relationship formally marked in some languages (e.g. Chinese). If a possessed item is seen as being in a permanent or necessary relationship to its possessor, the relationship is said to be 'inalienable' (e.g. *the dog's head, the town centre*), otherwise it is ALIENABLE.

inanimate see ANIMATE

inceptive, inchoative Terms used in the GRAMMATICAL analysis of VERBS, to refer to a type of ASPECTUAL relationship in which the beginning of an action is specified. In LANGUAGES which mark 'inceptive' (or 'inchoative') aspects, the MEANINGS might be translated into English by 'be about to' or 'be on the point of' – for example, Latin *-escere*. A contrast is sometimes drawn with TELIC verbs.

inclusion (inclu-ded, -sive) (1) A SEMANTIC relationship which identifies the SENSE relation of HYPONYMY; e.g. to say that a *car* is a kind of *vehicle* is to say that the class of cars is 'included' within that of vehicles.

(2) In GRAMMATICAL analysis, **included** is mainly used to refer to a LINGUISTIC FORM which occurs as a CONSTITUENT of a CONSTRUCTION: it is in the 'included position'. For example, the CLAUSE *parked in the street* is in the included position in the SENTENCE *The car parked in the street was a Hillman*.

(3) With reference to PRONOUNS, **inclusive** is used (in contrast with EXCLUSIVE) to refer to a first-PERSON role where the speaker and addressee (or the speaker and someone else) are both included, e.g. *we* = 'me and you'.

(4) In SEMANTICS, a term derived from formal logic (in contrast with EXCLUSIVE) to refer to a type of DISJUNCTION: in an inclusive interpretation, the disjunction is true if either, or both, of the propositions is true. In *Either X is happening or Y is happening*, an inclusive interpretation allows ('includes') both options.

(5) In SOCIOLINGUISTICS, and increasingly in general usage, **inclusive language** refers to the use of words which avoid the social stereotypes associated with particular social groups, especially in relation to ethnicity and sex. For example, because a noun such as *spokesman*, though traditionally GENERIC, could be given an excluding interpretation (i.e. referring to males only), it would be replaced in an inclusive approach by such nouns as *spokesperson*.

incompatibility (incompatible) A term used in SEMANTICS as part of the study of the SENSE relations between LEXICAL ITEMS. It refers to sets of items where the choice of one item excludes the use of all the other items from that set (unless there is to be a contradiction). Colour terms provide a well-studied example: to say *the car is red* excludes *the car is green/blue*, etc. – and the set of items which contrast in this way are said to be 'incompatible'. Incompatibility has been less investigated than other sense relations (such as ANTONYMY and SYNONYMY), but some linguists have pointed to the existence of different types of many-member (as opposed to binary) sets, such as ranks (e.g. military), scales (e.g. value judgements) and cycles (e.g. seasons).

incorporating A type of LANGUAGE sometimes distinguished in COMPARATIVE LINGUISTICS using STRUCTURAL (as opposed to DIACHRONIC) criteria, and focusing on the characteristics of the WORD: 'polysynthetic' or **incorporating languages** demonstrate MORPHOLOGICALLY complex, long word forms, as in the CONSTRUCTIONS typical of many American Indian languages, and encountered occasionally in English, in coinages such as *anti/dis/establish/ment/arian/ism/s*. Some linguists, however, prefer to see such constructions handled as a complex of 'incorporated' AGGLUTINATIVE and FUSIONAL characteristics, and do not regard this category of language as typologically distinct. As always in such classifications, the categories are not clear-cut: different languages will display the characteristic of 'incorporation' to a greater or lesser degree.

incorporation (incorporate) In the study of WORD FORMATION, a general term for any kind of MORPHOLOGICAL element found within a WORD (especially, within a VERB). PRONOUNS and PARTICLES are among the elements which may be incorporated, but the term is specifically used for **noun incorporation**, where a noun STEM is used within a verb to form a complex verb. The process carries a variety of functions, such as narrowing the SEMANTIC range of the verb, or varying the INFORMATION structure of the sentence. Incorporation has been much discussed in linguistic theory because of its unclear status in relation to the LEXICON (where it can be handled as a process of DERIVATION) or the SYNTAX (where it can be handled as a result of MOVEMENT TRANSFORMATIONS).

indefinite(ness) A term used in GRAMMAR and SEMANTICS to refer to an entity (or class of entities) which is not capable of specific identification; it is contrasted with DEFINITE. Indefiniteness in English is usually conveyed through the use of the indefinite ARTICLE, *a*, or an indefinite PRONOUN (such as *one*, *some*, etc.). 'Non-definite' is often used as a synonym, but some linguists make a difference between 'non-definite' and 'indefinite' reference. However, the distinction between definite and indefinite is not a straightforward one, given the many LINGUISTIC and EXTRALINGUISTIC CONTEXTUAL variables which operate.

indeterminacy (indeterminate) A term used in LINGUISTICS to refer to a state of affairs in linguistic study in which there is uncertainty on the part of a NATIVE-SPEAKER, or disagreement between native-speakers, as to what is GRAMMATICAL or ACCEPTABLE; or in which there is uncertainty on the part of a linguist, or between several linguists, as to how and where a boundary line between different types of STRUCTURE might best be drawn. Indeterminacy poses a major difficulty for linguistic theories which attempt to define the limits of grammaticality in an unequivocal way (as in GENERATIVE grammar). It is a major focus of attention in NON-DISCRETE or FUZZY GRAMMAR, and several analytical notions have been proposed to handle the phenomenon (e.g. GRADIENCE, SQUISH).

index see AFFIX, INDEXING

indexical (1) (**indices**) A term used by some LINGUISTS to refer to features of speech or writing which reveal the personal (biological, psychological or social) characteristics of a LANGUAGE user, as in VOICE QUALITY or handwriting. More generally, the term may be used to refer to the membership-identifying characteristics of a group, such as regional, social or occupational 'indices'.

(2) (**indexicality**) The philosophical use of this term (either alone, or in the phrase **indexical expression**) is sometimes encountered in LINGUISTICS to refer to those features of language which refer directly to characteristics of the SITUATION within which an UTTERANCE takes place; their meaning is thus relative to that situation. Linguists more regularly refer to these features as DEICTIC features.

indexing (index, indices) An application of the general use of this term in GENERATIVE LINGUISTICS to refer to the numerical or literal markers attached to a set of items in a SENTENCE, to show identity or difference of REFERENCE. The indices are known more explicitly as **referential indices**. In recent work, **indexing rules** ASSIGN numerical or literal indices to NOUN PHRASES in a sentence to ensure that the correct SEMANTIC relations of CO-REFERENCE are represented – a process which has come to be known as CO-INDEXING. The CONDITIONS which restrict the application of indexing rules are known as BINDING conditions.

indicative A term used in the GRAMMATICAL CLASSIFICATION of SENTENCE types, and usually seen in contrast to IMPERATIVE, SUBJUNCTIVE, etc., MOODS. It refers to VERB forms or sentence/CLAUSE types used in the expression of STATEMENTS and QUESTIONS, e.g. *the horse is walking*. With reference to statements, the term 'declarative' may be used.

indirect (1) A term used in GRAMMATICAL description to refer to one of the two types of OBJECT ELEMENT which can function in CLAUSE STRUCTURE, the other being labelled DIRECT; traditionally considered a DATIVE function. **Indirect objects** in English usually appear before the direct object (e.g. *the woman gave the boy a book*), but may also follow it (e.g. *the woman gave a book to the boy*). This traditional use of the term applies to the 'recipient' NOUN PHRASE in DITRANSITIVE constructions regardless of its position. By contrast, GENERATIVE grammar (especially RELATIONAL GRAMMAR), uses the term in a more restricted way, only for the COMPLEMENT of the PREPOSITION (usually *to*), as in *The woman gave a book to the boy.* In relational grammar, the indirect object can be promoted and become a direct object, while the original direct object becomes a CHÔMEUR.

(2) The opposition between direct and indirect is also used to identify the two main ways of reflecting a person's speech: **indirect speech** (or 'reported speech') refers to the use of a grammatical CONSTRUCTION where the WORDS of the speaker are SUBORDINATED to a VERB in a main CLAUSE, e.g. *she said that she had a cold*, where the 'direct speech' would have been *I have a cold.*

(3) In the classification of SPEECH ACTS, the term refers to an UTTERANCE whose linguistic FORM does not directly reflect its communicative purpose, as when *I'm feeling cold* functions as a request for someone to close a door. If, on the other hand, someone produced the same sentence to express, literally, the

fact that he or she was feeling cold, then the speech act would be direct – an assertion.

inessive A term used in GRAMMATICAL DESCRIPTION to refer to a type of INFLECTION which expresses the meaning of location or position within a place. The inessive CASE is found in Finnish, for example, along with ADESSIVE, ALLATIVE and several other cases expressing 'local' temporal and spatial meanings.

infelicitous utterance see FELICITY CONDITIONS

infinitive (infinitival) A traditional term for the non-FINITE FORM of the VERB usually cited as its UNMARKED or BASE form, e.g. *go, walk, kick*, though some LANGUAGES mark it SYNTACTICALLY or MORPHOLOGICALLY. In English, the infinitive form may be used alone or in conjunction with the PARTICLE *to* (the ***to*** **infinitive**), e.g. *he saw her go v. he wants to go*. The form without *to* is sometimes known as the **bare** or **zero infinitive**. In GOVERNMENT-BINDING THEORY, the term **infinitive** (or **infinitival**) **clause** is used for constructions with *to*-infinitive.

infix(-ing, -ation) A term used in MORPHOLOGY referring to an AFFIX which is added within a ROOT or STEM. The process of **infixation** is not encountered in European LANGUAGES, but it is commonly found in Asian, American Indian and African languages (e.g. Arabic).

INFL An abbreviation used in early GOVERNMENT-BINDING THEORY for INFLECTION, later replaced by I.

inflection(al) (inflexion(al), inflect) (1) A term used in MORPHOLOGY to refer to one of the two main CATEGORIES or processes of WORD FORMATION (**inflectional morphology**), the other being DERIVATION(AL). These terms also apply to the two types of AFFIX involved in word formation. Inflectional affixes signal GRAMMATICAL relationships, such as plural, past TENSE and possession, and do not change the grammatical CLASS of the STEMS to which they are attached; that is, the words constitute a single PARADIGM, e.g. *walk, walks, walked*. A word is said to 'inflect for' past tense, plural, etc. In traditional (pre-linguistic) grammatical studies, the term 'accidence' was used in this sense.

(2) **inflection (INFL, I)** A term used in GOVERNMENT-BINDING THEORY (at first symbolized as INFL, later as I) for an abstract CONSTITUENT which subsumes various grammatical properties – in particular, tense, PERSON and NUMBER (the latter two being separately grouped as AGREEMENT features, or AGR). In X-BAR theory, I is like the LEXICAL categories N, V, A and P in that it is a ZERO-level category with two PHRASAL PROJECTIONS, I′ and I″. I″, the maximal projection of I, is usually referred to as **inflection phrase (IP)**. It is equivalent to S in earlier GB and certain other theories.

(3) In the phrase **inflecting language** ('inflectional' or 'inflected' languages), the term refers to a type of LANGUAGE established by COMPARATIVE LINGUISTICS using STRUCTURAL (as opposed to DIACHRONIC) criteria, and focusing on the characteristics of the WORD. In this kind of language, words display grammatical relationships morphologically: they typically contain more than one MORPHEME but, unlike AGGLUTINATIVE languages, there is no one-to-one correspondence between these morphemes and the linear SEQUENCE of MORPHS. In languages such as Latin, Greek and Arabic, the inflectional forms of words may represent

several morphological OPPOSITIONS, e.g. in Latin *amo* ('I love'), the form simultaneously represents tense, ACTIVE, first person singular, INDICATIVE. This 'fusing' of properties has led to such languages being called FUSIONAL, and has motivated the WORD-AND-PARADIGM MODEL of analysis. As always in such classifications, the categories are not clear-cut: different languages will display the characteristic of inflection to a greater or lesser degree.

informant Someone who acts as a source of DATA for LINGUISTIC analysis, usually a NATIVE-SPEAKER of a LANGUAGE. Linguists may act in this way, but more usually an attempt is made to construct or verify hypotheses by referring directly to a range of informants, who provide, it is hoped, a representative sample of the language one is investigating. In fieldwork on previously unstudied languages, the informant is of fundamental importance, and several sophisticated techniques for ELICITING relevant but natural data from informants have now been devised. Informants' judgements about the ACCEPTABILITY of sentences are known as INTUITIONS (especially in GENERATIVE GRAMMAR). Since the early 1980s, some linguists have preferred to use the term **consultant**, reflecting the collaborative nature of the work.

information LINGUISTICS has made several uses of this fundamental concept, both in a general sense, and also as formalized in statistical terms, derived from the mathematical theory of COMMUNICATION. Ideas derived from information theory (as formulated originally by Claude Shannon and Warren Weaver in their book *The Mathematical Theory of Communication* (1949)) have been applied in PHONETICS (e.g. in analysing the amount of information carried by the various features of the sound wave), GRAMMAR (e.g. in studies of the predictability of various parts of a SENTENCE) and SEMANTICS (e.g. in applying the notion of 'choice' between alternatives in the analysis of semantic CONTRASTS, as in DYNAMIC semantics). The concept of REDUNDANCY, for example, ultimately derives from this approach.

In its general sense, the term is used by several linguists as a basis for a theoretical account of the STRUCTURE of messages. It is postulated that speech can be seen as displaying an 'information structure', encoding the relative salience of the elements in a message, with formally identifiable 'units of information'. INTONATION provides the main signal for such UNITS. The TONE UNIT represents an information unit, and the NUCLEAR tone marks the information FOCUS. Many sentences will be single units of information, e.g. *the box on the table is ready for pòsting/*, but altering the intonation, in this view, alters the number of informational units, e.g. *the box on the táble/ is ready for pòsting/*. Even if one tone unit is retained, altering the TONICITY will change the information structure, e.g. *the bòx on the table is ready for posting/* (i.e not the envelope). The further analysis of information structure is complex and controversial: a common next step is to distinguish between GIVEN and NEW information. Analysts who use this approach (e.g. HALLIDAYAN linguists) usually distinguish between information structure and THEMATIC and grammatical structure.

***-ing* form** A term used in English GRAMMATICAL description to refer to the FORM of the VERB ending in *-ing*, e.g. *going, smoking*. Many such forms can be used without change as NOUNS (e.g. *smoking is prohibited*), and the purpose of the term is to provide a neutral DESCRIPTIVE label for this feature of English, thus avoiding the use of such traditional notions as 'gerund', which were originally devised for Latin grammar. In classical TRANSFORMATIONAL GRAMMAR, *-ing* noun forms were transformationally derived from the related verb forms.

ingressive A term used in the PHONETIC classification of speech sounds, referring to all sounds produced using an inwards-moving AIRSTREAM MECHANISM. The opposite category is EGRESSIVE, which is the normal mode for speech production. Ingressive sounds are often heard incidentally, as when one speaks while breathing in, when out of breath, or vocalizes upon a sudden intake of breath when expressing pain or surprise. Two types of ingressive sound are used as part of the PHONEMIC systems of some LANGUAGES: IMPLOSIVE CONSONANTS such as [ɠ], [ɗ], [ɓ], made by an inward flow of air in conjunction with GLOTTAL vibration; and VELARIC consonants, which constitute such CLICK sounds as [ǀ] (as in 'tut tut'), made by an inward flow of air in conjunction with contact made at the velum.

inherent features A term used in some MODELS of GENERATIVE GRAMMAR (cf. ASPECTS) to refer to one of the types of (BINARY) FEATURES which are contained in a LEXICAL entry (the others being CONTEXTUAL and RULE features), and which provides information about the essential characteristics of an ITEM likely to affect its SYNTACTIC functioning, e.g. [+human], [+abstract], [+male]. These features are involved at several points in an analysis, e.g. in specifying SELECTIONAL restrictions and in some non-lexical TRANSFORMATIONS.

inherit(ance) A term used in several domains of LINGUISTICS to refer to the passing on of information from one part of a structural REPRESENTATION to another. For example, in SEMANTICS, the relationship between subtype and TYPE (e.g. *fish* and *food*) can be characterized as the subtype inheriting all the properties of its supertypes. In GENERATIVE GRAMMAR, inheritance refers to the preservation of ARGUMENT structure under certain conditions (e.g. a NOMINALIZATION of a VERB, such as *running*, preserves the arguments of the input verb). In some models of NON-LINEAR PHONOLOGY, information can be inherited between certain types of unit in a PROSODIC HIERARCHY.

initial The usual way of referring to the first ELEMENT in a LINGUISTIC UNIT, especially in PHONOLOGY. For example, the PHONEME /k/ occurs 'in initial position' (or 'initially') in the word *cat*; the word *the* occurs in initial position in the PHRASE *the big house*. Other positions are referred to as MEDIAL and FINAL. Other linguistic features which occur in this position are sometimes labelled accordingly, e.g. 'initial STRESS' (i.e. stress on the first SYLLABLE in a WORD).

initialism see ABBREVIATION

initial symbol The first, undefined term in a GENERATIVE GRAMMAR, employed in early PHRASE-STRUCTURE GRAMMARS, which appears on the left-hand side of the first REWRITE RULE. Standing for SENTENCE, the highest-level CONSTRUCTION recognized by the grammar, it has been symbolized as Σ, S′ or CP. The contrast implied is with TERMINAL symbols, the items which occur in a terminal STRING generated by the grammar. Other starting-points than sentence have occasionally been suggested.

initiator (initiation) A term in PHONETICS for those VOCAL ORGANS which are the source of air movement. The lungs are the normal initiators for speech, but other AIRSTREAM MECHANISMS can be used. Initiation, from an aerodynamic point of view, is comparable to a bellows or piston.

innate(ness) An application of the philosophical use of this term in PSYCHOLINGUISTICS, referring to the view that the child is born with a biological predisposition to learn LANGUAGE. The **innateness hypothesis** argues that the rapid and complex development of children's GRAMMATICAL COMPETENCE can be explained only by the hypothesis that they are born with an innate knowledge of at least some of the UNIVERSAL STRUCTURAL principles of human language. This view has received considerable support in GENERATIVE linguistics (cf. language ACQUISITION DEVICE), but controversy abounds over the nature of the early linguistic knowledge which might be attributable to the child, and whether this knowledge can be specified independently of other (e.g. cognitive) factors.

insert(ion) A basic SYNTACTIC operation within the framework of TRANSFORMATIONAL GRAMMAR which introduces a new STRUCTURAL ELEMENT into a STRING; specific types of example include '*DO*-insertion', 'NEGATIVE (*neg*-) insertion', '*there*-insertion' (which inserts an EMPTY *there* in SUBJECT position in STATEMENTS, e.g. *there was a cat in the garden*) and 'lexical insertion' (which inserts LEXICAL ITEMS at particular places in grammatical structure).

instantaneous A term sometimes used in the DISTINCTIVE FEATURE theory of PHONOLOGY, as part of the phrase 'instantaneous release', referring to a sound released suddenly, without the ACOUSTIC turbulence of a FRICATIVE, as in PLOSIVE CONSONANTS. Its opposite is DELAYED RELEASE, used to characterize AFFRICATES.

institutional linguistics A developing branch of LINGUISTICS in which the focus is on the language used in professional contexts, such as law, medicine, education, and business. As other domains of linguistic enquiry (e.g. SOCIOLINGUISTICS, STYLISTICS) also study such contexts, the term is not in widespread use.

instrumental In languages which express GRAMMATICAL relationships by means of INFLECTIONS, this term refers to the FORM taken by a NOUN PHRASE (often a single noun or PRONOUN), when it expresses such a notion as 'by means of' (as in Russian). The term has a special status in CASE grammar, where it refers to the SEMANTIC case of the inANIMATE entity causally involved in a verb's action (e.g. *the key* in *the key opened the door* or *the door was opened with a key*), and is contrasted with AGENTIVE, DATIVE, etc. It is also used in some predicative constructions in Russian, e.g. *Ona krasivoy devushkoy* 'She is a pretty girl'.

instrumental phonetics see PHONETICS

intensifier (intensifying) A term used in some GRAMMATICAL classifications of WORDS to refer to a CLASS of ADVERBS which have a heightening or lowering effect on the MEANING of another ELEMENT in the SENTENCE, e.g. *very, terribly, definitely, hardly, kind of.*

intension(al) A term used in philosophy and logic, and now often used as part of a theoretical framework for LINGUISTIC SEMANTICS, to refer to the set of defining properties which determines the APPLICABILITY of a term. For example, 'legs', 'flat surface', etc., define the intension of *table*, and an **intensional definition** would be based on such notions, e.g. 'A table is something with legs, a flat surface, etc.' It is opposed to EXTENSION.

intensity see LOUDNESS

intensive A term used in some GRAMMATICAL analyses to refer to STRUCTURES where there is a close SEMANTIC identity between ELEMENTS of structure, such as between SUBJECT and COMPLEMENT (e.g. *she is a dentist*), between OBJECT and complement (e.g. *they called him Fred*) or in APPOSITION (e.g. *John the butcher . . .*). The verbs involved in **intensive constructions** are called **intensive verbs** or 'linking verbs'. In GOVERNMENT-BINDING THEORY some of these constructions are analysed as SMALL CLAUSES. The term is opposed to EXTENSIVE.

interaction An application of the general use of this term in SOCIOLINGUISTICS, to refer to the study of speech in face-to-face communication (**interactional sociolinguistics**). The approach deals chiefly with the norms and strategies of everyday conversation, and is characterized by detailed TRANSCRIPTIONS of taped interactions, with particular reference to features which have been traditionally neglected in the analysis of conversation, such as PROSODY, facial expression, silence, and rhythmical patterns of behaviour between the participants. In contrast to other kinds of CONVERSATION ANALYSIS, particular attention is paid to the social factors which help to shape the interaction, such as the desire by the participants to maintain politeness (cf. FACE) or to recognize mutual rights and obligations.

interchangeability A suggested defining property of a SEMIOTIC SYSTEM, including human LANGUAGE, to refer to the system's ability to be mutually transmitted and received by members of the same species. Some animal signals, by contrast, lack this property – for example, female calls which are not shared by the male members of the species.

interclausal grammar see ROLE AND REFERENCE GRAMMAR

interdental A term used in the PHONETIC classification of CONSONANT sounds, referring to a sound made by the TIP of the TONGUE between the teeth, as in English *th* /θ/ and /ð/.

interface In the MINIMALIST PROGRAMME, a term describing the status of the two LEVELS of REPRESENTATION recognized in the approach: LOGICAL FORM (LF) and PHONETIC FORM (PF). Their role is to connect linguistic representations to interpretation elsewhere: LF interfaces with the conceptual systems of cognition, and PF interfaces with articulatory and perceptual systems of speech production/perception.

interference A term used in SOCIOLINGUISTICS and foreign-language learning to refer to the ERRORS a speaker introduces into one LANGUAGE as a result of contact with another language; also called **negative transfer**; cf. CONTRASTIVE (2). The most common source of error is in the process of learning a foreign language, where the native tongue interferes; but interference may occur in other CONTACT situations (as in MULTILINGUALISM).

interjection A term used in the TRADITIONAL CLASSIFICATION of PARTS OF SPEECH, referring to a CLASS of WORDS which are UNPRODUCTIVE, do not enter into SYNTACTIC relationships with other classes, and whose FUNCTION is purely EMOTIVE, e.g. *Yuk!, Strewth!, Blast!, Tut tut!* There is an unclear boundary between these ITEMS and other types of EXCLAMATION, where some REFERENTIAL MEANING may be involved, and where there may be more than one word, e.g. *Excellent!, Lucky devil!, Cheers!, Well well!* Several alternative ways of analysing these items have been suggested, using such notions as MINOR SENTENCE, FORMULAIC LANGUAGE, etc.

interlanguage The linguistic SYSTEM created by someone in the course of learning a foreign LANGUAGE, different from either the speaker's first language or the target language being acquired. It reflects the learner's evolving system of RULES, and results from a variety of processes, including the influence of the first language ('transfer'), CONTRASTIVE interference from the target language, and the OVERGENERALIZATION of newly encountered rules.

inter-level A term used in HALLIDAYAN LINGUISTICS referring to a LEVEL of analysis lying in between the main levels recognized by the theory. In this view, PHONOLOGY would be seen as an inter-level relating PHONIC/GRAPHIC SUBSTANCE and linguistic FORM.

interlingua(l) (1) A term used in machine translation for a proposed intermediate REPRESENTATION constructed to facilitate the automatic translation of one language into another. In an interlingual approach, the source language is given a highly abstract representation which captures all the SYNTACTIC and SEMANTIC information necessary for translation into several target languages. The interlingua would usually be a specially constructed FORMAL language, but other ARTIFICIAL LANGUAGES have been proposed (such as Esperanto), and in theory a natural language could also be used. The difficulty of developing a model of syntactic or semantic UNIVERSALS has limited the applicability of this approach.

(2) See LINGUA FRANCA.

intermediate (1) A term used in the PHONETIC classification of VOWEL QUALITIES, to refer to a vowel which falls between two adjacent CARDINAL vowels. The vowel which occurs in the centre of the cardinal vowel area (cf. SCHWA) is also sometimes referred to as an 'intermediate vowel'.

(2) In X-BAR theory, a 'small' phrase – larger than the lexical category (zero-level projection) and smaller than the maximal projection (usually X-double-bar, or XP) – is called an **intermediate projection**.

internal adequacy see ADEQUACY

internalize A term used in GENERATIVE LINGUISTICS to refer to the process whereby speakers come to possess knowledge of the STRUCTURE of their LANGUAGE. The term is primarily used in the context of language ACQUISITION, where children are said to 'internalize' RULES, as when the use of such FORMS as **mans* and **mices* shows that a plural formation RULE has been acquired. COMPETENCE, on this account, can be seen as a SYSTEM of internalized rules..

internalized language see I-LANGUAGE

internal reconstruction see RECONSTRUCTION

International Phonetic Association (IPA) An organization founded in 1886 by a group of European phoneticians (Paul Passy (1859–1940) and others) to promote the study of PHONETICS. In 1889 it published the **International Phonetic Alphabet** which, in modified and expanded form, is today the most widely used system for transcribing the sounds of a LANGUAGE (cf. TRANSCRIPTION). See p. xvii of this dictionary.

interpersonal A term sometimes used in SEMANTICS as part of a classification of types of MEANING. It refers to those aspects of meaning which relate to the establishing and maintaining of social relations, e.g. social roles, STYLISTIC LEVEL, the expression of personality. Some scholars also subsume EXPRESSIVE meaning under this heading. An alternative view sees the LINGUISTIC expression of social relationships as being a matter of SOCIOLINGUISTIC or PRAGMATIC FUNCTION, and not semantics.

interpretive A term used in GENERATIVE LINGUISTICS to refer to a mode of relationship between LEVELS OF REPRESENTATION. Its original use can be defined with reference to the STANDARD THEORY of generative GRAMMAR. Here, the SEMANTIC RULES which relate SYNTACTIC DEEP STRUCTURE to the semantic COMPONENT, and the PHONOLOGICAL rules which relate syntactic SURFACE STRUCTURES to the phonological component, are both 'interpretative', i.e. they 'interpret' the output of the syntactic structures by ASSIGNING them a (semantic or PHONETIC) representation, which is the basis from which the MEANING and pronunciation of the sentence is derived. In the **interpretive semantics** view, associated with Noam CHOMSKY and others, it is thus the level of syntax which contains all the generative POWER of the grammar. In the early 1970s, the term came to characterize any MODEL of this general sort, as opposed to those which claimed that it was the syntax, and not the semantics, which was interpretative – the view of GENERATIVE SEMANTICS.

interrogative A term used in the GRAMMATICAL classification of SENTENCE types, and usually seen in contrast to DECLARATIVE. It refers to VERB FORMS or sentence/CLAUSE types typically used in the expression of QUESTIONS, e.g. the inverted order of *is he coming?*, or the use of an 'interrogative word' (often subclassified as interrogative ADJECTIVES, e.g. *which*; ADVERBS, e.g. *why*; and PRONOUNS, e.g. *who*).

interruptability A term used in GRAMMAR to refer to a defining property of the WORD, seen as a grammatical UNIT, where it appears in the form **uninterruptability**. A more positive name for this criterion is COHESIVENESS.

interrupted A term sometimes used in the DISTINCTIVE FEATURE theory of PHONOLOGY to refer to sounds produced with a complete CLOSURE of the VOCAL TRACT, as in PLOSIVES. Its opposite is CONTINUANT, used to characterize FRICATIVES, VOWELS, etc.

intervocalic A term used in PHONETICS to refer to a CONSONANT sound used between two VOWELS, as in the /t/ of *attack*. The phonetic characteristics of consonants in this position are often different from those in other positions, e.g. the amount of VOICING in a voiced consonant is likely to be greater.

intonation A term used in the study of SUPRASEGMENTAL PHONOLOGY, referring to the distinctive use of patterns of PITCH, or melody. The study of intonation is sometimes called **intonology**. Several ways of analysing intonation have been suggested: in some approaches, the pitch patterns are described as CONTOURS and analysed in terms of LEVELS of pitch as pitch PHONEMES and MORPHEMES; in others, the patterns are described as TONE UNITS or tone groups, analysed further as contrasts of NUCLEAR tone, TONICITY, etc. The three variables of pitch range, height and direction are generally distinguished. Some approaches, especially within PRAGMATICS, operate with a much broader notion than that of the tone unit: **intonational phrasing** is a structured HIERARCHY of the intonational CONSTITUENTS in conversation. A formal category of **intonational phrase** is also sometimes recognized: an UTTERANCE span dominated by BOUNDARY TONES.

Intonation performs several functions in language. Its most important function is as a signal of GRAMMATICAL structure, where it performs a role similar to punctuation in writing, but involving far more contrasts. The marking of SENTENCE, CLAUSE and other boundaries, and the contrast between some grammatical structures, such as QUESTIONS and statements, may be made using intonation. For example, the change in meaning illustrated by 'Are you asking me or telling me' is regularly signalled by a contrast between RISING and FALLING pitch, e.g. *He's going, isn't he?* (= I'm asking you) opposed to *He's going, isn't he!* (= I'm telling you). A second role of intonation is in the communication of personal attitude: sarcasm, puzzlement, anger, etc., can all be signalled by contrasts in pitch, along with other PROSODIC and PARALINGUISTIC features. Other roles of intonation in language have been suggested, e.g. as one of the ways of signalling social background.

Intonation patterns can be seen as a sequence of pitch levels, or 'tones', but this use of 'tone' has to be distinguished from that encountered in the phrase TONE LANGUAGE, where it refers to the use of pitch to make contrasts of meaning at WORD level.

intransitivity see TRANSITIVITY

intrinsic A term used in GENERATIVE GRAMMAR, referring to a type of CONSTRAINT imposed on the ORDERING of RULES (as opposed to a CONDITION where such rules are allowed to apply in a random order). An **intrinsic ordering** is one where the FORMAL or logical properties of a SYSTEM of rules dictate the SEQUENCE in which the rules apply: one rule (B) cannot apply until after another rule (A) has operated, because A supplies B with the properties B needs for its operation. Intrinsic ordering is opposed to EXTRINSIC ordering, where the order of application is not motivated by such considerations of formal consistency; the rules could logically occur in any order, but some ordering has to be imposed (taking into account the DATA of the LANGUAGE) in order for a correct output to emerge.

intrusion A term used occasionally in PHONETICS and PHONOLOGY to refer to the addition of sounds in CONNECTED SPEECH which have no basis in the pronunciation of the SYLLABLES or WORDS heard in isolation. The most well-known example in English (RECEIVED PRONUNCIATION) is of the /r/ which is introduced as a LINKING FORM after a VOWEL, when the following word begins with a vowel, where there is no historical justification for it (i.e. there is no *r* in the spelling). Examples such as *law(r) and order, India(r) and Pakistan*, and (within word) *draw(r)ings* are common, and attract much criticism, though the frequency with which such forms are heard (the critics not excluded) indicates that the tendency of this ACCENT to link words in this way is deep-rooted. But one may hear other cases of intrusion, such as the introduction of an unstressed, SCHWA vowel between CONSONANTS in such words as *athletics* /aθəletɪks/.

As with the opposite effect, ELISION, traditional rhetoric had devised a classification of types of intrusion in terms of the position of the extra sound in a word: in word-INITIAL position, it was termed *prothesis*, in word-MEDIAL position *anaptyxis* or *epenthesis*, and in word-FINAL position *paragoge*. In phonetic analyses of modern languages, too, reference to a 'prothetic' vowel or an 'epenthetic' vowel is often encountered.

intuition (intuitive) A term in LINGUISTICS referring to the judgement of SPEAKERS about their LANGUAGE, especially in deciding whether a SENTENCE is ACCEPTABLE or not, and how sentences are interrelated. It is sometimes referred to as TACIT knowledge, or *Sprachgefühl*. Native-speaker intuitions are always a crucial form of evidence in linguistic analysis, but they are given a special theoretical status in GENERATIVE GRAMMAR, where in his later work Noam CHOMSKY sees them as part of the DATA which the grammar has to account for. It is important, in discussion of this topic, to distinguish the intuitions of the native-speaker from those of the linguist – a distinction which can be easily confused when linguists are investigating their own language. Linguists' intuitions concerning the accuracy or elegance of their analyses are quite different in kind from those of non-linguists, whose intuitions concern the sameness, difference and relatedness of MEANINGS.

invariable A term sometimes used in the GRAMMATICAL classification of WORDS to refer to one of two postulated major WORD-CLASSES in LANGUAGE, the other being VARIABLE. Invariable or **invariant** words are said to be those which are used without any MORPHOLOGICAL change, e.g. *under, but, them*. Variable words, by contrast, INFLECT, e.g. *house/houses, sit/sat* . . .

invariance (invariant) A principle in some approaches to PHONOLOGY whereby each PHONEME is seen as having a set of defining PHONETIC FEATURES, such that whenever a phoneme occurs the corresponding features will occur. Along with the conditions of LINEARITY and BIUNIQUENESS, the invariance principle establishes a view of phonemic analysis which has been criticized by GENERATIVE phonologists, as part of a general attack on TAXONOMIC phonemics.

invariant (in grammar) see INVARIABLE

inventory A term used in LINGUISTICS and PHONETICS to refer to an unordered listing of the ITEMS belonging to a particular LEVEL or area of DESCRIPTION in a LANGUAGE; e.g. the listing of the PHONEMES of English would constitute that language's 'phonemic inventory'.

inversion A term used in GRAMMATICAL analysis to refer to the process or result of

SYNTACTIC change in which a specific SEQUENCE of CONSTITUENTS is seen as the reverse of another. In English, for example, one of the main ways of forming QUESTIONS is by inverting the order of SUBJECT and AUXILIARY, e.g. *Is he going?*

IO The abbreviation for INDIRECT OBJECT in RELATIONAL GRAMMAR and some other models of grammatical description.

IP (1) The abbreviation for an ITEM-AND-PROCESS MODEL of DESCRIPTION in MORPHOLOGY.

(2) In X-BAR theory, the abbreviation for INFLECTION phrase.

IPA An abbreviation which is used for both the INTERNATIONAL PHONETIC ASSOCIATION and the International Phonetic Alphabet of that association.

irrealis see REALIS

irregular(ity) A term used in LINGUISTICS to refer to a linguistic FORM which is an exception to the pattern stated in a RULE. For example, VERBS such as *took, went, saw*, etc., are irregular, because they do not follow the rule which forms the past TENSE by adding *-ed*. GRAMMAR is concerned with the discovery of REGULAR PATTERNS in linguistic DATA: lists of 'irregularities' are usually avoided, and handled by incorporating the exceptional information into a dictionary entry.

-ise/ize (-d, -isation/-ization) (1) In PHONETICS, a SUFFIX used to identify the place of ARTICULATION of a secondary STRICTURE, as in 'labialized', 'velarization' (cf. SECONDARY ARTICULATION). For example, [tʲ] would be described as a 'palatalized t'. Both dynamic and static interpretations are used: a sound is described as 'labialized' both (a) during the process of labialization, and (b) once that process is over.

(2) In HISTORICAL LINGUISTICS and SOCIOLINGUISTICS, a SUFFIX used to characterize a change of a sound from one place of ARTICULATION to another: for example, a change from [k] to [c] or [t] to [c] could be described as a process of 'palatalization'. This sense needs to be kept clearly distinct from (1) above: the palatalization of [t] as [tʲ] is very different from [t] as [c].

island A term originally used in TRANSFORMATIONAL GRAMMAR to refer to a structure out of which CONSTITUENTS cannot be moved by any MOVEMENT RULE; more generally, a constituent across whose boundary certain relations between two ELEMENTS cannot be held. For example, the constituents of a RELATIVE CLAUSE cannot be moved out of the clause: in the sentence *I saw the person* ***who bought my car***, the relative-clause constituents cannot be moved to other positions in the sentence without producing an unacceptable sentence – as in **I saw my car the person who bought.* Other structures which may have been proposed as islands are NOUN-COMPLEMENT clauses (e.g. *The fact* ***that Mary was angry*** *surprised me*), SUBJECT noun clauses (e.g. ***What she told me*** *was this*), CO-ORDINATE structures (e.g. *I saw* ***Jules and Jim***) and constructions to which the A-OVER-A principle applies. The ISLAND CONDITION in X-BAR SYNTAX asserts that constituents can be extracted out of complement phrases, but not out of subject/ADJUNCT phrases. See also WH-.

iso- A PREFIX used in DIALECTOLOGY as part of the labelling of the various types of

LINGUISTIC information which can be displayed on maps ('linguistic atlases'). The most widely used notion is that of the **isogloss** (or 'isograph', or 'isoglottic line'), a line drawn on a map to mark the boundary of an area in which a particular linguistic feature is used. A number (or 'bundle') of isoglosses falling together in one place suggests the existence of a dialect boundary. Further distinctions can be made in terms of the kind of linguistic feature being isolated: an **isophone** is a line drawn to mark the limits of a PHONOLOGICAL feature: an **isomorph** marks the limits of a MORPHOLOGICAL feature; an **isolex** marks the limits of a LEXICAL ITEM; an **isoseme** marks the limits of a SEMANTIC feature (as when lexical items of the same phonological form take on different MEANINGS in different areas). Other distinctions have been suggested, based on the same principle. An alternative terminology talks of isophonic/isomorphic/ . . . 'lines'. An **isopleth** is a more general notion, being used by some SOCIOLINGUISTS to refer to a line which marks the limits of a linguistic feature seen in association with relevant sociocultural features. An **isolect** is a term used by some sociolinguists to refer to a linguistic VARIETY (or LECT) which differs minimally from another variety (i.e. a single isogloss, whether of a regional or a social kind, differentiates them).

isochrony/isochronism A term used in PHONETICS and PHONOLOGY to refer to the rhythmic characteristic of some LANGUAGES. In isochronous RHYTHM, the STRESSED SYLLABLES fall at approximately regular intervals throughout an UTTERANCE. This is 'subjective' isochrony, based on the perception of the listener – a more realistic interpretation of this notion than that of 'objective' isochrony, where the intervals would be measurably identical. One implication of this is that the theory predicts that unstressed syllables between stresses will be uttered in similar periods of time. If there are several unstressed syllables, accordingly, they will be articulated rapidly, to get them into the time span available. In such sentences as *The ˈconsequences of his ˈaction are ˈseveral*, the speed of ARTICULATION of the five syllables after *ˈcon-* will be greater than the two following *ˈac-*. Isochrony is said to be a strong tendency in English, for example, which is accordingly referred to as a STRESS-TIMED (as opposed to a 'syllable-timed') language. The UNITS of rhythm in such languages, i.e. the distances between stressed syllables, are called FEET (cf. FOOT) by some phoneticians. The theory is not without its critics, who doubt the extent of the principle's applicability, given the many variations in TEMPO heard in speech.

isolated A type of OPPOSITION recognized in PRAGUE SCHOOL PHONOLOGY, distinguished from PROPORTIONAL. The opposition between English /v/ and /l/ is isolated, because there are no other segments that are contrasted in this particular way, i.e. VOICED LABIO-DENTAL FRICATIVE *v.* voiced LATERAL. The opposition between /f/ and /v/, however, is proportional, because there are other oppositions in the language which work in parallel, e.g. /s/ *v.* /z/, /θ/ *v.* /ð/.

isolating (isolation) A type of LANGUAGE established by COMPARATIVE LINGUISTICS using STRUCTURAL (as opposed to DIACHRONIC) criteria, and focusing on the characteristics of the WORD: in **isolating languages**, all the words are invariable (and SYNTACTIC relationships are primarily shown by WORD ORDER). Vietnamese, Chinese and many South-East Asian languages are often cited as good instances of isolating languages. As always with such general classifications, the CATEGORIES are not clear-cut: different languages will display the characteristics of 'isolation' to a greater or lesser degree. An alternative term is ANALYTIC, seen as opposed to SYNTHETIC types of language (AGGLUTINATIVE and INFLECTING), where words contain more than one MORPHEME.

isomorphism (isomorphic) A property of two or more STRUCTURES whose CONSTITUENT parts are in a one-to-one correspondence with each other, at a given level of abstraction. For example, a SYNTACTIC and a SEMANTIC analysis would be isomorphic if for each syntactic UNIT there were a corresponding semantic unit, e.g. SUBJECT+VERB+OBJECT : ACTOR+action+goal. Likewise, a structural isomorphism may occur between LANGUAGES or DIALECTS, e.g. in VOCABULARY (the kinship terms in language X may be isomorphic with those in language Y).

item A term used in LINGUISTICS to refer to an individual linguistic FORM, from the viewpoint of its occurrence in an inventory and not in a CLASSIFICATION. For example, the vocabulary of a LANGUAGE, as listed in a dictionary, can be seen as a set of 'LEXICAL items' (e.g. the headwords in this dictionary). GRAMMATICAL and PHONOLOGICAL UNITS may also be listed as items, though this is less common, as they are more readily analysable into classes.

item and arrangement (IA) A MODEL of description used in MORPHOLOGY for the analysis of WORDS (and sometimes in SYNTAX for larger GRAMMATICAL UNITS). In this approach, words are seen as linear SEQUENCES ('arrangements') of MORPHS ('items'), e.g. *The boys kicked the ball* will be analysed as *the+boy+s+kick+ed +the+ball.* Problem cases, where this notion of sequence would not easily apply, constituted a main part of discussion in LINGUISTICS of the 1940s and 1950s, e.g. whether *mice* can be seen as *mouse* + plural. The chief alternatives to this way of proceeding are the ITEM-AND-PROCESS and WORD-AND-PARADIGM models.

item and process (IP) A MODEL of description used in MORPHOLOGY for the analysis of WORDS. In this approach, the relationships between words are seen as processes of DERIVATION; e.g. the 'item' *took* is derived from the item *take* by a 'process' involving VOWEL change. For some LINGUISTS this label is applicable to any approach which makes use of derivational processes in its formulation, such as GENERATIVE grammar; but its original use was in the context of morphology.

iteration (iterative) A term sometimes used in LINGUISTICS as an alternative to RECURSION – the repeated application of a RULE in the GENERATION of a SENTENCE. Iterative rules are especially used in PHONOLOGY, where a particular process (such as vowel HARMONY or STRESS assignment) needs to be applied repeatedly in a word or phrase.

iterative A term used in the GRAMMATICAL analysis of ASPECT, to refer to an event which takes place repeatedly, e.g. 'jump several times'. Iterative in this context often contrasts with SEMELFACTIVE.

iterativity (iterative) In some versions of METRICAL PHONOLOGY, a PARAMETER which determines the extent to which a FOOT structure may be repeatedly applied. In

non-iterative systems, words have a single foot at the EDGE. In **iterative** (or **bidirectional**) systems, there is a non-iterative foot assignment at one edge and an iterative foot assignment at the other.

-ize see -ISE/-IZE

J

Jakobsonian Characteristic of, or a follower of, the linguistic principles of the American LINGUIST Roman **Jakobson** (1896–1983), a principal founder of the PRAGUE SCHOOL, and a major influence on contemporary linguistics. Two terms in particular are associated with his name, 'Jakobsonian DISTINCTIVE FEATURE theory' refers to the use he and other scholars made of the notion of distinctive feature in the mid-1950s, in which features are defined primarily in ACOUSTIC terms. In this dictionary, the main reference to this approach is cited as 'Jakobson and Halle' (i.e. R. Jakobson and M. Halle, *Fundamentals of Language* (1956)). In LANGUAGE ACQUISITION, the **Jakobsonian hypothesis** concerns the order in which he predicted OPPOSITIONS between sounds would appear (and also be lost, in cases of language breakdown).

jaw setting In PHONETICS, a term used in the classification of the characteristic jaw (or mandible) positions adopted during speech. In a neutral jaw position, a small vertical gap is just visible between the biting surfaces of the upper and lower teeth. In various degrees of 'close' jaw settings, this gap disappears, until one reaches clenched teeth; in 'open' jaw settings, several degrees of opening are possible.

junction see NEXUS (1)

juncture (1) A term used in PHONOLOGY to refer to the PHONETIC boundary features which may demarcate GRAMMATICAL UNITS such as MORPHEME, WORD or CLAUSE. The most obvious junctural feature is silence, but in CONNECTED SPEECH this feature is not as common as the use of various MODIFICATIONS to the beginnings and endings of grammatical units. Word division, for example, can be signalled by a complex of PITCH, STRESS, LENGTH and other features, as in the potential contrast between *that stuff* and *that's tough*. In a SEGMENTAL phonological TRANSCRIPTION, these appear identical, /ðætstʌf/, but there are several phonetic modifications which can differentiate them in speech. In *that stuff* the /s/ is strongly ARTICULATED and the /t/ is unaspirated, whereas in *that's tough* the /s/ is relatively weak and the /t/ is ASPIRATED. In rapid speech such distinctions may disappear: they are only potentially CONTRASTIVE.

There have been several attempts to establish a typology of junctures. A commonly used distinction is between 'open' or 'plus' juncture (the features used at a word boundary, before silence), as illustrated in the above example (usually transcribed with a plus sign ⟨+⟩), and 'close' juncture (referring to the normal TRANSITIONS between sounds within a word). To handle the special cases of an open transition within a word, as in *co-opt*, the notion of 'internal open juncture' may be used. A more general distinction sometimes used to handle these possibilities is that between 'open' and 'close' transition.

In some American analyses of the INTONATION patterns of larger grammatical units than the word, several types of juncture are distinguished: 'single-bar' or 'sustained' juncture is recognized when the pitch pattern stays level within an UTTERANCE (transcribed with a single oblique ⟨/⟩ or level arrow <→>; 'double-bar' or 'rising' juncture is recognized when the pitch pattern rises before a silence (transcribed with a double slash ⟨//⟩ or a rising arrow ⟨↗⟩); a 'terminal', 'double-cross', 'falling', or 'fading' juncture is recognized when the pitch pattern falls before a silence (transcribed with a double cross ⟨#⟩ or a falling arrow ⟨↘⟩).

(2) A term used in ROLE AND REFERENCE GRAMMAR to describe that part of the grammar which deals with how sub-CLAUSAL units combine. It is seen in association with a theory of NEXUS – the type of SYNTACTIC relationship which obtains between the units in the juncture.

jussive A term sometimes used in the GRAMMATICAL analysis of VERBS, to refer to a type of MOOD often equated with an IMPERATIVE (*leave!*), but in some languages needing to be distinguished from it. For example, in Amharic, a jussive paradigm is used for wishes ('May God give you strength'), greetings, and certain other contexts, and this is formally distinct from the imperative.

K

Katz–Postal hypothesis A proposed property of TRANSFORMATIONS claimed by the American LINGUISTS Jerrold Katz and Paul Postal in 1964 in their book *An Integrated Theory of Linguistic Descriptions*, which had considerable influence on subsequent discussions of the relationship between SYNTACTIC and SEMANTIC analysis. Essentially, the hypothesis argued that all transformations should not change MEANING (they should be MEANING-PRESERVING). In relation to the MODEL of GRAMMAR expounded by Noam CHOMSKY in *Aspects of the Theory of Syntax* (1965), it came to be argued that whenever two SENTENCES differ in meaning they will differ in DEEP STRUCTURE; and that accordingly, from a consideration of deep structure, the grammatical meaning of a sentence can be deduced, which can then provide the input to the semantic COMPONENT. The removal of meaning-changing transformations, on this view, would thus simplify the functioning of the semantic RULES. There are, of course, several areas of syntax which provide apparent COUNTER-EXAMPLES to this hypothesis (such as TAG QUESTIONS, or the introduction of CONJUNCTIONS), and these provided the grounds of much subsequent discussion as to the validity of this and similarly motivated hypotheses. Considerable effort was made to apply the hypothesis to such cases, by reformulating the analyses (usually by adding extra ELEMENTS to the UNDERLYING structures involved).

kernel A term used in early GENERATIVE GRAMMAR to refer to a type of STRUCTURE produced by the PHRASE-STRUCTURE RULES of a grammar. The output of these rules is a 'kernel STRING'. The basic type of SENTENCE generated from this string without any OPTIONAL TRANSFORMATIONS (as defined in the *Syntactic Structures* MODEL, e.g. NEGATIVE or PASSIVE) is a **kernel sentence** – corresponding to the SIMPLE, ACTIVE, AFFIRMATIVE DECLARATIVE (SAAD) sentences of LANGUAGE. The term **kernel clause** is also sometimes used.

key (1) A term used by some SOCIOLINGUISTS as part of a classification of variations in spoken interaction: it refers to the tone, manner or spirit in which a SPEECH ACT is carried out, e.g. the contrast between mock and serious STYLES of activity. In a more restricted sense, the term is used by some LINGUISTS to subsume the various LEVELS of FORMALITY found in speech. One proposal analyses speech in terms of five such keys: 'frozen', 'formal', 'consultative', 'casual' and 'intimate'.

(2) See DOWNSTEP.

kinesics (kine, -me) A term in SEMIOTICS for the systematic use of facial expression and body gesture to communicate MEANING, especially as this relates to the use of LANGUAGE (e.g. when a smile or a frown alters the interpretation of a SENTENCE). In language ACQUISITION studies, the notion is present, under the heading of 'developmental' kinesics. Some analysts have applied the full EMIC terminology to this area, distinguishing 'kinemes', 'kines' and 'ALLOkines'; but the extent to which one can handle 'body language' in these terms is controversial, as analytic criteria are less clear than in PHONOLOGY, and kinesic TRANSCRIPTIONS raise several problems of interpretation.

kinetic A term sometimes used in PHONOLOGY, applied to TONES which vary in PITCH range; also called 'dynamic' or 'contour' tones, and contrasted with 'static' or 'level' tones.

kinship terms The system of LEXICAL ITEMS used in a LANGUAGE to express personal relationships within the family, in both narrow and extended senses. The FORMAL analysis of such terminology is often carried on using COMPONENTIAL analysis.

L

L The abbreviation for the 'low' variety in DIGLOSSIA and for a 'low' tone in PHONOLOGY.

label(-led, -ling) A term in GRAMMATICAL analysis for the explicit marking of the parts or stages in a STRUCTURAL analysis of a SENTENCE. For example, the main structural divisions in the sentence *People ran* can be signalled using such methods as BRACKETING or a TREE diagram, e.g. [[people] [ran]]; but this analysis is made more meaningful if a structural description is added (ASSIGNED) to the brackets, e.g. $[[\text{people}]_N[\text{ran}]_V]_S$ where N = NOUN, V = VERB and S = sentence. Such a convention is known as a **labelled bracketing**. In a tree diagram NODES can be labelled similarly.

labial(-ize, -ization) A general term in the PHONETIC classification of speech sounds on the basis of their PLACE OF ARTICULATION: it refers to active use of one lip (as in LABIO-DENTAL sounds, such as [f]) or both lips (as in BILABIAL CONSONANTS, such as [b], or ROUNDED VOWELS, such as [u]). In an empty sense, all ORAL sounds are labial, in that the airflow has to pass through the lips: the important qualification in the above definition is that the lips are *actively* involved. From a position of rest, there must be a marked movement to qualify as a labial sound, and it is lip-rounding which is the most common and noticeable feature. Similary, **labialization** is a general term referring to a SECONDARY ARTICULATION involving any noticeable lip-rounding, as in the initial [k] of *coop*, or *sh-* [ʃ] of *shoe*, which are here 'labialized', because of the influence of the labialization in the following vowel [u]. Labialization is applied both to cases where the lip-rounding is an essential feature of a sound's identity, as in [u], and to cases where the lip-rounding is found only in specific contexts, as in the [k] example above – in *kill*, there is no labialization. The DIACRITIC for labialization is [$_w$], underneath the main symbol, but a raised [ʷ] is often used. The term has developed a special status in recent phonological theory, especially in various NON-LINEAR models. For example, in ARTICULATOR-BASED FEATURE THEORY, it refers to a single-valued NODE involving the lips as an active articulator. In CONSTRICTION-based models, it is defined as a constriction formed by the lower lip. See also -ISE/IZE.

labio-dental(-ize, -ization) A term used in the PHONETIC classification of speech sounds on the basis of their PLACE OF ARTICULATION: it refers to a sound in which one lip is actively in contact with the teeth. The usual way is for the lower lip to articulate with the upper teeth, as in [f] and [v]. The opposite effect, upper lip against lower teeth, is possible in theory, but not recognized in the usual phonetic classifications. The term is also applied to articulations where the lip approaches close to the teeth, but without actual contact, as in the sound [ʋ], which is a VOWEL-like sound midway between [w] and [v]. See also -ISE/-IZE.

labio-velar(-ize, -ization) A term used in the PHONETIC classification of speech sounds on the basis of their PLACE OF ARTICULATION: it refers to a sound made at the velum (cf. VELAR) with the simultaneous accompaniment of lip-ROUNDING. A 'labio-velar SEMI-VOWEL' occurs in English as /w/, e.g. *well, wasp*; some ACCENTS preserve a VOICELESS PHONEME /ʍ/ for words written with *wh*, and thus CONTRAST such pairs as *Wales* and *whales*. See also -ISE/-IZE.

LAD The usual abbreviation for LANGUAGE ACQUISITION DEVICE.

lag A term used in ACOUSTIC PHONETICS as part of the study of VOICE-onset time variations in INITIAL PLOSIVE CONSONANTS; **voicing lag** refers to the occurrence of voicing after the plosive release (BURST); it contrasts with 'voicing LEAD'.

lambda (λ) (1) A notion developed in mathematical logic and used as part of the conceptual apparatus underlying FORMAL SEMANTICS. The **lambda operator** is a device which constructs expressions denoting functions out of other expressions (e.g. those denoting truth values) in a process called LAMBDA ABSTRACTION. The process of relating equivalent lambda expressions is known as **lambda conversion**. Several kinds of **lambda calculus** have been devised as part of a general theory of functions and logic, functions here being defined as sets of unordered pairs (graphs). The approach has proved attractive to linguists because of its ability to offer a powerful system for formalizing exact meanings and semantic relationships, and lambda notions have helped to inform a number of linguistic theories, notably MONTAGUE GRAMMAR and CATEGORIAL GRAMMAR.

(2) In ACOUSTICS, the symbol for wavelength.

laminal (lamin-a(r), -o) A term used in PHONETIC classification, referring to a sound made with the BLADE or 'lamina' of the TONGUE in contact with the upper lip, teeth or alveolar ridge, as in ALVEOLAR (sc. 'lamino-alveolar') or DENTAL (sc. 'lamino-dental') sounds.

landing site see MOVEMENT

language The everyday use of this term involves several different senses, which LINGUISTICS is careful to distinguish. At its most specific level, it may refer to the concrete act of speaking, writing or signing (cf. SIGN language) in a given situation – the notion of PAROLE, or PERFORMANCE. The linguistic SYSTEM underlying an individual's use of language in a given time and place is identified by the term IDIOLECT – and this is often extended to the SYNCHRONIC analysis of the whole of a person's language (as in 'Shakespeare's language'). A particular VARIETY, or LEVEL, of speech/writing may also be referred to as 'language' (e.g. 'scientific language', 'bad language'), and this is related to the SOCIOLINGUISTIC or STYLISTIC restrictiveness involved in such terms as 'trade language' (cf. PIDGIN), the teaching of 'languages for special purposes' (in APPLIED

LINGUISTICS), etc. In COMPUTATIONAL LINGUISTICS, a variety may be referred to as a 'sublanguage'. In such phrases as 'first language', 'the English language', the sense is the abstract system underlying the collective totality of the speech/writing behaviour of a community (the notion of LANGUE), or the knowledge of this system by an individual (the notion of COMPETENCE). In recent CHOMSKYAN linguistics, a distinction is drawn between language viewed as an element of the mind (I-LANGUAGE) and language viewed independently of the mind (E-LANGUAGE). The notion of language may be seen both in a synchronic sense (e.g. 'the English language today') and a DIACHRONIC sense (e.g. 'the English language since Chaucer'). Higher-order groupings can be made, as in such notions as 'the Romance languages', 'CREOLE languages'. All of these examples would fall under the heading of 'natural languages' – a term which contrasts with the artificially constructed systems used to expound a conceptual area (e.g. 'formal', 'logical', 'computer' languages) or to facilitate communication (e.g. Esperanto).

In contrast with these instances of individual languages, DIALECTS, VARIETIES, etc., there is also the abstract sense of 'language', referring to the biological faculty which enables individuals to learn and use their language – implicit in the notion of 'language ACQUISITION DEVICE' in PSYCHOLINGUISTICS. At a comparably abstract level 'language' is seen as a defining feature of human behaviour – the UNIVERSAL properties of all speech/writing systems, especially as characterized in terms of 'design features' (e.g. PRODUCTIVITY, DUALITY, LEARNABILITY) or 'language universals' (FORMAL, SUBSTANTIVE, etc.). Linguistics does not, however, follow the popular application of the term to human modes of communication other than by speech and writing (cf. such phrases as 'body language', 'eye language'), on the grounds that the behaviours involved are different in kind (as the criteria of productivity and duality suggest). Nor is 'language' a term generally applied to natural animal communication (cf. ZOÖSEMIOTICS).

The term enters into several technical phrases, most of which are self-evident, e.g. 'language teaching', 'language learning', 'language change'. Some, however, require a minimum of elucidation. For example, **first language** (sc. mother-tongue) is distinguishable from **second language** (a language other than one's mother-tongue used for a special purpose, e.g. for education, government) distinguishable in turn from **foreign language** (where no such special status is implied) – though the distinction between the latter two is not universally recognized (especially not in the USA). **Language laboratory** is a term used in foreign-language learning to refer to a specially equipped classroom (a set of booths containing recording and playback facilities, capable of being monitored at a central console) which provides students with a means of listening and responding instantly to UTTERANCES made in the foreign language. **Language pathology** (or **speech pathology**) is the study of all forms of involuntary, abnormal linguistic behaviour, especially when associated with medical conditions. **Language planning** is a term used in sociolinguistics to refer to a systematic attempt to solve the communication problems of a community by studying the various languages or dialects it uses and developing a realistic policy concerning their selection and use; often referred to as **language engineering**. In particular, the study of language change within a sociolinguistic perspective has motivated a wide range of terms: the concern to preserve the use of a language or the traditional form of a language is referred to as **language loyalty** or **language maintenance**; the gradual or sudden move from the use of one language to another is known as **language shift**; the feelings people have about their own language or the language(s) of others are called **language attitudes**; the situation which arises when a language ceases to be used by a person or community is called **language loss** or (when there is no doubt that the process is irreversible) **language death**; and the increased use of a language in a given area over a period of time is known as **language spread** or **language diffusion**. All of these notions are the result of **language contact**.

language awareness A term used especially in EDUCATIONAL LINGUISTICS, to refer to an informed, sensitive and critical response to the use of language by oneself and others, including the awareness of relevant terminology ('metalinguistic awareness'). A particular impetus was given to the task of promoting linguistic awareness in the early 1990s, when new perspectives on language teaching in schools came to be adopted in several countries.

langue A term introduced into LINGUISTICS by the Swiss linguist Ferdinand de SAUSSURE, to distinguish one of the senses of the word 'LANGUAGE' (the others being *langage* and PAROLE). It refers to the language SYSTEM shared by a community of speakers, and is usually contrasted with parole, which is the concrete act of speaking in actual SITUATIONS by an individual (cf. also COMPETENCE and PERFORMANCE).

larynx (laryng-eal(ization), -oscope, -ograph) The part of the windpipe, or trachea, containing the VOCAL CORDS. The larynx, or 'voice box', is a casing of muscle and cartilage, which at the front is most noticeable in the protruberance in the adult male neck known as the 'Adam's apple'. Its functions are both biological and LINGUISTIC. Under the former heading, the larynx acts as a valve to shut off the lungs, e.g. to aid the process of exertion. Under the latter heading, the larynx is involved in the production of several types of sound effect (e.g. VOICING, PITCH, whisper, GLOTTAL stop, glottalic sounds): these functions are described more fully under VOCAL CORDS. Speech sounds made in the larynx are sometimes referred to as **laryngeals**, and this term has come to be used in some models of NON-LINEAR PHONOLOGY, where a **laryngeal node** may be represented within the FEATURE HIERARCHY, within which is grouped a series of **laryngeal features** representing various states of the vocal cords (e.g. spread *v.* constricted, voiced *v.* unvoiced, stiff *v.* slack). **Laryngealization** refers to variation in the mode of vibration of the vocal cords, over and above their normal vibratory mode in the production of voice, as in CREAKY voice. Laryngealized sounds are sometimes used CONTRASTIVELY with non-laryngealized sounds in LANGUAGE, e.g. in Hausa. The traditional method of examining the inside of the larynx is by using the **laryngoscope**, a mirror placed at an angle inside the mouth: several high-speed films of vocal-cord activity have been made using this technique. The fibre-optic laryngoscope allows a more direct and flexible inspection to be made: the fibres are inserted through the nose, and thus interfere less with normal speech. The **laryngograph** is a device for recording vocal-cord vibrations visually, using electrodes placed against the appropriate part of the neck. See also -ISE/-IZE.

latent consonant In PHONOLOGY, a term used to describe a CONSONANT pronounced only under certain circumstances; opposed to **fixed** consonants, which are always pronounced. The notion has been used especially in French phonology, in relation to such phenomena as LIAISON.

lateral(-ly) A term used in the PHONETIC classification of CONSONANT sounds on the basis of their MANNER OF ARTICULATION: it refers to any sound where the air escapes around one or both sides of a CLOSURE made in the mouth, as in the various types of *l* sound. Air released around only one side of the TONGUE produces **unilateral** sounds; around both sides **bilateral** sounds. Lateral sounds may be VOICED, as in *lady, pool*, or VOICELESS, as in *play*, where the [l] has been devoiced due to the influence of the preceding voiceless consonant: [l̥]. An independent voiceless *l* sound occurs with Welsh *ll*, as in *Llandudno*, but here there is much accompanying friction, and the sound is best described as a 'lateral FRICATIVE' [ɬ]. /t/ and /d/ followed by /l/ in English are often released 'laterally', the phenomenon of 'lateral PLOSION': the air escapes round the sides of the tongue, the closure between tongue and ALVEOLAR ridge remaining, as in *bottle, cuddle*. It is possible to say the final SYLLABLE of such words without moving the front of the tongue from its contact at all.

In some DISTINCTIVE FEATURE approaches to PHONOLOGY, the term 'lateral' is specifically opposed to **non-lateral** (i.e. sounds which do not have a lateral release, as described above), these being postulated as two of the contrasts needed in order to specify fully the sound system of a language. In CHOMSKY and Halle's theory, for example, 'lateral' is classified as a CAVITY feature, along with NASAL, under the specific heading of SECONDARY APERTURES.

law see SOUND CHANGE

lax One of the features of sound set up by JAKOBSON and Halle in their DISTINCTIVE FEATURE theory of PHONOLOGY, to handle variations in MANNER OF ARTICULATION. Lax sounds are those produced with less muscular effort and movement, and which are relatively short and indistinct, compared to tense sounds (cf. TENSION). Examples are VOWELS articulated nearer the CENTRE of the vowel area (as in *bit, put*).

layer see METRICAL GRID

layering A term used by some LINGUISTS to refer to the successive HIERARCHICAL LEVELS in an IMMEDIATE-CONSTITUENT analysis. In TAGMEMIC GRAMMAR, it refers to the inclusion of a tagmemic CONSTRUCTION within another construction at the same level, as in *the car in the road*, where the PHRASE is within a phrase. Here it contrasts with LOOPBACK and LEVEL SKIPPING.

lead A term used in ACOUSTIC PHONETICS as part of the study of VOICE-onset time variations in INITIAL PLOSIVE CONSONANTS: **voicing lead** refers to the occurrence of voicing before the plosive release (BURST); it contrasts with 'voicing LAG'.

learnability A suggested defining property of human LANGUAGE (contrasting with the properties of other SEMIOTIC SYSTEMS), referring to the way any language can in principle be acquired by any normal child given the opportunity to do so. More specifically, the term is used in linguistics with reference to the mathematical investigation of the IDEALIZED learning procedures needed for the ACQUISITION of GRAMMARS (**learnability theory** or 'learning theory'). Because the emphasis is on the way in which grammars can be induced from linguistic input, the approach is also characterized as 'grammar induction' or 'grammatical inference'.

lect(al) A term used by some SOCIOLINGUISTS to refer to a collection of LINGUISTIC phenomena which has a functional identity within a SPEECH COMMUNITY, but without specifying the basis on which the collection was made (e.g. whether the lect was regional (cf. DIALECT), social (cf. SOCIOLECT), etc.). Different levels of identity are recognized within the variety continuum – in particular, BASILECT, MESOLECT and ACROLECT. GRAMMARS which take lectal variation into account are referred to as PANLECTAL or POLYLECTAL.

left-associative grammar A term used in COMPUTATIONAL LINGUISTICS for a type of GRAMMAR which operates with a regular order of LINEAR compositions. This approach, based on the building up and cancelling of VALENCIES, aims to avoid the irregular ordering introduced by CONSTITUENT STRUCTURE analysis which, it claims, results in computational inefficiency. Left-associative PARSERS are distinctive in that the history of the parse doubles as the linguistic analysis.

left-branching A term used in GENERATIVE GRAMMAR to refer to a CONSTRUCTION whose DERIVATION involves a series of structural operations which would be represented as increasing complexity of the left-hand side of a TREE diagram. The type of RULE involved can be represented by $X \rightarrow (X) + Y$. For example, the phrase *my friend's aunt's pen* is a 'left-branching' or 'left recursive' structure; it contrasts with the RIGHT-BRANCHING character of *the pen of the friend of my aunt.* Within classical TRANSFORMATIONAL grammar, the **left branch constraint/condition** asserts that no noun phrase on the left branch of another noun phrase may be extracted from that noun phrase. The condition accounts for the unacceptability of English sentences such as * *How many did you read – books?*, in which an AP has been extracted out of the NP headed by *books.*

left dislocation In GRAMMATICAL description, a type of SENTENCE in which one of the CONSTITUENTS appears in INITIAL position and its CANONICAL position is filled by a PRONOUN or a full LEXICAL NOUN PHRASE with the same REFERENCE, e.g. *John, I like him/the old chap.* In TRANSFORMATIONAL grammar, left dislocation sentences have been contrasted with TOPICALIZATION sentences. The former are analysed as BASE-generated and the latter as involving MOVEMENT.

left-linear grammar see LINEAR GRAMMAR

lemma (1) In LEXICOLOGY, the item which occurs at the beginning of a dictionary entry; more generally referred to as a **headword**. It is essentially an abstract representation, subsuming all the formal LEXICAL variations which may apply: the verb *walk*, for example, subsumes *walking, walks* and *walked.*

(2) A term used in PSYCHOLINGUISTICS referring to the SYNTACTIC and SEMANTIC properties of a word represented in the mental LEXICON. The PHONETIC shape of the word is thought to be represented separately. The distinction can be seen in various kinds of speech production ERROR; for example, malapropisms (e.g. saying *illiterate* but meaning *obliterate*) illustrate the possibility that the correct lemma can be activated but with an incorrect phonetic shape.

length (long) (1) A term used in PHONETICS to refer to the physical duration of a sound or UTTERANCE, and in PHONOLOGY to refer to the relative DURATIONS of sounds and SYLLABLES when these are linguistically contrastive; also referred to as QUANTITY. Sometimes the term is restricted to phonological contexts, the phonetic dimension being referred to as 'duration'. Phonologically 'long' and 'short' values are conventionally recognized, for both VOWELS and CONSONANTS. LANGUAGES often have one degree of phonological length, and may have more than one. Long vowels (transcribed with the DIACRITIC [ː]) occur in Arabic and Finnish; long (or 'double') consonants in Lithuanian and Luganda. A further contrast of length ('over-long' or 'extra-long') is also sometimes encountered with vowels. In English, the so-called distinction between long and short vowels (as in *beat/bit*) is not strictly a contrast in length, as QUALITY variations are always involved. See also COMPENSATORY LENGTHENING, MORA, WEIGHT.

(2) The notion of physical length has also been used in PSYCHOLINGUISTIC, SOCIOLINGUISTIC and STYLISTIC studies of GRAMMAR and VOCABULARY, in an attempt to quantify variations in the apparent COMPLEXITY of SENTENCES, WORDS, etc. Notions such as **sentence length** and **mean length of utterance** have been studied in terms of the number of CONSTITUENT words, MORPHEMES, SYLLABLES, etc., which they contain. These quantifications have been criticized by many LINGUISTS, on the grounds that there is no necessary correlation between the length of a linguistic UNIT and its STRUCTURAL or FUNCTIONAL COMPLEXITY.

lenis A general term used in the PHONETIC classification of CONSONANT sounds on the basis of their MANNER OF ARTICULATION: it refers to a sound made with a relatively weak degree of muscular effort and breath force, compared with some other sound (known as FORTIS). The distinction between LAX and TENSE is used similarly. The labels 'weak' and 'strong' are sometimes used for the contrast involved, but these are more prone to ambiguity. In English, it is the VOICED CONSONANTS ([b], [d], [v], [z], etc.) which tend to be produced with lenis articulation (their voiceless counterparts being relatively strong), and often, when the voicing distinction is reduced, it is only the degree of articulatory strength which maintains a contrast between sounds. The term 'lenis' is sometimes used loosely to refer to weak vowel articulation also, but this is not a standard practice.

lenition A term used in PHONOLOGY to refer to a weakening in the overall strength of a sound, whether DIACHRONICALLY or SYNCHRONICALLY; opposed to **fortition**. Typically, lenition involves the change from a STOP to a FRICATIVE, a fricative to an APPROXIMANT, a voiceless sound to a VOICED sound, or a sound being reduced to zero. For example, the initial MUTATION in Celtic languages shows lenition in such cases as Welsh *pen* 'head' becoming *ben* '(his) head'.

level (1) A general term in LINGUISTICS to refer to a major dimension of STRUCTURAL organization held to be susceptible of independent study. The most widely recognized 'levels of analysis' are PHONOLOGY, GRAMMAR and SEMANTICS, but often PHONETICS is distinguished from phonology, LEXIS from semantics, and MORPHOLOGY and SYNTAX are seen as separate levels within grammar. PRAGMATICS is also sometimes described as a level. Some linguistic MODELS make even more specific divisions, identifying MORPHOPHONOLOGY, for example, as a separate level. An analogous notion is found in all theories, e.g. the COMPONENTS of a GENERATIVE grammar, or the STRATA of STRATIFICATIONAL grammar. There is considerable difference of opinion concerning not only the number but also the way these levels should be interrelated in a linguistic theory. BLOOMFIELDIAN linguistics, for example, saw analysis as a matter proceeding unidirectionally from the 'lower' levels of phonetics through the progressively 'higher' levels of phonology, morphology and syntax towards semantics. In this approach, the 'mixing of levels' was disallowed: phonology, for example, was to be analysed without reference to higher levels of description. In HALLIDAYAN linguistics, phonology is seen as an **inter-level**, linking the level of phonic/graphic SUBSTANCE with that of grammatical/lexical FORMS. 'Double ARTICULATION' theories recognize the main levels only. When criteria of analysis from different levels coincide in establishing a linguistic UNIT (as when phonological and grammatical criteria are found to agree in identifying the WORDS in a language), the term 'CONGRUENCE of levels' is sometimes used.

(2) In GENERATIVE linguistics, the term is used to refer to the different types of REPRESENTATION encountered within the DERIVATION of a SENTENCE. For example, DEEP- and SURFACE-STRUCTURE 'levels of representation' are commonly recognized, as are SYSTEMATIC PHONEMIC and PHONETIC levels. Linguistic operations, such as TRANSFORMATIONS, can be described as taking place at certain 'levels of depth'. In X-BAR theory, categories are analysed at ZERO- or word level and at PHRASE level.

(3) The different STRUCTURAL layers within a linguistic HIERARCHY are often referred to as 'levels'; e.g. within grammar one might talk of the levels (or RANKS) of SENTENCE, CLAUSE, phrase, WORD and MORPHEME. This view is a central feature of TAGMEMIC analysis. In METRICAL PHONOLOGY, metrical trees display different levels of structure ('prosodic levels').

(4) The various degrees of progress which it is anticipated linguistics can achieve are referred to as 'levels' (or 'criteria') of ADEQUACY.

(5) Within PHONETICS and PHONOLOGY, 'level' may be used to characterize (a) the degree of PITCH height of an UTTERANCE, or SYLLABLE, e.g. 'average pitch level', 'four pitch levels', or (b) the degree of loudness of a sound, e.g. 'three levels of STRESS'. 'Level tone' is used by some INTONATION analysts to refer to a NUCLEAR tone which has neither a FALLING nor a RISING component (as in the tone of boredom or sarcasm in English, e.g. *r̄ēally*). 'Level stress' is sometimes used to refer to COMPOUNDS where the two items have a major stress feature, e.g. *washing machine.*

(6) In STYLISTICS and SOCIOLINGUISTICS, 'level' is often used to refer to a mode of expression felt to be appropriate to a type of social SITUATION, e.g. 'FORMAL level', 'intimate level'. Sometimes, several such stylistic levels are distinguished within the range of formality (e.g. 'frozen', 'casual', 'deliberative').

levelling (level) In HISTORICAL LINGUISTICS, the gradual loss of a linguistic distinction, so that forms which were originally CONTRASTIVE become identical. For example, Old English NOUNS generally distinguished NOMINATIVE and ACCUSATIVE cases, but in Modern English these have been levelled to a single form.

level-skipping A term used in TAGMEMIC GRAMMAR to refer to a process of SYNTACTIC CONSTRUCTION where a LEVEL has been omitted. In such cases, a FILLER from a lower-level construction is used in a higher-level one, as when a GENITIVE ending (from the MORPHEME level) is attached to a PHRASE, rather than a WORD (e.g. *the King of Spain's daughter*). It is contrasted with LOOPBACK and LAYERING.

lexeme A term used by some LINGUISTS to refer to the minimal DISTINCTIVE UNIT in the SEMANTIC SYSTEM of a LANGUAGE. Its original motivation was to reduce the AMBIGUITY of the term WORD, which applied to orthographic/PHONOLOGICAL, GRAMMATICAL and LEXICAL LEVELS, and to devise a more appropriate term for use in the context of discussing a language's vocabulary. The lexeme is thus postulated as the abstract unit underlying such sets of grammatical VARIANTS as *walk, walks, walking, walked*, or *big, bigger, biggest*. IDIOMATIC phrases, by this definition, are also considered lexemes (e.g. *kick the bucket* (= 'die')). Lexemes are the units which are conventionally listed in dictionaries as separate entries.

lexical-functional grammar (LFG) A LINGUISTIC theory in which the role of the LEXICON is central, and grammatical FUNCTIONS are taken as PRIMITIVE. The SYNTACTIC STRUCTURE of a SENTENCE consists of a CONSTITUENT structure (**c-structure**) and a FUNCTIONAL structure (**f-structure**), which represent superficial GRAMMATICAL RELATIONS. In this approach, the LEXICAL COMPONENT is assigned much of the role formerly associated with the syntactic component of a TRANSFORMATIONAL grammar.

lexical noun phrase (lexical NP) A term used in recent GENERATIVE GRAMMAR to refer to a type of NOUN PHRASE (ANAPHOR, PRONOMINAL or R-EXPRESSION) with PHONOLOGICAL content which is of particular importance for the theory of BINDING. Unlike anaphors and pronominals, lexical NPs are FREE in all POSITIONS in the SENTENCE; their REFERENCE is typically independent of other NPs. A contrast can be drawn with non-lexical noun phrases (PRO, *pro, t*).

lexical phonology A theory of PHONOLOGY in which MORPHOLOGICAL and PHONOLOGICAL RULES are brought together within a single framework. The approach is based on the insight that much of the phonology operates together with the WORD-FORMATION rules in a CYCLIC fashion to define the class of LEXICAL items in a language. The morphological sub-theory is 'level-ordered': AFFIXES are differentiated, not by the use of BOUNDARY-MARKERS (as in earlier phonological theory), but by being divided into distinct subsets (numbered 'levels' or 'strata') within the LEXICON, where the division of the word-formation rules corresponds to a division among the phonological rules. The phonological sub-theory is divided into a 'lexical' (sometimes called a 'cyclic') COMPONENT and a 'post-lexical' (sometimes called a 'post-cyclic') component, the latter also being referred to as the 'PHRASAL phonology', as its rules operate across word boundaries, making use of SYNTACTIC structure.

lexical representation language A model used in SEMANTICS to REPRESENT basic LEXICAL entries and characterize systematic lexical processes. A notion of 'types' is used to structure lexical entries, which are represented as FEATURE structures (a 'typed feature structure language'), and specify how they combine by means of GRAMMAR rules, or CONSTRAINTS on PHRASAL types. The types are organized in a conceptual HIERARCHY as a lattice framework, with the top being the most general type and the bottom indicating inconsistency. The model is not restricted to lexical representation (despite its name), being also used for SYNTAGMATIC description.

lexicon In its most general sense, the term is synonymous with VOCABULARY. A dictionary can be seen as a set of lexical ENTRIES. The lexicon has a special status in GENERATIVE GRAMMAR, where it refers to the COMPONENT containing all the information about the STRUCTURAL properties of the LEXICAL ITEMS in a LANGUAGE, i.e. their specification SEMANTICALLY, SYNTACTICALLY and PHONOLOGICALLY. In later MODELS (cf. ASPECTS), these properties are formalized as FEATURES, and put in square brackets, e.g. WORD-CLASS assignments include NOUN [+N], etc. Given this component, the TERMINAL symbols in PHRASE-MARKERS can then be related directly to the lexicon through the use of lexical TRANSFORMATIONS; e.g. any item in the lexicon specified by [+D] can be attached to the NODE D, and so on. The **mental lexicon** is the stored mental representation of what we know about the lexical items in our language.

lexicostatistics A technique used in GLOTTOCHRONOLOGY with which one attempts to make quantitative comparisons between the rates of change within sets of LEXICAL ITEMS in hypothetically related LANGUAGES, and thus to deduce the distance in time since the languages separated. Other types of lexical comparison (e.g. to determine the mutual intelligibility of languages) may also be referred to by this label.

lexis (lexic-al (-ize, -ist), -ology, -ography) A term used in LINGUISTICS to refer to the vocabulary of a LANGUAGE, and used adjectivally in a variety of technical phrases. A UNIT of vocabulary is generally referred to as a **lexical item**, or LEXEME. A complete inventory of the lexical items of a language constitutes that language's dictionary, or LEXICON – a term particularly used in GENERATIVE GRAMMAR: items are listed 'in the lexicon' as a set of **lexical entries**. The way lexical items are organized in a language is the **lexical structure** or **lexical system**. A group of items used to identify the network of contrasts in a specific semantic or **lexical field** (e.g. cooking, colour) may also be called a 'lexical SYSTEM'. Specific groups of items, sharing certain FORMAL or semantic features, are known as **lexical sets**. The absence of a lexeme at a specific STRUCTURAL place in a language's lexical field is called a **lexical gap** (e.g. *brother v. sister, son v. daughter*, etc., but no separate lexemes for 'male' *v.* 'female' *cousin*). In comparing languages, it may be said that one language may **lexicalize** a contrast, whereas another may not – that is, the contrast is identified using lexemes, as in the many terms for 'hole' available in some Australian Aboriginal languages. The mutual restriction governing the CO-OCCURRENCE of sets of lexical items is known as **lexical selection** (e.g. ANIMATE NOUNS being compatible with animate VERBS). **Lexical density** is a measure of the difficulty of a text, using the ratio of the number of different words (the 'word types') to the total number of words (the 'word tokens'): the 'type-token ratio'.

The insertion of particular lexemes at particular places in grammatical structures is carried out by a process of **lexical substitution** or **lexical transformation**, using **lexical insertion rules. Lexical redundancy rules** are used in generative grammar to simplify the specification of lexical entries, e.g. by omitting to specify SUB-CATEGORIZATION FEATURES which may be predicted on the basis of other features. Some generative models also recognize the so-called **'lexicalist' hypothesis**, in which a class of lexical rules governing word formation is distinguished from the set of syntactic transformations. Essentially, the hypothesis bans category-changing rules from the grammar – disallowing a verb or adjective from being transformed into a noun, etc. The terms **lexical syntax** and **lexical phonology** are also encountered in the generative literature: the former refers to an approach which incorporates syntactic rules within the lexicon; the latter is an approach where some of the PHONOLOGICAL rules are transferred to the lexicon, and integrated with the MORPHOLOGICAL component. In earlier GOVERNMENT-BINDING THEORY, N, V and A (but not P) were lexical categories, as their members were proper governors. In recent GB, the lexical categories are N, V, A and P, and C and I are non-lexical.

Lexis may also be seen in contrast with GRAMMAR, as in the distinction between 'grammatical WORDS' and **lexical words**: the former refers to words whose sole function is to signal grammatical relationships (a role which is claimed for such words as *of, to* and *the* in English); the latter refers to words which have **lexical meaning**, i.e. they have semantic CONTENT. Examples include **lexical verbs** (*v.* auxiliary verbs) and **lexical noun phrases** (*v.* non-lexical NPs, such as PRO). A similar contrast distinguishes **lexical morphology** from derivational MORPHOLOGY. HALLIDAYAN linguistics makes a theoretical distinction between grammar and lexis, seen as two subdivisions within linguistic FORM: lexis here is studied with reference to such formal concepts as COLLOCATION, and not in semantic terms. **Lexicology** is a term sometimes used to refer to the overall study of a language's vocabulary (including its history); the psychological study of word meaning (e.g. the linguistic expression of spatial relations) is known as **psycholexicology**. It is distinguished here from **lexicography**, which is the art and science of dictionary-making. Lexicography could accordingly be seen as a branch of 'applied lexicology'. The term 'lexicologist' is less widely used: someone interested in vocabulary would normally be considered a species of semanticist. See also AMBIGUITY, CYCLE (2), STRESS.

LF In government-binding theory, the abbreviation for LOGICAL FORM.

LFG The abbreviation for LEXICAL FUNCTIONAL-GRAMMAR.

liaison A term used in PHONOLOGY to refer to one type of TRANSITION between sounds, where a sound is introduced at the end of a WORD if a certain CONTEXT follows. It is a notable feature of French, e.g. the final *t* of *c'est* is pronounced when followed by a VOWEL. It may be heard in English where a 'linking /r/' is often found in words ending with an *r* in the spelling, when they occur before words beginning with a vowel, e.g. *hear* /hɪə/ usually becomes /hɪər/ in such phrases as *here are.*

licensing (license-r) In recent GOVERNMENT-BINDING THEORY, a notion introduced in formulating conditions on REPRESENTATION: every element in a WELL-FORMED structure must be licensed in one of a small number of ways. For example, an element that assigns SEMANTIC ROLES is licensed if it has recipients in appropriate SYNTACTIC positions; a syntactically defined PREDICATE is licensed if it has a SUBJECT.

The term as used in AUTOSEGMENTAL PHONOLOGY applies to the analysis of

SYLLABLE structure. **Prosodic licensing** is a condition that all SEGMENTS must be part of a higher-level unit (the syllable), or else they are contingently EXTRASYLLABIC. **Autosegmental licensing** presents the view that certain PROSODIC units are **licensers**, which license a set of phonological features (AUTOSEGMENTS). The syllable NODE is a **primary licenser**; the CODA node and certain word-FINAL MORPHEMES are **secondary licensers**. A given licenser can license only one occurrence of the autosegment in question. All autosegmental material must be licensed at the WORD level; elements not licensed at this level will be DELETED. The notion of licensing has also been put to use in some other NON-LINEAR models of phonology.

light syllable see WEIGHT

line see ASSOCIATION LINE

linear(ity) (1) A term used in LINGUISTICS to describe the characteristic REPRESENTATION of LANGUAGE as a unidimensional SEQUENCE of ELEMENTS or RULES. The assumption is made that it is possible to order rules in a sequence, and to adhere strictly to this ordering in constructing DERIVATIONS without any loss of GENERALITY (compared to an unordered set of rules or a set ordered on a different principle, e.g. one of simultaneous application). It is also claimed that linear ordering makes it possible to formulate grammatical processes that would otherwise not be expressible with complete generality.

(2) In PHONOLOGY, **linearity** is an organizational principle, whereby each occurrence of a PHONEME is associated with a specific sequence of PHONES (minimally, one phone) which realize that phoneme. If phoneme A precedes phoneme B, then phone(s) A′ will precede phone(s) B′. Linearity is thus one of the preconditions of BIUNIQUENESS. The principle has been criticized by GENERATIVE phonologists, as part of a general attack on TAXONOMIC phonemics.

linear grammar A term used in COMPUTATIONAL LINGUISTICS for a type of GRAMMAR which describes only LINEAR or non-HIERARCHICAL aspects of STRINGS; also known as **regular grammar**. If the NON-TERMINAL symbol is the leftmost symbol on the right-hand side of a RULE, the grammar is a **left-linear grammar**; if it is the rightmost, it is a **right-linear grammar**. For example, a right-linear grammar has rules of the form A→aB, B→b. See also FINITE-STATE GRAMMAR.

linear phonology see NON-LINEAR PHONOLOGY

linear precedence rule (LP rule) A type of RULE in GENERALIZED PHRASE-STRUCTURE GRAMMAR of the form X < Y, specifying that X must precede Y. Together with IMMEDIATE DOMINANCE rules and various general PRINCIPLES, LP rules generate PHRASE-MARKERS.

linear prediction A technique used in SPEECH SYNTHESIS and SPEECH RECOGNITION to represent ACOUSTIC PHONETIC knowledge in a way which is capable of computational processing. In **linear prediction coefficient (LPC)** synthesis, a speech signal is defined by a set of coefficients (predictors), which try to predict the signal from its past time domain values. These coefficients are then used to produce a REPRESENTATION of the SPECTRUM of the signal. The approach is based on the analysis of RESONANCES in the VOCAL TRACT, and is thus especially useful in its ability to identify FORMANT locations (though sounds involving NOISE features are less accurately modelled), producing syntheses of high quality.

lingua franca A term used in SOCIOLINGUISTICS, and often in everyday speech, to refer to an auxiliary LANGUAGE used to enable routine communication to take place between groups of people who speak different native languages; also sometimes called an **interlingua**. English is the world's most common lingua franca, followed by French; but other languages are also widely used. In East Africa, for example, Swahili is the lingua franca; in many parts of West Africa, Hausa is used.

lingual (linguo-) A general term sometimes used in the PHONETIC classification of speech sounds, referring to a sound made with the TONGUE. A 'lingual roll/trill', for example, is the trilled [r] made with the TIP of the tongue against the ALVEOLAR ridge. The term **linguo-** is occasionally used as a PREFIX in the definition of PLACE OF ARTICULATION (e.g. 'linguolabial', where the tongue would be in contact with the lips, as in 'blowing raspberries'), but usually more specific prefixes are used (e.g. APICO-, LAMINO-).

linguist The normal term for a student or practitioner of the subject of LINGUISTICS. 'Linguistician' is often cited for this purpose, but it is never used by professional linguists about themselves. Ironically, confusion sometimes arises from the earlier, and still current, sense of someone proficient in several languages.

linguistic A term which has to be used with care because of its ambiguity: it can be (1) the adjective from LANGUAGE, as in such phrases as 'linguistic philosophy', 'linguistic skill' and 'linguistic minority', or (2) the adjective from LINGUISTICS, where it refers to an approach characterized by the scientific attributes of that subject, as in 'linguistic analysis'. In such phrases as 'linguistic intuition', however, either sense could apply: (a) intuitions about language, or (b) 'intuitions about how to analyse language linguistically'. Similarly, a 'linguistic atlas' may or may not be based on the techniques, findings, etc., of linguistics.

linguistic anthropology see ANTHROPOLOGICAL LINGUISTICS

linguistically significant generalization A term used especially in GENERATIVE GRAMMAR to refer to the kind of analytic statement which it is hoped the grammatical analysis will provide. The aim of the grammar is not just to generate all and only the grammatical SENTENCES of a language, but to do this in such a way that those relationships felt to be significant by NATIVE-SPEAKERS are expressed in an economical and GENERAL way. For example, a grammar which generated ACTIVE sentences separately from PASSIVE ONES, or QUESTIONS from STATEMENTS, and which failed to show these are interrelated, would be missing linguistically significant generalizations. This was one of the reasons for the introduction of TRANSFORMATIONS into linguistic analysis. The extent to which a grammar expresses the linguistically significant generalizations about a language would be one measure of the grammar's ADEQUACY.

linguistic atlas see DIALECT

linguistic determinism see RELATIVITY

linguistic environment see ENVIRONMENT

linguistic geography see DIALECT, GEOLINGUISTICS

linguistic historiography The study of the history of ideas in LINGUISTICS and LANGUAGE study. The subject traces the origins of thinking about language from Classical times, using Greek, Roman, Indian, Arabic, and other sources, continuing with the various schools of thought in the Middle Ages and the emergence of 'traditional' accounts of pronunciation, spelling, GRAMMAR, LEXICOGRAPHY and USAGE, down to the antecedents of present-day scientific and popular views of language and languages. All languages are in principle included, though most work has been carried out on European languages, where historical records are most in evidence. The subject also includes debate on the methodological and philosophical foundations of historiography, including its relationship to the history and philosophy of science.

linguistic philosophy see PHILOSOPHICAL LINGUISTICS

linguistic relativity see RELATIVITY

linguistics The scientific study of LANGUAGE. As an academic discipline, the development of this subject has been recent and rapid, having become particularly widely known and taught in the 1960s. This reflects partly an increased popular and specialist interest in the study of language and communication in relation to human beliefs and behaviour (e.g. in theology, philosophy, information theory, literary criticism), and the realization of the need for a separate discipline to deal adequately with the range and complexity of linguistic phenomena; partly the impact of the subject's own internal development at this time, arising largely out of the work of the American linguist Noam CHOMSKY and his associates, whose more sophisticated analytic techniques and more powerful theoretical claims gave linguistics an unprecedented scope and applicability.

Different branches may be distinguished according to the linguist's focus and range of interest. A major distinction, introduced by Ferdinand de SAUSSURE, is between **diachronic** and **synchronic linguistics**, the former referring to the study of language change (also called **historical linguistics**), the latter to the study of the state of language at any given point in time. In so far as the subject attempts to establish general principles for the study of all languages, and to determine the characteristics of human language as a phenomenon, it may be called **general linguistics** or **theoretical linguistics**. When it concentrates on establishing the facts of a particular language system, it is called **descriptive linguistics**. When its purpose is to focus on the differences between languages, especially in a language-teaching context, it is called **contrastive linguistics**. When its purpose is primarily to identify the common characteristics of different languages or language families, the subject goes under the heading of **comparative** (or **typological**) **linguistics**.

When the emphasis in linguistics is wholly or largely historical, the subject is traditionally referred to as COMPARATIVE PHILOLOGY (or simply PHILOLOGY), though in many parts of the world 'philologists' and 'historical linguists' are people with very different backgrounds and attitudes. The term **structural linguistics** is widely used, sometimes in an extremely specific sense, referring to the particular approaches to SYNTAX and PHONOLOGY current in the 1940s and 1950s, with their emphasis on providing DISCOVERY PROCEDURES for the analysis of a language's SURFACE STRUCTURE; sometimes in a more general sense, referring to any SYSTEM of linguistic analysis that attempts to establish explicit systems of RELATIONS between linguistic UNITS in surface structure. When the emphasis in language study is on the classification of structures and units, without reference to such notions as DEEP STRUCTURE, some linguists, particularly within GENERATIVE grammar, talk pejoratively of **taxonomic linguistics**.

In recent years the term **linguistic sciences** has come to be used by many as a single label for both linguistics and PHONETICS – the latter being considered here as a strictly pre-language study. Equally, there are many who do not see the divide between linguistics and phonetics being as great as this label suggests: they would be quite happy to characterize the subject as **linguistic science**. 'Linguistics' is still the preferred name.

The overlapping interest of linguistics and other disciplines has led to the setting up of new branches of the subject in both pure and applied contexts, such as **anthropological linguistics, biolinguistics, clinical linguistics, computational linguistics, critical linguistics, educational linguistics, ethnolinguistics, institutional linguistics, mathematical linguistics, neurolinguistics, philosophical linguistics, psycholinguistics, quantitative linguistics, sociolinguistics, statistical linguistics**. When the subject's findings, methods, or theoretical principles are applied to the study of problems from other areas of experience, one talks of **applied linguistics**; but this term is often restricted to the study of the theory and methodology of foreign-language teaching. See also AREA, CORPUS.

linking (1) A term used in PHONOLOGY to refer to a sound which is introduced between LINGUISTIC UNITS, usually for ease of pronunciation. In English, the 'linking /r/' is the most familiar example of this process, as when the *r* in *car* is pronounced before a VOWEL, or when an /r/ is introduced without there being justification in the writing (e.g. *Shah of*... /ʃɑːrəv ... /). In French, a linking /t/ is introduced in the third-PERSON QUESTION form of VERBS, when this ends in a vowel, e.g. *il a* 'he has' → *a-t-il*. In SYNTAX, the COPULA *be*, and sometimes such verbs as *seem, become*, etc., may be referred to as 'linking' verbs.

(2) (**link-ed, de-, linkage**) In models of NON-LINEAR PHONOLOGY, a FORMAL means of relating UNITS (nodes, features, particles, etc.) within a HIERARCHICAL REPRESENTATION; the disassociation of a unit from a SEGMENT is called **delinking**. A delinked unit occurs on a TIER on its own. Units which are linked to more than one segment (as in the various kinds of ASSIMILATION, or in certain kinds of GEMINATION) are said to show **multiple linking** (or be **multilinked**). Various CONDITIONS have been proposed to ensure the WELL-FORMEDNESS of ASSOCIATION lines in STRUCTURAL DESCRIPTIONS, such as the **linking constraint**, which requires that all association lines be interpreted exhaustively.

LIPOC An abbreviation for 'language-independent preferred order of constituents' – a LINGUISTIC tendency recognized in FUNCTIONAL GRAMMAR, according to which CONSTITUENTS are ORDERED in terms of their CATEGORIAL COMPLEXITY.

liquid A term used by some PHONETICIANS in the classification of speech sounds, referring collectively to all the APICO-ALVEOLAR sounds of the types [l] and [r].

little *pro* see PRO

l-marking A term used in recent GOVERNMENT-BINDING THEORY, distinguishing a category which is the COMPLEMENT of a V, N, A or P ('l-marked') from one which is the complement of C or I. The symbol 'l' derives from 'lexical category'.

loan A LINGUISTIC UNIT (usually a LEXICAL ITEM) which has come to be used in a LANGUAGE or DIALECT other than the one where it originated. Several types of loan process have been recognized, such as **loan words** (where both FORM and MEANING are borrowed, or 'assimilated', with some adaptation to the PHONOLOGICAL system of the new language, e.g. *sputnik*); **loan blends** (where the meaning is borrowed, but only part of the form, e.g. *restaurant* with a simulated French ending /ˈrestərɔ̃/; **loan shifts** (where the meaning is borrowed, and the form is native, e.g. *restaurant* as /ˈrestrənt/); and **loan translations** (where the MORPHEMES in the borrowed word are translated item by item, e.g. *superman* from *Übermensch* – also known as a CALQUE).

loc The usual abbreviation for LOCATIVE.

local A type of TRANSFORMATION, introduced by Noam CHOMSKY (in *Aspects of the Theory of Syntax*), which affects only a sub-STRING DOMINATED by a single CATEGORY symbol: the applicability of the RULE is thus determined by the PHRASE STRUCTURE of the string, not just by the SEQUENCE of elementary symbols of which the string is composed. For example, the way in which the rules of the transformational CYCLE in PHONOLOGY are applied to assign STRESS depends on the way the FORMATIVES are categorized, e.g. as NOUN, VERB, ADJECTIVE, etc., in the phrase-structure TREE. See also LOCALITY.

localism (localist, -ic) An approach to LINGUISTIC analysis which proposes that expressions of location (in space and time) are more basic to a GRAMMATICAL or SEMANTIC analysis than are other types of expressions, which are viewed as derived. In this 'localist' view, distinctions such as TENSE, ASPECT, possession and existence are interpreted as having underlying locational features, as is most evident in such relations as *John has a dog/John's dog* . . . , and *there are four legs on that table/that table has four legs.*

locality A term used in PHONOLOGY, especially in some NON-LINEAR models, to refer to the domain of application of a RULE. In one formulation, the **locality condition** states that phonological rules apply between elements ADJACENT on a given TIER. Non-linear phonology is especially interested in locality because its ability to handle non-adjacent SEGMENTS (as in vowel HARMONY) is one of its chief claims. Non-linear principles enable long-distance rules to operate between segments which are adjacent at a particular level of REPRESENTATION, even though the segments are not adjacent at all levels. **Locality theory** develops this approach into a general theory of phonological adjacency requirements. It is defined by a **universal locality condition**, which requires elements to be local within a plane (the 'adjacency parameter', which then allows rules to impose further CONSTRAINTS on the maximal distance between interacting segments) and by a principle of **transplanar locality** (which bans certain types of relations across featural planes).

location see HOLD

locative (loc) In LANGUAGES which express GRAMMATICAL relationships by means of INFLECTIONS, this term refers to the FORM taken by a NOUN PHRASE (often a single noun or PRONOUN), when it typically expresses the idea of location of an entity or action. English does not have a locative CASE form, using such PREPOSITIONS as *at* instead. Structures which express locational MEANING may also be referred to as locative, e.g. in *The woman was standing at a bus stop, at a bus stop* could be called a 'locative PHRASE'. Some LINGUISTS see locative CONSTRUCTIONS as having particular importance in developing a LINGUISTIC theory, interpreting such notions as 'being', 'having', etc., as involving a fundamental locative feature. The term is also given special status in CASE grammar.

locus A term used in ACOUSTIC PHONETICS to refer to the apparent point of origin of a FORMANT for a given PLACE OF ARTICULATION, as displayed on a SPECTROGRAM. The formants which identify VOWELS are bent in characteristic directions, depending on the CONSONANTS adjacent to them; but for any single consonant these bends, or TRANSITIONS, all point in the same direction, at a hypothetical natural frequency range for the consonant. It is this hypothetical point of origin which is referred to as the 'locus' of the consonant.

locutionary A term used in the theory of SPEECH ACTS to refer to an act of making a MEANINGFUL UTTERANCE. The point of the term is in its contrast with ILLOCUTIONARY and PERLOCUTIONARY acts, where there is more involved than merely 'speaking'.

logical form (LF) A term used in GOVERNMENT-BINDING THEORY to refer to the initial REPRESENTATION of SENTENCE MEANING, which results from the SEMANTIC interpretation of CASE-MARKED S-STRUCTURES. It includes information about such matters as element FOCUS and QUANTIFIER representation. It is complemented in the semantic COMPONENT by a further LEVEL of semantic interpretation, known as 'full semantic representation', which is required to determine such matters as PRAGMATIC inference and the conditions governing a sentence's APPROPRIATE use.

logocentrism (logocentric) In literary STYLISTICS, a term referring to a LANGUAGE- or WORD-centred view of literature or other behaviour. The notion is associated with the STRUCTURALIST approach to analysis, which focused on the study of the language of a text to the exclusion of the author's individuality, the social context, and the historical situation. A reaction to this view in the late 1960s came to be called POST-STRUCTURALISM. Here, language is seen as a system whose value shifts in response to non-linguistic factors. A range of viewpoints drew attention to the multiple MEANINGS of words, stressing the role of mental processes in interpreting linguistic relationships, and denying the possibility of objectivity in textual interpretation. In particular, the methods of **deconstruction**, developed by Jacques Derrida (1930–), aimed to show the inherent contradictions and paradoxes in logocentric approaches.

logophoric see PRONOUN

London School see FIRTHIAN

long (sound) see LENGTH (1)

longitudinal An application of the general use of this term in the field of child language ACQUISITION, referring to one of the two main procedures used in order to study the process of LANGUAGE development. A longitudinal study follows the course of language acquisition in a single child or group over a period of time. This method contrasts with a CROSS-SECTIONAL study, where the language of a group of children of the same or different ages is compared at a given point in time.

loopback (backlooping) A term in TAGMEMIC GRAMMAR for the inclusion of a higher-LEVEL CONSTRUCTION within the SLOTS of a lower-level construction, as in the use of RELATIVE CLAUSES within the NOUN PHRASE (e.g. *the girl who was talking . . .*). It is distinguished from LEVEL-SKIPPING and LAYERING.

loss (of language) see LANGUAGE

loudness The attribute of auditory sensation in terms of which a sound may be ordered on a scale from soft to loud. It is an AUDITORY PHONETIC feature, corresponding to some degree with the ACOUSTIC features of **intensity** (measured in decibels (dB)), which in the study of speech is based on the size of the vibrations of the VOCAL CORDS, as a result of variations in air pressure. There is, however, no direct or parallel correlation between loudness (or 'volume') and intensity: other factors than intensity may affect our sensation of loudness; e.g. increasing the FREQUENCY of vocal-cord vibrations may make one sound seem louder than another.

The linguistic use of loudness is of particular interest to the PHONOLOGIST, and this is studied under the heading of STRESS.

low (1) One of the features of sound set up by CHOMSKY and Halle in their DISTINCTIVE FEATURE theory of PHONOLOGY, to handle variations in PLACE OF ARTICULATION (CAVITY features). Low sounds are a type of TONGUE-BODY feature, and defined ARTICULATORILY, as those produced by lowering the TONGUE to below the level it holds in neutral position; OPEN VOWELS and the GLOTTAL FRICATIVES are [+low]. Its opposite is **non-low [−low]** or HIGH, referring to sounds produced without any such lowering; it thus covers MID and CLOSE vowels, and most CONSONANTS.

(2) A term which describes the less formal variety in DIGLOSSIA; opposed to 'high'.

lower category A term used in GENERATIVE GRAMMAR to refer to the introduction into a SENTENCE DERIVATION of a CATEGORY which has already been used once in the derivation. In a TREE-diagram representation of the derivation, the category that has been introduced later will appear to be lower down the tree than the earlier (HIGHER) category. Lower, or EMBEDDED, sentences (CLAUSES, VERB PHRASES, NOUN phrases, etc.) can be illustrated by *the car* ***which I left in the street*** *has been stolen*. It has occasionally been suggested that there are no lowering TRANSFORMATIONS, but lowering operations have been assumed in recent GOVERNMENT-BINDING THEORY.

lowering see RAISING (2)

loyalty (language) see LANGUAGE

LP An abbreviation for LINEAR PRECEDENCE in GENERALIZED PHRASE-STRUCTURE GRAMMAR.

ludic A term sometimes used in LINGUISTICS to refer to LANGUAGE whose primary function is to be part of play, as in the nonsense, repetitive rhythms, and rhymes heard in children's games all over the world. Adults too may play with language, such as by adopting silly tones of voice or by twisting words into unorthodox shapes to create a humorous effect (cf. LUDLING, VERBAL PLAY).

ludling A term used in an approach to the FORMAL definition of LANGUAGE games (e.g. play languages, speech disguises, secret languages); from Latin *ludus* ('play') + *lingua* ('language'). The focus is on the distinctive structure such games display. In particular, their MORPHOLOGICAL system is limited to a small number of operations superimposed on ordinary language (e.g. INFIXATION, SYLLABLE reversal), its AFFIXES are very few (often only one), and the added elements have no meaning. Ludling operations are seen as extensions of ordinary language processes (cf. RESTRICTED LANGUAGE), and their study has proved attractive in NON-LINEAR approaches to PHONOLOGY and morphology, where they are often referred to as part of the evidence supporting a particular theoretical construct (e.g. the notion of a SKELETAL TIER).

M

M The abbreviation for MOT in METRICAL PHONOLOGY; also sometimes for a MODAL verb.

macrolinguistic(s) A term used by some LINGUISTS, especially in the 1950s, to identify an extremely broad conception of the subject of linguistic enquiry. LINGUISTICS is seen in its overall relation to PHONETIC and EXTRALINGUISTIC experience. It is divided into three main subfields: PRELINGUISTICS (whose primary subject-matter is PHONETICS), MICROLINGUISTICS (whose primary subject-matter is PHONOLOGY, MORPHOLOGY and SYNTAX) and METALINGUISTICS (whose subject-matter is the relationship between LANGUAGE and all extralinguistic features of communicative behaviour, e.g. including what would now be called SOCIOLINGUISTICS). Some sociolinguists (e.g. Joshua Fishman (b. 1926)) distinguish between the broad concerns of 'macrosociolinguistics' (e.g. MULTILINGUALISM, language planning) and the detailed investigation of 'microsociolinguistics' (e.g. speech events, conversations).

macro-phylum see FAMILY

main A term used in GRAMMATICAL analysis as part of the CLASSIFICATION of CLAUSE types; opposed to SUBORDINATE or DEPENDENT. **A main clause** is an independent clause, i.e. it can stand on its own as a SENTENCE. The term is also used to identify the more important STRUCTURAL member of a SEQUENCE of ITEMS all belonging to the same CLASS, e.g. 'main VERB' (*v.* AUXILIARY verb).

maintenance (of a language) see LANGUAGE

major (1) A term used by some LINGUISTS in the CLASSIFICATION of SENTENCE types to refer to the most PRODUCTIVE sentence patterns in a LANGUAGE. In English, the SUBJECT+PREDICATE (NP+VP) pattern is the **major sentence** (or FAVOURITE) type, e.g. *The elephant is running, A book is on the table.* Other types may be referred to as MINOR.

(2) In some models of FEATURE GEOMETRY, a term which forms part of a binary PHONOLOGICAL distinction corresponding to the PHONETIC contrast between primary and SECONDARY ARTICULATION; opposed to **minor**. It is argued that, in CONSONANTS involving multiple articulations, only one degree of CLOSURE is distinctive (the 'major articulator'); the other is predictable (the 'minor

articulator'), and thus its degree of closure need not be specified in the phonological REPRESENTATION.

major class feature One of the five main dimensions of classification in CHOMSKY and Halle's DISTINCTIVE FEATURE theory of PHONOLOGY (the others being CAVITY features, MANNER-OF-ARTICULATION features, SOURCE features and PROSODIC features). The term refers to the main types of sound produced by the open *v.* closed possibilities of VOCAL TRACT variation. There are three such features, all defined as OPPOSITIONS: SONORANT *v.* non-sonorant (OBSTRUENT), VOCALIC *v.* non-vocalic, and CONSONANTAL *v.* non-consonantal. Using these features, sounds can be subdivided into the major classes of VOWELS, CONSONANTS, OBSTRUENTS, SONORANTS, GLIDES and LIQUIDS.

mandibular setting see JAW SETTING

manifest(ation) A term used by some linguists to refer to the physical expression of an abstract LINGUISTIC UNIT, e.g. PHONEMES are 'manifested' in PHONIC SUBSTANCE as PHONES, MORPHEMES as morphs. Any UNDERLYING FORM may be seen as having a corresponding manifestation in substance. In TAGMEMICS, the term has a special status, referring to the ETIC (physical) expression of EMIC (abstract) units (the **manifestation mode**). Elsewhere, the term REALIZATION is widely used.

manner (1) **(of articulation)** One of the main parameters in the PHONETIC or PHONOLOGICAL classification of speech sounds, referring to the kind of ARTICULATORY process used in a sound's production. The distinction between CONSONANT and VOWEL is usually made in terms of manner of articulation. Within consonants, several articulatory types are recognized, based on the type of CLOSURE made by the VOCAL ORGANS. If the closure is complete, the result is a PLOSIVE, AFFRICATE or NASAL. If the closure is partial, the result is a LATERAL. If the closure is intermittent, the result is a ROLL (TRILL), or FLAP. And if there is narrowing without complete closure the result is a FRICATIVE. Within VOWELS, classification is based on the number of auditory qualities distinguishable in the sound (PURE VOWEL, DIPHTHONG, TRIPHTHONG), the position of the soft PALATE, and the type of lip position (see ROUNDING). Sounds which are vowel-like in manner of articulation, but consonantal in function, are classified as SEMI-VOWELS or FRICTIONLESS CONTINUANTS.

The term has special status in DISTINCTIVE FEATURE theory in PHONOLOGY, where it constitutes one of the five main dimensions in terms of which features of speech sound are analysed (the others being MAJOR CLASS FEATURES, CAVITY features, SOURCE features and PROSODIC features). The features subsumed under this heading, all analysed as OPPOSITIONS, are: CONTINUANT, RELEASE features (INSTANTANEOUS and DELAYED), SUPPLEMENTARY MOVEMENTS (SUCTION and PRESSURE) and TENSE.

(2) Several linguists use this term in the classification of LANGUAGE VARIETIES (more fully, **manner of discourse**), referring to the relations among the participants in a language activity, especially the LEVEL of FORMALITY they adopt (colloquial, formal, etc.). Alternative labels which have been proposed for this area are STYLE or TENOR of discourse.

(3) **Manner adverbials** are usually recognized in GRAMMATICAL description,

e.g. *in an X manner/way, quickly, angrily* – all able to answer the question 'how?' Certain other SEMANTIC CLASSES of ADVERBIAL are closely related (e.g. instrument, means), and sometimes subsumed under the heading of manner. Some GENERATIVE linguists see adverbials of manner as particularly significant, proposing a relationship between them and the PASSIVE construction.

(4) A term identifying one of the MAXIMS OF CONVERSATION: the 'maxim of manner' states that a person's contribution to a conversation should ideally be perspicuous – for example, avoiding obscurity and AMBIGUITY.

map(-ping, -ped) This term, used to characterize a feature of MODEL construction in scientific enquiry, has been applied in several areas of LINGUISTICS and PHONETICS. **Mapping** refers to the correspondence between the ELEMENTS defined in a model of a situation, and the elements recognized in the situation itself. If these elements are in a one-to-one correspondence, at a given level of abstraction, then the mapping is said to be ISOMORPHIC; if there is a superficial or selective correspondence (again, at a given level of abstraction), the mapping is 'homomorphic'. For example, one could evaluate the extent to which an isomorphic relationship existed between SYNTACTIC and SEMANTIC LEVELS of REPRESENTATION of SENTENCE STRUCTURE. In TRANSFORMATIONAL GRAMMAR, the term is used specifically to refer to the process whereby a particular stage in the DERIVATION of a sentence is formally related to a subsequent stage, e.g. an input phrase is 'mapped' by a set of transformations on to a derived PHRASE-MARKER.

marginal auxiliary see AUXILIARY (1)

margins The collective term for the sound SEGMENTS which form the boundaries of a SYLLABLE. In the WORD *cup*, for example, the CONSONANTS [k] and [p] constitute the syllable margins, as opposed to the VOWEL, which constitutes the syllable CENTRE.

markedness (mark-ing, -ed) An analytic principle in LINGUISTICS whereby pairs of linguistic FEATURES, seen as OPPOSITIONS, are given different values of POSITIVE (**marked**) and NEUTRAL or NEGATIVE (**unmarked**). In its most general sense, this distinction refers to the presence versus the absence of a particular linguistic feature. There is a formal feature marking plural in most English nouns, for example; the plural is therefore 'marked', and the singular is 'unmarked'. The reason for postulating such a relationship becomes clear when one considers the alternative, which would be to say that the opposed features simply operate in parallel, lacking any directionality. Intuitively, however, one prefers an analysis whereby *dogs* is derived from *dog* rather than the other way round – in other words, to say that '*dogs* is the plural of *dog*', rather than '*dog* is the singular of *dogs*'. Most of the theoretical discussion of markedness, then, centres on the question of how far there is intuitive justification for applying this notion to other areas of language (cf. *prince/princess, happy/unhappy, walk/walked*, etc.).

One of the earliest uses of the notion was in PRAGUE SCHOOL PHONOLOGY, where a sound would be said to be marked if it possessed a certain DISTINCTIVE FEATURE (e.g. VOICE), and unmarked it if lacked it (this unmarked member being the one which would be used in cases of NEUTRALIZATION). In GENERATIVE phonology, the notion has developed into a central criterion for formalizing the relative NATURALNESS of alternative solutions to phonological problems. Here, evidence from frequency of occurrence, HISTORICAL LINGUISTICS and language ACQUISITION is used to support the view that marking is a basic principle for assigning UNIVERSAL (and possibly innate) values to PHONETIC features (by contrast with the language-specific, phonological approach of the Prague School). The distinctive features are each assigned marking values, e.g. [+voice] is seen as marked, [−voice] as unmarked. SEGMENTS, in this view, can then be seen as combinations of marked or unmarked features, and thus be compared with each other, e.g. /a/ is the maximally unmarked vowel because it is [−high], [−back] and [−round]; /ɔ/ is more complex because it is [+low] and [+round], and so on. In recent phonological theory (e.g. in UNDERSPECIFICATION theory), the notion of markedness has taken on a critical status. Based on the view that the unmarked value of a feature is the normal, neutral state of the relevant articulator, some approaches assert that only one value need be present in the UNDERLYING REPRESENTATION; the other can be predicted by a CONTEXT-free RULE which mirrors the relevant markedness statement. For example, [ ] → [−nasal] would represent the notion that segments are normally oral. The rule would insert [−nasal] by default only in segments lacking a nasal value. Such rules are known as 'markedness based context-free redundancy rules'.

Several other interpretations of the notion of marking are found in the literature, where the concept of 'presence *v.* absence' does not readily apply. One interpretation relates marking to frequency of occurrence, as when one might say a FALLING INTONATION pattern was unmarked, compared with a RISING one, because it is more common. Another is found in the SEMANTIC analysis of LEXICAL ITEMS, where pairs of items are seen as unmarked and marked respectively, on the grounds that one member is more specific than the other (e.g. *dog/bitch*, where the latter is marked for sex – one can say *male/female dog*, but these ADJECTIVES are inapplicable with *bitch*). A third, related sense occurs when the DISTRIBUTION of one member of an opposition is restricted, compared with the other: the restricted item is then said to be marked – several COMPARATIVE SENTENCES illustrate this, e.g. *How tall is John?* (where *How short is John?* is abnormal). In recent GENERATIVE linguistics, a more general **theory of markedness** has emerged. Here, an unmarked property is one which accords with the general tendencies found in all languages; a marked property is one which goes against these general tendencies – in other words, it is exceptional (a RELATIVE UNIVERSAL). See also AGREEMENT.

marker A term used by some GENERATIVE LINGUISTS as part of a (controversial) two-way classification of the SEMANTIC COMPONENTS of LEXICAL ITEMS. Markers are those components of the meaning of a lexical item which are systematic for the language, i.e. the relations into which the item enters are systematic, in that the analysis of other lexical items makes reference to them. For example, [animate] is a marker, as can be seen by SELECTIONAL restrictions on the CO-OCCURRENCE of [+animate] lexical items with [−animate] ones, e.g. **the stone slept*. Components of meaning which do not operate in this way are called DISTINGUISHERS.

Markov process A term introduced into linguistics by Noam CHOMSKY in *Syntactic Structures* referring to the mathematical characterization of a FINITE-STATE GRAMMAR. A. A. Markov (1856–1922) was a Russian mathematician who helped to develop the theory of stochastic processes, introducing the notion of chained events (a 'Markov chain'). See also AUTOMATON, HIDDEN MARKOV MODEL.

mass A term used in the GRAMMATICAL classification of NOUNS; opposed to COUNT. The term refers to those nouns which the speaker treats as continuous entities, having no natural bounds (contrasting with the separable 'countable' quality of count nouns); but the distinction is not made on SEMANTIC grounds alone; the contrasting pattern of co-occurrence with DETERMINERS, QUANTIFIERS, etc., is the main evidence, e.g. **an anger v. some anger* shows this to be a mass noun. There is no logical reason why nouns should be count or mass: a concept may be countable in one language, but mass in another, as in the case of *information*, which is mass in English, but countable in French (*des informations*).

matched guise A technique used in SOCIOLINGUISTICS to obtain information about unconsciously held LANGUAGE attitudes. The output of one person capable of speaking in two 'guises' (authentically sounding alternative ACCENTS, DIALECTS or LANGUAGES) is presented to listeners who rate the speech in terms of such scales as intellectual capability and social solidarity. Because other variables (such as subject-matter) can be kept constant, the technique offers a larger measure of experimental control than is usual in sociolinguistic research.

matching A term used in GOVERNMENT-BINDING THEORY as a CONDITION required by the (sub-)theory of BINDING. The matching condition states that, if two NOUN PHRASES are ASSIGNED the same INDICES, their FEATURES (of NUMBER, GENDER, etc.) must be compatible.

mathematical linguistics A branch of LINGUISTICS which studies the mathematical properties of LANGUAGE, usually employing concepts of a statistical or algebraic kind. A contribution has also come from INFORMATION theory (e.g. quantification of such notions as REDUNDANCY and FUNCTIONAL load) and from computational analysis (e.g. the use of ALGORITHMS). The main application of mathematical notions has been in the FORMALIZATION of linguistic theory, as developed in relation to GENERATIVE linguistics; but several other areas of language study have been investigated using these methods. Statistical studies of the DISTRIBUTION and frequency of linguistic ITEMS have led to the development of several empirical laws and specific techniques, e.g. in authorship studies (cf. stylostatistics in STYLISTICS) and COMPARATIVE language study (cf. LEXICOSTATISTICS).

matrix (1) A term derived from mathematics to refer to a rectangular array of entities (usually symbols) made up of rows and columns, and used in all branches of LINGUISTICS as an aid in DESCRIPTION or analysis. In PHONOLOGY, for example, DISTINCTIVE FEATURES are usually described within a matrix, where the columns are SEGMENTS and the rows are features: the cells of the matrix are then filled with pluses or minuses (or, in some cases, zero) corresponding to whether a feature is or is not used.

(2) A term used in linguistics, and especially in GENERATIVE GRAMMAR, to refer

to the superordinate SENTENCE within which another sentence is EMBEDDED, e.g. *The student who shouted left*, where *The student left* is the **matrix sentence**, and *The student shouted* is the embedded sentence.

(3) See SOURCE (4).

maxims of conversation A term derived from the work of the philosopher H. P. Grice (1913–88), and now widely cited in PRAGMATICS research. The maxims are general principles which are thought to underlie the efficient use of LANGUAGE, and which together identify a general CO-OPERATIVE PRINCIPLE. Four basic maxims are recognized. The **maxim of quality** states that speakers' contributions ought to be true – specifically, that they should not say what they believe to be false, nor should they say anything for which they lack adequate evidence. The **maxim of quantity** states that the contribution should be as informative as is required for the current purposes of the exchange, and should not be unnecessarily informative. The **maxim of relevance** states that contributions should be relevant to the purpose of the exchange. The **maxim of manner** states that the contribution should be perspicuous – in particular, that it should be orderly and brief, avoiding obscurity and AMBIGUITY. The ideas underlying the maxims have since been developed within RELEVANCE THEORY.

m-command The usual abbreviation for 'maximal-command'. See COMMAND (2).

MDP An abbreviation often used in language ACQUISITION studies for MINIMAL-DISTANCE PRINCIPLE.

meaning(ful) The basic notion is used in LINGUISTICS both as a datum and as a criterion of analysis: linguists study meaning, and also use meaning as a criterion for studying other aspects of LANGUAGE (especially through such notions as CONTRASTIVITY and DISTINCTIVENESS). The topic of 'meaning' in the context of language, however, necessitates reference to non-linguistic factors, such as thought, situation, knowledge, intention and use. It is the difficulty in drawing clear dividing-lines between such notions that indicates why so many other academic disciplines are involved in the study of meaning along with linguistics – philosophers and logicians especially, but also psychologists, sociologists, literary critics, theologians and others. Linguists' primary interests are distinguished by the attention they pay to the analysis of meaning in the context of everyday speech (rather than, say, in the context of literature, or abstract reasoning), by their comparative interests (comparing the way meaning is structured in a range of languages, and how meaning changes over time), and by their attempt to integrate meaning with the other COMPONENTS of a general linguistic theory (especially with GRAMMAR). These emphases characterize the linguistic study of meaning, SEMANTICS. There has been continuing debate, in recent decades (especially in GENERATIVE grammar), about the place of semantics in relation to SYNTAX, when considering the DERIVATION of sentences.

Linguistics shares with other disciplines the concern to isolate the several factors which contribute to the total interpretation, or signification, of a message, as this provides the essential perspective within which the specifically intra-linguistic properties of meaning can be identified. These factors – the 'meanings of meaning' as they are sometimes called – have been variously labelled; and, while it is impossible to generalize about usage (in view of the many technical senses these labels have in various theories), labels do cluster around three major themes. When the emphasis is on the relationship between language, on the one hand, and the entities, events, states of affairs, etc., which are external to speakers and their language, on the other, terms such as 'REFERENTIAL/DESCRIPTIVE / DENOTATIVE / EXTENSIONAL / factual / objective meaning' have been used. When the emphasis is on the relationship between language and the mental state of the speaker, two sets of terms are used: the personal, emotional aspects are handled by such terms as 'ATTITUDINAL/AFFECTIVE/CONNOTATIVE/EMOTIVE/EXPRESSIVE meaning'; the intellectual, factual aspects involve such terms as 'COGNITIVE/IDEATIONAL meaning'. When the emphasis is on the way variations in the EXTRALINGUISTIC situation affect the understanding and interpretation of language, terms such as 'CONTEXTUAL/FUNCTIONAL/interpersonal/social/SITUATIONAL' have been used. 'Contextual', along with 'TEXTUAL meaning', is also used to refer to those factors which affect the interpretation of a sentence which derive from the rest of the DISCOURSE or TEXT within which the sentence occurs.

Within linguistics, the role each linguistic LEVEL plays in the total interpretation of a sentence is often referred to as the 'meaning' of that level. The main levels involved are 'LEXICAL meaning', the meaning of lexical ITEMS; and 'GRAMMATICAL meaning' (or 'STRUCTURAL meaning'), the meaning of grammatical structures. This approach has been extended by some linguists (e.g. FIRTHIANS) to include other linguistic levels, e.g. 'PHONETIC meaning' (cf. SOUND-SYMBOLISM), 'PHONOLOGICAL meaning' (as in the structural use of alliteration or rhyme in poetry). The term 'semantic meaning' may be used whenever one wants to emphasize the content, as opposed to the form or reference, of linguistic units. Specific aspects of the content of sentences may be singled out for special attention, e.g. the notion of 'PROPOSITIONAL meaning'. A 'meaning POSTULATE' is a notion used in MODEL-THEORETIC SEMANTICS which restricts the possible interpretations of an object language (L) by describing lexical meanings in terms of analytically true sentences in L.

meaning-changing (-preserving) A theoretical distinction introduced in early GENERATIVE GRAMMAR between two types of TRANSFORMATIONS. If the operation of a transformation involves a change in the MEANING between input and DERIVED SENTENCES, the transformation is said to be 'meaning-changing'; in 'meaning-preserving' transformations, there is no such change (cf. KATZ–POSTAL HYPOTHESIS). An example of the former would be in deriving IMPERATIVE sentences from an UNDERLYING (DECLARATIVE) STRUCTURE by using a *you*-DELETION transformation (e.g. *see* from *you see*); here is a plain contrast between declarative and imperative 'meanings', and the reason for the appearance of this contrast in the grammar is the use of the transformation. On the other hand, if the imperative is derived from an underlying structure where its 'imperativeness' has been represented, then the application of the *you*-deletion transformation would no longer change the structure's meaning, but simply make tangible an element of meaning which was already present (viz. Imp. + *see* → *see*). Other examples of meaning-changing transformations include NEGATIVE placement (e.g. *Not much shrapnel hit the soldier v. Much shrapnel did not hit the* *soldier*) and subject raising (e.g. *It is certain that nobody will pass the test* v. *Nobody is certain to pass the test*).

mean length of utterance (MLU) A measure introduced by the American psychologist Roger Brown (b. 1925) into LANGUAGE ACQUISITION studies, which computes the LENGTH of an UTTERANCE in terms of MORPHEMES. The technique is then used to show the increasing length of a child's utterances over time, as a base-line for carrying out studies on the developmental complexity of SENTENCE STRUCTURE.

medial The usual way of referring to an ELEMENT occurring within a LINGUISTIC UNIT, other than in INITIAL and FINAL positions. The term is especially used in PHONOLOGY, e.g. the PHONEME /i/ occurs 'in medial position' (or 'medially') in the word *seat*.

medium A term used in the study of COMMUNICATION to refer to the functionally distinct dimensions in which a message is transmitted. In LINGUISTICS, the basic media are speech and writing, but others are not excluded (e.g. signing). Of these, speech is generally held in linguistics to be the 'primary medium', writing the 'secondary' or 'derived' medium, and the analysis of the differences between these media in STRUCTURAL and FUNCTIONAL terms is an important topic in linguistics. The term is usually distinguished from 'channel' (as used in communication theory), which refers to the physical means whereby a (spoken or written) message is transmitted, such as a wire, air, light, etc.

mellow One of the features of sound set up by JAKOBSON and Halle in their DISTINCTIVE FEATURE theory of PHONOLOGY, to handle variations in PLACE OF ARTICULATION; its opposite is STRIDENT. Mellow sounds are defined ARTICULATORILY and ACOUSTICALLY, as those involving a less complex or 'smooth-edged' CONSTRICTION at the point of articulation, and marked by acoustic energy of relatively low FREQUENCY and intensity, compared with strident sounds. PLOSIVES and NASALS are examples.

melodic tier In some models of NON-LINEAR PHONOLOGY, a term referring to a level in a PROSODIC HIERARCHY at which ARTICULATORY GESTURES can be REPRESENTED, distinct from SKELETAL or SYLLABIC tiers. For example, a LONG VOWEL would be analysed as a single melody unit but would occupy two slots at the skeletal tier; and a CONTOUR segment would occupy a single skeletal slot but correspond to two articulatory gestures at the melodic tier. Several other items have also been used as names for this level of representation (cf. TIER).

mentalese In LINGUISTICS, the concepts, and combinations of concepts, postulated as a 'language of thought' (LOT), differing in various ways from the GRAMMAR of natural language. A thought, in this context, is conceived as an intentional state of mind representing something about the world, including the various beliefs, hopes, and other PROPOSITIONAL attitudes held by the thinker. The approach is of special relevance in COMPUTATIONAL LINGUISTICS, where mental processes can be modelled as sequences of mental states and transitions.

mentalism (mentalistic) In LINGUISTICS, the influence of this school of thought (that mental states and processes exist independently of their manifestations of behaviour, and can explain behaviour) is most marked in the work of Noam CHOMSKY, especially in his notions of COMPETENCE and INNATENESS, and in his general views of the relationship between LANGUAGE and mind. In this respect, **mentalistic linguistics** is opposed to the BEHAVIOURISM of earlier psychological work on language.

merge In the MINIMALIST PROGRAMME, an operation which forms larger units out of those already constructed. Specifically, it is a process which combines LEXICAL elements in the NUMERATION with partial TREES – a basic operation, along with MOVE, in the process of tree construction.

merger (merge) A term used in LINGUISTICS, especially in HISTORICAL LINGUISTICS, to refer to the coming together (or CONVERGENCE) of linguistic UNITS which were originally distinguishable. In cases of two PHONEMES coming together, the phrase **phonemic merger** is often used (the opposite phenomenon being referred to as 'phonemic split'). For example, the /æː/ and /eː/ vowels in Old English have now merged in modern English /iː/, as in *meet* and *clean*. Analogous terms include COALESCENCE, FUSION and NEUTRALIZATION.

meronym(y) A term used in SEMANTICS as part of the study of the SENSE relations which relate LEXICAL ITEMS. 'Meronymy' is the relationship which obtains between 'parts' and 'wholes', such as *wheel* and *car* or *leg* and *knee*. 'X is a part of Y' contrasts especially with the 'X is a kind of Y' relationship (HYPONYMY).

mesolect(al) A term used by some SOCIOLINGUISTS, in the study of the development of CREOLE languages, to refer to the intermediate linguistic VARIETIES (or LECTS) which fall between ACROLECT and BASILECT. Because of the range of variety covered by this notion, a further distinction is often drawn between the 'upper' mesolect (i.e. that closest to the acrolect), the 'lower' mesolect (i.e. that closest to the basilect) and the 'mid' mesolect (equidistant from the two); but the extent to which these distinctions can be drawn in a non-arbitrary way is disputed.

metagrammar A term used in recent LINGUISTIC theory to refer to a GRAMMAR which contains a set of METARULES.

metalanguage (metalinguistic(s)) (1) LINGUISTICS, as other sciences, uses this term in the sense of a higher-level language for describing an object of study (or 'object language') – in this case the object of study is itself language, viz. the various language samples, INTUITIONS, etc., which constitute our linguistic experience. The subject of this dictionary is **linguistic metalanguage**. 'Metalinguistics' is the study of metalanguage, in this general sense. Other 'meta' notions will also be encountered, such as METARULE and METADISCOURSE. See also LANGUAGE AWARENESS.

(2) The general term **metalinguistics** has a more specific sense within linguistics, where some linguists have used it, especially in the 1950s, to refer to the overall relation of the linguistic system to the other systems of behaviour in the associated culture (cf. the similar notion of CONTEXT OF SITUATION). In this view, only such a total account will constitute the full statement of the MEANINGS of the linguistic FORMS.

metadiscourse A term used in the study of DISCOURSE for those features in the organization or presentation of a text which help the reader to interpret or evaluate its content. They include features of textual organization (e.g. headings, spacing, and connectives such as *first* and *next*) as well as such interpersonal elements as HEDGES (*perhaps*), attitude markers (*frankly*), and dialogue features (*see Figure 1*).

metanalysis A term sometimes used in HISTORICAL LINGUISTICS, referring to the formation of a new LEXICAL item through a wrong analysis of an existing word boundary; for example in early English *a naddre* came to be heard in the popular mind as *an adder*, which has become the modern form. It is a kind of folk ETYMOLOGY.

metaphony A term used in PHONOLOGY for a process of ASSIMILATION which affects non-adjacent VOWELS in a word. The notion thus subsumes such processes as vowel HARMONY and the type of phonological change which takes place when a vowel changes its quality under the influence of a following vowel ('umlaut'), and is used both in SYNCHRONIC and DIACHRONIC contexts.

metaphor see COGNITIVE METAPHOR

metarule A term used in recent LINGUISTIC theory to refer to a type of RULE which defines some rules in a GRAMMAR on the basis of the properties of others already present in the grammar. Metarules are particularly important in GENERALIZED PHRASE-STRUCTURE GRAMMAR, where they derive IMMEDIATE DOMINANCE rules from immediate dominance rules. They allow the capturing of certain GENERALIZATIONS which are handled by TRANSFORMATION in transformational grammar; for example, the relation between active and PASSIVE sentences is captured by a metarule deriving rules for passive VPs from rules for active VPs. Metarules, it has been said, in effect provide a grammar which can be used for generating a grammar – in other words, a METAGRAMMAR.

metathesis A term used in LINGUISTICS to refer to an alteration in the normal SEQUENCE of ELEMENTS in a SENTENCE – usually of sounds, but sometimes of SYLLABLES, WORDS, or other UNITS. 'Metatheses' are well recognized in HISTORICAL LINGUISTICS (e.g. Old English *brid* becoming *bird*), but they can also be seen in PERFORMANCE ERRORS – in such TONGUE-SLIPS as *aks* for *ask*, or in the phenomenon of 'spoonerisms' (cf. *the dear old queen* becoming *the queer old dean*).

metonym(y) A term used in SEMANTICS and STYLISTICS, referring to a figure of speech in which the name of an attribute of an entity is used in place of the entity itself. People are using metonyms when they talk about *the bottle* (for the drinking of alcohol) or *the violins* (in *The second violins are playing well*).

metric see SIMPLICITY

metrical grid A FORMALISM used in some approaches to METRICAL PHONOLOGY to display HIERARCHIC patterns of SYLLABIC PROMINENCE, presented graphically in columns (for relative prominence) and rows (for rhythmical structure). Each syllable is assigned a position on a metrical grid, strong syllables being assigned progressively higher 'layers' in the grid. For example, the grids for *thirteen men* and *antique settee* would be:

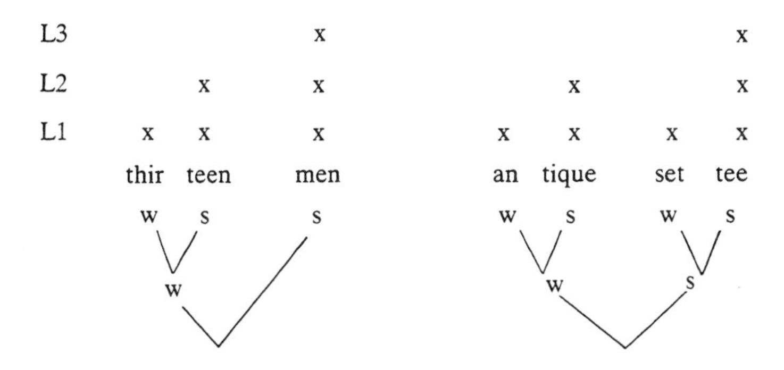

At the bottom layer (L1), or row, each TERMINAL NODE of the TREE is aligned with a grid placeholder (marked by x); this layer is the grid's 'terminal set'. A second layer is used to reflect the relative strength of *-teen* and *men*, as opposed to *thir-*; and a third layer is used to reflect the relative strength of *men* as opposed to *-teen*. Grid elements at the same layer are said to be 'adjacent'. Adjacent elements are 'alternating' if, at the next lower layer, the elements corresponding to them (if any) are not adjacent (as in the *antique settee* example); they are 'clashing' if their counterparts one layer down are adjacent (as in the *thirteen men* example). The relationship between trees and grids proved controversial: some phonologists argued that the formalisms are equivalent, and that only grids need be represented (an 'autonomous' grid, 'grid-only' phonology); some argued that only trees need be represented ('tree-only' phonology); and some argued that both are required, because they have different functions (trees representing STRESS, grids representing RHYTHM). Grid construction is carried out using a set of PARAMETERS (e.g. QUANTITY SENSITIVITY). The rhythmical basis of the grid is provided by the rule of **perfect grid**: a foot-layer mark is added on top of alternating syllable-layer marks. **Bracketed grid theory** is a metrical grid with CONSTITUENCY markers added, introduced to formalize a constituent structure view of rhythm. Various notations have been proposed.

metrical phonology A theory of PHONOLOGY in which phonological STRINGS are REPRESENTED in a HIERARCHICAL manner, using such notions as SEGMENT, SYLLABLE, FOOT and WORD (cf. also PROSODIC phonology). Originally introduced as a hierarchical theory of STRESS, the approach now covers the whole domain of syllable structure and phonological boundaries. Stress patterns are considered to reflect, at least in part, relations of PROMINENCE between SYNTACTIC and MORPHOLOGICAL CONSTITUENTS. The UNDERLYING metrical STRUCTURE of words and PHRASES may be represented in the form of a metrical TREE, whose NODES reflect the relative metrical strength between SISTER constituents, as in the following examples (w = weak, s = strong):

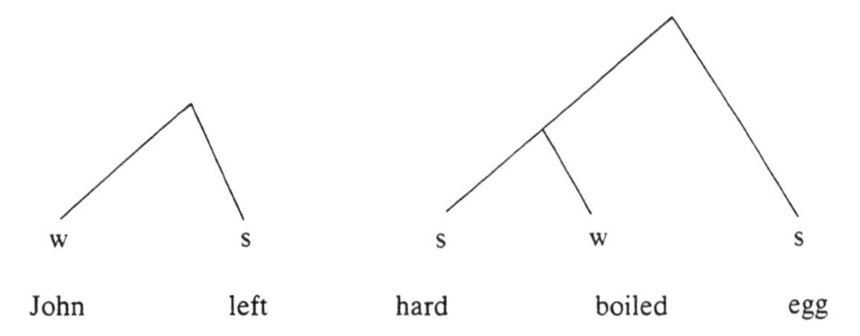

Patterns of syllabic prominence can also be formally represented through the use of METRICAL GRIDS. Later developments of the theory represent phonological relations in terms of PARAMETERS.

metrics (metrical) The traditional sense of this term – the study of versification – is interpreted in LINGUISTICS as the analysis of metrical structure using the whole range of linguistic techniques, especially those belonging to SEGMENTAL and SUPRASEGMENTAL PHONOLOGY. It has developed a special sense in the context of METRICAL PHONOLOGY.

microlinguistic(s) A term used by some linguists, especially in the 1950s, to refer to the main areas of LINGUISTICS, especially PHONOLOGY, MORPHOLOGY and SYNTAX, these being seen as constituting a sharply defined field of study differentiable from PRELINGUISTICS and METALINGUISTICS. In this frame of reference, it was seen as a branch of MACROLINGUISTICS. More broadly, the term can be used to distinguish complementary views of a subject, one being strictly linguistic, the other being wider; for example, a study of MEANING which concentrates on DENOTATIVE meaning and does not take SOCIOLINGUISTIC, etc., factors into account might be called 'microlinguistic' (as opposed to 'macrolinguistic') semantics.

The term 'microlinguistic' is sometimes used outside this framework in a general sense, to refer to any analysis of linguistic data involving a maximum depth of detail. Likewise, the term 'microsociolinguistic' (opposed to 'macro-') is sometimes found.

mid A term used in the threefold PHONETIC classification of vertical TONGUE movement in VOWEL sounds, the others being HIGH and LOW. It refers to vowels made in the middle area of ARTICULATION, as in *get, say, go* or *got*. Relatively high mid-vowels are sometimes described as **mid-close**; relatively low mid-vowels as **mid-open**. See also CLOSE (1), OPEN (1).

minimal(ity) A term which is widely used in recent LINGUISTICS, especially as part of the discussion of the FORMAL properties of REPRESENTATIONS. For example, in GENERATIVE phonology, 'lexical minimality' assumes that UNDERLYING representations must reduce to some minimum the phonological information used to distinguish LEXICAL items. The notion of a 'minimal word' is required in some models of NON-LINEAR PHONOLOGY. In PROSODIC MORPHOLOGY, for instance, a 'prosodic word' must satisfy a **minimality condition**: according to the prosodic HIERARCHY, any instance of a prosodic word must contain at least one FOOT, and every foot must contain at least two MORALS (in QUANTITY sensitive languages) or two SYLLABLES (in quantity insensitive languages). A **minimality condition** is also defined in GOVERNMENT-BINDING THEORY, formalizing the view that an element governed by one relationship will not be governed by another; in terms of a theory of BARRIERS, NODES become barriers for an element if they immediately DOMINATE the nearest GOVERNOR of that element. **Relativized minimality** is the view that what counts as a governor is related to what is being governed: an element will minimally govern its TRACE if there is no other typical potential governor that is closer to the trace.

minimal-distance principle (MDP) A term used in PSYCHOLINGUISTICS, referring to a principle assumed to be generally applicable in the analysis of COMPLEMENT structures of the type *Mary wants Jim to go*, where the SUBJECT of the complement CLAUSE is *Jim*, i.e. the nearest NOUN PHRASE to the left of the complement VERB. Most complement-taking verbs conform to this principle (e.g. *like, hope, make*), which is used especially in child language studies to explain apparent anomalies in the ACQUISITION of complements and other similar types of STRUCTURE. For example, in *Mary promised Jim to go*, the subject of *go* is *Mary*: this breaks the minimal-distance principle, and it is hypothesized that children will have greater difficulty learning structures involving such verbs, since they constitute exceptions to the general rule.

minimal free form A term introduced into LINGUISTICS by the American linguist Leonard BLOOMFIELD as part of his definition of WORD. The phrase can be glossed as 'the smallest linguistic FORM which can stand on its own as an UTTERANCE'.

minimalist program(me) (MP) A recent development in GENERATIVE linguistic thinking, which emphasizes the aim of making statements about language which are as simple and general as possible. All REPRESENTATIONS and DERIVATIONAL processes should be as ECONOMICAL as possible, in terms of the number of devices proposed to account for language phenomena (the 'principle of economy') – in effect, an application of Occam's razor. There should be no REDUNDANT or superfluous elements in the representation of sentence structure: each element must play a role and must be interpreted (the 'principle of full interpretation'). The four LEVELS of representation recognized in standard GOVERNMENT-BINDING THEORY (D-structure, S-structure, logical form (LF), and phonetic form (PF)) are reduced to two: LF and PF, referred to as INTERFACE levels. Minimally, the mapping of sounds to meanings requires no more than a lexicon and a computational (SYNTACTIC) procedure which gives lexical elements a PHONOLOGICAL and a SEMANTIC identity. The grammar is modelled as a COMPUTATIONAL SYSTEM containing a NUMERATION of LEXICAL items, to which operations of MOVE and MERGE apply in order to build up a STRUCTURAL DESCRIPTION. All INFLECTED words are formed in the lexicon. Operations are driven by MORPHOLOGICAL necessity, with features being checked for their applicability. Economy constraints, such as PROCRASTINATE and GREED, are used to compare derivations involving the same lexical resources and reject those which do not conform. The derivation eventually splits into phonetic and semantic representations (following SPELL-OUT), which must CONVERGE to produce grammatical sentences.

minimal link condition see MOVEMENT (1)

minimal pair (test) One of the DISCOVERY PROCEDURES used in PHONOLOGY to determine which sounds belong to the same class, or PHONEME. Two WORDS which differ in meaning when only one sound is changed are referred to as a 'minimal pair', e.g. *pin v. bin, cot v. cut,* and linguists or native speakers who make these judgements are said to be carrying out a 'minimal pair test'. A group of words differentiated by each having only one sound different from all others, e.g. *big, pig, rig . . .* is sometimes called a 'minimal set'.

minor (1) A term used by some LINGUISTS in the classification of SENTENCE types to refer to a sentence (a **minor sentence**) with limited PRODUCTIVITY (e.g. *Please, Sorry*) or one which lacks some of the CONSTITUENTS of the LANGUAGE'S MAJOR (or FAVOURITE) sentence type (e.g. VOCATIVES, ELLIPTICAL CONSTRUCTIONS).
(2) For **minor articulation** in FEATURE geometry, see MAJOR (2).

minority language A LANGUAGE used in a country by a group which is significantly smaller in number than the rest of the population; also called a **linguistic minority** or **language minority**. Those who speak the language may be nationals of the country, but they have distinguishing ethnic, religious, or cultural features which they wish to safeguard. Most countries have several minority languages within their borders.

misderivation A term used by some PSYCHOLINGUISTS to refer to a type of TONGUE-SLIP where the wrong AFFIX is attached to a WORD, as in *kingness for kingship.*

mismatch see OVERLAPPING (2)

mistake see ERROR (2)

MIT The abbreviation for Massachusetts Institute of Technology, used in LINGUISTICS as a label characterizing GENERATIVE linguistic theory and method. The 'MIT school' is so called because of the influence of the work of Noam CHOMSKY and his associates at MIT since the late 1950s.

MLU The abbreviation for MEAN LENGTH OF UTTERANCE.

modal(ity) A term used in GRAMMATICAL and SEMANTIC analysis to refer to contrasts in MOOD signalled by the VERB and associated categories. In English, modal contrasts are primarily expressed by a subclass of AUXILIARY verbs, e.g. *may, will, can.* This subclass is symbolized as M in the PHRASE-STRUCTURE RULES of a GENERATIVE grammar. Modal verbs share a set of morphological and syntactic properties which distinguish them from the other auxiliaries, e.g. no *-s, -ing*, or *-en* forms. In CASE grammar, **modality** refers to one of the two major CONSTITUENTS of a sentences's DEEP STRUCTURE, the other being PROPOSITION.

mode (1) A term used in the HALLIDAYAN classification of LANGUAGE VARIETIES, referring to the MEDIUM of the language activity which determines the role played by the language in a situation. Mode (more fully, **mode of discourse**) primarily includes the choice of speech *v.* writing (along with other possible subdivisions, such as reading aloud, speech from notes, etc.), but also includes choice of format (as in newspapers, commentary, poetry, etc.). The main terms with which it contrasts are FIELD and STYLE.

(2) A term used in TAGMEMIC analysis to label the various dimensions recognized by the theory, e.g. the distinction between PHONOLOGICAL, LEXICAL and GRAMMATICAL 'modes' (which constitute the main components of the theory), and between FEATURE, MANIFESTATION and DISTRIBUTION 'modes' (which are used to handle the UNITS of linguistic description).

model (1) This central notion of scientific enquiry has been applied in several areas of LINGUISTICS and PHONETICS. A model is a specially designed representation of concepts or entities, used to discover or explain their structure or function. All models involve the MAPPING in a new conceptual dimension of a set of ELEMENTS recognized in the situation being modelled. For example, the PHONOLOGIST builds models of the organization of the speech continuum, using such contrasts as PHONEMES (sc. the 'phonemic model of analysis') or DISTINCTIVE FEATURES (sc. the 'distinctive feature model'); the GRAMMARIAN uses TREE diagrams, BRACKETS and other such devices to help model SYNTACTIC STRUCTURE. One of the earliest uses of the term in linguistics was by the American linguist, Charles Hockett (b. 1916), in a discussion of models of DESCRIPTION in MORPHOLOGY – a distinction being made between the 'ITEM-AND-ARRANGEMENT model' and the 'ITEM-AND-PROCESS model' (and later, the 'WORD-AND-PARADIGM model'). In discussion of GENERATIVE grammar, and related developments in linguistic theory, the term is often used in the sense of 'formal representation of a theory', as when one contrasts the '*Syntactic Structures* model' of generative grammar with the '*Aspects* model'. Sometimes, though, the term 'model' is used synonymously with 'theory' by some authors; usage is not entirely consistent. However, there is now increasing awareness of the role of models in linguistic enquiry, and of their strengths and limitations in generating testable hypotheses.

(2) In several areas of APPLIED LINGUISTICS, one encounters the traditional sense of a model as someone or something used as an exemplar of a level of language achievement. For example, foreign-language teaching may use a NATIVE-SPEAKER, or a STANDARD DIALECT, as a model of the language to be learned; speech therapists may use themselves as models for language-disordered patients; English teachers may use a certain piece of writing as a model of attainment for their class.

model-theoretic semantics A version of TRUTH-CONDITIONAL SEMANTICS developed by Richard Montague (1930–70) and others. A MODEL is defined relative to a LANGUAGE, and provides three kinds of information: (a) the individuals which are taken to be the domain of DISCOURSE; (b) an arbitrary number of world-time pairs; and (c) the reference and extension values at each world-time pair for the LEXICAL items in the language – such as what individuals' names or their PREDICATE terms refer to in all possible worlds. In **possible-worlds semantics**, the truth conditions of a sentence are the ways the world has to be if a sentence is true.

modification (modif-y, -ier) (1) A term used in SYNTAX to refer to the STRUCTURAL dependence of one GRAMMATICAL UNIT upon another – but with different restrictions in the scope of the term being introduced by different approaches. Some reserve the term for structural dependence within any ENDOCENTRIC PHRASE; e.g in *the big man in the garden*, both *the big* and *in the garden* 'modify' *man* – PREMODIFICATION and POST-modification respectively. Some LINGUISTS reserve the term for the premodifying structures only: in HALLIDAYAN grammar, for example, the above phrase would have the structure M–H–Q, standing for modification–HEAD–QUALIFICATION. TRADITIONAL grammar reserved the term for ADVERBIAL units which were dependent on the VERB, and this tradition is sometimes encountered.

(2) The term is also used in MORPHOLOGY to refer to a process of change within the ROOT or STEM of a FORM, as in the VOWEL changes between the singular and plural of some nouns in English (*man* ~ *men*), or in cases of SUPPLETION. In this, and related senses, the term is also found in HISTORICAL LINGUISTICS.

(3) In PHONETICS, factors which influence the airflow in the VOCAL TRACT are often referred to as **modifications**, e.g. the movement of the soft PALATE, the degree of CLOSURE of the GLOTTIS. The term is also sometimes used to refer to any factors which alter the typical actions of the VOCAL ORGANS in producing the PHONEMES of a language, as in PROSODIC features, SECONDARY ARTICULATIONS, and TRANSITIONS between sounds.

(4) Also in phonetics, the range of DIACRITIC marks which indicate variations in VOWEL and CONSONANT quality are referred to as **modifiers**, in the INTERNATIONAL PHONETIC ALPHABET.

modular(-ity, module) A term used in recent discussion of LANGUAGE in two slightly different ways. On the one hand, it is proposed, especially in J. A. Fodor's *The Modularity of Mind*, that the mind is modular in the sense that it consists of a number of different systems (**modules**) each with its own distinctive properties, such as the language system and the vision system. On the other hand, it is suggested, especially in GOVERNMENT-BINDING THEORY, that the language system itself is modular in the sense that it consists of a number of different subsystems which interact in specific ways.

modulation (modulate) A term sometimes used in LINGUISTICS to refer to the SUPRASEGMENTAL alterations introduced into an UTTERANCE for a particular attitudinal or social effect, e.g. whispering, shouting.

mono- A PREFIX used in PHONETICS and LINGUISTICS when one wants to contrast the unitary manifestation of a linguistic concept with a multiple one. Examples of this contrast are: **monosyllabic** WORDS (or 'monosyllables') *v.* POLYSYLLABLES; **monomorphemic** words (i.e. consisting of a single MORPHEME) *v.* bimorphemic, etc.; **monosystemic** PHONOLOGY (consisting of a single SYSTEM of PHONEMES) *v.* POLYSYSTEMIC; **monosemy** (consisting of a single MEANING) *v.* POLYSEMY; and so on.

monogenesis (monogenetic) In HISTORICAL LINGUISTICS, the hypothesis that all human LANGUAGES originate from a single source; contrasts with **polygenesis**, where language is thought to have emerged more or less spontaneously in several places. The terms are also used in discussing the similarities among PIDGINS and CREOLES: monogenetic theories assume the diffusion of a single pidgin to other areas via migration; polygenetic theories assume that the development of a pidgin in one community is independent of the development of a pidgin in another.

monophthong(-ize, -ization) A term used in the PHONETIC classification of VOWEL sounds on the basis of their MANNER OF ARTICULATION: it refers to a vowel (a PURE VOWEL) where there is no detectable change in quality during a SYLLABLE, as in English *cart, cut, cot.* Vowels which change in quality are known as DIPHTHONGS (or TRIPHTHONGS). In some DIALECT and DIACHRONIC studies, a process of **monophthongization** can be found, i.e. a change in VOWEL QUALITY from a diphthong to a monophthong.

monosemy see POLYSEMY

monostratal A term sometimes used in LINGUISTIC theory to refer to a GRAMMAR which contains only a single LEVEL of REPRESENTATION (roughly equivalent to the TRANSFORMATIONAL notion of SURFACE STRUCTURE). The contrast is intended with GENERATIVE grammars which recognize more than one level – typically, DEEP STRUCTURE as well as surface structure.

monovalent see PRIVATIVE (2), VALENCY

Montague grammar A movement in LINGUISTIC theory in the mid-1970s which owes its impetus to the thinking of the American logician Richard Montague (1930–70). The approach uses a conceptual apparatus derived from the study of the SEMANTICS of FORMAL (logical) LANGUAGES, and applies it to the analysis of natural languages. The GRAMMAR contains a SYNTACTIC and a SEMANTIC COMPONENT, which are strictly related, in that there is a one-to-one correspondence between CATEGORIES set up at the two levels. The syntax is introduced through CATEGORIAL RULES which define syntactic categories, and build up a PHRASE-STRUCTURE grammar. The corresponding semantic rules construct a PROPOSITIONAL interpretation of these sentences, using the notions of truth-conditional predicate logic. The approach has been modified and extended in several ways – notably in relation to GENERALIZED PHRASE-STRUCTURE GRAMMAR. Approaches showing Montague's influence are sometimes characterized as 'Montagovian'.

mood (modal, -ity) A term used in the theoretical and descriptive study of SENTENCE/CLAUSE types, and especially of the VERBS they contain. Mood ('modality', or 'mode') refers to a set of SYNTACTIC and SEMANTIC CONTRASTS signalled by alternative PARADIGMS of the verb, e.g. INDICATIVE (the UNMARKED form), SUBJUNCTIVE, IMPERATIVE. Semantically, a wide range of meanings is involved, especially attitudes on the part of the speaker towards the factual content of the utterance, e.g. uncertainty, definiteness, vagueness, possibility. Syntactically, these contrasts may be signalled by alternative INFLECTIONAL forms of a verb, or by using AUXILIARIES. English mainly uses **modal auxiliaries**, e.g. *may, can, shall, must*, but makes a little use of inflection (e.g. *If I were you v. I was . . .*). The semantic analysis of **modal verbs**, and the study of their distribution in everyday speech, is a topic which has attracted a great deal of recent attention in LINGUISTICS, and several classifications involving such notions as necessity, possibility, certainty, etc., have been proposed. The results of such studies have implications for fields other than linguistics; for example, theoretical modal distinctions involving such notions have been a major concern of logicians. See also ALETHIC, DEONTIC, EPISTEMIC.

mora(-ic) A term used in traditional studies of METRICS to refer to a minimal unit of metrical time or weight, and now used in some models of NON-LINEAR PHONOLOGY (e.g. METRICAL and PROSODIC phonology) as a separate level of phonological representation. The analysis of SEGMENTS into moras is usually applied only to the syllabic NUCLEUS and CODA (the RHYME), and not to the ONSET ('onset/rhyme asymmetry'). Moraic structure accounts for many of the phenomena described in other models by such notions as the SKELETAL TIER. In the prosodic HIERARCHY, the moraic level is symbolized by μ ('mu'). The notion of **mora counting** is used to handle languages where there is an opposition between heavy (two-mora, or **bimoraic**) syllables and light (one-mora, or **monomoraic**) syllables, and the equivalence between various types of heavy syllable. In Latin, for example, a long vowel was equivalent to two short vowels or to a short vowel plus consonant.

morpheme (morph, -emics) The minimal DISTINCTIVE UNIT of GRAMMAR, and the central concern of MORPHOLOGY. Its original motivation was as an alternative to the notion of the WORD, which had proved to be difficult to work with in comparing LANGUAGES. Words, moreover, could be quite complex in STRUCTURE, and there was a need for a single concept to interrelate such notions as ROOT, PREFIX, COMPOUND, etc. The morpheme, accordingly, was seen primarily as the smallest functioning unit in the composition of words.

Morphemes are commonly classified into **free forms** (morphemes which can occur as separate words) and **bound forms** (morphemes which cannot so occur – mainly AFFIXES): thus *unselfish* consists of the three morphemes *un, self* and *ish*, of which *self* is a free form, *un-* and *-ish* bound forms. A word consisting of a single (free) morpheme is a **monomorphemic** word; its opposite is **polymorphemic**. A further distinction may be made between 'lexical' and 'grammatical morphemes'; the former are morphemes used for the construction of new words in a language, such as in COMPOUND words (e.g. *blackbird*), and affixes such as *-ship, -ize*; the latter are morphemes used to express grammatical relationships between a word and its CONTEXT, such as plurality or past TENSE (i.e. the INFLECTIONS on words). Grammatical morphemes which are separate words are called (*inter alia*) FUNCTION WORDS.

As with all EMIC notions, morphemes are abstract units, which are realized in speech by DISCRETE units, known as **morphs**. The relationship is generally referred to as one of EXPONENCE, or REALIZATION. Most morphemes are realized by single morphs, as in the example above. Some morphemes, however, are realized by more than one morph according to their position in a word or sentence, such alternative morphs being called **allomorphs** (cf. ALLO-) or **morphemic alternants/variants**. Thus the morpheme of plurality represented orthographically by the *-s* in e.g. *cots, digs* and *forces* has the allomorphs represented phonetically by {-s}, {-z} and {-iz} respectively (morphemes are usually symbolized using brace brackets). In this instance the allomorphs result from the phonetic influence of the sounds with which the singular forms of the words terminate, the process being referred to as one of 'phonological conditioning'.

The study of the arrangement of morphemes in linear sequence, taking such factors into account, is **morphotactics**.

The application of morphemic ideas to the analysis of languages was particularly extensive in the 1940s and 1950s in post-BLOOMFIELDIAN linguistics, when the approach came to be called **morphemics**, and several analytical difficulties emerged. The English plural morpheme illustrates some of these. When the plurality is simply added to the root, as in the above examples, the correspondence between morpheme and morph is straightforward. But in cases like *mouse* ~ *mice* and *sheep* ~ *sheep* it is more problematic. Several solutions have been proposed to handle such cases: in the case of *sheep*, for example, a **zero morph** of plurality may be recognized, to preserve the notion of 'sheep+ plural', this being symbolized as Ø. Other concepts which have proved to be of importance in 'morphemic analysis' include (1) the **empty morph**, set up to handle cases where a FORMAL feature in a word cannot be allocated to any morpheme, and (2) the **portmanteau morph**, set up to handle cases where a formal feature can be allocated to more than one morpheme. A **submorpheme** is a term sometimes used to refer to a part of a morpheme that has recurrent form and meaning, such as the *sl-* beginning of *slimy, slug*, etc.

morpheme-structure rules/conditions Terms used in GENERATIVE PHONOLOGY, to refer to the processes which have attempted to cope with REDUNDANCY in carrying out an analysis. When SEGMENTS CO-OCCUR, the presence of a FEATURE characterizing one segment may make it unnecessary to specify a certain feature in another segment: the CONSTRAINTS involved are handled by MORPHEME-structure (or 'LEXICAL-redundancy') rules. For example, given an English morpheme which has an AFFRICATE in INITIAL position, it is predictable that the following segment will be a VOWEL. It would then be possible to leave the features for vowels (e.g. [−consonantal], [+sonorant]) blank in the UNDERLYING FORM of the morpheme, the appropriate values being filled in automatically by the application of the relevant morpheme-structure rule at some subsequent point in the DERIVATION. Several problems with this view led to a subsequent proposal to handle these redundancies in terms of **morpheme-structure conditions**, which state more explicitly the processes constraining the correspondences between segments, without recourse to the blank-filling procedure.

morphology (morphological) The branch of GRAMMAR which studies the STRUCTURE or FORMS of WORDS, primarily through the use of the MORPHEME construct. It is traditionally distinguished from SYNTAX, which deals with the RULES governing the combination of words in SENTENCES. It is generally divided into two fields: the study of INFLECTIONS (**inflectional morphology**) and of WORD FORMATION (**lexical** or **derivational morphology**) – a distinction which is sometimes accorded theoretical status (**split morphology**). When emphasis is on the technique of analysing words into morphemes, particularly as practised by American STRUCTURALIST linguists in the 1940s and 1950s, the term **morphemics** is used. 'Morphemic analysis' in this sense is part of a SYNCHRONIC linguistic study; **morphological analysis** is the more general term, being applied to DIACHRONIC studies as well. Morphological analysis may take various forms. One approach is to make a DISTRIBUTIONAL study of the morphemes and morphemic variants occurring in words (the analysis of **morphotactic arrangements**), as in ITEM-AND-

ARRANGEMENT MODELS of description. Another approach sets up **morphological processes** or **operations**, which see the relationships between word forms as one of replacement (e.g. replace the /ei/ of *take* with the /ʊ/ of *took*), as in ITEM-AND-PROCESS models.

In early GENERATIVE linguistics, morphology and syntax are not seen as two separate LEVELS; the syntactic RULES of grammar apply to the structure of words, as they do to PHRASES and sentences, and morphological notions emerge only at the point where the output of the syntactic component has to be given a PHONOLOGICAL REPRESENTATION (via the MORPHOPHONOLOGICAL rules). **Natural morphology** is an approach which aims to describe and explain UNIVERSAL tendencies in word formation (such as the preference to derive NOUNS from VERBS, rather than the reverse). **Prosodic morphology** is a theory of how morphological and phonological determinants of linguistic form interact. In **affixal** (as opposed to **non-affixal**) **morphology**, the only permissible morphological operation is the combining of affixes and stems. Morphologically driven processes have become increasingly recognized within generative linguistics in recent years; for example, morphological features play a central role in the MINIMALIST PROGRAMME.

morphophoneme The basic unit recognized in a MORPHOPHONEMIC LEVEL of analysis. It is usually symbolized by the use of a capital letter within brace BRACKETS, e.g. {F}, {T}. One of the original examples used in order to justify establishing this entity was the ALTERNATION between /f/ and /v/ in some English plurals, such as *knife* ~ *knives*. There is no predictable alternation between /f/ and /v/ for English WORDS in general, but only in this specific GRAMMATICAL CONTEXT. This fact, it is argued, can be captured by setting up a morphophoneme {F}, as in {naɪF}: in a singular context this is realized as /f/, in a plural context as /v/. Each morphophonemic symbol thus represents the class of PHONEMES which occurs within a particular set of grammatical ENVIRONMENTS. In recent linguistic theory, the term SYSTEMATIC PHONEME is more widespread.

morphophonemics (morpho(pho)nology) A branch of LINGUISTICS referring to the analysis and classification of the PHONOLOGICAL factors which affect the appearance of MORPHEMES, or, correspondingly, the GRAMMATICAL factors which affect the appearance of PHONEMES. In the European tradition, **morphophonology** (or 'morphonology') is the preferred term; in the American tradition, it is **morphophonemics**. In some theories, morphophonemics is seen as a separate level of linguistic structure intermediate between grammar and phonology (cf. MORPHOPHONEME). In early versions of GENERATIVE grammar, **morphophonemic rules** were distinguished as a separate COMPONENT in the DERIVATION of SENTENCES, whereby a TERMINAL STRING of morphemes would be converted into their correct phonological form. In later generative theory, the term SYSTEMATIC PHONEMICS became standard.

morphosyntactic (morphosyntax) A term used in LINGUISTICS to refer to GRAMMATICAL categories or properties for whose definition criteria of MORPHOLOGY and SYNTAX both apply, as in describing the characteristics of WORDS. The distinctions under the heading of NUMBER in NOUNS, for example, constitute a morphosyntactic category: on the one hand, number CONTRASTS affect syntax (e.g. singular subject requiring a singular verb); on the other hand, they require morphological definition (e.g. add *-s* for plural). Traditional properties such as singular, PERFECT, INDICATIVE, PASSIVE, ACCUSATIVE, third PERSON are examples.

morphotactics see MORPHEME, TACTICS

mot (M) (as in French, *mot* 'word') A term sometimes used in METRICAL PHONOLOGY for a PROSODIC level assigned to LEXICAL category WORDS. For example, there would be two mots (prosodic words) in the phrase *the fat cat*:

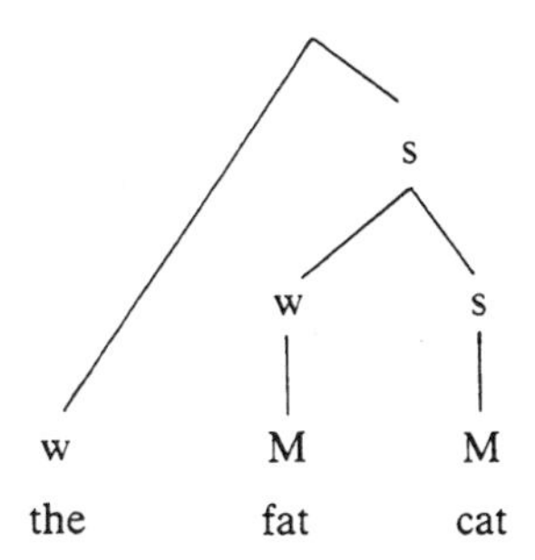

mother A term used in GENERATIVE GRAMMAR to refer to a relation between NODES in a PHRASE-MARKER. If one node X IMMEDIATELY DOMINATES another node Y, then X is the mother of Y, and Y is the DAUGHTER of X.

motherese A term commonly used in the study of child LANGUAGE ACQUISITION for the distinctive way in which mothers talk to their young children. Its features include simplified GRAMMAR, exaggerated INTONATION patterns, DIMINUTIVE forms of words (e.g. *doggie*), a repetitive style and a tendency to expand the child's reduced utterances. A correlative notion of **fatherese** has also been proposed; but both notions are often now subsumed under the broader concept of **caretaker speech** (also known as **caregiver speech**), which includes grandparents, nannies and other carers, as well as parents. The term BABY-TALK, formerly widely used for this phenomenon, is not now usual in PSYCHOLINGUISTICS.

mother-in-law languages see AVOIDANCE LANGUAGES

motor theory A term used in PHONETICS and PSYCHOLINGUISTICS to refer to a theory of SPEECH PERCEPTION which proposes that the brain of the listener constructs a MODEL of the ARTICULATORY ('motor') movements being produced by the speaker. It is not usually interpreted as someone having to 'talk in parallel' (i.e. subvocally) while listening – a view for which there is little support – but, rather, as an abstract mechanism, or model, which can help explain the indirect correspondences between the features of the ACOUSTIC signal and the SEGMENTS the listener actually perceives.

move alpha (move α) A term used in GOVERNMENT-BINDING THEORY to refer to a single, UNIVERSAL MOVEMENT RULE, which subsumes all specific movement rules; also called **alpha movement**. The rule permits the movement of any PHRASAL or LEXICAL CATEGORY from one part of a SENTENCE to another in such a way that the operation involves SUBSTITUTION or (Chomsky-) ADJUNCTION. The application of the TRANSFORMATION is restricted by the SUBJACENCY principle of BOUNDING (sub-)theory, and its output is subject to a variety of FILTERS, PRINCIPLES, etc. stated by other (sub-)theories of GB.

movement (1) (**move**) A term often used within the framework of TRANSFORMATIONAL GRAMMAR to refer to a basic kind of transformational operation. **Movement transformations** have the effect of moving CONSTITUENTS (usually one at a time) from one part of a PHRASE-MARKER to another (the 'landing site'), as in the formation of PASSIVE sentences. An alternative term is REORDERING or PERMUTATION. In some approaches this notion is broken down into the more basic operations of ADJUNCTION and DELETION. Two main types of **movement rules** have been used: *WH*-movement and NP-movement (as when such PASSIVE sentences as *The cup was put on the table* are said to DERIVE from — *was put the cup on the table* by NP-movement of *the cup*). Other such RULES have been proposed from time to time, such as DATIVE movement (to handle such alterations as *X gave Y to Z* and *X gave Z Y*) and *though* movement (to handle such sentences as *good writer though she is*...); but the need for these has been disputed. The possibility that all movement rules may be reflexes of a single, universal rule (referred to as MOVE ALPHA) has also now been proposed. In later formulations, the category which has been moved leaves behind an EMPTY NODE, or TRACE: this approach is known as the 'trace theory of movement rules'. A moved constituent and its CO-INDEXED trace form a **movement chain**. In the MINIMALIST PROGRAMME, **move** is an operation which moves elements about in the process of TREE construction. Movement is constrained in various ways. Only the shortest movements of an element are acceptable (**shortest move**) into the nearest relevant position (the **minimal link condition**). Movements should be delayed until absolutely necessary (PROCRASTINATE). And movements must satisfy the requirements of the moved element (GREED).
(2) See HOLD.

MP The abbreviation for MINIMALIST PROGRAMME, and also for MORPHOPHONEMIC, in the term 'MP-RULES' in natural generative PHONOLOGY.

mu (**μ**) see MORA

multidimensional scaling A statistical technique which has been applied in PSYCHOLINGUISTICS to quantify the MEANINGS of related LEXICAL ITEMS and define the SEMANTIC space within which these items work. INFORMANTS rate numerically a set of items (e.g. kinship terms, colours) in terms of their mutual similarity; the more similar the average ratings are, the closer these items are placed in the hypothetical space. In this inductive manner, it is hoped to establish classificatory criteria for lexical sets which might otherwise not emerge, and to develop more illuminating models of semantic STRUCTURE than are available using conventional analytic techniques.

multilateral A type of OPPOSITION recognized in PRAGUE SCHOOL PHONOLOGY, distinguished from BILATERAL. The opposition between English /t/ and /v/ is multilateral, because there are several possibilities of CONTRAST involving the same set of FEATURES, e.g. /d/ *v.* /f/. The opposition between /t/ and /d/, however, is bilateral, because these are the only units in the system which are ALVEOLAR/PLOSIVE, and they are differentiated by the single feature of VOICING.

multilingual(ism) A term used in SOCIOLINGUISTICS to refer, in the first instance, to a SPEECH community which makes use of two or more LANGUAGES, and then to the individual speakers who have multilingual ability. 'Multilingualism' (or 'plurilingualism') in this sense may subsume BILINGUALISM, but it is often contrasted with it (i.e. a community or individual in command of *more* than two languages). A further distinction is sometimes made between a multilingualism which is internal to a speech community (i.e. for routine domestic communicative purposes), and one which is external to it (i.e. an additional language being used to facilitate communication with other nations, as in the use of a LINGUA FRANCA). Sociolinguistic studies have emphasized both the frequency and complexity of the phenomenon: on the one hand, there are very few speech communities which are totally monolingual (because of the existence of linguistic minority groups within their boundaries); on the other hand, the multilingual abilities demonstrated are of several levels of proficiency, and raise different kinds of political, educational and social problems, depending on the numbers, social standing and national feeling of the groups concerned.

murmur see BREATHY

mutation A term used in LINGUISTICS, especially in HISTORICAL LINGUISTICS, to refer to the change in a sound's QUALITY owing to the influence of sounds in adjacent MORPHEMES or WORDS. For example, in the period when Old English was developing, the influence of an /i/ VOWEL in certain circumstances caused other vowels to 'mutate' in the direction of the CLOSE vowel, e.g. **foti* became *feet*. The term is also occasionally used in SYNCHRONIC CONTEXTS, as in the mutation of various INITIAL CONSONANTS in Welsh after certain words, e.g. *pen* 'head' → *fy mhen* 'my head'.

mutual intelligibility A criterion used in LINGUISTICS, referring to the ability of people to understand each other. If two VARIETIES of speech are mutually intelligible, they are strictly DIALECTS of the same LANGUAGE; if they are mutually unintelligible, they are different languages. The criterion seems simple, but there are many problem cases. Two varieties may be partially intelligible – for example, because they share some vocabulary. Also, political or cultural factors may intervene, causing two mutually intelligible varieties to be treated as different languages (e.g. Swedish and Danish) or two mutually unintelligible varieties to be treated as the same language (e.g. the so-called 'dialects' of Chinese).

N

N The usual abbreviation for NOUN.

narrative An application of the everyday use of this term, as part of the linguistic study of DISCOURSE, which aims to determine the principles governing the structure of narrative TEXTS. A narrative is seen as a recapitulation of past experience in which language is used to structure a sequence of (real or fictitious) events. The structural study of narrative is known as **narratology**. Structural elements are proposed, such as those which initiate a narrative (e.g. a summarizing abstract, a story orientation) or those which close it (a closing summary, a narrator's evaluation). There is a focus on such notions as theme, plot, character, role, and point of view, especially in studies of literary narrative.

narrow (1) A term used in the classification of types of PHONETIC TRANSCRIPTION. A 'narrow' transcription is more detailed than a 'broad' transcription.

(2) A term used in the description of types of VOWEL, referring to a vowel which is articulated with less PHARYNX width than another with the same TONGUE and lip configuration; it is opposed to WIDE.

narrowing In HISTORICAL LINGUISTICS, a term used in the classification of types of SEMANTIC change, referring to a restriction of meaning in a LEXICAL item; opposed to EXTENSION. For example, in Old English *mete* 'meat' referred to food in general, whereas today it refers to only one kind of food.

nasal(-ized, -ization, -ity) A term used in the PHONETIC classification of speech sounds on the basis of MANNER OF ARTICULATION: it refers to sounds produced while the soft PALATE is lowered to allow an audible escape of air through the nose. Both CONSONANTS and VOWELS may be articulated in this way. Nasal consonants occur when there is a complete CLOSURE in the mouth, and all the air thus escapes through the nose. Examples in English are the final consonants of *ram, ran, rang* [ram, ran, raŋ], where the closures are in BILABIAL, ALVEOLAR and VELAR positions respectively. Several other nasal sounds are possible, e.g. in PALATAL positions [ɲ], as in Spanish *mañana*. VOICELESS nasal sounds also occur, as when a nasal consonant follows [s] in English, e.g. *small, snooze*. In nasal (or **nasalized**) vowels, air escapes through nose and mouth simultaneously; the vowels are transcribed with [˜], above the symbol, e.g. [ã]. Nasal vowels are opposed to ORAL vowels in a language, as in French and Portuguese. English has no distinct nasal vowels, but **nasalization** is often heard on English vowels, when they display the articulatory influence of an adjacent nasal consonant, as in *mat* or *hand*. The vowel in a word like *man* may be articulated with the soft palate lowered throughout, because of this influence. Such cases, where the nasality comes from other sounds, would be referred to as 'nasalized' vowels; the term 'nasal vowel', on the other hand, suggests that the nasality is an essential identifying feature of the sound. A 'nasalized consonant', likewise, would refer to a consonant which, though normally oral in a language, was being articulated in a nasal manner because of some adjacent nasal sound. Stop consonants (and sometimes fricatives) may be articulated with a **pre-nasal** onset or **post-nasal** release, depending on the timing of the velic closure relative to the oral closure: Swahili, for example, has a series of **pre-nasalized** stops. The opposite term is **denasalized**, which would be applied only to sounds which normally were articulated with a nasal component (as when one speaks through a blocked nose). In certain clinical conditions, such as cleft palate, abnormal degrees of nasalization may be present: excessively nasal (or **hypernasal**) speech is here opposed to reduced nasality (or **hyponasal** speech).

Other nasal effects may be heard in a language. A PLOSIVE sound, for example, when followed by a nasal articulated in the same position, may be released through the nose instead of the mouth, and the resulting auditory effect is one of 'nasal plosion', as in *sudden* [sʌdn̩], which is rather more likely than [sʌdən]. 'Nasal twang' is not a term with a precise phonetic definition, as it refers to any degree of nasal effect in a speaker or ACCENT, seen in contrast with speech which is more oral in character.

The opposition between 'nasal' and 'oral' is given a special technical status in the DISTINCTIVE FEATURE theory of PHONOLOGY, where it works alongside other two-way CONTRASTS as part of the complete specification of a sound system. In CHOMSKY and Halle's theory, for example, it is classified as a CAVITY feature, and grouped along with LATERAL under the specific heading of SECONDARY APERTURES. See also -ISE/-IZE.

native-speaker A term used in LINGUISTICS to refer to someone for whom a particular LANGUAGE is a 'native language' (also called 'first language', 'mother-tongue'). The implication is that this language, having been acquired naturally during childhood, is the one about which a speaker will have the most reliable INTUITIONS, and whose judgements about the way the language is used can therefore be trusted. In investigating a language, accordingly, one is wise to try to obtain information from 'native-speaking' informants, rather than from those who may have learned it as a SECOND or foreign language (even if they are highly proficient). Many people do, however, develop a 'native-like' command of a foreign language, and in BILINGUALISM one has the case of someone who has a native command of two languages. The term has become a sensitive one in those parts of the world where *native* has developed demeaning connotations.

natural gender see GENDER

natural generative phonology see PHONOLOGY

natural kind terms In the SEMANTIC analysis of NOUNS, a type of general term for entities which have an identity in nature (as opposed to artefactual, abstract, and other general terms). They include SORTAL terms (e.g. *lion*), where a notion of individuation is involved, and mass terms (e.g. *water*), where there is no such notion. The distinction can be seen, for example, by using a divisibility criterion: if water is divided into parts, each part may still be labelled water, without any change in meaning; whereas the parts of a lion are not the lion.

natural language processing (NLP) In COMPUTATIONAL LINGUISTICS, the computational processing of TEXTUAL materials in natural human languages. The aim is to devise techniques which will automatically analyse large quantities of spoken (transcribed) or written text in ways which are broadly parallel to what happens when humans carry out this task. The field emerged out of machine translation in the 1950s, and came to be much influenced by research in artificial intelligence. Recent work has concentrated on devising 'intelligent programs' (or 'expert systems') which will simulate aspects of human behaviour, such as the way people use their knowledge of the world and their ability to draw inferences in order to make interpretations and reach conclusions. A more specifically linguistic contribution involves detailed SYNTACTIC, SEMANTIC, and DISCOURSE analysis, often on a much larger scale than hitherto, and using the large amounts of lexical data currently available in computer CORPORA.

natural morphology see MORPHOLOGY

naturalness/natural class A notion introduced into (especially GENERATIVE) LINGUISTIC theory to refer to the PHONETIC plausibility of an analysis, which is seen as an important criterion in evaluating analyses alongside such other criteria as SIMPLICITY. An analysis, it is argued, must make phonetic sense, if it is to have any explanatory role in relation to the speaker's behaviour, e.g. such factors as relative ease of ARTICULATION must be taken into account. One of the first steps in defining naturalness more formally is to recognize the notion of 'natural class'. A set of SEGMENTS is said to constitute a natural class if fewer phonetic FEATURES are needed to specify the set as a whole than to specify any one member of the set. The set of VOICED PLOSIVE segments in English are a natural class, on this basis: /b/, /d/ and /g/ all share the features of VOICING, INSTANTANEOUS RELEASE and INTERRUPTED; but, to specify any one of these, further features would be required (e.g. /d/ would be CORONAL, in addition).

The term in this sense applies to any set of speech segments which can be shown to have a highest common factor in this way; but as it stands the criterion needs to be supplemented by others, as it is too general (e.g. it would allow for all sounds in a language to be considered a natural class, on the grounds that they are all PULMONIC EGRESSIVE). Several other relevant criteria have been suggested, e.g. that the set of sounds all turn up in the same PHONOLOGICAL RULES, undergoing similar processes together. Also, there are several difficulties in working with the notion in terms of features, e.g. the more natural solution is not always the simpler. The notion of naturalness has thus been developed to take into account the relative naturalness of (1) segments (mainly through the use of the MARKING convention), (2) sound SYSTEMS (by computing the relative complexity of its units, this being defined in terms of marking values) and (3) phonological rules (based on the tendency for some phonological processes to be more frequent and phonetically more expected than others, e.g. /i/

becoming /u/ rather than /ɯ/, or certain types of ASSIMILATION or SYLLABLE structures being preferred). These developments are continuing.

natural phonology see PHONOLOGY

negation (negative) A process or construction in GRAMMATICAL and SEMANTIC analysis which typically expresses the contradiction of some or all of a sentence's meaning. In English grammar, it is expressed by the presence of the 'negative PARTICLE' *not* or *n't* (the CONTRACTED negative); in LEXIS, there are several possible means, e.g. PREFIXES such as *un-*, *non-*, or words such as *deny.* Some LANGUAGES use more than one particle in a single CLAUSE to express negation (as in French *ne . . . pas*). The use of more than one negative form in the same clause (as in 'double negatives') is a characteristic of some English DIALECTS, e.g. *I'm not unhappy* (which is a STYLISTICALLY MARKED mode of assertion) and *I've not done nothing* (which is not acceptable in STANDARD English).

In recent LINGUISTICS, a topic of particular interest has been the range of sentence STRUCTURE affected by the position of a negative particle, e.g. *I think John isn't coming v. I don't think John is coming*: such variations in the SCOPE of negation affect the logical structure as well as the semantic analysis of the sentence. The opposite 'pole' to negative is POSITIVE (or AFFIRMATIVE), and the system of contrasts made by a language in this area is often referred to as POLARITY. **Negative polarity** items are those words or phrases which can appear only in a negative environment in a sentence, e.g. *any* in *I haven't got any books* (*cf.* *I've got any books*).

negative transfer see INTERFERENCE

neo-Firthian see FIRTHIAN

neogrammarian(s) A follower of, or characteristic of the principles of, a nineteenth-century school of thought in COMPARATIVE PHILOLOGY, initiated by the German scholars K. Brugmann (1849–1919) and S. A. Leskien (1840–1916). Their main tenet was that sound laws admitted no exceptions (the **neogrammarian hypothesis**). Their nickname in German *Junggrammatiker* ('young grammarians') arose from the attitude of older scholars who, while not necessarily rejecting the principle, objected to the forceful way in which it was promulgated.

neologism see NONCE

nesting (nested) A term used in LINGUISTICS to refer to the INSERTION of one or more linguistic UNITS (usually PHRASES or CLAUSES) within the STRUCTURE of an ENDOCENTRIC phrase. A phrase such as *the table in the corner with the candlesticks near the window* shows several MODIFYING phrases RECURSIVELY 'nested' (cf. EMBEDDED).

network grammar A term used for a class of GRAMMARS which have developed out of the concerns of COMPUTATIONAL LINGUISTICS and artificial intelligence, to show how LANGUAGE understanding can be simulated. A **network** is a state-and-path REPRESENTATION of a SENTENCE – 'states' being the points at which a new condition can be introduced, in putting together a CONSTRUCTION, and 'paths' being the transitions between states, which are dependent on a condition being met. Two main types of network grammar have been proposed: PROCEDURAL GRAMMARS and augmented TRANSITION NETWORK GRAMMARS. These grammars extract and store information from a TEXT, and use the results to decide what grammatical and SEMANTIC structures lie behind it. The grammatical breakdown of a text is known as a PARSE, which contains SYNTACTIC, semantic and REFERENTIAL information. In this approach, the analysis is presented pictorially (using rectangles, circles and lines) as well as in words and formulae.

neural network see CONNECTIONISM

neurolinguistics A branch of LINGUISTICS, sometimes called **neurological linguistics**, which studies the neurological basis of LANGUAGE development and use, and attempts to construct a MODEL of the brain's control over the processes of speaking, listening, reading, writing, and signing. The main approach has been to postulate the stages of a 'neural programme', which would explain the observed phenomena of temporal ARTICULATORY co-ordination, SEQUENCING, and other features of SPEECH PRODUCTION. Central to this approach has been the research findings from two main areas: the study of CLINICAL LINGUISTIC conditions (such as aphasia, dysarthria, stuttering), in an attempt to deduce the nature of the underlying system from the analysis of its various stages of breakdown; and the study of speech production in PARAMETRIC articulatory phonetic terms – especially of the 'normal' ERRORS which are introduced into speech (e.g. TONGUE-SLIPS, HESITATIONS).

neutral (1) A term used in the classification of lip position in PHONETICS, referring to the visual appearance of the lips when they are held in a relaxed position, with no lip-ROUNDING, and a medium lowering of the jaw, as in the vowels of *pet* or *bird*. It is contrasted with SPREAD, OPEN and rounded lip positions.

(2) A term used in the classification of VOWEL sounds, to refer to a LAX vowel made in the centre of the vowel ARTICULATION area, with the TONGUE neutral with respect to FRONT, BACK, HIGH or LOW positions. The most widely encountered vowel of this quality is heard in the first vowel of *asleep, balloon*, or the last vowel in *mother, cover*. It is usually referred to as SCHWA [ə]. Several terms for this quality have been proposed, including 'central', 'medium' and 'murmured' vowel.

neutralization (neutraliz-e, -able) A term used in PHONOLOGY to describe what happens when the distinction between two PHONEMES is lost in a particular ENVIRONMENT. For example, in English, the contrast between ASPIRATED (voiceless) and unaspirated (VOICED) PLOSIVES is normally crucial, e.g. *tip v. dip*, but this contrast is lost, or 'neutralized', when the plosive is preceded by /s/, as in *stop, skin, speech*, and as a result, there are no pairs of words in the language of the type /skɪn/ *v.* /*sgɪn/. From a PHONETIC point of view, the explanation lies in the phonetic change which happens to /k/ in this position: the /k/ lacks aspiration and comes to be physically indistinguishable from /g/. In the original PRAGUE SCHOOL formulation of this notion, 'neutralizable' was seen as a type of OPPOSITION, and contrasted with CONSTANT.

new A term used by some LINGUISTS in a two-part analysis of utterances on the basis of INFORMATION structure; 'new' information is opposed to GIVEN. (The contrast between FOCUS and PRESUPPOSITION makes an analogous distinction.) 'New', as its name suggests, refers to information which is additional to that already supplied by the previous CONTEXT of speaking; 'given', by contrast, refers to the information already available. In the clearest cases, new information is identified by INTONATIONal emphasis within the TONE UNIT, the NUCLEAR tone (or primary STRESS) signalling its focus, e.g. *I've got thrèe books in my bag* v. *I've got three books in my bàg*, and so on. Several problems arise in determining the scope of the new information, with reference to the previous CONTEXT, however, which have been the subject of much discussion, e.g. A: *What can you see?* B: *I can see* ˈ*three mèn*, where the *three* is plainly part of the new information, but does not carry the nuclear tone.

nexus (plural **nexi**) (1) In the approach to GRAMMAR of Otto Jespersen (1860–1943), a term which describes the kind of relationship which exists between SUBJECT and PREDICATE (*the dog barks*); it is distinguished from a **junction**, which is a relationship between a primary word and an ADJUNCT (e.g. *the barking dog*). Several other notions were derived from this basic terminology, e.g. 'nexus-word', 'nexus-question'.

(2) A term used in ROLE AND REFERENCE GRAMMAR to describe that part of the grammar which deals with the SYNTACTIC relationships obtaining between sub-CLAUSAL units. It is seen in association with a theory of JUNCTURE.

NGP The abbreviation for 'natural generative PHONOLOGY'.

NLP The abbreviation for NATURAL LANGUAGE PROCESSING.

no-crossing constraint A CONSTRAINT used in NON-LINEAR PHONOLOGY which states that ASSOCIATION lines linking two elements on one TIER with two elements on another tier may not cross. In the figure, (a) is possible; (b) is not.

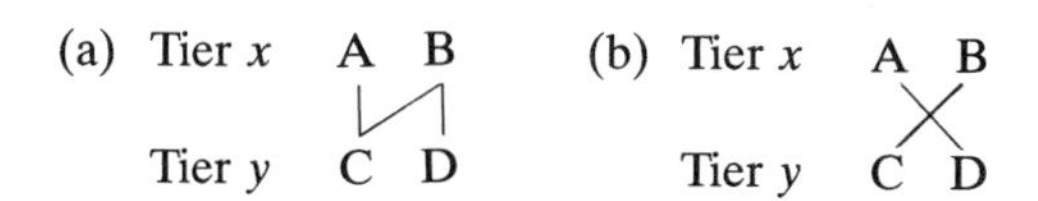

node A term used in GENERATIVE GRAMMAR to refer to any point in a TREE from which one or more BRANCHES emanate. A 'family' metaphor is often used in the discussion of nodes. A node which immediately DOMINATES another is called a 'mother' node; the dominated node is its 'daughter'; if two nodes are directly dominated by the same node, they are 'sister' nodes. A node which is separated from its mother in a derivation is said to have been 'orphaned'. The topmost node of the tree diagram is the 'root'. Nodes which do not dominate other CATEGORIES (i.e. they are at the bottom of the tree) are **terminal nodes**; nodes which do dominate other categories are **non-terminal nodes**. The notion has achieved special status in various models of FEATURE geometry. See also BOUNDING THEORY, CONNECTIONISM, EMPTY (1), GOVERN (2).

noise In ACOUSTIC PHONETICS, a complex sound wave with irregular (aperiodic) vibrations (cf. PERIOD). Noise is an important feature of speech, being part of the acoustic definition of several consonant sounds and voice qualities, such as FRICATIVES and BREATHY voice.

NOM An abbreviation for NOMINATIVE case.

nominal(ization) A term used in some GRAMMATICAL descriptions as a substitute for NOUN (e.g. 'nominal group' = 'noun phrase'). In a more restricted sense, it refers to WORDS which have some of the attributes of nouns but not all, e.g. ***the poor*** *are many*, where the HEAD word of this PHRASE does not pluralize (**the poors*). **Nominalization** refers to the process of forming a noun from some other WORD-CLASS (e.g. *red+ness*) or (in classical TRANSFORMATIONAL grammar especially) the DERIVATION of a noun phrase from an underlying CLAUSE (e.g. *Her answering of the letter . . .* from *She answered the letter*). The term is also used in the classification of RELATIVE clauses (e.g. *What concerns me is her attitude*). Some linguistic theories use the term in a more general sense, as in COGNITIVE GRAMMAR, where 'nominals' ('things', chiefly noun phrases) are distinguished from relational expressions.

nominative (NOM) In languages which express GRAMMATICAL relationships by means of INFLECTIONS, this term refers to the FORM taken by a NOUN PHRASE (often a single noun or PRONOUN) when it is the SUBJECT of a VERB. It is usually the first form to be listed in a grammatical PARADIGM, or in a dictionary, and is often the UNMARKED form (cf. OBLIQUE), e.g. in Latin, *homo* ('man') is nominative singular (cf. *hominem, hominis*, etc.) The term is also used in recent GENERATIVE grammar, to refer to the CASE assigned to the subject NP in a FINITE CLAUSE. In the phrase **nominative island condition**, it refers to a type of CONSTRAINT on the freedom of MOVEMENT of items occurring inside a clause containing a nominative-marked subject. In GOVERNMENT-BINDING THEORY, NOM CASE is assigned to the NP GOVERNED by I with AGR, i.e. to the subject in a finite clause.

non-agentive see PASSIVE

non-anterior see ANTERIOR

non-areal see AREA

non-back (sounds) see BACK

non-branching see BRANCH

non-causative see CAUSATIVE

nonce A LINGUISTIC FORM which a speaker consciously invents or accidentally uses on a single occasion is known as a **nonce word** or a **nonce formation** (which may involve UNITS larger than the WORD). Many factors account for their use, e.g. a speaker cannot remember a particular word, so coins an alternative approximation (as in *linguistified*, heard recently from a student who felt he was getting nowhere with linguistics), or is constrained by circumstances to produce a new form (as in newspaper headlines). Nonce formations have occasionally come to be adopted by the community – in which case they cease by definition to be 'nonce' (forms used 'for the (n)once'), and become **neologisms**.

non-collective see COLLECTIVE

non-configurational languages Languages with fairly free WORD ORDER and seemingly 'FLAT' CONSTITUENT structure, such as Japanese and the Dravidian and Australian languages; contrasted with CONFIGURATIONAL LANGUAGES. Both types have received a great deal of attention in GOVERNMENT-BINDING THEORY, where non-configurational languages are also known as **W* (w-star) languages**.

non-consonantal see CONSONANT

non-continuant see CONTINUANT

non-continuous see CONTINUOUS

non-conventional implicature see IMPLICATURE

non-core rule see CORE (1)

non-coronal see CORONAL

non-count see COUNT

non-covered see COVERED

non-defining see RELATIVE

non-discrete see DISCRETE

non-discrete grammar The name given to a LINGUISTIC MODEL suggested by the American linguist John Robert Ross (b. 1938) in the early 1970s (as an alternative to the EXTENDED STANDARD THEORY of TRANSFORMATIONAL GRAMMAR), which analyses LANGUAGE as a series of DISCRETE contrasts (e.g. grammatical *v.* ungrammatical, applicability *v.* non-applicability of RULES). In non-discrete grammar, however, such notions as grammaticality, rule applicability, CLASS membership, etc., are seen as matters of degree. Accounting for the existence of marginally grammatical sentences, SEMI-SENTENCES, and so on, is conceived as a major aim of linguistic theory, and INDETERMINACY of this kind is seen as an essential feature of COMPETENCE. The idiosyncratic terminology which this model uses (e.g. SQUISH, 'nouniness', 'clausematiness', etc.) has endeared it to some, and been a source of irritation to others. Its emphasis on the analysis of problematic DATA has been welcomed, but so far there has been relatively little development of the approach in linguistics as a whole, and its theoretical significance is controversial.

non-distributed see DISTRIBUTED

non-echo see ECHO

non-equivalent see EQUIVALENT

non-factive see FACTIVE

non-favourite see FAVOURITE

non-finite see FINITE

non-headed see HEAD

non-high see HIGH

non-lateral see LATERAL

non-linear phonology In PHONOLOGY, any model which avoids a linear REPRESENTATION of the phonological structure of a word. 'Linear', in this context, refers to a representation of structure as a series of SEGMENTS occurring in a strict horizontal sequence, each segment being analysed (vertically) as an unordered column of FEATURES – [s], for example, being [−syllabic], [−voice], [−nasal], [+coronal], etc. A recognized weakness of these two-dimensional matrices is their inability to handle features which extend over DOMAINS greater than an individual segment (e.g. certain properties of TONES, vowel HARMONY); another is their inability to represent structure relationships (functional or 'natural' classes) within columns of features. The result has been the development of non-linear models, such as Firth's PROSODIC PHONOLOGY, and (since the 1970s) such models as METRICAL PHONOLOGY, AUTOSEGMENTAL PHONOLOGY and DEPENDENCY PHONOLOGY. In these approaches, features which extend over domains greater than a single segment are taken out of feature matrices and represented on separate levels (TIERS) of their own. There is now a large class of non-linear models in contemporary phonology.

non-low see LOW

non-native varieties A term used in SOCIOLINGUISTICS and foreign language teaching, to refer to VARIETIES of a LANGUAGE which have emerged in speech communities where most of the speakers do not have the language as a mother tongue. The notion has been chiefly used in the context of English as a world language, and specifically in relation to the kind of English which has grown up in India, Singapore, and many of the countries of Africa.

non-perfective see PERFECT

non-primitive see PRIMITIVE

non-productive see PRODUCTIVE

non-progressive see PROGRESSIVE (1)

non-restrictive see RESTRICTIVE

non-rhotic see RHOTIC

non-rounded see ROUNDING

nonsense In several contexts in LINGUISTICS and PHONETICS, this term is used in a rather more restricted sense than in everyday use. In phonetics, it is applied to the invented phonetic SEQUENCES ('nonsense words') used as part of EAR-TRAINING exercises. In linguistics it refers, first, to SENTENCES which may be GENERATED by a GRAMMAR (i.e. they are grammatical), but which are not SEMANTICALLY ACCEPTABLE, e.g. **The stone is sleeping, *He drank the car in a table.* Such meaningless sentences are often called 'anomalous'. The term is also used in grammar, as part of a technique for identifying PRODUCTIVE grammatical UNITS. Often used here is an extract from Lewis Carroll's *Jabberwocky*, where phrases such as *all mimsy were the borogoves* display WORD-CLASS identities clearly, e.g. *mimsy* (adjective) and *borogoves* (nouns). The technique is also used in language ACQUISITION, e.g. in language production tasks, to see if the child has acquired a grammatical unit (as in the WUGS experiment).

non-segmental see SUPRASEGMENTAL

non-sibilant see SIBILANT

non-sonorant see SONORANT

non-standard see STANDARD

non-strident see STRIDENT

non-tense see TENSION

non-terminal see NODE, TERMINAL

non-verbal communication see COMMUNICATION

non-vocalic see VOCALIC

non-voiced see VOICE

non-volition see VOLITION

no-ordering condition see ORDER (1)

norm(ative) The general sense of this term is used in LINGUISTICS to refer to a standard practice in speech or writing. The 'norm' in question may apply to groups of varying size within a SPEECH community, or to the community as a whole. For example, several kinds of scientific English make use of impersonal CONSTRUCTIONS much more frequently than is the case in conversational English, which may be seen as the norm for purposes of STYLISTIC comparison. Often, the norms of different groups conflict, and **normative rules** may be imposed by one group on another (e.g. stating the 'correct' use of *whom, shall* or *will*; insisting on PREPOSITIONS at the end of SENTENCES). A collection of such rules is known as a **normative grammar**: such GRAMMARS were particularly current in the eighteenth and nineteenth centuries, and this tradition still exercises considerable influence. In contrast with this PRESCRIPTIVE concern to maintain an imagined set of linguistic standards, linguistics emphasizes the description of actual USAGE in the community, and SOCIOLINGUISTICS emphasizes the need to take into account the relative APPROPRIATENESS of different VARIETIES of language in different situations.

notation(al) A term used in LINGUISTICS and PHONETICS to refer to any system of GRAPHIC representation of speech (as in a 'PHONEMIC notation', where the term TRANSCRIPTION is widely used). Specifically, it refers to the set of symbols which represent a mode of linguistic analysis, as in the 'PHRASE STRUCTURE notation' in GENERATIVE GRAMMAR. An analytic convention, in this sense, which is introduced into an analysis to facilitate the formulation of a statement, such as a RULE, is often called a 'notational device', e.g. the use of ( ) to indicate OPTIONALITY in generative syntax. See also ALPHA NOTATION, BRACKETING.

notional A characteristic of much TRADITIONAL grammatical analysis, which assumed that there existed EXTRALINGUISTIC categories in terms of which the UNITS of GRAMMAR could be defined. Well-known notional definitions are of the NOUN as the name of a 'person, place or thing', of the VERB as a 'doing word', of a SENTENCE as a 'complete thought', and so on. A grammar which makes regular use of such definitions is a **notional grammar**. LINGUISTICS is critical of the notional approach in so far as the 'notions' involved are incapable of systematic and consistent exposition, and replaces it with an emphasis on FORMAL criteria.

noun (N) A term used in the GRAMMATICAL classification of WORDS, traditionally defined as the 'name of a person, place or thing', but the vagueness associated with the notions of 'name' and 'thing' (e.g. is *beauty* a thing?) has led LINGUISTIC descriptions to analyse this class in terms of the FORMAL and FUNCTIONAL criteria of SYNTAX and MORPHOLOGY. In linguistic terms, then, nouns are ITEMS which display certain types of INFLECTION (e.g. of CASE or NUMBER), have a specific DISTRIBUTION (e.g. they may follow PREPOSITIONS but not, say, MODALS), and perform a specific syntactic function (e.g. as SUBJECT or OBJECT of a sentence). Nouns are generally subclassified into COMMON and PROPER types, and analysed in terms of NUMBER, GENDER, CASE and COUNTABILITY.

The CONSTRUCTIONS into which nouns most commonly enter, and of which they are the HEAD word, are generally called **noun phrases** (NP) or 'nominal groups'. The structure of a noun phrase consists minimally of the noun (or noun substitute, such as a PRONOUN); the constructions preceding and following the noun are often described under the headings of PREMODIFICATION and POST-modification respectively. There are many derived notions, including COMPLEX NPs, HEAVY NPs and NP-MOVEMENT. **Noun incorporation** is found in some languages (such as Iroquoian languages), where a generic noun (e.g. 'vehicle') is syntactically included within a verb, thereby cross-classifying a specific noun (e.g. 'car') that is governed by the verb. See also COLLECTIVE, INCORPORATION, TRACE, WH-.

NP The usual abbreviation for NOUN PHRASE.

NP-movement One of the two major MOVEMENT PROCESSES assumed in EXTENDED STANDARD THEORY and early GOVERNMENT-BINDING THEORY, the other being *WH*-movement. NP-movement moves a NOUN PHRASE from one ARGUMENT position to another. It is involved in the formation of PASSIVE and (subject) RAISING sentences. What kinds of NP-movement are possible is largely determined by THETA (sub-)THEORY and BINDING (sub-)THEORY, while CASE (sub-)THEORY makes NP-movement obligatory in certain circumstances.

nucleus (nuclear) (1) A term used by some INTONATION analysts, particularly those working within the British tradition, to refer to the SYLLABLE in a TONE UNIT which carries maximal PROMINENCE, usually due to a major PITCH change. The **nuclear syllable** is also referred to as the TONIC syllable. In GENERATIVE PHONOLOGY, the analogous notion is **nuclear stress**, with the relevant STRESS-ASSIGNMENT RULE referred to as the **nuclear-stress rule**. In the normal, unemphatic version of the sentence *The lady saw the **tramp***, the last word is nuclear, and will carry one of the possible nuclear tones in English. The **nuclear tone** is the most prominent pitch movement in a tone unit. In English, analyses of nuclear tones vary, but most recognize such contrasts as FALLING (transcribed with ` above or before the SYLLABLE in question), RISING ´, rising-falling ˆ, falling-rising ˇ and level ¯. Others are possible, including distinctions within these types, such as 'high' *v.* 'low' fall.

(2) In GRAMMAR and SEMANTICS, the term is sometimes used to refer to the essential SUBJECT–PREDICATE or NP–VP STRUCTURE of a simple SENTENCE. **Nuclear predications** play a central role in FUNCTIONAL GRAMMAR.

null An application in GENERATIVE GRAMMAR of the mathematical use of this term, with the general meaning of EMPTY or ZERO, as in 'null subject' (a phonologically empty constituent, PRO) or 'null element'. In some recent models of PHONOLOGY, a 'null SEGMENT' is one carrying a full SURFACE specification, but behaving as if it lacks (some or all) FEATURE values. An example is the EPENTHETIC VOWEL when this is analysed not as an UNDERLYING segment, but as a vowel inserted late in the DERIVATION, and attached to an empty PLACE-holder.

number A GRAMMATICAL CATEGORY used for the analysis of WORD-CLASSES displaying such CONTRASTS as **singular, plural, dual** (two), **trial** (three), **paucal** (few), etc., as in English *boy v. boys, he walks v. they walk.* The contrasts generally correspond to the number of real-world entities referred to, but LINGUISTIC discussion has drawn attention to the problems involved in proposing any such straightforward one-to-one correlation. A NOUN, for example, may 'look' singular, but refer to a multiplicity of entities (e.g. *the committee are agreed*, cf. COLLECTIVE), and nouns which 'look' plural may refer to a single entity (e.g. *billiards*). There are in addition several analytical difficulties in relating the notion of number to that of COUNTABILITY (to explain the absence of such forms as **a butter*).

numeration In the MINIMALIST PROGRAMME, the set of items taken from the LEXICON for the purpose of building a STRUCTURAL DESCRIPTION. The COMPUTATIONAL SYSTEM selects elements from the numeration and combines them into structures.

object(ive) A term used in the analysis of GRAMMATICAL FUNCTIONS to refer to a major CONSTITUENT of SENTENCE or CLAUSE structure, traditionally associated with the 'receiver' or 'goal' of an action, as in *The cat bit* ***the dog***. Traditional analysis distinguishes a **direct** versus an **indirect object**, to allow for sentences such as *The teacher gave a letter to the girl/The teacher gave the girl a letter*, which is marked in English by a contrast using PREPOSITIONS and WORD ORDER, and in INFLECTING languages by different CASES (typically, the object case being ACCUSATIVE, the indirect object case being DATIVE). In GENERATIVE GRAMMAR, the direct object is called simply 'object', and contrasted with indirect object. A further distinction is that between 'objective GENITIVE' (i.e the genitive functions as object, as in *the writing of the questions* = 'X wrote the questions'), and 'subjective genitive' (i.e. the genitive functions as subject, as in *the shouting of the people* = 'people shout'). Much discussion in LINGUISTICS has focused on clarifying the notion of 'receiving' an action, in relation to the other ELEMENTS of clause structure (SUBJECT, COMPLEMENT, etc.), distinguishing various kinds of VERB–object relationship, both in terms of SURFACE and UNDERLYING structure. Examples of problem sentences are *John is easy to please* (where *John* is the underlying object of *please*) and *The plants are selling well* (where in reality it is the plants which are the 'logical receivers' of the action).

In the study of inflected languages, **objective** may be used as an alternative to ACCUSATIVE; e.g. in English the contrast between subject and object forms of PRONOUNS (e.g. *she* ~ *her*) is sometimes referred to as a distinction between SUBJECTIVE and objective case. Some linguists talk about the 'object of a preposition' to refer to the NOUN PHRASE in *around the corner*. The term 'objective' has a special status in CASE GRAMMAR, where it refers to the semantically most neutral case, i.e. a noun whose role in the action is identified by the SEMANTIC interpretation of the verb itself. In GOVERNMENT-BINDING THEORY, objective Case is assigned to any noun phrase governed by a TRANSITIVE verb. See also APPLICATIVE, RAISING.

object language see METALANGUAGE

obligatory One of the two types of TRANSFORMATIONAL RULE postulated by Noam CHOMSKY in his book *Syntactic Structures* (1957), the other being OPTIONAL. An **obligatory transformation** is one which *must* apply at a given stage in a DERIVATION, when its STRUCTURAL DESCRIPTION is met, if a WELL-FORMED SENTENCE is to result, e.g. the rule which attaches AFFIXES to their BASE forms. In later versions of transformational grammar, the range of this notion changes as SURFACE STRUCTURES come to be derived from DEEP STRUCTURES by obligatory transformations, and the notion of optional selection comes to be replaced by choices made between the rules of the base COMPONENT.

obligatory contour principle (OCP) In some models of GENERATIVE PHONOLOGY, a principle which disallows adjacent identical elements in a REPRESENTATION. It was originally proposed for TONE languages, where it excluded sequences of identical adjacent tones (e.g. a sequence of High–High–Low would simplify to High–Low). The principle was later extended to SEGMENTAL phonology, especially in NON-LINEAR models, where it disallows any two identical FEATURES or NODES which are adjacent on a given TIER. Violations of this principle are handled through various processes, such as DISSIMILATION or the insertion of an EPENTHETIC vowel (as in the vowel which separates a sequence of two CORONAL SIBILANTS in such English plural forms as *buses*).

oblique In languages which express GRAMMATICAL relationships by means of INFLECTIONS, this term refers to the FORM taken by a NOUN PHRASE (often a single NOUN or PRONOUN) when it refers collectively to all the CASE forms of a word except that of the UNMARKED case, or NOMINATIVE.

observational adequacy see ADEQUACY

obsolescence (1) In HISTORICAL LINGUISTICS, a term used to describe the gradual loss of a LEXICAL item because changes in the language or in the external world eliminate the opportunity or motivation for its use. Examples in English would be the terms referring to vehicles from a previous era, such as *landau* or *hansom*. These words have not gone completely out of use, as they will be heard from time to time at vintage rallies and in other special contexts, but most people would not use them. When a word does go totally out of general use, it is said to be **obsolete**.

(2) In SOCIOLINGUISTICS, a term used to describe the gradual loss of a LANGUAGE, which takes place when its transmission between generations ceases, and the number of its native speakers diminishes.

obsolete see OBSOLESCENCE

obstruent A term used in the PHONETIC classification of speech sounds to refer to sounds involving a CONSTRICTION which impedes the flow of air through nose or mouth, as in PLOSIVES, FRICATIVES and AFFRICATES. In the DISTINCTIVE FEATURE approach of CHOMSKY and Halle, the term is used in the same sense, but its status is that of PHONOLOGICAL opposition to SONORANT.

obviative A term used in LINGUISTICS to refer to a fourth-PERSON FORM used in some languages (e.g. some North American Indian languages). This form (of a PRONOUN, VERB, etc.) usually contrasts with the third person, in that it is used to refer to an entity distinct from that already referred to by the third-person form – the general sense of 'someone/something else'.

occlusion (occlusive) A term used in PHONETICS referring to the duration of the

CLOSURE which is made while a PLOSIVE CONSONANT is being articulated. Plosives are sometimes referred to as 'occlusives'.

OCP The abbreviation for OBLIGATORY CONTOUR PRINCIPLE.

oesophageal A term used in PHONETICS for sounds or VOICE initiated at or below the oesophagus; also spelled **esophageal**. An oesophageal technique of voice PRODUCTION is often taught to patients following laryngectomy.

off-/on-glide Terms used in PHONETICS to refer to the AUDITORY effect of ARTICULATORY movement at points of TRANSITION between sounds. An **off-glide** is a movement which occurs as the VOCAL ORGANS leave the position taken up by one speech sound and travel towards the position required for the next sound (or towards a position of rest). An **on-glide** is the correlative movement which occurs as the vocal organs approach their TARGET position for the articulation of a sound either from a previous sound, or from the position of rest.

offset see ONSET

onomasiology A term sometimes used in SEMANTICS to refer to the study of sets of associated concepts in relation to the LINGUISTIC FORMS which designate them, e.g. the various ways of organizing LEXICAL ITEMS conceptually in thesauri.

onomastics A branch of SEMANTICS which studies the ETYMOLOGY of institutionalized ('proper') names, such as the names of people ('anthroponymy' or 'anthroponomastics') and places ('toponymy' or 'toponomastics'). In a looser usage, 'onomastics' is used for personal names and 'toponymy' for place names.

onset (1) A term used in PHONETICS and PHONOLOGY to refer to the initial functional element in a linguistic UNIT. The notion has been especially used in relation to the description of SYLLABLE structure, but it is also sometimes found in other contexts, such as in relation to INTONATION or RHYTHM units. A distinction is sometimes drawn between 'simple' syllabic onsets (containing only one segment) and 'complex' onsets (containing more than one segment). The **maximal onset principle** (or 'CV rule') states that a . . .VCV. . . string is universally syllabified as . . .V.CV. . . . In MORAIC phonology, onsets are thought not to contribute to syllable weight (unlike RHYMES – the notion of 'onset/rhyme assymetry').

(2) In PHONETICS, a term used in the ARTICULATORY description of SEGMENTS, referring to a phase (the **onset phase**) at the beginning of a segment during which the VOCAL ORGANS are approaching the maximal degree of CONSTRICTION (the 'medial phase'). Onset phase specifically contrasts with **offset phase**, which shows the movement of the vocal organs towards the medial phase of the next segment.

ontogeny (ontogene-tic, -sis) The application of this general term in LINGUISTICS refers to the chronological ACQUISITION, development and decay of LANGUAGE in the individual, as opposed to in the SPEECH COMMUNITY as a whole (PHYLOGENY). It is particularly encountered in child language studies.

opaque (opacity) (1) A term used in GENERATIVE PHONOLOGY to refer to the extent to which the applications of a given RULE to a given FORM cannot be seen in the PHONETIC OUTPUT at the end of the DERIVATION. The **opacity** of a rule is contrasted with its TRANSPARENCY.

(2) In the context of recent generative SYNTAX, the term refers to a set of CONDITIONS specifying the grammatical CONTEXTS in which an expression cannot be FREE. For example, in the construction *They believe* [*each other are intelligent*], *each other* is an opaque context, and cannot be CO-INDEXED with an item outside it. The structure is ILL FORMED because the ANAPHOR *each other* has to be BOUND with its GOVERNING category (the EMBEDDED TENSED CLAUSE), but there is no appropriate NP present to enable this to happen. By contrast, *each other* is in a transparent context in *They believe* [*each other to be intelligent*]; here, it can be co-indexed with an NP outside the clause (*they*).

(3) In SEMANTICS, the notion of **referential opacity** (as opposed to transparency) applies to a construction or context which fails to preserve its truth-functional status when substituted by certain types of CO-REFERENTIAL expression.

(4) A term used in NON-LINEAR PHONOLOGY, as part of the characterization of the DOMAIN within which ASSIMILATION RULES apply: in long-distance assimilations (such as VOWEL HARMONY), intervening CONSONANTS are said to be either **opaque** or **transparent**. An 'opaque' segment is one already characterized by the NODE or FEATURE which is being SPREAD by an assimilation rule, and thus blocks the application of the rule; a segment which permits the application of a rule is said to be 'transparent'. In cases where a feature of vowel A may spread to vowel B if segment P intervenes but not segment Q, P is transparent to the application of the rule, whereas Q is opaque.

open (1) A term used in the four-level PHONETIC classification of vertical TONGUE movement in VOWEL sounds based on the CARDINAL VOWEL SYSTEM, the others being CLOSE, 'half-close' and 'half-open'. It refers to a vowel made with the tongue in the lowest possible position, i.e. the mouth as wide open as possible, as in [a] and [ɑ]: the most open vowels in English are in words like *cat* and *cart*. The area of articulation immediately above 'open' is known as **half-open** or **mid-open**, as in [ɛ] and [ɔ] (the nearest English vowels being in words like *get* and *got* respectively). In a three-level classification of vowel sounds, the lowest group are known as 'low' vowels (as opposed to 'high' and 'mid').

(2) A term used in the classification of lip positions, referring to the visual appearance of the lips when they are held relatively wide apart, but without any noticeable ROUNDING, as in such sounds as the [ɑ] in *part*. It is contrasted with SPREAD, NEUTRAL and rounded positions. A similar notion is involved in the classification of JAW SETTINGS.

(3) A term used in the two-way classification of SYLLABLE structure, referring to a syllable which ends in a VOWEL, as opposed to the CLOSED syllable, which ends in a CONSONANT. This feature is sometimes referred to as a 'free' syllable. The open syllable is the first syllable type to be productively used by children, in the early stages of PHONOLOGICAL development. It also constitutes a syllable type (consonant+vowel) which seems to be a UNIVERSAL feature of LANGUAGE.

(4) A term sometimes used in the GRAMMATICAL CLASSIFICATION of WORDS to refer to one of two postulated major word-classes in language, the other being CLOSED. An **open class** is one whose membership is in principle indefinite or

unlimited. New items are continually being added, as new ideas, inventions, etc., emerge. NOUNS, VERBS, ADJECTIVES and ADVERBS are open-class items, whereas CONJUNCTIONS, PRONOUNS, etc., are closed. The distinction is not quite as clear-cut as it seems, as the class of PREPOSITIONS in English, for example, is relatively open (e.g. *in accordance with, on account of,* and many more), and within the so-called open classes of words there are several closed sub-systems, e.g. AUXILIARY verbs. But the contrast between 'open' and 'closed' is widely recognized.

(5) In language ACQUISITION studies of the two-word stage of grammatical development, the term refers to the variable ELEMENT in a CONSTRUCTION, the other being referred to as the PIVOT. For example, in the set *daddy there, cat there, drink there, there* is the pivot word (a member of a small, 'closed' class), and *daddy*, etc., are members of an **open class**.

(6) A term used in the classification of types of JUNCTURE or TRANSITION, referring to the features which help to define a word boundary, before silence; also known as 'plus juncture'. 'Open juncture' is opposed to 'close juncture'; 'open transition' to 'close transition'.

operator (1) In FORMAL SEMANTICS, a symbol or expression denoting a process which has to be performed. For example, operators such as NEGATION and CONJUNCTION form SYNTACTIC (or SEMANTIC) expressions out of other syntactic (or semantic) expressions. 'Variable binding operators' combine a variable and an expression to form a compound expression, as in the universal and existential QUANTIFIERS, or the use of LAMBDA.

(2) In some approaches to English GRAMMAR (notably QUIRK GRAMMAR), the first AUXILIARY VERB to be used in a verb phrase. It is so called because it performs an 'operation' on the CLAUSE, such as marking the change from STATEMENT to QUESTION. For example, in *The cat has been eating, has* is the operator (cf. *Has the cat been eating?*).

(3) In ROLE AND REFERENCE GRAMMAR, any of a set of formal items which govern the behaviour of units in inter-CLAUSAL construction. Examples include ASPECT, which affects the VERB; MODALITY, which affects the CORE part of the clause; and TENSE, which affects the clause PERIPHERY.

opposition A term used in LINGUISTICS to refer to linguistically important differences between UNITS. The term is used primarily in PHONOLOGY, where contrasts between DISTINCTIVE FEATURES of sound, or between the presence and absence of a feature, are referred to as oppositions. The difference between /p/ and /s/, for example, can be seen as a combination of two oppositions – PLACE and MANNER OF ARTICULATION. One of the first attempts to classify the oppositions in this sense was in the PRAGUE SCHOOL's theory of **distinctive oppositions**, as first formulated in Nikolai Trubetzkoy's *Principles of Phonology* (1939). The main types of opposition recognized are:

(1) **bilateral** *v.* **multilateral**: the opposition between English /t/ and /d/, for example, is *bilateral*, because these are the only units in the system which are ALVEOLAR/PLOSIVE, and they are differentiated by the single feature of VOICING; the opposition between say, /t/ and /v/, however, is *multilateral*, because there is more than one parameter of contrast, e.g. /d/ *v.* /f/.

(2) **proportional** *v.* **isolated**: the opposition between /f/ and /v/ in English is

proportional, because there are other oppositions in the language which work in parallel, e.g. /s/ *v.* /z/, /ʃ/ *v.* /ʒ/; on the other hand, the opposition between, say, /v/ and /l/ is *isolated* – there are no other segments that are contrasted in this particular way, i.e. VOICED LABIO-DENTAL FRICATIVE *v.* voiced LATERAL.

(3) **privative, gradual** and **equipollent**: a *privative* opposition is a BINARY one, where one member is seen as MARKED by the presence of a feature, which its opposite member lacks (i.e. it is 'unmarked'), as in the /p/ *v.* /b/ distinction in English; in a *gradual* opposition, degrees of difference in a language are recognized along a scale of some kind, as in a language with four front vowels /i/, /e/, /ɛ/ and /æ/ where (according to Trubetskoy) it would not be desirable to analyse the four degrees of vowel height in terms of privative pairs, such as 'high' *v.* 'low'; in an *equipollent* opposition, the members are seen as logically equivalent to each other, contrasted neither gradually nor by a binary feature; e.g. the distinction between /p/ and /k/ cannot be analysed, according to Trubetskoy, as a difference along a single phonetic continuum, nor can /p/ be seen as 'non-velar', or /k/ as 'non-bilabial'.

(4) **constant** and **neutralizable**: a *constant* opposition exists when its members can occur in all possible positions, e.g. wherever /p/ might be found in a language, a contrast with /b/ will also be found; in English, the /t/ *v.* /d/ distinction is *neutralizable*, because in some positions there is no such contrast, the opposition being realized by the same sound, as when /t/ follows initial /s/, e.g. *stick* does not contrast with **sdick*.

optative A term sometimes used in GRAMMATICAL description, to refer to a category of MOOD which expresses a desire, hope, or wish. It is chiefly known from Classical Greek. Optative expressions in English use the MODAL VERBS or the SUBJUNCTIVE: *May they get home safely, Heaven help us!*

optimality theory In recent PHONOLOGICAL theory, and specifically in relation to PROSODIC MORPHOLOGY, a theory of the relationship between proposed underlying and output representations. In this approach, an input representation is associated with a large class of candidate output representations, and various kinds of filter are used to evaluate these outputs and select the one which is 'optimal' (i.e. most well-formed). The selection takes place through the use of a set of well-formedness constraints, ranked in a hierarchy of relevance on a language-particular basis, so that a lower-ranked constraint may be violated in order to satisfy a higher-ranked one. The candidate representation which passes the highest ranked constraint is the output form (special tests are needed to deal with the possibility of tied candidates).

optional One of two types of TRANSFORMATIONAL RULE postulated by Noam CHOMSKY in his book *Syntactic Structures* (1957), the other being OBLIGATORY. **Optional transformations** may apply at a certain stage in a DERIVATION; but it is not essential for the WELL-FORMEDNESS of the SENTENCE that they do so, e.g. the transformation from POSITIVE to NEGATIVE, ACTIVE to PASSIVE, or DECLARATIVE to INTERROGATIVE. In later versions of transformational GRAMMAR, the range of this notion changes, as more structural rules come to be incorporated into the BASE component of the grammar, and are thus handled by obligatory rules. A few rules handling STYLISTIC alternatives remain optional.

oral (1) In phonetics, 'oral' is opposed to NASAL, referring either to the ARTICULATORY area of the mouth, as in the phrases 'oral CAVITY, 'oral chamber', or to the specific sounds that are made there. The opposition is usually with the nasal cavity (and with nasal sounds), but the PHARYNX, oesophagus and lungs are also excluded from the notion of 'oral'. In the DISTINCTIVE FEATURE theory of PHONOLOGY, 'oral' is specifically opposed to 'nasal', these being postulated as two of the contrasts needed in order to specify fully the sound SYSTEM of a language. In some models of FEATURE GEOMETRY, an 'oral cavity NODE' is introduced, corresponding to the articulatory notion of an oral cavity CONSTRICTION. It is represented between the ROOT node and the PLACE node, thus DOMINATING place and [+/−CONTINUANT] nodes.

(2) The usual adjective for the manifestation of LANGUAGE in its spoken, as opposed to its written form. The term **oracy** has been coined, on analogy with 'literacy', to refer to ability in speech and listening comprehension, but this term is used more in discussion of language skills and curricula in mother-tongue education, and will not generally be found in technical studies in LINGUISTICS and PHONETICS.

order(-ing, -ed) (1) A term used in LINGUISTICS to refer to the pattern of relationships constituting or UNDERLYING a LINEAR SEQUENCE of linguistic UNITS. Sometimes, no distinction is made between the sequential arrangement of observable FORMAL ELEMENTS (defined, for example, in terms of SURFACE STRUCTURE) and the abstract pattern of relationships assumed to underlie the surface arrangement: notions such as 'WORD ORDER', 'MORPHEME order', 'SUBJECT–VERB–OBJECT order', etc., are often seen in this way. Usually, however, a systematic distinction is made between these two LEVELS of analysis, the former being referred to as SEQUENCE, and the latter as 'order'. That there is no necessary one-to-one correspondence between surface sequence and underlying order can be shown in such sentences as *She took off her hat/She took her hat off/Her hat she took off*, etc., where the same basic subject–verb–object order is REALIZED in different surface sequences. This notion – that there is an underlying abstract 'ordering' of elements from which several surface arrangements can be derived – is a fundamental insight of TRANSFORMATIONAL GRAMMAR. In this approach, also, the term **ordering** is used to refer to the application of the RULES of a grammar in a given succession, a crucial principle which prevents the generation of unACCEPTABLE STRINGS, and enables SIMPLER analyses to be made. Several specific ordering conventions have been suggested (cf. the notions of CYCLICAL, LINEAR, CONJUNCTIVE, DISJUNCTIVE, BLEEDING, FEEDING, EXTRINSIC and INTRINSIC ordering). In natural generative PHONOLOGY, the **no-ordering condition** requires that no extrinsic ordering of rules be permitted. See also BRACKETING PARADOX, RULE-ORDERING PARADOX.

(2) In PSYCHOLINGUISTICS, the phrase **order of mention** refers to a use of language where the order of events in the outside world is paralleled by the order in the sequence of SEMANTIC UNITS within the utterance. For example: *After John shut the door, he spoke* follows order of mention; *Before John spoke, he shut the door* does not.

ordinal A term used in some models of GRAMMATICAL description referring to the class of numerals *first, second*, etc., by contrast with the CARDINAL numbers *one, two*, etc.

other-repair see REPAIR

output A use of the general sense of this term in GENERATIVE GRAMMAR to refer to a SENTENCE which is produced after the application of a RULE or set of rules.

overcorrection see HYPERCORRECTION

overextension A term used in language ACQUISITION studies to refer to one type of relationship between adult and child MEANING, as expressed in LEXICAL ITEMS. In overextension, the child's lexical item has a wider range of APPLICATION than the equivalent term in adult language, e.g. when *dog* is used for other animals apart from dogs. The term is usually contrasted with UNDEREXTENSION.

overgeneralization A term used in language ACQUISITION studies, referring to the process whereby children extend their use of a GRAMMATICAL feature to CONTEXTS beyond those found in the adult language, e.g. 'overgeneralizing' the regular past-TENSE FORM in such items as **goed, *wented, *goned.*

overgenerate (overgeneration) A term used in GENERATIVE LINGUISTICS to characterize a RULE which generates ungrammatical structures as well as GRAMMATICAL ones.

overlapping (overlap) (1) A term used in PHONOLOGY to refer to the possibility that a PHONE may be assigned to more than one PHONEME (**phonemic overlapping**). The notion was introduced by American STRUCTURAL LINGUISTS in the 1940s. The overlapping (or 'intersection') of phonemes was said to be 'partial' if a given sound is assigned to phoneme A in one PHONETIC CONTEXT and to phoneme B in another; it would be 'complete' if successive occurrences of the sound in the *same* context are assigned sometimes to A, and sometimes to B (cf. the notion of NEUTRALIZATION). An example of partial overlap is found between /r/ and /t/ in some DIALECTS of English, where both are realized by the TAP [ɾ] in different contexts: /r/ → [ɾ] after DENTAL FRICATIVES, as in *through*; /t/ → [ɾ] between VOWELS, as in *bitter*. An example of complete overlap occurs in the case of [ə], which may stand for most occurrences of English STRESSED vowels, when they occur in unstressed positions (e.g. *telegraph – telegraphy*, where the first and third vowels reduce to [ə]). The notion of complete overlap was generally rejected, on the grounds that it would lead to an unacceptable INDETERMINACY in phonemics which would destroy the principle of phonemic analysis as an independent LEVEL. One would not be able to tell, on the basis of pronunciation alone, which phoneme a phone belonged to. The need to preserve some kind of phonemic integrity for successive instances of the same sound led to the maxim 'Once a phoneme, always a phoneme', and to the notion of BIUNIQUENESS (or one-to-one correspondence between phones and phonemes). However, even partial overlap provides considerable difficulties for the notion of INVARIANCE, which is fundamental to the biuniqueness hypothesis, as has been argued by CHOMSKY, among others. It is evident that it is not always possible to predict the phoneme a phone belongs to, simply by considering its phonetic properties.

(2) A term used in language ACQUISITION studies to refer to one type of relationship between adult and child MEANING, as expressed in LEXICAL ITEMS. 'Overlapping' meanings, or 'overlap', as the name suggests, occur when the meaning of a lexical item for the child is not identical with that for the adult (cf. OVEREXTENSION and UNDEREXTENSION). In cases of no overlap ('mismatch'), a child's lexical item has no point of contact at all with the meaning of that item in the adult language, e.g. one child used *door* to mean 'walk'.

overt (1) A term used in LINGUISTIC analysis to refer to the relationships between linguistic FORMS which are observable in the SURFACE STRUCTURE of a SENTENCE; opposed to COVERT. Examples of overt relations include WORD ORDER, CONCORD and PHONOTACTIC SEQUENCE. The term is also sometimes used of elements (e.g. an 'overt subject' in PRO-DROP LANGUAGES) and processes (e.g. *WH*-MOVEMENT).

(2) A term used in SOCIOLINGUISTICS as part of the analysis of the way linguistic FORMS carry social prestige: in **overt prestige**, forms are valued which follow the NORMS recommended by powerful groups or institutions within society (such as public schools, broadcasting institutions and usage manuals). An example would be the forms associated with Standard English. This kind of prestige is overt because the forms are openly and publicly recognized as socially desirable. An opposition is drawn with COVERT prestige, where VERNACULAR DIALECT forms are positively valued, emphasizing local solidarity and identity.

overtone see HARMONIC

P

P (1) The usual abbreviation for PHRASE, in such combinations as NP (= NOUN phrase), VP (= VERB phrase), PP (= PREPOSITIONAL phrase), etc.

(2) An abbreviation sometimes used for PREDICATOR, PREPOSITION and PARTICIPLE, in various approaches to SYNTAX.

(3) In natural generative PHONOLOGY, the abbreviation for 'phonological' in the term 'P-RULES'.

palatal(ization) A term used in the PHONETIC classification of speech sounds on the basis of their PLACE OF ARTICULATION: it refers to a sound made when the FRONT of the TONGUE is in contact with or approaches the hard PALATE. Slavic languages usually illustrate a range of palatal sounds; in German, *ich* ('I') exemplifies a VOICELESS palatal [ç]; in English, palatal sounds are heard only in restricted contexts, as variants of a PHONEME, e.g. /k/ is normally described as VELAR, but the *k* in such words as *keep* is often quite palatal in its articulation, because of the influence of the following FRONT VOWEL. One may also hear palatal GLIDES in such words as *cute* [kj-] or *huge* [ç]. 'Palatal' is sometimes used with reference to vowels or SEMI-VOWELS articulated in the hard-palate area (front CLOSE vowels), as in the [iː] of *seat* or the initial sound of *yet* [j̥], formerly [j]; but the commoner use is in relation to CONSONANTS.

Palatalization is a general term referring to any articulation involving a movement of the tongue towards the hard palate. It may be used to describe the altered articulation illustrated by *k* above, but its more common use is in relation to SECONDARY ARTICULATIONS. Here, the primary place of articulation is elsewhere in the mouth; for example, a [t] sound, normally made in ALVEOLAR position, is said to be 'palatalized' if during its articulation the front of the tongue is raised towards the hard palate: in the case of [t], the palatalization would be most noticeable when the plosive was released, as a palatal GLIDE would then be heard before the onset of the next main sound. Several languages, such as Russian, have sets of palatalized consonants operating as phonemes. Because of the auditory effect involved, the labels SOFT and HARD are often used to describe the contrasting qualities of palatalized and non-palatalized CONSONANTS respectively. (These labels have no relation to their use in the terms 'hard palate' and 'soft palate', which are anatomically based: see PALATE.) In phonetic TRANSCRIPTION, there are several ways of representing palatalization;

for instance [ţ], [ṫ], [tʲ] and [t'] have all been used to represent a palatalized [t]. See also -ISE/-IZE.

palate (palatal, palatogra-phy, -m) The arched bony structure which forms the roof of the mouth, and which is much used for the ARTICULATION of speech sounds. The delimitation and classification of the PALATAL area has not been without controversy, as is shown by the several different classificatory systems for describing the types of pathological condition known as cleft lip and palate. In one such system, the whole of the upper oral area (including lips and alveolum) is referred to as palatal, on the grounds that this constituted a single embryological process. In PHONETICS, a much more restricted sense is used: here, the term applies to the whole area from behind the ALVEOLAR ridge to the UVULA. It is divided into two parts: the **hard palate**, which is the immobile bony area immediately behind the alveolar ridge, and the **soft palate** or 'velum', which is the mobile fleshy continuation of this, culminating in the uvula. Only sounds articulated in the area of the hard palate are called 'palatal' sounds; soft-palate sounds are either VELAR or UVULAR. The soft palate is particularly important in the production of speech, as it is under muscular control which enables it to be raised (closing the upper part of the PHARYNX) for the production of ORAL sounds, or lowered (keeping the passage to the nose open) for the production of NASAL sounds. Poor control of the soft palate (which may result from several neurological or anatomical conditions, such as cleft palate) leads to abnormal nasal resonance or friction.

It is difficult to see or sense what is going on inside the mouth when the TONGUE is making contact with the palate. **Palatography** is the instrumental study of articulation in this area. Several techniques have been tried to produce accurate pictures of TONGUE contact with the palate – **palatograms**. An early technique involved spraying the roof of the mouth with a dark powdery substance; an articulation would then be made, which, if in the palatal or alveolar area, would rub off some of the substance: the roof of the mouth would then be photographed to pinpoint the place of articulation. Apart from the inconvenience of this method, its biggest drawback is that it was static: it disallowed any observation of the movement of the tongue in connected speech. More recently, ELECTROPALATOGRAPHIC techniques have been devised which enable a continuous record to be made of the tongue contact in this area. The potential of the device used, known as an **electropalatograph**, is very great, but the research is still in its infancy.

palato-alveolar A term used in the PHONETIC classification of CONSONANT sounds on the basis of their PLACE OF ARTICULATION: it refers to a sound made by a double movement of the TONGUE towards the area between the ALVEOLAR ridge and hard PALATE: the BLADE of the tongue (or the TIP and blade together) makes contact with the alveolar ridge, while the FRONT of the tongue is raised in the direction of the hard palate. Examples in English are the *sh-* [ʃ] of *ship* and the *-s-* [ʒ] of *treasure*. Several other varieties of sound may be articulated in this part of the mouth by slightly varying the position and shape of the tongue, e.g. ALVEO(LO)-PALATAL sounds, which are important in some LANGUAGES, such as Polish.

pandialectal A term used primarily in DIALECTOLOGY and SOCIOLINGUISTICS to characterize any LINGUISTIC FEATURE, RULE, etc., which is applicable to all the dialects of a LANGUAGE.

panlectal A term used by some SOCIOLINGUISTS to refer to a general MODEL of GRAMMAR within which all individual VARIETIES (or LECTS) can be interrelated, thus providing a model of a speaker's passive COMPETENCE. A somewhat less ambitious undertaking is known as a POLYLECTAL grammar.

paradigmatic (paradigm) (1) A basic term in LINGUISTICS for the set of substitutional relationships a linguistic UNIT has with other units in a specific CONTEXT. **Paradigmatic relations** can be established at all LEVELS of analysis, e.g. the selection of /p-/ as opposed to /b-/, /n-/, etc., in the context /-it/, or of *the* as opposed to *a, this, much*, etc., in the context — *cake*. Paradigmatic RELATIONS, together with SYNTAGMATIC relations, constitute the statement of a linguistic unit's identity within the language system. CLASSES of paradigmatically related elements are often referred to as SYSTEMS, e.g. the 'PRONOUN system', 'CASE system'. A set of GRAMMATICALLY conditioned FORMS all derived from a single ROOT or STEM is called a **paradigm**.

(2) In PSYCHOLINGUISTICS, the term is used to refer to a class of ASSOCIATIVE responses which people make when hearing a stimulus word, viz. those which fall into the same WORD-CLASS as the stimulus. A **paradigmatic response** or **association** would be *girl* following *boy, white* following *black*, etc. The SYNTAGMATIC association, by contrast, involves a change of word-class in the response.

paradox see BRACKETING PARADOX, RULE-ORDERING PARADOX

paragrammatism see AGRAMMATISM

paralanguage (paralinguistic) A term used in SUPRASEGMENTAL PHONOLOGY to refer to variations in TONE of voice which seem to be less systematic than PROSODIC features (especially INTONATION and STRESS). Examples would include the controlled use of BREATHY or CREAKY voice, spasmodic features (such as giggling while speaking), and the use of secondary ARTICULATION (such as lip-ROUNDING or NASALIZATION) to produce a tone of voice signalling attitude, social role, or some other language-specific meaning. Some analysts broaden the definition of paralanguage to include KINESIC features; some exclude paralinguistic features from LINGUISTIC analysis.

parallel distributed processing see CONNECTIONISM

parameter (parametric) A term used in GOVERNMENT-BINDING THEORY for a specification of the variations that a principle of GRAMMAR manifests among different LANGUAGES. In recent GB, it is suggested that there are no RULES of grammar in the traditional sense, but only PRINCIPLES which can take a slightly different form in different languages. For example, a HEAD parameter specifies the positions of heads within PHRASES (e.g. head-first in English, head-last in Japanese). The ADJACENCY parameter of CASE theory specifies whether case assigners must be adjacent to their NOUN phrases (e.g. to the left in English, to the right in Chinese). The PRO-DROP (or 'null subject') parameter determines whether the

SUBJECT of a CLAUSE can be suppressed. Determining the values of parameters for given languages is known as **parameter-setting**. The overall approach has been called the 'principles and parameters' theory of UNIVERSAL grammar, and has since come to be applied outside of syntactic contexts, notably in characterizing PHONOLOGICAL relations. Later versions of METRICAL PHONOLOGY, for example, recognize a series of parameters governing the way metrical FEET should be represented, such as QUANTITY SENSITIVITY and DIRECTIONALITY. See also HEAD.

parametric phonetics An approach to PHONETICS which sees speech as a single physiological SYSTEM, in which the range of ARTICULATORY variables (or 'parameters') in the VOCAL TRACT is seen as being continually in operation, interacting in various ways along the time dimension to produce a continuum of sound which listeners SEGMENT according to the RULES of their LANGUAGE. It thus contrasts with the traditional view of speech, where articulation is seen in advance as a sequence of speech 'postures', or segments, each of which is independently definable with reference to a set of isolatable FEATURES (PLACES OF ARTICULATION, MANNER OF ARTICULATION, etc.). This 'static' model contrasts with the DYNAMIC parametric model, which has led to fresh interest in the nature of NEUROLINGUISTIC control mechanisms.

paraphrase A term used in LINGUISTICS for the result or process of producing alternative versions of a SENTENCE or TEXT without changing the MEANING. One SENTENCE may have several paraphrases, e.g. *The dog is eating a bone, A bone is being eaten by the dog, It's the dog who is eating a bone*, and so on. Most SEMANTIC theories would treat all these sentences as having a single semantic REPRESENTATION (though variations in FOCUS and PRESUPPOSITION could differentiate them). Linguists use syntactic paraphrase as a major procedure for establishing certain types of TRANSFORMATIONAL relations.

parasite vowel see ANAPTYXIS

parasitic gap A term in recent GENERATIVE GRAMMAR for a syntactic GAP in a SENTENCE which is possible only because the sentence contains an ordinary gap; it is therefore dependent or 'parasitic' upon the ordinary gap. The following example involves a parasitic gap, indicated by *p*, and an ordinary gap, indicated by *e*: *Which film did he criticize e without seeing p?*. The parasitic gap is possible only because the ordinary gap is present; hence, the following is ungrammatical: **He criticized Henry V without seeing p.*

paratactic (parataxis) A term used in TRADITIONAL GRAMMATICAL analysis, and often found in DESCRIPTIVE LINGUISTIC studies, to refer to CONSTRUCTIONS of equal status which are linked solely through juxtaposition and punctuation/INTONATION. 'Paratactic constructions' are opposed to HYPOTACTIC ones, where a subordinate relationship is expressed. **Parataxis** is illustrated by *She bought tea, coffee, eggs and milk* or *I came; I saw; I conquered.*

paratone A coherent formal sequence of INTONATION units, analogous to the concept of 'paragraph' in writing. The term is not widely used.

parole A term introduced into LINGUISTICS by the Swiss linguist Ferdinand de SAUSSURE (1857–1913), to distinguish one of the senses of the word 'LANGUAGE' (the others being *langage* and LANGUE). It refers to the concrete UTTERANCES produced by individual speakers in actual situations, and is distinguished from *langue*, which is the collective LANGUAGE SYSTEM of a SPEECH community. An analogous term is PERFORMANCE.

paronym(y) A term sometimes used in SEMANTIC analysis to refer to the relationship between WORDS derived from the same ROOT. It is especially applied to a word formed from a word in another LANGUAGE with only a slight change: French *pont* and Latin *pons* are paronyms, and the relationship between them is one of paronymy.

parsing (parse(r)) (1) In TRADITIONAL GRAMMAR, this term refers to the pedagogical exercise of labelling the grammatical ELEMENTS of single SENTENCES, e.g. SUBJECT, PREDICATE, past TENSE, NOUN, VERB; in the USA, also called **diagramming**. LINGUISTICS, by contrast, is less concerned with labels, and more with the criteria of analysis which lead to the identification of these elements, and with the way in which speakers use these elements to relate sentences in the LANGUAGE as a whole. Modern grammatical FORMALISMS have begun to develop the properties of several parsing mechanisms, and the notion of parsing has proved to be central to work in COMPUTATIONAL LINGUISTICS, especially NATURAL LANGUAGE PROCESSING.

(2) The term **parse** identifies a central feature of the procedures of NETWORK GRAMMARS, where it refers to the grammatical breakdown of a TEXT (a 'parse') in terms of SYNTACTIC, SEMANTIC and REFERENTIAL information, as presented in the form of a **parse tree**.

part In SYNTAX, an abbreviation sometimes used for the category PARTICLE.

participant role (1) A term used in LINGUISTICS, especially in PRAGMATICS, to refer to the FUNCTIONS which can be ascribed to people taking part in a linguistic interaction. Typical roles are speaker and addressee, but several other roles can be recognized, such as the recipient (as opposed to the target) of a message, or the message's source (as opposed to its speaker).

(2) The term is also sometimes used in GRAMMAR, as an alternative to CASE, to refer to the SEMANTIC functions attached to CLAUSE ELEMENTS, such as AGENT, RECIPIENT and AFFECTED.

participle (participial) A traditional GRAMMATICAL term referring to a word derived from a VERB and used as an ADJECTIVE, as in *a laughing face*. It is thus distinct from the traditional notion of **gerund**, where the word derived from a verb is used as a NOUN, as in *smoking is forbidden*. In LINGUISTICS the term is generally restricted to the non-FINITE forms of verbs other than the INFINITIVE, viz. present and past, as in *I am going* and *I have walked* respectively, but, even here, there is a strong tendency to avoid the use of the traditional labels 'present' and 'past' participles, with their Latinate associations of time (inapplicable, for example, in a passive sentence like *I shall be kicked*, where the participle can hardly be 'past'), and to use instead a neutral set of terms, such as *-ING* FORMS or *-ED/-EN* FORMS.

particle (1) A term used in GRAMMATICAL description to refer to an INVARIABLE ITEM with grammatical FUNCTION, especially one which does not readily fit into a standard classification of PARTS OF SPEECH; often abbreviated as **PRT** or **part**. In English, for example, the marker of the INFINITIVE, *to*, is often called a particle because, despite its surface similarity to a PREPOSITION, it really has nothing in common with it. Likewise, the unique characteristics of *not* have prompted some to label it a 'NEGATIVE particle', and the units in PHRASAL VERBS are often called 'verbal particles'.

(2) A term used in TAGMEMIC analysis to refer to a linguistic UNIT seen as a DISCRETE entity, definable in terms of FEATURES. It is contrasted with WAVE (where the unit's CONTEXTUAL variability is analysed) and FIELD (where its DISTRIBUTION is described).

particle phonology An approach to PHONOLOGY which focuses on the analysis of the internal structure of phonological SEGMENTS. For example, in the analysis of VOWELS, three privative features (**particles**) are recognized – [a] representing OPENNESS, [i] representing FRONTNESS, and [u] representing ROUNDING – and segments are seen to be composed of one or more particles. An [e] vowel, for example, would be analysed as a combination of [i] + [a]. The approach is similar to that used in DEPENDENCY PHONOLOGY, though differences include the number of PRIMITIVES recognized and the treatment of vowel height. The approach claims to have advantages in the handling of such processes as ASSIMILATION and the relationship between MONOPHTHONGS and DIPHTHONGS.

partitive A term used in GRAMMAR and SEMANTICS to refer to a part or quantity, such as *piece*, *ounce*, and *bar* (of soap). Some partitive forms are very general in meaning, occurring with almost any quantifiable LEXICAL item (e.g. *some*); others are restricted to a single lexical item, or to a very small set (e.g. *blade* – of grass).

part of speech The TRADITIONAL term for a GRAMMATICAL CLASS of WORDS. The main 'parts of speech' recognized by most school grammars derive from the work of the ancient Greek and Roman grammarians, primarily the NOUN, PRONOUN, VERB, ADVERB, ADJECTIVE, PREPOSITION, CONJUNCTION and INTERJECTION, with ARTICLE, PARTICIPLE and others often added. Because of the inexplicitness with which these terms were traditionally defined (e.g. the use of unclear NOTIONAL criteria), and the restricted nature of their definitions (reflecting the characteristics of Latin or Greek), LINGUISTS tend to prefer such terms as WORD-class or FORM-class, where the grouping is based on FORMAL criteria of a more UNIVERSALLY applicable kind.

passive (passiviz-e, -ation) A term used in the GRAMMATICAL analysis of VOICE, referring to a SENTENCE, CLAUSE or VERB FORM where the grammatical SUBJECT is typically the recipient or 'goal' of the action denoted by the verb, e.g. *The letter was written by a doctor*. It is contrasted with ACTIVE, and sometimes with other forms, e.g. 'middle' (as in Greek). A full linguistic statement of the CONSTRAINTS affecting these relationships is a complex matter. In English, for example, there are active sentences that do not have passive counterparts (e.g. *The boy fell, They have a car*), passive sentences which have an unclear active counterpart (e.g. *The house was sold*), and so on. In addition, there is the problem that the central type of passive construction (using the verb *to be*, e.g. *She was pushed*) is closely related to other types of construction (cf. *She got* *pushed, She was interested*), and a boundary line is sometimes difficult to establish. Constructions such as *Plums are selling well* are sometimes described as **pseudo-passives**. Constructions such as *They were interested in history*, which have both verbal and adjectival properties, are sometimes called **semi-passives**. Passive constructions which take an agent are **agentive passives** (e.g. *She was chased (by the dog)*), as opposed to 'non-AGENTIVE' or 'agentless' passives, where there is no need for (and sometimes no possibility of) an agentive phrase being added, since the speaker does not have a 'performer' of the action in mind (e.g. *The city is industrialized now*). In GENERATIVE grammar, the TRANSFORMATION of a sentence from its active to its passive form is known as **passivization**. A verb or sentence which undergoes such a process is said to **passivize**. Two kinds of passive may be distinguished: verbal and ADJECTIVAL.

passive vocabulary see VOCABULARY

past anterior In GRAMMAR, a TENSE form used in some languages to express the rapid completion of a past action. In French, for example, it is chiefly used instead of the PLUPERFECT in past NARRATIVE after time CONJUCTIONS or when the MAIN VERB is in the PAST HISTORIC. It is formed by combining the past historic tense of an AUXILIARY verb with the past PARTICIPLE of a LEXICAL verb: *Dès qu'elle eut mangé, elle sortit* 'As soon as she had eaten, she left'.

past definite see PAST HISTORIC

past historic In GRAMMAR, a PAST TENSE form of a VERB, used in some languages to refer to a completed action; also sometimes called the **past definite**. In French, for example, it is used in the written language as part of past NARRATIVE description as well as in the reporting of completed past events: *Hier, Marie se leva et sortit* 'Yesterday, Marie got up and went out'.

past perfect see PERFECT

past tense In GRAMMAR, a TENSE form which refers to a time of action prior to the moment of utterance. Languages make different distinctions within this period, such as whether the reference is recent or distant, or whether the action is completed or not. French, for example, recognizes IMPERFECT, PAST HISTORIC, PERFECT, pluperfect, and PAST ANTERIOR tenses, as well as FUTURE and CONDITIONAL perfect forms. A range of past tenses is also traditionally recognized in English grammar, following the influence of Latin descriptive MODELS, though only a single past tense form is represented INFLECTIONALLY (*I walked*), other past time reference using AUXILIARY verbs (*I have walked*) and past time ADVERBIALS (*yesterday, last year*).

path A term used in GENERATIVE GRAMMAR referring to an unbroken series of BRANCHES and NODES moving in a single direction with respect to the top of a TREE diagram. The term is also used by some linguists as part of the grammatical analysis of a sentence: an entity takes a path from a source to a GOAL, e.g. in *John rowed along the river, along* is 'path'.

patient A term used by some LINGUISTS as part of the GRAMMATICAL analysis of a SENTENCE: it refers to the entity which is affected by the action of the VERB, e.g. *The dog bit **the man***. GOAL and RECIPIENT have been used as alternative terms.

pattern In the general sense of 'a systematic arrangement of UNITS', this term is found in LINGUISTICS and PHONETICS, without any special implication. Certain theoretical implications may be added in some contexts, however. For example, in language teaching, **pattern drills** (or 'structure drills') refer to the use of a SUBSTITUTION-frame technique for the practice of a particular STRUCTURE. Also, in PHONOLOGY, the term has been used to refer specifically to any neatness of arrangement that can be demonstrated in a sound SYSTEM – a UNIT such as a PHONEME being seen as a point in a pattern of sound relationships. It is felt that a phonemic pattern ought to be regular and symmetrical, and that the demonstration of **pattern congruity** in an analysis is a desirable feature. Whether a sound cluster should be analysed as one phoneme or two, for example, may depend on the parallel patterns that can be demonstrated between this CLUSTER and other phonemes; e.g. English /ʧ/ and /ʤ/ on this criterion would be analysed as single phonemes, as a STOP+FRICATIVE analysis would receive little support elsewhere in the system. The phrase 'gap/hole in the pattern' is often used to refer to a lacuna which spoils the symmetry of an analysis, as when a series of unrounded VOWELS might have a corresponding series of ROUNDED vowels except for one case.

paucal see NUMBER

pause The general sense of this term applies in LINGUISTICS, PHONETICS and PSYCHOLINGUISTICS, where an attempt is made to give a precise account of the types and DISTRIBUTION of 'pausal phenomena' and to draw conclusions concerning their FUNCTION in speech. A distinction has been drawn between **silent pauses** and **filled pauses** (e.g. *ah, er*), and several functions of pause have been established, e.g. for breathing, to mark GRAMMATICAL boundaries, and to provide time for the planning of new material. Investigations of pausal phenomena have been particularly relevant in relation to developing a theory of SPEECH PRODUCTION. In GRAMMAR, the notion of **potential pause** is sometimes used as a technique for establishing the WORD UNITS in a LANGUAGE – pauses being more likely at word boundaries than within words.

PCF see PHONETICALLY CONSISTENT FORM

peak In PHONETICS and PHONOLOGY, a term used to characterize a relatively high level of PROMINENCE; opposed to **valley** or **trough**. In METRICAL GRID theory, peaks (*v.* troughs) are RHYTHM prominences. A TROCHAIC rhythm starts with a left-edge peak or a right-edge trough; an IAMBIC rhythm starts with a left-edge trough or a right-edge peak. See also SONORITY.

pedagogical linguistics see EDUCATIONAL LINGUISTICS

pejoration see DETERIORATION

percentage symbol (%) In some approaches to INTONATIONAL PHONOLOGY, in the analysis of BOUNDARY TONES, a symbol which shows that a tone ASSOCIATES with the EDGE syllable of a phrase (H%, L%).

perception (perceptual) The general sense of this term is found in PHONETICS and PSYCHOLINGUISTICS, where it refers to the process of receiving and decoding SPEECH input. The process requires that listeners take into account not only the

ACOUSTIC CUES present in the speech signal, but also their own knowledge of the sound patterns of their LANGUAGE, in order to interpret what they hear. The term is usually contrasted with PRODUCTION.

percolation (percolate) In GRAMMAR, a process whereby a feature associated with the HEAD of a CONSTRUCTION comes to be associated with the construction as a whole. It has come to be used chiefly in GENERATIVE MORPHOLOGY for the analysis of WORDS in terms of heads. For example, in a word like *goodness*, it is the *-ness* AFFIX which gives NOUN status to the word as a whole (not the other constituent, *good*, which is ADJECTIVAL). The affix therefore has to be seen as the head and assigned to the noun category. As a consequence, this category has to 'percolate' through to the word as a whole (analogous to the way that a head noun in a PHRASE confers noun phrase status on the whole phrase).

perf An abbreviation often used for PERFECTIVE.

perfect(ive) (perf) A term used in the GRAMMATICAL description of VERB FORMS, referring to a contrast of a temporal or durative kind, and thus sometimes handled under the heading of TENSE (e.g. 'perfect', 'future perfect', 'pluperfect') and sometimes under ASPECT (e.g. 'perfective', 'non-perfective'). It is illustrated in English by the contrast between *I go* and *I have gone*, or between *I have gone* and *I had gone* (traditionally called the **pluperfect**, also now **past perfect**). LINGUISTS prefer an aspectual analysis here, because of the complex interaction of durational, completive and temporal features of meaning involved; TRADITIONAL grammars, however, refer simply to 'perfect tense', etc., and thus imply a meaning which is to some degree an oversimplification. 'Perfect', in these contexts, refers to a past situation where the event is seen as having some present relevance; in **perfective** aspect, by contrast, a situation is seen as a whole, regardless of the time contrasts which may be a part of it. Perfective then contrasts with **imperfective** or **non-perfective**, which draws attention to the internal time-structuring of the situation. The terminological distinction between 'perfect' and 'perfective' is often blurred, because grammarians writing on English have often used the latter term to replace the former, presumably because they wish to avoid its traditional associations. But this can lead to confusion in the discussion of those LANGUAGES (such as the Slavic languages) where both notions are required. In such languages as Russian and Polish, for example, a contrast between perfective and imperfective is fundamental to verb classification, and is formally marked MORPHOLOGICALLY. For example, the PREFIX про- ('pro-') before the verb 'read' produces a 'perfective verb' where the meaning is that the action (of reading) is completed; in the 'imperfective verb', which lacks the prefix, there is no such implication.

perfect grid see METRICAL GRID

performance (1) A term used in LINGUISTIC theory, and especially in GENERATIVE GRAMMAR, to refer to LANGUAGE seen as a set of specific UTTERANCES produced by NATIVE-SPEAKERS, as encountered in a CORPUS; analogous to the SAUSSUREAN concept of PAROLE. It is opposed, in this sense, to the idealized conception of language known as COMPETENCE. The utterances of performance will contain features irrelevant to the abstract RULE system, such as hesitations and unfinished structures, arising from the various psychological and social difficulties acting upon the speaker (e.g. lapses of memory, or biological limitations, such as PAUSES being introduced through the need to breathe). These features must be discounted in a grammar of the language, which deals with the systematic process of SENTENCE CONSTRUCTION. The possible implication of this view, that performance features are unimportant, has been strongly criticized in recent years, and the factors which contribute to **performance grammars** are now of considerable interest, especially in PSYCHOLINGUISTICS. See also GRAMMAR (5).

(2) A technique used in PHONETICS whereby aspiring practitioners of the subject are trained to control the use of their VOCAL ORGANS so as to be able to produce the whole range of human speech sounds. The correlative technique of discriminating and identifying sounds is known as EAR-TRAINING.

performative A term used by the philosopher J. L. Austin (1911–60), and now found in GRAMMATICAL and SEMANTIC analysis, to refer to a type of SENTENCE where an action is 'performed' by virtue of the sentence having been uttered, e.g. *I apologize, I baptize you . . . I promise . . .* The original distinction was drawn between **performative utterances** and CONSTATIVE UTTERANCES: the latter are descriptive statements which can be analysed in terms of truth-values; performatives, on the other hand, are expressions of activity which are not analysable in truth-value terms. **Performative verbs** (*apologize*, etc.) have a particular significance in SPEECH-ACT theory, as they mark the ILLOCUTIONARY force of an utterance in an explicit way. Some TRANSFORMATIONAL analysts have even proposed a 'performative analysis' of sentences, such that a performative VERB is present in UNDERLYING structure, e.g. an underlying (deletable) verb such as 'I assert that . . .'; but the advantages of adopting such a procedure have still to be fully explored.

period(ic) A term derived from the study of the physics of sound, and used in ACOUSTIC PHONETICS, referring to the time it takes for a CYCLE of pressure variation in a sound wave to repeat itself. The shorter the period, the more cycles there will be in a given unit of time, and thus the higher the FREQUENCY. Waveforms which show a repeating pattern of vibration are **periodic** waves; those which do not are **aperiodic**. Speech makes use of both types of waveform: VOWEL sounds have periodic waveforms; FRICATIVES, for example, involve aperiodic waveforms.

periodicity A term used in METRICAL PHONOLOGY for the repetition of ELEMENTS in a METRICAL GRID. For example, in the grid for *the car returned*, the bottom level elements occur four times (*the – car – re – turned*) and the elements at the next level, higher in the grid, occur twice (*car – turned*). The notion thus has relevance for accounts of a speaker's sense of an utterance's RHYTHMICAL structure.

peripheral (periphery) (1) An application of the general sense of this term in LINGUISTICS, to refer to UNITS or PROCESSES which operate at the margins of a STRUCTURE or within a REPRESENTATION. For example, EXTRAMETRICALITY is restricted to the peripheral elements in a STRING, and several kinds of EDGE phenomena have been noted. The term has a particular application in some phonological studies of Australian Aboriginal languages, where it refers to

ARTICULATIONS made at the FRONT or BACK of the mouth (as distinct from APICAL and LAMINAL articulations), and is thus equivalent to non-CORONAL.

(2) In ROLE AND REFERENCE GRAMMAR, a term used to identify one of the two basic concepts used in analysing CLAUSE structure; opposed to **core**. The peripheral layer contains a range of optional ADJUNCTIVAL elements.

periphrasis (periphrastic) A term used in GRAMMATICAL DESCRIPTION to refer to the use of separate WORDS instead of INFLECTIONS to express the same grammatical relationship. In English, for example, the COMPARISON of ADJECTIVES involves both inflection (e.g. *happier, happiest*) and periphrasis (e.g. *more happy, most happy* – the 'periphrastic forms'), though most adjectives use only one or other of these possibilities (cf. **more big, *interestinger*).

perlocutionary A term used in the theory of SPEECH ACTS to refer to an act which is performed when an UTTERANCE achieves a particular effect on the behaviour, beliefs, feelings, etc., of a listener. Examples of **perlocutionary acts** (or **perlocutionary effects**) include utterances which frighten, insult, ridicule, sympathize, persuade, etc. A distinction may then be made between the intended and the actual perlocutionary effect of an utterance (e.g. a speaker may intend to persuade X to do Y, but may succeed in getting X to do Z). The term is contrasted with LOCUTIONARY (the act of 'saying') and ILLOCUTIONARY (where the act is defined with reference to the speaker's purpose).

permutation A term often used within the framework of TRANSFORMATIONAL GRAMMAR to refer to a basic kind of transformational operation. 'Permutation transformations' have the effect of moving CONSTITUENTS (usually one at a time) from one part of a PHRASE-MARKER to another, as in the formation of PASSIVE SENTENCES. An alternative term is MOVEMENT or REORDERING. In some approaches this notion is broken down into the more basic operations of ADJUNCTION and SUBSTITUTION.

perseveration A term used by some PSYCHOLINGUISTS to refer to a type of TONGUE-SLIP where an earlier LINGUISTIC UNIT is carried over, as when *stop the car* might become *stop the star*.

person(al) A category used in GRAMMATICAL description to indicate the number and nature of the participants in a SITUATION. The contrasts are DEICTIC, i.e. refer directly to features of the situation of UTTERANCE. Distinctions of person are usually marked in the VERB and/or in the associated PRONOUNS ('personal' pronouns). Usually a three-way contrast is found: **first person**, in which speakers refer to themselves, or to a group usually including themselves (e.g. *I, we*); **second person**, in which speakers typically refer to the person they are addressing (e.g. *you*); and **third person**, in which other people, animals, things, etc. are referred to (e.g. *he, she, it, they*). Other formal distinctions may be made in languages, such as 'inclusive' *v.* 'exclusive' *we* (e.g. speaker, hearer and others *v.* speaker and others, but not hearer); FORMAL (or 'honorific') *v.* informal (or 'intimate'), e.g. French *vous v. tu*; male *v.* female; definite *v.* indefinite (cf. *one* in English); and so on. There are also several stylistically restricted uses, as in the 'royal' and authorial uses of *we*. Other word-classes than personal pronouns may show person distinction, as with the REFLEXIVE and possessive pronouns in

English (*myself*, etc., *my*, etc.). Verb constructions which lack person contrast, usually appearing in the third person, are called **impersonal**. An OBVIATIVE contrast may also be recognized.

PF The abbreviation in GOVERNMENT-BINDING THEORY for PHONETIC FORM.

phantom segment see GHOST SEGMENT

pharyngeal(-ize, -ization, pharynx) A term used in the PHONETIC classification of CONSONANT sounds on the basis of their PLACE OF ARTICULATION: it refers to a sound made in the **pharynx**, the tubular cavity which constitutes the throat above the LARYNX. Pharyngeal consonants occur in Arabic, for example. They do not occur as speech sounds in English, but similar effects can be heard in stage whispers, as when *hey*, said forcefully in a whisper, is produced with a pharyngeal 'rasp'. The general term **pharyngealization** refers to any articulation involving a constriction of the pharynx. A 'pharyngealized' [s], for example, is a SECONDARY ARTICULATION produced by simultaneously constricting the pharynx while making the [s] articulation; the auditory result would be a sound with a somewhat central and husky resonance (transcribed [sˤ]). Pharyngealized sounds are transcribed with [~] placed through the letter. See also GUTTURAL, -ISE/-IZE.

phase A term used by some GRAMMARIANS to refer to the CONTRAST between PERFECT and non-perfect in the VERB PHRASE (of English, in the first instance). The term is intended to distinguish these forms from the PROGRESSIVE/non-progressive contrast within ASPECT, and also from contrasts of TENSE and VOICE.

phatic communion A term introduced by the anthropologist Bronislaw Malinowski (1884–1942) and used subsequently by many LINGUISTS to refer to LANGUAGE used for establishing an atmosphere or maintaining social contact rather than for exchanging information or ideas (e.g. comments on the weather, or enquiries about health). 'Phatic language' (or the 'phatic function' of language) is of particular relevance to the SOCIOLINGUISTIC analysis of linguistic FUNCTIONS.

philology (philologist) The traditional term for the study of LANGUAGE history, as carried on by 'COMPARATIVE philologists' since the late eighteenth century. The study of literary texts is also sometimes included within the term (though not in Britain), as is the study of texts as part of cultural, political, etc., research.

philosophical linguistics A little-developed branch of LINGUISTICS which studies, on the one hand, the role of LANGUAGE in relation to the understanding and elucidation of philosophical concepts, and, on the other hand, the philosophical status of linguistic theories, methods and observations. When these topics are studied by philosophers, rather than linguists, the terms **linguistic philosophy** and the **philosophy of language** are used. When the term 'philosophical' is used in association with the various fields of linguistic enquiry, a contrast is usually intended with 'linguistic', e.g. 'philosophical GRAMMAR' (i.e. NOTIONAL, as opposed to DESCRIPTIVE grammar), 'philosophical SEMANTICS' (which includes such matters as the truth and validity of PROPOSITIONS, normally taken for granted by linguistic semantics).

philosophical semantics see SEMANTICS

phon(a)esthetics (phon(a)esth-eme, -esia) A term sometimes used in LINGUISTICS to refer to the study of the aesthetic properties of sound, especially the SOUND SYMBOLISM attributable to individual sounds. Cases such as the [iː] vowels in a LANGUAGE signalling smallness (cf. *teeny, weeny,* etc.) have been suggested as evidence for a limited sound/MEANING correspondence in language ('phonaesthesia' or SYNAESTHESIA), the sound units concerned being referred to as 'phonaesthemes'. The branch of STYLISTICS which studies such EXPRESSIVE effects (e.g. the onomatopoeia of poetry) is known as phonoSTYLISTICS.

phonation A general term used in PHONETICS to refer to any vocal activity in the LARYNX whose role is one neither of INITIATION nor of ARTICULATION. The various kinds of VOCAL-CORD vibration (VOICING) are the main phonatory activities, and the study of **phonation types** is aimed at accounting for the various laryngeal possibilities, such as BREATHY and CREAKY voice. Some phoneticians would also include under this heading the MODIFICATIONS in phonation which stem from variations in the length, thickness and tension of the vocal cords, as displayed in the various REGISTERS of speech (e.g. falsetto, soprano). See also ARTICULATORY SETTING.

phone A term used in PHONETICS to refer to the smallest perceptible DISCRETE SEGMENT of sound in a stream of speech ('phonic continuum' or PHONIC SUBSTANCE). From the viewpoint of segmental PHONOLOGY, phones are the physical REALIZATION of PHONEMES; phonic varieties of a phoneme are referred to as ALLOphones.

phonematic unit One of the two analytic categories used in the FIRTHIAN theory of PROSODIC PHONOLOGY, the other being the PROSODY. Phonematic UNITS comprise CONSONANTS and VOWELS, occurring in LINEAR SEQUENCE, which cannot be handled in terms of prosodies. Despite the resemblance of the term to PHONEME, the two terms are conceptually quite different, as no attempt is made with this unit to analyse speech totally into a single system of phonological OPPOSITIONS, valid for all places in structure (as is the case with the phoneme), and some features which would be included in a phonemic analysis would not be included in an analysis into phonematic features (e.g. lip-ROUNDING).

phoneme (phonemic(s)) The minimal unit in the sound SYSTEM of a LANGUAGE, according to traditional PHONOLOGICAL theories. The original motivation for the concept stemmed from the concern to establish patterns of organization within the indefinitely large range of sounds heard in languages. The PHONETIC specifications of the sounds (or PHONES) heard in speech, it was realized, contain far more detail than is needed to identify the way languages make CONTRASTS in MEANING. The notion of the phoneme allowed linguists to group together sets of phonetically similar phones as VARIANTS, or 'members', of the same underlying unit. The phones were said to be REALIZATIONS of the phonemes, and the variants were referred to as **allophones** of the phonemes (cf. ALLO-). Each language can be shown to operate with a relatively small number of phonemes; some languages have as few as fifteen phonemes; others as many as eighty. An analysis in these terms will display a language's **phonemic inventory, structure** or **system**. No two languages have the same phonemic system.

Sounds are considered to be members of the same phoneme if they are phonetically similar, and do not occur in the same ENVIRONMENT (i.e. they are in

COMPLEMENTARY DISTRIBUTION) – or, if they do, the substitution of one sound for the other does not cause a change in meaning (i.e. they are in FREE VARIATION). A sound is considered 'phonemic', on the other hand, if its substitution in a word does cause a change in meaning. In a **phonemic transcription**, only the phonemes are given symbols (compared with phonetic TRANSCRIPTIONS, where different degrees of allophonic detail are introduced, depending on one's purpose). Phonemic symbols are written between oblique brackets, compared with square brackets used for phonetic transcriptions; e.g. the phoneme /d/ has the allophones [d] (i.e. an ALVEOLAR VOICED variant), [d̥] (i.e. an alveolar devoiced variant), [d̪] (i.e. a DENTAL variant) in various complementary positions in English words. Putting this another way, it is not possible to find a pair of words in English which contrast in meaning solely on account of the difference between these features (though such contrasts may exist in other languages). The emphasis on transcription found in early phonemic studies is summarized in the subtitle of one book on the subject: 'a technique for reducing languages to writing'. The extent to which the relationship between the phonemes and the GRAPHEMES of a language is regular is called the 'phoneme–grapheme correspondence'.

On this general basis, several approaches to **phonemic analysis**, or **phonemics**, have developed. The PRAGUE SCHOOL defined the phoneme as a BUNDLE of abstract DISTINCTIVE FEATURES, or OPPOSITIONS between sounds (such as VOICING, NASALITY), an approach which was developed later by JAKOBSON and Halle, and GENERATIVE phonology. The approach of the British phonetician Daniel Jones (1881–1967), viewed the phoneme as a 'family' of related sounds, and not as oppositions. American linguists in the 1940s also emphasized the phonetic reality of phonemes, in their concern to devise PROCEDURES of analysis, paying particular attention to the DISTRIBUTION of sounds in an UTTERANCE. Apart from the question of definition, if the view is taken that all aspects of the sound system of a language can be analysed in terms of phonemes – that is, the SUPRASEGMENTAL as well as the SEGMENTAL features – then 'phonemics' becomes equivalent to phonology (= **phonemic phonology**). This view was particularly common in later developments of the American STRUCTURALIST tradition of linguistic analysis, where linguists adopting this 'phonemic principle' were called **phonemicists**. Many phonologists, however (particularly in the British tradition), prefer not to analyse suprasegmental features in terms of phonemes, and in recent years approaches have developed which do without the phoneme altogether ('non-phonemic phonology', as in PROSODIC and DISTINCTIVE FEATURE theories).

The term **phonemic clause** is a unit which has been used primarily in PSYCHOLINGUISTIC research into the distribution and function of PAUSES: it refers to a GRAMMATICAL structure produced within a single INTONATION CONTOUR, and bounded by JUNCTURES. The term **phonemic tier** is often used in AUTOSEGMENTAL PHONOLOGY for the TIER containing segments specified for the features that identify CONSONANTS and VOWELS (other than [± syllabic], which is specified on the SKELETAL TIER); also called the **segmental tier**. See also AUTONOMOUS (2), MERGER, ZERO.

phonetically consistent form (PCF) In child language ACQUISITION, a vocalization which is recognizable, recurrent, and apparently meaningful, but which does not seem to equate with a WORD in the adult language; also called a **proto-word** or (less commonly) **vocable**. As the term suggests, phonetically consistent forms have ARTICULATORY stability, but they are nonetheless phonetically less well controlled than words. Their meanings may also not be REFERENTIAL, but relate to social activities or emotional states.

phonetic form (PF) A term used in GOVERNMENT-BINDING THEORY for the output of the PHONOLOGICAL COMPONENT of a GRAMMAR, or the phonological component itself. The term is given a revised status in the MINIMALIST PROGRAMME.

phonetics (phonetic, -ian) The science which studies the characteristics of human sound-making, especially those sounds used in speech, and provides methods for their DESCRIPTION, CLASSIFICATION and TRANSCRIPTION. Three branches of the subject are generally recognized: (a) **articulatory phonetics** is the study of the way speech sounds are made ('articulated') by the vocal organs; (b) **acoustic phonetics** studies the physical properties of speech sound, as transmitted between mouth and ear; (c) **auditory phonetics** studies the perceptual response to speech sounds, as mediated by ear, auditory nerve and brain. The term **instrumental phonetics** is used for the study of any of these aspects of the subject using physical apparatus, such as devices for measuring airflow, or for analysing sound waves. People engaged in the study of phonetics are known as **phoneticians**.

Phonetic categories are generally defined using terms which have their origins in other subjects, such as anatomy, physiology and acoustics. CONSONANT sounds, for example, are described with reference to anatomical place of articulation (as in DENTAL, PALATAL, etc.), or to their physical structure (the frequency and amplitude characteristics of the sound waves). Because these methods of analysis are equally valid for all human speech sounds, regardless of the LANGUAGE or speaker, the subject is often referred to as **general phonetics**. This term also reflects the aim of the phonetician to discover universal principles governing the nature and use of speech sounds. **Experimental phonetics** is another term which reflects the general nature of this 'pure' scientific endeavour.

Work in phonetics can, accordingly, be classified into two broad types: (a) general studies of the articulation, acoustics or perception of speech, and (b) studies of the phonetic properties of specific languages. In this latter sense, it is evident that a further dimension will be required, in order to study how the sounds are used within the pronunciation SYSTEM of a language. This 'functional' approach to phonetics is usually carried on under the heading of PHONOLOGY. However, in so far as phoneticians have a specific interest in the study of individual (groups of) languages or DIALECTS, it might then be argued that phonetics is a branch of LINGUISTICS.

It is this twofold character of phonetic enquiry which gives rise to a difficulty: is phonetics an autonomous subject, or is it to be seen as a branch of linguistics? In terms of methods, it is certainly very different, and phonetic research of type (a) above often has little to do with the aims of linguistic analysis. But phonetic research of type (b) is plainly part of linguistic enquiry – some would say, an indispensable foundation. Depending on their traditions, emphases and aims, then, some university departments have been called 'Departments of Linguistics', some have been called 'Departments of Linguistics and Phonetics' – a distinction which should not be taken to mean that phonetics is not taught in the former! One compromise has been to talk of the 'linguistic sciences' – that is, linguistics and phonetics.

phonetic setting see ARTICULATORY SETTING

phonic substance A term used by some PHONETICIANS and LINGUISTS to refer to speech seen as a set of physically definable ACOUSTIC, ARTICULATORY or AUDITORY properties. The importance of this notion is that it constitutes an empirical datum to which theories of LANGUAGE must ultimately relate. To be plausible, an account of the English sound SYSTEM, for example, needs to correlate well with the PHONETIC facts (as defined in acoustic, articulatory or auditory terms); and 'phonic' (or 'phonetic') substance is a convenient label to summarize this physical level of investigation. The analogous term for the written language is GRAPHIC SUBSTANCE.

phonologize (phonologization) A term used in historical PHONOLOGY for a PROCESS whereby sounds which were formerly ALLOPHONES develop a CONTRASTIVE status (become PHONEMIC) through the loss of their CONDITIONING ENVIRONMENTS.

phonology (phonolog-ical, -ist) A branch of LINGUISTICS which studies the sound SYSTEMS of LANGUAGES. Out of the very wide range of sounds the human vocal apparatus can produce, and which are studied by PHONETICS, only a relatively small number are used DISTINCTIVELY in any one language. The sounds are organized into a system of CONTRASTS, which are analysed in terms of PHONEMES, DISTINCTIVE FEATURES, or other such 'phonological UNITS', according to the theory used. The aim of phonology is to demonstrate the patterns of distinctive sound found in a language, and to make as general statements as possible about the nature of sound systems in the languages of the world. Putting this another way, phonology is concerned with the range and function of sounds in specific languages (and often therefore referred to as 'functional phonetics'), and with the rules which can be written to show the types of phonetic relationships that relate and contrast words and other linguistic units. The student of phonology is known as a **phonologist**.

In linguistic theories, phonology is seen in one of two main ways: (a) as a LEVEL of linguistic organization, contrasted with the levels of PHONETICS, GRAMMAR and SEMANTICS in the first instance, (b) as a COMPONENT of a GENERATIVE grammar (the **phonological component**), contrasted with various other components (e.g. SYNTACTIC/semantic in early generative grammar; COVERT in the MINIMALIST PROGRAMME). Within phonology, two branches of study are usually recognized: SEGMENTAL and SUPRASEGMENTAL. **Segmental phonology** analyses speech into DISCRETE segments, such as phonemes; **suprasegmental** or **non-segmental phonology** analyses those features which extend over more than one segment, such as INTONATION CONTOURS. Another distinction is made between DIACHRONIC and SYNCHRONIC phonology, the former studying patterns of sound change in the history of language, the latter studying sound patterns regardless of the processes of historical change. **Experimental phonology** aims to integrate research in experimental phonetics, experimental psychology and phonological theory to provide a hypothesis-based investigation of phonological phenomena (of the kind which is standard in the experimental sciences).

The history of phonology is largely taken up with the development of ideas concerning the phoneme, as originally propounded in PRAGUE SCHOOL and BLOOMFIELDIAN phonological theory, and the subsequent alternative views proposed, especially in generative and PROSODIC phonology, both of which reject the concept of the phoneme. In prosodic phonology, the notions of PHONEMATIC UNIT and PROSODY are proposed. In early versions of GENERATIVE phonology, different LEVELS of REPRESENTATION (such as the SYSTEMATIC PHONEMIC and the SYSTEMATIC PHONETIC) are recognized, and an AUTONOMOUS phonemic level rejected. The purpose of the phonological component of a generative GRAMMAR is to take the output of the syntactic component and interpret it phonetically, making reference only to the SURFACE-STRUCTURE properties of the FORMATIVES involved. These surface-structure properties include a specification of the segmental (VOWEL/CONSONANT) structure of the formatives (which comes from the LEXICON), and a specification of the SYNTACTIC FEATURES involved (which comes from the syntactic RULES). The phonological rules of the component apply to the segmental representation, using the principle of the TRANSFORMATIONAL CYCLE. At the end of this cycle, all the BRACKETS marking structure have been removed, STRESSES have been assigned, and the resulting STRING of elements is represented as a set of phonetic segments (defined in terms of DISTINCTIVE features).

Recent phonological theory has been much taken up with the question of how far phonological rules can be explained in synchronic phonetic (typically, ARTICULATORY) terms, and how far other constraints (e.g. of a syntactic, MORPHOLOGICAL or historical kind) require explanations involving more abstract notions. Earlier models of 'abstract' phonology, which presented solutions involving underlying forms that are not realized on the phonetic surface, are thus opposed to models which are more 'concrete' in character. Several alternatives to traditional generative phonology have been proposed. For example, **natural phonology** stresses the importance of natural processes – a set of UNIVERSAL, OBLIGATORY, inviolable rules which govern the phonology of a language. They are said to be 'natural' because they are phonetically plausible, in terms of the properties of the VOCAL TRACT, as evidenced by their tendency to appear similarly in a wide range of languages. Natural phonological processes are held to be INNATE, and represent the CONSTRAINTS which a child has to follow when learning a language. These constraints disallow the production of all but the simplest pronunciation patterns in the first stages of development; they later have to be modified or suppressed, as the child learns to produce more advanced forms. In this approach, a distinction is drawn with 'acquired' rules, which are learned and language-specific.

Many phonological models have been proposed in recent years. They include **natural generative phonology (NGP)**, which requires that phonological rules and representations bear a direct relation to surface linguistic forms. This differs from natural phonology in certain respects (in particular, it allows less abstractness in its underlying representation). Its aim is to formulate the strongest possible (universal) constraints on phonological rules, all of which make generalizations about the surface forms of the language. **Atomic phonology** aims to specify the most limiting conditions on the application of the phonological rules; these restrictions are then taken to constitute the 'atomic rules' for phonological processes (such as DEVOICING), and variations are predicted through the use of universal principles. It is not limited to phonetic explanations, and adopts a methodology which appeals to TYPOLOGICAL investigations for determining the constraints on rules. **Metrical phonology** is an approach which emphasizes the relationship between segments, SYLLABLES and prosodic processes, such as RHYTHM and stress (see separate entry). **Autosegmental phonology** is an approach within the generative tradition in which phonological features are assigned to units larger than the segment – as in FIRTHIAN **prosodic phonology** (see separate entries). **Phonological scaling** is an abstract account of phonology which aims to determine automatically, on the basis of a universal strength scale, the behaviour of segments or segment classes in all possible structural positions. See also ARTICULATORY PHONOLOGY, DEPENDENCY PHONOLOGY, PARTICLE PHONOLOGY.

phonological space A term used in PHONOLOGY to refer to a theoretical space in which a system of phonological CONTRASTS can be thought to operate. For example, changes affecting a VOWEL SYSTEM (such as the English Great Vowel Shift) can be conceived of as operating in a space where such relations as 'above' and 'below' or 'in front of' and 'behind' are phonologically relevant.

phonostylistics see STYLISTICS

phonotactics A term used in PHONOLOGY to refer to the sequential ARRANGEMENTS (or 'tactic behaviour') of phonological units which occur in a language – what counts as a phonologically well-formed word. In English, for example, CONSONANT sequences such as /fs/ and /spm/ do not occur INITIALLY in a word, and there are many restrictions on the possible consonant+VOWEL combinations which may occur, e.g /ŋ/ occurs only after some short vowels /ɪ, æ, ʌ, ɒ/. These 'sequential constraints' can be stated in terms of 'phonotactic RULES'. In recent phonological theory, 'generative phonotactics' is the view that no phonological principles can refer to morphological structure; any phonological patterns which are sensitive to morphology (e.g. affixation) are represented only in the morphological component of the grammar, not in the phonology.

phrasal verb A type of VERB consisting of a SEQUENCE of a LEXICAL element plus one or more PARTICLES e.g. *come in, get up, look out for*. Subtypes may be distinguished on SYNTACTIC grounds (for instance, the particles may be classified into PREPOSITIONAL or ADVERBIAL types), and the definition of 'phrasal' varies somewhat within different descriptions. But the overall syntactic and SEMANTIC unity of these sequences is readily demonstrable, using TRANSFORMATIONAL and SUBSTITUTION criteria (cf. *She* ***got up*** *at six/She* ***rose*** *at six/What time did she* ***get up****?*, etc.).

phrase (phrasal) A term used in GRAMMATICAL analysis to refer to a single ELEMENT of STRUCTURE typically containing more than one WORD, and lacking the SUBJECT-PREDICATE structure typical of CLAUSES. Traditionally, it is seen as part of a structural HIERARCHY, falling between clause and word, several types being distinguished, e.g. 'ADVERB phrase' (e.g. *very slowly, . . .*), 'ADJECTIVAL phrase' (e.g. *the house, old and derelict,* . . .), 'PREPOSITIONAL phrase' (e.g. *in the morning,* . . .). In GENERATIVE grammar, the term has a broader function, being used as part of a general characterization of the initial stage of analysis (PHRASE-STRUCTURE GRAMMAR, PHRASE-MARKER, PROJECTION) and of the analytic units involved (NOUN phrase, VERB phrase). In recent GOVERNMENT-BINDING THEORY, clauses are a special kind of phrase, as CP=S′ and IP=S. See also DETERMINER, *WH*-.

phrase-marker (PM) A term used in GENERATIVE LINGUISTICS to refer to the STRUCTURAL REPRESENTATION of SENTENCES in terms of a LABELLED BRACKETING, as ASSIGNED by the RULES of the GRAMMAR. Phrase-markers EXPLICITLY specify the HIERARCHICAL structure of sentences, at the various stages of their DERIVATION, and analyse them into a LINEAR SEQUENCE of MORPHEMES, or FORMATIVES. They are usually presented in the form of a TREE diagram.

phrase-structure (PS) grammar A type of GRAMMAR discussed by Noam CHOMSKY in his book *Syntactic Structures* (1957) as an illustration of a GENERATIVE DEVICE. Phrase-structure grammars contain RULES (**PS-rules**) which are capable not only of generating STRINGS of LINGUISTIC ELEMENTS, but also of providing a CONSTITUENT analysis of the strings, and hence more information than FINITE-STATE GRAMMARS. They are not, however, as POWERFUL as TRANSFORMATIONAL grammars, as the latter are more capable of displaying certain types of INTUITIVE relationship between SENTENCES, and may ultimately be demonstrable as SIMPLER. In a related sense, the 'phrase-structure COMPONENT' of a transformational grammar specifies the HIERARCHICAL structure of a sentence, the linear sequence of its constituents, and indirectly (through the notion of DOMINANCE) some types of SYNTACTIC RELATIONS.

The main difference between the phrase-structure grammars (PSGs) of Chomsky as opposed to the IMMEDIATE-CONSTITUENT analysis of earlier linguists is that Chomsky's MODEL is FORMALIZED as a system of generative rules, and aims to avoid the emphasis on DISCOVERY PROCEDURES characteristic of the earlier approach. In their original formulation, PSGs took the form of a set of REWRITE RULES (with the abbreviations expanded here), such as:

Sentence → Noun Phrase+Verb Phrase
Verb Phrase → Verb+Noun Phrase
Noun Phrase → Determiner+Noun

Various distinctions have been made in the classification of phrase-structure grammars, of which the main division is into **context-free** and **context-sensitive** types: a grammar consisting wholly of context-free rules (rules which are of the form 'Rewrite X as Y', i.e. regardless of CONTEXT) is much less powerful than a grammar containing context-sensitive rules (rules which are of the form 'Rewrite X as Y in the context of Z'). In recent linguistic theory several approaches to syntax have been developed which are equivalent to PSGs, but do not employ PS rules, and are thus able to capture generalizations missed by ordinary PSGs. Examples include GENERALIZED PHRASE-STRUCTURE GRAMMAR and HEAD-DRIVEN PHRASE-STRUCTURE GRAMMAR. The MINIMALIST PROGRAMME introduces a major simplification of the notion ('bare phrase structure').

phylogeny (phylogene-tic, -sis) The application of this general term in LINGUISTICS refers to the historical (or DIACHRONIC) development and decay of LANGUAGE in SPEECH communities, or as represented in historical TEXTS. The term contrasts with ONTOGENY, for the study of development in the individual, as carried on in language ACQUISITION.

phylum see FAMILY

pidgin(ize) A term used in SOCIOLINGUISTICS to refer to a LANGUAGE with a markedly reduced GRAMMATICAL STRUCTURE, LEXICON and STYLISTIC range, compared with other languages, and which is the native language of no one. Structures which have been reduced in this way are said to be 'pidginized'. Pidgins are formed by two mutually unintelligible SPEECH communities attempting to communicate, each successively approximating to the more obvious features of the other's language. Such developments need considerable motivation on the part of the speakers, and it is therefore not surprising that **pidgin languages** flourish in areas of economic development, as in the pidgins based on English, French, Spanish and Portuguese, in the East and West Indies, Africa and the Americas. Pidgins become CREOLIZED when they become the mother-tongue of a community.

pied piping A term used in GENERATIVE LINGUISTICS for one of the PROCESSES involved in DERIVING such SENTENCES as *To whom did you turn for help?*: the PREPOSITION OPTIONALLY moves to the front of the CLAUSE, following its *WH*-NOUN phrase OBJECT – just as, the analogy suggests, the rats in the traditional tale followed the Pied Piper out of Hamelin. A contrast can be drawn with cases where the preposition is left behind (STRANDED), as in *Who did you turn to for help?*.

pitch The attribute of auditory sensation in terms of which a sound may be ordered on a scale from 'low' to 'high'. It is an AUDITORY PHONETIC feature, corresponding to some degree with the acoustic feature of FREQUENCY, which in the study of speech is based upon the number of complete cycles of vibration of the VOCAL CORDS. Frequency is measured in hertz (Hz), e.g. 440 Hz = 440 cps (cycles per second). The frequency of a sound can be determined automatically using a 'FUNDAMENTAL FREQUENCY analyser', or **pitch meter**. There is however no direct or parallel correlation between pitch and frequency: other factors than frequency may affect our sensation of pitch (measured in units known as *mels*). Variations of pitch are more easily produced using VOICED sounds, because of their regular wave-form. It is, however, possible to hear pitch contrasts in voiceless sounds; and, even in whispered speech, impressions of FALLING, RISING, etc., pitches can be heard, reflecting the changing configurations of the VOCAL TRACT.

The linguistic use of pitch is of particular interest to the PHONOLOGIST, and this is studied under the headings of INTONATION and TONE. However, the term **pitch accent** is used phonologically in the description of tone languages in which the distribution of tone within words is highly restricted (as in Japanese). The notion has also been applied to English, where some phonological models analyse intonation CONTOURS as a sequence of one or more pitch accents, each associated with a STRESS-prominent SYLLABLE in a word.

pivot A term introduced into language ACQUISITION studies of the 1960s, to refer to a primitive WORD-CLASS thought to characterize the early two-word combinations produced by children. Analysis of these combinations suggested that children used a few words very frequently, and in a fixed position, e.g. *my daddy, my car, my drink; shoe gone, car gone*, etc. These common elements were seen as 'pivots' on which the rest of a SENTENCE (the 'OPEN-class' word) depended, the STRUCTURE of the whole SENTENCE being seen as either Pivot+ Open or Open+Pivot. This analysis is no longer popular, for several reasons (e.g. it fails to relate to the analysis of adult grammatical structures, ignores the SEMANTIC structure of such sentences, and seems to apply to only certain types of sentence in certain children).

place (of articulation) One of the main parameters used in the PHONETIC classification of speech sounds, referring to where in the vocal apparatus a sound is produced. It is usual to represent this parameter horizontally, though as a result this dimension does omit some of the variations which can only be identified transversely, e.g. whether one or both sides of the tongue is involved in an ARTICULATION (see LATERAL). The conventionally recognized places or 'points' of articulation for CONSONANTS correspond to main anatomical divisions, viz. LABIAL, LABIO-DENTAL, DENTAL, ALVEOLAR, PALATAL, VELAR, UVULAR, PHARYNGEAL, GLOTTAL, but other places relative to these are also recognized, such as POST-alveolar and RETROFLEX. The analogous traditional classification of VOWELS is made in terms of AUDITORY criteria, using the horizontal scale of FRONT and BACK, and the vertical scale of CLOSE and OPEN; but because of the lack of a clear anatomical correlate it has been less usual to talk about vowels in terms of articulatory 'places' or 'points', except in a loose way. However, the notion of place, for both consonants and vowels, has come to the fore in recent (NON-LINEAR) phonological models, where a specific **place node** may be represented in the FEATURE HIERARCHY, and used as a constituent under which consonant and vowel (or vowel-like) features are organized. For example, some ARTICULATOR-BASED models recognize a place node (with no phonetic content) for CONSTRICTION location, represented by **C-place** for consonants and **V-place** for VOCOIDS. Some approaches also characterize segments which lack oral articulatory targets as **placeless**: examples would be glottal stop, schwa, and [h]. See also GESTURE.

plain One of the features of sound set up by JAKOBSON and Halle in their DISTINCTIVE FEATURE theory of PHONOLOGY, to handle variations in MANNER OF ARTICULATION, its opposite being FLAT OR SHARP, depending on the contrast involved. 'Plain' is defined articulatorily and ACOUSTICALLY: in contrast to flat, it refers to sounds involving a relatively wide mouth opening, and a relatively strong high-frequency component of the sound spectrum, as in sounds lacking lip-ROUNDING; in contrast to sharp, it refers to sounds lacking any PALATALIZATION feature.

plane (planar) A term used for an autonomous dimension of structural REPRESENTATION in some models of NON-LINEAR PHONOLOGY and MORPHOLOGY. Several derived notions are found in planar phonology. **Planar segregation** permits units to be on separate planes under specified conditions: for example, CONSONANT and VOWEL features can be located on independent phonological planes (so that the relation of [LABIAL] in a consonant to C-PLACE would define a different plane from that of [labial] in a vowel to V-place). **Plane** (or **planar**) **conflation** combines two planes into a single level of representation. **Plane copying** transfers information from one plane to another.

planning see LANGUAGE

plateauing A term used in AUTOSEGMENTAL PHONOLOGY for a type of RULE in which a sequence of high–low–high VOWELS is changed to high–high–high. The rule applies regardless of whether the sequence appears in the same WORD or in separate words.

pleonastic pronoun The use of a PRONOUN which has no NOUN REFERENCE, as seen in ***It** seems that Mary has left* or ***It**'s raining*. The term is derived from the traditional language of usage criticism, where a **pleonasm** was seen as a species of tautology – the use of more words than is strictly necessary to convey a particular sense.

plereme (1) A term used by some LINGUISTS to refer to the minimal UNITS of MEANING in COMPONENTIAL SEMANTIC analysis – what are often called 'semantic FEATURES' or 'semantic COMPONENTS'. In GLOSSEMATICS, the term refers to the minimal unit of meaningful EXPRESSION (cf. MORPHEME).

(2) (**pleremic**) In the study of writing systems, a SIGN which denotes both MEANING and FORM; opposed to **ceneme**. Examples include Egyptian hieroglyphs and Chinese characters.

plosive (plosion) A term used in the PHONETIC classification of CONSONANT sounds on the basis of their MANNER OF ARTICULATION: it refers to a sound made when a complete CLOSURE in the VOCAL TRACT is suddenly released; the air pressure which had built up behind the closure rushes out with an explosive sound, hence the term. Examples in English are [p, b, t, d, k, g, ʔ]. 'Plosion' is the term used to refer to the outwards movement of air upon release. Plosive consonants are one type of STOP consonant. It is also possible, using a different AIRSTREAM MECHANISM than the one which produces an outwards flow of lung air, to produce plosives (IMPLOSIVES) where the air upon release moves inwards.

pluperfect see PERFECT

plurisegmental A term used by some PHONETICIANS to refer to a vocal effect which extends over more than one sound SEGMENT in an UTTERANCE, such as an INTONATION CONTOUR. The term SUPRASEGMENTAL is more widely used.

plus juncture see JUNCTURE

PM An abbreviation sometimes used in GENERATIVE LINGUISTICS, standing for PHRASE-MARKER.

pneumotachograph In PHONETICS, an instrument which measures air flow from mouth and nose independently and simultaneously, as part of the technique of AEROMETRY. A face mask is placed over the nose and mouth, and separate meters monitor the air flow.

poetics A term used in LINGUISTICS to refer to the application of linguistic theory and method to the analysis of poetry. However, some linguists (such as Roman JAKOBSON) have given the term a broader interpretation, including within the 'poetic function' of LANGUAGE any aesthetic or creative linguistic use of the spoken or written MEDIUM. See also ETHNOPOETICS.

polarity (1) A term used by some LINGUISTS for the SYSTEM of POSITIVE/NEGATIVE CONTRASTIVITY found in a LANGUAGE. The distinction between 'positive' and 'negative polarity' may be expressed SYNTACTICALLY (e.g. *not* in English), MORPHOLOGICALLY (e.g. *happy v. unhappy*) or LEXICALLY (e.g. *high v. low*).

(2) A term sometimes used in the study of TONE languages, referring to cases where a tone is always opposite that of a preceding or following tone (**tonal polarity**).

politeness phenomena In SOCIOLINGUISTICS and PRAGMATICS, a term which characterizes linguistic features mediating norms of social behaviour, in relation to such notions as courtesy, rapport, deference and distance. Such features include the use of special DISCOURSE markers (*please*), appropriate tones of voice, and acceptable forms of ADDRESS (e.g. the choice of intimate *v.* distant PRONOUNS, or of first *v.* last names).

poly- see MONO-, and POLY- entries below

polygenesis see MONOGENESIS

polylectal A term used by some SOCIOLINGUISTS to refer to a proposed MODEL of GRAMMAR which would account for many of the VARIETIES (LECTS) of LANGUAGE used by the individual (and, by extension, in the community as a whole). The contrast intended is with grammars which ignore regional and social variations, and which analyse language as if it were in a hypothetical homogeneous state. A further contrast can be drawn with a PANLECTAL grammar, in which *all* varieties would be taken into account.

polysemy (polysem-ia, -ic, -ous) A term used in SEMANTIC analysis to refer to a LEXICAL ITEM which has a range of different MEANINGS, e.g. *plain* = 'clear', 'unadorned', 'obvious' . . .; opposed to **monosemy** (or **univocality**). A large proportion of a language's vocabulary is **polysemic** (or **polysemous**). The theoretical problem for the LINGUIST is how to distinguish polysemy or **polysemia** (one FORM – several meanings) from HOMONYMY (two lexical items which happen to have the same PHONOLOGICAL form). Several criteria have been suggested, such as ETYMOLOGY (the antecedents of homonymous items would be formally distinct) and the closeness of the relationship between the meanings in question (the meanings of homonymous items would be further apart, or unrelated – cf. the related sense of *plain* above with the homonyms *plane* = 'carpenter's tool' and *plane* = 'aeroplane'). But all such criteria involve analytic problems, and the distinction between polysemy and homonymy thus remains a source of theoretical discussion in LINGUISTICS.

polysyllable (polysyllabic) A term used in PHONETICS and PHONOLOGY to refer to a WORD consisting of more than one SYLLABLE. 'Polysyllabic' or 'multisyllabic' words are contrasted with MONOSYLLABLES.

polysynthetic A type of LANGUAGE sometimes distinguished in COMPARATIVE LIN-

GUISTICS using STRUCTURAL (as opposed to DIACHRONIC) criteria, and focusing on the characteristics of the WORD: 'polysynthetic' or 'incorporating' languages demonstrate MORPHOLOGICALLY complex, long word-forms, as in the constructions typical of many American Indian languages, and encountered occasionally in English, in coinages such as *anti/dis/establish/ment/arian/ism/s*. The term is opposed to SYNTHETIC and ANALYTIC type languages. Some linguists, however, prefer to see such constructions handled as a complex of AGGLUTINATIVE and FUSIONAL characteristics, and do not regard this category of language as typologically distinct. As always in such classifications, the categories are not clear-cut: different languages will display the characteristic of 'polysynthesis' to a greater or lesser degree.

polysystemic(ism) A term used to identify an approach to LINGUISTIC analysis proposed by J. R. FIRTH, in which different linguistic SYSTEMS are set up at different places in STRUCTURE, no attempt being made to identify the systems with each other. The approach has been developed primarily in relation to PHONOLOGY, where it is known as PROSODIC analysis. 'Polysystemic' is opposed to 'monosystemic', as in phonemic theories of phonology, where a single basic phonological unit is used (the PHONEME), and the set of phonemes is seen as a single system of CONTRASTS, applicable to the analysis and TRANSCRIPTION of LINEAR SEQUENCES of speech sounds, regardless of the GRAMMATICAL or LEXICAL structures involved. In polysystemicism, on the other hand, different phonological systems are set up as required at different places in the structure of SYLLABLES, WORDS and other UNITS, and within different areas of the vocabulary or grammar. There is little emphasis on transcription, and a correspondingly greater emphasis on relating phonology to other levels of linguistic structure. In this approach, the set of sounds needed to define the contrastive possibilities at the beginning of words in a language may be quite different from those required in the middle or at the end of words. There is little evidence of the need for this analysis in English (apart from occasional contrasts such as /ŋ/ and /h/, which do not occur in the same ENVIRONMENTS), but several languages, such as many in South-East Asia, have been fruitfully analysed in these terms.

popular etymology see ETYMOLOGY

portmanteau A term used in MORPHOLOGICAL analysis referring to cases where a single morph can be analysed into more than one MORPHEME, as in French *au*, *aux*, etc. (= **à le*, **à les*, 'to the').

Port Royal The name given to a group of seventeenth-century scholars, based at the convent of Port Royal, south of Versailles, who, following the ideas of Descartes, developed a view of LANGUAGE in which grammatical CATEGORIES and STRUCTURES were seen as relatable to UNIVERSAL logical patterns of thought (an influential work was the *Grammaire générale et raisonnée* of C. Lancelot, A. Arnauld and others, published in 1660). The ideas of this school of thought became widely known in the 1960s, when CHOMSKY drew certain parallels between them and his own conception of the relationship between LANGUAGE and mind.

position(al) (1) A term used in LINGUISTICS to refer to the FUNCTIONALLY

CONTRASTIVE places within a linguistic UNIT, e.g. PHONEMES within the SYLLABLE or WORD, MORPHEMES within the word, words within the SENTENCE. It is common to talk of ELEMENTS occurring in INITIAL, MEDIAL or FINAL 'positions' within the higher-order unit. A 'positional variant' refers to the FORMAL variations introduced into a linguistic unit (usually a phoneme or morpheme) because of the CONDITIONING influence of its linguistic CONTEXT. See also ARGUMENT.

(2) In phonetics, the term is used to refer to the arrangement of the VOCAL ORGANS during the ARTICULATION of a sound: the various articulators (lips, TONGUE, etc.) are said to be in certain positions, based on their PLACE and MANNER OF ARTICULATION.

positional mobility A term often used in GRAMMAR to refer to a defining property of the WORD, seen as a grammatical UNIT. The criterion states that the CONSTITUENT elements of complex words are not capable of rearrangement (e.g. *unsuccessful* cannot vary to produce *full-un-success*, etc.), thus contrasting with the way words themselves are mobile in SENTENCES, i.e. they can occur in many contrasting positions.

positive (1) A term used in GRAMMATICAL description to refer to a type of SENTENCE or VERB which has no marker of negation, i.e. it is expressing an assertion. The positive or AFFIRMATIVE 'pole' of this contrast is opposed to NEGATIVE, and the grammatical system involved is often referred to under the heading of POLARITY.

(2) The UNMARKED term in the three-way grammatical description of ADJECTIVES and ADVERBS into DEGREES, specifying the extent of their application. The positive or 'absolute' degree implies no comparative quality, and contrasts with such terms as COMPARATIVE and SUPERLATIVE. In English, the adjective with no formal MODIFICATION is used as the positive form, and this is generally the case in languages.

possession see ALIENABLE

possessive pronoun see PRONOUN

possible worlds semantics see MODEL-THEORETIC SEMANTICS

post- A PREFIX used commonly in PHONETICS and LINGUISTICS, referring to relative POSITION in a SEQUENCE; opposed to PRE-. In phonetics, it refers to an ARTICULATION a little behind a recognized PLACE OF ARTICULATION, e.g. 'post-ALVEOLAR', 'post-PALATAL'. The terms 'post-VOCALIC', 'post-CONSONANTAL', however, do not refer to points of articulation, but to sounds occurring in a specific SYLLABIC position, viz. after a VOWEL/CONSONANT respectively. In GRAMMAR, the term is found in relation to several contexts, such as POSTMODIFICATION, 'post-determiner', 'post-article', 'post-verbal', etc.

post-alveolar see POST- (1)

post-aspiration see ASPIRATION

post-creole continuum A term used in SOCIOLINGUISTICS to describe the result of a STANDARD LANGUAGE exerting an influence on a CREOLE (where both are VARIETIES of the same language). People alter their creole speech in the direction of the standard, and a whole range of varieties emerge, which form a continuum between the standard and the creole. Terms which have been devised to refer to different parts of the continuum include ACROLECT (an educated variety very close to the standard), BASILECT (the variety closest to the original creole) and MESOLECT (intermediate varieties).

post-cyclic A term used for a type of RULE recognized in the EXTENDED STANDARD THEORY of TRANSFORMATIONAL GRAMMAR, to refer to a type of transformation which applies after CYCLIC transformations have been completed. Post-cyclic rules are intended to handle such cases as INVERSION of SUBJECT and AUXILIARY VERB in INTERROGATIVE CLAUSES, where cyclic rules do not seem to apply.

post-determiner see POST- (2)

post-lexical see LEXICAL PHONOLOGY

postmodification (postmodify) A term used in some grammatical DESCRIPTIONS to refer to all the ITEMS which occur after the HEAD of a PHRASE (an ENDOCENTRIC phrase), e.g. *The cars **in the garage** are expensive.* In English, three main types of postmodifying structure are recognized: PREPOSITIONAL phrases (e.g. *the cars **in the garage** . . .*), FINITE (RELATIVE) CLAUSES (e.g. *the car **which was in the garage** . . .*) and non-finite (INFINITIVE or PARTICIPIAL) clauses, e.g. *the car **parked in the street** . . ., the car **to buy** . . .*

postposition (postpose) A term used in the grammatical classification of WORDS, referring to the CLOSED set of items which follow NOUN phrases (or single nouns or PRONOUNS) to form a single CONSTITUENT of structure. The analogous construction in English involves PREPOSITIONS. Many languages make regular use of postpositions, e.g. Japanese, Hindi. The word *ago* (e.g. *two years ago*) is also sometimes classified as a postposition.

post-structuralism see LOGOCENTRISM

postulates An application in LINGUISTICS of the general use of this term in the branch of logic known as axiomatics. It refers to a set of initial PROPOSITIONS which a theory assumes to be true; these initial statements, and subsequent deductions made from them, are collectively known as the 'postulational method' (cf. AXIOMATIC). In linguistics, several 'sets of postulates' have been proposed, in attempts to systematize ideas about LANGUAGE, the best known being those propounded by the American linguists Leonard BLOOMFIELD (in 1926) and Bernard Bloch (in 1948).

potential pause A term often used in GRAMMAR to refer to a defining property of the WORD, seen as a grammatical UNIT. The criterion states that, in normal speech, PAUSES are not introduced within the STRUCTURE of the word but are always possible (and often present) at word boundaries.

power(ful) A term used in the formal evaluation of GRAMMARS, and particularly found in discussion of GENERATIVE theories. Basically, grammar A would be said to be more powerful than grammar B if it can generate more LANGUAGES (SENTENCES, etc.) than B. A further distinction is often introduced, between 'weak' and 'strong' generative power. In the notion of 'weak' generative power, a grammar (or RULE, or set of rules, etc.) is said to be more powerful than another if it GENERATES more grammatical sentences. In the notion of 'strong' generative power, a grammar is said to be more powerful if it assigns to these sentences a set of STRUCTURAL DESCRIPTIONS which more satisfactorily shows their relationships. It is important, however, that a grammar should not become too powerful, in the sense that it generates sentences which are ungrammatical, structural descriptions which are intuitively implausible, or a characterization of natural language that is too broad (e.g. including features of non-language systems). FORMAL constraints therefore have to be built into grammatical MODELS to restrict the power of grammars in specific ways, and much current discussion is focused on this subject.

pr An abbreviation sometimes used for PREPOSITION.

pragmalinguistics A term sometimes used within the study of PRAGMATICS, to refer to the study of LANGUAGE use from the viewpoint of a language's STRUCTURAL resources; it contrasts with those pragmatic studies which examine the conditions on language use which derive from the social SITUATION (sometimes referred to as SOCIOPRAGMATICS). The former approach might begin with the PRONOUN system of a language, and examine the way in which people choose different forms to express a range of attitudes and relationships (such as deference and intimacy). The latter approach might begin with the social backgrounds of the participants in an INTERACTION, and examine the way in which different factors (such as age, sex, class) lead people to choose particular pronouns.

pragmatics A term traditionally used to label one of the three major divisions of SEMIOTICS (along with SEMANTICS and SYNTACTICS). In modern LINGUISTICS, it has come to be applied to the study of LANGUAGE from the point of view of the users, especially of the choices they make, the CONSTRAINTS they encounter in using language in social interaction, and the effects their use of language has on the other participants in an act of communication. The field focuses on an 'area' between semantics, SOCIOLINGUISTICS, and EXTRALINGUISTIC CONTEXT; but the boundaries with these other domains are as yet incapable of precise definition. At present, no coherent pragmatic theory has been achieved, mainly because of the variety of topics it has to account for – including aspects of DEIXIS, conversational IMPLICATURES, PRESUPPOSITIONS, SPEECH ACTS and DISCOURSE structure. Partly as a consequence of the potentially vast scope of the subject, several conflicting definitions have arisen. In a narrow linguistic view, pragmatics deals only with those aspects of context which are FORMALLY encoded in the STRUCTURE of a language; they would be part of a user's **pragmatic competence**. At the opposite extreme, it has been defined as the study of those aspects of meaning not covered by a semantic theory. In this connection, some semanticists see the subject as contrasting with TRUTH-CONDITIONAL SEMANTICS: it is suggested that the difficulties which arise in relation to the latter (e.g. how to handle the notion of presupposition) are more readily explicable with reference to pragmatics. More inclusively, it has been characterized as the study of the principles and practice of conversational PERFORMANCE – this including all aspects of language USAGE, understanding and APPROPRIATENESS. Especial attention has been paid to the range of **pragmatic particles** which are found in speech (e.g. *you know, I mean, sort of,* TAG questions) which play an important role in controlling the pragmatic nature of an interaction.

Several derivative terms have been proposed in order to classify the wide range of subject-matter involved. **Pragmalinguistics** has been used by some to refer to the more linguistic 'end' of pragmatics, wherein one studies these matters from the viewpoint of the structural resources available in a language. **Sociopragmatics**, by contrast, studies the way conditions on language use derive from the social situation. **General pragmatics** is the study of the principles governing the communicative use of language, especially as encountered in conversations – principles which may be studied as putative UNIVERSALS, or restricted to the study of specific languages. **Literary pragmatics** applies pragmatic notions (especially to do with NARRATIVE) to the production and reception of literary texts. **Applied pragmatics** focuses on problems of interaction that arise in contexts where successful communication is critical, such as medical interviews, judicial settings, counselling, and foreign language teaching.

Prague School The name given to the views and methods of the Linguistic Circle of Prague and the scholars it influenced. The circle was founded in 1926 by Vilém Mathesius (1882–1946), a professor of English at Caroline University, and included such LINGUISTS as Roman JAKOBSON and Nikolai Trubetskoy (1890–1938). The 'Praguean' influence has been widespread and long-lasting, as the frequent reference to it throughout this dictionary testifies. Its main emphasis lay on the analysis of LANGUAGE as a SYSTEM of FUNCTIONALLY related UNITS, an emphasis which showed SAUSSUREAN influence. In particular, it led to the distinction between the PHONETIC and the PHONOLOGICAL analysis of sounds, the analysis of the PHONEME into DISTINCTIVE FEATURES, and such associated notions as BINARITY, MARKING and MORPHOPHONEMICS. Since the 1950s, Prague School ideas have been received and developed, particularly with reference to the SYNTAX, SEMANTICS and STYLISTICS of English and Slavonic languages, and illustrated in the work of Josef Vachek (b. 1909), Jan Firbas (b. 1921) and others. Of particular note here is the formulation of a theory of FUNCTIONAL SENTENCE PERSPECTIVE, wherein sentence analysis is seen as a complex of functionally contrastive CONSTITUENTS. A representative reader is J. Vachek (ed.), *A Prague School Reader in Linguistics* (1964), but the early book by Trubetskoy, *Grundzüge der Phonologie* (1939), translated in 1969 as *Principles of Phonology*, is seminal.

pre- A PREFIX used commonly in PHONETICS and LINGUISTICS, referring to relative POSITION in a SEQUENCE; opposed to POST-. In phonetics, it usually refers to an ARTICULATION a little in front of a recognized PLACE OF ARTICULATION, e.g. 'pre-PALATAL', 'pre-VELAR'. The terms 'pre-VOCALIC', 'pre-CONSONANTAL', however, do not refer to points of articulation, but to sounds occurring in a specific SYLLABIC position, viz. before a VOWEL/CONSONANT respectively; 'pre-head' has a similar force within the TONE GROUP; 'pre-ASPIRATION' and 'pre-NASALIZATION' illustrate temporal uses of the term. In LINGUISTICS, the term is found in relation to several GRAMMATICAL contexts, such as PREDETERMINER, 'pre-article', 'pre-verbal', PRE-LEXICAL, PRELINGUISTIC, PREMODIFICATION – and, of course, PREPOSITION.

precede(nce) A term used in GENERATIVE LINGUISTICS to refer to a type of relationship between pairs of NODES in a PHRASE-MARKER. One node 'precedes' another when it occurs anywhere to the left of the other in the phrase-marker: if it occurs immediately to the left of a node X, the node 'immediately precedes' X. In GENERALIZED PHRASE-STRUCTURE GRAMMAR, **linear precedence rules** take the form X < Y (i.e. X must precede Y). The 'horizontal' relationship of precedence should be distinguished from the 'vertical' relationship between nodes, known as DOMINANCE.

predeterminer A term used in some MODELS of grammatical DESCRIPTION, referring to a CLASS of ITEMS which occur before a DETERMINER in the NOUN PHRASE, e.g. *all/both/half* in *all the people*, etc.

predicate (predicat-ion, -ive, -or) (1) A term in the analysis of GRAMMATICAL FUNCTIONS, to refer to a major CONSTITUENT of SENTENCE structure, traditionally associated with a two-part analysis in which all obligatory constituents other than the SUBJECT are considered together. For example, *Sue walked/Sue kicked the ball/Sue went on holiday* . . . would all be seen as Subject (*Sue*)+Predicate constructions. These sentences would also be labelled 'predicative' in a classification of EXOCENTRIC constructions. There are several points of contact here with the philosophical analysis of propositions in terms of **predication** (i.e. properties being 'predicated' of entities), and recent linguistic discussion has focused on the extent to which there are parallels between the SYNTACTIC and the SEMANTIC dimensions of analysis (using such distinctions as GIVEN/NEW and TOPIC/COMMENT). Parallels between the syntactic and semantic dimensions of the analysis have been one of the central areas of interest in recent GOVERNMENT-BINDING THEORY. The focus has been on VERBLESS subject–predicate constructions, as in *Martha considers **Mary intelligent***. The mainstream analysis involves the assumption that *Mary intelligent* is a constituent, the so-called SMALL CLAUSE. (The category label of this constituent is a subject of controversy.) A rival analysis (the so-called PREDICATION THEORY) holds that *Mary* and *intelligent* are two separate constituents.

In FUNCTIONAL GRAMMAR, the term has a central status: here, a predicate is taken to be the basic element of a predication; it is listed in the LEXICON in the form of a **predicate frame**, from which **nuclear predications** are formed by inserting appropriate terms into the ARGUMENT positions. **Full predications** are then formed from NUCLEAR predications through the use of SATELLITES (e.g. MANNER, LOCATIVE).

At a more detailed level, in syntax, distinctions are sometimes made between **predicative** and 'non-predicative' functions of words; e.g. the ADJECTIVE in *the house is **big*** is predicative, whereas in *the **big** house* it is ATTRIBUTIVE. However, terminology varies a great deal here, depending on the model of description used. The term **predicator** has also been suggested by some theorists to refer to the verbal element in Subject–Verb–Object constructions, viz. Subject–Predicator–Object, on the grounds that this avoids using 'verb' in both a functional and a FORMAL sense (cf. 'a subject may have a noun as its exponent' with the undesirability of 'a verb may have a verb as its exponent').

(2) The term is also used in linguistics, where notions from the logical system of **predicate calculus** are sometimes used as a framework for aspects of

GRAMMATICAL and SEMANTIC analysis. A logical calculus presents a set of logical laws or truths in systematic deductive form: in predicate calculus, rules for representing the internal structure of simple PROPOSITIONS (especially for handling QUANTIFICATION) are presented (usually axiomatically) in a FORMAL notation. A 'predicate' is that term in a proposition which provides information about the individual or entity, e.g. *the car is* ***stolen/big/beautiful*** . . . : it is seen as a device whereby simple propositions can be formed out of names. A simple proposition is then said to be a FUNCTION of its component name(s), the name(s) being its ARGUMENT(s). The terms 'one-place/two-place, etc., predicates' are then used, depending on the number of arguments contained within the proposition; e.g. *Jules saw Jim* is a two-place predicate, *Jules* and *Jim* being arguments of the predicate *saw*. MODELS based on this principle are used in several linguistic theories, e.g. CASE GRAMMAR, DEPENDENCY GRAMMAR.

predication theory A sub-theory of some versions of GOVERNMENT-BINDING THEORY, whose central principle is that a PREDICATE requires a SUBJECT. This accounts for the obligatory occurrence of expletive or DUMMY *it* in sentences like *It's raining* and *It's possible that John is ill.* Not only VERB PHRASES but expressions like *drunk* in *John arrived drunk* are regarded as predicates in this context.

prefabricated language see FORMULAIC LANGUAGE

prefix(-ing, -ation) A term used in MORPHOLOGY referring to an AFFIX which is added initially to a ROOT or STEM. The process of **prefixation** is common in English, for forming new LEXICAL items (e.g. *para-, mini-, un-*), but English does not INFLECT words using prefixes. Languages which do inflect in this way include German (e.g. the *ge-* of PERFECTIVE forms), Greek, and many American Indian languages (e.g. the Athapaskan family).

prehodiernal see HODIERNAL

pre-lexical A term used in some MODELS of GENERATIVE GRAMMAR (cf. ASPECTS) to refer to the first stage in a two-stage generation of DEEP STRUCTURES. In this stage PHRASE-MARKERS are generated in which the TERMINAL NODES are expressed as a △ (DELTA) ELEMENT. In the second stage, LEXICAL ITEMS are inserted into these positions, in the form of COMPLEX SYMBOLS (i.e. 'lexical TRANSFORMATIONS').

prelinguistic(s) (1) A term used by some linguists, especially in the 1950s, to refer to the ARTICULATORY and ACOUSTIC study of sound, as opposed to the strictly LINGUISTIC studies of PHONOLOGY, etc. (MICROLINGUISTICS). In this frame of reference, it was seen as a branch of MACROLINGUISTICS. The term 'prelinguistic' is sometimes used outside this framework to refer to any construct which needs to be taken into account as a preliminary consideration before linguistic analysis proceeds, e.g. the obtaining of adequate DATA samples.

(2) In the study of PERFORMANCE MODELS of language, the term has also been used with reference to hypothetical stages in SPEECH PRODUCTION which precede those involved with language organization. Psychological factors, such as cognitive awareness and attention, could be seen as prelinguistic in this sense.

(3) In language ACQUISITION, the period immediately preceding the emergence of linguistic patterning in children's VOCALIZATION is considered a 'prelinguistic' stage of development, viz. much of the second half of the first year of life.

premodification (premodify) A term used in some MODELS of GRAMMATICAL description to refer to all the ITEMS which occur before the HEAD of a PHRASE (an ENDOCENTRIC phrase). e.g. ***All those big red foreign*** *cars have been sold.* DETERMINERS and ADJECTIVES are the main CLASSES occurring in premodifying position in English, but there are several other categories involved in the full description of this complex area, e.g. QUANTIFIERS, INTENSIFIERS.

prep An abbreviation sometimes used for PREPOSITION.

preparatory conditions see FELICITY CONDITIONS

preparatory *it* see ANTICIPATORY (3)

prepose A term used in GENERATIVE GRAMMAR to refer to the MOVEMENT of a CONSTITUENT to a POSITION earlier in the SENTENCE, e.g. an ADVERB is preposed in ***Yesterday*** *I bought a bike;* a verb is preposed in *I thought they'd be complaining, and* ***complaining*** *they were.* See also *WH*-.

preposition(al) (pr, prep) A term used in the GRAMMATICAL classification of WORDS, referring to the set of ITEMS which typically precede NOUN PHRASES (often single nouns or PRONOUNS), to form a single CONSTITUENT of STRUCTURE. The resulting **prepositional phrase** (**PP**) (or **prepositional group**) can then be described in terms of DISTRIBUTION (e.g. their use following a noun, as in *the man* ***in the corner***) or SEMANTICALLY (e.g. the expression of possession, direction, place). Prepositional sequences of the type illustrated by *in accordance with* are often called **complex prepositions.** POSTpositions refer to structures where a PARTICLE, similar in function to a preposition, is placed after a noun, as in Japanese. Many linguists subscribe to a broader view of prepositions. To form a prepositional phrase, prepositions can combine not only with an NP but also a PP (e.g. *since before breakfast*), a CLAUSE (e.g. *since they finished their breakfast*) or nothing (e.g. *I haven't seen him since*). In this account, it is possible to talk of 'TRANSITIVE' and 'intransitive' prepositions.

prerequisites A term used in LINGUISTICS to refer to the concepts on which an analysis at a specific linguistic LEVEL depends. Its main application is in the context of PHONOLOGICAL PROCEDURES, where the American STRUCTURALIST view of the 1940s – that phonological analysis should proceed solely on the basis of PHONETIC criteria – came to be opposed by a view which stressed the importance of 'GRAMMATICAL prerequisites' – the PRESUPPOSITIONS about the identity of such notions as WORD and SENTENCE which had to be made before techniques such as the MINIMAL PAIR test could be used.

prescriptive (prescriptiv-ism, -ist) A term used by LINGUISTS to characterize any approach which attempts to lay down RULES of CORRECTNESS as to how LANGUAGE should be used. Using such criteria as purity, logic, history or literary excellence, **prescriptivism** aims to preserve imagined standards by insisting on NORMS of USAGE and criticizing departures from these norms. **Prescriptive grammars** of English include such recommendations as: *I* should be used after the VERB *be*, e.g. *It is I; whom* should be used as the RELATIVE PRONOUN in OBJECT FUNCTION, e.g. *the man whom I saw*; and so on. A distinction is sometimes made between prescriptive and PROSCRIPTIVE rules, the latter being rules which forbid rather than command. Linguistics has been generally critical of the **prescriptivist** approach, emphasizing instead the importance of DESCRIPTIVELY accurate studies of usage, and of the need to take into account SOCIOLINGUISTIC variation in explaining attitudes to language. More recently, there has been interest in studying prescriptivism objectively, as a sociocultural phenomenon. The term 'prescriptive' is sometimes used in sociolinguistics (e.g. the 'prescriptions' of a sociolinguistically realistic language-planning programme), but on the whole the term is pejorative in linguistic contexts.

prespecification (prespecify) In PROSODIC MORPHOLOGY, in the analysis of REDUPLICATIONS, the name given to a special type of relation between an element on the MELODIC TIER and TEMPLATE position. Invariant prior linking of a melodic element to a template position is said to supplant the RULE-governed linking of an element to the same position (i.e. the element has been 'prespecified'). The notion is not accepted in all accounts of melodic invariance.

pressure One of the features of sound set up by CHOMSKY and Halle in their DISTINCTIVE FEATURE theory of PHONOLOGY, under the heading of SUPPLEMENTARY MOVEMENTS, to handle variations in MANNER OF ARTICULATION. It refers to articulatory movements of the GLOTTIS or VELUM (cf. VELAR) where the airflow is directed outwards, as in EJECTIVES. See also STOP.

presupposition (presuppose) The philosophical uses of this term will be found in SEMANTIC discussion, viz. a condition which must be satisfied if a particular state of affairs is to obtain, or (in relation to language) what a speaker assumes in saying a particular sentence, as opposed to what is actually asserted. It is also analysed as a certain type of logical relationship between statements, contrasting with ENTAILMENT. Some linguists have come to use the term in a narrower sense, in a two-part analysis of sentences which contrasts the INFORMATION assumed (or 'presupposed') by the speaker, and that which is at the centre of the speaker's communicative interest; in this sense, 'presupposition' is opposed to FOCUS. (The contrast between GIVEN and NEW information makes an analogous distinction.) For example, in one interpretation of this notion, the sentence *Where's the salt?* is said to presuppose that the salt is not present to the speaker, that there is someone whom the speaker thinks might know where the salt is, and so on. This total study of the factors in the communicative context which affect the meaning of an utterance has attracted increasing interest from linguists in recent years, partly in SEMANTICS and partly under the heading of PRAGMATICS. Controversial aspects of analysing language in these terms abound, in particular over the extent to which the notion of presupposition can or ought to be restricted to certain kinds of logical or behaviourally demonstrable factors.

prevarication A suggested defining property of human LANGUAGE (contrasting with the properties of other SEMIOTIC SYSTEMS), referring to the way languages can be used to misinform, as in lying, irony, etc.

primary articulation see SECONDARY ARTICULATION

primitive (prime) An application in LINGUISTICS and PHONETICS of the general use of this term in scientific investigation, where certain constructs are taken as 'given' by a theory, the purpose of the theoretical exposition being to explicate them. The PROPOSITIONS which contain such undefined terms are referred to as POSTULATES or AXIOMS. Examples of terms often taken as primitive include 'utterance', 'acceptable', 'sound', 'meaningful', 'mouth', 'vocalization', 'distinctiveness', etc. – though any of these might become the focus of controversy in an investigation, and could not thereby be assumed to have primitive status. The distinction between primitive and **non-primitive** terms is of particular importance in attempts to FORMALIZE linguistic theory, and has been much discussed in GENERATIVE GRAMMAR. In early versions of this MODEL, the terms which appear in the STRUCTURAL DESCRIPTIONS of a SENTENCE are primitive, e.g. 'sentence', 'NOUN PHRASE', 'VERB phrase', '+', '→' ('REWRITE'); terms such as SUBJECT, OBJECT, SUBORDINATE, CO-ORDINATE, etc., are DERIVED or non-primitive. In X-BAR theory, noun phrases and verb phrases are not primitives: NP is a phrase headed by a noun, VP is a phrase headed by a verb, a noun is defined as [+N, −V], a verb is defined as [−N, +V], and the features N and V are primitives. In recent GOVERNMENT-BINDING THEORY, S is not a primitive, but an IP. Subject, etc. are derived notions in TRANSFORMATIONAL and PHRASE-STRUCTURE GRAMMARS, but primitives in RELATIONAL and LEXICAL FUNCTIONAL GRAMMARS.

principal parts In GRAMMAR, a TRADITIONAL term referring to the FORMS of a VERB required to determine which CONJUGATION it belongs to. The notion was important in Latin grammars, where the principal parts of *amo*, for example, included the first PERSON form of the PRESENT INDICATIVE (*amo* 'I love'), the INFINITIVE *amare* ('to love'), the first person form of the PERFECT indicative (*amavi* 'I have loved'), and the 'supine' (*amatum*), which was a type of VERBAL NOUN ('loving'). Verbs like *amo* ('first conjugation verbs') could thus be quickly distinguished from verbs belonging to other conjugations. The term is not usually found in modern LINGUISTIC analysis, but will be encountered in studies of LINGUISTIC HISTORIOGRAPHY.

principles A term used in recent GRAMMATICAL theory for grammatical statements that are much broader in their scope than ordinary RULES, such as the PROJECTION principle of GOVERNMENT-BINDING (GB) THEORY and the FOOT-feature principle of GENERALIZED PHRASE-STRUCTURE GRAMMAR. Principles are particularly important in GB, where it has been suggested that there are no rules, in the traditional sense, but only principles which can take a slightly different form in different LANGUAGES. A specification of the range of forms that a principle can take is known as a PARAMETER. The overall approach is known as the **principles and parameters** theory of UNIVERSAL grammar. See also PROJECTION.

privative (1) A type of OPPOSITION recognized in PRAGUE SCHOOL PHONOLOGY, distinguished from GRADUAL and EQUIPOLLENT. A privative opposition is a BINARY one, where one member is seen as MARKED by the presence of a FEATURE, which its opposite member lacks (i.e. it is 'unmarked'), as in the /p/ *v.* /b/ DISTINCTION in English, where the latter is seen as marked for VOICING.

(2) **(privativity)** A term used in some recent models of NON-LINEAR PHONOLOGY, notably UNDERSPECIFICATION theory, referring to a FEATURE which can take only one value; also called **monovalent** and opposed to EQUIPOLLENT. For example, the features of NASALITY, ASPIRATION, and GLOTTALIZATION have all

been proposed as privative, in that all processes which affect them (e.g. ASSIMILATION refer only to their [+] values. The extent to which privativity can be applied in the analysis of other (possibly all) features is a topic in contemporary phonological debate.

privilege of occurrence A term used in LINGUISTICS to refer to the FORMAL ENVIRONMENT in which a linguistic ITEM may be used. Items which share the same 'privileges of occurrence' belong to the same CLASS, e.g. *black, nice, big, angry*, etc., in the CONTEXT *the – dog*.

pro A term used in GOVERNMENT-BINDING THEORY for a non-ANAPHORIC NULL (phonologically EMPTY) PRONOMINAL; known also as 'little pro', to distinguish it from 'big PRO' (see following entry). Usually associated with SUBJECT position in FINITE CLAUSES in PRO-DROP LANGUAGES, it is identified through the MORPHOLOGICAL FEATURES present in the sentence.

PRO A term used in GOVERNMENT-BINDING THEORY for a BASE-generated SUBJECT of certain INFINITIVES; known also as 'big PRO', to distinguish it from 'little pro' (see previous entry). Within the GB classification of NOUN PHRASES, PRO is analysed as both a PRONOMINAL and an ANAPHOR. It can be controlled by some NP within a sentence, or have arbitrary reference: the former possibility is illustrated by *John tried PRO to please Mary*, where PRO is controlled by *John;* and the latter by *It is easy PRO to please Mary*. Constructions with PRO are known as CONTROL constructions, and are to be distinguished from RAISING constructions. Some grammarians refer to both as CATENATIVE constructions. In GENERALIZED PHRASE-STRUCTURE GRAMMAR and LEXICAL FUNCTIONAL GRAMMAR, control constructions involve a bare VP and not clauses with a PRO subject.

procedural grammar A label given to a type of NETWORK GRAMMAR which sees analysis as a set of PROCEDURES (i.e. instructions for analysing or building up a CONSTRUCTION) for interpreting what we hear – such as recognizing WORDS in TEXT, trying them out as parts of constructions, comparing them with conclusions already made, and so on.

procedural semantics see SEMANTICS

procedure A term used in LINGUISTICS referring to a particular way of arriving at a linguistic analysis or decision. Different views about the goals of a linguistic theory can be clarified by phrasing the question in terms of procedures, of which three types have attracted particular interest, since their first formulation by Noam CHOMSKY:

(a) **discovery procedure**: a technique which can be automatically or 'mechanically' applied to a sample of LANGUAGE and which would produce a CORRECT analysis. Attempts to develop such a procedure characterized the work of many BLOOMFIELDIAN linguists, and were strongly criticized in early formulations of GENERATIVE GRAMMAR. It is argued that it is never possible to identify with certainty all the factors which lead a linguist in the direction of a particular analysis. Nor is it desirable to seek such a procedure, as the analysis itself can be evaluated regardless of the means by which it was obtained.

(b) **decision procedure:** a technique which could be automatically applied to a series of grammars of a language, to decide which was the best grammar. It is suggested that such a goal is impossible, in the present state of linguistic knowledge, and that linguists must content themselves with relative and not absolute decisions, as in (c) below.

(c) **evaluation procedure:** a technique which provides criteria for choosing the better of two analyses of a set of DATA, as when it is argued that one analysis is simpler, more plausible or more elegant than another. In generative linguistics, a few (controversial) procedures have been suggested (cf. SIMPLICITY) which attempt to FORMALIZE the properties of alternative DESCRIPTIONS so that precise evaluations can be made.

process Any approach to LINGUISTIC DESCRIPTION which sees some ELEMENTS (STRUCTURES, etc.) as being the result of a change operating on some other element in the LANGUAGE. The process of change may be real (as in ATTESTED processes of DIACHRONIC change) or part of the abstract system of relationships found in a particular MODEL of description (as when plural NOUNS are derived from singulars by a process of pluralization). This notion is fundamental to the ITEM-AND-PROCESS model of linguistic description, and several important terms in contemporary linguistics reflect a process approach, e.g. DERIVATION, REWRITE RULE, BLEND and the many terms ending in *-ization*, such as LABIALIZATION, PASSIVIZATION. In PSYCHOLINGUISTICS, considerable discussion has taken place concerning the extent to which the linguistic processes encountered in a linguistic model can be related to processes of a psychological kind (cf. PERFORMANCE GRAMMAR, CORRESPONDENCE hypothesis).

processing An application in PSYCHOLINGUISTICS and NEUROLINGUISTICS of a term used in psychology for the range of activities which take place in the brain during LANGUAGE production and comprehension. Any LEVEL of language can be considered in processing terms ('lexical processing', 'phonological processing', etc.), and processing MODELS aim to represent the input/output relationship between these levels, both for speaking/listening and reading/writing. An analogous use of the term is found in COMPUTATIONAL LINGUISTICS, where it refers to the automated handling of linguistic information.

proclitic see CLITIC

pro-constituent A term used in recent GENERATIVE LINGUISTICS, usually abbreviated to PRO, and analogous to PRO-FORM in other approaches, referring to an ELEMENT which SUBSTITUTES for a LEXICAL item elsewhere in a SENTENCE. The application of the term varies, depending on the grammatical MODEL involved. In GOVERNMENT-BINDING THEORY, for example, the symbol PRO is associated with a BASE-generated SUBJECT of certain INFINITIVES.

procrastinate In the MINIMALIST PROGRAMME, a general ECONOMY constraint which states that all MOVEMENTS in a DERIVATION should be delayed as long as possible. An operation should take place only when it is needed, and not before. The principle prefers derivations which postpone movements until after SPELL-OUT, so that the results of the movements do not affect PHONETIC FORM.

pro-drop A term used in GOVERNMENT-BINDING THEORY for a PARAMETER which determines whether the SUBJECT of a CLAUSE can be suppressed. Italian is a **pro-drop language**, in this sense, because it can have subjectless sentences (e.g. *E* *pericoloso* 'It is dangerous'); by contrast, English is a **non-pro-drop language**, as the translation of the Italian sentence indicates. Other properties of pro-drop languages have been suggested, such as that they have a rich system of VERB-AGREEMENT, and free INVERSION of subject and verb. Pro-drop languages are also known as 'NULL subject' languages.

production (productive) The general sense of this term is found in PHONETICS and PSYCHOLINGUISTICS, where it refers to the process of planning and executing the act of SPEECH. The study of **speech production** includes not only the neuroanatomical and neurophysiological activities involved in speaking, but also the construction and testing of MODELS of the neural control system in the brain's organization of speech. A particular strategy is to analyse certain characteristics of speech output (e.g. PAUSE, TONGUE-SLIPS, DYNAMIC features), as a means of inferring the properties of this system. Production is usually contrasted with speech PERCEPTION and COMPREHENSION.

productivity (productive, non-/un-) A general term used in LINGUISTICS to refer to the CREATIVE capacity of LANGUAGE users to produce and understand an indefinitely large number of SENTENCES. It contrasts particularly with the 'unproductive' communication systems of animals, and in this context is seen by some linguists as one of the design features of human language. The term is also used in a more restricted sense with reference to the use made by a language of a specific feature or pattern. A pattern is **productive** if it is repeatedly used in language to produce further instances of the same type (e.g. the past-TENSE AFFIX *-ed* in English is productive, in that any new VERB will be automatically assigned this past-tense form). **Non-productive** (or **unproductive**) patterns lack any such potential; e.g. the change from *mouse* to *mice* is not a productive plural formation – new NOUNS would not adopt it, but would use instead the productive *s*-ending pattern. **Semi-productive** forms are those where there is a limited or occasional creativity, as when a PREFIX such as *un-* is sometimes, but not universally, applied to words to form their opposites, e.g. *happy* → *unhappy*, but not *sad* → **unsad*.

pro-form A term used in some models of GRAMMATICAL description to refer collectively to the ITEMS in a SENTENCE which substitute for other items or CONSTRUCTIONS. The central class of examples (from which the term is derived by analogy) is PRONOUNS, which substitute for NOUN PHRASES. Other pro-forms replace ADJECTIVE phrases (e.g. *so* in *John is very tall and so is Mary*), PREPOSITIONAL phrases (e.g. *then, there*), VERB phrases (e.g. *do* in *I like films and John does too*), and even whole CLAUSES or sentences (e.g. *so* as in *I said so*). Terminology such as 'pro-verb', 'pro-nominal', 'pro-locative', 'pro-NP', etc., is therefore likely to be encountered.

prog An abbreviation often used for PROGRESSIVE.

progressive (1) **(prog)** A term used in the GRAMMATICAL description of VERB FORMS, referring to a contrast of a temporal or durative kind, and thus sometimes handled under the heading of TENSE and sometimes under ASPECT. The usual contrast recognized is between 'progressive' or 'continuous' (e.g. *I am going*) and **non-progressive** or 'simple' (e.g. *I go*). LINGUISTS prefer an aspectual analysis here, because of the complex interaction of durational, completive and temporal features of meaning involved; TRADITIONAL grammars, however, merely refer to 'simple tense forms', etc., and thus imply a meaning which is to some degree an oversimplification.

(2) A term used in PHONETICS and PHONOLOGY as part of the classification of types of ASSIMILATION. In **progressive assimilation** one sound influences the following sound, as when [s] becomes [ʃ] following [ʤ], in such phrases as *Goodge Street*. It is opposed to REGRESSIVE and COALESCENT assimilations.

project(ion) A term used in GENERATIVE LINGUISTICS to characterize the capability of a GRAMMAR to extend the analysis of any given set of SENTENCES so that it applies also to the potentially infinite number of sentences in the LANGUAGE as a whole. The main means of doing this is the generative RULE. In some MODELS of generative grammar, a more restricted sense is found: **projection rules** are established as part of the SEMANTIC COMPONENT, their function being to assign a semantic INTERPRETATION to each STRING of FORMATIVES generated by the SYNTACTIC component. A central principle of GOVERNMENT-BINDING THEORY is the **projection principle**, which projects the properties of LEXICAL entries on to the STRUCTURE of the sentence. It states that the SUBCATEGORIZATION requirements of lexical items must be satisfied at all levels of REPRESENTATION. It eliminates the need for rules combining lexical items with their COMPLEMENTS, and requires a TRACE to be left when a complement is removed. In X-BAR syntax, **phrasal projections** (or **bar projections**) refer to the different types of phrasal expansion of any word-level category: a SINGLE-BAR projection into a 'small' X-bar phrase, and a DOUBLE-BAR projection into a 'large' X double-bar phrase. All full phrases (e.g. AP, NP, PP) are **maximal projections** – levels above which the properties of the lexical entries for the HEADS have no influence. See also INTERMEDIATE (2).

prominence (prominent) A term used in AUDITORY PHONETICS to refer to the degree to which a sound or SYLLABLE stands out from others in its ENVIRONMENT. Variations in LENGTH, PITCH, STRESS and inherent SONORITY are all factors which contribute to the relative prominence of a UNIT. An abstract sense of the term is often used in PHONOLOGY; for example, in METRICAL PHONOLOGY, it refers to the relative weight between CONSTITUENTS in a metrical TREE, defined in terms of the values of *s* ('stronger than') and *w* ('weaker than').

promotion (1) A term used in RELATIONAL GRAMMAR for a class of relation-changing PROCESSES which make a NOUN PHRASE more prominent. In the process of **advancement**, an NP which bears a particular grammatical relation to some VERB comes to bear another grammatical relation to that verb, which is higher up the relational HIERARCHY. In the process of **ascension**, an NP which is part of a larger NP comes to bear the grammatical relation previously borne by the larger NP.

(2) The term is also found in some models of FEATURE GEOMETRY, to refer to an alteration in the status of a construct (e.g. a feature, an articulation) from a lower to a higher level. For example, a minor ARTICULATION (such as PALATALIZATION) may be assigned MAJOR status under certain conditions.

pronominalization (pronominal, -ize) A term used in classical TRANSFORMATIONAL

GRAMMAR to refer to a RULE which replaces a LEXICAL NOUN PHRASE with a PRONOUN. In more recent approaches within GENERATIVE grammar, pronouns are BASE-generated. In GOVERNMENT-BINDING THEORY, the term **pronominal** is used for a type of noun phrase (along with ANAPHORS and R-EXPRESSIONS) of particular importance as part of a theory of BINDING. Pronominals include the class of PERSONAL pronouns, and little and big PRO. A pronominal NP must be FREE in its GOVERNING CATEGORY.

pronoun A term used in the GRAMMATICAL classification of WORDS, referring to the CLOSED set of ITEMS which can be used to substitute for a NOUN PHRASE (or single noun). There are many types of pronoun, with terminology varying somewhat between grammars. **Personal pronouns** include *I, you*, etc., in their variant FORMS (e.g. *I/me*); in their form *my/mine*, the term **possessive pronoun** is often used. Other classes of pronoun regularly recognized include: **demonstrative pronouns**, e.g. *this/that* (in certain of their uses); **interrogative pronouns**, e.g. certain uses of *who/which/what*; **reflexive pronouns**, e.g. *myself/yourself*; **indefinite pronouns**, e.g. *anyone/nobody*; **relative pronouns**, e.g. *who/whom/-that*; and **resumptive** or **shadow pronouns**, e.g. *him* in *John, I like him*. A **logophoric pronoun** refers to a person whose speech or thought is represented in discourse. Some linguists use the term 'lazy pronoun' for a usage (quite common in informal speech) where there is an imprecise match between the pronoun and its ANTECEDENT: for example, in *X wears her hat every day of the week. Y wears it only on Sundays*, the *it* in the second sentence should more precisely be *hers*. The grammatical statement of pronominal distribution in a language is usually quite complex. It is often discussed with reference to the more general notions of PRO-FORM and DEIXIS.

prop A term used in some GRAMMATICAL descriptions to refer to a meaningless ELEMENT introduced into a structure to ensure its GRAMMATICALITY, e.g. the *it* in *it's a lovely day*. Such words are also referred to as EMPTY, because they lack any SEMANTICALLY independent MEANING. SUBSTITUTE WORDS, which refer back to a previously occurring element of structure, are also often called 'prop words', e.g. *one* or *do* in *he does, he's got one*, etc.

proper A term used primarily in the GRAMMATICAL classification of NOUNS, opposed traditionally to a set of terms including COMMON, abstract, etc., but in LINGUISTIC analysis usually contrasting with 'common' alone. The alternative term, **proper name**, reflects its traditional SEMANTIC definition: the name of an individual person, place, etc. Modern grammars aim to provide a FORMAL treatment of these distinctions: proper nouns, for example, cannot be used with DETERMINERS in the way common nouns can, cf. *the/a boy* with **the/a London*, etc. In GOVERNMENT-BINDING THEORY, **proper government** is government by a LEXICAL CATEGORY.

proportional A type of OPPOSITION recognized in PRAGUE SCHOOL PHONOLOGY, distinguished from ISOLATED. The opposition between /f/ and /v/ in English is proportional, because there are other oppositions in the language which work in parallel, e.g. /s/ and /z/, /ʃ/ and /ʒ/; on the other hand, the opposition between say, /v/ and /l/ is isolated – there are no other segments that are contrasted in this particular way, i.e. VOICED LABIO-DENTAL FRICATIVE *v.* voiced LATERAL.

proposition(al) A term derived from philosophy, where its status is controversial, and often used in LINGUISTICS as part of a GRAMMATICAL or SEMANTIC analysis. It refers to the UNIT of MEANING which constitutes the subject-matter of a STATEMENT in the form of a SIMPLE DECLARATIVE sentence. Two 'terms' are involved in the analysis of propositions: the expression of a single action or state (a PREDICATE), and one or more entities ('names') which delimit the effects of this action or state. The logical system of **propositional calculus** may then be used as a framework for aspects of grammatical and semantic analysis. A logical calculus presents a set of logical laws or truths in systematic deductive form; in propositional calculus, rules for determining the relations between combinations of propositions are presented (usually AXIOMATICALLY) in a formal notation. Particular emphasis is placed on the analysis of the logical CONNECTIVES used in forming these combinations (negation, conjunction, disjunction and implication), and on the possible truth-values which 'single' or 'complex' propositions may have.

In linguistics, the interest is primarily in the way in which different linguistic FORMS can be shown to express the same proposition (e.g. *The cat ate the meat, The meat was eaten by the cat*, and so on), and how a single linguistic form can be analysed in terms of several propositions (e.g. *Those nice red apples cost a lot* expresses the propositions that 'the apples cost a lot', 'the apples are nice' and 'the apples are red'). The notion of 'proposition' is fundamental to CASE GRAMMAR, where it is used as one of the two main UNDERLYING CONSTITUENTS of sentences (Sentence → Modality+Proposition): each proposition is analysed in terms of a predicate word and its associated ARGUMENTS (i.e. case roles). Also of interest is the distinction to be made between the **propositional meaning** of a sentence on the one hand, and the use made of the sentence (e.g in various SPEECH-ACT situations) on the other. Linguists are not primarily concerned with the evaluation of a proposition in terms of truth-values, nor with the question of the referential or cognitive status of the notion. The notion of **propositional attitude** captures the point that propositions are not just bearers of truth, but means of enabling the speaker to express such attitudes as belief, hope, and doubt, as in '*A* believes that *p*'. If *p* is an object of belief and *q* is not, then *p* and *q* cannot be the same proposition. The verbs are called 'verbs of propositional attitude', and attitude reports of this kind help to provide a frame of reference for studying the nature of propositional meaning. See also ANALYTIC (2).

proscriptive A term used by LINGUISTS to characterize any approach which attempts to lay down RULES of CORRECTNESS, emphasizing how LANGUAGE should *not* be used. For example, the view that 'SENTENCES should not end with PREPOSITIONS' is a 'proscriptive RULE'. These NORMATIVE statements are usually made within the overall context of a PRESCRIPTIVE GRAMMAR.

prosodic phonology see PROSODY

prosody (prosod-ic (feature), -eme) A term used in SUPRASEGMENTAL PHONETICS and PHONOLOGY to refer collectively to variations in PITCH, LOUDNESS, TEMPO and RHYTHM. Sometimes it is used loosely as a synonym for 'suprasegmental', but in a narrower sense it refers only to the above variables, the remaining suprasegmental features being labelled PARALINGUISTIC. The narrow sense is close to the traditional use of the term 'prosody', where it referred to the characteristics and analyses of verse structure. The term **prosodic features** is preferred in LINGUISTICS, partly to enable a distinction to be drawn with the traditional use. In some recent approaches to phonology, the term **sentence prosody** is used to group together intonation, phrasal rhythmic patterning and more general features of prosodic phrasing.

In the theory of phonology proposed by J. R. FIRTH (**prosodic phonology**), the notion of prosody is given special status. It is distinguished in this approach from PHONEMATIC UNIT: the latter is a SEGMENTAL unit, such as consonant or vowel, whereas **prosodies** are features extending over stretches of UTTERANCE (one talks of 'sentence prosodies', 'syllable prosodies', etc.) – a notion which has taken on a more central role in recent thinking (cf. below, and also the concept of 'semantic prosody' in lexicology: see SEMANTICS). Not only would pitch, STRESS and JUNCTURE patterns be subsumed under the heading of prosody, but such features as SECONDARY ARTICULATIONS would also be included, e.g. lip-ROUNDING or NASALIZATION, when these are used to account for phonotactic restrictions, or to characterize GRAMMATICAL structure (as in the notion of 'VOWEL harmony'). Another feature of Firth's prosodic analysis is its POLYSYSTEMIC principle: it permits different phonological systems to be set up at different places in grammatical, lexical or phonological structure: e.g. the contrasts which occur at the beginning of a WORD may not be the same as those which occur at the end, and this fact is given special attention in this approach.

In PHONEMIC phonology, linguistically contrastive prosodic features are often referred to as **prosodemes**. In GENERATIVE phonology, prosodic features are considered to be one of the five main dimensions of classification of speech sounds (the others being MAJOR CLASS FEATURES, CAVITY features, MANNER-OF-ARTICULATION features and SOURCE features). Recently, the term has been applied to a model of MORPHOLOGY in which non-LINEAR phonological REPRESENTATIONS play a central role. Using notation derived from AUTOSEGMENTAL PHONOLOGY, the approach is based on the view that information about the CANONICAL pattern of SEGMENTS in a FORM (the **prosodic template**) is represented on a different tier from information about the kinds of segments occurring in the form. In METRICAL PHONOLOGY, one of the levels of structure in a metrical TREE is referred to as a **prosodic level**. In **prosodic morphology**, the focus is specifically on the way in which morphological and phonological determinants of linguistic form interact, and the notion of prosody becomes more powerful, as it is seen to determine the structure of morphological templates. This approach makes reference to the **prosodic morphology hypothesis** (templates are defined in terms of the units in a **prosodic hierarchy** – MORA, SYLLABLE, FOOT, and **prosodic word**) and the notion of **prosodic circumscription** (the domain to which morphological operations apply is circumscribed by prosodic as well as morphological criteria). In an alternative account, **p-structure** (i.e. 'prosodic structure') is seen as a LEVEL at which syntactic and phonological components interact, with its own hierarchical organization of four domains – phonological word, phonological phrase, intonational phrase, and utterance – the properties of which are specified by **prosodic hierarchy theory** ('hierarchy' here referring to a higher level of structural organization than in the case of prosodic morphology). Some model of a prosodic hierarchy is assumed in most modern phonological frameworks.

protasis see APODOSIS

prothesis (prothetic) A term used in PHONETICS and PHONOLOGY to refer to a type of INTRUSION, where an extra sound has been inserted initially in a WORD: a type of EPENTHESIS. The phenomenon is common both in historical change (e.g. Latin *spiritus* → French *esprit*) and in CONNECTED SPEECH (e.g. *left turn* pronounced as /ᵊleft tɜːn/).

proto- A prefix used in HISTORICAL LINGUISTICS to refer to a LINGUISTIC FORM or STATE of a LANGUAGE said to be the ancestor of ATTESTED forms/languages, e.g. Proto-Indo-European, Proto-Romance. More recently, some linguists have begun to use the term analogously in the context of language ACQUISITION, to refer to the emerging linguistic system of the young child, in such uses as 'proto-conversation', 'proto-sentence' (cf. PHONETICALLY CONSISTENT FORM).

prototype A term used in SEMANTICS and PSYCHOLINGUISTICS for a typical member of the EXTENSION of a referring expression (cf. REFERENT). For example, a sparrow would be a prototype of bird, whereas an ostrich (because of its atypical characteristics, notably its inability to fly) would not. The notion has been particularly fruitful in studies of child language ACQUISITION, where it has been used to help explain the order of emergence of complex sets of related LEXICAL items, such as types of chair, drinking utensil or vehicle. **Prototype semantics** involves the development of criteria for the definition of prototypical meaning, with particular reference to the way that the 'radial set' of overlapping meanings interrelate, and the nature of category membership and boundaries.

proxemics A term used in SEMIOTICS to refer to the study of variations in posture, inter-personal distance and tactile contact in human COMMUNICATION. These variations in interpersonal space are often culture-specific, and can be analysed in terms of sex, age, intimacy, social role and other such factors.

PRT In SYNTAX, an abbreviation sometimes used for the category PARTICLE.

PS(G) The usual abbreviation for PHRASE STRUCTURE (GRAMMAR).

pseudo-cleft sentence A term used in GRAMMATICAL description to refer to a CONSTRUCTION which resembles a CLEFT SENTENCE, in that a single CLAUSE has been divided into two separate sections, each with its own VERB, but with the essential difference that the two sections can be analysed as having a MAIN clause-SUBORDINATE clause relationship. For example, the sentence *You are a fool* is related to *What you are is a fool* or (an 'inverted' pseudo-cleft) *A fool is what you are.*

pseudo-intransitive see TRANSITIVITY

pseudo-passive see PASSIVE

pseudo-procedure A term sometimes used in LINGUISTICS and PHONETICS to refer to an analytic procedure which claims to work in a certain way, but which is in fact incapable of doing so, e.g. to assume that PHONOLOGICAL distinctions can be established by scrutinizing the ACOUSTIC patterns displayed on a SPECTROGRAM, or that it is possible to do GRAMMATICAL analysis without reference to MEANING.

psycholexicology see LEXIS

psycholinguistics A branch of LINGUISTICS which studies the correlation between linguistic behaviour and the psychological processes thought to underlie that behaviour. There are two possible directions of study. One may use LANGUAGE as a means of elucidating psychological theories and processes (e.g. the role of language as it affects memory, perception, attention, learning, etc.), and for this the term **psychological linguistics** is sometimes used. Alternatively, one may investigate the effects of psychological constraints on the use of language (e.g. how memory limitations affect SPEECH PRODUCTION and COMPREHENSION). It is the latter which has provided the main focus of interest in linguistics, where the subject is basically seen as the study of the mental processes underlying the planning, production, perception and comprehension of speech. The best-developed branch of the subject is the study of language ACQUISITION in children, but several other topics have attracted considerable interest (e.g. the notion of linguistic COMPLEXITY, the relationship between linguistic and cognitive UNIVERSALS, the study of reading). See also DEVELOPMENTAL LINGUISTICS.

pulmonic In PHONETICS the usual adjective to describe activity associated with the lungs. The pulmonic AIRSTREAM MECHANISM, for example, refers to the use of the lungs to initiate an airflow for SPEECH PRODUCTION. Most human speech involves pulmonic sounds.

punctual(ity) A term used in the GRAMMATICAL analysis of ASPECT, to refer to a momentary event, thought of as having no temporal duration; it thus contrasts with DURATIVE or CONTINUOUS events, where a period of time is involved.

pure vowel A term used in PHONETICS referring to a VOWEL sound with no perceived change in quality during a SYLLABLE, as in *pot* or *pit*. Alternatively known as a MONOPHTHONG, its opposite is 'gliding vowel' (cf. GLIDE) or DIPHTHONG.

purism (purist) A term used pejoratively in LINGUISTICS to characterize a school of thought which sees a LANGUAGE as needing preservation from the external processes which might infiltrate it and thus make it change, e.g. the pressures exercised by other DIALECTS and languages (as in LOAN WORDS) and the variations introduced by colloquial speech. This 'purist' concern is considered misplaced by linguists, who point to the inevitability of language change, as a reflex of social, cultural and psychological development.

push chain see CHAIN (3)

Q

Q An abbreviation often used for QUESTION and QUANTIFIER.

qualia structure In LEXICAL SEMANTICS, a mode of REPRESENTATION which builds on the logical connection between SENSES to arrive at a richer semantic representation for NOUNS and ADJECTIVES. The 'qualia' (singular **quale**) refer to modes of explanation for the object. This kind of approach is used to account for such matters as how a hospital can be both an institution and a building, or a window both an aperture and a physical object.

qualification (qualifier, qualify) A term used in SYNTAX to refer to certain types of STRUCTURAL DEPENDENCE of one grammatical UNIT upon another. In some TRADITIONAL GRAMMARS, for example, dependent ITEMS in a NOUN PHRASE (such as ADJECTIVES, PREPOSITIONAL phrases) were said to 'qualify' the noun. In HALLIDAYAN grammar, on the other hand, the term is reserved for structures following the HEAD of the noun phrase: *the car in the street* would be analysed in terms of M–H–Q, standing for MODIFICATION–head–qualification.

quality (1) (**qualitative**) A term used in AUDITORY PHONETICS and PHONOLOGY to refer to the characteristic resonance, or TIMBRE, of a sound, which is the result of the range of FREQUENCIES constituting the sound's identity. Variations in both VOWELS and CONSONANTS are describable in terms of quality, e.g. the distinction between [i], [e], etc., would be called a 'qualitative' difference. In this sense, the term 'quality' is generally opposed to QUANTITY or LENGTH. Voices are also described as having a characteristic 'quality', though this notion has no linguistic status (cf. VOICE QUALITY).

(2) A term identifying one of the MAXIMS OF CONVERSATION: the 'maxim of quality' states that a person's contribution to a conversation should ideally be true – for example, people should not say what they believe to be false.

quantal theory see QUANTUM

quantifier (quantification) (Q) A term used in SEMANTIC or logical analysis, referring to a set of ITEMS which express contrasts in quantity, such as *all, some, each*. The status of some of these items has particular significance in the construction of logical systems, and the distinctions made in logic between **universal quantification** (i.e. 'for all X, it is the case that . . .') and **existential quantification** (i.e. 'for some X, it is the case that . . .') may be found in semantic studies. In some MODELS OF GRAMMATICAL description, quantifiers refer to a class of items expressing contrasts in quantity occurring with restricted DISTRIBUTION in the NOUN PHRASE, e.g. *much/many, several, a lot of.* **Adverbs of quantification** (e.g. *usually, seldom*) may also be recognized, especially in semantic studies. The rule of **quantifier-floating** has been proposed by some TRANSFORMATIONAL LINGUISTS, to handle the mobile properties of quantifiers in SENTENCES, as in *All the people arrived v. The people all arrived.* **Quantifier-raising** is a process assumed in GOVERNMENT-BINDING THEORY which applies in the mapping from S-STRUCTURE to LOGICAL FORM and moves a quantified noun phrase such as *everyone* into CLAUSE-INITIAL position, giving structures similar to those assumed in logic.

quantitative linguistics A branch of LINGUISTICS which studies the frequency and DISTRIBUTION of linguistic UNITS using statistical techniques. The subject has both a pure and an applied side: the former aims to establish general principles concerning the statistical regularities governing the way WORDS, sounds, etc., are used; the latter investigates the way statistical techniques can be used to elucidate linguistic problems (such as FUNCTIONAL LOAD, STYLISTIC DISTINCTIVENESS, authorship identity). Considerable use is made of CORPORA.

quantity (1) (**quantitative**) A term used in PHONOLOGY to refer to the relative DURATIONS of sounds and SYLLABLES when these are linguistically contrastive; also referred to as LENGTH. The term is particularly used in historical studies of VOWEL and syllable length, and is contrasted with the notion of QUALITY; but it also applies to CONSONANTS, as seen in such notions as 'long' *v.* 'short' consonants and GEMINATION.

(2) A term identifying one of the MAXIMS OF CONVERSATION: the 'maxim of quantity' states that a person's contribution to a conversation should ideally be just as informative as is required for the purposes of an exchange – for example, avoiding verbosity.

quantity sensitivity In METRICAL PHONOLOGY, a FOOT-shape PARAMETER governing the DISTRIBUTION of light and heavy SYLLABLES in TERMINAL NODES of feet. In **quantity-insensitive** feet, all syllables are treated as equally light or equally heavy; there are no restrictions. In **quantity-sensitive** feet, heavy syllables may not occur in RECESSIVE positions, and are STRESSED. **Quantity-determined** feet are quantity sensitive, with the additional requirement that DOMINANT terminal nodes must dominate heavy syllables. Quantity sensitivity may also be formalized using MORAS (as in METRICAL GRID theory).

quantum (quantal) In PHONETICS, a term sometimes used for a zone of ARTICULATORY performance within which the results of minor articulatory variation are not auditorily perceptible. However, a small shift outside of this zone will produce a large acoustic change. For example, when a CONSTRICTION reaches a critical cross-sectional area, there is a sudden shift as the sound moves from an APPROXIMANT to a FRICATIVE mode of articulation. It is argued that articulation is evolutionarily organized to make maximum use of the vocal tract's ability to produce such changes, which are thus critical in the development of PHONOLOGICAL DISTINCTIVENESS. The notion is central to the **quantal theory** of speech proposed by US phonetician K. N. Stevens.

question (Q) A term used in the classification of SENTENCE FUNCTIONS, typically used to elicit information or a response, and defined sometimes on GRAMMATICAL and sometimes on SEMANTIC or SOCIOLINGUISTIC grounds. SYNTACTICALLY, in English, a question is a SENTENCE with INVERSION of the SUBJECT and first VERB in the verb PHRASE (YES–NO QUESTIONS, such as ***Is he going*?**), commencing with a **question word** (*WH*-questions, such as ***Where*** *is he*?), or ending with a question TAG (e.g. *He's going*, ***isn't he***?). Some would include the use of sentences with a rising INTONATION to be a class of question. Semantically, questions express a desire for more information, usually requesting a reply from the listener (exceptions include 'rhetorical questions' (e.g. *Isn't that awful?*)). The term is usually contrasted with three other major sentence functions: STATEMENT, COMMAND and EXCLAMATION. In grammatical discussion, questions are usually referred to as INTERROGATIVE in form. See also DIRECT (2).

Quirk grammar The approach to grammatical description pioneered by British linguist (Charles) Randolph **Quirk** (1920– , Lord Quirk) and his associates, and published in a series of reference GRAMMARS during the 1970s and 1980s, notably *A Comprehensive Grammar of the English Language* (1985). It is a synthesis of knowledge about the grammatical structure of English, bringing together information from a range of DESCRIPTIVE approaches, informed by copious illustration from CORPUS materials, and paying special attention to STYLISTIC and regional VARIETIES. Terminology generally falls within the European tradition of reference grammars (CLAUSE, SUBJECT, VERB, OBJECT, etc.), but a number of novel terms are introduced, such as comment clause, ECHO utterances, and the distinction between CONJUNCT, DISJUNCT, and SUBJUNCT.

quotative In DISCOURSE ANALYSIS, a term used for a form which introduces a piece of DIRECT speech (e.g. *she said, he goes*). A **zero quotative** is the reporting of direct speech with neither a reporting verb nor an attributed speaker.

R

R An abbreviation in BINDING theory, used as part of the phrase **R(eferring)-expression** (see R-EXPRESSION); also a symbol used in METRICAL PHONOLOGY to identify the ROOT or topmost NODE of a metrical TREE.

radix (radical) see ROOT (2)

raising (raise) (1) A type of RULE recognized in some MODELS of TRANSFORMATIONAL GRAMMAR. In a 'raising-to-object' (or **object-raising** rule, the LINEAR CONSTITUENTS in a STRING consisting of a main CLAUSE+COMPLEMENT clause (e.g. *he believes John to be honest*) are BRACKETED so that the SUBJECT of the complement clause appears to have been 'raised' to become the OBJECT of the HIGHER clause (*he believes it+John is honest* becoming *he believes John+to be honest*). In a **subject-raising** rule, an underlying subject complement clause has the subject taken from it and 'raised' to be the subject of the main clause. For example, in relating such sentences as *it seems that the man is angry* to *the man seems angry*, one may begin with:

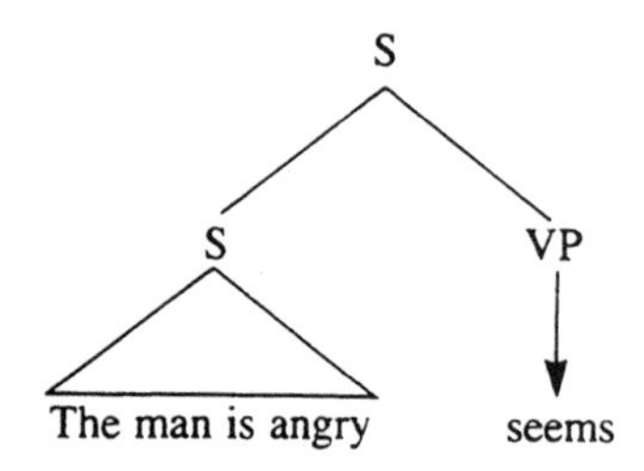

Subject-raising (in association with other transformational operations, omitted here) places *the man* as subject of *seems*, producing (*the man) (seems) (to be angry*). The FORMALIZATION of such rules is controversial, as is the extent of their application (they are both GOVERNED rules, applying to small classes of verb only). In GOVERNMENT-BINDING THEORY, classical TG object-to-subject raising constructions are analysed in terms of EXCEPTIONAL CASE MARKING, and classical TG subject-raising constructions in terms of NP-MOVEMENT. In PHRASE-STRUCTURE GRAMMAR and LEXICAL FUNCTIONAL GRAMMAR, both are regarded as types of CONTROL constructions. Sometimes raising constructions are referred to as

CATENATIVE constructions. Other syntactic applications of the term 'raising' may also be encountered (e.g. 'PREDICATE-raising', 'NEGATIVE raising', 'QUANTIFIER raising').

(2) In PHONETICS and PHONOLOGY, a vertical process affecting TONGUE height; opposed to **lowering**. For example, in the study of VOWEL HARMONY, a vowel might be said to 'raise' (e.g. from mid to high) in the context of a following high vowel. In the course of language change, a vowel in an originally low position might be raised to a relatively high position.

rank In HALLIDAYAN LINGUISTICS, this term is used to refer to one of the SCALES of analysis which interrelates the CATEGORIES of the theory, viz. the HIERARCHICAL arrangement of linguistic UNITS within a linguistic LEVEL. The GRAMMATICAL **rank scale**, for instance, recognizes SENTENCE–CLAUSE–GROUP–WORD–MORPHEME in a relationship of inclusion (i.e. a sentence consists of one or more clauses, etc.). Other scales in this approach are labelled EXPONENCE and DELICACY. The term **rank shift** is used to refer to a linguistic process when a given unit is 'shifted' down the rank scale, so that it operates within the structure of a lower unit (or one of equal rank); e.g. a clause working within a group (as in RELATIVE clauses, e.g. *the lady* ***who came in*** *asked* . . .) is said to be a 'rank-shifted' clause.

rate An application of the general sense of this term in PHONETICS and PHONOLOGY to refer to speed of speaking; alternatively known as TEMPO. LANGUAGES and people vary in their overall rate of ARTICULATION (measured in such terms as SYLLABLES per second, WORDS per minute, incidence of PAUSES). Within a given NORM, however, it is possible to vary one's rate for particular SEMANTIC or social effects, e.g. the 'meditative' sense of *we-e-ll*, produced very slowly. Rate thus forms part of the CONTRASTIVITY studied by SUPRASEGMENTAL phonology.

r-colouring see RETROFLEX

readjustment rules A class of RULES in GENERATIVE GRAMMAR which help to relate the SYNTACTIC COMPONENT to the PHONOLOGICAL component. The rules make modifications in SURFACE STRUCTURES by effecting individual changes in the shapes of certain FORMATIVES in the context of other formatives. The output of these rules then provides the input to the phonological rules. For example, readjustment rules would take the formative 'past' (i.e. past TENSE) and generally replace it by *d*; however, in such cases as *sing*, the rules would provide a special FEATURE specification to ensure that *i* would be converted to *a*.

realis In LINGUISTICS, a term used in the study of EPISTEMIC MODALITY: in a **realis** ('real') assertion, a proposition is strongly asserted to be true, the speaker being ready to back up the assertion with evidence or argument. It is opposed to an **irrealis** ('unreal') assertion, where the proposition is weakly asserted to be true, but the speaker is not ready to support the assertion. Realis VERB forms include the past TENSE ('X did Y'); irrealis forms include certain MODALS ('X may do Y'). Realis ADVERBS include *fortunately* and *sadly*; irrealis adverbs include *maybe* and *hopefully*.

realistic grammar A term used in recent LINGUISTIC theory to refer to any approach to grammatical analysis which aims to be psychologically real, in that it contributes to the explanation of such areas of linguistic behaviour as comprehension and memory. A contrast is intended between this approach and earlier, FORMAL characterizations of GRAMMAR on the basis of INTUITION alone: the intention is to 'realize' a TRANSFORMATIONAL grammar within a psychological MODEL of language use, so that the model genuinely represents users' knowledge of their language. Such a grammar would also be 'realizable', i.e. define explicit REALIZATIONS which would MAP grammatical RULES and CATEGORIES on to processing operations and informational units, as defined by the psychological model. In this way, it is hoped that realistic grammars, through the use of psycholinguistic as well as linguistic criteria, will provide further insight into the nature of COMPETENCE, as well as help to evaluate the merits of competing formal grammars (cf. ADEQUACY).

realization (realize) (1) The physical expression of an abstract LINGUISTIC UNIT; e.g. PHONEMES are 'realized' in PHONIC SUBSTANCE as PHONES, MORPHEMES as MORPHS. Any UNDERLYING FORM may be seen as having a corresponding realization in substance. Alternative terms are ACTUALIZATION, MANIFESTATION, EXPONENCE and REPRESENTATION, though the latter two are not restricted to expression solely at a physical level.

(2) **Realization grammar** is a label sometimes used for a GRAMMAR which derives all SENTENCES from their corresponding SEMANTIC representation. In STRATIFICATIONAL grammar, **realizational analysis** is one of two main types of linguistic patterning (the other being TACTIC analysis), which involves the setting-up of four basic types of operation: 'horizontal grouping' (e.g. *d+o+g* → *dog*), 'horizontal splitting' (e.g. French *des* realizes *de* + *les*), 'vertical grouping' (two or more lower-LEVEL UNITS realize one higher-level unit, e.g. the various forms of the plural MORPHEME), and 'vertical splitting' (two or more higher-level units are realized by one lower-level unit, e.g. *-s* realizing both plural and possessive).

reanalysis (reanalyse) (1) In the study of language change, a development which alters the STRUCTURE or FUNCTION of a linguistic FORM. For example, when two words COALESCE as a COMPOUND , their separate identities need to be reanalysed as a whole (*hair* noun + *cut* verb → *haircut* noun). Any level of language could be affected: for example, a LEXICAL item (such as a main verb) might develop into a GRAMMATICAL item (such as an auxiliary verb), a PHONOLOGICAL change might require a reanalysis of the SYLLABLE divisions in a word, or a SEGMENT of one word might be assigned to another (English *a naddre* → *an adder*). See also ANALOGY.

(2) A term used in GENERATIVE (especially TRANSFORMATIONAL) GRAMMAR for a process which enables a sequence of SYNTACTIC CATEGORIES to be taken together as a single unit; sometimes known as **restructuring**. For example, the SENTENCE [$_{NP}$ the lady] [$_{V}$ took] [$_{NP}$ account] [$_{PP}$ of [$_{NP}$ his answer]] might be reanalysed as [$_{NP}$ the lady] [$_{V}$ took account of] [$_{NP}$ his answer]. The factors which govern the application of such RULES are little understood.

reassociation see ASSOCIATION LINE

recategorization see CATEGORY

received pronunciation (RP) The name given to the regionally neutral ACCENT in British English, historically deriving from the prestige speech of the Court and the public schools. The term indicates that its prestige is the result of social factors, not linguistic ones. RP is in no sense linguistically superior or inferior to other accents: but it is the accent which tends to be associated with the better-educated parts of society, and is the one most often cited as a norm for the description of British English, or in teaching that DIALECT to foreigners. The BBC originally adopted RP for its announcers because it was the form of pronunciation most likely to be nationally understood, and to attract least regional criticism – hence the association of RP with the phrase 'BBC English'. These days, the BBC, as indeed educated speech at large, displays considerable regional variation, and many modified forms of RP exist (**modified RP**). RP no longer has the prestigious social position it once held. In the eyes of many (especially of the younger generations), regionally marked forms of accent are more desirable. The present-day situation is plainly one of rapid change.

recessive In METRICAL PHONOLOGY, a term used to refer to the non-DOMINANT elements in a FOOT. In left-dominant feet, all right NODES are recessive, and in right-dominant feet all left nodes are recessive. Recessive nodes do not BRANCH.

recipient A term used by some LINGUISTS as part of the GRAMMATICAL or SEMANTIC analysis of a SENTENCE in terms of CASES or PARTICIPANT ROLES: it usually refers to the ANIMATE being passively implicated by the happening or state expressed by the VERB (e.g. *I gave you the cheque*). It is typically the role of the INDIRECT OBJECT, but other ELEMENTS may act as recipient – such as the SUBJECT in such sentences as *John has seen a vision*. Alternative terms include PATIENT, DATIVE and AFFECTED, but different approaches vary in their use of these terms.

reciprocal (1) A term used in PHONETICS and PHONOLOGY as part of the classification of types of ASSIMILATION. In reciprocal (or 'coalescent') assimilation, each of two adjacent ARTICULATIONS influences the other. An example is the fusion of [d] and [j] to produce [ʤ] in such phrases as *could you*.

(2) In some models of GRAMMATICAL description, the term is used to refer to classes which express the meaning of mutual relationship, e.g. 'reciprocal PRONOUNS', such as *each other*, or 'reciprocal VERBS', such as *meet*. In GOVERNMENT-BINDING THEORY, reciprocal pronouns, along with REFLEXIVE pronouns and NP-TRACES, form the class of ANAPHORS.

recognition see SPEAKER RECOGNITION, SPEECH RECOGNITION

reconstruct(ion) (1) A method used in HISTORICAL LINGUISTICS and COMPARATIVE PHILOLOGY in which a hypothetical SYSTEM of sounds or FORMS representing an earlier, non-extant state of a LANGUAGE ('PROTO-forms' in a 'proto-language') is established deductively from an analysis of the attested sounds and forms of extant TEXTS. This process of **comparative reconstruction** is dependent on the existence of good written records or several known related languages. When these do not exist, as in many African and American Indian languages, it is still possible to hypothesize about the historical development of the languages by analysing the STRUCTURAL regularities and irregularities of their contemporary states, and deducing UNDERLYING forms which might reflect earlier states – a process of **internal reconstruction**.

(2) In GOVERNMENT-BINDING THEORY, a PROCESS that occurs in the MAPPING

from S-STRUCTURE to LOGICAL FORM, moving certain CONSTITUENTS back to their D-STRUCTURE positions. It allows examples like *which picture of herself did Mary buy?* to be analysed as ordinary cases of ANAPHORA, in which the ANAPHOR is C-COMMANDED by its ANTECEDENT.

recoverable (recoverability) A term used in SYNTACTIC theory to refer to sentences where elements which have been ELIDED (or DELETED) are capable of being retrieved, by taking the linguistic CONTEXT into account. In recent GENERATIVE GRAMMAR, it refers to a CONDITION governing the application of DELETION RULES, which specifies that only elements which do not have SEMANTIC content can be deleted.

recursive (-ness, recursion) A term used in GENERATIVE LINGUISTICS to refer to RULES which are capable of repeated application in generating a SENTENCE, to the STRUCTURES thus generated, and to the languages characterized by such rules. There is no limit, for example, to the number of ADJECTIVES which may be used before a NOUN in English, or the number of ADVERBS which may MODIFY a VERB. Such sequences would be introduced by the repeated ('recursive') application of the appropriate adjective- or adverb-insertion rules in the relevant section of the GRAMMAR. The importance of the notion is that recursive rules are the main FORMAL means of accounting for the CREATIVITY of LANGUAGE: by using this device, an infinite set of sentences can be generated from a finite set of rules. A simple illustration of how this can be formalized is in the following rules:

NP → Det + N (+ Prep Phrase)
Prep Phrase → Prep + NP

These rules say, in effect, that there is in principle no limit to the number of PREPOSITIONAL PHRASES which may occur following a noun in a noun phrase, e.g. *the man in a coat on a bus with his wife* . . . The phenomenon is also known as 'iteration'. The term has also been used to define an extension of TRANSITION NETWORK GRAMMARS – **recursive transition networks (RTNs)**.

reduce (reduction) (1) A term used in the PHONOLOGICAL classification of VOWEL sounds, referring to a vowel which can be analysed as a CENTRALIZED VARIANT of a vowel in a related form. For example, the pronunciation of /ɒv/ becomes /əv/ when unstressed; the STRESSED vowels in ˈ*telegraph* become reduced in the related word *te*ˈlegraphy /ˈteləgrɑːf/ → /təˈlegrəfɪ/.

(2) A further phonological use of the term is found in the context of phonological RULES, where it refers to a process of simplification which affects certain types of sound sequence. The most important category is **consonant-cluster reduction** (e.g. *clock* becoming /gɒk/), which is common in early child language.

(3) In GRAMMAR, the term usually refers to a CLAUSE (a **reduced clause**) which lacks one or more of the ELEMENTS required to enable it to be used as a FULL, independent construction, e.g. *to see the book*. Such clauses may be referred to as 'abbreviated', ELLIPTICAL or CONTRACTED; but different approaches often introduce distinctions between these terms. Other units are sometimes referred to as 'reduced', such as PHRASES (e.g. ***phone's** ringing*) and WORDS (e.g. *it**'s** him*).

redundancy (redundant) A term derived from INFORMATION theory and applied to the analysis of the range of features used in making LINGUISTIC contrasts. A FEATURE (of sound, GRAMMAR, etc.) is redundant if its presence is unnecessary in order to identify a linguistic unit. For example, the contrast between the /p/ and /b/ PHONEMES of English, as in *pin v. bin*, may be defined in terms of VOICING, muscular TENSION and ASPIRATION; but only one of these features is necessary to specify the contrast involved, and, once this decision has been made (e.g. voicing), the other features would be seen as redundant, in respect of this contrast. Features of sound (grammar, MEANING) which are not considered redundant are DISTINCTIVE. It should be noted that circumstances may arise which will affect the GENERALITY of an analysis; for instance, in other positions in the word, other features may become less redundant (e.g. muscular tension in final position, as in such contrasts as *rip v. rib*), and in some VARIETIES of speech (such as public speaking, or in very noisy situations) the speaker may need to use all the available features in order to be ACCEPTABLE or intelligible.

Similar principles apply to the analysis of grammar and SEMANTICS in terms of redundancy. In grammar, for example, SENTENCES such as *The bird flies* display redundancy, in that both the SUBJECT and the VERBS are MARKED for singularity: in theory, it would be possible for English to use, for example, *the bird fly v. the birds fly* to keep a singular/plural distinction clear. In semantics, the issue is more complex: what to one person might appear a totally unnecessary (and hence redundant) use of a word or phrase may to someone else provide an additional nuance, and thus be distinctive. In GENERATIVE linguistics, the notion of redundancy has been formalized in terms of RULES (**redundancy rules**) which simplify the form of descriptions. Any feature which can be predicted on the basis of other features is said to be redundant. For example, in generative PHONOLOGY, when certain features of a SEGMENT are predictable (because of the occurrence of other features in some CO-OCCURRING segment), the specification of these features is unnecessary: such redundant feature specifications would be left blank in the UNDERLYING representation of MORPHEMES (the rules subsequently involved in inserting the redundant features being referred to as 'LEXICAL-redundancy rules' or MORPHEME-STRUCTURE RULES). Redundancy rules are also important in UNDERSPECIFICATION theories of phonology. In generative SYNTAX, the lexical-redundancy rules apply to such processes as SUB-CATEGORIZATION (thus simplifying the feature specification of a syntactic CATEGORY) and WORD FORMATION (enabling one WORD-CLASS to be DERIVED from another).

Various mathematical methods are available to demonstrate the nature and extent of redundancy in linguistic analysis.

reduplication (redupli-cate, -cative, -cant) A term in MORPHOLOGY for a process of repetition whereby the form of a PREFIX/SUFFIX reflects certain PHONOLOGICAL characteristics of the ROOT. This process may be found in Greek, where the initial CONSONANT of the root is reduplicated in certain GRAMMATICAL CONTEXTS (PERFECTIVE forms); e.g. /'luːoː/ (λύω), 'I loose', becomes /'leluka/ (λέλυκα), 'I have loosed'. In English the nearest one gets to this is in 'reduplicative compound' words, such as *helter-skelter, shilly-shally.* The phonological processes involved in reduplication have been a particular focus of PROSODIC morphology, which distinguishes the base form of the reduplication from the repeating element (the **reduplicant**), as well as PREFIXING and SUFFIXING types.

referent (referen-ce, -tial, referring) (1) A term used in philosophical LINGUISTICS and SEMANTICS for the entity (object, state of affairs, etc.) in the external world to which a linguistic EXPRESSION relates: for example, the referent of the WORD *table* is the object 'table'. The term is found both as part of a two-term analysis of MEANING (e.g. words ~ things) and in three-term analyses (e.g. words ~ concepts ~ things). Several limitations in the notion of **referential meaning** have been pointed out, such as that several words have no obvious referents (e.g. *the, should, since*), and that the same referent may be referred to by several different linguistic expressions, none of which may be SYNONYMOUS (e.g. (pointing to a book) *that is a book/the answer/my authority/a disgrace* . . .). Other terms have been suggested in an attempt to avoid these limitations, e.g. DENOTATION, EXTENSION. In linguistics, care is usually taken to distinguish knowledge of the world from knowledge of language: the extralinguistic notion of **reference** is contrasted with the intralinguistic notion of SENSE, a property arising from the meaning relations between LEXICAL ITEMS and SENTENCES.

(2) In GRAMMATICAL analysis, the term **reference** is often used to state a relationship of identity which exists between grammatical UNITS, e.g. a PRONOUN 'refers' to a NOUN or noun PHRASE. When the reference is to an earlier part of the DISCOURSE, it may be called 'back-reference' (or ANAPHORA); correspondingly, reference to a later part of the discourse may be called 'forward-reference' (or CATAPHORA). In SWITCH REFERENCE languages, the verb indicates whether the subjects of successive clauses are the same or different. In GOVERNMENT-BINDING THEORY, the term **referential expression**, usually abbreviated to **R-expression**, has special meaning as part of the classification of NPs. Similarly, **arbitrary reference** is a term used in that theory for the reference of the understood subject represented by PRO.

reference grammar see GRAMMAR (1)

referential indices A term used in GENERATIVE GRAMMAR (since ASPECTS) to refer to markers attached to a set of items in a SENTENCE to show identity or difference of REFERENCE. For example, both the sentences (a) *The dog saw the dog* and (b) *The dog saw itself* could, on one analysis, be derived from the same UNDERLYING structure *The dog saw the dog*. To mark the difference, sentence (a) would be marked as *The* dog_i *saw the* dog_j, whereas (b) would be *The* dog_i *saw the* dog_i. Items marked with the same referential-index variable are CO-REFERENTIAL; with different indices they are 'non-co-referential'. In yet more recent work, the term CO-INDEXING is used.

referring-expression see R-EXPRESSION

reflexive(-ness, reflexiv-ity, -ization) (1) A term used in GRAMMATICAL description to refer to a VERB or CONSTRUCTION where the SUBJECT and the OBJECT relate to the same entity. English uses reflexive PRONOUNS to express this relationship (e.g. *he kicked* ***himself***), but the same verbal MEANING is often present without the pronoun (e.g. *I shaved (myself)*). Other LANGUAGES use a variety of FORMS for the expression of reflexive meaning, such as SUFFIXES, CASE endings and

WORD order. In TRANSFORMATIONAL grammar, **reflexivization** refers to a RULE which introduces the reflexive pronouns into a sentence – in one formulation by changing the syntactic feature on the object personal PRONOUN from [−reflexive] to [+reflexive], when it is CO-REFERENTIAL with the subject, e.g. *she saw her → she saw herself.* In GOVERNMENT-BINDING THEORY, reflexives, together with NP-TRACES and PRO, are BASE-generated ANAPHORS – a class of NPs.

(2) **Reflexiveness** ('reflectiveness' or 'reflexivity') is also a suggested defining property of human LANGUAGE (contrasting with the properties of other SEMIOTIC SYSTEMS) whereby language can be used to 'talk about' language. The development of this METALANGUAGE leads to the terminology and notation which this dictionary is attempting to elucidate. If a linguistic form is used as a CITATION FORM it is said to be used 'reflexively', as in *The cat is a noun phrase.*

regional accent see ACCENT (1)

regional dialect see DIALECT

register (1) A term used in PHONETICS to refer to the VOICE QUALITY produced by a specific physiological constitution of the LARYNX. Variations in the length, thickness and tension of the VOCAL CORDS combine to produce (in singing) the differences between soprano, contralto, tenor, bass, etc. voices, and also (within one person) such differences as between 'head' (falsetto') and 'chest' voice. Some phoneticians use the term in a functional way in relation to speech, to refer to types of PHONATION which the speaker varies in a controlled manner (as in CREAKY and BREATHY voice). See also DOWNSTEP.

(2) In STYLISTICS and SOCIOLINGUISTICS, the term refers to a VARIETY of LANGUAGE defined according to its use in social SITUATIONS, e.g. a register of scientific, religious, FORMAL English. In HALLIDAYAN linguistics, the term is seen as specifically opposed to varieties of language defined according to the characteristics of the users (viz. their regional or class DIALECT), and is given a subclassification into FIELD, MODE and MANNER of DISCOURSE.

register tone language A term introduced by Kenneth Pike (1912–) as part of a classification of TONE languages. In a register tone system (e.g Yoruba), the critical feature is the relative height of the SYLLABIC PITCHES, and not the direction in which they move. LEVEL pitches are central, and if the language makes use of changing pitches, the end-points of the FALLS or RISES are identified with one of the level pitches. The notion contrasts with a 'CONTOUR tone language' (e.g. Mandarin Chinese), where the critical feature is the nature of the gliding tone rather than its relative pitch height. Mixed register/contour tone systems (e.g. Trique) can also be found.

regressive A term used in PHONETICS and PHONOLOGY as part of the classification of types of ASSIMILATION. In **regressive** (or 'anticipatory') **assimilation**, a sound changes because of the following sound, as when [t] becomes [p] in *hot pies.* It is opposed to PROGRESSIVE and COALESCENT assimilations.

regular(ity) A term referring to LINGUISTIC FORMS when they are in conformity with the general RULES of a LANGUAGE, i.e. they are predictable. In English, for example, NOUNS such as *boy, girl, dog* are regular, in that they follow the rules governing the majority of nouns (e.g. take plurals in *-s*); nouns such as *mouse* and *sheep* are 'irregular', or 'exceptions'. In TRADITIONAL GRAMMARS, the notion was interpreted MORPHOLOGICALLY, e.g. 'regular verbs' were those whose VARIANT forms were in the majority, for a given CLASS. In linguistics, the notion includes both SYNTACTIC and morphological predictability. In HISTORICAL LINGUISTICS, regularity is a major explanatory principle, in that one attempts to show systematic CORRESPONDENCES between languages and STATES of a language, which can be formulated in general terms. COMPARATIVE PHILOLOGISTS called such general correspondences SOUND LAWS, and much controversy took place in the late nineteenth century, when it was argued (by the NEOGRAMMARIANS) that sound laws admitted no exceptions which could not be explained by reference to other laws. The attempt to deal with exceptions by seeing them as variants of a general rule (conditioned by regional, social or other factors) is a major preoccupation of contemporary linguistics.

regular grammar A term used in COMPUTATIONAL LINGUISTICS for a type of GRAMMAR which describes only the LINEAR (non-HIERARCHICAL) aspects of a STRING of symbols. Such grammars allow only RULES with a single NON-TERMINAL symbol on the left-hand side, and at most one non-terminal symbol (e.g. NOUN, VERB) and one TERMINAL on the right-hand side. See also FINITE-STATE GRAMMAR.

reiteration A term used in HALLIDAYAN analysis of the COHESIVE characteristics of LANGUAGE to refer to the repeated use of a LEXICAL ITEM, or the use of a SYNONYMOUS lexical item, as a means of linking the various parts of a TEXT. An example is the use of *car* and *monstrosity* in the sequence *John saw a car. The car was very old. 'What a monstrosity!' he said.* There are other means of lexical linkage, e.g. COLLOCATION.

relation(-s, -al) A general term used in PHONETICS and LINGUISTICS to refer to the linguistically significant connections between two or more ELEMENTS in a LANGUAGE, such as EQUIVALENCE, CONTRAST, INCLUSION, GOVERNMENT. In GRAMMATICAL analysis, for example, the FUNCTIONAL role which a NOUN PHRASE has in relation to a VERB can be identified by using such terms as SUBJECT, OBJECT, AGENT, COMPLEMENT, etc. These 'relational' notions are central to some theories (e.g. CASE grammar, RELATIONAL GRAMMAR), and of marginal importance in others (e.g. ASPECTS-type grammars). In SEMANTICS, the correspondences between LEXICAL items of similar, opposed etc., MEANINGS are referred to as **sense relations**, and classified under such headings as SYNONYMY and ANTONYMY. At the most general level, 'linguistic relations' can be classified into SYNTAGMATIC and PARADIGMATIC types. Several other applications will also be encountered within particular theories (e.g. COGNITIVE GRAMMAR).

relational grammar A development of GENERATIVE LINGUISTIC thinking of the mid-1970s which takes as central the notion of GRAMMATICAL RELATIONS (such as SUBJECT and OBJECT), rather than the categorial terms of standard PHRASE-MARKERS (e.g. NP, VP). TRANSFORMATIONS in this view are replaced by operations performed on unordered RELATIONAL networks – and formal representations of SENTENCES which show the grammatical relations that elements of a sentence bear to each other, and the syntactic level(s) at which these relations hold. The approach is in marked contrast with most other versions of generative grammar, where the emphasis is on SYNTACTIC CATEGORIES such as NP and VP, and on LINEAR ORDERING, syntactic relations being specifiable only derivatively.

relative (1) (**relativization**) A term used in GRAMMATICAL DESCRIPTION to characterize PRONOUNS which may be used to introduce a POST-MODIFYING CLAUSE within a NOUN PHRASE, and by extension to the clause as a whole. **Relative pronouns** in English include *who, which, whom, whose* and *that* (cf. *WH-*), as used in such **relative clauses** as *the man who went was . . . When* and *where* are sometimes called **relative adverbs**, when linking a relative clause to a MAIN clause (e.g. *I remember the day (when) I first saw John, I remember the street where I lived as a child*). Several detailed CLASSIFICATIONS of relative pronouns and clauses have been made, distinguishing such types as **adnominal** (e.g. *The answer which I received . . .*), **nominal** (*What interests me is his motive . . .*), **sentential** (e.g. *It's said she's back in the country – which I just don't believe*) and **zero** or **contact** relatives (e.g. *There's the bus I caught*). Widely recognized in TRADITIONAL as well as in LINGUISTIC grammars is the contrast between **restrictive** (or **defining**) and **non-restrictive** (or **non-defining**) types of relative: *The Bible which I own was given to me by my grandmother v. The Bible, which I often read, is my favourite book*. In classical TRANSFORMATIONAL GRAMMAR, the process of forming a relative-clause CONSTRUCTION is known as **relativization**. See also RESUMPTIVE.

(2) A term used in recent linguistic theory to refer to a type of UNIVERSAL. A **relative universal** is one which characterizes a general tendency in a language, and allows for exceptions; it contrasts with ABSOLUTE universal.

(3) A term used in HISTORICAL LINGUISTICS, referring to one way of characterizing the temporal relationship between language changes: to say that one change occurs before another is a statement of **relative chronology**. A contrast is intended with **absolute chronology**, where it is possible to state the specific time-periods when the changes took place.

relativity A term used to identify an influential view of the relationship between LANGUAGE and thought, generally known as **linguistic relativity**, which asserts, in its strongest form, that language determines the way people perceive and organize their worlds. This view (of 'linguistic determinism') was first expounded by the German ethnologist Wilhelm von Humboldt (1767–1835): in the twentieth century it came to be known as the SAPIR–WHORF HYPOTHESIS.

relativized minimality see MINIMAL

release A term used in PHONETICS to refer to the type of movement made by the VOCAL ORGANS away from a point of ARTICULATION, particularly with reference to PLOSIVES. English plosives, for example, may be released with or without ASPIRATION, or as a LATERAL or NASAL (as in *button* and *bottle*).

In the DISTINCTIVE FEATURE approach to PHONOLOGY of CHOMSKY and Halle, DELAYED and INSTANTANEOUS (or ABRUPT) types of release are recognized.

relevance theory A theory of communication and cognition which claims that human cognition is geared to the maximizing of relevance (cf. MAXIMS OF CONVERSATION). New information is relevant if it interacts with old information to produce various CONTEXTUAL effects, and the more contextual effects it produces the more relevant it is. On the other hand, the more processing effort it involves the less relevant it is. The theory claims that all communicative acts carry a guarantee of optimal relevance – a guarantee that they have enough contextual effects and require no unnecessary processing effort – and that they are interpreted in the light of this guarantee.

relexification A term used in SOCIOLINGUISTICS to refer to a theory concerning the origins of, and relationships between, PIDGIN (and CREOLE) LANGUAGES. The **relexification hypothesis** proposes that the range of English, French, Spanish, etc. pidgins is derived from the first widely used pidgin language, Portuguese pidgin, in the fifteenth century in West Africa, by a process whereby the GRAMMAR of this language was retained but new LEXICAL ITEMS were introduced from the other European languages. This view, it is maintained, provides a satisfactory explanation for the grammatical similarities noted between pidgin languages, and for the many lexical similarities which seem to derive from an original West African source or from Portuguese (e.g. *savvy?* – possibly from *sabe* 'know').

relic area see AREA

remote structure A term sometimes used in GENERATIVE LINGUISTICS to refer to what is more usually known as DEEP STRUCTURE.

renewal of connection see CONNECTION

reordering (1) A term often used within the framework of TRANSFORMATIONAL GRAMMAR to refer to a basic kind of transformational operation. **Reordering transformations** have the effect of moving CONSTITUENTS (usually one at a time) from one part of a PHRASE-MARKER to another, as in the formation of PASSIVE sentences, the placement of NEGATIVES and AFFIXES. An alternative term is MOVEMENT or PERMUTATION. In GOVERNMENT-BINDING THEORY, reordering involves either ADJUNCTION or SUBSTITUTION.

(2) The term is also used in transformational analysis of LINGUISTIC change, referring to differences in the historical SEQUENCE of RULES which must be postulated in order to explain the divergences between DIALECTS, FORMS, etc. The matter has been discussed mainly with reference to PHONOLOGY, and various types of rule-ordering relationships have been suggested, e.g. the distinction between FEEDING and BLEEDING rule-ordering.

repair (1) A term used in CONVERSATION ANALYSIS and DISCOURSE analysis to refer to the attempt made by participants in a conversation to make good a real or imagined deficiency in the interaction (e.g. a mishearing or misunderstanding). Some repairs are **self-initiated** (made by a speaker without prompting from the listener), as in the spontaneous use of *I mean*; some are **other-initiated** (prompted by the listener), as in the use of ECHO QUESTIONS such as *He said what?* Repairs may also be classified as **self-repairs** (made by the speakers themselves) and **other-repairs** (made by the listeners).

(2) In PHONOLOGY, a term sometimes used to refer to the process of altering a REPRESENTATION so that it conforms to the structural principles of a model. For example, in METRICAL PHONOLOGY, various strategies are available to ensure that degenerate FEET are 'repaired' (e.g. lengthening, reparsing).

repertoire (repertory) A term used in SOCIOLINGUISTICS to refer to the range of

LANGUAGES or VARIETIES of a language available for use by a speaker, each of which enables the speaker to perform a particular social role. The term may also be applied collectively to the range of LINGUISTIC varieties within a SPEECH community.

replacive A term sometimes used in MORPHOLOGY to refer to a MORPH postulated to account for such problematic internal ALTERNATIONS as *man* ~ *men, take* ~ *took*, etc. The 'replacive morph' would be stated as *a* → *e*, etc. – a 'solution' which recent morphological theory has generally discounted.

represent(ation) A term used, especially in GENERATIVE LINGUISTICS, to refer to the relationship of correspondence existing between the successive levels of analysis which are recognized in generating a SENTENCE. The DATA of LANGUAGE are 'represented' as a configuration of ELEMENTS at a given level (e.g. 'SEMANTIC/PHONOLOGICAL/DEEP-STRUCTURAL/SYSTEMATIC PHONETIC . . . representation' of a sentence), and the RULES of the grammar assign STRUCTURAL DESCRIPTIONS to these representations. For example, in a phonetic representation, an UTTERANCE might be analysed in terms of a MATRIX where the various rows are labelled by phonetic FEATURES and the columns are successive SEGMENTS. The notion has become a central issue in recent phonological theory, where the question of the nature and organization of representations has characterized a great deal of work in NON-LINEAR PHONOLOGY. Different approaches can be distinguished by their principles of representation – for example, by the way they handle word PHONOTACTICS, phonological ALTERNATIONS, or phonological CONTRASTS – and the issue of representation is at the centre of several models, notably UNDERSPECIFICATION theory.

representative A term used in the theory of SPEECH ACTS to refer to a type of UTTERANCE where speakers convey their belief about the truth of a PROPOSITION, as in *I state/hypothesize . . .*

resonance (resonate) A term derived from the physics of sound, and used in ACOUSTIC PHONETICS to refer to those vibrations of air movement in the VOCAL TRACT which are set in motion by a source of PHONATION. The main **resonance chambers** of the vocal tract are the mouth, nose and PHARYNX, and these CAVITIES, in their various shapes, act to strengthen some of the FREQUENCIES present in the source of sound, producing the range of human sounds.

resonant A term used by some PHONETICIANS to refer to speech sounds produced at the GLOTTIS with a relatively wide articulatory channel, so that no subsequent audible friction is produced, e.g. VOWELS, LATERALS, NASALS, FRICTIONLESS CONTINUANTS. The analogous term in DISTINCTIVE FEATURE theory is SONORANT. In this respect, the category can be opposed to OBSTRUENT, where CLOSURE or narrowing is the essential characteristic.

REST The usual abbreviation for REVISED EXTENDED STANDARD THEORY.

restricted (1) A term used by the sociologist Basil Bernstein (b. 1924) to refer to one of two VARIETIES (or CODES) of LANGUAGE use, introduced as part of a general theory of the nature of social systems and social roles, the other being ELABORATED. **Restricted code** was thought to be used in relatively informal situations, stressing the speaker's membership of a group, was very reliant on CONTEXT for its meaningfulness (e.g. there would be several shared expectations and assumptions between the speakers), and lacked STYLISTIC range. Linguistically, it was highly predictable, with a relatively high proportion of such features as PRONOUNS, TAG QUESTIONS, and use of gestures and INTONATION to convey MEANING. Elaborated code, by contrast, was thought to lack these features. The correlation of restricted code with certain types of social-class background, and its role in educational settings (e.g. whether children used to this code will succeed in schools where elaborated code is the norm – and what should be done in such cases), brought this theory considerable publicity and controversy, and the distinction has since been reinterpreted in various ways.

(2) The phrase **restricted language** is used by some LINGUISTS (especially FIRTHIANS) to refer to a reduced linguistic SYSTEM used for a special communicative purpose, as in the language of heraldry, or air-traffic control. Alternatively, the notion may be characterized with reference to 'restricted CONTEXTS'.

restrictive A contrast recognized in the GRAMMATICAL analysis of PHRASES, referring to the semantic relationship of a MODIFYING structure to its accompanying HEAD word. In **restrictive modification**, the LINGUISTIC identity of the head is dependent upon the accompanying modification; if it is not, the modification being inessential, the term **non-restrictive** is used. The contrast is illustrated by the two meanings of the sentence *Look at John's black dog*; with the emphasis on *dog*, the implication is that John has one dog with him, which happens to be black (i.e. the modification is non-restrictive); but with the emphasis on *black* the implication is that John has more than one dog with him, and our attention is being drawn to the black one (i.e. the blackness is crucial to the identity of the dog, and the modification is thus restrictive). Several areas of grammar illustrate this contrast, such as RELATIVE clauses and APPOSITIONAL constructions.

restructuring see REANALYSIS

result (-(at)ive, -ing, -ant) A term used in GRAMMAR and SEMANTICS to refer to a CLAUSE or ELEMENT whose MEANING expresses the notion of consequence or effect. Several features of grammar have a use which has been variously labelled 'resultative', 'resulting' or 'resultant', such as ADVERBIALS (e.g. *at last, as a result*), certain types of ATTRIBUTIVE constructions (e.g. *He became sad*), OBJECTS where the REFERENT exists only because of the activity of the VERB (e.g. *She's writing **a letter***) and clauses introduced by the CONJUNCTIONS *so* or *so that* (e.g. *I went **so that I could see what was happening***). In later CASE grammar, the term replaced FACTITIVE, used to refer to an object or being which results from an action or state.

resumptive A term used in GRAMMATICAL analysis to refer to an element or structure which repeats or in some way recapitulates the meaning of a prior element. The chief examples are **resumptive pronouns** (e.g. *Mary, I know **her***) and **resumptive relative clauses** (e.g. *The chairman announced the result, an announcement **which had been long awaited***).

resyllabify see SYLLABLE

retract(ed) A term used in PHONETICS to refer to the backwards movement of an

ARTICULATOR, especially the BACK of the TONGUE towards the velum. 'Retracted' sounds are heard in VELARIZATION, or the CENTRALIZATION of FRONT VOWELS.

retroflex(-ion, -ed) A term used in the PHONETIC classification of CONSONANT sounds on the basis of their PLACE OF ARTICULATION: it refers to a sound made when the TIP of the TONGUE is curled back in the direction of the front part of the hard PALATE – in other words, just behind the ALVEOLAR ridge. The degree of **retroflexion** varies considerably between sounds and DIALECTS. The quality of *r* sounds traditionally associated with American English, and with many rural British English dialects (especially in the South West), illustrates one main group of retroflex sounds, and this quality may also be heard on any VOWELS preceding a **retroflexed** *r* (the vowel is said to be '*r*-COLOURED' or 'rhotacized'), as the tongue may begin to move to a retroflex position while the vowel is still being articulated. Other common retroflex consonants are the retroflexed correlates of [t] and [d] – [ʈ] and [ɖ] – heard in many Indian LANGUAGES, such as Hindi, and also in the English spoken by NATIVE-SPEAKERS of such languages. [n], [l], [s] and [z] may also be retroflexed.

reversal (1) A term used by some PSYCHOLINGUISTS to refer to a type of TONGUE-SLIP where two LINGUISTIC UNITS are interchanged, as when *rabbits and chickens* might become *chabbits and rickens*. Traditionally, such errors are referred to as METATHESES or spoonerisms.

(2) A term used in METRICAL PHONOLOGY for the switching of weak and strong NODES encountered in such phrases as *thirteen men*, so that ˘// becomes /˘/; also known as **iambic reversal**, the **rhythm rule**, or (after one of the original examples used to discuss the phenomenon) the **thirteen men rule**. The METRICAL GRID, as a consequence, has a structure which is alternating rather than clashing.

revised extended standard theory (REST) The name given to the revised version of the EXTENDED STANDARD THEORY, proposed by Noam CHOMSKY in the mid-1970s, following the adoption of the TRACE convention on the application of MOVEMENT RULES. There are several aspects to the 'revision': the BASE COMPONENT of the GRAMMAR now incorporates the LEXICAL hypothesis and the X-BAR convention; the notion of SURFACE STRUCTURE is supplemented by the notion of SHALLOW structure (cf. S-STRUCTURE), which provides the INPUT to the SEMANTIC rules (as opposed to the DEEP STRUCTURES of standard theory); there are two semantic components and two LEVELS of semantic REPRESENTATION (LOGICAL FORM and full semantic representation); and the DESCRIPTIVE POWER and number of TRANSFORMATIONS is much reduced.

rewrite rule (rewriting rule) A type of RULE in GENERATIVE GRAMMAR, which takes the form X → Y. The symbol to the left of the arrow represents a single STRUCTURAL ELEMENT; the symbol to the right of the arrow represents a STRING of one or more elements: and the arrow is an instruction to replace (or 'expand') X by Y. Such rules are conventionally read as 'Rewrite X as Y'; see further, PHRASE-STRUCTURE GRAMMAR, ENVIRONMENT.

R-expression An abbreviation for **referring expression**, a category in the three-way classification of NOUN PHRASES in BINDING theory, the other two being

ANAPHORS and PRONOMINALS. According to principle C of binding theory, R-expressions must be FREE.

rheme (rhematic) In the PRAGUE SCHOOL approach to LINGUISTICS of recent years, this term is distinguished from THEME, as part of an analysis of the INFORMATION structure of messages, within an overall theoretical framework known as FUNCTIONAL SENTENCE PERSPECTIVE. The rheme is defined as the part of a sentence which adds most to the advancing process of communication (it has the highest degree of COMMUNICATIVE DYNAMISM); in other words, it expresses the largest amount of extra MEANING, in addition to what has already been communicated. The theme, by contrast, carries the lowest degree of communicative dynamism. Various transitional expressions, neither 'thematic' nor 'rhematic', are also recognized.

rhetoric (-ian, -al) In classical approaches to LANGUAGE, the study of effective or persuasive speaking and writing, especially as practised in public oratory. Several hundred **rhetorical figures** were recognized by classical rhetoricians, classifying the way words could be arranged in order to achieve special STYLISTIC effects. Some of these notions have continued in modern stylistic analysis, such as METAPHOR, simile, personification and paradox. On the whole, however, the complex terminology of the ancients has been considered too cumbersome for continued use, and its Latin/Greek provenance of limited applicability to modern languages. But the study of rhetoric has been given a new lease of life in modern courses on communication, where the aim is to understand the processes underlying successful argument and persuasion. Special applications have emerged: for example, **contrastive rhetoric** is a hypothesis that the organization of written text (chiefly, formal expository prose) is significantly different between languages. It works within a weak version of the SAPIR–WHORF HYPOTHESIS, and involves an application of DISCOURSE ANALYSIS. A chief objective is educational (cf. CONTRASTIVE ANALYSIS): to help foreign-language learners handle the discourse structures of advanced texts.

rhetorical question see QUESTION

rhotic A term used in English PHONOLOGY referring to DIALECTS or ACCENTS where /r/ is pronounced following a VOWEL, as in *car* and *cart*. VARIETIES which do not have this feature are **non-rhotic** (such as RECEIVED PRONUNCIATION). Vowels which occur after RETROFLEX consonants are sometimes called **rhotacized**.

rhyme In METRICAL PHONOLOGY, a term referring to a single CONSTITUENT of SYLLABLE structure comprising the NUCLEUS (the non-consonantal SEGMENTS) and CODA (the final sequence of CONSONANTAL segments); sometimes also called the **rime** (using a less common US spelling to reinforce its technical interpretation in this context) or **core**. The notion postulates a close relationship between these two elements of the syllable, as distinct from the syllable ONSET (the initial consonant sequence). Stress is assigned to syllables using only the elements of the STRING DOMINATED by rhyme NODES (i.e. onsets are ignored); this principle is called **rhyme projection**.

rhythm An application of the general sense of this term in PHONOLOGY, to refer to the perceived regularity of PROMINENT UNITS in speech. These regularities may be stated in terms of patterns of STRESSED *v.* unstressed SYLLABLES, syllable LENGTH (long *v.* short) or PITCH (high *v.* low) – or some combination of these variables. Maximally regular patterns, such as are encountered in many kinds of poetry, are referred to as 'metrical'.

rhythm rule see REVERSAL

right-branching A term used in GENERATIVE GRAMMAR to refer to a CONSTRUCTION whose DERIVATION involves a series of structural operations which would be represented in increasing complexity of the right-hand side of a TREE diagram. The type of rule involved can be represented by X → Y + (X). For example, the phrase *the book of the wife of the major* . . . is a 'right-branching' or 'right-recursive' structure; it contrasts with *the major's wife's book*, which is LEFT-BRANCHING, and also with the notion of SELF-EMBEDDING.

right dislocation In GRAMMATICAL description, a type of SENTENCE in which one of the CONSTITUENTS appears in FINAL position and its CANONICAL position is filled by a PRONOUN with the same REFERENCE, e.g. *I know her, Julie; He's always late, that chap.*

right-linear grammar see LINEAR GRAMMAR

right node raising A term used in GENERATIVE GRAMMAR for the type of CO-ORDINATE CONSTRUCTION illustrated by *John likes, and Bill hates, writing letters.* It is also known as **shared constituent co-ordination**. Some grammatical approaches handle this kind of construction using the notion of ELLIPSIS.

rim The edges of the TONGUE, the extent of whose contact with the roof of the mouth can affect the quality of several sounds, such as [s] and [l].

rime see RHYME

rising/rise (1) A term used in classifying the LINGUISTIC uses of PITCH, referring to a movement from relatively low to relatively high. Rising tones of various kinds (e.g. 'high/low rising', 'rising-falling') may be encountered in the study of INTONATION systems and of TONE LANGUAGES.

(2) A term used in a two-way classification of DIPHTHONGS, referring to cases where the second element of the diphthong receives the maximum PROMINENCE.

role In LINGUISTICS, an application of the general sense of this term to refer to the FUNCTION of an element in a SENTENCE or DERIVATION. It is particularly used in the analysis of SYNTACTIC or SEMANTIC functions, such as AGENT or LOCATIVE. See also THETA ROLE.

role and reference grammar A FUNCTIONALLY orientated framework for GRAMMATICAL DESCRIPTION, in which the choice of a grammatical structure is determined by an interaction of SEMANTIC (i.e. **role**) factors and PRAGMATIC or CONTEXTUAL (i.e. **reference**) factors. The focus is on the STRUCTURE of the CLAUSE, analysed into a 'core' layer (a 'nuclear' VERB and its associated ARGUMENTS) and a 'periphery' (e.g. ADJUNCTS), and supplemented by a theory of JUNCTURE (how sub-clausal UNITS combine) and a theory of NEXUS (the types of SYNTACTIC relationship between the units in the juncture). These elemental units are used in an 'interclausal grammar' to analyse the variety of clausal, sentential, and larger constructions found in languages. The approach is LEXICALLY based and makes no use of DERIVATIONS. It functions by establishing the contextual conditions which govern the pairing of meaning REPRESENTATIONS to structural REALIZATIONS.

roll(ed) A term used in the PHONETIC classification of CONSONANT sounds on the basis of their MANNER OF ARTICULATION. Also known as a 'rolled' consonant, or a TRILL, it refers to any sound made by the rapid tapping of one organ of articulation against another. (VOCAL-CORD vibration is not included in such a definition.) Several ACCENTS of English use an ALVEOLAR rolled [r], as in Welsh and Scots. French and German are examples of languages where UVULAR rolled [R] can be heard.

root (1) A term often used in LINGUISTICS (and traditionally used in HISTORICAL LINGUISTICS) as part of a classification of the kinds of ELEMENT operating within the STRUCTURE of a WORD. A root is the BASE FORM of a WORD which cannot be further analysed without total loss of identity. Putting this another way, it is that part of the word left when all the AFFIXES are removed. In the word *meaningfulness*, for example, removing *-ing*, *-ful* and *-ness* leaves the root *mean*. Roots (sometimes referred to as 'radicals') may be classified in several different ways. They may be 'free' MORPHEMES, such as *mean* (i.e. they can stand alone as a word), or they may be 'bound' morphemes, such as *-ceive* (e.g. *receive, conceive, deceive*). From another point of view, roots are sometimes classified as 'simple' (i.e. compositionally unanalysable in terms of morphemes) or 'complex'/'compound' (i.e. certain combinations of simple root forms, as in *blackbird, careful*, etc.), though for the latter the term STEM is commonly used. From a SEMANTIC point of view, the root generally carries the main component of MEANING in a word. From a historical viewpoint, the root is the earliest form of a word, though this information is not relevant to a SYNCHRONIC analysis (and may not always coincide with the results of it). The term **root-inflected** is sometimes applied to a type of language where the INFLECTIONS affect the internal PHONOLOGICAL structure of the root, as in Arabic, where roots are defined as a sequence of CONSONANTS (CvCvC), and variation in the intervening VOWELS signals such GRAMMATICAL differences as present *v.* past TENSE. By contrast, a language such as Chinese may be said to be **root-isolating**, i.e. the root morphemes are invariable, and grammatical relationships are signalled by other means, such as WORD ORDER.

(2) The furthest-back part of the TONGUE, opposite the PHARYNGEAL wall, not normally involved in the production of speech sounds; also called the **radix** (articulations may therefore be described as **radical**). It is however involved in advanced tongue root (ATR) articulation – a movement which expands the front-back diameter of the pharynx, used phonologically in some (e.g. African) languages as a factor in contrasts of VOWEL HARMONY.

(3) In GENERATIVE GRAMMAR, the term is sometimes used to refer to the topmost NODE in a TREE diagram. In NON-LINEAR PHONOLOGY, the **root node** is the one which DOMINATES all other FEATURES in the HIERARCHY; for example in METRICAL PHONOLOGY, it refers to the topmost node in a metrical tree. In TRANSFORMATIONAL grammar it also refers to a type of transformation which applies only to full SENTENCE STRUCTURE and not to EMBEDDED sentences. A **root**

transformation applies in the formation of *YES–NO* QUESTIONS, for instance, where only the main CLAUSE is affected (e.g. *He said that there was trouble* → *Did he say that there was trouble?*).

root-and-pattern A term applied to the MORPHOLOGY of certain languages (notably Semitic languages), referring to the way in which a stable CONSONANTAL sequence (the 'root') appears in several related WORDS of varying SEGMENTAL shape; for example, from such Arabic forms as *katab* 'write' and *kaatib* 'writing' one may identify a root pattern *k-t-b*. The notion has attracted particular attention in NON-LINEAR PHONOLOGY, because it is a motivation for the SKELETAL TIER of representation. In this context, the phenomenon is handled by the mapping of consonantal roots to skeletal TEMPLATES, each template defining the basic shape for a particular morphological category.

rounding (rounded) A term used in the classification of lip position in PHONETICS, referring to the visual appearance of the lips when they assume a **rounded** shape, as in the 'close rounding' of [u] and the more 'open rounding' of [ɔ]. Each of the VOWEL positions on the CARDINAL VOWEL diagram has both a rounded and an **unrounded** form, e.g. [i] *v.* [y], [e] *v.* [ø]. Lip position is, in fact, of particular PHONOLOGICAL significance in the analysis of VOWEL and SEMI-VOWEL qualities.

The opposition rounded/non-rounded has special status in CHOMSKY and Halle's DISTINCTIVE FEATURE theory of PHONOLOGY, where it handles variations in PLACE OF ARTICULATION (CAVITY features), specifying lip position. 'Rounded' sounds are defined articulatorily, as those produced with a narrowing of the lips, as in [w], [u], etc. Its opposite is **non-rounded**, referring to sounds produced without any such narrowing, as in English FRONT VOWELS.

RP The abbreviation for RECEIVED PRONUNCIATION.

RTN The abbreviation for 'recursive TRANSITION NETWORK' GRAMMAR.

rule A term used in LINGUISTICS, and especially in GENERATIVE GRAMMAR, to refer to a formal statement of correspondence between linguistic ELEMENTS or STRUCTURES. In the case of **generative rules**, there is more involved than a set of descriptive statements summarizing one's observations; generative rules are predictive, expressing a hypothesis about the relationships between SENTENCES which will hold for the LANGUAGE as a whole, and which reflect the NATIVE-SPEAKER'S COMPETENCE. In the classical account, a grammar is seen as a set of REWRITE RULES which will generate all and only the grammatical sentences of a language. The rules may be subclassified in terms of the COMPONENTS of the grammar in which they appear (e.g. 'phonological rules', 'syntactic rules', 'lexical rules').

Several types of rules have been recognized. The most basic types are PHRASE-STRUCTURE rules, of the form X → Y, and TRANSFORMATIONAL rules, of the form A => B, where A and B are STRINGS of structural elements. In *Syntactic Structures* (1957) a distinction was made between OPTIONAL and OBLIGATORY rules. Other types of rule commonly cited include RECURSIVE, GLOBAL, MOVEMENT, READJUSTMENT, VARIABLE, lexical INSERTION and lexical REDUNDANCY rules (see LEXIS). In some later MODELS of generative grammar, the notion of a **rule**

schema is introduced. This is a means of specifying a set of rules without having to list them individually, e.g. $S \rightarrow S^n$, where ^{n} refers to any number of sentences (greater than 1) that can be the result of this rule (as in CO-ORDINATE sentences, which may be of any length). In GENERALIZED PHRASE-STRUCTURE GRAMMAR, reference is made to IMMEDIATE DOMINANCE rules and LINEAR PRECEDENCE rules. In GOVERNMENT-BINDING THEORY there has been a shift away from the notion of rules to that of PRINCIPLES and PARAMETERS.

The linguistic sense thus contrasts with the traditional use of the term, where rules are recommendations for correct usage, as in 'a preposition is not to be used at the end of a sentence'. No PRESCRIPTIVE or PROSCRIPTIVE implication is present in the linguistic sense of 'rule'. See also CATEGORY, CONSTRUE, CYCLE, DEPENDENCY GRAMMAR, EXPRESSION (2), FORMATION RULE, NORM, NUCLEUS, PROJECTION, SANDHI, WORD FORMATION.

rule features A term used in classical TRANSFORMATIONAL GRAMMAR (cf. ASPECTS) to refer to one of the types of (BINARY) FEATURES which are contained in a LEXICAL entry (the others being INHERENT features and CONTEXTUAL features), and which provides information as to whether a lexical ITEM is exceptional with reference to the applicability of a non-lexical TRANSFORMATION (e.g. PASSIVIZATION). This type of feature is symbolized as [–Passive], [–Equi], etc. If a rule does have lexical exceptions, it is said to be GOVERNED (otherwise ungoverned).

rule-ordering paradox In recent PHONOLOGICAL theory, a term used to characterize violations of the CONDITION on consistent RULE ORDERING stipulated in early GENERATIVE phonology. Approaches which permit such violations require $A < B$ in some derivations and $B < A$ in others.

rule-to-rule A term sometimes used in theoretical LINGUISTICS, arising out of MONTAGUE GRAMMAR, to refer to a view of LANGUAGE (the 'rule-to-rule hypothesis') which maintains that each SYNTACTIC RULE in a grammar is associated with a SEMANTIC rule which determines the MEANING of the CONSTITUENT whose FORM is specified by the syntactic rule.

S

Σ see SIGMA

S The usual abbreviation for SENTENCE or SUBJECT; and sometimes for SURFACE or SHALLOW, in such contexts as S-STRUCTURE.

S′ An abbreviation used in GENERATIVE GRAMMAR for a CLAUSE introduced by a SUBORDINATING CONJUNCTION or COMPLEMENTIZER. In recent GOVERNMENT-BINDING THEORY, it is assumed that such clauses are headed by the complementizer, and hence they are labelled CP (see CP).

SAAD An abbreviation sometimes used to refer to the KERNEL SENTENCES GENERATED by a GRAMMAR – standing for SIMPLE–ACTIVE–AFFIRMATIVE–DECLARATIVE.

sandhi A term used in SYNTAX and MORPHOLOGY to refer to the PHONOLOGICAL MODIFICATION of GRAMMATICAL FORMS which have been juxtaposed. The term comes from a Sanskrit word meaning 'joining'. **Sandhi forms** are forms which have undergone specific modifications in specific circumstances (i.e. various **sandhi rules** have applied). ASSIMILATION and DISSIMILATION are two widespread tendencies which could be classified under this heading. The merit of the sandhi notion is that it can be used as a very general term within which can be placed a wide range of structural tendencies that otherwise it would be difficult to interrelate. In languages where sandhi forms are complex, a distinction is sometimes made between **external sandhi** (sandhi RULES which operate across word boundaries) and **internal sandhi** (rules which operate within words). See also TONE.

Sapir–Whorf hypothesis A theory of the relationship between LANGUAGE and thought expounded in its most explicit form by the American anthropological linguists Edward Sapir (1884–1939) and Benjamin Lee Whorf (1897–1941). Also known as the theory of linguistic RELATIVITY, the hypothesis states (in the words of Whorf) that 'we dissect nature along lines laid down by our native languages . . . by the linguistic systems in our minds.' The differences in world-view imposed by different languages have, however, proved extremely difficult to elucidate or test experimentally, and the fact of successful BILINGUAL translation weakens the force of the theory's claims; as a result, the Sapir–Whorf hypothesis has made little impact on contemporary PSYCHOLINGUISTICS.

satellite A term used in FUNCTIONAL GRAMMAR to refer to those elements which turn a NUCLEAR PREDICATION into a full predication. Satellites specify further properties of the nuclear state of affairs expressed in a SENTENCE – such as MANNER, TEMPORAL and LOCATIVE.

satem language see CENTUM LANGUAGE

Saussurean Characteristic of, or a follower of, the principles of Ferdinand de **Saussure** (1857–1913), especially as outlined in his posthumous *Cours de linguistique générale* (Paris, 1913), first translated by W. Baskin as *Course in General Linguistics* (New York, 1959). His conception of LANGUAGE as a SYSTEM of mutually defining entities was a major influence on several schools of LINGUISTICS (e.g. the PRAGUE SCHOOL, GENEVA SCHOOL, GLOSSEMATICS), and most of the theoretical distinctions he introduced have become foundations of linguistic study. Chief among these are the notions of LANGUE and PAROLE, SYNTAGMATIC and PARADIGMATIC, SYNCHRONIC and DIACHRONIC, and SIGNIFIANT and SIGNIFIÉ.

SC An abbreviation used in GENERATIVE GRAMMAR to refer to STRUCTURAL CHANGE. In GOVERNMENT-BINDING THEORY, it is an abbreviation for SMALL CLAUSE, especially in contexts where linguists want to avoid taking a stand on what the correct label for this constituent is!

scalar expressions In SEMANTICS and PRAGMATICS, expressions which involve scales in their interpretation. They include logical QUANTIFIERS (e.g. *all, some*), quantifying DETERMINERS (e.g. *few, half*), quantifying time expressions (e.g. *always, often*), scalar ADVERBS (*almost, only, more than*), and scalar PREDICATES (e.g. *love, like; must, shall*). The nature of such scales is controversial, being conceived both in terms of strength (e.g. '*all* is stronger than *some*') and of direction (*almost* and *more* activate a scale which is in a positive direction, by contrast with the negative direction of *only* and *less than*).

scale-and-category grammar A LINGUISTIC theory devised by the British linguist M. A. K. HALLIDAY in the early 1960s in which the STRUCTURE of LANGUAGE is seen as an intersecting set of scales and CATEGORIES operating at different LEVELS. Several levels of oganization are recognized. At the level of SUBSTANCE, the physical DATA of speech or writing are defined in PHONIC or GRAPHIC terms. The organization of substance into linguistic CONTRASTS is carried out at the level of FORM; GRAMMAR and LEXIS being the two main subdivisions. PHONOLOGY is seen as an 'inter-level' connecting the level of substance and form. CONTEXT is a further 'inter-level', connecting the level of form with the extralinguistic SITUATION. Linguistic analysis in this view proceeds by establishing four theoretical 'categories' – UNITS, STRUCTURES, CLASSES and SYSTEMS – and interrelating these by the 'scales' of RANK, EXPONENCE and DELICACY. (This use of 'scale' should not be confused with that found in phonology, in relation to STRENGTH values.) In the late 1960s, parts of this approach were superseded by a SYSTEMIC MODEL of analysis.

scansion (scan) An application in some approaches to NON-LINEAR PHONOLOGY of a term used in traditional METRICS (where it refers to the analysis of verse RHYTHM) for the analysis of certain rhythmic properties of speech. A phonological REPRESENTATION can be 'scanned' to determine its properties – in particular, to determine whether it satisfies the LOCALITY condition at various levels in the FEATURE HIERARCHY. In one approach, two kinds of scansion are recognized: in **minimal scansion**, a RULE scans a TIER which contains a target NODE/feature; in **maximal scansion**, a rule scans the highest level of SYLLABIC structure providing access to a target node/feature. In METRICAL PHONOLOGY, the **level of scansion** is the highest grid level where EURHYTHMY is relevant as a component of the phonology. It is typically one level down from the level of the STRESS peak.

SCC The abbreviation for 'strict CYCLE condition'.

schwa/shwa (pronounced [ʃwɑː]) The usual name for the NEUTRAL VOWEL [ə], heard in English at the beginning of such WORDS as *ago, amaze*, or in the middle of *afterwards*. It is a particularly frequent vowel in English, as it is the one most commonly heard when a STRESSED vowel becomes unstressed, e.g. *telegraph* becoming *telegraphy* /ˈteləgrɑːf/ *v.* /təˈlegrəfi/. It is also the usual pronunciation of the vowel in such words as *the, a, an, and*. The term 'schwa' comes from the German name of a vowel of this CENTRAL quality found in Hebrew.

scope A term used in SYNTAX, SEMANTICS and PRAGMATICS to refer to the stretch of LANGUAGE affected by the meaning of a particular form; in formal terms, if an OPERATOR combines with an expression (E.O), E is the 'scope' of O. For example, in English, the scope of NEGATION normally extends from the negative word until the end of the CLAUSE; this therefore allows such SEMANTIC contrasts as *I deliberately didn't ask her* (= 'I did not ask her') and *I didn't deliberately ask her* (= 'I did ask her, but accidentally'). ADVERBIALS, INTERROGATIVE forms and QUANTIFIERS are among the features where it is necessary to refer to the notion of scope. Sentences where there is AMBIGUITY deriving from alternative scope interpretations are sometimes referred to as **scope ambiguities**.

scrambling In SYNTAX, an optional RULE which permutes major CONSTITUENTS in free WORD-ORDER languages (e.g. Latin); for example, the STRING A+B+C+D could become A+C+B+D. The factors which influence scrambling (e.g. the elements which are affected, and the direction in which they move) may be STYLISTIC in character. A distinction is drawn between 'short-distance scrambling' (within a CLAUSE) and the less usual 'long-distance scrambling' (across a clause boundary).

SD An abbreviation used in GENERATIVE GRAMMAR to refer to STRUCTURAL DESCRIPTION.

secondary aperture One of the types of sound feature set up by CHOMSKY and Halle in their DISTINCTIVE FEATURE theory of PHONOLOGY, to handle variations in PLACE OF ARTICULATION (CAVITY features). It subsumes NASAL and LATERAL features, both defined as OPPOSITIONS.

secondary articulation In a sound produced with two points of ARTICULATION, this term refers to the point of articulation involving the lesser degree of STRICTURE, e.g. LABIALIZATION, PALATALIZATION; opposed to **primary articulation**. See also the distinction between 'major' and 'minor' in the context of PHONOLOGY (cf. MAJOR (2)).

secondary response A term introduced into LINGUISTICS by Leonard BLOOMFIELD to refer to UTTERANCES people make about their LANGUAGE. The term includes not only the METALINGUISTIC utterances of linguistics but also the loosely organized, yet fairly uniform system of popular pronouncements about language, e.g. 'bad grammar', 'correct pronunciation'. It is distinguished from 'primary' response (the use of language as such) and TERTIARY RESPONSE (the evaluation of secondary responses).

second language see LANGUAGE

segment(-al, -ation, -ator) A term used in PHONETICS and LINGUISTICS primarily to refer to any DISCRETE UNIT that can be identified, either physically or auditorily, in the stream of speech. 'Segmentation' can take place using either physical or auditory criteria: in the former case, ACOUSTIC or ARTICULATORY change-points can be identified as boundaries of segments; in the latter case, perceptible changes in QUALITY or QUANTITY, often showing the influence of the language's PHONEMIC units, are the basis of division. The term is especially used in phonetics, where the smallest perceptible discrete unit is referred to as a PHONE. A feature which begins or ends within one of the phases of articulation of a segment is called a **subsegmental** feature (cf. ONSET). 'Segment' has developed an abstract sense in GENERATIVE PHONOLOGY, where it is used for a mental unit of phonological organization – one of a series of minimal units which, however, are not strung together in a simple LINEAR way. In this model, no physical reality is being segmented.

A **segmentator** is a device used in instrumental phonetics which plays back a recording of speech at varying small time intervals, thus allowing a more detailed study of the segments produced.

In phonology, a major division is often made into segmental and SUPRASEGMENTAL (or 'non-segmental') categories. **Segmental phonology** analyses the speech into distinctive units, or PHONEMES (= 'segmental phonemes'), which have a fairly direct correspondence with phonetic segments (alternative approaches involve analysis in terms of DISTINCTIVE FEATURES and PROSODIES). **Suprasegmental** or **non-segmental phonology** analyses those features of speech which extend over more than one segment, such as INTONATION or (in some theories) VOWEL harmony.

The above terminology has been applied analogously to the study of written texts, where GRAPHS and GRAPHEMES are some of the segments identified. The term is also found in the analysis of higher linguistic units, such as MORPHEMES or WORDS, as in STRUCTURALIST analyses of GRAMMAR (cf. IMMEDIATE-CONSTITUENT analysis).

segmental tier see PHONEME

segmented discourse representation theory see DISCOURSE REPRESENTATION THEORY

selectional feature/restriction/rule A term in GENERATIVE GRAMMAR for a type of CONTEXTUAL FEATURE, i.e. a SYNTACTIC feature which specifies the conditions relating to where in a DEEP STRUCTURE a LEXICAL ITEM can occur. Selectional features specify the restrictions on the permitted combinations of lexical items within a given GRAMMATICAL context. These restrictions are stated with reference to the relevant INHERENT features in an adjacent or nearby COMPLEX SYMBOL (within the same structural unit, i.e. they must be CLAUSE-MATES). For example, a VERB which requires an ANIMATE SUBJECT NOUN PHRASE (cf. **the stone slept*) would have the restriction stated as part of its feature specification, e.g. as [+[+Animate]].

selective listening A term derived from the notion of selective attention in psychology, and used in PSYCHOLINGUISTICS to refer to the process whereby people are able to pick out certain aspects of a speech signal and to ignore others. The COCKTAIL PARTY PHENOMENON characterizes the problem – how a person is able to attend selectively to one out of several simultaneously occurring conversations. Analysis of the factors which affect this ability (e.g. the SEMANTIC content of the conversations, the speed of the speech) suggests several conclusions which are of major importance in developing a theory of speech perception – for instance, that CONNECTED SPEECH cannot be perceived as a series of isolated SEGMENTS.

self-embedding A term used in GENERATIVE GRAMMAR to refer to a CONSTRUCTION whose DERIVATION involves structural operations of the form X→Y+(X)+Z; also known as **centre-embedding**. Self-embedding constructions can be illustrated from RELATIVE CLAUSES, such as *The dog that the cat scratched ran away*. Here, the SENTENCE which UNDERLIES the relative clause (*The cat scratched the dog*) is embedded within the sentence *The dog ran away*. The process can continue indefinitely, but the ACCEPTABILITY of this construction deteriorates with the number of self-embeddings, cf. *?The dog that the cat that the man bought scratched ran away*. These problems have stimulated considerable discussion concerning the psychological mechanisms that need to be assumed to explain linguistic behaviour, reference being made to alternative processes of sentence formation, such as RIGHT-BRANCHING and LEFT-BRANCHING constructions.

self-repair see REPAIR

semantics (semantic, -ity) A major branch of LINGUISTICS devoted to the study of MEANING in LANGUAGE. The term is also used in philosophy and logic, but not with the same range of meaning or emphasis as in linguistics. **Philosophical semantics** examines the relations between linguistic expressions and the phenomena in the world to which they refer, and considers the conditions under which such expressions can be said to be true or false, and the factors which affect the interpretation of language as used. Its history of study, which reaches back to the writings of Plato and Aristotle, in recent years includes the work of such philosophers and logicians as Charles Peirce (1839–1914), Rudolf Carnap (1891–1970) and Alfred Tarski (1902–83), particularly under the heading of SEMIOTICS and the 'philosophy of language'. 'Logical' or 'pure' semantics is the study of the meaning of expressions in terms of logical systems of analysis, or calculi, and is thus more akin to formal logic or mathematics than to linguistics. An influential approach is **Davidsonian semantics** (proposed by the British philosopher Donald Davidson (b.1917)), which argues that a theory of truth for a natural language constitutes a theory of meaning for that language. The meaning of any sentence is derivable from axioms which assign semantic properties to its constituents, and sentence structures are linked by valid inferential relations.

In linguistics, the emphasis is on the study of the semantic properties of natural languages (as opposed to logical 'languages'), the term 'linguistic semantics' often being employed to make the distinction clear (though this is not a convention needed in this dictionary, where the term 'semantics' is used without qualification to refer to its linguistic sense). Different linguists' approaches to meaning nonetheless illustrate the influence of general philosophical or psychological positions. The 'behaviourist' semantics of Leonard BLOOMFIELD, for example, refers to the application of the techniques of the BEHAVIOURIST movement in psychology, restricting the study of meaning to only observable and measurable behaviour. Partly because of the pessimism of this approach, which concluded that semantics was not yet capable of elucidation in behavioural terms, semantics came to be much neglected in post-Bloomfieldian linguistics, and has received proper attention only since the 1960s.

Of particular importance here is the approach of **structural semantics**, which displays the application of the principles of STRUCTURAL linguistics to the study of meaning through the notion of **semantic relations** (SENSE or 'meaning' relations such as SYNONYMY and ANTONYMY). 'Semantic meaning' may here be used, in contradistinction to 'GRAMMATICAL meaning'. The linguistic structuring of 'semantic space' is also a major concern of GENERATIVE linguistics, where the term 'semantic' is widely used in relation to the grammar's organization (one section being referred to as the **semantic component**) and to the analysis of SENTENCES (in terms of a **semantic representation**) and of LEXICAL ITEMS (in terms of **semantic features**). However, the relation between SYNTAX and semantics in this approach is a matter of controversy. Other terms used to distinguish features of meaning in this and other theories include 'semantic MARKERS/DISTINGUISHERS/properties' and (in an unrelated sense to the above) 'semantic components' (cf. COMPONENTIAL). The **semantic-feature hypothesis** (SFH) is an application of this notion in the study of language ACQUISITION, where the order of appearance of a child's lexical items is held to be governed by the type and complexity of the semantic FEATURES they contain. There have also been attempts in recent years to analyse meaning in terms of the truth-functional relations which obtain between semantic representations of sentences (TRUTH-CONDITIONAL SEMANTICS, MODEL-THEORETIC SEMANTICS). The influence of mathematical and computational models is also evident: **state-transition semantics**, for example, is an analysis of natural language meanings in terms of a series of states and state transitions in a language user (cf. AUTOMATA).

Semantic field theory is an approach which developed in the 1930s; it took the view that the VOCABULARY of a language is not simply a listing of independent items (as the head words in a dictionary would suggest), but is organized into areas, or FIELDS, within which words interrelate and define each other in various ways. The words denoting colour are often cited as an example of a semantic field: the precise meaning of a colour word can be understood only by placing it in relation to the other terms which occur with it in demarcating the colour spectrum.

Other areas of semantics include the DIACHRONIC study of word meanings (ETYMOLOGY), the SYNCHRONIC analysis of word USAGE (LEXICOLOGY), and the compilation of dictionaries (LEXICOGRAPHY). For example, in corpus-based lexicology, a word is sometimes said to have a **semantic prosody** if it typically co-occurs with other words that belong to a particular semantic set; for example, *utterly* co-occurs regularly with words of negative evaluation (e.g. *utterly appalling*). The term 'semantic' has many other uses, however. In the phrase **semantic differential**, it has in fact very little to do with linguistic semantics, being a technique devised by psychologists to find out the emotional reactions of speakers to lexical items, and thus suggest the main AFFECTIVE dimensions in terms of which a language's concepts are organized. In the phrase **semantic triangle**, it refers to a particular MODEL of meaning proposed by C. K. Ogden (1889–1957) and I. A. Richards (1893–1979) in the 1920s, which claimed that meaning is essentially a threefold relationship between linguistic FORMS, concepts and REFERENTS. In the phrase **procedural semantics**, it refers to an approach in PSYCHOLINGUISTICS which models the notion of 'sense' in terms of a set of mental operations that decide on the applicability of a lexical item to an entity, state of affairs, etc. And the term **semanticity** has a much broader sense, being suggested as a very general defining property of language (and other SEMIOTIC SYSTEMS), viz. the ability of the system to convey meaning, by virtue of the associative ties which relate the system's signals to features of the external world. See also GENERAL (1), PROTOTYPE.

semasiology see SEMIOTICS

seme A term used by some European LINGUISTS (e.g. Eugene Coseriu (b. 1921)), to refer to minimal DISTINCTIVE SEMANTIC FEATURES operating within a specific semantic FIELD, e.g. the various defining properties of *cups v. glasses*, such as 'having a handle', 'made of glass'. In this approach, semes contrast with CLASSEMES, which are features of a much more general kind, e.g. 'male', 'animate'.

semeiology see SEMIOTICS

semelfactive A term used in the GRAMMATICAL analysis of ASPECT, to refer to an event which takes place once only, as commonly happens with such verbs as *sneeze, knock*, etc. It is regularly contrasted with ITERATIVE.

sememe (sememic(s)) A term used in some SEMANTIC theories to refer to a minimal UNIT of MEANING. For some, a sememe is equivalent to the meaning of a MORPHEME; for others it is a FEATURE of meaning, equivalent to the notion of 'semantic COMPONENT' or 'semantic feature' in some theories. The term **sememics** is used as part of the description of strata in STRATIFICATIONAL GRAMMAR; the 'sememic stratum', which handles the SYSTEMS of semantic relationship between LEXICAL ITEMS, is here distinguished from the HYPERSEMEMIC stratum, at which is analysed the relationship between LANGUAGE and the external world. **Semotactics**, in this approach, involves the study of the SEQUENTIAL arrangement of sememes.

semi-auxiliary see AUXILIARY (1)

semi-consonant see CONSONANT

semilingual(ism) A term sometimes used in SOCIOLINGUISTICS and language teaching, referring to people who have ACQUIRED two or more LANGUAGES, but who lack a native level of proficiency in any of them. The situation is likely to arise with people who have moved between countries a great deal in their early years. Semilingualism has been little studied, and is controversial, as it suggests that there are people who do not have a true mother tongue; however, many people do claim to be semilingual.

semiotics (semiotic) The scientific study of the properties of signalling systems, whether natural or artificial. In its oldest sense, it refers to the study within philosophy of sign and symbol systems in general (also known as **semiotic, semiology, semasiology, semeiology, significs**). In this approach, LINGUISTIC, psychological, philosophical and sociological characteristics of communicative systems are studied together. The philosophers Charles Peirce (1834–1914), Charles Morris (b. 1901) and later Rudolf Carnap (1891–1970) saw the field as divisible into three areas: SEMANTICS, the study of the relations between linguistic expression and the objects in the world which they refer to or describe; SYNTACTICS, the study of the relation of these expressions to each other; and PRAGMATICS, the study of the dependence of the meaning of these expressions on their users (including the social situation in which they are used).

In recent years, the study of semiotics has come to be applied to the analysis of patterned human COMMUNICATION in all its sensory modes, i.e. hearing, sight, taste, touch and smell. Semiotic studies in this sense vary in the degree to which they have progressed: this emphasis has been taken up mainly by anthropologists, linguists, psychologists and sociologists. The branch of the subject which has received most study is the VOCAL–AUDITORY mode, primarily through the subjects of PHONETICS and LINGUISTICS. The study of visual communication is known as KINESICS. The study of touch behaviour (and associated phenomena, such as body orientation and distance between people) is often called PROXEMICS. Gustatory (taste) and olfactory (smell) systems of communication have received more study in relation to animal communication. The extension of the subject to the analysis of animal systems of communication is known as ZOÖSEMIOTICS.

Particularly in Europe, semiotic (or **semiological**) analysis has developed as part of an attempt to analyse all aspects of communication as SYSTEMS of signals (**semiotic systems**), such as music, eating, clothes and dance, as well as language. In this area, the French writer Roland Barthes (1915–80) has exercised particular influence.

semi-productive see PRODUCTIVITY

semi-sentence A term used by some GRAMMARIANS to refer to SENTENCES whose GRAMMATICALITY or ACCEPTABILITY is doubtful, but where there is sufficient plausibility of interpretation to make one unhappy about a definite judgement of ungrammaticality. For example, in certain CONTEXTS (e.g. poetry) a sentence might seem acceptable, which elsewhere would be rejected as ungrammatical (e.g. the breaking of SELECTIONAL RULES in *all the moon long . . .*).

semi-vowel A term used in the classification of CONSONANT sounds on the basis of their MANNER OF ARTICULATION: it refers to a sound functioning as a consonant but lacking the PHONETIC characteristics normally associated with consonants (such as FRICTION or CLOSURE); instead, its QUALITY is phonetically that of a VOWEL; though, occurring as it does at the MARGINS of a SYLLABLE, its DURATION is much less than that typical of vowels. The common examples in English are

[w] and [j], as in *wet* and *yet* respectively. Some phoneticians refer to these sounds as a type of APPROXIMANT.

semology A major COMPONENT recognized in STRATIFICATIONAL GRAMMAR, comprising the stratal SYSTEMS of SEMEMICS and HYPERSEMEMICS (or SEMANTICS). The component deals with the statement of MEANINGS, both in terms of semantic FEATURES, and in terms of REFERENTIAL/COGNITIVE meaning.

semotactics see SEMEME

sense In SEMANTICS, this term is usually contrasted with REFERENCE, as part of an explication of the notion of MEANING. Reference, or DENOTATION, is seen as EXTRALINGUISTIC – the entities, states of affairs, etc. in the external world which a linguistic EXPRESSION stands for. Sense, on the other hand, refers to the SYSTEM of linguistic relationships (**sense relations**) which a LEXICAL ITEM contracts with other lexical items – the PARADIGMATIC relationships of SYNONYMY, ANTONYMY, etc., and the SYNTAGMATIC relationships of COLLOCATION.

sentence The largest STRUCTURAL UNIT in terms of which the GRAMMAR of a LANGUAGE is organized. Innumerable definitions of sentence exist, ranging from the vague characterizations of TRADITIONAL grammar (such as 'the expression of a complete thought') to the detailed structural descriptions of contemporary LINGUISTIC analysis. Most linguistic definitions of the sentence show the influence of the American linguist Leonard BLOOMFIELD, who pointed to the structural autonomy, or independence, of the notion of sentence: it is 'not included by virtue of any grammatical construction in any larger linguistic form'. Recent research has attempted to discover larger grammatical units (of DISCOURSE, or TEXT), but so far little has been uncovered comparable to the sentence, whose constituent structure is stateable in FORMAL, DISTRIBUTIONAL terms.

Linguistic discussion of the sentence has focused on problems of identification, classification and generation. Identifying sentences is relatively straightforward in the written language, but is often problematic in speech, where INTONATION and PAUSE may give uncertain clues as to whether a sentence boundary exists. Classification of sentence structure proceeds along many different lines, e.g. the binary constituent procedures of IMMEDIATE-CONSTITUENT analysis, or the HIERARCHICAL analyses of HALLIDAYAN and other grammars (sentences being seen as composites of CLAUSES, which in turn are analysed into PHRASES, etc.). In GENERATIVE grammar, likewise, there are several models of analysis for sentence structure, with competing views as to the direction in which a sentence DERIVATION should proceed. Certain analytic problems are shared by all approaches, e.g. how to handle ELLIPTICAL sentences (or 'sentence fragments'), such as *To town* (in answer to *Where are you going?*); how to handle cross-reference between sentences, such as *She's writing* ('sentence CONNECTIVITY'); and how to handle the MINOR, non-PRODUCTIVE sentence types in a language (e.g. *Yes, Please, How do you do?*).

Most analysts agree on the need to recognize a FUNCTIONAL classification of sentences into STATEMENT, QUESTION, COMMAND and EXCLAMATORY types. There is also widespread recognition (albeit with varying terminology) of a formal classification into DECLARATIVE, INTERROGATIVE, IMPERATIVE and EXCLAMATIVE types. Most analyses also recognize some such classification of 'sentence patterns' into simple *v.* complex or compound types, i.e. consisting of one SUBJECT-PREDICATE unit, as opposed to more than one. Whether one calls this subject–predicate unit a CLAUSE, a 'simple' sentence, or uses some other term depends on one's model of analysis – but something analogous to this unit emerges in all theories, e.g. NP+VP, ACTOR–ACTION–GOAL, Subject–Verb–Object. Likewise, the number of formal sentence types recognized, and how they are best defined, has been and remains controversial. Several linguists insist on making a systematic distinction between sentence (a theoretical unit, defined by a grammar) and UTTERANCE (a physical unit, a matter of speech production or PERFORMANCE): in this view, utterances can be analysed in terms of sentences, but utterances do not 'consist of' sentences.

sentence accent see ACCENT (2)

sentential relative clause A type of RELATIVE CLAUSE which modifies the whole of the preceding SENTENCE, instead of only a NOUN. An example is *John loves flying –* ***which amazes me***.

sequence (sequencing) An application of the general sense of this term in LINGUISTICS and PHONETICS, referring to the observable succession of UNITS in an UTTERANCE or TEXT. This sequence may be LINEAR, where the dependencies are made between successive, adjacent units (*the–big–cat–is* . . .), but it may involve non-linear relationships, as in AGREEMENT between WORDS which are separated by other STRUCTURES. Sometimes a specific sequential correspondence is given a separate label, as in the traditional term 'sequence of TENSES', referring to the dependencies between tense forms in successive CLAUSES (e.g. *if he enters, he will win*, but not * . . . *he had won*), or the 'sequencing' patterns analysed in dialogue (as in the greeting ritual in conversational openings) which form part of the subject-matter of DISCOURSE analysis and text linguistics. **Sequencing** is also occasionally used, especially in psychologically influenced studies, to refer to the influence successive structures exercise upon each other (as seen, for example, in the difficulty some language-disordered patients have in sequencing appropriately a set of linguistic units). This use is quite different from the term 'sequencing' in language teaching, where it refers to the order in which a graded series of items is presented to the learner. The structure of linguistic sequences constitutes the province of SYNTAGMATIC analysis. The term is often distinguished from the more abstract notion of ORDER.

serial relationship A term sometimes used in LINGUISTICS, and especially in QUIRK GRAMMAR, to refer to a theory which recognizes GRADIENCE between SYNTACTIC CATEGORIES. In a matrix of the type:

	A	B	C
a	+	–	–
b	+	+	–
c	+	+	+

B would be said to be 'serially related' to A and C. An analogous notion is that of syntactic BLENDING.

serial verb In SYNTAX, a type of CONSTRUCTION for a sequence of VERBS or verb

PHRASES within a CLAUSE (or a sequence of clauses) in which the syntactic relationship between the items is left unmarked. The verbs share a semantic ARGUMENT, but there is no CONJUNCTION or INFLECTION to mark CO-ORDINATION or SUBORDINATION: for example, in the Yoruba sentence *O ra eran je* ('3rd-person buy meat eat') 'meat' is simultaneously the object of both verbs. The verbs may both be MAIN verbs or vary in their syntactic status (e.g. one might function more like an AUXILIARY or a PARTICLE). Serial verb construction is not an important feature of English, though it can be seen in such sentences as *I'll go see* (cf. CATENATIVE).

series A term used in PHONETICS and PHONOLOGY to refer to any set of CONSONANT sounds which has at least one phonetic FEATURE in common, and is distinguished in terms of PLACE OF ARTICULATION. For example, the VOICED PLOSIVE 'series' includes [b] – [d] – [g], the nasal series [m] – [n] – [ŋ], etc.

set expression see FORMULAIC LANGUAGE

setting see ARTICULATORY SETTING

SFH The usual abbreviation in language ACQUISITION studies for semantic-feature hypothesis (cf. SEMANTICS).

SGML The abbreviation for STANDARD GENERALIZED MARKUP LANGUAGE.

shadow pronoun see RESUMPTIVE PRONOUN

shared constituent co-ordination see RIGHT NODE RAISING

shallow A term used in the REVISED EXTENDED STANDARD THEORY of GENERATIVE GRAMMAR, to refer to a LEVEL of REPRESENTATION distinct from (SYNTACTIC) SURFACE STRUCTURE. Shallow structure differs from surface structure principally in the way it is followed within the grammar by certain types of FORMAL operation other than PHONOLOGICAL RULES – FILTERS, DELETION and STYLISTIC rules. The term has also been used in the work of some generative grammarians to refer to the output of CYCLIC TRANSFORMATIONS, whereas in REST it refers to the output of POST-CYCLIC transformations. In GOVERNMENT-BINDING THEORY, shallow structure is known as **S-structure**.

sharp One of the features of sound set up by JAKOBSON and Halle in their DISTINCTIVE FEATURE theory of PHONOLOGY, to help handle SECONDARY ARTICULATIONS – in this case, PALATALIZATION. 'Sharp' CONSONANTS are defined both ARTICULATORILY and ACOUSTICALLY as sounds produced with the TONGUE being raised towards the hard PALATE during their articulation, and with a relatively wide area behind the stricture; there is a consequent greater intensity of some of the higher frequencies of the sound spectrum. All palatalized consonants are [+sharp]. Its opposite term is PLAIN, which lacks these features, and thus corresponds to the whole range of non-palatalized sounds. The feature is not used in the CHOMSKY and Halle system.

shift see CHAIN (3), LANGUAGE, LOAN, RANK, SOUND CHANGE, SYNTAGMATIC (2)

short (sound) see LENGTH (1)

sibilant (sibilance) A term in the PHONETIC classification of sounds on the basis of

MANNER of ARTICULATION. It refers to a FRICATIVE sound made by producing a narrow, GROOVE-like STRICTURE between the BLADE of the TONGUE and the back part of the ALVEOLAR ridge. These sounds, such as [s] and [ʃ], have a high-frequency hiss characteristic. Sounds which lack this feature could be called **non-sibilant**. See also STRIDENCY.

sigma (Σ) A symbol often used for the initial element in a GENERATIVE GRAMMAR, corresponding to SENTENCE, or for a STRESS FOOT in METRICAL PHONOLOGY.
(σ) A symbol used for SYLLABLE in metrical phonology.

sign (1) **(signif-y, -iant, -ié, -ics, -ication)** Several restricted applications of this general term are found in philosophical and LINGUISTIC studies of MEANING, the former especially discussing the types of possible contrast involved in such notions as 'signs', 'symbols', 'symptoms' and 'signals'. Sometimes 'sign' is used in an all-inclusive sense, as when SEMIOTICS is defined as 'the science of signs' (or **significs**). In linguistic discussion, the most widespread sense is when linguistic EXPRESSIONS (WORDS, SENTENCES, etc.) are said to be 'signs' of the entities, states of affairs, etc., which they stand for (or, often, of the concepts involved). This relationship between sign and thing, or sign and concept, is traditionally known as **signification**. The term **linguistic sign** is often used when a distinction is needed with other categories of sign (e.g. visual, tactile). The Swiss linguist Ferdinand de SAUSSURE introduced a terminological distinction which has exercised a major influence on subsequent linguistic discussion: **signifiant** (or 'signifier', or 'significans') was contrasted with **signifié** (or 'concept signified', 'significatum'), and the ARBITRARINESS of the relationship between the FORM and MEANING of signs was emphasized.
(2) In such phrases as **sign language** and **sign system**, the term has a very restricted sense, referring to the system of manual communication used by certain groups as an alternative to ORAL communication. Such groups include policemen (in traffic control), drivers, monks vowed to silence, television studio directors, and so on; but the main application of the term is in relation to the deaf, where the linguistic properties of the various natural and contrived deaf sign languages (e.g. American Sign Language, British Sign Language, Paget–Gorman Sign System) began to receive systematic investigation by linguists in the 1970s (cf. CHEROLOGY).
(3) A more restricted sense of **significant** is found in linguistics, referring to the linguistic status of a spoken or written FEATURE: a feature is significant if it is CONTRASTIVE, i.e. where by substituting it for another feature a difference in meaning is obtained. For example, the distinction between VOICED and voiceless is significant for many English CONSONANTS; WORD ORDER is significant in many types of SENTENCE.

significs see SEMIOTICS

silent pause see PAUSE

silent stress see STRESS

simple A term sometimes used in GRAMMATICAL classification, especially of VERB FORMS, referring to the UNMARKED member of an OPPOSITION, e.g. 'simple present' = the non-PROGRESSIVE ASPECT of the present-TENSE form (as in *I go*); 'simple tense' = a VERB without any AUXILIARIES (as in *I take/took*); 'simple past' = the past-tense form of the verb without auxiliary modification (as in *I took*). The term tends to be avoided in contemporary LINGUISTICS, because of its undesirable psychological associations, but the oppositions between simple and complex/compound SENTENCES (viz. whether containing one CLAUSE or more than one), and simple and compound/complex PREDICATES (viz. a predicate consisting wholly of a verb) are sometimes used. See COMPLEX for examples in other domains.

simplicity (metric) A measure proposed by GENERATIVE LINGUISTIC theory which would automatically assign factors to competing linguistic analyses that would determine which of them was the most satisfactory. Simplicity is here defined quantitatively, in terms of the number of constructs (symbols, RULES, etc.) used in formulating an analysis; this is also often referred to as an ECONOMY measure. Perhaps the most widespread criterion is the number of FEATURES required in order to state a PHONOLOGICAL GENERALIZATION, and much thought has been given by generative phonologists to ways in which such generalizations can be more economically stated, using various kinds of notational abbreviation, e.g ALPHA NOTATION. But the measure relies on a notion of simplicity which still requires much theoretical and methodological elucidation. It is proving extremely difficult to evaluate simultaneously the many variables entering into an analysis, especially the closer that analysis gets to the language as a whole. A simplification made in one part of the analysis may lead to unexpected consequences, in terms of great complexity (or COST) elsewhere. There is also the regular possibility that adult NATIVE-SPEAKERS, and children learning a language, will not always prefer the simpler of the two solutions; and little progress has been made in relating simplicity to other aspects of intuitive evaluation, such as NATURALNESS. Simplicity, then, and its FORMALIZATION, remains a controversial topic.

sincerity conditions see FELICITY CONDITIONS

single-bar A term used in the most widely assumed version of X-BAR theory referring to a small PHRASAL CATEGORY, distinguished from a full phrasal (DOUBLE-BAR) category.

single-base A type of TRANSFORMATIONAL RULE recognized in early MODELS of transformational GRAMMAR, where the rule operates with an input of one TERMINAL STRING. Single-base transformations are also known as SINGULARY transformations, and are opposed to DOUBLE-BASE types, where more than one string is involved.

singular see NUMBER

singulary A type of TRANSFORMATIONAL RULE recognized in early MODELS of transformational GRAMMAR, where the rule operates with an input of one TERMINAL STRING. Singulary, or SINGLE-BASE, transformations are contrasted with GENERALIZED types, where more than one string is involved.

sister A term used in GENERATIVE GRAMMAR to refer to a relation between NODES in a PHRASE-MARKER. A set of nodes will be called sisters if they are all immediately DOMINATED by the same (MOTHER) node.

sister-adjunction (-adjoin) A type of SYNTACTIC operation in classical TRANSFORMATIONAL GRAMMAR, referring to a RULE which places certain elements of STRUCTURE in adjacent POSITIONS, with the aim of specifying how these structures fit together in larger units. To 'sister-adjoin' elements, a CONSTITUENT A is joined to B immediately under a mother NODE. A contrast was drawn with CHOMSKY-ADJUNCTION, where A is joined to B by creating a new B node, which immediately dominates both A and B. In GOVERNMENT-BINDING THEORY, the only type of adjunction is Chomsky-adjunction.

situation(al) In LINGUISTICS, this term is generally used to refer to the EXTRALINGUISTIC setting in which an UTTERANCE takes place – referring to such notions as number of participants, level of FORMALITY, nature of the ongoing activities, and so on. Linguistics emphasizes the need to study LANGUAGE in its situation (or CONTEXT, or **context of situation**), for a full statement of MEANING to be obtained. SOCIOLINGUISTICS is primarily concerned to correlate systematic variations in language with variations in social situation; and the term 'situation' may be used in a restricted sense to refer to the socially distinctive characteristics of the setting in which language is used. The **situational meaning** of an utterance, in this sense, would be equivalent to its sociolinguistic interpretation, e.g. religious, political, informal 'situations'.

situation semantics An approach to the SEMANTIC analysis of LANGUAGES developed during the 1980s as an alternative to possible-worlds-based MODEL-THEORETIC SEMANTICS. It assumes a richer ontology than model-theoretic semantics, treating properties, relations, facts and situations as real objects. Sentences are analysed as denoting not truth values but situations (sets of facts which consist of a location, a relation and a truth value). The approach is also more concerned than model-theoretic semantics with the ways in which the interpretation of sentences depends on the CONTEXT.

skeletal tier A term used in AUTOSEGMENTAL PHONOLOGY for the TIER where units are represented as CONSONANTS and VOWELS within SYLLABIC STRUCTURE; also known as the **CV-tier** or **skeleton**. The intention is to represent information about the length and arrangement of segments independently of their articulatory characteristics. In the original formalization, this tier is specified for the FEATURE [±syllabic], where vowels (V) are (+syllabic] and other units (C) are [−syllabic]; SEGMENTS may also be unspecified (symbolized as X). If these distinctions are interpreted structurally, corresponding to location within the syllable, the C-position is the ONSET (where only non-syllabic material can be found), the V-position is the NUCLEUS (where only syllabic material can be found), and the X-position is the CODA (where either is possible). There are analogous notions in other models of NON-LINEAR PHONOLOGY, e.g. the syllabic representation which forms part of the prosodic HIERARCHY in PROSODIC morphology. See also X-TIER.

slash A term used in GENERALIZED PHRASE-STRUCTURE GRAMMAR for a FEATURE (symbolized using a 'slash' notation as in 'S/NP') which is used in the analysis of UNBOUNDED DEPENDENCY constructions to indicate what category is missing.

slip of the tongue see TONGUE-SLIP

slit A term used by some PHONETICIANS to refer to a type of FRICATIVE where air is released over the surface of the ARTICULATORS through a narrow, horizontal opening; also called **flat**. Such fricatives (e.g. [f], [θ], [ç]) are contrasted with GROOVE fricatives, where a hollowing of the active articulator is involved (e.g. [s], [ʃ]).

slot (1) A term used in GRAMMATICAL analysis to refer to a place in a CONSTRUCTION into which a CLASS of ITEMS can be INSERTED. For example, in the SENTENCE *The children – home*, the 'slot' marked by the dash can be 'filled' by *came, are, went*, etc. – a subclass of VERBS. Approaches characterized by this emphasis are sometimes referred to as **slot-and-filler** MODELS. The analysis of SENTENCE STRUCTURE in terms of slots is a major feature of TAGMEMIC grammar, where the notion is used to identify the filler items (e.g. 'SUBJECT slot', 'OBJECT slot').

(2) A term used in AUTOSEGMENTAL PHONOLOGY for an ELEMENT on the SKELETAL TIER. These elements are also known as **V-slots** and **C-slots**, referring to the segments to which VOWELS and CONSONANTS must associate if they are to be realized (cf. ASSOCIATION LINE).

sluicing A term sometimes used in SYNTAX for a type of ELLIPSIS, in which an INTERROGATIVE item is interpreted as a complete question, the omitted material being retrieved from the previous discourse. The DELETION leaves a *WH*-phrase, as in *Somebody just left. Guess who.*

small clause A term used in GOVERNMENT-BINDING THEORY for a CLAUSE that contains neither a FINITE VERB nor an INFINITIVAL *to*; often abbreviated as **SC**. Lacking both C and I, its STRUCTURE can be defined as [NP XP], where XP is an AP, NP, etc. Examples include *John considered* [*Mary foolish*], *Mary considered* [*John a fool*], *I want* [*him off my boat*] and *I saw* [*him do it*].

social accent see ACCENT (1)

social dialectology see DIALECTOLOGY

social function see FUNCTION (3)

sociolect A term used by some SOCIOLINGUISTS to refer to a linguistic VARIETY (or LECT) defined on social (as opposed to regional) grounds, e.g. correlating with a particular social class or occupational group.

sociolinguistics A branch of LINGUISTICS which studies all aspects of the relationship between LANGUAGE and society. **Sociolinguists** study such matters as the linguistic identity of social groups, social attitudes to language, STANDARD and non-standard forms of language, the patterns and needs of national language use, social VARIETIES and LEVELS of language, the social basis of MULTILINGUALISM, and so on. An alternative name for the subject (which suggests a greater concern with sociological rather than linguistic explanations of the above) is the **sociology of language**.

The term overlaps to some degree with ETHNOLINGUISTICS and ANTHROPOLOGICAL LINGUISTICS, reflecting the overlapping interests of the correlative disciplines involved – sociology, ethnology and anthropology. The study of DIALECTS is sometimes seen as a branch of sociolinguistics, and sometimes differentiated from it, under the heading of DIALECTOLOGY, especially when regional dialects are the focus of study. When the emphasis is on the language of face-to-face interaction, the approach is known as **interactional sociolinguistics** (cf. INTERACTION). **Sociological linguistics** is sometimes differentiated from sociolinguistics, particularly in Europe, where the term reflects a concern to see language as an integral part of sociological theory. Also sometimes distinguished is SOCIOHISTORICAL LINGUISTICS, the study of the way particular linguistic functions and types of variation develop over time within specific languages, speech communities, social groups and individuals.

sociopragmatics A term sometimes used within the study of PRAGMATICS, to refer to the way conditions on LANGUAGE use derive from the social SITUATION. It contrasts with a view of pragmatics in which language use is studied from the viewpoint of the STRUCTURAL resources available in a language (sometimes referred to as PRAGMALINGUISTICS).

soft consonant An impressionistic term sometimes used in the PHONETIC descriptions of particular LANGUAGES, referring to a CONSONANT which is PALATALIZED. Russian is a language which has several such soft (as opposed to HARD) consonants. In Russian the ь symbol ('soft sign') marks the palatalization (or 'softening') of the preceding consonant.

soft palate see PALATE

sonagraph (sonagram) The commercial name of the most widely used model of sound SPECTROGRAPH, its visual displays being referred to as 'sonagrams' (cf. 'spectrograms').

sonorant One of the MAJOR CLASS FEATURES of sound set up by CHOMSKY and Halle in their DISTINCTIVE FEATURE theory of PHONOLOGY, to handle variations in MANNER OF ARTICULATION. Sonorant sounds are defined articulatorily, as those produced with a relatively free airflow, and a VOCAL CORD position such that spontaneous VOICING is possible, as in VOWELS, LIQUIDS, NASALS and LATERALS. Its opposite is **non-sonorant** (or OBSTRUENT), referring to sounds where there is a stricture impeding the airflow, as in PLOSIVES, FRICATIVES and AFFRICATES. An analogous term is RESONANT.

sonority (sonorous) A term in AUDITORY PHONETICS for the overall LOUDNESS of a sound relative to others of the same PITCH, STRESS and DURATION. Sounds are said to have an 'inherent sonority', which accounts for the impression of a sound's 'carrying further', e.g. [s] carries further than [ʃ], [a] further than [i]. The notion has also been used in attempts to define the SYLLABIC STRUCTURE of UTTERANCES. For example, the notion is important in AUTOSEGMENTAL (and specifically METRICAL) PHONOLOGY. In a **sonority scale**, or **sonority hierarchy**, the most sonorous elements are assigned the highest value, and the least sonorous the lowest value. The centre of a syllable (the syllabic NUCLEUS) is defined as the place where sonority is greatest (the **sonority peak**). Patterns of sonority sequence have been noted, leading to such observations as the **sonority sequencing generalization**: in any syllable, there is a SEGMENT constituting a sonority peak which is preceded and/or followed by a sequence of segments with progressively decreasing sonority values. The notion of **visual sonority** is used in the phonological analysis of the various features of SIGN language.

sortal(ity) A property of a word that necessarily applies to an entity throughout its existence; for example, *cow* is **sortal**, whereas *ill* is not. The term derives from 'sort', in the sense of 'species'. Sortal terms include NATURAL KIND TERMS (*cow*), artefactual terms (*car*), and abstract terms (*number*). Multi-word items are not excluded (*black-and-white cow*).

sound change/law/shift Terms used in HISTORICAL LINGUISTICS to describe the changes in a LANGUAGE'S SOUND SYSTEM over a period of time. Many types of **sound change** have been recognized, e.g. whether the change affects the total number of PHONEMES (as when two phonemes MERGE into one, or one phoneme splits into two) or affects only the ALLophones of a phoneme. Particular attention is paid to the nature of the ENVIRONMENTS which can be shown to restrict (or 'condition') the sound change. When a series of related sound changes takes place at a particular stage of a language's history, the change is known as a **sound shift**, e.g a VOWEL shift (as took place between Middle and Early Modern English – the Great Vowel Shift) or a CONSONANT shift (as in several of the changes between Latin and English). A regular series of changes is traditionally referred to in COMPARATIVE PHILOLOGY as a **sound law** – one hypothesis about such 'laws' (the NEOGRAMMARIAN hypothesis) being that they had no exceptions, i.e. at a given time all WORDS containing a sound in a given PHONETIC environment would change in the same way, and any which did not could be explained by reference to a further law. Several apparent exceptions to the initial statement of such laws came to be explained by investigations which were carried out working on this premise.

sound-symbolism A term used in SEMIOTICS to refer to a direct association between the FORM and the MEANING of LANGUAGE: the sounds used reflect properties of the external world, as in cases of onomatopoeia (e.g. *cuckoo, murmur, crash*) and other forms of SYNAESTHESIA (e.g. *sl-* in such words as *slimy, slither*).

sound system A term for the network, or SYSTEM, of PHONETICALLY REALIZED CONTRASTS which constitute the PHONOLOGY of a LANGUAGE, DIALECT, etc.

source (1) The term is used in the phrase **source feature** to refer to one of the five main dimensions of classification in CHOMSKY and Halle's DISTINCTIVE FEATURE theory of PHONOLOGY (the others being MAJOR CLASS FEATURES, CAVITY features, MANNER-OF-ARTICULATION features, and PROSODIC features). The term subsumes the feature OPPOSITIONS of HEIGHTENED SUBGLOTTAL PRESSURE, VOICE and STRIDENT.

(2) In ACOUSTIC PHONETICS, the term refers to the waveform of the vibrating LARYNX. Its SPECTRUM is rich in HARMONICS, which gradually decrease in AMPLITUDE as their FREQUENCY increases. The various RESONANCE chambers of the VOCAL TRACT, especially the movements of the tongue and lips, then act on the laryngeal source in the manner of a filter (cf. FILTERED SPEECH), reinforcing certain harmonics relative to others. The combination of these two elements is known as the **source-filter model** of vowel production.

(3) In the study of COMMUNICATION, the term refers to a point of origin of a message, as opposed to its 'destination'. More specifically, in SEMANTICS, the term is used as part of a LOCALISTIC theory of MEANING: an entity takes a 'path'

from a 'source' to a 'goal'. In CASE GRAMMAR, it refers to the place from which something moves.

(4) In HISTORICAL LINGUISTICS, the term is used to characterize a language from which a particular feature (such as a LOAN word) comes (the 'source language'); the receiving language is known as the 'matrix' language.

(5) In translating and interpreting, the term describes the language from which a message originates (the 'source language'); the 'target' language is the one into which the translation takes place.

space grammar see COGNITIVE GRAMMAR

speaker recognition/identification/verification In PHONETICS and COMPUTATIONAL LINGUISTICS, the acoustic analysis of a speech sample to infer the identity of the speaker (cf. ACOUSTIC PHONETICS). In **speaker verification**, a sample of speech is acoustically analysed to check a claimed identity against a stored reference sample stored in the computer. This technique is used, for example, in such situations as controlling access to buildings. In **speaker identification**, a speech sample from a known speaker is compared to one obtained from an unknown speaker, to determine whether the same person is involved. This technique has been most commonly used in criminal cases, where the visual analysis of spectrograms (VOICEPRINTING) has been used to investigate whether the speaker in a tape-recording is the same as a suspect.

spec The abbreviation for SPECIFIER.

specialization A suggested defining property of SEMIOTIC SYSTEMS, such as human LANGUAGE, referring to the extent to which the use of a signal and the behaviour it evokes are directly linked. Animal communication is said to lack specialization, in that a signal triggers a behaviour; language, by contrast, is highly specialized, as the behavioural consequences of using a LINGUISTIC signal are less predictable (and often unpredictable).

specification see UNDERSPECIFICATION

specified-subject condition A term used in EXTENDED STANDARD THEORY to refer to a type of CONSTRAINT on the application of TRANSFORMATIONAL or INTERPRETIVE rules; replaced in GOVERNMENT-BINDING THEORY by conditions A and B of BINDING theory. The constraint states that when a SUBORDINATE CLAUSE or NOUN PHRASE contains a specified subject (a LEXICAL, NP, PRONOMINAL or TRACE, but not PRO), no other (non-subject) CONSTITUENT can be moved out of that clause.

specifier (spec) A category in the X-BAR theory of PHRASE STRUCTURE. Specifiers are normally seen as combining with a SINGLE-BAR category to form the related DOUBLE-BAR category. For example, in *John is a student, a* is the specifier of the NOUN, *student*, and in *She is very happy, she* is the specifier of the ADJECTIVE, *happy*. **Spec/head agreement** is agreement between the head of a phrase and the element which occupies the specifier of that phrase.

spectrograph (spectrogram) An instrument used in ACOUSTIC PHONETICS which provides a visual representation of the acoustic features that constitute the sounds in an UTTERANCE. The original 'sound spectrograph' produced a three-dimensional visual record, or 'spectrogram', of an utterance, in which time is displayed horizontally, frequency vertically, and intensity by the relative blackness of the marks, on a sheet of sensitized paper. Today, spectrographic information can be generated electronically and displayed on a screen.

spectrum (spectra, -l) A term derived from the study of the physics of sound, and used in ACOUSTIC PHONETICS, referring to the set of acoustic components which identify a complex sound wave. A spectral analysis is a graph in which one axis displays the FREQUENCY of each HARMONIC and the other displays AMPLITUDE. Several devices are available to measure and display spectra, but the one most commonly used in phonetics is the SPECTROGRAPH.

speech For the most part, the term is used in LINGUISTICS in its everyday sense, providing the subject with its primary DATA. There are two main interpretations of these data, which are complementary rather than opposed. One interpretation is from the viewpoint of PHONETICS: here, speech is seen as a MEDIUM of transmission for LANGUAGE – the **spoken medium** or PHONIC SUBSTANCE of language (as opposed to writing). It is in this context that the term is used as part of the label for the many devices available in instrumental phonetics, e.g. the **speech stretcher** (which presents a slowed but otherwise undistorted recording of speech). **Speech science** is the study of all the factors involved in the production, transmission and reception of speech; also called **speech sciences** or **speech and hearing science**. As well as phonetics, the study includes such subjects as anatomy, physiology, neurology and acoustics, as applied to speech.

The other interpretation is from the viewpoint of linguistics, where **spoken language** (PERFORMANCE, or PAROLE) can be analysed in PHONOLOGICAL, GRAMMATICAL and SEMANTIC, as well as phonetic terms. It is in this sense that terms such as **speech community** are used, referring to any regionally or socially definable human group identified by a shared linguistic SYSTEM. The term SPEECH ACT, also, has a more abstract sense than its name suggests (see separate entry); it is not in fact an 'act of speaking', but the activity which the use of language performs or promotes in the listener (respectively, the ILLOCUTIONARY force and the PERLOCUTIONARY effect of the language). Similarly, the **speech event** is seen as the basic unit for the analysis of spoken interaction, i.e. the emphasis is on the role of the participants in constructing a DISCOURSE of verbal exchanges.

In recent years, phonetics and PSYCHOLINGUISTICS have come to pay increasing attention to constructing MODELS of the neurophysiological mechanisms hypothesized to underlie speech behaviour. In this respect, two main branches of speech analysis have developed: **speech production**, involving the planning and execution of acts of speaking; and **speech perception**, involving the perception and interpretation of the sound sequences of speech. The term **speech recognition** (or **speech reception**) is used to identify the initial stage of the decoding process involved in speech perception – and also to the automatic decoding of speech by machine (**automatic speech recognition (ASR)**). **Speaker recognition** is the analysis of speech to infer the identity of the speaker or to check a claimed identity (**speaker verification**). The whole activity of the perception and production of speech is known as **speech processing**. See also DIRECT (2), DISPLACED, LANGUAGE.

speech act A term derived from the work of the philosopher J. L. Austin (1911–60), and now used widely in LINGUISTICS, to refer to a theory which analyses the role of UTTERANCES in relation to the behaviour of speaker and hearer in interpersonal communication. It is not an 'act of speech' (in the sense of PAROLE), but a communicative activity (a LOCUTIONARY act), defined with reference to the intentions of speakers while speaking (the ILLOCUTIONARY force of their utterances) and the effects they achieve on listeners (the PERLOCUTIONARY effect of their utterances). Several categories of speech act have been proposed, viz. DIRECTIVES (speakers try to get their listeners to do something, e.g. begging, commanding, requesting), COMMISSIVES (speakers commit themselves to a future course of action, e.g. promising, guaranteeing), EXPRESSIVES (speakers express their feelings, e.g. apologizing, welcoming, sympathizing), DECLARATIONS (the speaker's utterance brings about a new external situation, e.g. christening, marrying, resigning) and REPRESENTATIVES (speakers convey their belief about the truth of a PROPOSITION, e.g. asserting, hypothesizing). The verbs which are used to indicate the speech act intended by the speaker are sometimes known as PERFORMATIVE verbs. The criteria which have to be satisfied in order for a speech act to be successful are known as FELICITY CONDITIONS.

speech recognition In PHONETICS and COMPUTATIONAL LINGUISTICS, the recognition of human SPEECH through computer analysis; also called **automatic speech recognition** (**ASR**). The task involves the matching of an input acoustic signal with a vocabulary (of sounds, syllables, words, etc.) stored in the computer's memory. A standard technique for matching individual words is to use stored waveforms (or features/parameters of waveforms) against which an input signal is matched ('template matching'). The computer requires a period of training, in which it receives examples of spoken words provided by (single or multiple) speakers, and averages these to derive a CANONICAL waveform. The variable RATE of speech inputs needs to be taken into account, most often using the technique of 'dynamic time warping', in which SEGMENTS in the input signal are aligned with those in the template. The more challenging aim of ASR is to handle continuous speech. Here the computer is provided with information about typical patterns of phonetic and PHONOLOGICAL segmentation, as well as MORPHOLOGICAL and SYNTACTIC information. More advanced simulations, such as those provided by CONNECTIONIST models, are also used.

speech synthesis In PHONETICS and COMPUTATIONAL LINGUISTICS, the process of generating artificial SPEECH signals, using a MODEL of the linguistically important ACOUSTIC or ARTICULATORY properties. The devices involved are known as **speech synthesizers**. **Acoustic domain analogs** or **terminal analogs** replicate the acoustic properties of the VOCAL TRACT in terms of its output. The tract is represented using a SOURCE-filter model, and several devices have been devised to synthesize speech in this way, such as the early channel vocoders, the spectrogram-based FORMANT synthesizers, and the more recent LINEAR PREDICTION coefficient (LPC) synthesizers. **Articulatory analogs** replicate the anatomical geometry of the vocal tract between the LARYNX and the lips, insofar as information about the DYNAMIC properties of the phonatory and articulatory parameters is available. A further technique is called **text-to-speech** synthesis, in which written texts are automatically transformed into their spoken equivalents (cf. TEXT-TO-SPEECH).

speed (of speech) see RATE

spell-out In the MINIMALIST PROGRAMME, an operation which distinguishes the PHONETIC REPRESENTATION within a STRUCTURAL DESCRIPTION from other kinds of information. The operation motivates the distinction between PHONETIC FORM (PF) and LOGICAL FORM (LF). Semantic information is not allowed in PF representations, and phonological information is not allowed in LF representations. Movements which occur before spell-out will affect the pronunciation of a sentence; those which occur afterwards will not.

spirant(-ize, -ization) see FRICATIVE

spoken medium see SPEECH

Sprachbund see AREA

Sprachgefühl see INTUITION

spread(ing) (1) A term in the classification of lip position in PHONETICS, referring to the visual appearance of the lips when they are held fairly close together and stretched sideways, as in a slightly open smile. Lip-spreading is noticeable in CLOSE VOWELS, as in the [i] of *see*, and is contrasted with NEUTRAL, OPEN and ROUNDED lip positions.

(2) (**-ing**) in some models of NON-LINEAR PHONOLOGY, a term used to refer to the ASSOCIATION (or LINKING) of a FEATURE or NODE belonging to one SEGMENT with an ADJACENT segment; the disassociation of a feature or node from a segment is called **delinking**. The notion is of particular importance in the study of ASSIMILATION, where the effect of spreading produces an output REPRESENTATION with multilinked nodes, and DISSIMILATION, where a feature or node is delinked from a segment, and the orphaned node is later deleted. AUTOSEGMENTAL spreading also accounts for COMPENSATORY LENGTHENING in a CV framework.

(3) In AUTOSEGMENTAL PHONOLOGY, a type of RULE which extends the association of a TONE in a given direction, e.g. a high tone associated with an initial VOWEL comes to be associated wtih the following vowel(s) (cf. ASSOCIATION LINE). Spreading is indicated by an arrow in the autosegmental rule, pointing to the right for unbounded rightward spreading, and to the left for unbounded leftward spreading:

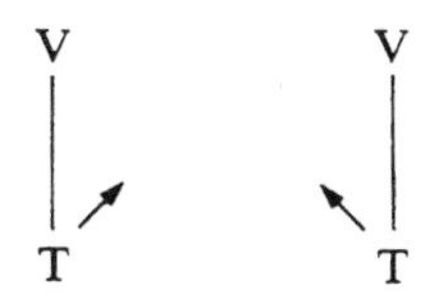

(4) In the phrase **language spread**, the increased use of a LANGUAGE in a given area over a period of time; also called 'language diffusion'.

split ergative see ERGATIVE

squish A term introduced into LINGUISTIC analysis by the American linguist John Robert Ross (b. 1938) in the early 1970s, as part of his notion of NON-DISCRETE

GRAMMAR; it refers to a continuum along which LEXICAL ITEMS can be placed, the poles being VERB and NOUN. Lexical items are seen as displaying degrees of verb-ness or noun-ness, and SYNTACTIC RULES are seen as applying with varying PRODUCTIVITY to different parts of the continuum. For example, nouns used as PREMODIFIERS in noun PHRASES fall between the CLASSES of noun and ADJECTIVE (e.g. *the railway station, the town clock*), in that some but not all rules which apply to nouns can be used (cf. *the town's clock, *the towns clock*, etc.). INDETERMINATE or FUZZY categories are the focus of attention. What remains unclear, in this approach, is the extent to which these cases are sufficiently different from other problems of classification to warrant a radical reformulation of linguistic theory.

S-structure A term used in GOVERNMENT-BINDING THEORY to refer to an alternative conception of SURFACE or SHALLOW STRUCTURE, which has been enriched by the inclusion of EMPTY elements (such as TRACES and PRO) relating to a sentence's DEEP STRUCTURE (or D-STRUCTURE). S-structure is what is produced after TRANSFORMATIONS and CASE RULES, but before DELETION rules and FILTERS; it is the INPUT to the rules of SEMANTIC interpretation. It contrasts with surface structure, which follows deletion and filtering, and which is the input to the PHONOLOGICAL component.

stability A term used in AUTOSEGMENTAL PHONOLOGY for an effect which stems from the principle of autonomy of TIERS in the phonological REPRESENTATION: operations which apply to a SEGMENT on one tier (e.g. DELETION) will not affect any AUTOSEGMENT with which that segment was formerly associated. For example, a tone can be deleted without its corresponding vowel being deleted, and vice versa.

standard(ization) A term used in SOCIOLINGUISTICS to refer to a prestige VARIETY of LANGUAGE used within a SPEECH COMMUNITY. 'Standard languages/dialects/varieties' cut across regional differences, providing a unified means of communication, and thus an institutionalized NORM which can be used in the mass-media, in teaching the language to foreigners, and so on. Linguistic FORMS or DIALECTS which do not conform to this norm are then referred to as **sub-standard** or (with a less pejorative prefix) **non-standard** – though neither term is intended to suggest that other dialect forms 'lack standards' in any linguistic sense. The natural development of a standard language in a speech community (or an attempt by a community to impose one dialect as a standard) is known as **standardization**.

Standard Generalized Markup Language (**SGML**) In COMPUTATIONAL LINGUISTICS, the use of a scheme currently being developed in literary and linguistic computing for putting texts into machine-readable form, using a single encoding system (cf. CODE). The scheme avoids the need for researchers to write special programs to convert texts from one encoding format to another.

standard theory/model A term used in GENERATIVE LINGUISTICS to refer to the MODEL of generative GRAMMAR proposed by Noam CHOMSKY in his 1965 book, *Aspects of the Theory of Syntax*. The importance of this formulation is such that, despite extensive subsequent modifications and alternatives provided by

Chomsky and others, it is still viewed by many as the main statement concerning the aims and form of a TRANSFORMATIONAL GRAMMAR. It is usually contrasted with the EXTENDED STANDARD THEORY developed by Chomsky in later modifications of his own work, the REVISED EXTENDED STANDARD THEORY, GOVERNMENT-BINDING THEORY, and the various 'non-standard' versions of generative grammar (e.g. GENERATIVE SEMANTICS), which differ radically from the *Aspects* model.

starred form A term used in LINGUISTICS to refer to a linguistic CONSTRUCTION that is UNACCEPTABLE or UNGRAMMATICAL, and marked thus by the use of an initial ASTERISK, e.g. **a boys have gone*. The term **asterisked form** is an alternative. In HISTORICAL LINGUISTICS, starred forms indicate historical RECONSTRUCTIONS, the forms cited not being attested in any written records. In AUTOSEGMENTAL PHONOLOGY, a 'starred ASSOCIATION' is an association which resists modification by subsequent rules.

state (1) A term used in LINGUISTICS to refer to the condition of a LANGUAGE at a hypothetical point or period of time, e.g. Middle English, sixteenth century, 1920s. States of languages (cf. ÉTAT DE LANGUE) thus constitute the subject-matter of SYNCHRONIC linguistics.
(2) See STATIVE.
(3) See AUTOMATON.

statement A term used in the classification of SENTENCE FUNCTION, and defined sometimes on GRAMMATICAL and sometimes on SEMANTIC or SOCIOLINGUISTIC grounds. SYNTACTICALLY, a statement is in English typically a sentence which contains a SUBJECT occurring before a VERB, e.g. *The train is coming*. Semantically, it is used primarily to convey information. The term is usually contrasted with three other major sentence functions: QUESTION, COMMAND, EXCLAMATION. In grammatical discussion, statements are usually referred to as DECLARATIVE or INDICATIVE in form.

static (1) A term sometimes used in PHONOLOGY, applied to TONES which do not vary in PITCH range; also called **level** tones. A contrast is usually drawn with DYNAMIC tones.
(2) See STATIVE.

statistical linguistics A branch of LINGUISTICS which studies the application of statistical techniques in linguistic theory and description. The study includes the analysis of frequency and DISTRIBUTION of linguistic UNITS in TEXTS with the aim of identifying the DISTINCTIVE characteristics of the speaker or writer (as in STYLOstatistics); but attempts have also been made to establish general laws concerning the statistical characteristics of languages, such as the relationship between WORD types (e.g. the word *up*) and word tokens (e.g. the number of instances of the word *up* in a sample), the relative frequency of ITEMS in different samples, the quantification of such notions as REDUNDANCY in statistical terms, and so on. See also QUANTITATIVE LINGUISTICS, UNIVERSAL.

stative (stat-ivity, -ic, state) A term used in GRAMMATICAL classification referring to one of two main ASPECTUAL categories of VERB use, the other being DYNAMIC. The distinguishing criteria for **stativity** are mainly SYNTACTIC; for example, **stative, static** or **state verbs** do not usually occur in a PROGRESSIVE form (e.g. **I* *am knowing*, **He is concerning*), nor in the IMPERATIVE (e.g. **know!*). On SEMANTIC grounds, they can be said to express states of affairs, rather than actions, i.e. the expression of relational processes (e.g. *be, belong to, involve, seem*) or of inactive perceptual or cognitive processes (e.g. *know, mean, realize, suppose*). The classification is complicated by the existence of verbs which have both a stative and a dynamic use, e.g. *smell*.

status planning see CORPUS (2)

stem A term often used in LINGUISTICS as part of a classification of the kinds of ELEMENTS operating within the structure of a WORD. The stem may consist solely of a single ROOT MORPHEME (i.e. a 'simple' stem, as in *man*), or of two root morphemes (e.g. a 'compound' stem, as in *blackbird*), or of a root morpheme plus a DERIVATIONAL AFFIX (i.e. a 'complex' stem, as in *manly, unmanly, manliness*). All have in common the notion that it is to the stem that inflectional affixes are attached.

stereotype (1) A term used by some GRAMMARIANS for a sequence of WORDS which resembles a PRODUCTIVE grammatical STRUCTURE but which in fact has been learned as a single unit and has little or no productivity. Proverbs, quotations, aphorisms and several types of idiom can be classed as grammatical stereotypes: the sentence *Jack and Jill went up the hill*, for example, might be used by a young child who is not yet at the stage of producing CO-ORDINATIONS or past TENSES in spontaneous speech. Stereotyped constructions are particularly common in the speech of those suffering from language handicap.

(2) In SEMANTICS, a term sometimes used for the set of characteristics which describe a PROTOTYPE. For example, a stereotyped feature of cars is that they have four wheels.

stock see FAMILY

stop A term used in the PHONETIC classification of speech sounds on the basis of their MANNER OF ARTICULATION. It refers to any sound which is produced by a complete CLOSURE in the VOCAL TRACT, and thus traditionally includes the class of PLOSIVES. Both NASAL and ORAL sounds can be classified as stops, though the term is usually reserved for the latter. A distinction is sometimes made between 'simple' and 'complex' stops, depending on whether the closure is made at one place or at two places simultaneously (e.g. the [g͡b] COARTICULATION heard in some African languages, or CONSONANTS produced with a simultaneous GLOTTAL stop). Other classifications of stop consonants involve taking into account the direction of airflow, whether INGRESSIVE or EGRESSIVE: 'ingressive stops' are often referred to as **suction stops**, 'egressive stops' as **pressure stops**.

In the DISTINCTIVE FEATURE theory of PHONOLOGY, the term 'stop' is sometimes used in opposition to CONTINUANT.

stranding (stranded) A term used in some GRAMMARS to refer to an ELEMENT which is left unattached after it has been MOVED out of a CONSTRUCTION, or after the rest of the construction has been moved. For example, a PREPOSITION is commonly left stranded, after the NOUN PHRASE within the prepositional phrase has been moved, as in *Who did you give the book* ***to***?; the AUXILIARY verb *did* is stranded after the ELLIPSIS of the second CLAUSE in *He asked her to arrive before six, but she **didn't**.*

stratificational (strat-um, -al) A LINGUISTIC theory devised by the American linguist Sydney M. Lamb (b. 1929), as expounded initially in *Outline of Stratificational Grammar* (1962), which models LANGUAGE as a SYSTEM of several related layers (or 'strata') of STRUCTURE. Six strata are recognized for English and many other languages: the component of PHONOLOGY comprises the HYPOPHONEMIC (or PHONETIC) and PHONEMIC strata; GRAMMAR comprises MORPHEMIC and LEXEMIC strata; and SEMOLOGY comprises the SEMEMIC and HYPERSEMEMIC (or SEMANTIC) strata. Each stratum is organized in terms of a set of 'stratal systems', and each system deals with an aspect of linguistic structure which has to be stated independently of the structures operating at other strata. Two types of PATTERNing are recognized: TACTIC analysis (the patterns of sequential arrangement within each stratum) and REALIZATIONAL analysis (the relationship between UNITS operating at higher and lower LEVELS between strata). A parallel terminology is used for each stratum: there is a 'hypophonemic / phonemic / morphonemic / lexemic / sememic / hypersememic' system consisting of various structural patterns (e.g. 'hypophonotactic/phonotactic', etc.), defined in terms of 'hypophonemes/phonemes', etc., and realized as 'hypophons/phons/morphons/lexons', etc.

stray A term used in various models of NON-LINEAR PHONOLOGY, describing a unit (e.g. a SYLLABLE, a SEGMENT) which falls outside the conventions of a REPRESENTATION and which therefore needs to be handled in a special way. For example, in METRICAL PHONOLOGY a stray syllable produced by destressing (cf. STRESS) needs to be adjoined to another NODE in the word TREE (**stray syllable adjunction**). **Stray erasure** is a procedure which DELETES SEGMENTS which cannot be incorporated into a WELL-FORMED syllable. It is particularly used in relation to CONSONANTS, where it accounts for certain types of syllable shortening and consonant deletion. For example, its application is suggested in cases like *hymn/hymnal*, where /mn/ is an unacceptable CODA sequence. However, an underlying representation of /him.n/ would result in an **unsyllabified** /n/, which (in one solution) could then be deleted by stray erasure.

strength A term used in PHONOLOGY, referring to a UNIVERSAL scale (or scales) of values on which units (SEGMENTS or classes of segments) can be arrayed: the behaviour of segments in DIACHRONIC or SYNCHRONIC processes is claimed to be derivable from their rank on the scale. In one approach, for example, VELARS are assigned a lower rank on this scale (are 'weaker') than DENTALS, which are in turn weaker than LABIALS. The approach aims to determine mechanically, on the basis of a strength scale for segments and for structural POSITIONS, the relative probability of any segment occurring in any position, e.g. the hypothesis that strong segments will dominate in strong positions, and weak segments in weak positions. However, the number and nature of phonological scales of this kind is controversial.

stress(-ed, de-) A term used in PHONETICS to refer to the degree of force used in producing a SYLLABLE. The usual distinction is between **stressed** and **unstressed** syllables, the former being more PROMINENT than the latter (and marked in

TRANSCRIPTION with a raised vertical line, [ˈ]. The prominence is usually due to an increase in LOUDNESS of the stressed syllable, but increases in LENGTH and often PITCH may contribute to the overall impression of prominence. In popular usage, 'stress' is usually equated with an undifferentiated notion of 'emphasis' or 'strength.'

From the viewpoint of PHONOLOGY, the main function of stress is to provide a means of distinguishing degrees of emphasis or contrast in SENTENCES (**sentence stress**), as in *The* ***big*** *man looks angry*; the term **contrastive stress** is often used for this function. Many pairs of WORDS and word sequences can also be distinguished using stress variation (**lexical stress** or **word stress**), as in the contrast between *An increase in pay is needed* and *I'm going to increase his pay* – /ˈɪŋkriːs/ *v.* /ɪŋˈkriːs/ – or the distinction between *ˈblack ˈbird* and *ˈblack-bird*. The analytical question here, which has attracted a great deal of attention in recent years, is how many degrees of stress need to be recognized in order to account for all such contrasts, and to show the interrelationships between words derived from a common root, such as *ˈtelegraph*, *teleˈgraphic* and *teˈlegraphy*. In the American STRUCTURALIST tradition, four such degrees are usually distinguished, and analysed as stress PHONEMES, namely (from the strongest to weakest) (1) 'primary', (2) 'secondary', (3) 'tertiary' and (4) 'weak'. These contrasts are, however, demonstrable only on words in isolation, as in the compound $\overset{1}{\text{e}}\overset{4}{\text{le}}\overset{3}{\text{va}}\overset{4}{\text{tor}}$ $\overset{2}{\text{o}}\overset{4}{\text{pe}}\overset{3}{\text{ra}}\overset{4}{\text{tor}}$ – one of several such phrases originally cited to justify analyses of this kind.

Alternative views recognized different kinds and degrees of stress, the simplest postulating a straight stressed *v.* unstressed contrast, referring to other factors (such as INTONATION and VOWEL QUALITY) to explain such sequences as *elevator operator*. In DISTINCTIVE FEATURE theories of phonology, the various degrees of stress are assigned to the syllables of words by means of the repeated application of RULES (such as 'lexical', 'compound', and 'NUCLEAR' stress rules). Some analysts maintain there is a distinction to be made between linguistic contrasts involving loudness (which they refer to as 'stress') and those additionally involving pitch (which they refer to as ACCENT). All the examples given above, they would argue, are matters of accent, not stress, because contrasts in pitch variation are normally involved. Similar problems arise in the analysis of TONE languages.

In cross-language comparison, it is useful to note variations in the typical place within the word where the stressed syllable falls. Some languages have a 'fixed' stress (or accent), e.g. Welsh, where the stressed syllable is almost always the penultimate, in polysyllabic words. Others, such as English, have a 'free' or 'movable' stress (accent).

In the context of RHYTHM studies, the notion of a STRESS-TIMED language is often cited, i.e. one where the stresses fall at roughly regular intervals within an UTTERANCE. In analysing such a language in this way, the notion of **silent stress** is sometimes invoked, to handle cases where the omission of a stressed syllable in colloquial speech can nonetheless be 'felt'; a regularly cited case in the abbreviated version of *thank you* /kjʊ/, which is said to be the unstressed residue of an unspoken stressed+unstressed combination. A sequence of syllables constituting a rhythmical unit, containing one primary stress, is known as a **stress group**. In METRICAL PHONOLOGY a **stress-foot** is a STRING containing as its first ELEMENT a stressed syllable, followed by zero or more unstressed syllables symbolized by Σ. The most prominent element in the stress foot is called the HEAD. It should be noted that 'foot', in this context, refers to an UNDERLYING unit, whose phonetic interpretation varies according to the theoretical approach. **Destressing**, in this approach, is a RULE which eliminates stresses produced by foot construction. See also CONTOUR.

stress-timed A very general term used in PHONETICS to characterize the pronunciation of LANGUAGES displaying a particular type of RHYTHM; it is opposed to SYLLABLE-TIMED languages. In stress-timed languages, it is claimed that the STRESSED SYLLABLES recur at regular intervals of time, regardless of the number of intervening unstressed syllables, as in English. This characteristic is referred to as 'isochronism', or ISOCHRONY. However, it is plain that this regularity is the case only under certain conditions, and the extent to which the tendency towards regularity in English is similar to that in, say, other Germanic languages remains unclear.

strict cycle condition see CYCLE

stricture A general term used in PHONETICS to refer to an ARTICULATION which restricts the airstream to some degree, ranging from a complete CLOSURE to a slight narrowing. See also ARTICULATOR-BASED FEATURE THEORY.

stridency In PHONETICS, a scale used to characterize sounds (specifically, FRICATIVES) in auditory terms on the basis of their perceived PITCH and LOUDNESS; also called **sibilance**. Sounds such as [s] are higher on a stridency scale, being relatively high-pitched and intense (they display more energy at higher FREQUENCIES); sounds such as [f] are much lower (displaying more energy at lower frequencies).

strident One of the SOURCE FEATURES of sound set up by CHOMSKY and Halle in their DISTINCTIVE FEATURE theory of PHONOLOGY, to handle variations in the SIBILANCE of a sound. Strident sounds are defined ARTICULATORILY and ACOUSTICALLY as those sounds produced by a relatively complex STRICTURE, and marked by relatively high frequency and intensity, as in [f], [s] and [ʃ]. The opposite term in JAKOBSON and Halle's approach is MELLOW; in Chomsky and Halle's later system it is **non-strident**: these are sounds produced by a less complex stricture, and marked by noise of relatively low frequency and intensity, such as in PLOSIVES and NASALS. All vowels are also [–strident]. The allocation of segments to these categories has been controversial (e.g. whether [f] is + or – strident).

string A term used in LINGUISTICS, and especially in GENERATIVE GRAMMAR, to refer to a linear SEQUENCE of ELEMENTS of determinate length and constitution. Formal analysis also permits the notion of a string consisting of just one short element, and also one consisting of no elements (cf. ZERO in linguistic description) – the EMPTY or NULL string. **A substring** is any part of a string which is itself a string. For example, the following SENTENCE can be seen as a string of elements: *the+cat+sit+Past+on+the+mat*. Within this, several substrings could be recognized, e.g. *the+cat, the+cat+sit+Past*, etc.

strong adequacy see ADEQUACY

strong form One of two possible pronunciations for a WORD, in the context of CONNECTED SPEECH, the other being WEAK. The strong form is that which is the result of a word being STRESSED. For example, most of the GRAMMATICAL WORDS of English occur in both forms, e.g. *I want bacon and eggs v. I want bacon – AND eggs.*

structural(-ism, -ist) A term used in LINGUISTICS referring to any approach to the analysis of LANGUAGE that pays explicit attention to the way in which linguistic features can be described in terms of STRUCTURES and SYSTEMS (**structural** or **structuralist linguistics**). In the general SAUSSUREAN sense, structuralist ideas enter into every school of linguistics. Structuralism does, however, have a more restricted definition, referring to the BLOOMFIELDIAN emphasis on the processes of SEGMENTING and CLASSIFYING the physical features of UTTERANCE (i.e. on what Noam CHOMSKY later called SURFACE STRUCTURES), with little reference to the abstract UNDERLYING structures (Chomsky's DEEP STRUCTURES) of language or their MEANING. It is this emphasis which the Chomskyan approach to language strongly attacked; for GENERATIVE linguistics, accordingly, the term is often pejorative.

The contribution of this notion in linguistics is apparent in the more general concept of **structuralism**, especially as formulated in the work of the French anthropologist, Claude Lévi-Strauss (b. 1908), and others. Here, any human institution or behaviour (e.g. dancing, courtship, religion) is considered analysable in terms of an underlying network of relationships, and the structures demonstrated referrable to basic modes of thought. The crucial point is that the elements which constitute a network have no validity apart from the relations (of equivalence, contrast, etc.) which hold between them, and it is this network of relations which constitutes the structures of the system.

Within linguistics, 'structural' will be found in several contexts in PHONOLOGY, GRAMMAR and SEMANTICS. **Structural(ist) grammar**, as a general term, is now a largely dated conception of grammatical analysis, though the emphases which characterized it may still be seen in several areas of APPLIED LINGUISTIC studies (e.g. in the structural drills of foreign-language teaching), and the term 'structural' is often given a special status as part of the exposition of a grammatical MODEL, e.g. the notion of STRUCTURAL DESCRIPTION in TRANSFORMATIONAL GRAMMAR. **Structural semantics** is an influential contemporary position, which is still in its early stages of analysing the SENSE relations that interconnect LEXEMES and SENTENCES.

structural ambiguity A term used in LINGUISTICS to refer to a CONSTRUCTION with more than one GRAMMATICAL interpretation in terms of CONSTITUENT analysis. A much-used example is *old men and women*, which is 'structurally ambiguous': it may be analysed as [*old men*] *and women* (i.e. only the men are old) or *old* [*men and women*] (i.e. both the men and women are old). In GENERATIVE grammar, this phenomenon is sometimes referred to as 'CONSTRUCTIONAL homonymity'.

structural change (SC) A term used in (especially classical) TRANSFORMATIONAL GRAMMAR to refer to the operations involved in applying a transformational RULE, i.e. the changes between the input and the output PHRASE-MARKERS. In the transformation of ACTIVE into PASSIVE SENTENCES, for example, the structural change is complex, involving the REORDERING of the two NOUN PHRASES, and the INSERTION of new forms of the VERB, and the AGENT marker *by* (e.g. *The dog bit the cat v. The cat was bitten by the dog*).

structural description (SD) A term used in (especially classical) TRANSFORMATIONAL GRAMMAR to refer to an analysis of a TERMINAL STRING in terms of a labelled BRACKETING. In transformational analysis, the SD identifies the input to a transformational RULE: it specifies which PHRASE-MARKERS are to be affected by the rule, i.e. which will 'satisfy' or 'meet' the CONDITIONS of the rule. The terms 'structural analysis' and 'structure index' are also used.

structural dialectology see DIALECT

structure In its most general sense, and especially as defined by STRUCTURALIST studies of human institutions and behaviour, the term applies to the main abstract characteristic of a SEMIOTIC SYSTEM. A LANGUAGE, for example, is a structure, in the sense that it is a network of interrelated UNITS, the MEANING of the parts being specifiable only with reference to the whole. In this sense, the terms 'structure' and 'system' are often synonymous (and the phrase 'structured system' which is sometimes encountered – as in 'language is a structured system' – is a tautology). More specifically, the term is used to refer to an isolatable section of this total network, as in discussion of the structure of a particular GRAMMATICAL area (e.g. TENSES, PRONOUNS), and here 'structure' and 'system' are distinguished: one might talk of the 'structure' of a particular 'system'.

However, this application of the term to PARADIGMATIC relationships is not as widespread as the SYNTAGMATIC conception of 'structure'. Here a particular sequential pattern of linguistic ELEMENTS is referred to as 'a structure', definable with reference to one of the various 'structural LEVELS' recognized in a theory, e.g. 'PHONOLOGICAL structure', 'SYNTACTIC structure', 'MORPHOLOGICAL structure', 'SEMANTIC structure'. For example, CLAUSE structure can be defined in terms of STRINGS of such elements as SUBJECT, VERB, OBJECT, or NOUN PHRASE, verb phrase; SYLLABLE structure can be defined in terms of strings of CONSONANTS and VOWELS. The set of items which CONTRAST at a particular 'place' in a structure is then referred to as a system. This is the way in which the term is used in HALLIDAYAN linguistics, for example, where it has a special status, as the name of one of the four major CATEGORIES recognized by the theory (the others being 'unit', 'system' and 'CLASS'): the category of structure accounts for the ways in which an occurrence of one syntactic unit can be made up out of occurrences of the unit below it (e.g. which kinds of GROUP structure can constitute which kinds of clause structure). In this sense, the MORPHEME has no structure, being the minimal unit in grammar. A narrower use of the term is found in the phrase **structure index**, sometimes used in TRANSFORMATIONAL GRAMMAR to refer to the FORMAL description of the input string to a transformational RULE – also known as a STRUCTURAL DESCRIPTION. A **structure-preserving** CONSTRAINT is one which imposes the condition that a CONSTITUENT can be MOVED only into another CATEGORY of the same structural type, which has been independently generated. Transformations to which this constraint applies are known as 'structure-preserving transformations'. See also HIERARCHY, TREE.

structure dependency A principle used in GENERATIVE LINGUISTICS which asserts that the speaker's knowledge of LANGUAGE relies on the STRUCTURAL relationships between ELEMENTS in the SENTENCE rather than on the LINEAR sequence of items. The principle imposes strong constraints on the notion of 'possible grammatical rule', and is an essential feature of a theory of UNIVERSAL GRAMMAR.

structure preservation A principle in LEXICAL PHONOLOGY which states that CONSTRAINTS on possible UNDERLYING SEGMENTS in the inventory of a language, and constraints on AUTOSEGMENTAL associations, hold throughout the DERIVATION during the lexical part of the phonology. These constraints are dropped during the post-lexical part of the phonology.

stylistics (styl-e, -istic, -o-) A branch of LINGUISTICS which studies the features of SITUATIONally distinctive uses (VARIETIES) of LANGUAGE, and tries to establish principles capable of accounting for the particular choices made by individual and social groups in their use of language. **General stylistics** deals with the whole range (or REPERTOIRE) of non-DIALECTAL varieties encountered within a language; **literary stylistics** deals with the variations characteristic of literature as a genre and of the 'style' of individual authors. **Applied stylistics** is often used for the study of contextually distinctive varieties of language, especially with reference to the style of literary and non-literary texts. The quantification of stylistic patterns is the province of **stylostatistics** (or **stylometry**) – a field which usually studies the statistical structure of literary texts, often using computers. The study of the expressive or aesthetic function of sound is sometimes called **phonostylistics**.

The term 'stylistics' is occasionally used in a very broad sense, to include all situationally distinctive language – that is, including the variations of regional, social and historical dialects. It is more common, however, to see **style** used in a highly restricted sense – though the extremely broad and ambiguous reference of the term in everyday use has not made its status as a technical linguistic term very appealing. For example, in the HALLIDAYAN classification of language varieties, style (more fully, 'style of DISCOURSE') refers to the relations among the participants in a language activity, especially the level of FORMALITY they adopt (colloquial, formal, etc.). Alternative terms used by some linguists, presumably to avoid the ambiguity of an additional sense for the term 'style', include MANNER and TENOR. The main terms with which it contrasts in the Hallidayan model are MODE and FIELD. A similar conception of style in terms of 'vertical' formality level is found in many SOCIOLINGUISTIC studies. In some contexts (such as GENERATIVE GRAMMAR), **stylistic rules** refer to optional processes which highlight an element in a sentence.

sub-categorization (sub-categorize) An application of the general use of this term in LINGUISTICS and especially in GENERATIVE GRAMMAR, to refer to the further subclassification of a SYNTACTIC CATEGORY. In the ASPECTS MODEL, the function of **strict sub-categorization** features is to specify a class of restrictions operating on the choice of VERBS (and other elements) in DEEP STRUCTURE. Related notions include CATEGORY and SELECTIONAL features. The category verb is sub-categorized in terms of its sister-NODES within the verb phrase – whether or not it permits a following NOUN-PHRASE OBJECT. This distinction might be summarized using a **sub-categorization frame**, which specifies the range of sister constituents which a LEXICAL ITEM takes, as in such cases of verb COMPLEMENTATION as '*go* –[–NP]', '*kick* +[–NP]'.

subgenre see GENRE

subgesture see GESTURE

subjacency A term used in EXTENDED STANDARD THEORY and GOVERNMENT-BINDING THEORY to refer to a type of CONDITION which restricts the application of a TRANSFORMATIONAL RULE; it is the main principle of BOUNDING theory. The **subjacency condition** states that a CONSTITUENT cannot be moved (in any single application) across more than one bounding NODE. For example, in the sentence *The story that* [[*the quarrel about pay*$_{NP}$] *was wrong*$_{S}$] *is irrelevant*, the brackets mark the place of the constituent boundaries NP and S. To move the phrase *about pay* to the right of *wrong* is possible, because only one bounding node has been crossed; but it is not possible to move this phrase to the right of *irrelevant*, according to the subjacency condition, because then both the NP and S nodes would be crossed. It has been argued that it is possible to subsume several earlier CONSTRAINTS under this condition, which is claimed to be more GENERAL and NATURAL as a consequence.

subject(ive) A term used in the analysis of GRAMMATICAL FUNCTIONS to refer to a major CONSTITUENT of SENTENCE or CLAUSE structure, traditionally associated with the 'doer' of an action, as in ***The cat*** *bit the dog*. The oldest approaches make a twofold distinction in sentence analysis between subject and PREDICATE, and this is still common, though not always in this terminology; other approaches distinguish subject from a series of other elements of STRUCTURE (OBJECT, COMPLEMENT, VERB, ADVERBIAL, in particular). Linguistic analyses have emphasized the complexity involved in this notion, distinguishing, for example, the 'grammatical' from the UNDERLYING or 'logical' subject of a sentence, as in *The cat was chased by the dog*, where *The cat* is the grammatical and *the dog* the logical subject. Not all subjects, moreover, can be analysed as doers of an action, as in such sentences as *Dirt attracts flies* and *The books sold well*. The definition of subjects in terms of SURFACE grammatical features (using WORD ORDER or INFLECTIONAL criteria) is usually relatively straightforward, but the specification of their function is more complex, and has attracted much recent discussion (e.g. in RELATIONAL GRAMMAR). In GENERATIVE grammar, subject is sometimes defined as the NP immediately DOMINATED by S. While NP is the typical formal realization of subject, other categories can have this function, e.g. clause (S-bar), as in *That oil floats on water is a fact*, and PP, as in *Between 6 and 9 will suit me*. The term is also encountered in such contexts as RAISING and the SPECIFIED-SUBJECT CONDITION.

In the study of inflected languages, **subjective** may be used as an alternative to NOMINATIVE; e.g. in English the contrast between subject and object forms of PRONOUNS (e.g. *he* ~ *him*) is sometimes referred to as a distinction between subjective and objective case. The term 'subjective GENITIVE' is also used (as in *the playing of the musicians* = 'musicians play'), in contrast with the OBJECTIVE genitive (as in *the building of the house* = 'X built the house'). See also COMPLEMENT, RAISING.

subjunct A term used in QUIRK GRAMMAR to refer to a subclass of ADVERBIALS along with ADJUNCTS, DISJUNCTS and CONJUNCTS. In early work 'subjuncts' were grouped within the category of 'adjuncts'; in later work, however, they were felt to be sufficiently different in SEMANTIC and SYNTACTIC behaviour to warrant their 'equal' status with the other subclasses. Subjuncts include a wide range of adverbials which have a subordinate role in comparison with other CLAUSE ELEMENTS. They include several classes of item, such as the expression of viewpoint (e.g. ***Morally**, that is wrong*), courtesy (e.g. *Come in, **please***) and emphasis (e.g. *actually, frankly*).

subjunctive A term used in the GRAMMATICAL classification of SENTENCE types, and usually seen in contrast to INDICATIVE, IMPERATIVE, etc., MOODS. It refers to VERB forms or sentence/CLAUSE types used in the expression of many kinds of SUBORDINATE clause, for a range of attitudes including tentativeness, vagueness, uncertainty. In modern English, the examples which come nearest to the subjunctive occur in 'hypothetical' constructions of the type *if she **were** going* (cf. *if she was going*), in certain formulae (e.g. *So **be** it!*), and in some clauses introduced by *that* (especially in American English, e.g. *I insist that he **go** to town*). In many LANGUAGES, it is more PRODUCTIVE, e.g. in French.

sublanguage see LANGUAGE

submorpheme see MORPHEME

subordination (subordinat-e, -ing, -or) A term used in GRAMMATICAL analysis to refer to the process or result of linking LINGUISTIC UNITS so that they have different SYNTACTIC status, one being dependent upon the other, and usually a constituent of the other; **subordinate** is sometimes contrasted with SUPERORDINATE. (In this respect, it is usually distinguished from CO-ORDINATE linkage, where the units are equivalent.) **Subordinate clauses** are illustrated in the SENTENCE *John left when the bus arrived*: the marker of linkage is *when*, a **subordinating conjunction** (or **subordinator**). A wide range of subordinates exists in English, e.g. *although, since, because, while, after*. Some grammarians analyse certain subordinators (e.g. *before, since, until*) as PREPOSITIONS with sentential COMPLEMENTS. In ENDOCENTRIC PHRASES, the term 'subordinate' is also used to refer to the words which modify the HEAD; e.g. in *all the very big cars, all the very big* is subordinate to *cars*, and *very* is subordinate to *big*.

subsegment see SEGMENT

substance A term used in LINGUISTICS to refer to the undifferentiated raw material out of which LANGUAGE is constructed – the sound waves of speech (PHONIC SUBSTANCE), the marks of writing (GRAPHIC SUBSTANCE). 'Substance' is here opposed to FORM – the abstract pattern of relationships imposed on this substance by a language. In SAUSSUREAN theory, MEANING too is conceived as having substance, namely, the conceptual store of thoughts, feelings, etc., which exist independently of language. In modern linguistics, however, the term tends to be restricted to the PHONETIC and GRAPHETIC MEDIA (as in HALLIDAYAN theory, where 'substance' is recognized as a separate LEVEL).

sub-standard see STANDARD

substantive (substantival) (1) A term used in LINGUISTIC theory to refer to a category of linguistic UNIVERSAL; opposed to FORMAL. **Substantive** (or **substantival) universals** are the PRIMITIVE ELEMENTS which a GRAMMAR establishes in order to analyse linguistic DATA, e.g. S, NP, VP, [+ human], [+ high] in GENERATIVE grammar, or SUBJECT, VERB, OBJECT, etc., in RELATIONAL MODELS.

(2) In some DESCRIPTIVE grammars, **substantive** is a term used in the CLASSIFICATION of WORDS, referring to the class of NOUNS (traditionally defined as 'substances', i.e. names of persons, places, things, etc.), and also to those ITEMS which function as nouns, though lacking some of the formal characteristics of that class (cf. the 'substantival function' of ADJECTIVES, in *the poor, the rich*, etc.). The set of PRONOUNS may also be included in this class.

substitution (substitut-e, -able, -ability) A term used in LINGUISTICS to refer to the process or result of replacing one ITEM by another at a particular place in a STRUCTURE. In GRAMMAR, the structural CONTEXT within which this replacement occurs is known as a **substitution frame**, e.g. *The – is angry*, and the set of items which can be used PARADIGMATICALLY at a given place is known as a **substitution class**. A WORD which refers back to a previously occurring element of structure (such as the PRONOUN *he* in *The man came in. He was smiling.*) may be called a **substitute word**. In GOVERNMENT-BINDING THEORY, substitution is one of the two main types of MOVEMENT process (the other being ADJUNCTION); it involves the moved category replacing an EMPTY category of the same kind in accordance with the STRUCTURE-preserving CONSTRAINT. In language teaching, exercises to improve the ability of learners to carry out this process of replacement are known as **substitution drills** (or 'pattern drills').

substrate (substratum) A term used in SOCIOLINGUISTICS and HISTORICAL LINGUISTICS to refer to a LINGUISTIC VARIETY or set of FORMS which has influenced the STRUCTURE or use of a more dominant variety or LANGUAGE within a community. A **substrate language** (**linguistic substrate** or **substratum**) is particularly evidenced when a language is imposed on a community, as a result of political or economic superiority, as can be seen in the many varieties of English spoken throughout the world which incorporate characteristics of a mother-tongue, e.g. in India, West Africa. The opposite effect is known as a SUPERSTRATUM.

substring see STRING

subtractive bilingualism see BILINGUALISM

subtree see TREE

suction One of the features of sound set up by CHOMSKY and Halle in their DISTINCTIVE FEATURE theory of PHONOLOGY, under the heading of SUPPLEMENTARY MOVEMENTS, to handle variations in MANNER OF ARTICULATION. It refers to articulatory movements of the GLOTTIS or velum (cf. VELAR) where the airflow is directed inwards, as IMPLOSIVES and CLICKS. See also STOP.

suffix(-ing, -ation) A term used in MORPHOLOGY referring to an AFFIX which is added following a ROOT or STEM. The process of **suffixation** or **suffixing** is common in English, both for the DERIVATIONAL formation of new LEXICAL items (e.g. *-ize, -tion*) and for expressing GRAMMATICAL relationships (INFLECTIONAL endings such as *-s, -ed, -ing*).

superfix/suprafix A term used in PHONETICS and PHONOLOGY to refer to a vocal effect which extends over more than one sound SEGMENT in an UTTERANCE, such as a PITCH, STRESS or JUNCTURE pattern, particularly when this is seen in the context of a specific GRAMMATICAL STRUCTURE. The term SUPRASEGMENTAL is however now widely used instead.

superfoot A term in METRICAL PHONOLOGY for a NODE which DOMINATES the two rightmost FEET in a metrical TREE; symbolized by Σ'. For example, in the tree structure for *reconciliation*, the node governing the two stress feet (Σ) *cil-i* and *a-tion* is a superfoot.

superheavy syllable see WEIGHT

superlative A term used in the three-way GRAMMATICAL description of ADJECTIVES and ADVERBS into DEGREES, specifiying the extent of their application. The superlative form is used to express a comparison between more than two entities, and contrasts with COMPARATIVE, where only two entities are involved, and POSITIVE, where no comparison is implied. In English there is both an INFLECTION (*-est*) and a PERIPHRASTIC construction (*most*) to express this notion (e.g. *biggest, most interesting*).

superordinate A term sometimes used in GRAMMATICAL DESCRIPTION to refer to a linguistic UNIT higher up a HIERARCHY than another (SUBORDINATE) unit. For example, in *John saw where Mary lived, John saw* (or, *John saw X*) is the superordinate CLAUSE while *where Mary lived* is the subordinate clause. The term is also used in other areas of LINGUISTICS to refer to higher-order units, such as the more inclusive LEXICAL item in HYPONYMY (*flower* is the superordinate label for *tulip*, *daffodil*, etc.).

superstratum A term used in SOCIOLINGUISTICS and HISTORICAL LINGUISTICS to refer to a LINGUISTIC VARIETY or set of FORMS which has influenced the STRUCTURE or use of a less dominant variety or LANGUAGE within a community. A **linguistic superstratum** is usually the result of political, economic or cultural dominance, as illustrated by the influence of English, French, Arabic, etc., on the languages of the world at various periods in history. One of the most noticeable features of superstratal influence is the increased use of LOAN words.

supplementary movements One of the types of sound feature set up by CHOMSKY and Halle in their DISTINCTIVE FEATURE theory of PHONOLOGY, to handle variations in MANNER OF ARTICULATION. They are subdivided into SUCTION and PRESSURE types, a distinction made on the basis of the INGRESSIVE or EGRESSIVE GLOTTAL or VELAR movement involved in sounds with two simultaneous CLOSURES, as in IMPLOSIVES, EJECTIVES and CLICKS.

suppletion (suppletive) A term used in MORPHOLOGY to refer to cases where it is not possible to show a relationship between MORPHEMES through a general RULE, because the forms involved have different ROOTS. A **suppletive** is the grammar's use of an unrelated FORM (i.e. with a different root) to complete a PARADIGM, as in the present–past-TENSE relationship of *go* ~ *went*, or the COMPARATIVE form *better* in relation to *good*.

suprafix see SUPERFIX

supraglottal A general term used in PHONETICS to refer to the whole area of the VOCAL TRACT above the GLOTTIS.

suprasegmental A term used in PHONETICS and PHONOLOGY to refer to a vocal effect which extends over more than one sound SEGMENT in an UTTERANCE, such as a PITCH, STRESS or JUNCTURE pattern. In its contrast with 'segmental', it is seen as one of two main classes into which phonological UNITS can be divided. In American STRUCTURALIST theories, suprasegmentals were analysed as PHONEMES and sequences of such features as MORPHEMES, but not all phonologists analyse these features in EMIC terms. Alternative terms are PLURISEGMENTAL, non-segmental and SUPERFIX.

surface structure A central theoretical term in TRANSFORMATIONAL GRAMMAR, opposed to DEEP STRUCTURE. The 'surface structure' of a SENTENCE is the final stage in the SYNTACTIC REPRESENTATION of a sentence, which provides the input to the PHONOLOGICAL COMPONENT of the grammar, and which thus most closely corresponds to the structure of the sentence we articulate and hear. Analysing a surface STRING of MORPHEMES through CONSTITUENT analysis is a universal procedure which indicates many important facts about LINGUISTIC structure; but it by no means indicates everything, e.g. it cannot explain how we recognize certain AMBIGUOUS sentences, or how we INTUITIVELY relate sentences which have different surface FORMS but the same basic MEANING (e.g. *Cats chase mice* and *Mice are chased by cats*). For such reasons, linguists in the late 1950s postulated a deep or 'underlying' structure for sentences – a LEVEL of structural organization in which all the factors determining structural interpretation are defined and interrelated. The standard view is that a grammar operates by generating a set of abstract deep structures, subsequently converting these UNDERLYING REPRESENTATIONS into surface structures by applying a set of TRANSFORMATIONAL RULES. This two-level conception of grammatical structure is still widely held, though it has been much criticized in recent GENERATIVE studies. An alternative conception is to relate surface structure directly to a SEMANTIC level of representation, bypassing deep structure altogether. More recently, a modified conception known as S-STRUCTURE has been introduced. The term 'surface grammar' is sometimes used as an informal term for the superficial properties of the sentence.

svarabhakti vowel see ANAPTYXIS

switch reference A means of showing the SEMANTIC relationship between CLAUSE elements (typically, the SUBJECTS) in a CHAIN of clauses. In a given chain, the VERB of each clause except the last indicates MORPHOLOGICALLY whether its subject is the same as the subject of the following clause, or different from it (cf. REFERENCE). Switch-reference marking has been noted in several Australian Aboriginal languages.

syllable (syllab-ic, re- -(if)ication, -ify) A UNIT of pronunciation typically larger than a single sound and smaller than a WORD. A word may be pronounced 'syllable at a time', as in *ne-ver-the-less*, and a good dictionary will indicate where these **syllabic divisions** occur in writing, thus providing information about how a word may be hyphenated. The notion of syllable, in short, is very real to NATIVE-SPEAKERS, and is often used in a quasi-technical sense in everyday conversation (e.g. *Shall I put it in words of one syllable?*). **Syllabification** is the term which refers to the division of a word into syllables; **resyllabification** refers to a REANALYSIS which alters the location of syllable boundaries. A word containing a single syllable is called a **monosyllable**; if it contains more than one, the term **polysyllable** is used (or 'monosyllabic word'/'polysyllabic word' respectively).

Providing a precise definition of the syllable is not an easy task, and there are several theories in both PHONETICS and PHONOLOGY which have tried to clarify matters. From a phonetic viewpoint, attempts have been made to define the syllables of a LANGUAGE on the basis of the articulatory effort needed in order to produce them. The 'pulse' or 'motor' theory of syllable production proposed by the psychologist R. H. Stetson (1892–1950) argued that each syllable corresponds to an increase in air pressure, air from the lungs being released as a series of chest pulses. This can often be readily felt and measured, particularly in emphatic speech; but it is also often difficult to detect such a pulse in adjacent syllables, as when two VOWELS co-occur, e.g. *going* (which is two syllables, but usually said in a single muscular effort). An alternative phonetic approach attempts to define the syllable in auditory terms: the PROMINENCE theory argues that, in a STRING of sounds, some are intrinsically more 'sonorous' than others, and that each 'peak' of SONORITY corresponds to the centre of a syllable. These peaks are best illustrated by vowels, which have the greater carrying-power. The less sonorous sounds provide 'valleys' of prominence, and are best illustrated by the closures and narrowings which produce consonants. This approach gives a useful general guideline, but it does not always indicate clearly where the boundary between adjacent syllables falls, e.g. in *busker*, the problem of whether to split the word as *bus-ker, bu-sker* or *busk-er* is not answerable using arguments based on perceived sonority. The problem remains, even if other acoustic features than sonority (such as pitch or length) are incorporated within the notion of prominence, but has been specifically addressed in recent phonological theories (notably METRICAL PHONOLOGY).

Phonetic approaches of this kind attempt to provide a definition of the syllable valid for all languages, and it is possible that more valid definitions in terms of speech production or perception will emerge. Phonological views of the syllable, on the other hand, focus on the ways sounds combine in individual languages to produce typical SEQUENCES. Here, two classes of sounds are usually established: sounds which can occur on their own, or at the centre of a sequence of sounds, and sounds which cannot occur on their own, or which occur at the edges of a sequence of sounds. The former include such sounds as [i], [a], [u], etc., and are generally referred to as VOWELS; the latter include such sounds as [p], [g], [f], [ʧ], etc., and are generally referred to as CONSONANTS. A consonant–vowel (CV) sequence is a pattern which seems to be found in all languages: because the syllable is not 'closed' by another consonant, this type of syllable is often called an **open syllable** type. A CVC pattern is also very common in English. In such a case, the following terminology is widely used:

the opening segment of a syllable = the **onset**,

the closing segment of the syllable = the **coda**,
the central segment of the syllable = the **centre** or **nucleus**.

A useful collective term for the opening and closing segments is the MARGINS (or EDGES) of the syllable. In METRICAL PHONOLOGY, the nucleus and coda are viewed as a single constituent of syllable structure, called the **rhyme** (or **rime**), and syllables are distinguished phonologically in terms of their WEIGHT.

Using such methods, syllables can be defined in terms of the way the sound SEGMENTS of a language function. In this way, for instance, one can identify the various CLUSTERS of segments which may occur at syllable margins, such as CV (*say*), CCV (*play*), CCCV (*stray*), etc. Exceptional syllables can also be identified, such as those where certain consonants occur alone to form the syllable – the NASALS and LATERALS in words such as *button* [bʌtn̩] and *bottle* [bɒtl̩], where [̩] indicates that the final consonant is a **syllabic consonant**.

The notion of syllable is widely used elsewhere in phonology, e.g. in relation to PROSODY and cross-linguistic studies of RHYTHM (cf. SYLLABLE-TIMED language). In the DISTINCTIVE FEATURE theory of phonology proposed by CHOMSKY and Halle, **syllabic** is used to replace the earlier term 'vocalic', referring to all segments constituting a syllabic nucleus. Vowels, liquids and nasals would be [+ syllabic] ([+ syll]); all other segments would be [– syll].

In later approaches to phonology, the notion of syllable has become increasingly important, especially in models of NON-LINEAR PHONOLOGY. Here, syllabification (and resyllabification) are interpreted in relation to questions of REPRESENTATION – how and at what point syllable structure is assigned to strings in a DERIVATION, and which phonological rules are involved in syllabification. Several models recognize a prosodic HIERARCHY in which the syllable plays a role: in PROSODIC MORPHOLOGY, for example, it is a level above the MORA and below the FOOT.

See also CODA, ONSET (1), TAUTOSYLLABIC.

syllable-timed A very general term used in PHONETICS to characterize the pronunciation of LANGUAGES displaying a particular type of RHYTHM; it is opposed to STRESS-TIMED languages. In syllable-timed languages, the SYLLABLES are said to occur at regular intervals of time, as in French; this characteristic is sometimes referred to as 'isosyllabism'. However, very little work has been done on the accuracy or general applicability of such properties, and the usefulness of the typology is questionable.

synaesthesia A term used in SEMANTICS to refer to a direct association between the FORM and the MEANING of LANGUAGE. For example, the *sl-* sound combination is often felt to express unpleasantness (cf. *slimy, slither*, etc., – and Lewis Carroll's *slithy*). Such SOUND-SYMBOLIC units are sometimes called PHONAESTHEMES.

synchronic One of the two main temporal dimensions of LINGUISTIC investigation introduced by the Swiss linguist Ferdinand de SAUSSURE, the other being DIACHRONIC. In **synchronic linguistics**, languages are studied at a theoretical point in time: one describes a 'state' of the language, disregarding whatever changes might be taking place. For example, one could carry out a synchronic description of the language of Chaucer, or of the sixteenth century, or of modern-day English. Most synchronic descriptions are of contemporary language states, but their importance as a preliminary to diachronic study has been stressed since Saussure. Linguistic investigations, unless specified to the contrary, are assumed to be synchronic.

syncope A term used in COMPARATIVE PHILOLOGY, and sometimes in modern PHONOLOGY, to refer to the DELETION of a VOWEL within a WORD; often contrasted with APHAERESIS and APOCOPE. Examples include the modern British English pronunciations of such words as *secretary* /ˈsekrɪtri/, where American English has /ˈsekrɪteri/. Some authors extend the notion to include internal CONSONANT deletion.

syncretism (syncretize) A term originally used in HISTORICAL LINGUISTICS (referring to the merging of forms following the loss of INFLECTIONS), and now often used SYNCHRONICALLY to refer to identity between two forms of the same LEXEME, e.g *walked* in *I walked* (where it is past TENSE) and *I've walked* (where it is past PARTICIPLE). The distinction is here 'syncretized', or 'neutralized'.

syndeton (syndetic) A term from Greek RHETORICAL tradition, and sometimes used in modern GRAMMAR, to refer to the use of CONJUNCTIONS to link parts of a SYNTACTIC construction, as in *They spoke rapidly and quietly.* It contrasts with **asyndeton**, which describes the omission of conjunctions, especially in order to achieve an economical or dramatic form of expression, as in *They spoke rapidly, quietly.*

synonym(-y, -ous) A term used in SEMANTICS to refer to a major type of SENSE relation between LEXICAL ITEMS: lexical items which have the same MEANINGS are synonyms, and the relationship between them is one of **synonymy**. For two items to be synonyms, it does not mean that they should be identical in meaning, i.e. interchangeable in all CONTEXTS, and with identical CONNOTATIONS – this unlikely possibility is sometimes referred to as 'total synonymy'. Synonymy can be said to occur if items are close enough in their meaning to allow a choice to be made between them in *some* contexts, without there being any difference for the meaning of the sentence as a whole. Linguistic studies of synonymy have emphasized the importance of context in deciding whether a set of lexical items is synonymous. For example, in the context *What a nice – of flowers*, the items *range, selection, choice*, etc., are synonymous; but in the context *Her – of knowledge is enormous*, only *range* can be used, along with a different set of synonyms, e.g. *breadth*. Synonymy is distinguished from such other sense relations as ANTONYMY, HYPONYMY and INCOMPATIBILITY.

syntagmatic (1) (**syntagm-a, -eme**) A fundamental term in LINGUISTICS, originally introduced by the Swiss linguist Ferdinand de SAUSSURE to refer to the SEQUENTIAL characteristics of speech, seen as a STRING of CONSTITUENTS (sometimes, but not always) in LINEAR order. The relationships between constituents ('syntagms' or 'syntagmas') in a CONSTRUCTION are generally called **syntagmatic relations**. Sets of syntagmatically related constituents are often referred to as STRUCTURES. Syntagmatic relations, together with PARADIGMATIC relations, constitute the statement of a linguistic UNIT's identity within the LANGUAGE SYSTEM. For example, the function of /p/ in English PHONOLOGY can be summarized by identifying its syntagmatic relationships (e.g. *p-it, ni-p, a-p-t* . . .) and the paradigmatic relationships it contracts with other elements (e.g. *p-it, b-it, n-it* . . .). Syntagmatic relationships can be established at all LEVELS of analysis. In TAGMEMIC GRAMMAR, however, the term **syntagmeme** is used in a restricted sense, referring to a unit in a grammatical HIERARCHY seen from the viewpoint of the ELEMENTS (or tagmemes) it includes; e.g. the SENTENCE is a syntagmeme for the CLAUSES that constitute it.

(2) In PSYCHOLINGUISTICS, the term is used to refer to a class of ASSOCIATIVE responses which people make when hearing a stimulus word, viz. those which fall into a different WORD-CLASS from the stimulus, in that the response word could precede or follow the stimulus word in a sentence. A **syntagmatic response** or **association** would be *drive* following *car, sheep* following *black*, etc. The **syntagmatic/paradigmatic shift** refers to a change in the patterns of response noted in children at around age seven, when the earlier pattern (of primarily syntagmatic associations) develops into the more adult-like pattern primarily involving PARADIGMATIC associations.

syntax (syntactic(s)) A traditional term for the study of the RULES governing the way WORDS are combined to form SENTENCES in a language. In this use, syntax is opposed to MORPHOLOGY, the study of word structure. An alternative definition (avoiding the concept of 'word') is the study of the interrelationships between ELEMENTS of SENTENCE STRUCTURE, and of the rules governing the arrangement of sentences in SEQUENCES. In this use, one might then talk of the 'syntax of the word'. In GENERATIVE linguistics, the **syntactic component** is one of three major organizational units within a grammar (the others being PHONOLOGICAL and SEMANTIC), containing rules for the generation of **syntactic structures** (e.g. PHRASE-STRUCTURE rules, TRANSFORMATIONAL rules). The exact nature of the **syntactic rules** within this component varies from one grammatical theory to another. Syntactic structures (PATTERNS, or CONSTRUCTIONS) are analysable into sequences of **syntactic categories** or **syntactic classes**, these being established on the basis of the **syntactic relationships** linguistic ITEMS have with other items in a construction. Some recent studies propose an analysis whereby categories are analysed as sets of **syntactic features**, to permit a greater degree of generalization across categories. For example, using the features V (= verbal) and N (= nominal), the suggestion has been made that the four categories of verb, noun, adjective and preposition can be analysed respectively as:

$$\begin{bmatrix}+\text{V}\\-\text{N}\end{bmatrix}, \begin{bmatrix}-\text{V}\\+\text{N}\end{bmatrix}, \begin{bmatrix}+\text{V}\\+\text{N}\end{bmatrix} \text{ and } \begin{bmatrix}-\text{V}\\-\text{N}\end{bmatrix}.$$

This kind of approach is referred to as **feature-based syntax**. Both positive and negative SUB-CATEGORIZATION features can be used, either singly or in combination, depending on the syntactic facts and on the analytic principles proposed. The study of the field as a whole is known as **syntactic theory**. Studying the sequential arrangements of syntax is sometimes referred to as 'syntactics', but there is a possibility of confusion here with the earlier use of this term as one of the three major divisions of SEMIOTICS (along with PRAGMATICS and SEMANTICS). The adjective form of 'syntax' in modern linguistics is 'syntactic', as in the above examples: 'syntactical' these days sounds quaint. See also AUTONOMOUS (3), BLEND, FRAME.

synthesis see SPEECH SYNTHESIS

synthetic (1) A type of LANGUAGE sometimes distinguished in COMPARATIVE LINGUISTICS using STRUCTURAL (as opposed to DIACHRONIC) criteria, and focusing on the characteristics of the WORD: in **synthetic languages**, words typically contain more than one MORPHEME (as opposed to ANALYTIC languages, where words are typically monomorphemic). Two types of synthetic language are usually recognized: AGGLUTINATIVE and INFLECTING – with POLYSYNTHETIC sometimes additionally distinguished. Examples include Latin, Greek, Arabic, Turkish. As always in such classifications, the categories are not clear-cut: different languages will display the characteristic of 'synthesis' to a greater or lesser degree.

(2) Some use is made in SEMANTICS of the sense of 'synthetic' found in logic and philosophy, where a **synthetic proposition/sentence** is one whose truth can be verified only by using empirical criteria, e.g. *It's raining, Those dogs are fierce.* The term contrasts with ANALYTIC, where the internal form of the PROPOSITION makes it necessarily true, without reference to external criteria.

system(-atic, -ic) In its most general sense, the term refers to a network of patterned relationships constituting the organization of LANGUAGE. Language as a whole is then characterized as a system (cf. the 'linguistic system of English', etc.) – and often as a HIERARCHICALLY ordered arrangement of systems. In one view, the 'language system' is constituted by the phonological, grammatical and semantic systems; the PHONOLOGICAL system comprises the SEGMENTAL and SUPRASEGMENTAL systems; the segmental system comprises the VOWEL and CONSONANT systems; and so on. Within this totality, the term 'system' may be applied to any finite set of FORMALLY or SEMANTICALLY connected UNITS (referred to variously as the 'terms' or 'members' of the system), where the interrelationships are mutually exclusive (i.e. two members of the same system cannot co-occur) and mutually defining (i.e. the meaning of one member is specifiable only with reference to others). For example, the set of personal PRONOUNS in a language constitutes a system, according to these criteria. First, it is finite (in English, *I, you, he, she, it, we, they*); the system is 'closed', in the sense that new members are not normally created. Second, it is not possible to use more than one at a given place in STRUCTURE (cf. **I you came*, etc.). Third, it is easier to define a member by referring to the other members of the system, rather than independently; e.g. *I* is 'the pronoun which is not *you/he/she/it/we/they*'. Other 'grammatical systems' would include DETERMINER/TENSE/MOOD/PREPOSITIONAL/NEGATION, etc. The term would not normally be applied to OPEN-class items, such as NOUNS, ADJECTIVES, SENTENCES, etc., unless it meant the set of formal grammatical relationships subsumed under that heading, e.g. the 'noun system' would mean the set of SYNTAGMATIC and PARADIGMATIC relationships which define the CLASS of nouns. The analysis is also applicable in principle to the study of MEANINGS, and the term 'SEMANTIC system' is often used; but in the present state of knowledge it is often difficult to model the interrelationship between semantic units according to criteria such as the above. A similar problem sometimes applies in grammatical analysis, where a full 'systemic' statement is difficult to establish in certain areas (e.g. ADVERBIALS, APPOSITION), partly because of the INDETERMINACY of the notions involved.

In HALLIDAYAN linguistics, the notion of system receives a special status. In SCALE-AND-CATEGORY grammar, it is one of the four central categories recognized by the theory (the others being UNIT, STRUCTURE and CLASS): 'systems' are finite sets of paradigmatically related items functioning in classes. In the later development of this approach, **systemic grammar**, the notion of system is made a central explanatory principle, the whole of language being conceived as a 'system of systems'. Systemic here should not be confused with 'systematic' (in either its general or technical uses; see below): systemic grammar is concerned to establish a network of systems of relationships, in the above sense, which will account for all the semantically relevant choices in the language as a whole.

The adjective **systematic** is often used in linguistics in its everyday sense, but in certain contexts (usually in relation to PHONETICS and PHONOLOGY) it receives a restricted definition. In GENERATIVE grammar, it has been used to refer to two LEVELS of REPRESENTATION in the phonological COMPONENT of the grammar: SYSTEMATIC PHONEMIC and SYSTEMATIC PHONETIC levels are distinguished, the implication being that the terms of these analyses are being seen as in systemic correspondence with other aspects of the grammar (e.g. the MORPHOLOGICAL relationships between items).

system architecture A computing term used in COMPUTATIONAL LINGUISTICS, referring to the set of superordinate principles which define the operations of a LANGUAGE processing system. System architectures specify the components of such a system, the structural relations between the components, and the way information can be controlled as it flows from one component to another during processing.

systematic phonemics A level of REPRESENTATION in GENERATIVE PHONOLOGY which sets up a single UNDERLYING form capable of accounting for the phonological variations which relate GRAMMATICAL STRUCTURES (e.g. words). In such pairs of words as *divine* ~ *divinity, obscene* ~ *obscenity*, there is plainly a regular relationship of some kind, but it is not an easy relationship to state explicitly. CHOMSKY and Halle, in their approach to this problem, argue that the ROOT MORPHEME in each pair of words can be given a single underlying representation (/divīn/ and /obsēn/ in the above cases), and that this, along with the rules which relate such representations to the SURFACE ALTERNANTS, accounts for the NATIVE-SPEAKER's awareness of the 'systematic' relationships which exist between grammar and phonology. (Such rules also often reflect sound changes which have taken place in the history of the language.) The units in these representations are referred to as **systematic phonemes**, as opposed to the 'autonomous' PHONEMES of traditional phonemic phonology, which are established without reference to grammatical structure. Some generative phonologists (such as Chomsky and Halle) prefer the term 'phonological' to refer to this level of representation, because of the undesirable associations of the term 'phonemic' with traditional phonemic theory.

systematic phonetics A level of REPRESENTATION in GENERATIVE PHONOLOGY which

T

t The abbreviation for TRACE.

T The abbreviation for TRANSFORMATION, in such phrases as 'T RULES'. See also T FORMS.

tacit A term used in GENERATIVE LINGUISTICS to characterize NATIVE-SPEAKERS' knowledge of their LANGUAGE (their COMPETENCE). It refers to the fact that their INTUITIONS about the way their language is constructed and functions are largely unconscious; it is usually used in the phrase **tacit knowledge**.

tactic(s) (taxis) A general term used in PHONETICS and LINGUISTICS to refer to the systematic arrangements of UNITS in LINEAR SEQUENCE at any linguistic LEVEL. The commonest terms based on this notion are: **phonotactics**, dealing with the sequential arrangements of sounds; **morphotactics** with MORPHEMES; and **syntactics** with higher grammatical units than the morpheme. Some linguistic theories give this dimension of analysis particular importance (e.g. STRATIFICATIONAL grammar, where several levels of tactic organization are recognized, corresponding to the strata set up by the theory, viz. 'hypophonotactics', 'phonotactics', 'morphotactics', 'lexotactics', 'semotactics' and 'hypersemotactics').

tag (1) A term used in GRAMMATICAL DESCRIPTION to refer to a QUESTION structure (a **tag question**) usually consisting of an AUXILIARY VERB plus PRONOUN, attached to the end of a STATEMENT in order to convey a NEGATIVE or POSITIVE orientation. It may be invariable, as in French *n'est-ce pas*, German *nicht wahr*, or VARIABLE, as in English. In all cases, the INTONATION in which the tag is uttered determines its FUNCTION – the contrast between 'asking' and 'telling', illustrated by English *she's late, isn't she?* ('I am asking you if she is late') *v. she's late, isn't she?* ('I am asking you to agree with me that she is late'). In English, in addition to this, the POLARITY of the tag is usually the reverse of that found in the MAIN CLAUSE: a positive clause takes a negative tag, and vice versa, e.g. *she's coming, isn't she/she isn't coming, is she*. Sometimes, two positive clauses are found (*she's coming, is she*), and, very rarely, two negatives (*she doesn't know, doesn't she*). Some grammars also recognize **tag statements** (e.g. *That was a lovely drink, that was; He's a nice man, is John*) and there are some close connections between this CONSTRUCTION and such 'reinforcing' patterns as *They're all the same, these phoneticians!* See also CHECKING, COPYING.

(2) A GRAMMATICAL label attached to a word in a computer CORPUS to indicate its CLASS, in a procedure known as **tagging**. Tags may be added manually or automatically (the latter at present with varying degrees of success).

tagmemics ((syn)tagmeme, tagma, -tics) A system of LINGUISTIC analysis developed by the American linguist Kenneth Lee Pike (b. 1912), and used by the Summer Institute of Linguistics for the training of linguists. LANGUAGE is seen as comprising three MODES – PHONOLOGY, LEXICON and GRAMMAR. The relationship phonology:PHONEME and lexicon:MORPHEME is paralleled by grammar:**tagmeme**. This basic grammatical UNIT consists of a 'functional slot' within a CONSTRUCTION frame, and a CLASS of substitutable items that can fill this SLOT ('fillers'). The identity of the tagmeme is in its correlation of FUNCTION and FORM, with both being explicitly labelled in the analysis (such functions as SUBJECT, PREDICATE, HEAD, MODIFIER and such forms as PRONOUNS, NOUN PHRASES, INFINITIVES). **Tagmemic analysis** involves a distinction between essential units (the tagmemes) and the non-essential units (the minimal ETIC units, called **tagmas**, which are analysed as **allotagmas** of the tagmeme). The identification and CLASSIFICATION of tagmas is the province of **tagmatics**. The constructions which result from the stringing together of tagmemes are known as **syntagmemes**. Grammatical units are organized hierarchically into LEVELS (MORPHEMES, WORDS, PHRASES, CLAUSES, SENTENCES, etc.).

Units of language description, at any level in this approach, can be analysed simultaneously as PARTICLE (in terms of FEATURES), WAVE (in terms of their status as VARIANTS MANIFESTED in different CONTEXTS) and FIELD (in terms of their DISTRIBUTION).

tail see TONE GROUP

tambre, tamber see TIMBRE

tap A term used in the PHONETIC classification of CONSONANT sounds on the basis of their MANNER OF ARTICULATION: it refers to any sound produced by a single rapid contact with the roof of the mouth by the TONGUE, resembling a very brief articulation of a STOP. It is commonly heard in many American English pronunciations of the medial /t/ or /d/ in *writer* and *rider*. Some phoneticians distinguish between taps and FLAPS in terms of the articulatory movements involved.

target (1) A term used in PHONETICS and PSYCHOLINGUISTICS to refer to a hypothetical ARTICULATORY state used as a reference point when describing SPEECH PRODUCTION in DYNAMIC terms. In CONNECTED SPEECH, the target articulatory features for a sound (e.g. ALVEOLAR, VOICING) may not be fully attained, because of the anticipatory influence of successive **target articulations**. The target MODEL postulates an idealized set of articulatory positions and a set of RULES which attempt to predict actual patterns of articulatory movement, taking into account such factors as speed of articulation, and the direction and distance between articulators. Similarly, models of SPEECH PERCEPTION have been proposed which use the construct of an **auditory target**, which enables the listener to identify the common factors in different ACCENTS, VOICE QUALITIES, etc.

(2) The LANGUAGE (or VARIETY, etc.) which is the focus of a linguistic process

of change is known as the **target language**, e.g. the language into which one is translating or interpreting, the language (or variety, etc.) being taught to foreign learners, and so on.

(3) In TRANSFORMATIONAL GRAMMAR, the CONSTITUENT affected by a transformation is sometimes referred to as the **target**. For example, the target for *WH*-MOVEMENT can be a NOUN PHRASE, as in *How many parcels will he send to London?*, a PREPOSITIONAL phrase, as in *In which book did you read about it?*, or certain other kinds of phrase. A similar use is found in GENERATIVE PHONOLOGY, where a rule can be triggered by one segment (the 'trigger segment') so as to apply to another (the 'target segment').

tautosyllabic A term sometimes use in PHONOLOGY to characterize a pattern of SEGMENTS which can be analysed as belonging to the same SYLLABLE. For example, the question of VCV syllabification can be discussed in terms of whether it is the VC or CV sequences which are best analysed as tautosyllabic.

taxeme A term introduced by the American linguist Leonard BLOOMFIELD, on analogy with the PHONEME, to refer to a single minimal feature of GRAMMATICAL ARRANGEMENT. Examples of taxemes include WORD ORDER, CONCORD, the grammatical use of PITCH, and the constituents of the ACTOR–ACTION–GOAL relationship. Combinations of taxemes, occurring as a conventional grammatical unit, are **tactic forms** (cf. TACTIC). Taxemes are distinguished in this approach from TAGMEMES, which are the smallest *meaningful* units of grammatical FORM.

taxis see TACTIC

taxonomic (taxonomy) An application of the general sense of this term in biosystematics, to refer to an approach to LINGUISTIC analysis and DESCRIPTION which is predominantly or exclusively concerned with CLASSIFICATION. The basis of classification may be DIACHRONIC, AREAL, TYPOLOGICAL, FUNCTIONAL, etc., and the entities being classified may be linguistic FEATURES, ITEMS, UNITS, STRUCTURES – or whole VARIETIES, DIALECTS or LANGUAGES. The notion of taxonomy has been fruitfully applied in many areas of linguistics (SOCIOLINGUISTICS, HISTORICAL LINGUISTICS and SEMANTICS, in particular). The limitations of a taxonomic approach in linguistic analysis have, however, been emphasized by GENERATIVE linguists, who have criticized the overreliance of STRUCTURALIST (or 'taxonomic') linguistics on PROCEDURES of SEGMENTATION and classification. In particular, the use of this label is intended to indicate the inability of structural linguistics to provide a level of explanation in terms of DEEP STRUCTURE. Such phrases as 'taxonomic PHONOLOGY', 'taxonomic SYNTAX', etc., when used in generative linguistics, invariably have a pejorative implication.

telegraphic speech A style of SPEECH production in which FUNCTION WORDS and INFLECTIONAL endings tend to be omitted; also called **telegrammatic speech**. The term derives from the written style used in the days when pay-by-the-word telegrams were a common method of communication (*Send cheque Brighton*), and is still used to describe any ELLIPTICAL written style (e.g. in newspaper headlines or want-ads); but in linguistics it is more commonly encountered in relation to the SENTENCE STRUCTURES found in young children's speech (*me kick* *ball*) and the reduced range of grammatical expression typical of one form of aphasia (cf. AGRAMMATISM).

telic(ity) A term used in the GRAMMATICAL analysis of ASPECT, to refer to an event where the activity has a clear terminal point. Telic verbs include *fall, kick*, and *make* (something). These verbs contrast with ATELIC verbs, where the event has no such natural end-point, as with *play* (in such a context as *the children are playing*).

template (templatic) (1) A term used in METRICAL PHONOLOGY for an abstract TREE structure which defines the basic STRUCTURAL possibilities of SYLLABLES in a language. For example, an influential formulation of English syllable structure involves a HIERARCHICAL analysis into an ONSET + NUCLEUS + CODA, with the latter two elements being grouped as a RHYME, and each element consisting of two SEGMENTS.

(2) The term also has a central status in PROSODIC MORPHOLOGY, where it refers to a fixed PHONOLOGICAL shape imposed on varying SEGMENTAL material. Templates are defined in the grammar and realized in the derivation in terms of the units in the prosodic HIERARCHY: MORA, SYLLABLE, FOOT, and prosodic WORD. The templatic target may be imposed on any morphological BASE (e.g. STEM, WORD, AFFIX). In REDUPLICATIVE constructions, for example, there might be a prefix with a constant CANONICAL shape (e.g. a heavy syllable), but a varying segmental shape (depending on the base to which it is attached). The **template satisfaction condition** states that the satisfaction of templatic constraints is obligatory and is determined by prosodic principles. This approach contrasts with segmentalist theories of template form, such as in (1) above.

(3) A general sense of the term ('a pattern established as a norm against which other patterns can be measured') also has a number of applications in specific LINGUISTIC or PHONETIC contexts. For example, in COGNITIVE GRAMMAR, connections between established patterns of neurological activity serve as templates for categorizing expressions. In automatic SPEECH RECOGNITION, templates are the stored, labelled SPECTRA (or the key features of spectra) against which an analysis of the signal to be recognized is matched (**template matching**).

tempo An application of the general sense of this term in PHONETICS and PHONOLOGY to refer to speed of speaking; alternatively known as RATE. Contrasts in the tempo of UTTERANCE are analysed in SUPRASEGMENTAL phonetics and phonology, along with PITCH and LOUDNESS variation, as part of the overall study of RHYTHM.

tenor A term used in HALLIDAYAN classification of LANGUAGE VARIETIES (more fully **tenor of discourse**), referring to the relations among the participants in a language activity, especially the LEVEL of FORMALITY they adopt (colloquial, formal etc.). Alternative labels which have been proposed for this area are STYLE or MANNER of discourse.

tense (1) A CATEGORY used in the GRAMMATICAL description of VERBS (along with ASPECT and MOOD), referring primarily to the way the grammar marks the time at which the action denoted by the verb took place. Traditionally, a distinction is made between past, present and future tenses, often with further divisions (perfect, pluperfect, etc.). In LINGUISTICS, the relationship between tense and time has been the subject of much study, and it is now plain that there is no easily stateable relationship between the two. Tense FORMS (i.e. variations in the MORPHOLOGICAL form of the verb) can be used to signal MEANINGS other than temporal ones. In English, for example, the past-tense form (e.g. *I knew*) may signal a tentative meaning, and not past time, in some contexts (e.g. *I wish I knew* – that is, 'know now'). Nor is there a simple one-to-one relationship between tense forms and time: the present tense in English may help to refer to future or past time, depending on CONTEXT (e.g. *I'm going home tomorrow, Last week I'm walking down this street . . .*). Furthermore, if tenses are defined as forms of the verb, it becomes a matter of debate whether a language like English has a future tense at all: constructions such as *I will/shall go*, according to many, are best analysed as involving MODAL AUXILIARY verbs, displaying a different grammatical FUNCTION (e.g. the expression of intention or obligation, which may often involve futurity). English illustrates many such problems, as do other languages, where tense forms, if they exist, regularly display analytic difficulties, because of overlaps between tense and other verbal functions, such as aspect or mood. Alternative terminology (e.g. 'past' *v.* 'non-past', 'future' *v.* 'non-future', 'now' *v.* 'remote') will often be needed.

(2) See TENSION.

tensed (un-) A term used in GENERATIVE GRAMMAR to refer to a CLAUSE which contains a VERB that expresses a TENSE contrast (i.e. it is FINITE); it contrasts with **untensed**. The **tensed-sentence (S) condition** in EXTENDED STANDARD THEORY states that a CONSTITUENT cannot be moved out of or into a tensed SUBORDINATE clause. In GOVERNMENT-BINDING THEORY, this CONDITION has been replaced by conditions A and B of BINDING theory.

tension (tense) A term used in the PHONETIC classification of speech sounds, referring to the overall muscular effort used in producing a sound. The contrasts are labelled variously, e.g. FORTIS *v.* LENIS, tense *v.* lax. This contrast is viewed as particularly important in DISTINCTIVE FEATURE theories of PHONOLOGY, where **tense** is one of the main features set up to handle variations in MANNER OF ARTICULATION. Tense sounds have been defined both ARTICULATORILY and ACOUSTICALLY: they are sounds produced with a relatively strong muscular effort, involving a greater movement of the (SUPRAGLOTTAL) VOCAL TRACT away from the position of rest (cf. FORTIS), and a relatively strong spread of acoustic energy. The VOWELS [i] and [u], for example, would be [+tense]; [ɪ] and [ʊ] would be [−tense]. ASPIRATED and long CONSONANTS (cf. LENGTH) would be [+tense]. The opposite term in JAKOBSON and Halle's system is LAX; in CHOMSKY and Halle's later system, the term **non-tense** is also used: these are sounds produced with less muscular effort and movement, and which are relatively short and indistinct, involving a relatively weak spread of acoustic energy as in CENTRALIZED vowels. Subglottal tension in Chomsky and Halle's system is handled by the feature HEIGHTENED SUBGLOTTAL PRESSURE.

term of address see ADDRESS

terminal A term used in GENERATIVE LINGUISTICS to identify certain characteristics of the output of the SYNTACTIC COMPONENT of the GRAMMAR. A **terminal element** or **terminal symbol** refers to the units employed in the syntactic REPRESENTATION of a SENTENCE, after all the RULES have been applied, viz. the MORPHEMES, FORMATIVES, FEATURES, such as *the, -en*, +, #, *man*. Terminal symbols are distinguished from **non-terminal** (or 'auxiliary') elements, which are used in formulating rules. The former are usually written in lower-case letters, the latter in upper-case (e.g. NP, VP). A NODE which does not DOMINATE other categories is a **terminal node**. A STRING consisting of terminal elements is known as a **terminal string**, i.e. the final string generated by a PHRASE-STRUCTURE grammar.

terminal analogs see SPEECH SYNTHESIS

termination see EXTRASYLLABIC (1)

tertiary response A term introduced into LINGUISTICS by Leonard BLOOMFIELD to refer to the views people display when their utterances about language (their SECONDARY RESPONSES) are themselves subjected to evaluation. For example, people who say, 'That dialect is ugly/primitive', etc., are making a secondary response; if this is disputed, then their attempt to explain the basis of their statement (or, indeed, their general emotional reaction) would constitute a tertiary response.

tessitura A term taken over by some PHONETICIANS from musical terminology and used to refer to the characteristic compass, or PITCH range, of a person's voice, when speaking normally. People are often impressionistically classified in this way (e.g. a 'very high-pitched' voice), as are languages.

test see ACCEPTABILITY, COMMUTATION, MINIMAL PAIR

text(-ual(ity), -ure, -linguistics) A pre-theoretical term used in LINGUISTICS and PHONETICS to refer to a stretch of language recorded for the purpose of analysis and description. What is important to note is that texts may refer to collections of written *or* spoken material (the latter having been transcribed in some way), e.g. conversation, monologues, rituals, and so on. The term **textual meaning** is sometimes used in SEMANTICS as part of a classification of types of MEANING, referring to those factors affecting the interpretation of a SENTENCE which derive from the rest of the text in which the sentence occurs – as when, at a particular point in a play or novel, a sentence or word appears whose significance can only be appreciated in the light of what has gone before.

In recent years, the study of texts has become a defining feature of a branch of linguistics referred to (especially in Europe) as **textlinguistics**, and 'text' here has central theoretical status. Texts are seen as language units which have a definable communicative function, characterized by such principles as COHESION, COHERENCE and informativeness, which can be used to provide a FORMAL definition of what constitutes their identifying **textuality** or **texture**. On the basis of these principles, texts are classified into text types, such as road signs, news reports, poems, conversations, etc. The approach overlaps considerably with that practised under the name of DISCOURSE analysis, and some linguists see very little difference between them. But usage varies greatly. Some linguists make a distinction between the notions of 'text', viewed as a physical 'product', and 'discourse', viewed as a dynamic process of expression and interpretation, whose function and mode of operation can be investigated using PSYCHOLINGUISTIC and SOCIOLINGUISTIC, as well as linguistic, techniques. A similar distinction sees 'text' as a notion which applies to SURFACE STRUCTURE, whereas 'discourse' applies to DEEP STRUCTURE. From the opposite viewpoint, some linguists have defined 'text' as an abstract notion, 'discourse' being its REALIZATION. Apart from these theoretical distinctions, there is also a tendency for texts to be thought of as monologues, usually written, and often very short (e.g. *no through road*), whereas discourses are often thought of as dialogues, usually spoken and of greater length.

text-to-speech A term used in PHONETICS and COMPUTATIONAL LINGUISTICS to refer to a system of SPEECH SYNTHESIS which can transform a conventional orthographic representation of LANGUAGE into its spoken equivalent. Such a system begins by carrying out a MORPHOLOGICAL and PHONOLOGICAL analysis of an input text, taking into account such matters as REGULAR *v.* irregular forms. Letter-to-sound RULES and other special features generate WORD-level phonological representations, which are then transformed into a PHONETIC REPRESENTATION (incorporating features of CONNECTED SPEECH, including sentence PROSODY). Synthesis takes place using a rule-based system, the output being provided by a terminal analog synthesizer.

T forms An abbreviation used in SOCIOLINGUISTICS as part of the study of terms of address in various LANGUAGES. Based on the distinction between *tu* and *vous*, the alternative forms of 'you' in French, and on similar CONTRASTS in many other languages (e.g. German *du/Sie*, Russian *ty/vy*), an OPPOSITION is set up between familiar (T) and formal (V) second-PERSON VERB and PRONOUN FORMS. Hypotheses are then developed concerning the system of FORMALITY in use in the languages.

TG The usual abbreviation for TRANSFORMATIONAL GRAMMAR.

that*-clause** A term used in some MODELS of GRAMMATICAL DESCRIPTION to refer to a DEPENDENT DECLARATIVE CLAUSE, introduced by *that*. The main types are: SUBJECT clauses, e.g. ***that she wrote** surprises me*; OBJECT clauses, e.g. *she said **that she wrote, APPOSITIONAL clauses, e.g. *your view, **that she'll write**, is rubbish*; subject COMPLEMENT clauses, e.g. *the trouble is **that it won't happen***; ADJECTIVAL complement clauses, e.g. *I'm certain **that he'll go***; and *that*-RELATIVE clauses, e.g. *The book **that I sold**...* The *that* may be omitted in some circumstances, e.g. *he said **he would come**.*

***that*-trace constraint/filter/phenomenon** A term in GENERATIVE GRAMMAR, originally in EXTENDED STANDARD THEORY, used in connection with such constructions as **Who do you know that — saw Bill?*, which involve extraction of a SUBJECT from a CLAUSE introduced by a COMPLEMENTIZER.

theme (themat-ic, -ization) A term used in LINGUISTICS as part of an analysis of the structure of SENTENCES (their **thematic structure**): it refers, not to the subject-matter of a sentence (its everyday MEANING), but to the way speakers identify the relative importance of their subject-matter, and is defined as the first major CONSTITUENT of a sentence (seen here as a STRING of constituents). There is no necessary correspondence with a FUNCTIONAL grammatical ELEMENT (though in English theme and SUBJECT often coincide) e.g. ***The man** is coming*, ***His hair** I can't stand*, ***Smith** her name was*, ***Under no condition** will he...* The process of moving an element to the front of the sentence in this way ('fronting'), to act as theme, is known as **thematization** (sometimes TOPICALIZATION) or **thematic fronting**. Some linguists systematically distinguish this notion from other ways of analysing the organization of the sentence structure of messages, such as the TOPIC/COMMENT distinction, or an analysis in terms of INFORMATION structure. In GOVERNMENT-BINDING THEORY, each ARGUMENT (i.e. subject or COMPLEMENT) of a PREDICATE is said to bear a particular **thematic role** (also known as THETA ROLE) in relation to its predicate, this being defined with reference to a restricted universal set of **thematic functions** (or **thematic relations**).

In the PRAGUE SCHOOL approach to linguistics of recent years, theme is opposed to RHEME, producing a distinction similar to that of topic/comment, but interpreted with reference to the theoretical framework of FUNCTIONAL SENTENCE PERSPECTIVE. In this theory, the theme is defined as the part of a sentence which adds least to the advancing process of communication (it has the lowest degree of COMMUNICATIVE DYNAMISM); in other words, it expresses relatively little (or no) extra meaning, in addition to what has already been communicated. The rheme, by contrast, carries the highest degree of communicative dynamism. Various transitional expressions, neither 'thematic' nor 'rhematic', are also recognized.

theory see AXIOM, GRAMMAR (2), LINGUISTICS, MODEL (1), POSTULATES, PRIMITIVE

***there*-insertion** A term used in TRANSFORMATIONAL GRAMMAR for a transformation which relates pairs of sentences by INSERTING a *there*-element, such as *A baby is in the bath* → *There is a baby in the bath*. The latter type of sentence is often referred to as EXISTENTIAL.

theta role A term used in GOVERNMENT-BINDING THEORY for a SEMANTIC role such as AGENT, PATIENT, LOCATIVE, SOURCE and GOAL; also known as a **thematic role**. It is often called a semantic CASE in other approaches.

theta theory One of the (sub-)theories of GOVERNMENT-BINDING THEORY. Its main principle is the **theta-criterion**, which requires that every ARGUMENT is assigned just one THETA ROLE and that every theta role is assigned to just one argument. Its main role is to determine the positions to which NP-MOVEMENT is possible.

thirteen men rule see REVERSAL

tier A term in HIERARCHICAL MODELS of PHONOLOGY (cf. NON-LINEAR PHONOLOGY) for a level of phonological REPRESENTATION. For example, in AUTOSEGMENTAL phonology, parallel tiers of phonological SEGMENTS are proposed, each tier consisting of a STRING of segments, and representing a sequence of ARTICULATORY gestures or ACOUSTIC TRANSITIONS. In a TONE language, for instance, tones are represented on one tier, which specifies FEATURES of tone and nothing else; other (non-tonal) features are represented on a separate tier. Features cannot appear on more than one tier, and thus tiers can be defined by the features found in them, as in the case of the PHONEMIC tier, the SKELETAL TIER and the X-TIER. The number of tiers varies between models. In PARTICLE PHONOLOGY, for example, there are five: syllabic, nucleus, timing, root and particle tiers. Terminology varies greatly among different models, as in the case of the tier handling information about articulation, which has been called a 'featural', 'gestural', 'melodic', 'segmental' and 'articulatory' tier.

timbre The attribute of auditory sensation in terms of which a listener can judge the dissimilarity between sounds of otherwise identical PITCH, LOUDNESS and LENGTH. Acoustically, the sensation of timbre derives from the set of HARMONICS involved in the production of a TONE. The best examples can be found in the characteristic timbres, or 'tonal qualities', of different instruments of the orchestra; but a similar set of timbres can be established to distinguish between the frequency characteristics of individual sounds (such as VOWELS, FRICATIVES) or individual speakers (as one of the features of VOICE QUALITY). The term is sometimes spelled **tambre** or **tamber**. An alternative term, more widely used in the context of SEGMENTAL studies, is QUALITY, as in VOWEL QUALITY.

timing (1) This general term is applied in PHONETICS and PSYCHOLINGUISTICS to the temporal constraints on the ARTICULATION and SEQUENCING of sounds in SPEECH PRODUCTION. Timing phenomena are therefore of relevance for an understanding of both SEGMENTAL and SUPRASEGMENTAL phonetics and PHONOLOGY: timing is involved in the co-ordination of musculature required to produce an individual sound, in the programming of PHONOTACTIC SEQUENCES, and in such notions as RHYTHM and INTONATION.

(2) The term is also found in some HIERARCHICAL models of PHONOLOGY, as the name of a tier of REPRESENTATION (though its application varies among theories). In PARTICLE PHONOLOGY, for example, the **timing tier** represents SYLLABLE WEIGHT (MORAS). In AUTOSEGMENTAL PHONOLOGY it describes a specific conception of the SKELETAL TIER (see X-TIER).

tip The end point of the TONGUE, also known as the APEX; used in the articulation of a few speech sounds, such as the TRILLED [r].

tip-of-the-tongue phenomenon The everyday sense of this phrase is found in PSYCHOLINGUISTICS, where the phenomenon is subjected to experimental investigation as part of a theory of SPEECH PRODUCTION. It is shown that people having a tip-of-the-tongue experience are able to recall certain general characteristics of the WORD, e.g. the number of SYLLABLES it has, its STRESS pattern; also some PHONETIC SEGMENTS are recalled more readily than others. These results suggest that words vary in the ACCESSIBILITY of their PHONOLOGICAL REPRESENTATION in the brain, and that certain features of word structure are stored independently of others.

TMA The abbreviation for the 'TENSE–MOOD–ASPECT' system encountered in the study of CREOLE languages.

token see TYPE (2)

tone (1) (**-me, -mics, -tics, a-tonal-ity**) A term used in PHONOLOGY to refer to the DISTINCTIVE PITCH level of a SYLLABLE. In the study of INTONATION, a sequence of tones constitutes a CONTOUR or TONE UNIT. In HALLIDAYAN analysis, the division of an utterance into tone groups is called **tonality**. The most PROMINENT tone in a tone unit may be referred to as a NUCLEAR tone. In many LANGUAGES, the tone carried by a WORD is an essential feature of the MEANING of that word (**lexical tone**), e.g. in Beijing Mandarin Chinese the word *ma* when pronounced in a level tone means 'mother', and in a FALLING-rising tone means 'horse' – two out of four possible tone contrasts in that language. Such languages, where word meanings or grammatical CATEGORIES (such as TENSE) are dependent on pitch level, are known as **tone languages**. The unit which carries the tone (e.g. syllable, MORA) is called the **tone-bearing unit**. Many languages of South-East Asia and Africa are tone languages, illustrating several types of tonal organization. In such languages, sequences of adjacent tones may influence each other phonetically or phonologically, e.g. a word which in isolation would have a low tone may be given a higher tone if a high-tone word follows: such a phenomenon is sometimes called **tone** (or **tonal**) **sandhi**. The organization of tonal structure within a NON-LINEAR PHONOLOGICAL model (the nature of tonal FEATURES and the location of tonal LINKAGE) is sometimes called **tonal geometry**. In PARTICLE PHONOLOGY, **tonality** refers to particles which represent PALATALITY and LABIALITY, and is distinguished from APERTURE. The historical development of a tonal language from an **atonal** one is known as **tonogenesis**.

The study of the phonetic properties of tone, in its most general sense, is sometimes referred to as **tonetics**. In the EMIC tradition of study, contrastive tones are classified as **tonemes**, and the study of such tones is known as **tonemics**. Features of tone, such as 'high', 'low', and 'mid', are proposed by DISTINCTIVE FEATURE theories of phonology. Tones which vary in PITCH range are often called 'contour', 'kinetic' or 'dynamic' tones; those which do not vary in range are 'static' or 'level' tones. See also CONTOUR, POLARITY (2), TONIC.

(2) In ACOUSTIC PHONETICS, a sound with sufficient regularity of vibration to provide a sensation of PITCH. Sounds which lack this regularity are characterized as NOISE. A **pure tone** is produced by a waveform whose pattern of vibration repeats itself at a constant rate; such tones are typically produced by electronic sources or tuning forks. When two or more tones of different FREQUENCIES combine, the result is a **complex tone**. Most sounds, including those of speech, involve complex tones, with different PERIODIC patterns.

tone group/unit A term used by some INTONATION analysts, particularly those working within the British tradition, to refer to a distinctive sequence of PITCHES, or TONES, in an utterance. The essential feature of a tone unit is the NUCLEAR tone, the most PROMINENT tone in the sequence; and this may be accompanied, depending on the length of the utterance, by other components, such as the **head** (i.e. the sequence of SYLLABLES between the first STRESSED syllable and the nuclear tone), **pre-head** (i.e. unstressed syllables at the very beginning of the tone unit) and **tail** (i.e. the syllables following the nuclear tone). This terminology can be illustrated by the sentence *the*|*man* ˈbought a|*nèw*|ˈclock|, where the sequence of pre-head/head/nucleus/tail is marked by vertical lines. A tone unit usually corresponds to a CLAUSE or SENTENCE, but may be used on any grammatical unit, e.g. in an extremely irritated version of the above sentence, there might be several tone units, as in *the mán*|*bóught*|*a néw*|*clòck*|.

tongue (1) From the PHONETIC point of view, the importance of the tongue is that it is the organ of articulation most involved in the production of speech sounds – all the VOWELS and the majority of the CONSONANTS (that is, excluding those made at the lips and in the throat). Different parts of the tongue are involved in articulating these sounds, and it has proved convenient to classify sounds with reference to these areas. From front to back, it is usual to distinguish the TIP (or APEX), BLADE (or FRONT), CENTRE (or 'top'), BACK (or DORSUM) and ROOT. The GROOVE running down the centre of the tongue is also significant, in that several sound contrasts can be made by altering its shape. Plotting tongue movements is difficult visually or kinaesthetically, but recent advances in phonetic instrumentation, such as the ELECTROPALATOGRAPH, can display many of these movements with accuracy.

(2) In CHOMSKY and Halle's DISTINCTIVE FEATURE theory of PHONOLOGY, **tongue-body features** constitute one of the categories set up to handle variations in PLACE OF ARTICULATION (CAVITY features). The placement of the body of the tongue is characterized with reference to three features, all seen as OPPOSITIONS: HIGH, LOW and BACK.

tongue-slip (slip of the tongue) The everyday sense of this phrase is found in PHONETICS and PSYCHOLINGUISTICS, where the phenomenon is studied as part of a theory of SPEECH PRODUCTION. Such slips seem not to be random; e.g. SEGMENTS occurring initially in SYLLABLES seem to interfere only with other syllable-initial segments. The suggestion is that tongue-slips are not just ERRORS of ARTICULATION, but are rather the results of incorrect neural programming ('slips of the brain', as some would say). The analysis of these errors motivates hypotheses about the properties of the NEUROLINGUISTIC control governing speech (cf. ACCESSIBILITY).

tonic(ity) A term used by some INTONATION analysts, particularly those working within the British tradition, to refer to the SYLLABLE in a TONE UNIT which carries maximal PROMINENCE, usually owing to a major PITCH change. The tonic syllable is also referred to as the 'NUCLEAR syllable', or 'nucleus', in this tradition. Most words in a tone unit can carry the **tonic syllable**, depending on the meaning intended, although the usual position for this is at or towards the end of a sequence. Compare the different emphases in *The* ***woman*** *was walking to town* with *The woman was walking to* ***town*** and *The woman was* ***walking*** *to town*. The change in **tonicity** gives the sentence different implications (e.g. '*The woman*, not the man, was walking . . .'), an important aspect of communication in conversation, where it draws attention especially to the NEW INFORMATION in a sentence.

top-down see BOTTOM-UP

topic (1) A term used in SEMANTICS and GRAMMAR as part of an alternative binary characterization of SENTENCE STRUCTURE to that traditionally found in the SUBJECT/PREDICATE distinction; the opposite term is COMMENT. The topic of a sentence is the entity (person, thing, etc.) about which something is said, whereas the further statement made about this entity is the comment. The usefulness of the distinction is that it enables general statements to be made about the relationships between sentences which the subject/predicate distinction (along with other contrasts of this type) obscures. The topic often coincides with the subject of a sentence (e.g. *A* ***visitor/*** *is coming to the door*), but it need not (e.g. *There's* ***the driver/*** *who gave you a lift*), and, even when it is a subject, it need not come first in a sentence (e.g. *John Smith* ***my name*** *is*). It is sometimes referred to as the 'psychological subject'. Some languages mark the topic of a sentence using PARTICLES (e.g. Japanese, Samoan). The topic/comment contrast is, however, sometimes difficult to establish, owing to the effects of INTONATION (which has a 'competing' INFORMATION-signalling function), and in many types of sentence the analysis is more problematic, such as in COMMANDS and QUESTIONS. **Topicalization** takes place when a CONSTITUENT is moved to the front of a sentence, so that it functions as topic, e.g. ***The answer*** *I'll give you in a minute* (cf. LEFT DISLOCATION).

(2) The phrase **topic sentence** is used in traditional studies of the structure of paragraphs, to refer to the sentence which introduces the paragraph's theme. Linguistic investigation of this and related notions is relatively recent, but TEXT analysis of paragraphs indicates that the SEMANTIC and SYNTACTIC complexities of paragraph structure are much greater than this simple judgement suggests.

total accountability A principle of LINGUISTIC analysis, introduced into STRUCTURALIST discussion in the 1940s, whereby everything that is stated at one LEVEL of DESCRIPTION is predictable from another. The principle is presented with reference to the relationship between PHONOLOGY and MORPHOLOGY: every MORPH (and thus every PHONEME) must be capable of being determined by the morphemes and TAGMEMES of which an UTTERANCE is composed. Notions such as EMPTY and PORTMANTEAU morphs require special discussion in relation to this principle.

***tough* movement** A term used in TRANSFORMATIONAL GRAMMAR, referring to a RULE which involves moving a NOUN PHRASE out of the PREDICATE of a COMPLEMENT SENTENCE. *Tough* is one of a CLASS of ADJECTIVES (others being *hard, easy, simple, difficult*, etc.) which have been the focus of discussion ever since Noam CHOMSKY's discussion of pairs such as *John is eager/easy to please.* Sentences such as *The ball was easy for John to catch* were said to be derived by *tough* movement from the structure ${}_{NP}[\mathit{it}_{S}[\mathit{for\ John\ to\ catch\ the\ ball}]_{S}]_{NP}$ *was easy*, via a rule which EXTRAPOSES the complement (*it was easy for John to catch the ball*). The rule of *tough* movement took the non-SUBJECT noun phrase from the extraposed complement (i.e. *the ball*) and substituted it for the initial subject PRONOUN of the sentence as a whole (i.e. *it*). Other formulations of this rule have been suggested, and the extent of the rule's application has been controversial.

trace (t) A term introduced into TRANSFORMATIONAL GRAMMAR of the mid-1970s to refer to a FORMAL means of marking the place a CONSTITUENT once held in a DERIVATION, before it was moved to another position by a transformational operation. The position from which the constituent was moved is known as a trace (*t* marks its place in the REPRESENTATION), which is said to be 'BOUND' by that constituent. The moved constituent and the EMPTY NODE it leaves behind are CO-INDEXED. For example, in a RULE which 'raises' the SUBJECT of an EMBEDDED CLAUSE to be the subject of the MAIN clause, the trace *t* marks the position of the embedded subject, e.g. *it is certain* [*the man to come*] → *the man is certain t to come.* (See also the *THAT*-TRACE CONSTRAINT.) In GOVERNMENT-BINDING THEORY, a distinction is made between traces of NOUN PHRASES moved by NP-MOVEMENT (**NP traces**), as in PASSIVE and RAISING sentences, and traces of categories moved by *WH*-movement (***wh*-traces**), as in *wh*-questions, relative clauses, etc. The former are ANAPHORS and the latter are VARIABLES. The distribution of traces is governed by the EMPTY CATEGORY PRINCIPLE. Several arguments have been proposed to support a **trace theory** of movement rules, e.g. that it facilitates the statement of the conditions which affect the SEMANTIC INTERPRETATION of SURFACE structures, and that it permits a more principled account of the operation of syntactic rules. The extent of the convention's applicability (whether *all* moved constituents leave traces), and the kinds of insight and problem which the theory raises, have been sources of controversy. See also FLOATING TRACE.

traditional A term used in LINGUISTICS, often pejoratively, in relation to GRAMMAR (**traditional grammar**), to refer to the set of attitudes, procedures and PRESCRIPTIONS characteristic of the prelinguistic era of language study, and especially of the European school grammars of the eighteenth and nineteenth centuries. The emphasis on such matters as CORRECTNESS, linguistic PURISM, literary excellence, the use of Latin models and the priority of the written language characterizes this approach, and is in contrast with the concern of linguistics for DESCRIPTIVE accuracy (APPROPRIATENESS, CRITERIA of analysis, comprehensiveness, EXPLICITNESS, etc.). On the other hand, several basic concepts of contemporary grammatical analysis have their origins in pre-twentieth-century linguistic traditions, such as the notions of HIERARCHY, UNIVERSALS and WORD CLASSIFICATION. The term 'traditional', too, has been applied to the major descriptive accounts of grammar in handbook form produced by several North European grammarians in the early twentieth century (e.g. Otto Jespersen's *Modern English Grammar on Historical Principles* (1909–40)) and even, these days, to the early period of generative grammar! The pejorative use of the term, therefore, needs to be invoked with caution.

transcription (-al, transcribe) A method of writing down speech sounds in a systematic and consistent way – also known as a 'notation' or 'script'. Two main kinds of transcription are recognized: PHONETIC and PHONEMIC. Square brackets enclose **phonetic transcription** (notation/script); oblique lines enclose **phonemic transcription** (notation/script). In the former, sounds are symbolized on the basis of their ARTICULATORY/AUDITORY identity, regardless of their FUNCTION in a LANGUAGE (sometimes called an **impressionistic** transcription). In the latter, the only UNITS to be symbolized are those which have a linguistic function, i.e. the phonemes. An **allophonic transcription** adds functional phonetic details. A phonemic transcription looks simplest of all, as in this only the units which account for differences of MEANING will be represented, e.g. /pin/, /pen/, pæn/. In a phonetic transcription, on the other hand, the aim is not to judge the functional significance of sounds, in the context of some language, but to identify the sounds as such. A phonetic transcription of the English word *pen*, for example, might be [pʰɛ̃n]: this indicates some quite subtle features of pronunciation, such as the ASPIRATION following the PLOSIVE, and the slight NASALIZATION of the VOWEL – features which are not phonemes in their own right. If necessary, such a transcription could be made more detailed still, to incorporate any other articulatory or auditory features found in the pronunciation. Phonetic transcriptions which are relatively detailed are called **narrow transcriptions**; those which are less detailed are called **broad transcriptions**. In the broadest possible transcription, only those phonetic SEGMENTS would be notated which correspond to the functionally important units in the language – in other words, it would be equivalent to a phonemic transcription, and some phoneticians do use 'broad' in the sense of 'phonemic'. But in principle it is important to appreciate that the two transcriptions of [pen] and /pen/ refer to very different entities: the first is a broad phonetic transcription, representing a sequence of concrete, physical articulations; the second is a phonemic transcription, representing a sequence of abstract, functional units, and reflecting a particular theoretical point of view.

It is also important to remember that there are several possible ways of transcribing sounds phonemically, depending on the analyst's views as to what the salient contrasting features are. The contrast between *seat* and *sit*, for example, might be shown as /siːt/ *v.* /sit/, or as /sit/ *v.* /sɪt/: in the former case, the transcription indicates that the CONTRAST between these words is due to the different LENGTH of the vowels; in the latter case, the transcription suggests that it is not length but the QUALITY of the vowels which differentiates the words, /sɪt/ using a more OPEN vowel than /sit/. It would also be possible to have a third view, /siːt/ *v.* /sɪt/, where both length and quality would be considered relevant. All these transcriptions will be found.

In any transcription (whether phonetic or phonemic), each distinguishable sound is given its own 'symbol'. The whole range of available phonetic symbols is known as a 'phonetic alphabet'. The most widely used such alphabet is the INTERNATIONAL PHONETIC ALPHABET.

Phonetic symbols are often the same as a letter of the alphabet, e.g. [b] as in *bit*, [k] as in *kettle*, but many new symbols have had to be invented to cope with the range of sounds heard in speech, e.g. [ʃ] for the *sh* sound in *ship*, [θ] for the *th* sound in *thin*. Most of the vowel sounds have had to be given a new symbol, to avoid overloading the five traditional vowel letters of the alphabet, and the generally 'alien' appearance of a phonetic transcription is largely due to this (see the range used in the CARDINAL VOWEL system, for example). See p. xvii of this dictionary.

transfer (1) In foreign language learning, the influence of a person's first language on the language being acquired. Transfer effects form part of a person's INTERLANGUAGE.

(2) In SEMANTICS, any process which enables the same linguistic expression to refer to different sorts of things. The notion includes various kinds of figurative language (such as METAPHOR).

transformation(al) (transform) A FORMAL LINGUISTIC operation which enables two levels of structural REPRESENTATION to be placed in correspondence. A **transformational rule (T rule, transformation** or **transform**) consists of a SEQUENCE of symbols which is rewritten as another sequence, according to certain conventions. The 'input' to the RULE is the STRUCTURAL DESCRIPTION ('structural analysis' or 'structure index'), which defines the class of PHRASE-MARKERS to which the rule can apply. The rule then operates a STRUCTURAL CHANGE on this input, by performing one or more of several basic operations. MOVEMENT (REORDERING or PERMUTATION) transformations modify an input structure by reordering the elements it contains. When this operation is seen as one of moving elements to adjoining positions in a phrase-marker, it is known as ADJUNCTION. INSERTION transformations add new structural elements to the input structure (as in element-COPYING, or the insertion of *by* in the PASSIVE transformation below). DELETION transformations eliminate elements from the input structure. There is a certain amount of variation in the names given to these operations, and opinions differ concerning their status as fundamental operations within the theory.

One of the earliest illustrations of the operation of a transformational rule was the one which converted ACTIVE sentences into passive ones, which can be formulated as follows:

$$NP_1\text{–Aux–V–}NP_2 \rightarrow NP_2\text{–Aux+}be\text{+}en\text{–V–}by\text{+}NP_1$$

(where *be* is a form of the verb *to be*, and *en* represents the past-participle ending of the LEXICAL verb). The rule is said to 'operate' on the first, UNDERLYING phrase-marker, converting it into a second, 'derived', phrase-marker. The STRING produced by the derived phrase-marker may then serve as the underlying string for further transformations, as the analysis of the SENTENCE proceeds. The sequence of phrase-markers assigned to a sentence constitutes its **transformational derivation** or **transformational history**.

A GRAMMAR which operates using this notion is a **transformational grammar (TG)**. This type of grammar was first discussed by Noam CHOMSKY in *Syntactic Structures* (1957) as an illustration of a GENERATIVE device more POWERFUL than FINITE-STATE grammars or PHRASE-STRUCTURE GRAMMARS. In this view, very many sentence types can be ECONOMICALLY derived by supplementing the CONSTITUENT analysis rules of phrase-structure grammars with rules for transforming one sentence into another. The rule of passivization above, for instance, is claimed to be a procedure both SIMPLER and INTUITIVELY more satisfactory than generating active and passive sentences separately in the same grammar. The arguments were persuasive, and as a result transformational grammars became the most influential type in the development of generative grammatical theory: indeed, the field as a whole came to be variously known as 'generative grammar', 'transformational-generative grammar' (or simply 'TG').

Several MODELS of transformational grammar have been presented since its first outline. The standard model, as presented by Chomsky in *Aspects of the Theory of Syntax* (1965), consists of three COMPONENTS: (a) a syntactic component, comprising a basic set of phrase-structure rules (sometimes called the BASE component), which together with lexical information provides the DEEP-STRUCTURE information about sentences, and a set of transformational rules for generating SURFACE STRUCTURES; (b) a PHONOLOGICAL component, which converts strings of syntactic elements into pronounceable utterance; and (c) a SEMANTIC component, which provides a REPRESENTATION of the meaning of the LEXICAL ITEMS to be used in the sentence. The ways in which these components should be interrelated (especially the relationships between semantics and syntax) have proved to be a source of continuing controversy, since the appearance of *Aspects*, and alternative models of analysis have developed (cf. especially the distinction between GENERATIVE and INTERPRETIVE semantics).

As a result of these developments, the status and classification of transformations varied a great deal in the 1960s and 1970s. A distinction introduced early on is that between OPTIONAL and OBLIGATORY transformations, the former referring to a rule which *may* apply at a given stage in a derivation, the latter to a rule which *must* apply, if a WELL-FORMED sentence is to result. On the other hand, the classification and terminology of transformations in *Syntactic Structures* is different in many respects from that encountered in *Aspects*. In the former, two types of transformation are recognized: SINGULARY (or SINGLE-BASE), where the rule operates on only one TERMINAL string; and GENERALIZED (or DOUBLE-BASE), where the rule combines two or more terminal strings, as in CONJOINING and EMBEDDING transformations (which handle CO-ORDINATION and SUBORDINATION respectively). In *Aspects*, however, other distinctions are introduced, some of which replace those found in the former book. Of particular importance is a distinction drawn in one of the models outlined in *Aspects* between LEXICAL and 'non-lexical' transformations: the former transform pre-lexical structures into deep structures containing COMPLEX SYMBOLS; the latter transform deep structures into surface structures. A further development is the much increased generality of transformations, culminating in the rule 'MOVE ALPHA' – essentially a licence to move anything anywhere, except that the movement must be an instance of either SUBSTITUTION or ADJUNCTION, and must obey SUBJACENCY.

The theoretical status of transformations in generative linguistics is still a matter of debate, e.g. how to restrict the power of transformations, or whether all transformations need to be meaning-preserving (cf. the KATZ–POSTAL hypothesis). Moreover, transformational grammars have come to be seen in contrast to non-transformational grammars, such as RELATIONAL GRAMMAR, LEXICAL FUNCTIONAL GRAMMAR and GENERALIZED PHRASE-STRUCTURE GRAMMAR. The potential fruitfulness of the notion, however, continues to be explored. See also CYCLE, REORDERING (1).

transition (1) A term used in PHONOLOGY to refer to the way adjacent sounds are linked. There are many ways in which the relationships between successive ARTICULATIONS may be described (cf. GLIDE, LIAISON): one general classification which has been suggested distinguishes between **close transitions** and **open transitions**, similar to the distinction between close and open JUNCTURE. Close transitions refer to those articulations where there is an articulatory continuity between successive sounds; in open transition, by contrast, there is a break in the continuity of the articulation. The distinction can be seen in the *s–s* sequences heard in *this sort* and *this assortment*, where the former illustrates a close and the latter an open transition.

(2) (**-al, transient**) The term is also used in ACOUSTIC PHONETICS for the acoustic change which takes place as the vocal organs move to and from the articulatory positions of CONSONANTS, especially PLOSIVES. The transitional features, or **transients**, can be clearly seen on a SPECTROGRAM, by the way the FORMANTS of the adjacent VOWELS are bent upwards or downwards, depending on which consonant is articulated.

transitional area see AREA

transition network grammar A label given to a type of NETWORK GRAMMAR which shows possible SURFACE-STRUCTURE patterns using diagrammatic models. When supplemented by features which enable it to handle such matters as AGREEMENT and ORDER displacement, it is known as an **augmented transition network (ATN) grammar**. See also AUTOMATON.

transitivity (transitive, intransitive) A category used in the GRAMMATICAL analysis of CLAUSE/SENTENCE CONSTRUCTIONS, with particular reference to the VERB's relationship to DEPENDENT elements of structure. The main members of this category are **transitive**, referring to a verb which can take a direct OBJECT (as in *he saw the dog*), and **intransitive**, where it cannot (as in **he went a ball*). Many verbs can have both a transitive and an intransitive use (cf. *we went a mile* v. *we went*), and in some languages this distinction is marked MORPHOLOGICALLY. More complex relationships between a verb and the elements dependent upon it are usually classified separately. For example, verbs which take two objects are sometimes called **ditransitive**, as in *she gave me a pencil*. There are also several uses of verbs which are marginal to one or other of these categories, as in **pseudo-intransitive** constructions (e.g. *the eggs are selling well*, where an AGENT is assumed – 'someone is selling the eggs' – unlike normal intransitive constructions, which do not have an agent transform: *we went*, but not **someone went us*). Some grammarians also talk about (in)transitive PREPOSITIONS. For example, *with* is a transitive preposition, as it must always be accompanied by a NOUN phrase COMPLEMENT (object), and *along* can be transitive or intransitive: cf. *She arrived with a dog* v. **She arrived with* and *She was walking along the river* v. *She was walking along.*

transparency (transparent) (1) A term used in several areas of LINGUISTICS to refer to an analysis which presents the relevant facts in a direct and perspicuous manner. In GENERATIVE PHONOLOGY, for example, it refers to the extent to which the applications of a given RULE to a given FORM can be seen in the PHONETIC OUTPUT at the end of the DERIVATION. Non-transparent rules are referred to as OPAQUE. The term has also developed special senses in SEMANTICS and generative SYNTAX.

(2) See OPAQUE (4).

tree (sub-) (1) A two-dimensional diagram used in GENERATIVE GRAMMAR as a convenient means of displaying the internal HIERARCHICAL STRUCTURE of SENTENCES as generated by a set of RULES. The 'root' of the **tree diagram** is at the top of the diagram, consisting of the INITIAL SYMBOL **S**. From this topmost point, or NODE, branches descend corresponding to the CATEGORIES specified by the rules (e.g. NP, VP). The internal relationships of parts of the tree are described using 'family tree' terminology: if two categories both derive from a single node, they are said to be 'sisters', and 'daughters' of the 'mother node' from which they derive. A subsection of a tree diagram, isolated for purposes of discussion, is referred to as a **subtree**, as in the enclosed area within the diagram on p. 398. The internal organization of a tree is sometimes referred to as **tree geometry**. In GENERALIZED PHRASE-STRUCTURE GRAMMAR, the term **local tree** refers to a tree of depth one, i.e. a tree in which every node other than the root is a daughter of the root. The S–NP–VP subtree in the diagram below would be a local tree, in this context. In PROCEDURAL GRAMMAR, a **structure tree** or **parse tree** is the result of applying the analytical procedures to a TEXT. In computer CORPUS research, a parsed corpus is known as a **treebank**. See also DEPENDENCY GRAMMAR, METRICAL GRID.

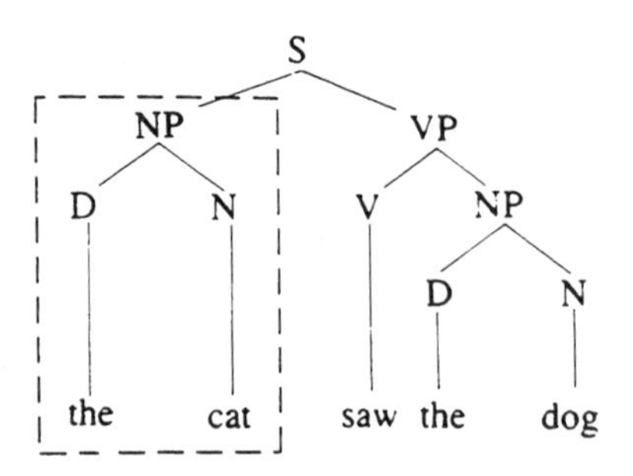

(2) In HISTORICAL LINGUISTICS, a representation of the genetic relationships between the members of a FAMILY of languages.

triadic A term used to characterize a theory of MEANING which postulates that there is an indirect relationship between LINGUISTIC FORMS and the entities, states of affairs, etc., to which they refer (i.e. REFERENTS). Instead of a direct two-way relationship (a DUALIST theory), a third step is proposed, corresponding to the mental concept or SENSE of the linguistic form. The best-known triadic MODEL is the 'semantic triangle' of C. K. Ogden (1889–1957) and I. A. Richards (1893–1979), presented in their book *The Meaning of Meaning* in 1923.

trial see NUMBER

triangle A NOTATIONAL device used in GENERATIVE GRAMMAR as part of a PHRASE-MARKER to represent a CONSTITUENT with a complex internal STRUCTURE, the details of which are not relevant for the point under discussion, as in the following TREE diagram:

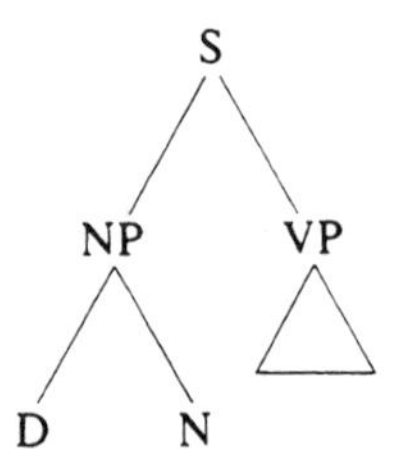

trill(ed) A term in the PHONETIC classification of CONSONANT sounds on the basis of their MANNER OF ARTICULATION: also known as a 'trilled' consonant, or a ROLL, 'trill' refers to any sound made by the rapid tapping of one organ of articulation against another. (VOCAL-CORD vibration is not included in such a definition.) Several ACCENTS of English use the trilled *r*, as in Welsh and Scots. French and German are examples of LANGUAGES which have a UVULAR trill. The trill may also be accompanied by audible friction, and would then be called a 'FRICATIVE trill'. BILABIAL trills are also possible, as when one makes a 'freezing' noise, *brrr* [B], or imitates a car engine.

triphthong (-al, -ization, -ize) A term used in the PHONETIC classification of VOWEL sounds on the basis of their MANNER OF ARTICULATION: it refers to a type of vowel where there are two noticeable changes in QUALITY during a SYLLABLE, s in a common pronunciation of English *fire* and *tower* /faɪə/ and /taʊə/. The distinction between triphthongs and the more common DIPHTHONGS is sometimes phonetically unclear.

trivalent see VALENCY

trochee A traditional term in METRICS for a unit of poetic RHYTHM comprising a single pair of STRESSED + unstressed syllables (as in *David*); also called a **trochaic foot**. In METRICAL PHONOLOGY, the notion is used as an informal name for BOUNDED left-DOMINANT FEET, which display this rhythmical structure. See also IAMB.

trough see PEAK

true generalization condition see GENERAL (2)

truncation (truncate) A term sometimes used in PHONOLOGY to refer to a process of WORD shortening which is phonologically predictable. Certain types of HYPOCORISTIC (pet-name), for example, have been shown to be truncated in a regular way. The process has attracted particular attention in PROSODIC MORPHOLOGY, where it is used to illustrate such processes as TEMPLATE-mapping and prosodic CIRCUMSCRIPTION.

truth-conditional semantics An approach to SEMANTICS which maintains that MEANING can be defined in terms of the conditions in the real world under which a SENTENCE may be used to make a true statement. It can be distinguished from approaches which define meaning in terms of the conditions on the use of sentences in communication, such as the function of the sentence in terms of SPEECH ACTS, or the speaker's beliefs about the sentence (cf. PRAGMATICS).

Turing machine see AUTOMATON

turn A term used in SOCIOLINGUISTICS as part of the study of conversational structure: conversation is seen as a sequence of **conversational turns**, in which the contribution of each participant is seen as part of a co-ordinated and RULE-governed behavioural interaction. Some of the rules governing **turn-taking** are obvious (e.g. that only one person should talk at a time); others are less easy to discover (e.g. the rules which decide who should speak next in a group discussion). How children learn the conventions governing turn-taking is an issue which has attracted considerable interest in language ACQUISITION.

type (1) **(-d)** A notion developed in mathematical logic and used as part of the conceptual apparatus underlying FORMAL SEMANTICS (notably, in LAMBDA calculus). A **type-theoretic** approach offers a mathematical perspective for the CATEGORIAL SYNTAX of natural language, using the notion of a HIERARCHY of types as a framework for semantic structure (as in MONTAGUE GRAMMAR). Basic (or primitive) types (e.g. 'entity', 'truth value', 'state') are distinguished from derived or complex types (e.g. functional types: an example is (*a*, *b*), i.e. all functions taking arguments in the *a* domain apply to values in the *b* domain). Types are used in several models of LEXICAL REPRESENTATION (notably, 'typed FEATURE structures') to refer to a superordinate category. The types are organized as a lattice framework, with the most general type represented at the top and inconsistency indicated at the bottom. Similarities in lattices specify compatibility between types. **Subtypes** INHERIT all the properties of all their **supertypes**: for example, in a typed feature structure hierarchy, the subtype *sausages* under the type *food* ('sausages are a type of food') means that *sausages* has all the properties specified by the type constraints on *food*, with some further properties of its own.

(2) In LEXICAL study, a term used as part of a measure of lexical density. The **type-token ratio** is the ratio of the total number of different words (**types**) to the total number of words (**tokens**) in a sample of text.

Type 0/1/2/3 grammars see CHOMSKY HIERARCHY

type-token ratio see TYPE (2)

typological linguistics (typology) A branch of LINGUISTICS which studies the STRUCTURAL similarities between LANGUAGES, regardless of their history, as part of an attempt to establish a satisfactory CLASSIFICATION, or typology, of languages. **Typological comparison** is thus distinguished from the historical comparison of languages – the province of COMPARATIVE PHILOLOGY and HISTORICAL LINGUISTICS – and its groupings may not coincide with those set up by the historical method. For example, in respect of the paucity of INFLECTIONAL endings, English is closer to Chinese than it is to Latin. One typological classification, proposed by the German linguist Wilhelm von Humboldt (1768–1835) in the early nineteenth century, established three main groups of languages on structural grounds: ISOLATING, AGGLUTINATIVE and FUSIONAL; a fourth category, POLYSYNTHETIC, has sometimes been suggested. The MORPHOLOGICAL orientation of this approach is, however, only one aspect of typological analysis, which can operate at all linguistic levels (e.g. a PHONOLOGICAL typology in terms of CONSONANT/VOWEL inventories or SYSTEMS, SYLLABLE structure, or SUPRASEGMENTAL patterns – as illustrated in such notions as 'TONE language' or 'CLICK language'). When one considers the many possible criteria of typological comparison, it is plain that no simple classification is likely to emerge, and that differences between languages are not clear-cut, but matters of degree.

U

UC The usual abbreviation for ULTIMATE CONSTITUENT.

ultimate constituent (UC) A term used in STRUCTURALIST GRAMMATICAL analysis to refer to the irreducible ELEMENTS which are the result of an IMMEDIATE-CONSTITUENT analysis. For example, in the SENTENCE *The girls stopped the bus*, the ultimate constituents would be *the+girl+s+stop+ed+the+bus*.

unaccented see ACCENT (2)

unacceptable see ACCEPTABLE

unaccusative A term used, especially in RELATIONAL GRAMMAR, for INTRANSITIVE VERBS whose SUBJECTS originate as OBJECTS. *Break* in *The vase broke* is such a verb, *the vase* being understood in the same way as it is in *John broke the vase*, where it is an object. Unaccusative verbs are also known as ERGATIVE verbs.

unanalysable see ANALYSABLE

unary A term used in some recent approaches to PHONOLOGY (e.g. DEPENDENCY PHONOLOGY, PARTICLE PHONOLOGY), characterizing the view that SEGMENTS can be represented as single elements (e.g. [round], [front]), as opposed to BINARY oppositions. The term is given special status in 'unary component theory'.

unassociated see ASSOCIATION LINE

unbounded dependency A term used in some recent theories of GRAMMAR (such as GENERALIZED PHRASE-STRUCTURE GRAMMAR) to refer to a CONSTRUCTION in which a SYNTACTIC RELATION holds between two CONSTITUENTS such that there is no restriction on the structural distance between them (e.g. a restriction which would require that both be constituents of the same CLAUSE). In English, CLEFT sentences, TOPICALIZATION, *WH*-QUESTIONS and RELATIVE clauses have been proposed as examples of constructions which involve this kind of DEPENDENCY; for instance, a topic, or topicalized constituent, may occur at the beginning of a MAIN clause, while the construction with which it is connected may be one, two or more clauses away, as in ***Every page*** *I read very carefully. He said I should read* ***every page*** *very carefully*, etc. In GOVERNMENT-BINDING THEORY, unbounded dependencies are analysed in terms of MOVEMENT. In GPSG, use is made of the feature SLASH. The term is increasingly used outside the generative context.

unchecked see CHECKED (1)

uncountable see COUNT

underextension A term used in LANGUAGE ACQUISITION studies to refer to one type of relationship between adult and child MEANING, as expressed in LEXICAL ITEMS. In underextension the child's lexical item has a narrower range of APPLICATION than the equivalent term in adult language, e.g. when *cat* is used to refer to only one specific cat.

underlying A term used in LINGUISTICS to refer to an abstract level of REPRESENTATION of a SENTENCE postulated in order to explain the patterns encountered in the empirical DATA of a LANGUAGE. The notion of **underlying forms** is central to GENERATIVE GRAMMAR where a stage of **underlying structure** is recognized in the DERIVATION of sentences. In early TRANSFORMATIONAL grammar, the **underlying phrase-marker** refers to the STRUCTURAL DESCRIPTION of a sentence which is the result of the PHRASE-STRUCTURE rules; this **underlying string** then acts as the input to the transformational rules, which thereby produces 'derived' phrase-markers. Later, the term DEEP STRUCTURE came to be used as a specific conception of underlying structure, in the context of *Aspects of the Theory of Syntax*, from which SURFACE STRUCTURES are transformationally derived. In GOVERNMENT-BINDING theory, the term D-STRUCTURE is used. The extent to which the various underlying representations of sentences have psychological reality has been and remains controversial.

underspecification (**underspecify**) (1) In recent FEATURE theories of PHONOLOGY, a term characterizing various approaches which see it as desirable that information should be omitted from underlying phonological REPRESENTATIONS. The representations should be minimally specified, or 'underspecified'. There is a departure from the concept of 'full' specification present in early GENERATIVE phonology: the view that the output of the phonological COMPONENT must contain fully specified BINARY feature matrices. Underspecification theory is concerned with the extent to which feature distinctions should appear in a phonological representation, not as a binary choice of [+feature] *v.* [−feature], but as a choice between [+feature] and no MARKING at all. It therefore looks in particular at which feature values are predictable and may thus be left unspecified in a representation without harming the surface form.

The approach is chiefly associated with LEXICAL PHONOLOGY, but there are several underspecification models, which vary over their conceptions of minimality. In **restricted** or **contrastive underspecification**, only REDUNDANT features are lexically unspecified (e.g. in English, VOICING would be specified for OBSTRUENTS, where it is CONTRASTIVE, but not for SONORANTS, where it is redundant). The approach limits the degree of underspecification in lexical forms by omitting only those feature values which are predictable on the basis of universal co-occurrence conditions. No other features may be underspecified. This contrasts with **radical underspecification**, which allows only one value to be specified in any given context in a representation. Moreover, such specifications are needed only when a rule would otherwise assign the wrong value to a feature. This approach omits from underlying representations not only the feature values which are predictable from co-occurrence conditions but also those which are predictable from context-free markedness statements. Default rules assign unmarked values. Other positions in underspecification theory are also possible, e.g. that the unmarked value is never introduced, so that all features are effectively single-valued (privative).

(2) The term is also used in relation to other LEVELS of language for any model which does not require the specification of all the factors potentially involved in an analysis. In SEMANTICS, for example, there are approaches to FORMALIZATION which do not completely specify all features of logical structure (e.g. in representing SCOPE ambiguities).

ungoverned see GOVERN (2)

ungradable see GRADABILITY

ungraded antonyms see ANTONYM

ungrammatical see GRAMMATICALITY

unification (unify) A term used for the central operation within a number of recent GRAMMATICAL theories, which have been termed 'unification-based approaches to grammar'. Unification is the merging of two DESCRIPTIONS to form a more specific description which is consistent with both. For example, a NOUN in description D1 might be specified for COUNTABILITY but not for CASE, whereas in D2 the same noun might be specified for case but not countability. The two descriptions could then be unified, and any operations which could be carried out on either of the original descriptions could then be performed on the unified description. The approach has advantages for grammatical analysis, in that it allows a grammar to specify CONSTRAINTS on the language without having to state the order in which the constraints are applied: regardless of the number of unifications it takes to fully specify a category, these unifications can be applied in any order. The approach thus has advantages for computational PARSING, in that it allows a parser to work with partial descriptions, gradually accumulating information about a grammatical category as it deals with different entries in the lexicon.

unified features A term used to characterize models of NON-LINEAR PHONOLOGY which integrate CONSONANTAL and VOWEL PLACE features in a single framework. In this approach, for example, LABIAL and CORONAL articulations are brought together into a single coronal TIER. However, consonants and vowels retain their identity, in that place features of consonants are immediately DOMINATED by the consonantal place NODE, and vowels by the vocalic place node. Thus the relation of [labial] in a consonant to C-place defines a different PLANE from that of [labial] in a vowel to V-place.

uniformitarian principle The application in HISTORICAL LINGUISTICS and SOCIOLINGUISTICS of a notion used in history and geology, as a guideline for RECONSTRUCTING LANGUAGE in its social context. The principle advocates that the linguistic forces which cause VARIATION today are similar to those which have operated in the past; it is therefore permissible to apply reasoning based on modern observations to the analysis of earlier states of a language.

unilateral (articulation) see LATERAL

uninterruptability see INTERRUPTABILITY

unit In a general, pre-theoretical sense, this term is often used in LINGUISTICS and PHONETICS to refer to any entity which constitutes the focus of an enquiry. In HALLIDAYAN linguistics, however, the term has a special status, referring to one of the four main CATEGORIES recognized by that theory (the others being STRUCTURE, CLASS and SYSTEM). The unit is the stretch of LANGUAGE that carries grammatical patterns, and within which grammatical choices are made. For example, the unit SENTENCE consists of one or more instances of the unit CLAUSE, and so on (cf. RANK). In some grammatical descriptions, the term 'unit NOUN' is preferred to COUNTABLE noun.

universal(ity) A term used in LINGUISTICS, and especially in GENERATIVE GRAMMAR, referring to a property claimed to be common for all LANGUAGES, to demonstrate the validity of which is a main goal of linguistic theory. **Universal grammar** is the term used to identify the main aim of those who hold that the ultimate purpose of linguistics is to specify precisely the possible form of a human grammar – and especially the restrictions on the form such grammars can take. In their broadest sense, then, **language universals** are equivalent to the general design features of human language identified by some linguists under such headings as DUALITY, CREATIVITY, REFLEXIVENESS and DISPLACEMENT. In this sense, universals provide a theory of the human language faculty – those properties of language which are biologically necessary – which is thought to be an important step in the task of understanding human intellectual capacities.

In the generative literature, two main types of universal are recognized. **Formal universals** are the necessary conditions which have to be imposed on the construction of grammars in order for them to be able to operate. They include such notions as the number of COMPONENTS, types of RULES, ORDERING conventions (e.g. CYCLES), types of TRANSFORMATIONS, and so on. **Substantive universals**, on the other hand, are the PRIMITIVE elements in a grammar, required for the analysis of linguistic data, e.g. NP, VP, [+grave], [+abstract]. Depending on the COMPONENT of the grammar in which they occur, universals are referred to as 'PHONOLOGICAL universals', 'semantic universals' (cf. 'universal SEMANTICS'), 'SYNTACTIC universals', etc. Some of these categories may actually be found in every language, but it is not crucial to the notion of substantive universal that they should be. All that is required is that they be constructs which need to be defined by linguistic theory to enable cross-language generalizations to be made, i.e. they are not terms established for the analysis of just one language, but are capable of general application. The **universal base** hypothesis in generative linguistics states that all languages can be generated by using the same set of basic rules – though whether these are seen as rules of the BASE syntactic component or as a set of semantic FORMATION RULES depends on the theory employed (cf. STANDARD THEORY and GENERATIVE SEMANTICS).

Other types of linguistic universal have been suggested. Quantitative studies have introduced the notion of **statistical universals**, i.e. constants of a statistical kind, such as a ratio of use between different structures. **Implicational universals** are generalized statements of the form 'if X, then Y', e.g. if a language has a WORD ORDER of a certain type, it will also have a VERB structure of a certain type. **Absolute universals** are properties which all languages share; there are no exceptions. **Relative universals** are general tendencies in language; there may be principled exceptions.

universal quantifier see QUANTIFIER

universe of discourse see DISCOURSE

univocality see POLYSEMY

unmarked A term used in LINGUISTICS in various senses, to refer to a property of language which is more neutral, common, expected or general than a corresponding property, which is said to be MARKED. Unmarked values in some approaches are also often called 'default' values, and can be handled by conditions that a category must meet if it can, but need not meet if it cannot, e.g. the default value for CASE might be ACCUSATIVE. The current use of the term in CORE grammar should be noted, as should its use in recent PHONOLOGICAL theory (e.g. UNDERSPECIFICATION theory).

unproductive see PRODUCTIVITY

unrounded see ROUNDING

unstressed see STRESS

untensed see TENSED

unvoiced see VOICE

update semantics see DYNAMIC (5)

usage The collective term for the speech and writing habits of a community, especially as they are presented DESCRIPTIVELY with information about preferences for alternative linguistic FORMS. LINGUISTS emphasize the importance of describing the facts of usage as a control on the claims made by GRAMMARS, and contrast this emphasis with the PRESCRIPTIVE attitudes of TRADITIONAL grammar, whose RULES often bore no relationship to what people actually did with their language. The many 'LEVELS of usage' which descriptive investigations encounter can be formally taken into account in several ways, such as by adding 'usage labels' (as in dictionary entries, e.g. 'slang', 'nautical'), or by the use of statistical statements about preferences, or (in GENERATIVE contexts) by the notion of VARIABLE rules.

utterance A term used in LINGUISTICS and PHONETICS to refer to a stretch of speech about which no assumptions have been made in terms of linguistic theory (as opposed to the notion of SENTENCE, which receives its definition from a theory of GRAMMAR). In principle, it is a physically definable, behavioural unit, capable of definition in everyday terms. One commonly used definition refers to a 'stretch of speech preceded and followed by silence or a change of speaker'. But it has proved very difficult to construct a satisfactory definition. The definition just given, for instance, applies equally to a one-word response and a sermon, and attempts have been made to produce a more restricted definition, using such features as PAUSE, RHYTHM, breath patterns, PITCH movement, etc. The analogous term in the study of writing is TEXT. See also CONTEXT.

uvular(-ize, -ization) A term used in the PHONETIC classification of CONSONANT sounds on the basis of their PLACE OF ARTICULATION: it refers to a sound made by the BACK of the tongue against the uvula. The *r* of STANDARD French is uvular, and this quality may be heard in some regional DIALECTS of English, especially in the north-east of England. It is transcribed as [ʀ]. Uvular PLOSIVE consonants are found in Arabic, for example, and are transcribed [q] and [ɢ] for the VOICEless and voiced types respectively. See also -ISE/-IZE.

V

V The usual abbreviation for VERB. See also V FORMS.

vagueness see AMBIGUITY

valency (valent) A term introduced by the French linguist Lucien Tesnière (1893–1954), which has been particularly influential in the development of models of DEPENDENCY GRAMMAR in Europe and Russia. The term is derived from chemistry, and is used in LINGUISTICS to refer to the number and type of bonds which SYNTACTIC ELEMENTS may form with each other. As in chemistry, a given element may have different valencies in different contexts. A **valency grammar** presents a MODEL of a SENTENCE containing a fundamental element (typically, the VERB) and a number of dependent elements (variously referred to as ARGUMENTS, expressions, COMPLEMENTS or **valents**) whose number and type is determined by the valency attributed to the verb. For example, the valency of *vanish* includes only the SUBJECT element (it has a valency of 1, **monovalent**), whereas that of *scrutinize* includes both subject and DIRECT OBJECT (a valency of 2, **bivalent**). A verb which takes no complements at all (such as *rain*) is said to have **zero valency** (be **avalent**). Valency deals not only with the number of valents with which a verb is combined to produce a WELL-FORMED sentence nucleus, but also with the classification of sets of valents which may be combined with different verbs. For example, *give* and *put* usually have a valency of 3 (**trivalent**), but the valents governed by the former (subject, direct object and INDIRECT object) are different from those governed by the latter (subject, direct object, and LOCATIVE ADVERBIAL). Verbs which differ in this way are said to be associated with different **valency sets**. The notion is similar to that used in CASE grammar, where cases are sometimes referred to as **valency roles**. See also ACTANT, CIRCONSTANT.

valley see PEAK

value (1) (**valeur**) A term introduced into LINGUISTICS by Ferdinand de SAUSSURE to refer to the FUNCTIONAL identity of an entity when seen in the context of a RULE-governed SYSTEM. In his view, LANGUAGE is a system of independent terms, in which the 'value' of each term results solely from the simultaneous presence of the others, related through the notions of SYNTAGMATIC and PARADIGMATIC association. The notion plays a central role in the later development of STRUCTURAL linguistics.

(2) The term is also used in GRAMMATICAL theory as part of a FEATURE specification, along with feature name. For example, in the specifications [V, −] and [BAR 2], the '−' and the '2' are the **feature values** of the features V and BAR respectively. **Multi-valued** features are often referred to as '*n*-ary' features.

variable (1) A term sometimes used in the GRAMMATICAL classification of WORDS to refer to one of two postulated major word-CLASSES in LANGUAGE, the other being INVARIABLE. 'Variable words' are said to be those which express grammatical relationships through a change of FORM, e.g. *boy/boys, walk/walking, nice/nicer*. Invariable words are unchanging, whatever their distribution, e.g. *in, on, and*.

(2) The term has been introduced into SOCIOLINGUISTICS by the American linguist William Labov (b. 1927) to refer to the UNITS in a language which are most subject to social or STYLISTIC variation, and thus most susceptible to change in the long term. Sets of PHONOLOGICAL, GRAMMATICAL and LEXICAL variables are described quantitatively with reference to such factors as social class, age and sex, and the results of this co-variation are stated in the form of **variable rules**. Variable RULES are GENERATIVE rules which have been modified so as to specify the socio-regional conditions under which they apply. The notion has been developed primarily in relation to hypotheses concerning the relationship between social variation and linguistic evolution.

(3) The term is also widely used in GRAMMAR and SEMANTICS in its general sense of a quantity which may assume any of a set of values. For example, a **category variable** (e.g. X) stands for any major word-level CATEGORY (e.g. N, P, Adj); a **bar variable**, in X-BAR SYNTAX, stands for any level of bar projection of X (e.g. X^n stands for X^o, X', X''). In GOVERNMENT-BINDING THEORY, variables form an important part of binding theory.

variant A term used in LINGUISTICS to refer to a linguistic FORM which is one of a set of alternatives in a given CONTEXT. The concept is fundamental to the notion of ALLO- (-PHONE, -MORPH, etc.), as illustrated by the **variant forms** of the past-TENSE MORPHEME (/-t/, /d/, /ɪd/, etc.). The choice of variants may be subject to contextual constraints (**conditioned variants**), or there may be no stateable CONDITIONS – the cases of **free variants** (cf. FREE).

variation see VARIABLE (2), VARIANT, VARIETY

variety A term used in SOCIOLINGUISTICS and STYLISTICS to refer to any SYSTEM of LINGUISTIC EXPRESSION whose use is governed by SITUATIONAL VARIABLES. In some cases, the situational DISTINCTIVENESS of the LANGUAGE may be easily stated, as in many regional and occupational varieties (e.g. London English, religious English); in other cases, as in studies of social class, the varieties are more difficult to define, involving the intersection of several variables (e.g. sex, age, occupation). Several classifications of language varieties have been proposed, involving such terms as DIALECT, REGISTER, MEDIUM and FIELD. For some sociolinguists, 'variety' is given a more restricted definition, as one kind of situational distinctive language – a specialized type of language used within a dialect, e.g. for occupational purposes.

velar(-ic, -ization, -ize, velum) A term used in the PHONETIC classification of CONSONANT sounds on the basis of their PLACE OF ARTICULATION: it refers to a sound made by the BACK of the tongue against the soft PALATE, or **velum** (the 'veil' of the palate). Examples in English are [k] and [g], and the *-ng-* sound [ŋ] as in *sing*. Velar FRICATIVE sounds are found in German and Greek, for example, and are transcribed [x] and [ɣ] for the VOICELESS and voiced types respectively. If the velum is raised to shut off the nasal tract, a 'velic closure' has been made.

Velar sounds are different from **velaric** sounds. The term 'velaric' refers to a quite different mode of speech production: instead of using an AIRSTREAM MECHANISM involving the lungs, velaric sounds use air generated by a closure in velar position. The back of the tongue is raised against the velum, and articulations are made further forward by the lips or front parts of the tongue. These sounds are usually called CLICKS, and have a distinctive role in some languages, such as Zulu. In English, they may be heard in the 'tut tut' sound, and in a few other contexts.

Velarization is a general term referring to any SECONDARY ARTICULATION involving a movement of the back part of the tongue towards the velum. For a sound to be 'velarized', of course, its primary place of articulation must be elsewhere in the mouth, e.g. a [z] sound, normally made in ALVEOLAR position, is said to be velarized if during its articulation the back of the tongue is raised towards the soft palate; this would give the sound a distinctive back (or 'dark') resonance. The term is usually applied to consonants other than velar consonants; it can be used with reference to VOWELS, but such variations in vowel articulation are usually described in different terms ('centralized', 'retracted', etc.). The velarization may be an essential feature of the sound's identity, contrasting with other **non-velarized** sounds, as in the distinction between velarized and non-velarized *s* in Arabic (transcribed [ᵴ] and [s] respectively). In English, velarization is dependent on context: syllable-final *l*, as in *cool*, is given a velar resonance; this can be compared with syllable-initial *l*, as in *leap*, where the back of the tongue is much further forward in the mouth (towards the palate). A loose auditory label for velar resonance sounds is 'dark' (DARK L, etc.), opposed to 'clear', used for the palatal-resonance sounds. The usual symbol for velarized consonants is [~], placed through the letter, as in [ᵵ], [ᵭ], [ɫ]. Some English dialects, such as those of the British Midlands (Birmingham, Wolverhampton, etc.), have several velarized sounds. See also -ISE/-IZE.

velum see VELAR

ventricular A term used in PHONETICS to describe a type of sound produced between the ventricular bands, or 'false' VOCAL FOLDS, which lie immediately above and parallel with the true vocal cords. It is not normally used in speech, but ventricular effects involving whisper and VOICE can be heard, the latter sometimes combining with GLOTTAL voice to produce a 'double' or 'diplophonic' voice.

verb(al) (V) A term used in the GRAMMATICAL classification of words, to refer to a class traditionally defined as 'doing' or 'action' words (a description which has been criticized in LINGUISTICS, largely on the grounds that many verbs do not 'act' in any obvious sense, e.g. *seem, be*). The FORMAL definition of a verb refers to an element which can display MORPHOLOGICAL contrasts of TENSE, ASPECT, VOICE, MOOD, PERSON and NUMBER. FUNCTIONALLY, it is the ELEMENT which, singly or in combination with other verbs (i.e. 'verb phrase'), is used as the minimal PREDICATE of a sentence, co-occurring with a SUBJECT, e.g. *she / wrote*. If the predicate contains other elements (e.g. OBJECT, COMPLEMENT, ADVERBIAL), then it is the verb which more than any other is the unit which influences the choice and extent of these elements; e.g. the verb *put* takes both an object and a LOCATIVE adverbial, as in *he put the book on the table*. In many grammatical theories, accordingly, the verb is considered the most important element in sentence structure.

The term **verb phrase** is used in two senses. Traditionally, it refers to a group of verbs which together have the same syntactic FUNCTION as a single verb, e.g. *is coming, may be coming, get up to*. In such phrases (**verbal groups, verbal clusters**), one verb is the main verb (the **lexical verb**) and the others are subordinate to it (**auxiliary verbs, catenative verbs**). A verb followed by a non-verbal PARTICLE (similar in form to a preposition or adverb) is generally referred to as a **phrasal verb**.

In GENERATIVE grammar, the verb phrase (VP) has a much broader definition, being equivalent to the whole of the predicate of a sentence, as is clear from the expansion of S as NP+VP in PHRASE-STRUCTURE GRAMMAR.

The adjective from 'verb', **verbal**, is often used in traditional grammatical description (though one must be careful not to confuse it with 'verbal' meaning 'spoken', as in 'verbal skill', 'verbalize', etc.), for instance 'verbal noun' (= a NOUN similar in form or meaning to a verb, e.g. *smoking*), 'verbal adjective' (= an ADJECTIVE similar in form or meaning to a verb, e.g. *interested*). See also COMMUNICATION, EXTENSIVE, FACTITIVE, MOOD, PERFORMATIVE, SERIAL VERB.

verbal duelling In SOCIOLINGUISTICS, a term which refers to the competitive use of LANGUAGE, within a game-like structure, with rules that are known and used by the participants. It is a genre of VERBAL PLAY – a ritual dialogue in which each speaker attempts to outdo an opponent by producing an utterance of increased verbal ingenuity. It has been noted, for example, in the ritual exchanges between warriors in classical epic texts as well as in the trading of insults between present-day street gangs.

verbal play In SOCIOLINGUISTICS, a term which refers to the playful manipulation of the elements of LANGUAGE, either in relation to each other, or in relation to the social or cultural contexts of language use; also called **speech play**. It is a LUDIC function of language which includes play languages, puns, VERBAL DUELLING, riddles, and many other genres.

verbless A type of CLAUSE recognized in some MODELS of GRAMMATICAL description (e.g. QUIRK GRAMMAR), in which the VERB is omitted (and often the SUBJECT as well), e.g. ***When ready**, we waited for the signal, Stay at home **if possible***. Some classical TRANSFORMATIONAL models of analysis would DERIVE such structures using a process of DELETION. In more recent GENERATIVE studies such constructions have been analysed as BASE-generated – a type of SMALL CLAUSE.

vernacular A term used in SOCIOLINGUISTICS to refer to the indigenous LANGUAGE or DIALECT of a SPEECH community, e.g. the vernacular of Liverpool, Berkshire,

Jamaica, etc. The study of 'black' or 'African-American English vernacular' in the United States has been the focus of several linguistic studies since the 1960s. PIDGIN languages are sometimes called **contact vernaculars**. Vernaculars are usually seen in contrast to such notions as STANDARD, LINGUA FRANCA, etc.

V forms An abbreviation used in SOCIOLINGUISTICS as part of the study of terms of address in various LANGUAGES. Based on the distinction between *tu* and *vous*, the alternative forms of 'you' in French, and on similar CONTRASTS in many other languages (e.g. German *du/Sie*, Russian *ty/vy*), an OPPOSITION is set up between formal (V) and familiar (T) second-PERSON VERB and PRONOUN FORMS. Hypotheses are then developed concerning the system of FORMALITY in use in the language.

via A term used in natural GENERATIVE PHONOLOGY, to refer to the (non-generative) RULES which link distinct UNDERLYING FORMS. For example, *divine/divinity* would be linked by a rule /aɪ/⟷/i/, though each form would be listed individually in the LEXICON.

visibility (visible) A term used in GOVERNMENT-BINDING THEORY for a CONDITION from which much of the content of the CASE FILTER can be derived. An ELEMENT is visible for theta-marking only if it is assigned Case. On the basis of this condition, a NOUN PHRASE can receive a THETA ROLE only if it is in a position to which Case is ASSIGNED, or is linked to such a position (as in *there is a lamp in the room*, where Case is transferred from *there* to *the lamp*).

vocable see PHONETICALLY CONSISTENT FORM

vocabulary LINGUISTICS uses this term in its everyday sense, reserving for its technical study the use of terms beginning with LEXI- (cf. LEXIS, LEXICON). A distinction is often made, especially in language learning, between **active** and **passive** vocabulary: the former refers to lexical items people use; the latter to WORDS which they understand, but do not themselves use. See also DEFINING VOCABULARY.

vocal–auditory channel A term used in the study of COMMUNICATION to refer to one of the human sensory modes which can be used for the transmission and reception of information. It provides the frame of reference within which the study of PHONETICS proceeds, and constitutes the majority of the subject-matter of LINGUISTICS (which of course is also concerned with the written LANGUAGE).

vocal cords/lips/bands/folds Two muscular folds running from a single point inside the front of the thyroid cartilage (Adam's apple) backwards to the front ends of the arytenoid cartilages. The vocal cords are very flexible, being shaped by the combined activities of the associated cartilages and muscles. The space between them is known as the GLOTTIS.

The vocal cords have several functions. Their main role in speech is to vibrate in such a manner as to produce VOICE, a process known as PHONATION. When the cords are not vibrating, two main alternative positions are available. They may be tightly closed ('adducted'), as when the breath is held – a process which produces a GLOTTAL stop upon release. Or they may remain open ('abducted'), so that the breath flowing through the glottis produces audible FRICTION, as in whispering and the [h] sound. Other 'phonation types' are possible, by varying the mode of vibration of the vocal cords in various ways, as in BREATHY and CREAKY voice. Varying the thickness, length and tension of the vocal cords also produces the different REGISTERS in voice production, such as the distinction between 'falsetto' and 'chest' voice. Lastly, by varying the rate and strength of vibration of the vocal cords, variations in PITCH and LOUDNESS can be introduced into speech.

The question of how precisely the vocal cords operate, from a physiological viewpoint, has been the subject of controversy, and is still not wholly understood. The most widely held theory maintains that the cords are set in vibration aerodynamically, solely by a reaction taking place between their elastic properties and the subglottal air-pressure involved – this is known as the 'myoelastic' theory of voice production. An alternative theory, developed in the 1950s, argued that the cords are set in motion as a result of periodic NEURAL stimulation and contraction of the muscles – this was known as the 'neurochronaxiac' theory.

vocalic One of the major CLASS FEATURES of sound set up by GENERATIVE phonologists in their DISTINCTIVE FEATURE theory of PHONOLOGY, its opposite being **non-vocalic**. Vocalic sounds may be defined ARTICULATORILY or ACOUSTICALLY in this approach: they are sounds where there is a free passage of air through the VOCAL TRACT, the most radical CONSTRICTION in the ORAL CAVITY not exceeding that found in [i] and [u], and the VOCAL CORDS being positioned so as to allow spontaneous VOICING; acoustically, there is a sharply defined FORMANT structure. Non-vocalic sounds lack one or other of these conditions. See also VOWEL.

vocalization A general term used in LINGUISTICS and PHONETICS to refer to an UTTERANCE viewed solely as a sequence of sound. No reference is made to its linguistic structure, and indeed, in such phrases as 'infant vocalization', there may be no such structure. In a somewhat more restricted sense, the term is sometimes used referring to the use of sound involving VOCAL-CORD vibration – a vocalization is then 'any voiced sound'.

vocal organs The collective term for all the anatomical features involved in the production of speech sounds, including the lungs, trachea, oesophagus, LARYNX, PHARYNX, MOUTH and nose.

vocal tract A general term used in PHONETICS to refer to the whole of the air passage above the LARYNX, the shape of which is the main factor affecting the QUALITY of speech sounds. It can be divided into the NASAL tract (the air passage above the soft PALATE, within the nose) and the ORAL tract (the mouth and pharyngeal areas, or CAVITIES). In a more general application, the term is used in the sense of VOCAL ORGANS, including all the features of the respiratory tract involved in the production of sounds, i.e. lungs, trachea and larynx as well.

vocative In LANGUAGES which express GRAMMATICAL relationships by means of INFLECTIONS, this term refers to the CASE FORM taken by a NOUN PHRASE (often a single noun or PRONOUN) when it is used in the function of address (including both ANIMATE and inanimate entities). English does not make this distinction inflectionally, but does so using an optional noun phrase, in certain positions, and usually with a distinctive INTONATION, as in *John, are you ready*?

vocoid A term invented by the American phonetician Kenneth Pike (b. 1912) to help distinguish between the PHONETIC and the PHONOLOGICAL notions of VOWEL. Phonetically, a vowel is defined as a sound lacking any CLOSURE or narrowing sufficient to produce audible FRICTION. Phonologically, it is a unit which functions at the centre of SYLLABLES. In cases such as [l], [r], [w] and [j], however, these criteria do not coincide: these sounds are phonetically vowel-like, but their function is CONSONANTAL. To avoid possible confusion, Pike proposed the term vocoid for sounds which are characterized by a phonetic definition such as the above; the term vowel is then reserved for the phonological sense. Its opposite is CONTOID. Since the 1980s, the term has become fashionable in FEATURE geometry models of phonology, where it is often used to designate one of the two chief classes of segments (the other being consonants).

voice (voic-ing, -ed, -eless, de-, un-) (1) A fundamental term used in the PHONETIC classification of speech sounds, referring to the auditory result of the vibration of the VOCAL CORDS. Sounds produced while the vocal cords are vibrating are **voiced** sounds, e.g. [b, z, a, i]; those produced with no such vibration are **voiceless** or **unvoiced**, e.g. [p, s, h]. A sound which is normally voiced, but which in a particular phonetic ENVIRONMENT is produced with less voice than elsewhere, or with no voice at all, is said to be **devoiced** (symbolized by a small circle beneath the symbol) – examples are the reduced voicing on voiced PLOSIVES in a word-final position as in *bib, bed* [bɪb̥], [bed̥].

This contrast is considered to be of primary significance in phonological analysis, and is used as a main parameter of classification both in PHONEMIC and DISTINCTIVE FEATURE theories of PHONOLOGY. **Voiced**, for example, is one of the SOURCE features of sound set up by CHOMSKY and Halle in their phonological theory. Voiced sounds are defined ARTICULATORILY, as those where the vocal cords are in a position which will enable them to vibrate in an airflow. Its opposite is **non-voiced** (or **voiceless**), referring to sounds where vocal-cord vibration is impossible, because of the wide gap between them.

Voice-onset time (VOT) is a term used in PHONETICS, referring to the point in time at which VOCAL-CORD vibration starts, following the release of a CLOSURE. In a fully VOICED PLOSIVE, for example, the vocal cords vibrate throughout; in a voiceless unaspirated plosive, there is a delay (or LAG) before voicing starts; in a voiceless aspirated plosive, the delay is much longer, depending on the amount of ASPIRATION. The amount of the delay, in relation to the types of plosive, varies from language to language.

(2) A CATEGORY used in the GRAMMATICAL description of SENTENCE or CLAUSE structure, primarily with reference to VERBS, to express the way sentences may alter the relationship between the SUBJECT and OBJECT of a verb, without changing the meaning of the sentence. The main distinction is between ACTIVE and PASSIVE, as illustrated by *The cat bit the dog* and *The dog was bitten by the cat*: in the first sentence, the grammatical subject is also the actor; in the second sentence the grammatical subject is the goal of the action – it is 'acted upon', and thus 'passive'. There will be certain differences in the emphasis or style of these sentences, which will affect the speaker's choice, but the factual content

of the two sentences remains the same. In other languages, further contrasts in voice may be encountered, e.g. the 'middle' voice of Greek (which included verbs with a REFLEXIVE meaning, e.g. *She cut herself*), and there are several other types of construction whose role in language is related to that of voice, e.g. 'reflexive', CAUSATIVE, 'impersonal' constructions. Voice contrasts may be formally marked in the verb (e.g. by INFLECTION, WORD ORDER or the use of special AUXILIARIES), or elsewhere in the sentence (e.g. by the use of passive 'agent'); the English passive can involve all three factors, as in *I was kicked by a bull.*

voice dynamics A term used by some PHONETICIANS as a collective term to refer to vocal effects other than VOICE QUALITY and SEGMENTAL features, e.g. LOUDNESS, TEMPO, RHYTHM, REGISTER. These effects are capable of differentiating MEANINGS and SPEECH communities, and are thus held to be within the purview of LINGUISTICS.

voice-onset time see VOICE (1)

voiceprint(ing) A display of a person's voice based upon a SPECTROGRAPHIC or similar output. The analogy is with the term 'fingerprint', and the claim is sometimes made that a person's voice is as individual as fingerprints. Several legal cases have in fact used voiceprints as evidence of SPEAKER IDENTIFICATION. But, while there are several idiosyncratic features in a spectrogram of a person's voice, it is not the case that such displays are always unequivocal indications of identity. It is difficult to visually compare and interpret sets of spectrographic features, and the limitations of the display techniques used must always be borne in mind.

voice/vocal qualifier A term used by some linguists as part of their analysis of the PARALINGUISTIC features of the voice. Examples are the expression of various emotional states, such as anger or sarcasm, by means of vocal effects such as a 'harsh' or 'tense' quality – effects which are sometimes specific to individual languages. The term VOICE QUALITY is sometimes used in a general sense to include these effects.

voice quality/set A term used in PHONETICS to refer to the permanently present, background, person-identifying feature of speech. All phonetic features contribute to this notion: an individual's voice quality derives from a combination of such factors as PITCH height, LOUDNESS level, TEMPO and TIMBRE of speaking. Labels for the many qualities that can be produced tend to be impressionistic and ambiguous, e.g. a 'cheery', 'haughty', 'sullen' voice. A terminological problem also arises because such labels may be used in both a non-linguistic way (as described above) and in a LINGUISTIC or PARALINGUISTIC context, as when someone who normally does not have a voice one would call 'sullen' deliberately adopts such a voice to communicate a particular emotional state. To classify such latter effects, terms such as VOICE QUALIFIER or 'paralinguistic feature' are available, but 'voice quality' is also commonly used.

volition(al) A term used in the SEMANTIC analysis of GRAMMATICAL CATEGORIES, referring to a kind of relationship between an AGENT and a VERB. A **volitional** verb or construction is one where the action takes place as a consequence of the agent's choice, e.g. *Mary left*. A **non-volitional** verb or construction is one where the agent has no determining influence on the action, e.g. *Mary slipped*. Many verbs allow both interpretations (e.g. *X hit Y* – accidentally or on purpose?). The notion has also had a contrastive role in the analysis of the meanings of certain AUXILIARY verbs in English: for example, the volitional sense of *will* in *I will go* (in the sense of 'it is my decision to go') is distinguished from other senses, such as characteristic action (*They'll sit there for hours*).

VOT The usual abbreviation for 'VOICE-onset time'.

vowel (vocalic) One of the two general CATEGORIES used for the classification of speech sounds, the other being CONSONANT. Vowels can be defined in terms of both PHONETICS and PHONOLOGY. Phonetically, they are sounds articulated without a complete CLOSURE in the mouth or a degree of narrowing which would produce audible FRICTION; the air escapes evenly over the centre of the TONGUE. If air escapes solely through the mouth, the vowels are said to be ORAL; if some air is simultaneously released through the nose, the vowels are NASAL. In addition to this, in a phonetic classification of vowels, reference would generally be made to two variables, the first of which is easily describable, the second much less so: (a) the position of the lips – whether rounded, spread, or neutral; (b) the part of the tongue raised, and the height to which it moves.

Relatively slight movements of the tongue produce quite distinct auditory differences in **vowel** (or **vocalic**) **quality**. Because it is very difficult to see or feel these movements, classification of vowels is usually carried out using ACOUSTIC or AUDITORY criteria, supplemented by details of lip position. There are several systems for representing vowel position visually, e.g. in terms of a 'vowel triangle' or a 'vowel quadrilateral' such as the CARDINAL VOWEL system.

These sounds are usually voiced, though some languages have been analysed as having 'voiceless' vowels, e.g. Portuguese. From a phonological point of view, vowels are those units which function at the CENTRE of syllables. In some approaches, the term 'vowel' is reserved for the phonological level of analysis; VOCOID is then used for the phonetic level (as opposed to CONTOID, for the phonetic equivalent of a consonant). The usefulness of this distinction is in relation to those sounds which are vowel-like in articulation, but which function as consonants in syllables: [r], for example, is phonetically very similar to a vowel, but it occurs at the margins of syllables, as in *red, car*. In such cases, it is sometimes clearer to talk of a 'vocoid with consonantal function'.

In establishing the **vowel system** of a language, several further dimensions of classification may be used. One criterion is in terms of the duration of the vowel (whether relatively 'long' or 'short' vowels are used). Another is whether, during an articulation, there is any detectable change in quality. If the quality of a vowel stays unchanged, the term **pure vowel**, or MONOPHTHONG, is used, e.g. the standard British pronunciation of *red, car, sit, seat*. If there is an evident change in quality, one talks instead of a **gliding vowel**. If two auditory elements are involved, the vowel GLIDE is referred to as a DIPHTHONG, e.g. *light, say, go*; if three elements, as a TRIPHTHONG, e.g. *fire, hour* (in some pronunciations). In the DISTINCTIVE FEATURE theory of phonology, the term VOCALIC is used as the main feature in the analysis of vowel sounds.

Yet another way of classifying vowels is in terms of the amount of muscular

W* languages An alternative form for NON-CONFIGURATIONAL LANGUAGES.

***wanna*-contraction** A term used in EXTENDED STANDARD THEORY and GOVERNMENT-BINDING theory for the process deriving *I wanna go home* from *I want to go home.* It has been suggested that restrictions on *wanna*-contraction and similar processes provide evidence for the view that PROCESSES leave behind TRACES.

wave (1) A term used in HISTORICAL LINGUISTICS and SOCIOLINGUISTICS as part of a DYNAMIC MODEL of LANGUAGE change: **wave theory** suggests that speech variations spread from a specific linguistic area, having maximum effect on adjacent languages, and progressively less effect on languages further away – in much the same way that waves in water radiate from a central point of contact.

(2) A term used in TAGMEMIC GRAMMAR as one mode of the analysis of linguistic UNITS: in the 'wave' mode, units at any LEVEL are analysed in terms of their status as VARIANTS MANIFESTED in different CONTEXTS, e.g. MORPHEMIC or TRANSFORMATIONAL processes. This mode is contrasted with the analysis of units in terms of PARTICLES and FIELDS.

weak adequacy see ADEQUACY

weak form One of two possible pronunciations for a WORD, in the context of CONNECTED SPEECH, the other being STRONG. The weak form is that which is the result of a word being UNSTRESSED, as in the normal pronunciation of *of* in *cup of tea*, and in most other GRAMMATICAL WORDS. Several words in English have more than one weak form, e.g. *and* [ænd] can be [ənd], [ən], [n], etc.

weather *it* A term sometimes used in GRAMMATICAL theory for the EXPLETIVE or DUMMY element in such sentences as *It was raining*. It is distinct from ANTICIPATORY *it*.

weight (1) In PHONOLOGY, a concept used to distinguish levels of syllabic PROMINENCE, based on the segmental constituency of SYLLABLES. Syllables can be metrically **heavy** or **light**: a light (or 'weak') syllable is one whose RHYME comprises a short-vowel NUCLEUS alone or followed by a CODA of no more than one short consonant (in terms of phonological LENGTH, a MORA); a heavy (or 'strong') syllable is any other type (its phonological length being greater than one mora). Syllables of structure CVVC or CVCC are sometimes referred to as 'superheavy'. The notion of weight has come to be important in several models of NON-LINEAR PHONOLOGY. See also COMPENSATORY LENGTHENING.

(2) In SYNTAX, a concept which relates the relative length/COMPLEXITY of different elements of SENTENCE STRUCTURE. For example, a CLAUSE as SUBJECT or OBJECT would be considered heavier than a LEXICAL NOUN PHRASE, which would be heavier than a PRONOUN. Such variations in length and complexity seem to influence the ORDER of elements in languages: for example, there is a preference for short > long linearization in right-branching (VO) languages, and for long > short in left-branching (OV) languages.

well formed (well-formedness) A term used in LINGUISTICS, especially in GENERATIVE GRAMMAR, to refer to the GRAMMATICALITY ('well-formedness') of a SENTENCE. A sentence is well formed if it can be generated by the RULES of a grammar; it is ILL-FORMED if it cannot be. The term applies equally to SYNTAX, SEMANTICS and PHONOLOGY.

wh- The usual abbreviation for a ***wh*-word** – a QUESTION WORD (INTERROGATIVE word) or RELATIVE item, such as *what, who, which, when, why, how,* etc. It is used generally in LINGUISTICS with reference to ***wh*-complements**, ***wh*-movement**, questions (***wh*-questions**) and relative CLAUSES (***wh*-relatives**). A *wh*-question is a term used in the grammatical sub-classification of question types to refer to a question beginning with a question word. These 'particular' or 'question word' questions are contrasted with *YES–NO* QUESTIONS. The term is commonly used in the context of GENERATIVE GRAMMAR. A ***wh*-NP** is a noun phrase introduced by a *wh*-word (e.g. *which car, what interest*). ***Wh*-movement** (***wh*-fronting** or ***wh*-preposing**) is used to refer to a TRANSFORMATIONAL RULE which moves a ***wh*-phrase** (***wh*-XP**) to INITIAL POSITION in the SENTENCE. For example, given a DEEP STRUCTURE of the sentence *Who did you see*? as 'You past see who', applying *wh*-movement would result in 'Who you past see'. In recent generative linguistics, several other transformations are subsumed under *wh*-movement. ***Wh*-islands** are constructions beginning with a *wh*-phrase, out of which it is not possible to move a constituent through a transformational rule (the ***wh*-island constraint**). In recent generative linguistics, several other types of construction are analysed in a way similar to *wh*-questions, such as *that*-relatives and COMPARATIVES; they are known as UNBOUNDED DEPENDENCIES. See also TRACE.

whistle(d)-speech A term used in LINGUISTICS to refer to a stylized form of COMMUNICATION, in which whistling substitutes for the TONES of normal SPEECH. In some DIALECTS (such as Mazatec, in Mexico) quite sophisticated conversations have been observed to take place using whistle-speech. An analogous system of communication is drum-signalling.

whiz*-deletion** A term sometimes used in GENERATIVE GRAMMAR to refer to a TRANSFORMATIONAL RULE which DELETES a RELATIVE PRONOUN and its associated VERB from a relative CLAUSE to produce a POST-modifying PHRASE, e.g. *the woman* ***who was *in the street* becoming *the woman in the street.*

Whorfian Characteristic of, or a follower of, the views of Benjamin Lee Whorf (1897–1941), especially as propounded in the **Whorfian hypothesis** (alternatively, the SAPIR–WHORF HYPOTHESIS), which states that our conceptual categorization of the world is determined (wholly or partly) by the STRUCTURE of our native LANGUAGE. In its strong form, the hypothesis is not accepted by most LINGUISTS.

wide A term used in the description of types of VOWEL, referring to a vowel which is articulated with greater PHARYNX width than another with the same TONGUE and lip configuration; it is opposed to **narrow**. The effect is achieved by drawing the root of the tongue forward and lowering the LARYNX. Twi and Akan (West Africa) use a contrast of this kind.

word A unit of expression which has universal intuitive recognition by NATIVE-SPEAKERS, in both spoken and written language. However, there are several difficulties in arriving at a consistent use of the term in relation to other CATEGORIES of linguistic description, and in the comparison of languages of different structural types. These problems relate mainly to word identification and definition. They include, for example, decisions over word boundaries (e.g. is a unit such as *washing machine* two words, or is it one, to be written *washing-machine*?), as well as decisions over status (e.g. is *the* a word in the same sense as is *chair*?). Regular definitions of words as 'units of meaning', or 'ideas' are of no help, because of the vagueness of such notions as 'idea'. As a result, several theoretical distinctions have been made.

Three main senses of 'word' are usually distinguished (though terminology varies):

(a) Words are the physically definable units which one encounters in a stretch of writing (bounded by spaces) or speech (where identification is more difficult, but where there may be PHONOLOGICAL clues to identify boundaries, such as a PAUSE, or JUNCTURE features). 'Word' in this sense is often referred to as the **orthographic word** (for writing) or the **phonological word** (for speech). A neutral term often used to subsume both is **word form**.

(b) There is a more abstract sense, referring to the common factor underlying the set of forms which are plainly VARIANTS of the same unit, such as *walk, walks, walking, walked*. The 'underlying' word unit is often referred to as a LEXEME. Lexemes are the units of VOCABULARY, and as such would be listed in a dictionary.

(c) This then leaves the need for a comparably abstract unit to be set up to show how words work in the GRAMMAR of a language, and 'word', without qualification, is usually reserved for this role (alternatively, one may spell out this implication, referring to 'MORPHEMIC/MORPHOSYNTACTIC/GRAMMATICAL' words, though the latter has an alternative sense). A word, then, is a grammatical unit, of the same theoretical kind as MORPHEME and SENTENCE. In a HIERARCHICAL model of analysis, sentences (clauses, etc.) consist of words, and words consist of morphemes (minimally, one free morpheme). **Word order** refers to the sequential arrangement of words in a language. Languages are sometimes classified in terms of whether their word order is relatively 'free' (as in Latin) or 'fixed' (as in English).

Several criteria have been suggested for the identification of words in speech (criteria which would also apply to the written language as well, if they were needed). One is that words are the most stable of all linguistic units, in respect of their internal structure, i.e. the CONSTITUENT parts of a complex word have little potential for rearrangement, compared with the relative POSITIONAL MOBILITY of the constituents of sentences and other grammatical structures (cf. *disestablishment*, where the sequence of *dis-establish-ment* is fixed, and *all boys like girls*, where many alternative sequences are possible, e.g. *boys all like girls*). A second criterion refers to the relative 'uninterruptibility' or COHESIVENESS of words, i.e. new elements (including pauses) cannot usually be inserted within them in normal speech: pauses, by contrast, are always potentially present at word boundaries. A criterion which has influenced linguists' views of the word since it was first suggested by Leonard BLOOMFIELD is the definition of word as a 'minimum free form', i.e. the smallest unit which can constitute, by itself, a complete utterance (it contrasts here with sentence, seen as the maximum free form recognized by most grammars). On this basis, *possibility* is a word, as is *possible* (contexts could be constructed which would enable such units to occur as single-element sentences, e.g. *Is that a probable outcome? Possible.*), but *-ity* is not (nor would any AFFIX be). Not all word-like units satisfy this criterion, however (e.g. *a* and *the* in English), and how to handle these has been the subject of considerable discussion.

Several general subclassifications of words have been proposed, such as the distinction between VARIABLE and invariable types, GRAMMATICAL (or FUNCTION) words *v.* LEXICAL words, CLOSED-CLASS *v.* OPEN-CLASS words, EMPTY *v.* FULL words. At a more specific level, **word-classes** can be established, by analysing the various GRAMMATICAL, SEMANTIC and PHONOLOGICAL properties displayed by the words in a language, and grouping words into classes on the basis of formal similarities (e.g. their INFLECTIONS and DISTRIBUTION). The results are analogous to the traditional notion of 'parts of speech', but word-classes usually display a wider range of more precisely defined classes, e.g. PARTICLES, AUXILIARIES, etc., alongside NOUNS, VERBS, etc., and lack the vagueness of many of the traditional NOTIONAL definitions (e.g. a noun as the 'name of a person, place or thing'). The study of the structure and composition of words (cf. WORD FORMATION) is carried on by MORPHOLOGY. The study of the ARRANGEMENTS of words in sentences is the province of SYNTAX. The notion of 'PROSODIC word' is central to some recent theories of phonological structure, as is the notion of a 'MINIMAL word' (one which contains at least two MORAS/SYLLABLES).

word accent see ACCENT (2)

word and paradigm (WP) A MORPHOLOGICAL MODEL of description which sees the WORD as the basic UNIT of analysis, operating within a set of variables which constitute a PARADIGM. This is the traditional model of description, as illustrated from Latin GRAMMARS (e.g. *amo, amas, amat* . . . constitutes the paradigm of the LEXEME *amo*). WP is seen as a major alternative to the two other main approaches to morphological analysis: ITEM AND PROCESS and ITEM AND ARRANGEMENT. In contrast to the traditional use of paradigms in LANGUAGE study, linguistics does not arbitrarily choose one form of a word (the 'leading form') as given, and derive the rest of the paradigm from this (the student usually learning it by rote); rather, the aim is to define a common factor (a ROOT or STEM) within the paradigm, neutral with respect to the variant forms of the paradigm, and to derive the VARIANT forms from this, e.g. using rules.

word formation In its most general sense, the term refers to the whole process of MORPHOLOGICAL variation in the constitution of WORDS, i.e. including the two main divisions of INFLECTION (word variations signalling GRAMMATICAL relationships) and DERIVATION (word variations signalling LEXICAL relationships). In a more restricted sense, word formation refers to the latter processes only, these being subclassified into such types as 'compositional' or 'compound' (e.g. *black bird* from the free elements *black* + *bird*), and 'derivational' (e.g. *national, nationalize*, etc., from the addition of the bound elements *-al, -ize*, etc.). Several possibilities of further subclassification are available in the literature on this subject. In GENERATIVE grammar, **word-formation rules** specify how to form one class of words out of another.

word grammar A GRAMMATICAL theory which claims that grammatical knowledge is largely a body of knowledge about WORDS. It regards DEPENDENCY as the central relation in grammar, and assumes that CONSTITUENCY is only important in connection with CO-ORDINATE structures.

word order A term used in GRAMMATICAL analysis to refer to the SEQUENTIAL arrangement of WORDS in larger linguistic UNITS. Some LANGUAGES (e.g. English) rely on word order as a means of expressing grammatical relationships within CONSTRUCTIONS; in others (e.g. Latin) word order is more flexible, as grammatical relations are signalled by INFLECTIONS. In recent GENERATIVE linguistics, languages with fairly fixed word order are called CONFIGURATIONAL LANGUAGES; those with fairly free word order are NON-CONFIGURATIONAL LANGUAGES.

word stress see STRESS

WP The usual abbreviation for the WORD-AND-PARADIGM model of description in GRAMMAR.

wugs A nonsense word invented in the late 1950s for a LANGUAGE ACQUISITION experiment into the learning of MORPHOLOGY. The drawing of a mythical animal (a *wug*) was presented to children, and the child was told: 'This is a wug'. Then the experimenter would point to a second picture, saying 'Now, there's another one. There are two of them. There are two—.' If the children had learned the plural ending, they would say *wugs*; if they had not, they would say *wug*. Using several such NONSENSE words in a range of morphological CONTEXTS, much basic information was obtained concerning the order and timing of the acquisition of GRAMMATICAL MORPHEMES.

X-bar ($\bar{X}$) A system of GRAMMATICAL analysis developed in GENERATIVE LINGUISTICS as an alternative to traditional accounts of PHRASE STRUCTURE and LEXICAL CATEGORIES. It is argued both that the rules of phrase-structure grammar need to be more constrained (cf. CONSTRAINT), and that more phrasal CATEGORIES need to be recognized. In particular, within the NOUN PHRASE, the need is felt to recognize intermediate categories larger than the noun but smaller than the phrase, e.g. *very fast* or *very fast car* in the phrase *the very fast car*. These intermediate categories, which have no status in previous phrase-structure models, are formally recognized in X-bar SYNTAX by a system of X-bars, each of which identifies a level of phrasal EXPANSION. Given a lexical category, X, X^0 = 'X with no bars' (i.e. 'zero-bar', the category itself); $\bar{X} = X^1$ = 'X-bar' = 'X-single-bar'; $\bar{\bar{X}} = X^2$ = 'X-double-bar'; $\bar{\bar{\bar{X}}} = X^3$ = 'X-treble-bar'; and so on. For example, the following TREE illustrates two levels of expansion for N ('N-bar' and 'N-double-bar'):

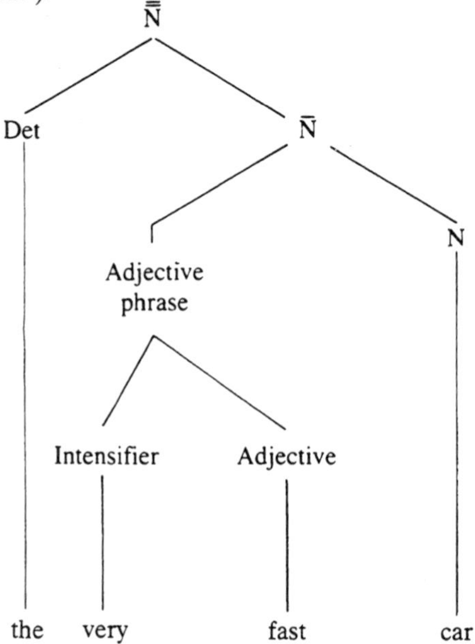

Each of the bar categories corresponding to X is known as a **bar-projection** of X.

The value of recognizing intermediate categories in this way is widely agreed, but discussion continues about the number of categories which need to be recognized, and how far it is possible to generalize rules of category formation throughout a grammar.

X-tier A term used in AUTOSEGMENTAL PHONOLOGY to describe a conception of the SKELETAL TIER in which the FEATURE [syllabic] is eliminated, SEGMENTS being specified for no features at all, thus contrasting with the CV-TIER approach; also known as the **timing unit** or **timing tier** theory. This approach is claimed to have advantages in removing REDUNDANCY (the overlap in FUNCTION between syllable position and whether a position is a C or a V).

Y

yers In the PHONOLOGY of Slavic languages (e.g. Polish), a term used to describe a type of very short VOWEL which appears only in certain contexts. It has been seen as an illustration of a GHOST SEGMENT, and the question of its REPRESENTATION has attracted particular attention in NON-LINEAR PHONOLOGY.

***yes-no* question** A term used in the GRAMMATICAL subclassification of types of QUESTION to refer to a question form where a grammatical reply would have to be of the type *yes* or *no*. It is formally marked by INVERTED SUBJECT–VERB order, e.g. ***is she** going?* These 'general' or 'inverted order' questions are contrasted with *WH*-questions.

Z

zero A term used in some areas of LINGUISTICS to refer to an abstract unit postulated by an analysis, but which has no physical realization in the stream of speech. Its symbol is Ø. In English MORPHOLOGY, for example, the pressure of the grammatical system to analyse plurals as Noun + plural has led some linguists to analyse unchanged nouns, such as *sheep* and *deer* as Noun + plural also, the plurality in these cases being realized as zero (a **zero morph**). A 'zero operation' of this kind is also called an 'identity operation', one where the input and the output of the operation are identical. Similarly, in other grammatical CONTEXTS where a given MORPHEME usually occurs, the absence of that morpheme under certain conditions may be referred to as zero, e.g. **zero infinitive**, referring to the absence of *to* before the verb in English; **zero article**, referring to the absence of a definite or indefinite ARTICLE before a noun; **zero connectors**, as in *he said he was coming*, where *that* is omitted; **zero valency**, referring in VALENCY grammar to verbs which take no COMPLEMENTS; and **zero relative** clauses, as in *the book I bought*... In cases such as *He's laughing, is he*, some linguists analyse the second part of the sentence as a REDUCED form of the verb phrase *is he laughing*, referring to the omitted part by the term **zero anaphora**. Zero is also found in PHONOLOGICAL analysis, e.g. in a conception of some types of JUNCTURE as **zero phonemes**, or to suggest a structural parallelism between SYLLABLE types (a CV sequence being seen as a CVC sequence, with the final C being zero).

Zero is especially encountered in the formulation of GENERATIVE RULES, where the term refers to an item deleted from a given context (a 'DELETION rule'). Such rules are of the type 'rewrite A as zero, in the context X–Y' (A → Ø/X–Y), and they apply in GRAMMAR, SEMANTICS and PHONOLOGY. In X-BAR SYNTAX, a **zero-level** or **zero-bar category** is a LEXICAL CATEGORY.

It is plain that the introduction of zero (sometimes referred to as the **null** element, deriving from the use of this term in mathematics) is motivated by the need to maintain a proportionality, or regular pattern, in one's analysis, or in the interests of devising an economic statement. It is also a notion which has to be introduced with careful justification; too many zeros in an analysis weaken its plausibility.

zoösemiotics A branch of SEMIOTICS that studies the features of human COMMUNICATION which, as the end products of an evolutionary series, are shared with animal systems of communication; opposed to 'anthroposemiotic' features, which are exclusively human. Under the heading of 'zoösemiotic features/systems' fall certain features of tone of voice (cf. PARALANGUAGE), facial expression, gesture, etc. (cf. KINESICS, PROXEMICS), as well as several mechanisms of animal communication which seem not to overlap with human signalling systems (e.g. chemical signals (pheromones), echolocation.